W9-BTP-836

Advance praise for *The Hauerwas Reader*

"Stanley Hauerwas is an unparalleled force for courage and generative thinking across the spectrum of Christian thought. Sometimes he heals and ener-
gizes, sometimes he (deliberately) infuriates. Always he claims attention and
redefines the theological task. For his allies as well as his adversaries, the publication of his papers is a welcome resource. It makes available much that is
needed for continuing work. Hauerwas draws us into the contemporary theological emergency and points us in fresh ways through it."
—WALTER BRUEGGEMANN, Columbia Theological Seminary

"The God met through the Jewish and Christian scriptures is always good but
rarely safe. No other living theologian—and not many throughout history—
has grasped that truth more excitingly than Stanley Hauerwas. This invaluable
guide will help varied readers see the Christian tradition through Hauerwas's
eyes and discover it is a treasure chest spiked with political, social, and spiritual dynamite."—RODNEY CLAPP, author of *Border Crossings* and *A Peculiar
People*

"Covering a range of ethical concerns from healthcare to warfare, these essays
show again how Stanley Hauerwas brings together Evangelical and Catholic
foundations for an ethics based on faith. The articles ring true, which is to say
they speak first of Christ and only then of life in Him."
—FRANCIS CARDINAL GEORGE, Archbishop of Chicago

"Texans and Christians are troublesome. At odds with enlightened liberal cos-
mopolitan pretensions, they embrace particularity. One cannot deduce either
Texas or Christianity from reason or from human nature. Hauerwas as a Texan
Christian has for three decades reminded us forcefully of the importance of
taking the troublesome particularity of Christianity seriously. These essays provoke, engage, and instruct. They are a superb selection from the work of one of
the most important theologians of our time. Everyone, whether Christian
or non-Christian, believer or atheist, should read these essays; they are key to
understanding the religious, moral, and metaphysical struggles of our age."
—H. TRISTRAM ENGELHARDT, JR., PH.D., M.D., Rice University, Baylor College of Medicine

"Stanley Hauerwas challenges, informs, provokes, and inspires anyone who reflects seriously on faith and life. *The Hauerwas Reader* is an invitation to accompany one of today's most provocative and creative thinkers on a transforming theological journey beyond our comfortable idolatries."
—BISHOP KENNETH L. CARDER, Mississippi Episcopal Area, The United Methodist Church

"For decades now Stanley Hauerwas has been the most eloquent voice proclaiming the morality of particularism and the immorality of universalism. In a liberal culture that voice is heard as both alien and unreasonable, accusations Hauerwas no doubt cherishes."—STANLEY FISH, author of *The Trouble with Principle*

"It would be hard to overestimate the value of Stanley Hauerwas's contributions to theological conversation and religious life in today's world. Alternately brilliant and exasperating, his work is indispensable in helping us find our way in a dark time. This wonderful reader is the best introduction to Hauerwas available."—ROBERT N. BELLAH, coauthor of *Habits of the Heart*

"This one-volume Hauerwas reader provides us with a rounded view of one of the greatest theological minds, who is equally one of the greatest ecclesial forces, of the postmodern era."—JOHN MILBANK

"The editors have made a happy and extensive selection from the mercurial essayist-theologian, which allows us to come to grips with his thought on a broad front. Stanley Hauerwas could not and would not accommodate himself to the ponderous demands of a Systematic Ethics; but if we think that we can see here a possible shape for that impossible book, it is a measure of how closely the editors have come to their author and discerned the ordered structures of his apparently disorderly mind. If somebody asks you why this man has been important to the moral thinking of a generation, thrust this collection at him. Then he will understand."—THE REVEREND OLIVER O'DONOVAN, Canon of Christ Church

"This collection is obviously a labor of love. Fortunately, it is also a labor of editorial care and precision. In addition to first-rate introductory material, the writings of a master provocateur are gathered here in a fresh, synthetic format. Re-reading these essays was humbling."—JEAN BETHKE ELSHTAIN, Laura Spelman Rockefeller Professor of Social and Political Ethics, University of Chicago

"If Kierkegaard knew Hauerwas, he would have seen that it is possible, after all, for one person to be a close friend of Jesus and of Socrates, at the same time. On behalf of all of us in the Abrahamite traditions, Hauerwas cracks open modern society's lazy moral speech and lets us see, lying neglected inside it, God's commanding word. In this way, he helps clear a space in contemporary America for Jews, and I trust Muslims, as well as Christians to narrate their stories of what God wants of us. If you don't know Hauerwas yet, this fine collection is the way to begin, along with its wonderful introductions and guides to Hauerwas's work. If you do know him, well, then, you already know that each reading and rereading will bring surprises. And blessings."
—PETER OCHS, Bronfman Professor of Modern Judaic Studies, University of Virginia

The Hauerwas Reader

The Hauerwas Reader

Stanley Hauerwas

Edited by John Berkman and Michael Cartwright

DUKE UNIVERSITY PRESS   *Durham and London* 2001

4th printing, 2005

© 2001 Duke University Press

Printed in the United States of America on acid-free paper ∞

Designed by Amy Ruth Buchanan

Typeset in Minion by Keystone Typesetting, Inc.

Library of Congress Cataloging-in-Publication Data appear
on the last printed page of this book.

Essay 12 is used by permission of Abington Press.

Contents

List of Abbreviations for Books by Stanley Hauerwas

(Not a comprehensive list of all books authored, coauthored, or edited by Hauerwas)

VV   *Vision and Virtue: Essays in Christian Ethical Reflection* (Notre Dame, IN: Fides Publishers, Inc., 1974).

CCL   *Character and the Christian Life: A Study in Theological Ethics* (San Antonio, TX: Trinity University Press, 1975). 2d ed., with a new introduction, 1985.

TT   *Truthfulness and Tragedy: Further Investigations in Christian Ethics* (Notre Dame, IN: University of Notre Dame Press, 1977).

CC   *A Community of Character: Toward a Constructive Christian Social Ethic* (Notre Dame, IN: University of Notre Dame Press, 1981).

PK   *The Peaceable Kingdom* (Notre Dame, IN: University of Notre Dame Press, 1983).

AN   *Against the Nations: War and Survival in a Liberal Society* (Minneapolis, MN: Winston Press, Inc., A Seabury Book, 1985). This book is now published by UNDP.

SP   *Suffering Presence: Theological Reflections on Medicine, the Mentally Handicapped, and the Church* (Notre Dame, IN: University of Notre Dame Press, 1986).

CET   *Christian Existence Today: Essays on Church, World, and Living in Between* (Durham, NC: Labyrinth Press, 1988).

RA   *Resident Aliens: Life in the Christian Colony*, with William Willimon (Nashville, TN: Abington Press, 1989).

NS   *Naming the Silences: God, Medicine, and the Problem of Suffering* (Grand Rapids, MI: Eerdmans, 1990). This book was reissued in 1993 under the title *God, Medicine, and the Problem of Suffering*.

AC   *After Christendom: How the Church Is to Behave If Freedom, Justice, and a Christian Nation Are Bad Ideas* (Nashville, TN: Abington Press, 1991).

US   *Unleashing the Scriptures: Freeing the Bible from Captivity to America* (Nashville, TN: Abington Press, 1993).

DF   *Dispatches from the Front: Theological Engagements with the Secular* (Durham, NC: Duke University Press, 1994).

IGC   *In Good Company: The Church as Polis* (Notre Dame, IN: University of Notre Dame Press, 1995).

WRAL   *Where Resident Aliens Live: Exercises for Christian Practice,* with William Willimon (Nashville, TN: Abington Press, 1996).

CAV   *Christians among the Virtues: Theological Conversations with Ancient and Modern Ethics,* with Charles Pinches (Notre Dame, IN: University of Notre Dame Press, 1997).

WW   *Wilderness Wanderings: Probing Twentieth-Century Theology and Philosophy* (Boulder, CO: Westview Press, 1997).

STT   *Sanctify Them in the Truth: Holiness Exemplified* (Nashville, TN: Abington Press, 1998).

TG   *The Truth about God: The Ten Commandments in Christian Life,* with William Willimon (Nashville, TN: Abington Press, 1999).

PPS   *Prayers Plainly Spoken* (Grand Rapids, MI: Brazos Press, 1999).

BH   *A Better Hope: Resources for a Church Confronting Capitalism, Postmodernity, and America* (Grand Rapids, MI: Brazos Press, 2000).

WGU   *With the Grain of the Universe: The Gifford Lectures for 2001* (Grand Rapids, MI: Brazos Press, 2001).

Acknowledgments

This *Reader* has been a long time coming. In the four years we have worked together preparing this volume, we have been assisted by an extraordinary company of people and have been shown a generosity in time and spirit that words cannot acknowledge. But to the extent that we can, we freely and joyfully acknowledge our debt of gratitude to a diverse company of strangers, friends, students, colleagues, and critics, without whose various labors this volume would be greatly impoverished, if possible at all.

Our first thanks must go to William Cavanaugh and James Fodor, who generously agreed to contribute an introductory essay and co-author the annotated bibliography, respectively.

We are extremely grateful to an extraordinary company of scholars who gave us feedback at various steps along the way. More than fifty persons responded to our two surveys of 225 theologians and ethicists as to what should go into *The Hauerwas Reader*. For advice on this, we gratefully acknowledge the assistance of Scott Bader-Saye, John Bowlin, David Burrell, William Cavanaugh, Dennis Doyle, Michael Duffy, Darrell Fasching, Michael J. Gorman, Jon P. Gunnemann, Vigen Guroian, Barry Penn Hollar, L. Gregory Jones, Emmanuel Katongole, Cathleen Kaveny, Philip Kenneson, Ted Koontz, Joseph Kotva, Stephen Lammers, Karen Lebacqz, Andrew Linzey, D. Stephen Long, Robin Lovin, Alasdair MacIntyre, James William McClendon Jr., David Matzko McCarthy, Gilbert Meilaender, John Milbank, Richard Miller, Debra Dean Murphy, Nancey Murphy, Elizabeth Newman, Douglas Ottati, Catherine Pickstock, William Placher, Jefferson Powell, John P. Reeder Jr., Warren Reich, Neville Richardson, Eugene Rogers, Michael Root, William Schweiker, Thomas Schaffer, David Smith, Glen Stassen, Kenneth Surin, Paul Wojda, Paul Wadell, Michael Westmoreland-White, Rowan Williams, and the late John Howard Yoder. Particularly comprehensive suggestions were gratefully received from Rodney Clapp, Reinhard Huetter, Peter Ochs, Samuel Wells, and especially

G. Scott Davis. We are also indebted to the six anonymous reviewers at Duke University Press for their comments on our original proposal.

While in the process of editing the essays for *The Hauerwas Reader,* we received valuable suggestions and assistance from David Cloutier, Joseph Mangina, Keith Meador, Charles Pinches, and Samuel Wells. Comments and critiques of the essays by Berkman and Cartwright were gratefully received from Kevin Armstrong, Michael Budde, Mary Wilder Cartwright, William Cavanaugh, Stephen Fowl, Stanley Hauerwas, Shalimar Holderly, L. Gregory Jones, Joseph Mangina, James William McClendon Jr., Gilbert Meilaender, Debra Dean Murphy, William Placher, Arne Rasmusson, Neville Richardson, Samuel Wells, and Michael Williams. William Cavanaugh would like to thank John Berkman, James Burtchaell, Michael Cartwright, Kelly Johnson, Daniel McFee, and Charles Pinches for anecdotes and helpful comments on his essay. We are also grateful for the careful feedback we received from two anonymous readers who submitted reports to Duke University Press on the manuscript as a whole.

We are very grateful that these scholarly friends and critics were able to identify mistakes, and we take responsibility for all errors that remain. If some discern that we have made errors of judgment, we accept responsibility for those as well. We also ask forgiveness of those who have assisted us in ways we have failed to acknowledge here.

We also want to express our appreciation to Reynolds Smith, senior editor at Duke University Press, for his enthusiastic support of this project over the past five years. More recently, Rebecca Johns-Danes has been particularly gracious and helpful as we executed this project. We feel fortunate to be able to publish *The Hauerwas Reader* with Duke University Press.

Many others contributed significant labors to enable this project to come to fruition. In the summer of 1998, Abraham Nussbaum labored extensively to transcribe and scan and proofread the original versions of the essays into electronic form, which served as the basis for the editing of the essays. Also, a special word of thanks to Shalimar Holderly, a member of the University of Indianapolis class of 2001, who worked on this project since the fall of 1997. Shalimar did a wonderful job of proofreading the manuscript at several stages, and she also contributed to preparing the indices.

In addition, a small grant from Dean Mary Moore of the University of Indianapolis made possible the initial survey in 1997. Debra Denning, secretary of the Philosophy and Religion Department at the University of Indianapolis, coordinated the mailings of the initial survey, assembled a database of responses, and handled details related to the follow-up survey. The labors of John Rziha, a graduate student of the Catholic University of America, facilitated the second survey. Theodore Whapham, another CUA graduate student, assisted with editing a number of the bibliographic annotations. Susan Downard, secretary for the Lantz Center for Christian Vocations in Indianapolis, provided timely and careful assistance in the preparation of the final manuscript. Michael Williams, Allegheny College '99, offered careful feedback about the entire manuscript. Thanks also to Perry Kea, who kindly and graciously shouldered some administrative burdens during the summer of 1999 so that Cartwright could complete his work on preparing the manuscript for publication.

Michael is also grateful to his wife, Mary, and children, Hannah, Erin, James, and Bethany, for the ways they cooperated with this effort by making adjustments at various times during the past two years to accommodate his schedule.

John wishes to thank his family for their love and support over these past three years. He is particularly grateful to Emily Berkman, who for the winter of 1996–1997 provided a cabin on the Big Rideau Lake in Portland, Ontario, where this project was hatched.

Finally, both Michael and John are grateful to God for the opportunity to have worked with Stanley Hauerwas on this project. Stanley never failed to offer his time to us most generously, whether it was to answer an unending stream of obscure and odd questions or to help us overcome various mundane problems with permissions and other bureaucratic difficulties. We are well aware of and extremely grateful for the trust he placed in us throughout the preparation of this volume. While offering us advice and suggestions whenever we asked, Hauerwas never sought in any way to dictate or even indicate a preference for what we ought to include in this volume. Furthermore, he graciously acceded to our editing his essays and kindly responded to interrogations about "obscure" passages. His extraordinary support enabled this project to go forward much more smoothly than otherwise could have been imagined. In seeking input from other scholars regarding the volume, we became powerfully aware of the great impact Hauerwas has had on the lives of this scholarly world. The widespread interest in this project is another testimony to the gift that Hauerwas's life and work are for so many of us.

PART I

Editorial Introductions

An Introduction to *The Hauerwas Reader*
John Berkman

At the turn of the new millennium, Stanley Hauerwas is perhaps North America's most important theological ethicist. He is certainly one of its most widely read and cited theological ethicists. No one in the field, however strongly they agree or disagree with his approach or his viewpoint, can afford to ignore him. Hauerwas is certainly the most prolific and comprehensive theological ethicist alive. He has authored or edited over thirty books and well over three hundred and fifty scholarly articles. He has been invited to lecture at literally hundreds of universities and churches in the United States and Canada as well as throughout Britain and Europe, in the Middle East, Australia, and Japan. Dozens of dissertations and theses have been written on his work, and doctoral students who have written under his guidance now hold positions in over forty universities throughout North America. He is one of those rare influential theologians who has spawned a new (both positive and pejorative) adjective: "Hauerwasian."

Hauerwas's work ranges incredibly widely. He has been at the forefront of the development of narrative theology.[1] He is clearly a seminal figure in the "recovery of virtue" in theological ethics.[2] He has been a singular voice in renewing the centrality of ecclesiology in the Protestant context, and a leading critic of the spirit of accommodationism that has led to the waning of mainline Protestantism. A leading moral and theological critic of political liberalism, he has blazed new trails with regard to what constitutes "public theology." Many believe his work in medical ethics to be the most important of all. He has written decisively not only on the "hot" issues (e.g., abortion, suicide, and euthanasia) but also on how the virtuous practice of medicine is to be sustained in the midst of the cacophony of pain, suffering, and death. In an age when ethicists are expected to specialize in some narrow subfield, Hauerwas

---

1. A representative sample of Hauerwas's contribution to—and criticism of—developing interest in narrative theology is represented by essays 6–9 and 11 in this volume.
2. On "the recovery of virtue," see essays 3, 10–12, 14–16, and 18 in this volume.

continues to see and insightfully evaluate the "big picture." He has simply refused to be limited to any narrow specialization. He has also somehow managed to avoid the status of theological gadfly, a common temptation for those who regularly run against the grain of the guild.

His influence is not limited to North America. He has been particularly influential in the United Kingdom, where he gave the Gifford Lectures in 2001.[3] One of his books was a series of lectures delivered in Australia (AC). His books have been translated into German and Japanese. Hauerwas has also achieved almost unheard of popular success with the little digest of his work published in 1989 entitled *Resident Aliens*. Having sold over 75,000 copies, *Resident Aliens* is probably the biggest-selling work by an academic theological ethicist since Joseph Fletcher's *Situation Ethics* in the 1960s. It can be hoped that history will smile more favorably on this popular work by Hauerwas.

Although Hauerwas is one of the most important late-twentieth-century theologians for the Church, it is the conviction of the editors that what Hauerwas has to say is not sufficiently accessible. The problem is not the lack of availability of Hauerwas's books, as almost all of his books remain in print. Rather, the difficulty is that Hauerwas writes almost too much for all but the most dedicated reader. Furthermore, his work appears in a somewhat unorganized manner, frustrating readers who like things laid out more tidily. With few exceptions, Hauerwas's books have been collections of "occasional" essays, and though the essays in the volumes are often thematically related, they rarely leave the reader with a sense of Hauerwas's overall project and vision. The "unfinished" nature of Hauerwas's work is not accidental, as Michael Cartwright explains in his "Reader's Guide." Although Hauerwas did write a "primer" for Christian ethics entitled *The Peaceable Kingdom* (1983), which, along with *A Community of Character* (1981) continue to constitute Hauerwas's most well-known scholarly books, they no longer adequately represent the scope or power of his thought, and thus a more adequate entryway into Hauerwas's work is needed.

It is out of this perceived need for a more adequate introduction to the work of Stanley Hauerwas that *The Hauerwas Reader* was born. This volume constitutes the most complete and representative selection of Hauerwas's work available in one volume. If one wishes to understand Hauerwas and intends to read only one of his books—whether to draw on it, to critique it, or

---

3. These lectures are titled "With the Grain of the Universe." For a summary of them and publication information, see the entry in the annotated bibliography at the end of this volume.

to do both—a thorough reading of these essays is one's best option. The volume strives to represent the different periods and phases of Hauerwas's work, the different subjects he has addressed, the different genres he writes in, and to represent both his constructive goals and his penchant for polemic.

Despite an unusually engaging and even humorous style of writing, Hauerwas is not an easy theologian to understand. This is not because his prose, like that of some theologians, is impenetrable. Rather, Hauerwas can be difficult to understand because he is often not interested in answering the questions that are typically posed, but rather seeks to "reframe" those very questions, as that is, according to Hauerwas, part of what is required by a response faithful to the gospel of Jesus Christ. One of Hauerwas's great strengths lies in exposing (what are often tacit) assumptions at work in contemporary secular and theological ethics which he takes to be incompatible with Christian faith.

Hauerwas is not a perfectionist. He never tries to utter the "final" word on a particular subject. He once was asked if he was going to spend his career defending the ideas of his first book; he said he would, if he could remember them! But this is not the strength and vigor of Hauerwas. That lies, rather, in the vision he has of what it means to live theologically, of teasing out the multifaceted implications of living in a way that God's existence and character make all the difference for how followers of Jesus Christ are to be and to live.[4]

A few critics are quick to write off Hauerwas because they believe he is not sufficiently "careful" or that he writes "too fast." These are not entirely illegitimate criticisms, but they somehow miss the point of what Hauerwas has to offer. Hauerwas's gift is not to give the Christian community tidy solutions and elegant phrases (though some do consider him to be the "king" of the theological one-liner); rather, he wants to transform the way his readers and listeners think and live. He is not unlike the tent evangelist; he will draw the lines and seek to have his readers and listeners live anew. Hauerwas leaves it to others to tidy things up and work out problematic details.

Who Is the Intended Audience?

Hauerwas writes for a large number of different audiences. In this volume alone, one finds essays addressed to the "guild" of theological ethics ("On

---

4. In 1997 Hauerwas wrote, "I have always hoped that my work might exhibit Cardinal Suhard's claim: 'To be a witness does not consist in engaging in propaganda nor even in stirring people up, but in being a living mystery. It means to live in such a way that one's life would not make sense if God did not exist'" (STT, 38).

Keeping Theological Ethics Theological," "Reforming Christian Social Ethics," "Vision, Stories, and Character"), essays directed at his own United Methodist Church ("On Being a Church Capable of Addressing a World at War," "Abortion, Theologically Understood"), to Mennonite undergraduates ("Why Truthfulness Requires Forgiveness"), to Catholic laypeople ("Christianity: It's Not a Religion, It's an Adventure"), to health care professionals ("Salvation and Health," "Should Suffering Be Eliminated?"), to his own theological mentor ("Why the 'Sectarian Temptation' is a Misrepresentation"), and to parents of teenagers ("Sex in Public: How Adventurous Christians Are Doing It").

In envisioning *The Hauerwas Reader,* the editors sought to produce a volume that would serve as an entryway into Hauerwas's thought for theologians and particularly for graduate students in ethics and theology. On the other hand, the editors also believe this volume is an appropriate next step for the many who have read Hauerwas's more popular works, such as *Resident Aliens,* and who are intrigued to read further. The editors have also deliberately chosen essays that are particularly accessible to undergraduates and seminarians without much background in theological ethics (e.g., "Christianity: It's Not a Religion, It's an Adventure," "The Interpretation of Scripture," "Abortion, Theologically Understood," "Why Truthfulness Requires Forgiveness," "The Radical Hope in the Annunciation," "A Story-Formed Community").

Finally, *The Hauerwas Reader* is also envisioned as a textbook, recognizing the significance of Hauerwas's work in four particular areas: theological metaethics (e.g., "virtue" or "character," "narrative," the possibility of a common or "natural law" morality), ecclesiology (e.g., discipleship, the methodological significance of the church), social ethics (e.g., church and culture, liberalism, war), and medical ethics (e.g., abortion, euthanasia, suffering, medicine as a "traditioned" practice). After an introductory historical and dogmatic section, *Who Are Christians? The Christian Story,* these four areas roughly correspond to the remaining four sections of *The Hauerwas Reader.*

For instance, in a course on virtue, essays 8, 10, and 11 provide not only Hauerwas's innovative views, but also an opportunity to analyze the evolution of Hauerwas's thinking between 1971 and 1980. By 1987, his views on these questions have evolved still further (see essay 3), with an increased emphasis on concretely displaying practices of particular communities. Of course, according to Hauerwas, the Christian's primary (though not only) community is the church. The church community is to provide in large part the context necessary, not merely for exercising the virtues, but also for shaping (and often redirecting) the very content of the virtues in the light of the telos of that community (see especially essay 14 and essay 19, section 3).[5] Essays 15, 16, and 18 display ways in which specific virtues function in distinctively Christian contexts.

In a course discussing the significance of "narrative ethics," Hauerwas's essays on the necessity of narrative construal of the self (essays 8, 11, and 10) and the Christian community (essays 6 and 7) could be brought together with "A Story-Formed Community: Reflections on *Watership Down*" (essay 9), Hauerwas's most elaborate display of the moral significance of narrative for construing the Christian life. The turn to the significance of narrative for theology in the 1970s and 1980s was not without its critics, and Hauerwas responds to James Gustafson—the most influential theological ethicist of the past generation and Hauerwas's own teacher and doctoral advisor—who sees the emphasis on narrative leading to a "tribalism" and an incorrigibly fideist theology that cannot respond to contemporary challenges (essay 4). On a different level, Hauerwas's rethinking of theological ethics led him to narrate first the history of Protestant Christian ethics in America (essay 2) and then later the development of theological ethics more generally, emphasizing the particular problems that modernity presents for a theological ethics (essay 1).

Hauerwas's philosophical conviction that a coherent moral life is necessarily narrative- and tradition-dependent, coupled with his theological conviction that the church is the community and tradition with which the Christian must foremost identify, requires that the church take center stage in Hauerwas's theological ethics.[6] His most careful attempt to describe the church in the light of these claims is "The Church as God's New Language" (essay 7). His account of the importance of the Church is also encapsulated in "Reforming Christian Social Ethics: Ten Theses" (essay 5) and more fully elaborated in the two central chapters of *The Peaceable Kingdom* (reprinted here as essays 6 and 19). Even Hauerwas's early essays, while placing less emphasis on the lived experience of specific Christian communities, emphatically argue for the narrative- and tradition-dependent character of a community's or society's practice of medicine (essay 30), prohibition of suicide (essay

---

5. In essay 3, Hauerwas notes that perhaps the biggest weakness of his early work on virtue and character is an inadequate emphasis on the telos of the Christian life.

6. Thus Hauerwas begins his programmatic essay on the church as follows: "Christian ethics would be unintelligible if it did not presuppose the existence and recognizability of communities and corresponding institutions capable of carrying the story of God" ("The Servant Community: Christian Social Ethics," essay 19 in this volume).

29), sexual norms (essay 23), practices in war (essays 17 and 10), and ability to live truthfully (essay 10). In Hauerwas's later work, his attention turns more toward showing how specific practices like the reading of Scripture (essay 12) and moral reasoning (essay 13), though often understood as individual practices, actually require appeals to forms of authority which in turn require embodiment in the ongoing tradition of church communities.

In a course on social ethics, an understanding of Hauerwas's approach would have to begin with his programmatic "The Servant Community: Christian Social Ethics" (essay 19) and his (Martin Luther–inspired) "Reforming Christian Social Ethics: Ten Theses" (essay 5). An adequate understanding of the context for these essays would require that they be read in conjunction with "Jesus and the Social Embodiment of the Peaceable Kingdom" (essay 6) and Hauerwas's history of the development of social ethics among American Protestants (essay 2). Hauerwas's understanding of just war and pacifism can be found in essays originally written in the 1980s in response to pastoral letters on the threat of nuclear war by the U.S. Catholic Bishops (essay 20) and the United Methodist Bishops (essay 21). Hauerwas's understanding of the problems that contemporary liberal democratic social orders present for the Christian is presented most explicitly in "A Christian Critique of Christian America" (essay 22). However, because habits of thought produced by political liberalism in the West hold an extraordinarily powerful grip over Western Christians, and because these habits of thought undermine the kinds of disciplined practices necessary to sustain Christian (and other) communities in a multitude of ways, Hauerwas eagerly confronts the problematic assumptions of liberalism in many if not most of his essays. Hauerwas engages the assumptions of political liberalism in essays on Jewish reflections on the Holocaust (essay 17), on the future of the family (essay 24), on the mentally handicapped (essay 28), on Christian sexual ethics (essay 23), on the practice of medicine (essays 27 and 30), on abortion (essays 26 and 31), on discrimination over sexual orientation (essay 25), and on the formation of character (essay 11). Similarly, Hauerwas's description of the virtues needed for contemporary Christian communities to faithfully thrive assumes that one element of such virtues is the ability to resist the moral habits that follow from the assumptions of political liberalism (e.g., essays 14, 15, 25, 26, 27, and 31).

Finally, in a course on medical ethics, Hauerwas's distinctive approach can be seen in the ways he challenges many of the reigning assumptions about questions of euthanasia (essay 29) and abortion (essay 31), as well as the supposed imperative to "eliminate suffering" (essay 28) and how to protect the dignity of the human person (essay 30). Hauerwas's treatment of various specific questions in medical ethics are interpreted in more programmatic fashion in "Salvation and Health: Why Medicine Needs the Church" (essay 27). For further explication of the claims about the church and the narrative construal of medicine presented there, the reader should refer back to the more general discussions of ecclesiology and narrative, suggestions for which are made above. Readers interested in elements of Hauerwas's vision of medicine Christianly conceived and practiced—both by practitioners of the medical art and the recipients of medical care—will want to read his discussions of the virtues of patience (essay 18), courage (essay 14), and peaceableness (essay 15), and his analysis of the place of the case method (i.e., casuistry) of moral decision making in medical ethics. To see the evolution in Hauerwas's general framework for discussing a question like physician-assisted suicide and euthanasia, compare his 1976 "Memory, Community, and the Reasons for Living" (essay 29) with his 1997 "Practicing Patience: How Christians Should Be Sick" (essay 18).

In a course on contemporary debates in theological ethics, Hauerwas's groundbreaking historical analyses of the field (essays 1 and 2), his engagements with Walter Rauschenbusch and the Niebuhr brothers (essay 2), Paul Ramsey (essays 21 and 30), James Gustafson (essay 4), Hans Frei (essay 7), Lawrence Kohlberg (essay 11), Gilbert Meilaender (essay 3), Rosemary Ruether, Eliezer Berkovits, and Michael Wyschograd (essay 17), David Hollenbach (essay 21), Richard John Neuhaus, Max Stackhouse, and Michael Novak (essay 22), Albert Jonsen and Stephen Toulmin (essay 13), and even a report commissioned by the Catholic Theological Society of America (essay 25)—all are key to understanding the current landscape in the discipline.

Having chosen to focus *The Hauerwas Reader* in the areas mentioned above, the editors are painfully aware that much had to be left out. For instance, there is nothing on Hauerwas's views on Christian education, and education and the university more generally.[7] There is little directly on friend-

---

7. See, for example, "How Christian Universities contribute to the Corruption of Youth" (1986) in CET; "The Politics of Witness: How We Educate Christians in Liberal Societies" (1991) in AC; "A Non-Violent Proposal for Christian Participation in the Culture Wars," *Soundings* 75, no. 4 (winter 1992): 477–92; "For Dappled Things" (1996) in STT. "Christians in the Hands of Flaccid Secularists: Theology and 'Moral Enquiry' in the Modern University" (1998) in STT; "Christian Schooling *or* Making Students Dysfunctional" (1998) in STT.

ship.[8] There is very little directly on the importance for Hauerwas of John Wesley and sanctification.[9] There is nothing indicating Hauerwas's views on questions surrounding reproductive technology or capital punishment,[10] and little that recognizes the remarkable emphasis in his writings on the mentally handicapped.[11] There is nothing on issues of race, gender, or the environment.[12] We have not included essays that make most explicit his deep debt to John Howard Yoder and to Alasdair MacIntyre.[13] Finally, we do not provide any of Hauerwas's analyses of postmodernity.[14] For more on these and other topics, see the annotated bibliography at the end of *The Hauerwas Reader*.

8. See, for example, "The Testament of Friends: How My Mind Has Changed," in *The Christian Century* 107, no. 7 (28 February 1990): 212–16; "Companions on the Way: The Necessity of Friendship" (1997) in *CAV*; "Gay Friendship: A Thought Experiment in Catholic Moral Theology" (1996) in *STT*; "Timeful Friends: Living with the Handicapped" (1998) in *STT*.

9. See, for example, "Sanctification and the Ethics of Character" (1975) in *CCL*; "Characterizing Perfection: Second Thoughts on Character and Sanctification" (1985) in *STT*.

10. See, for example, "Capital Punishment" (1996) in *The Dictionary of Theology and Society*, ed. Paul Clarke and Andrew Linzey (London: Routledge, 1996); "Capital Punishment: It's a Rite of Vengeance," *Notre Dame Magazine* 8, no. 4 (October 1979): 67–68; "Theological Reflections on in Vitro Fertilization," in *Report of Ethics Advisory Board of Department of Health, Education and Welfare* (Washington, D.C.: Government Printing Office, 1979), 5/1–20.

11. Hauerwas has authored over a dozen articles focused primarily on the mentally handicapped, and they have appeared in *VV* (1974), *TT* (1977), *SP* (1986), *DF* (1994), and *STT* (1998).

12. See, for example, "Ethics of Black Power," *Augustana Observer* 67, no. 14 (5 February 1969); "Remembering Martin Luther King Jr. Remembering" (1995) in *WW*; "Failure in Communication *or* A Case of Uncomprehending Feminism: A Response to Gloria Albrecht," *Scottish Journal of Theology* 50, no. 2 (1997): 228–39; "A Trinitarian Theology of the Chief End of All Flesh" (1992) in *IGC*; "Creation as Apocalyptic: A Tribute to William Stringfellow" (1995) in *DF*.

13. With regard to Yoder, see for example, "The Nonresistant Church: The Theological Ethics of John Howard Yoder" (1971) in *VV*; "Messianic Pacifism," Worldview 16, no. 6 (June 1973): 29–33; "Casuistry as a Narrative Art" (1983) in *PK*; "Can a Pacifist Think about War?" (1994) in *DF*; "When *The Politics of Jesus* Makes a Difference," *The Christian Century* 110, no. 28 (22 October 1993): 982–87. With regard to MacIntyre, see "Medicine as a Tragic Profession" (1977) in *TT*; "Review of Alasdair MacIntyre's *After Virtue*," *The Thomist* 46, no. 2 (April 1982): 313–21; "Authority and the Profession of Medicine" (1982) in *SP*; "The Renewal of Virtue and the Peace of Christ" (1997) in *CAV*; "The Non-Violent Terrorist: In Defense of Christian Fanaticism" (1998) in *STT*. Of course, the influence of Yoder and MacIntyre is apparent simply by referring to the index of *The Hauerwas Reader*.

14. See, for example, "Creation, Contingency, and Truthful Nonviolence: A Milbankian Reflection" (1997) in *WW*; "No Enemy, No Christianity: Preaching between 'Worlds'" (1998) in *STT*; "The Christian Difference, Or: Surviving Postmodernism" (1999) in *BH*.

Criteria for Inclusion of Essays in The Hauerwas Reader

With well over three hundred and fifty essays to choose from, written in a variety of styles and over a thirty-year period, the editors came up with a number of criteria for inclusion of essays in the volume. First of all, we sought to include a generous selection of essays in the four key areas mentioned above. Second, we avoided drawing more than three essays from any one of Hauerwas's books, both to provide a representative sampling and to respect the integrity of each of the already published books. We were committed to including some of Hauerwas's most famous and widely used essays (e.g., "On Keeping Theological Ethics Theological," "Jesus and the Social Embodiment of the Peaceable Kingdom," "A Story-Formed Community," "Self-Deception and Autobiography," "The Servant Community: Christian Social Ethics," and "Sex in Public," and also some that have never been published in any of Hauerwas's books (e.g., "On Being a Church Capable of Addressing a World at War," "Christianity: It's Not a Religion, It's an Adventure," "Abortion, Theologically Understood," and "The Radical Hope of the Annunciation: Why Both Single and Married Christians Welcome Children." Finally, it was decided not to include excerpts from *Resident Aliens,* as it already has a wide circulation and because the size of this volume allows the issues raised in that irrepressible volume to be taken up in a more leisurely and scholarly fashion.

Deciding what to include in *The Hauerwas Reader* also required finding a suitable structure for the essays as a whole. Given the unsystematic (even antisystematic) nature of Hauerwas's work, this was perhaps the most difficult and least satisfactory task engaged in by the editors. A large number of structures were proposed and debated at length. In the end, the editors decided to divide the volume into two main parts, which are further divided into thematic sections. Following the editorial introductions, part 2 has been entitled "Reframing Theological Ethics" to indicate that the distinctiveness of Hauerwas's way of doing theological ethics lies not so much in any novel solutions, but rather in the way he reorganizes and reframes what are to be understood as the significant questions for doing theological ethics.

One particular way Hauerwas reframes the issues in theological ethics is by the way he narrates particular elements of Christian history or of "the Christian story": the history of moral theology (essay 1), of Christian ethics in America (essay 2), and the significance of Jesus (essay 6) and the church (essay 7) for theological ethics. In this first section Hauerwas also narrates part of the story of his own development (essay 3) and of his theological disagreement with his mentor (essay 4). Finally, Hauerwas here stakes out his way of "reframing" Christian social ethics (essay 5).

In the second section of part 2, Hauerwas reframes the nature of Christian discipleship. Hauerwas provides his most extended argument for the centrality of narrative in theological ethics (essay 9), and shows the ever-present dangers of self-deception with regard to narrating our lives and the corresponding primacy of truthful narratives (essay 10). Hauerwas seeks to show that adequate understandings of the self must incorporate the importance of vision and character (essays 8 and 11), and show the importance of the tradition of the church for both faithfully interpreting the Christian Scriptures (essay 12) and evaluating moral problems (essay 13).

In the last section of part 2, Hauerwas seeks to display how training in particular virtues shapes and changes Christian disciples. Hauerwas begins by showing the uniqueness of the distinctively Christian conception of courage (essay 14); next he shows how Christian commitments to truthfulness cannot be sustained without accepting and offering forgiveness (essay 15); in another essay a commitment to peacemaking is seen not merely as one element of Christian life, but as central to all Christian life and worship (essay 16). In the fourth essay of this section, Hauerwas shows how the skill of "remembering well" sustains the ongoing life of the church (essay 17). In the final essay of this section the virtue of patience is shown to be essential for maintaining trust in God's providential care of his people (essay 18).

The various forms of "reframing" that go on in Hauerwas's work—particularly with regard to the relationship among authority, tradition, and the community of the church—create a host of "New Intersections in Theological Ethics," and part 3 of *The Hauerwas Reader* presents thirteen examples of such new intersections. The essays in these two sections are most accurately understood not as "applied ethics," but as examples of what might be involved in Christian disciples-in-community taking seriously the very practices through which they embody the hospitality of the church as servant community in the world.

We have grouped these new intersections in theological ethics into two sections. In "The Church's Witness: Christian Ethics after 'Public Theology,' " Hauerwas teases out some of the implications of doing Christian social ethics when one is seeking to resist many of the underlying moral assumptions of liberal democratic nation-states. This section begins with Hauerwas's programmatic understanding of the social role of the church (essay 19), follows with his examinations of war in relation to recent Catholic (essay 20) and Protestant (essay 21) thought, critiques accounts of the role of religion in liberal democracies (essay 22), and seeks to clarify the place of the family, the having of children, and sexuality in capitalist societies (essays 23 and 24). In the two final essays in this section (essays 25 and 26), Hauerwas's critique of an accommodationist church take two very different forms. One is a newspaper editorial evaluating the "gays in the military" debate of 1993; the other is an interview with a popular Catholic periodical in the wake of the Persian Gulf War of 1991.

The second section of part 3, "The Church's Hospitality: Christian Ethics after 'Medical Ethics,'" casts questions of the practice of medicine in relation to the purpose of life in theological perspective. The section begins with Hauerwas's programmatic statement on the significance of the church community for sustaining the ethos of medicine (essay 27), then shows how theological convictions (or the rejection of them) shape the very understanding of medicine's purposes (essay 28), and argues that much of medical ethics maintains (at least explicitly) an impoverished understanding of the self (essay 30). Finally, Hauerwas seeks to show how theological convictions should shape the unavoidably ethical descriptions Christians employ, and in so doing transform the way Christians see and respond to issues such as suicide and euthanasia (essay 29), the mentally handicapped (essay 28), and abortion (essay 31). In all of these essays, Hauerwas's goal is for Christians to see the questions of "medical ethics" in relation to central practices of the church, such as eucharist and baptism. Not surprisingly, Hauerwas has come to be regarded as one of the most significant "theological voices in medical ethics."[15]

How The Hauerwas Reader *Came to Be*

In 1997, the editors mailed a survey to about two hundred theologians and philosophers around the world familiar with Hauerwas's work, asking them what they thought should go into this volume. We received concrete suggestions from about sixty respondents, which were tabulated and critically evaluated. From that survey and analysis came a first draft of essays for inclusion in the reader. A year later we sent out a second survey, sending the proposed list of essays for the volume and soliciting suggestions of additional essays that

15. See Stephen Lammers, "On Stanley Hauerwas: Theology, Medical Ethics and the Church," in *Theological Voices in Medical Ethics* (Grand Rapids, MI: Eerdmans, 1993), 57–77.

ought to go in, and, if essays were added, what should be deleted. Again, we received about twenty-five responses with concrete suggestions and made some changes accordingly.

With our selection in hand, we sought publishers who would be interested in a volume large enough to adequately cover the key subject areas discussed above. In addition, we sought a publisher who would publish the book at a price that would enable wide distribution, inexpensive enough that graduate students would not hesitate to buy it and cost-conscious professors could justify requiring it for their courses.

The Editing Task

In deciding what essays to include in *The Hauerwas Reader,* many difficult choices had to be made. We were eager to include as much of Hauerwas's work as possible. Recognizing that Hauerwas does not always write in, say, as concise a form as possible, the editors chose to abridge some of the essays to allow the inclusion of a greater number of essays. This choice was made easier by the fact that Hauerwas's creativity often takes him in a number of different directions in an essay, and at times it takes him on what are digressions from his main point. Although many of these apparent tangents turn out to be making crucial but previously unseen connections, it remained the case that some of Hauerwas's essays could, without grievous loss, be streamlined. For instance, some essays contained an extraordinarily large number of extended footnotes; others contained illustrations that were then timely but are now dated or obscure. The editors believe they have not altered the substance, style, or tone of any of the essays in their work of editing, and will be grateful for any feedback from readers who think our editing work has invaded the integrity of earlier versions of the essays.

In a review of one of Hauerwas's early books, Paul Ramsey noted that Hauerwas was a very significant young theological ethicist, but that he needed to work on his "writing style." Hauerwas readily granted this criticism, but found it rather amusing coming from Paul "Never-waste-a-word" Ramsey, and this continued as somewhat of a standing joke between the two of them. One theologian has remarked that Hauerwas is one of those rare writers who is an excellent stylist while not being a terribly good writer. In examining a number of the pre-1986 essays, the editors determined that some editing for clarity was called for. This will be particularly noticeable in, for example, "On Keeping Theological Ethics Theological," "Jesus and the Social Embodiment of the Peaceable Kingdom," "Vision, Stories, and Character," and "The Servant Community: Christian Social Ethics." The essays have not been edited for content (i.e., the editors have not attempted to "update" any of the essays to bring them into line with Hauerwas's current views), but to clarify the occasional obscurity and ambiguity. All changes have been approved by Hauerwas.

Features and Tools

In addition to the thirty-one Hauerwas essays in the volume, there are a number of other features designed to assist readers. First, each essay is prefaced by a background and summary composed for this volume by the editors, providing the historical context and/or a brief statement of the main point(s) of each essay. Second, at the end of each essay a number of additional Hauerwas essays are listed under "Further Reading." These have been selected by the editors as essays that are complementary and pursue further one or more of the key themes of that essay. The essays are listed in (roughly) descending order of perceived significance in relation to the essay just read. Some of the "Further Reading" essays are also in *The Hauerwas Reader;* most of the others are briefly described in the annotated bibliography. Third, there are editorial footnotes scattered through the volume that provide additional context for what may now seem an obscure example, reveal implicit conversation partners, update bibliographical data, and so forth.

Fourth, the editors are extremely pleased that Professor William Cavanaugh of the University of St. Thomas in St. Paul, Minnesota, has authored "Stan the Man: A Thoroughly Biased Account of a Completely Unobjective Person" especially for *The Hauerwas Reader.* Cavanaugh's essay may be understood as an intellectual biography of—or, perhaps more accurately, as highbrow gossip about—Stanley Hauerwas. Everyone who knows Hauerwas knows that his work cannot be neatly separated from his person, and we believe that Professor Cavanaugh has succeeded marvellously in conveying why this is the universally shared view of Hauerwas.

Fifth, the thirty-one selections from the writings of Stanley Hauerwas are followed by coeditor Michael Cartwright's "Stanley Hauerwas's Essays in Theological Ethics: A Reader's Guide." Cartwright's guide furthers the goals of *The Hauerwas Reader* in three fundamental ways. First, he provides a compelling reading of Hauerwas from one who knows his work extremely well. Second, Cartwright outlines a number of additional angles and perspectives from which one can approach Hauerwas's work to get a sense of Hauerwas's larger project. Third, he introduces readers to a number of significant Hauerwas essays that could not be included in the *Reader.*

Sixth, John Berkman and James Fodor, with help from Michael Cartwright and Scott Bader-Saye, have composed an annotated bibliography. This bibliography is by no means exhaustive, seeking rather to provide a brief annotation regarding the main subject, argument, and particular significance of an additional one hundred or so essays by Hauerwas.[16] Our hope is that this will assist those who wish to find Hauerwas's views on a particular subject or theme. Because the subject matter or themes being taken up by Hauerwas in a particular essay often cannot be readily ascertained from its title, the editors hope that this bibliography will be of significant service. Finally, the volume also contains comprehensive Scripture, name, and subject indexes, uncommon in a Hauerwas book.

Finally, a word about abbreviations and dates used in *The Hauerwas Reader*. A list of abbreviations of all of Hauerwas's books referred to in this volume can be found immediately following the table of contents. Title pages and bibliographic entries have been assigned a date. This date represents in almost all cases the year of the essay's first publication. Most of Hauerwas's essays were first published in academic journals or in edited volumes of collected essays. These essays were then published in various of Hauerwas's books. Thus, for example, while we note that "Self-Deception and Autobiography" can be found in Hauerwas's 1977 book *Truthfulness and Tragedy* (i.e., *TT*), we put the date of 1974 next to the essay title because that was when the essay first appeared in the *Journal of Religious Ethics*.

The editors hope that this collection of Hauerwas's essays and the various and sundry scholarly tools will serve to elevate the debate as to the significance of the work of Stanley Hauerwas. Ideally, it will contribute to clearer and more thoughtful evaluations of his contribution, both to the church and to the academy. Hauerwas has undoubtedly charted much new territory. We look to some to trace his steps more carefully and precisely; to others to explore a direction in which Hauerwas has merely pointed; and finally, to others to articulate why Hauerwas's route is not to be followed. May these debates be of service to the pilgrim people of God.

---

16. The most comprehensive—though not exhaustive—bibliography of Stanley Hauerwas's published writings can be found in Samuel Wells, *Transforming Fate into Destiny: The Theological Ethics of Stanley Hauerwas* (London: Paternoster, 1998), 181–98.

Stan the Man: A Thoroughly Biased Account of a Completely Unobjective Person

William Cavanaugh

Anthologies of an academic's work do not usually include a characterization of the author as a person. Such is normally reserved for a given professor's Festschrift, when his or her former students produce a résumé-padding collection of their own essays, prefaced by some brief unctuous flattery of the beloved old gasbag. The assumption seems to be that academics' character and personality have little to do with the work they produce and need appear only in more "personal" tributes. If Stanley Hauerwas is correct, however, in saying that the only interesting arguments are ad hominem, then it is crucial to understand who Stanley *is* in order to understand what Stanley *thinks.* If ethics is not just about rules and choices but rather about the narrative-based formation of persons over time, then the story of Stanley Hauerwas will be an aid to cultivating the kind of moral vision that his work has developed. Put another way, to grasp what Stanley says, it is important to hear it in the accent in which it is said.

The accent, of course, is legendary. Many attempt it—his listeners commonly feel compelled to pass on his bons mots in a facsimile of his distinctive Texas twang—but such impersonations always fall short. For all his critiques of liberal individualism, Stanley Hauerwas is a unique and unrepeatable individual. For all his emphasis on community, Hauerwas blends into a crowd like a bull blends into a china shop. He is, in the fullest sense of the word, a *character,* and his personality illustrates one of the central paradoxes of tradition-based community; the more deeply one has been formed by a good community, the freer one is to be oneself. Conversely, one of the ironies of modern individualism is its tendency to produce uniformity, a trap from which we struggle to free ourselves through consumption of arbitrarily differentiated products, as in our pathetic trying to "have it your way" at Burger King. The genius of Stanley Hauerwas, in contrast, is manifested not in innovation but in putting himself under the authority of well-worn traditions and communities of ordinary folk. Hauerwas is famed for his brilliant insights, but his oft-repeated claim that "To have an original idea only means you forgot where you read it" is not merely a disingenuous attempt at modesty. Stanley does not waste time on modesty. He is too absorbed in the telos of his theological work to worry much about either modesty or its opposite. Hauerwas is a gregarious scholar who knows that his work achieves the depth it does only through sustained attention to the stories, friendships, insights, and criticisms of *others*. At his best, Stanley embodies Kierkegaard's dictum "The really 'exceptional' man is the truly ordinary man."

The Story of Stanley

The dirt of which Stanley Hauerwas is made is the black gumbo of north Texas. He did not know it at the time, but the town of Pleasant Grove, where he was born and raised, was poor. According to Stanley, he first realized his family was poor when he went to college. Back home he slept in the living room of a three-room house. Much of the yard was given over to the patch of black-eyed peas and okra that Stanley tended to help support the family. From his ninth year on, he worked summers with his father, Coffee Hauerwas, a bricklayer and a gentle man. Long before he laid eyes on the *Nicomachean Ethics*, the Aristotelian theme of formation as a craft through apprenticeship to a master was hammered into his soul on the job at his father's side. It was also here that, driven by fear of the appearance of nepotism, Stanley began to develop his legendary work habits. In his adult years Stanley has remarked, "I don't know where I'd be without the Protestant work ethic. I'm not any smarter than other people. I just outwork 'em." Books have replaced bricks, but Hauerwas has not ceased to see his work as a hardhat zone.

The life of the Hauerwas family revolved around Pleasant Mound United Methodist Church, whose roof was held up in part by Coffee Hauerwas's bricks. Pleasant Mound was not exceptional in its theology and practice. What the congregation there might make of Stanley's later writings on virtue and community is hard to say, though one can imagine that in that venue Hauerwas would not give Billy Graham a run for his money. Nonetheless it was at Pleasant Mound that Hauerwas first learned to identify community as that group of people with a *claim* on him, and thus realize that one's life is not entirely, or even primarily, one's own. Being formed in the Christian virtues is not a matter of choosing the right community, but rather acknowledging the fact that Christ is revealed in those with whom we have the great good fortune to be stuck.

At Pleasant Mound baptisms and confirmations were done and the Lord's Supper (infrequently) celebrated, but according to Stanley everyone knew that these had nothing to do with being a Christian. The real deal was getting saved on Sunday nights. The congregation would gather, sing hymns for hours, and wait to wear down the Spirit's patience. Stanley longed to join those declaring their salvation before the whole congregation, but was disappointed week after week. Finally, as Stanley describes it, he made a move to force God's hand. One sweaty Sunday night at age fifteen, Stanley joined those dedicating their lives to the ministry, figuring that if he were a minister, God would have to save him. This negotiation with the Spirit never resulted in his being ordained, but it set him on the path to academics and nearly killed his fledgling faith in the process.

Because of his dedication to the ministry, Hauerwas began to read. It was not a habit he had picked up at home, where the only books were a Bible and a set of Mark Twain. But he put himself under the tutelage of the associate pastor of Pleasant Mound and started to read on religion, mostly prim Protestant primers on the Christian life. In his senior year in high school, however, Stanley came across a book by one B. David Napier called *From Faith to Faith,* wherein he learned that the Bible was not true. In quick succession Stanley read *The Sun and the Umbrella* by Nels Ferré, a Swedish Barthian who argued that religion does more to hide God than reveal God. So he gave it up.

Losing one's religion was technically not allowed at Southwestern University in Georgetown, Texas, but mandatory chapel did nothing to save Stanley's faith. Rather, it was his encounter with a wonderfully cynical evangelical Methodist named John Score, who taught religion and philosophy, that would put him back on the road to the church, a road that in any case would do a lot of meandering. Score took Hauerwas through a four-semester course on the history of philosophy, and took him to see films and art exhibits in Dallas, opening up to Stanley a kind of culture that he had never seen before. It was Score as mentor who developed in Hauerwas a thirst for learning that has yet to be slaked. After graduation, Hauerwas went to Yale Divinity School, not entirely convinced that he was a Christian but convinced he needed to know more before he deserved an opinion on the subject.

Although he came from a different world than most Yalies, Hauerwas excelled by outworking 'em. He threw himself into his coursework and began to cobble together his distinctive vision out of various theological influences that were often at cross-purposes with one another. Stanley read Barth and, in Stanley's own words, was stunned to discover that Barth had stood against the

Nazis while the liberals had "given up the Jews" in Europe. Yet at the same time, the liberal Protestants he read had a great influence on Hauerwas's ideas on narrative, because they at least were still telling the story of Jesus, not just talking about Incarnation in the abstract. Hauerwas, along with almost everyone at Yale, assumed Reinhold Niebuhr's Christian realism was right, but he could not square Niebuhr with Barth's Christological emphasis. At the same time, Hauerwas was putting Wesley and Wittgenstein together, convinced that theology must be a practical discourse. Both Wesley and Wittgenstein were in the back of his mind when he read Aquinas's *Summa Theologica* from start to finish and realized that sanctification comes through activity, not mere experience. It would take years to untangle this unruly brawl of thinkers, but in so doing Hauerwas would produce some extraordinarily creative work.

I could attempt to trace the influence of various figures and books on Hauerwas's thought, but a more interesting question presses: What has New Haven to do with Pleasant Grove? Lest Stanley's life story be read as a Horatio Alger tale of poor-boy-makes-good, it is crucial to see that Pleasant Grove continued to haunt every conceptual move made by Hauerwas as his thought developed. Hauerwas went to Yale with the intention of studying systematic theology, sparked by a youthful quest for an overriding rational verification of Christian claims. As he learned from Julian Hartt, Wittgenstein, and others, however, the truth or falsity of theological claims is made manifest only in being lived out. It is for this reason that Hauerwas began to attend to the concrete practices of ordinary Christian lives, the way such lives are constituted by the narratives in which they are embedded, the virtues necessary to sustain character over time, and the communities capable of instilling these virtues. Though he may have gone to Yale to determine if Christianity were true, he discovered at Yale that Christianity is in fact verified or falsified in places like Pleasant Grove. And so Hauerwas began to attend to his own narrative as a theological resource, not in service to a debased kind of "identity politics," but as a practice that both resists the storylessness of Enlightenment rationality and simultaneously provides the basis for repentance from sin.

Hauerwas tells a painful story of visiting home during his Yale years (see *HR*, 245–47). His father had been building a deer rifle for Stanley during the off season, meticulously carving the stock and boring the barrel. It was beautifully made, as only a craftsman could do. When he presented it to Stanley, the son admired the craftsmanship, but proceeded to pronounce that in the future a wise social policy would mean that "someday we are going to have to take these goddamned things away from you people." From the standpoint of a universal and objective morality, Stanley believed his statement was both truthful and correct, but it was his realization that he had not done the right thing that led him to suspect the distortions involved in any supposedly universal morality. For it was not that he had failed to grasp some moral principle. His failure to respond appropriately to his father's loving gift was rather a sign that he had not yet developed the character necessary to acknowledge his debt to his parents. To do so he would need to learn to refuse to narrate his move from Pleasant Grove to Yale as a move from the particular to the universal.

Ph.D.s are often designed to educate people out of their particular commitments, to give them the illusion of universality, which is then used coercively to discount those who occupy "merely limited" and particular stories. The Yale school has been notorious for doing theology by typology (e.g., H. Richard Niebuhr's *Christ and Culture*), imagining that the academic's task is complete once he or she has located every position in its proper category. Hauerwas has contrarily claimed that being a Texan means to have an identity sufficiently particular to resist such universalization. Being from Pleasant Grove is therefore essential to his Christian formation, because it has given him the skills and virtues necessary to belong to a people set apart.

Hauerwas would have to use every one of those skills when he encountered John Howard Yoder. When Hauerwas began teaching at Notre Dame in 1970, he was still convinced that Reinhold Niebuhr's approach to Christian engagement with the political was right, needing just a little more Christology to buttress where it sagged. Then one day, a few months after arriving at Notre Dame, Hauerwas picked up some pamphlets on Barth and Niebuhr at the back of a church in Goshen, Indiana. The author was a Mennonite theologian named John Howard Yoder; the price was a quarter apiece. At Yale Hauerwas had read Yoder's pamphlet on Barth and thought, "This is the best critique of Barth I've read, but you'd have to be crazy to buy into this ecclesiology." Now, however, Hauerwas could no longer dismiss what he was reading, for he realized that something like Yoder's ecclesiology was necessary to make intelligible the Christological moves to which Hauerwas had been trying to arrive. Furthermore, this ecclesiology was unintelligible without a strong account of the nonviolence of Jesus.

And so Stanley Hauerwas began to stammer that he was a pacifist. As he says in the introduction to his book *The Peaceable Kingdom*, pacifism was a bitter pill to swallow, both because he wanted to do theology in a way that was broadly influential, and because he was not, by disposition, inclined to nonviolence. Indeed, of all the great Christian pacifists over the centuries—

Hippolytus, Francis of Assisi, Martin Luther King—Stanley Hauerwas is the one I would want on my side in a bar fight. Hauerwas is inclined by disposition to seek the margins of any group, but in part this stems from his unwillingness to step back from conflict. As a result, this ornery man's claim to be a pacifist serves two purposes. In the first place, it demonstrates that Jesus' nonviolence does not preclude, but rather requires, conflict with the principalities and powers that maintain the appearance of order through the threat of violence. In the second place, Stanley's public claim of pacifism illustrates the communal nature of virtue in the Christian community, for Stanley cannot claim peaceableness as his own native endowment. We make public commitments not to claim our own accomplishments and virtues, but to alert others to our commitments so that they can hold us to them. On our own there are few of us who can claim to have exorcised the violence within. It is therefore necessary to have a community of people committed to creating peace in order to keep each other faithful. Stanley Hauerwas declares aloud that he is a pacifist so that others will keep him from killing somebody.

Who exactly those others are has not always been easy to say. Not only do Protestant and Catholic influences cross-pollinate in Hauerwas's thought, but also his church affiliations have been many and transient. In New Haven a United Methodist church was his home for two years, followed by a period of no church at all. During his first teaching job, a brief stint at Augustana College in Illinois, he worshiped at a high Lutheran liturgy, but started going to Catholic Mass in a dorm when he moved to Notre Dame. After several years at Sacred Heart parish on the Notre Dame campus, Hauerwas began to take instruction in the Catholic faith, but his wife Ann's objections put an end to thoughts of becoming Catholic. Following a year at St. Augustine's, a largely African American Catholic congregation, Stanley and his son Adam finally ended up at Broadway United Methodist Church in South Bend.

What are we to make of this promiscuous pew-hopping, given Stanley's emphasis on constancy and constitutive community? On one level, we might recognize some incongruities between thought and practice; Stanley is fond of Oscar Wilde's contention that we are never more true to ourselves than when we are inconsistent. On a deeper level, however, I think that Stanley, like the proverbial Italian soldier, spent many years looking for someone to whom he could surrender. He developed strong ties to Broadway Methodist precisely because the pastor, John Smith, took his ministry seriously enough to boss Stanley around. When Hauerwas expressed his desire to join Broadway Methodist, Smith asked about his membership status in the Methodist Church.

Stanley told Smith that he had been ordained a deacon years ago, but wasn't sure what had happened to his membership in the meantime. Without blinking, Smith told the famous theologian that he wasn't much of a churchman, and he would have to attend classes at the church for a year. So he did. When Hauerwas left Notre Dame for Duke in 1984, his main reservation was leaving Broadway Methodist. He put his decision to stay or leave in the hands of the congregation, who prayed about it, discussed it, and finally told him, "You can go, but you have to teach them what you learned here." What Hauerwas continues to teach is that the church must take seriously the authority given it by the Holy Spirit if it is to save people from the tyranny of their own individual wills. It is a lesson Stanley continues to learn at Aldersgate United Methodist Church in Chapel Hill.

Hauerwas talks about Catholics like Jane Goodall talks about chimpanzees: he spent many years among them as an outsider, came to appreciate their strange practices and rituals, and grew to love them so much that he almost, but not quite, felt like one of them. It was during his fourteen years at Notre Dame that the set of practices called "church" became an important part of Hauerwas's vocabulary. Hauerwas became fascinated by a group of people who appeared to be so constituted by their communal practices that their understanding of God was ritually bound up with their relationships to one another. He relished the challenge to his Pietist upbringing posed by a sacramental sensibility that focused on the objective presence of God instead of the subjective holiness of the individual worshiper. This sensibility is manifested by what we used to call the "Catholic slob ethic": Catholics don't dress up for church because they figure God has to show up in the Eucharist no matter what they wear. During his Notre Dame years, Stanley imbibed the Catholic centrality of the Eucharist and became a weekly communicant. Ironically, however, he remained Protestant enough that, when refused the Eucharist by a priest because he was not Catholic, he simply got in another line.

Ultimately, Hauerwas left Notre Dame when a new chair of the theology department was brought in with a mandate from the university administration to make the department more denominationally Catholic. This move signaled the exit of Hauerwas and several other non-Catholic scholars, one of whom has since converted to Catholicism. Despite the acrimonious way in which some non-Catholics were made unwelcome, Hauerwas might have had a certain sympathy with the concern that the department at Notre Dame be in service to the Catholic Church. From Hauerwas's point of view, however, the move was incoherent because it construed "Catholic" in a liberal-Protestant way as a *denomination* that would take its place comfortably beside the other mainstream denominations whose purpose was to serve and edify the wider American culture that embraced them all. The irony is that Stanley was eased out of Notre Dame for being a "sectarian," when he thought that he had been contributing to a broader and more Catholic vision of truth. His claim that he did not know he was a Protestant until he was told so by the new department chair does, nevertheless, beg some questions about his ecclesial identity.

Hauerwas's move to a Methodist environment at Duke has not resolved the basic ecclesial ambiguity that runs like a geological fault line through his thought. Stanley Hauerwas remains deeply and creatively conflicted about his ecclesial identity: "I don't believe in Methodism, obviously. And yet I believe in my wife Paula's priesthood, and she's a Methodist, so I can't say I don't believe in Methodism."[1] Hauerwas's emphases on community, virtue, authority, and sacrament have marked him as a Catholic thinker and have brought many Catholic graduate students to him, in addition to several students who have converted to Catholicism under his influence. And yet Hauerwas claims that he cannot become Catholic as long as the Catholic Church will not recognize Paula's priesthood, which he says he has seen with his own eyes. Confounding the issue is the fact that Stanley's position would make Paula the only Methodist priest. Methodists do not believe in the ministerial priesthood; Stanley does.

Mennonite theologian Gerald Schlabach has recently said that Hauerwas's project is to call Catholics and Protestants to be more Anabaptist, and to call Anabaptists and Protestants to be more Catholic. The fact that he is not calling anyone to be more Protestant does not mean that he is not still the bearer of a Protestant soul. Protestant hymnody in particular has a special hold on Stanley. He causes the greatest consternation among his own Methodist brethren precisely as a rebellious son causes the most grief within his own family. The very fact of his ecclesial eclecticism shows that the Pietist habits of his youth are still with him; only a Protestant could move in and out of various churches—including the Catholic—with such ease. Nor is he without theological reasons for remaining in the Methodist fold. Hauerwas may not believe in Protestantism as such, but he remains Protestant as long as Protestant churches are necessary to remind the Catholic Church that it is not yet what it is called to be.

1. [For more explication of Hauerwas's self-understanding as a United Methodist, see pp. 665–70.]

Stan the Man

After years of academic work, the bricklayer's son from Pleasant Grove, Texas, is still evident to the naked eye. Stanley will answer a knock at his office door with the look of a busy workingman who has had to come down off some scaffolding to let you in. Lean and taut, Stanley is drawn to his work with an astonishing level of energy. He reads hungrily and omnivorously; all his graduate students know the frustration of recommending a new discovery to Stanley, inevitably to be told that he has already read it. For an alleged "sectarian," Stanley reads across an astounding variety of disciplines and is far better versed in the latest offerings of secular political science, literary criticism, social theory, and so on, than most of his supposedly more "world-affirming" critics. Stanley has the remarkable ability to sum up and critique the thesis of virtually any book he has ever read in two or three sentences (Oliver O'Donovan's *Resurrection and the Moral Order:* "Too much moral order, not enough resurrection"). Hauerwas reads with depth as well. Can anyone else claim to have read all of Trollope's forty-odd novels—that's Anthony Trollope, the very Victorian English novelist who used to discharge a quota of 10,000 words every morning before going to work as a *clerk* in a *post office*—and then to have read most of them *again*? The fact that I and most sane people would consider this particular feat a numbing exercise of senseless moil does not detract from the point that Stanley will read almost anything with a fascinated delight. Intellectual work is a labor of deep love for Hauerwas.

A friend and former student of Hauerwas tells of dropping a 110-page chapter of his dissertation at Stanley's office at 11:30 on a Saturday night, only to find it in his box, with extensive comments, at 12:30 Sunday afternoon. In the meantime, Stanley had also read and reviewed a book by Richard Neuhaus, gone to church, and, presumably, slept. Another of Stanley's students, upset at the process of preliminary exams, found Hauerwas simply puzzled: "All I remember about my prelims is that I couldn't wait to get in there and tell them what I'd learned." Hauerwas is unconvinced by St. Augustine that we will "rest in Thee," imagining instead a beatific vision characterized not by repose but by a never-satisfied desire pulling us deeper into the mystery of God.

All this passion does not come without a price; Stanley works with a physical intensity that sometimes leaves him exhausted. Those close to him have seen him engage a crowd with brilliance and fire, only to shut down afterward, completely spent. Contrary to what many believe, Stanley does not seek the limelight, but is pulled into it by the constant demands made on him. It is work he feels compelled to do for the sake of the Kingdom, and it is hard work.

What saves Hauerwas from overwork is his conviction that the mystery of God is found in the trivia of everyday life. He is a lover of novels, baseball, Mexican food, jogging, and, above all, conversation, punctuated by great sulphuric explosions of laughter, detonated primarily in astonished appreciation of his own jokes. As in everything, Stanley hurtles into the trivial with a mad passion. He is a fixture at the Durham Bulls minor league baseball games, eating burritos and shouting at the opposing teams. When he is not eating Flying Burritos at the park, he is at the restaurant of the same name, two or three times a week when in town. Jogging is another of Stanley's obsessions; in any place and any weather he faithfully performs his noontime run like a monk prays the Office.

This same passion drives his relationships with other people. A great many people are attracted by his energy and insight; a ten-minute chat with Stanley in his office will be interrupted at least twice by phone calls or visitors. He has no e-mail and resisted even voice mail for years in an attempt to limit the sheer volume of demands on his time. And yet Hauerwas is unfailingly generous with his time. He maintains a staggering correspondence with many hundreds (thousands?) of people, speaks to dozens of groups grand and lowly every year, and works very closely with his students and others who seek him out. To cite just one recent example: Hauerwas received a letter from a twenty-one-year-old Swarthmore graduate asking if he could talk with him about his work. Stanley found the means for him to spend the summer at Duke, doing odd jobs and talking theology. It is this openness to encounter with others that keeps Stanley's work so pastoral, and keeps him from writing about books as if they were people.

A complex dynamic seems to run through Stanley's relationships with those who want a piece of him: Hauerwas has a tendency to create disciples, and yet there are few things that annoy him more. His opening-day lecture to his Divinity School classes usually involves some form of the claim, "I don't want you to think for yourselves. I want to make you think like me." This is Stanley's attempt to disabuse his students of the Enlightenment illusion of individual sovereignty. In MacIntyrean fashion, Stanley believes that theology is a craft learned by putting oneself under the authority of a master of the tradition. And yet Stanley hated the first seminar paper I ever did at Duke

because it repeatedly saluted the Hauerwas party line without any real understanding of what was at stake. He returned it with the exasperated comment
"This sounds too much like me!" emblazoned on the final page. Tradition,
after all, is not identical repetition, but is defined by MacIntyre as an "ongoing
argument" over the goods and practices intrinsic to that tradition. Stanley
Hauerwas loves a good argument. Indeed, to be able to have an argument at all
is a significant moral achievement, for it presupposes some common understanding of the goods at issue.

Thus something like the reverse of Rodney King's famous appeal after the
L.A. riots is Stanley Hauerwas's plea: Can't we all just have an argument? I have
known Stanley for nearly two decades now, half of which I spent being scared
to death of him. What I gradually came to realize is that I was not disturbed by
his ferocity but rather by his lack of guile. His frank unwillingness to dis-
semble in the interests of "just getting along" came as a terrible shock to a nice
Midwesterner who hates the appearance of conflict more than the conflict
itself. Despite his confrontational image, however, Stanley does not seek to
create discord, but only refuses to just get along if it means covering over
conflicts that are already there. Christian pacifism must be an active peacemaking, the first step of which is to locate and truthfully name what is in
conflict. A Christian must recognize the tragic reality, however, that not all
conflicts are peacefully resolvable, which is why Christians must forswear the
use of coercion to enforce the truth.

At a recent Society of Christian Ethics meeting, Hauerwas found himself
on an elevator with one of his more persistent critics, a young academic with
whom he had had an exchange of views in print. Spying her nametag, Stanley
introduced himself, shook her hand, and then said, "I guess you and I don't
really have much to say to one another." She agreed, and they spent the rest of
the elevator ride in silence. Although the appearance of peacemaking might
have been created by some polite small-talk, in this instance Stanley—and his
critic too—recognized that the truth was better served by the forthright naming of a conflict not soon to be resolved.

Because of Stanley's openness and candor, he is perhaps not the best person
to whom to entrust a secret. This is one of the many ways one can tell that
Hauerwas does not work for the CIA. As he confesses in his essay "In Praise of
Gossip," he loves to share information about other people and considers it
part of an ethicist's task of illustrating how we might live our lives better,
provided it be free of malice. Stanley is just as forthcoming with observations
of his own strengths and faults as he is with those of others. For Stanley, doing

away with the lines between public and private is not just a feature of his political theory, but is something that he quite spontaneously lives in his everyday life. His capacity to transgress such boundaries has a way of drawing people together and creating community. Hauerwas will often send copies of the letters he receives—sometimes personal letters—to other of his correspondents in an effort to introduce them to one another. A great many new friendships have resulted.

Stanley's honesty and gregariousness make for friendships that are many and varied. He has many friends who are not Christians or even religious, but tend to fall into the category of those he considers "intellectually serious." It is hard to say exactly what Stanley means by this, other than to say that he is drawn to other restless souls. Stanley loves a virtuous pagan; at the same time, he genuinely mourns for those friends with whom he cannot pray. He is an extraordinarily devoted friend with a tender affection and a capacity for spiritual companionship that models the moral life itself. His profound readings of Aristotle and Aquinas on friendship are nurtured by a deep prayerfulness and a long, difficult experience of loving and being loved.

Stanley has a particularly close relationship with his son Adam, with whom he rode out the storm of a tragic twenty-five-year marriage to his first wife, Anne. Those who know Stanley know that his writings on suffering and perseverance are not unconnected to their experience during this period. Through it Adam and Stanley rode bikes together, went to church together, played endless hours of Frisbee, and developed a deep spiritual friendship that helped each name the silences of their life as a family.

Stanley Hauerwas has mellowed over the years I have known him. Gone is a certain rough edge that I saw during his years at Notre Dame. If we now have a kinder, gentler Hauerwas, much of the change is attributable to Stanley's wife, Paula Gilbert, whom he married in 1989. To hear Stanley address Paula with fond terms of endearment is to witness a happy man. Not only is Stanley very publicly in love, but his tremendous respect for Paula's ministry gives him a strong link to the pastoral concerns that are an ongoing font for his theological reflection.

It is essential that the reader understand Hauerwas as devoted and tender friend before we move on to that for which he is perhaps more famous. What the world needs to know about him (though he will probably want to kill me for saying so) is that Stanley Hauerwas is *sweet*. That he has a tendency to incite disagreements, to put it blandly, is attributable to the same passion and love of God that make him a faithful friend.

Everyone who has seen Hauerwas in action has a favorite story. Stanley confronts a medical researcher who is defending experiments on fetal tissue with the following question: "What if it were discovered that fetal tissue were a delicacy; could you eat it?" Stanley is asked to speak at a rally against the death penalty and declares, "I'm *for* the death penalty. I think they should build a guillotine on Wall Street and execute people for stock fraud." In the first case, Hauerwas's point was that no amount of benefit to medicine could justify experimenting on fetal tissue: either it is human and deserves respect, or the door is open to all kinds of uses. (The medical researcher was forced to admit that, given the researcher's own logic, there is no reason to forbid Hauerwas's ghastly suggestion.) In the second case, Hauerwas's point was that the death penalty is not justified by claiming it prevents crime. If such were the case, the death penalty would be much more profitably used against dispassionate white-collar crime than against murder, which is usually too entangled in personal vindication to be prevented by detached calculation. The real reason the death penalty is used is a desire for revenge, a temptation to which Christians must not succumb.

My tedious explanations of his points tend to dull the impact of Hauerwas's statements. Stanley will commonly eschew such explanations and let his audience figure it out. This omission often leads to more confusion and misunderstanding than is necessary; most of the crowd at the rally, for example, was left unaware that Hauerwas is opposed to the death penalty under any circumstances. Nevertheless, a deliberate part of Stanley's pedagogy is to force people to think by jolting them out of their customary positions. Troubling the waters is certainly part of Hauerwas's modus operandi, but he is not the Howard Stern of the theological world. His lessons are not easily forgotten because he makes his listener go through the process of making the logical connections for himself or herself. This at least partially explains Stanley's advice to one of his students: "Your job as a theologian is to cause ulcers in others and not suffer them yourself in the process."

For many people, Stanley's generous use of profanity is the jalapeño on the ulcer. Academic conferences, church groups, and classes alike are treated with some regularity to words that have never been found on the Queen's lips (at least not in public). Sometimes such profanity has a specific purpose: in a seminar Stanley once read from a Catholic moral theologian about the duty of Christianity to "penetrate and fecundate the symbol system of American society" and invites us to replace the words "penetrate and fecundate" with a certain four-lettered synonym. At other times, the profanity has a more random feel, such as in this quote captured by *Newsweek* magazine: "God is killing the church and we goddamn well deserve it." The latter incident caused a brief tempest in the church teapot (Stanley's defense: "At least I mentioned God's name twice"). For some, in fact, especially among more evangelical Protestants, Stanley's French is a considerable barrier to greater acceptance. Some see this as taking the Lord's name in vain, a violation of one of the Ten Commandments. Many evangelicals with a natural sympathy for Stanley's critiques of secularism and the centrality of Jesus in his thought have been turned away by what appears to be an easily correctable fault.

I confess that I tend to regard complaints about Stanley's swearing as I would complaints about, say, Santa Claus's weight problem. We all know what the AMA says about heart disease, but who wants a svelte Santa? My initial response, however, does not take seriously enough both the objections and Stanley's unwillingness to change his language. In some cases, the sharpness of Stanley's words is necessary for his message to penetrate ears that have become unaccustomed to hearing what is not nice. In the *Newsweek* quote, for example, Hauerwas's oath is *not* simply random but expresses the judgment that Christians have betrayed the Gospel and God may be damning us for it, a message that many wish to ignore by focusing on the swearing itself. On another level, however, Stanley swears simply because that's the way he has always talked. One colleague recalls being with Stanley when Coffee Hauerwas walked in and greeted his son with an affectionate stream of profanities. Stanley's colleague realized that his swearing is not an affectation meant to shock people but simply a manifestation of who he, as one particular Texan, is. That academic and ecclesiastical protocols should have to learn to accommodate such alien talk is perhaps not such a bad thing.

Unfortunately, Hauerwas's use of profanity and other idiosyncrasies of his personality allow some to excuse themselves from having to deal seriously with his work. Although his character is so much a part of his work, in some ways Hauerwas's character is so complex and so public that it often threatens to overwhelm and obscure the importance of his work. As he himself has said to me, "There's something about me that keeps some people from taking me seriously intellectually. They think my claims are so exaggerated they couldn't be true, and they don't want to do the homework necessary to understand me."

It is remarkable that a man who has given the Gifford Lectures should have to worry about being taken seriously. If some still dismiss Hauerwas too easily, I believe it is in part attributable to the fact that Stanley has chosen to do theology in a genre unfamiliar to many, a genre we might call "not-boring theology." Stanley is convinced that at least part of a theologian's job is to tell stories, and stories should be entertaining. Though some might take this as a sign of unsophistication, Stanley would argue that Wittgenstein and others have cured him of theology's self-defeating post-Enlightenment attempt to ground itself on anything but the biblical narrative. The only epistemologically secure "position" is the ever-moving position of the pilgrim people of God through time. With deep sophistication and skill, Hauerwas is able to guide his readers and listeners through the most difficult thickets of Western thought and theory, while simultaneously luring their attention toward the great adventure story that is the cross and resurrection of Jesus Christ. Stanley's entertaining character is not accidental to his ability to do theology well.

Some people have grown impatient with Hauerwas's reliance on short essays and await a magnum opus from his pen that will lay down his position in definitive form. Such a book or books is unlikely to be forthcoming, however, as Stanley does not believe that he has a position. Theologians are just expositors of what the church thinks; to have a position is to claim to know something the church does not. This is why Hauerwas relies on short essays done primarily over pastoral problems, such as marriage, education, war, and health. To write this way risks not being read for very long, because particular pastoral problems quickly shift. But Hauerwas claims that a theologian should not write for the ages, for to do so is to try to secure a position against the movement of the Spirit through time.

It is exactly this kind of insight that ironically has kept Hauerwas's older books in print for a quarter century already, with no sign of decreasing interest. His writings will continue to be read as the church tries to puzzle through what it means to be faithful in a world of violence. His most lasting impact, however, may be not the writings themselves but the friendships he has fostered and the communities he has helped to discern their ways through difficult times. God has done strange and wonderful things with Stanley Hauerwas, and those who love him for this fact love him dearly.

A couple of years ago I picked up Stanley in Minneapolis and drove him across the Mississippi River to my home in St. Paul. As we crossed the bridge Stanley suddenly interrupted our conversation with a lusty rendition of "Old Man River" in a baritone as muddy as the Mississippi itself. He sang the entire chorus and—though there was not much room for it, believe me—managed a dramatic crescendo at the end. It is an image of Stanley I treasure: head back, grinning, belting it out with joyful abandon. I once heard a priest tell his congregation, "If God gave you a good voice, sing out and thank Him. If God gave you a lousy voice, sing out and pay Him back." As a close personal friend of God, Stanley is used to such give and take. May he just keep rolling along.

Further Reading
"A Tale of Two Stories: On Being a Christian and a Texan: A Theological Entertainment" (1988) in CET
Introduction to PK (1983)
"A Homage to Mary and to the University called Notre Dame" (1995) in IGC
"Character, Narrative, and Growth in the Christian Life" essay 11 in this volume

PART II

Reframing Theological Ethics

Who Are Christians? The Christian Story

1. How "Christian Ethics" Came to Be (1997)

This essay provides the fullest account of how Hauerwas understands Christian ethics to have evolved as a discipline in relation to the practices of the Christian faith. After tracing developments from patristic writers Tertullian and Augustine, through the rise of medieval penitential manuals, to Aquinas and Luther, the essay explores how Christian ethics came to be seen as a problem in the context of the intellectual ferment of the Enlightenment. Hauerwas engages issues that emerged in the work of Kant, were given systematic theological expression in the writings of Schleiermacher, and received their strongest critique in Barth's Church Dogmatics. *For Hauerwas, like Barth, theological ethics proceeds from the first-order discourse (doctrine) of the Christian faith. Therefore, ethics is a part of the theological task, and Christian theology is first and foremost an activity of the church.*

The notion of Christian ethics is a modern invention. At one time Christian ethics did not exist. That does not mean that Christians did not think about how best to live their lives as Christians. There are obvious examples of such reflection in the New Testament as well as in the Church Fathers. That may well put the matter too lamely just to the extent that the New Testament and the early Christian theologians thought about little else than how Christians were to live their lives. For the ancients, pagan and Christian, to be schooled in philosophy or theology meant to submit one's life to a master in order to gain the virtues necessary to be a philosopher or a Christian.[1] Ethics, in such a

[Originally published as "On Doctrine and Ethics" in *The Cambridge Companion to Christian Doctrine*, ed. Colin Gunton (Cambridge, England: Cambridge University Press, 1997), 21–40. Reprinted with permission of Cambridge University Press. This essay was reprinted in STT. It has been edited for length.]
1. Robert Wilken provides a very helpful account of how such schools worked in his "Alexandria: A School for Training in Virtue," in *Schools of Thought in the Christian Tradition*, ed.

context, was not some "aspect" of life, but rather inclusive of all that constituted a person's life.[2]

That we do not find explicit treatises on Christian ethics in Scripture or in
the work of the Patristic writers does not mean they were unconcerned with
giving direction to the church. They simply did not distinguish between theology and pastoral direction as we now do. Tertullian's *On Patience* may well
have been the first treatise by a Christian on what we think of as a specifically
moral topic, but there is no indication that he would have understood this
treatise to be anything substantially different from his other theological and
pastoral work.[3] Augustine did the most to shape what would later be thought
of as Christian ethics. In his *On the Morals of the Catholic Church,* he suggested
that the fourfold division of the virtues familiar to pagan philosophers could
rightly be understood only as forms of love whose object is God. Thus,
"Temperance is love keeping itself entire and incorrupt for God; fortitude is
love bearing everything readily for the sake of God; justice is love serving God
only, and therefore ruling well all else, as subject to man; prudence is love
making a right distinction between what helps it towards God and what might
hinder it."[4]

Augustine's conflict with the Pelagians resulted in a particularly rich set of
treatises dealing with topics such as grace and free will, but also marriage and
concupiscence.[5] Equally important is Augustine's *City of God,* in which he

---

Patrick Henry (Philadelphia: Fortress Press, 1984), 15–30. This understanding of the relation
of theology to moral formation was not peculiar to Christianity but characteristic of all
serious study in the ancient world. For example, Pierre Hadot observes that for the ancients
philosophy, even in its most theoretical and systematic form, was "written not so much to
inform the reader of a doctrinal content but to form him to make him traverse a certain
itinerary in the course of which he will make spiritual progress. . . . For the Platonist, for
example, even mathematics is used to train the soul to raise itself from the sensible to the
intelligible" (*Philosophy as a Way of Life* [Oxford: Basil Blackwell, 1995], 64).

2. For example, Aristotle thought how a person laughed not unimportant for morality. See his
Nicomachean Ethics, trans. Martin Ostwald (Indianapolis: Bobbs Merrill, 1962), 1128a33–35.

3. Tertullian, "On Patience," in *The Ante-Nicene Fathers,* ed. Philip Schaff (Grand Rapids, MI:
Eerdmans, 1989), 707–17. For a further discussion of Tertullian's account of patience as well as
that of Cyprian, Augustine, and Aquinas, see my "Practicing Patience: How Christians Should
Be Sick," essay 18 of this volume. Robert Wilken rightly directs attention to the importance of
the lives of the saints for Christian reflection on the moral life in his *Remembering the
Christian Past* (Grand Rapids, MI: Eerdmans, 1995), 121–44.

4. Augustine, "On the Morals of the Catholic Church," in *Christian Ethics: Sources of the Living
Tradition,* ed. Waldo Beach and H. Richard Niebuhr (New York: Ronald Press, 1955), 115.

5. These treatises can be found in Philip Schaff, ed., *Nicene and Post-Nicene Fathers of the*

narrates all of human history as a conflict between the earthly and heavenly cities.[6] The earthly city knows not God and is thus characterized by order secured only through violence. In contrast, the heavenly city worships the one true God, making possible the collection of "a society of aliens, speaking all languages. She takes no account of any difference in customs, laws, and institutions, by which earthly peace is achieved and preserved—not that she annuls or abolishes any of those, rather, she maintains them and follows them, provided that no hindrance is presented thereby to the religion which teaches that the one supreme and true God is to be worshiped."[7] How to understand the relation between the two cities becomes the central issue for the development of what comes to be called Christian social ethics.

The Church Fathers and Augustine did much to shape the way Christians think about Christian living, but equally, if not more important, is the development of the penitential tradition. In 1 Corinthians 5 Paul had insisted that the Corinthians were to "root out the evil-doer from the community," but the question remained whether such an evildoer should be received back into the community after due repentance. This issue was not resolved until the Council of Nicaea in 325. Nicaea set a policy for the readmission of those excommunicated after appropriate periods of penance. This was particularly significant since often the sin they had committed had been apostasy during times of persecution. Sins involving idolatry, adultery, and/or homicide all required public penance which was quite onerous and available only once in a person's life.[8]

A major development occurred in this tradition largely by accident. Drawing on the monastic practice of spiritual direction of one monk by another, there developed in Ireland the practice of private confession to a priest with forgiveness of sins offered after appropriate penance. This practice resulted in the development of books called *Penitentials* that were meant as aids to confessors so that the appropriate penance would be given for the corresponding

---

Christian Church: Saint Augustine's Anti-Pelagian Works, vol. 5, trans. Benjamin Warfield (Grand Rapids, MI: Eerdmans, 1956).

6. Augustine, *The City of God*, trans. Henry Bettenson, introduced by David Knowles (New York: Penguin Books, 1972).

7. Ibid., 877–78.

8. I am indebted to John Mahoney's *The Making of Moral Theology: A Study of the Roman Catholic Tradition* (Oxford: Clarendon Press, 1987), and John A. Gallagher's *Time Past, Time Future: An Historical Study of Catholic Moral Theology* (New York: Paulist Press, 1990), for their accounts of the penitential tradition.

sin. Their organization was quite varied with little or no attempt at theological rationale. For example, *The Penitential of Theodore* stipulated the following with regard to avarice:

1. If any layman carries off a monk from the monastery by stealth, he shall either enter a monastery to serve God or subject himself to human servitude.
2. Money stolen or robbed from churches is to be restored fourfold; from secular persons, twofold.[9]

Penitentials differed markedly from one another, indicating different Christian practices at different times and places.

These books were carried by Irish missionaries across Europe and soon became the rule throughout Christendom. Though they were not explicitly theological, they depended on the continuing presumption that the church through baptism was to be a holy community. They were no doubt open to great misuse, but they also became the way the church grappled with the complexity of Christian behavior *through* the development of casuistry, that is, close attention to particular cases. From these beginnings there developed as part of the church's theological mission a special task called moral theology. Under the guidance of Pope Gregory VII the church's practice concerning moral questions was made more uniform through canon law and the development of *Summae Confessorum*. The latter were pastoral handbooks that gave theological order to the *Penitentials* so that priests might be given guidance in the administration of what had become the sacrament of penance.

Thus a clear tradition was established in the *Penitentials*, in canon law, and in the *Summae Confessorum* in which ethics was distinguished from theology and doctrine. There was, moreover, specialist training for each of these tasks, as canon lawyers, moral theologians, and theologians were given distinctive training for their different roles. However, these diverse tasks were, in fact, one insofar as their intelligibility depended on the practices of the church. Ethics was not something done in distinction from theology, since both theology and moral theology presumed baptism, penance, preaching, and Eucharist as essential for the corporate life of the church.

Perhaps nowhere is this inseparable unity between the ethical and the theological dimensions of Christian living better exemplified than in the great *Summa Theologica* of Thomas Aquinas. Though often characterized as a defender of "natural theology," Aquinas's *Summa is* first and foremost a work in

9. Gallagher, *Time Past, Time Future,* 7.

Christian theology. The structure of Aquinas's *Summa Contra Gentiles,* as well as the *Summa Theologica,* draws upon the image of God as artist, such that all created realities are depicted as exiting and returning to God.[10] In other words, Aquinas's great works evince a three-part structure. The story of creation begins in divine freedom; then Aquinas treats how all creation, and in particular that part of creation called human, returns to God; finally, in the third part he provides an account of the means of creation's return to God through Christ and the sacraments. The *Summa,* rather than being an argument for the independence of ethics, as it is sometimes characterized, is concerned to place the Christian's journey to God squarely within the doctrine of God.

Indeed, it has been argued that one of Aquinas's main purposes in writing the *Summa* was for the sake of the second part, which treats moral matters more specifically and directly. Aquinas thought the manuals far too haphazard in their presentation of the Christian moral life.[11] He therefore sought to place the discussion of morality in the context of a consideration of human nature and the virtues appropriate to our nature as creatures whose destiny was nothing less than to be friends with God. Drawing deeply on Aristotle's account of the virtues, Aquinas nonetheless argued that even the so-called natural virtues must be formed by charity if they are to be capable of directing us to God.

Aquinas's intentions, however, were subverted as it was not long before the *secunda pars,* the second part, was abstracted from its context in the *Summa* and used as if it stood on its own.[12] This kind of anthologizing in part accounts for the presumption by later commentators that law, and in particular

10. As Aquinas says in the *Summa Contra Gentiles,* "All creatures are compared to God as artifact to artist. Whence the whole of nature is like a certain artifact of the divine art. It is not, however, opposed to the nature of an artifact that the artist should work in a different way on his product even after he has given it its first form. Nor therefore is it against nature that God should work otherwise in natural things than the customary course of nature operates" (quoted in Thomas Hibbs, *Dialect and Narrative in Aquinas: An Interpretation of the Summa Contra Gentiles* [Notre Dame, IN: University of Notre Dame Press, 1995], 3, 10).

11. Leonard Boyle, OP, *The Setting of the Summa Theologica of St. Thomas* (Toronto: Pontifical Institute of Medieval Studies, 1981).

12. For an extraordinary account of why Aquinas's *Summa Theologica* must be read as a whole as well as evaluated as a whole, see Alasdair MacIntyre, *Three Rival Versions of Moral Enquiry: Encyclopedia, Genealogy, and Tradition* (Notre Dame, IN: University of Notre Dame Press, 1990), 133–37. MacIntyre argues, rightly I think, that integral to Aquinas's understanding of becoming a person of virtue, particularly the virtues of faith, hope, and love, is a recognition of our disobedience (140).

natural law, stands at the center of Aquinas's account. Yet Aquinas's under-standing of the moral life is one that assumes the primacy of the virtues for the shape of the Christian life. Aquinas's work was either misunderstood or ig-nored through subsequent centuries, even to the point that he was used to support positions almost diametrically opposed to his own views.

The developments of the late Middle Ages are not unimportant, but in many ways they are now lost due to the profound effect the Reformation had for shaping how Protestant and Catholic alike began to think about the Chris-tian life. It is not as if Luther and Calvin in their own work mark an entirely new way for thinking about the Christian life, but certainly the forces they unleashed changed everything. Neither Luther nor Calvin distinguished be-tween theology and ethics. Certainly Luther stressed the "external" character of our justification, yet in *The Freedom of a Christian* he equally maintained that "a Christian, like Christ his head, is filled and made rich by faith and should be content with this form of God which he has obtained by faith; only he should increase this faith until it is made perfect. For this faith is his life, his righteousness, and his salvation: it saves him and makes him acceptable, and bestows upon him all things that are Christ's."[13]

Yet the polemical terms of the Reformation could not help but reshape how ethics was conceived in relation to theology. Faith, not works, determines the Christian's relationship to God. Moreover works became associated with "ethics," particularly as ethics was alleged to be the way sinners attempt to secure their standing before God as a means to avoid complete dependence on God's grace. So for Protestants the Christian life is now characterized in such a way that there always exists a tension between law and grace. The law is needed, but we can never attain salvation through the law and the works of the law. A similar tension constitutes the Lutheran understanding of the Chris-tian's relation to what is now known as the "orders of creation," that is, marriage, the legal order, the state. Christians are called to love their neighbor through submission to such orders, recognizing that such service is not and cannot be that promised in the order of redemption.[14]

---

13. Martin Luther, *The Freedom of the Christian*, in *Martin Luther: Selections from His Writings*, ed. John Dillenberger (Garden City, NY: Anchor Books, 1961), 75.

14. Luther maintains that Christians must bear the "secular" sword even though they have no need for it for their own life, since the sword is "quite useful and profitable for the whole world and for your neighbor. Therefore, should you see that there is a lack of hangmen, beadles, judges, lords, or princes, and find that you are qualified, you should offer your services and seek the place, that necessary government may by no means be despised and

Calvin, and in particular later developments in Calvinism, were not as determined by the polemical context of the Lutheran reformation. However, justification by faith is no less central for Calvin, who equally insists that "actual holiness of life is not separated from free imputation of righteousness."[15] Accordingly, Calvinists stressed the importance of the sanctification of the Christian and the Christian community. Christians were expected to examine their lives daily so they might grow into holiness. This theme was retained in the Anglican tradition and was given particularly strong emphasis in the Wesleyan revival in England as well as other forms of Pietism.

Certainly the Protestant Reformation changed the language for how Christians understood "ethics," but far more important were changes in the ways Christians related to their world. In earlier centuries, the Christian understanding of life could be articulated in the language of natural law, but it was assumed that natural law was only intelligible as part of divine law as mediated by the church. What was lost after the Reformation was exactly this understanding of the church as the indispensable context in which order might be given to the Christian life. For example, with the loss of the rite of penance in Protestantism casuistry as an activity of moral theologians was lost. Such a loss did not seem to be a problem as long as it was assumed that everyone "knew" what it meant to be Christian. However, as it became less and less clear among Protestants what it "means" to be Christian there have increasingly been attempts to "do" ethics. The difficulty is that no consensus about what ethics is or how it should be done existed. As a result, theologians often turned to philosophy for resources in their search for an ethic—resources that ironically helped create the problem of how to relate theology and ethics because now it was assumed that "ethics" is an autonomous discipline that is no longer dependent on religious conviction.

How Ethics Became a Problem in Modernity

The birth of modernity is coincident with the beginnings of "ethics" understood as a distinguishable sphere or realm of human life. Faced with the

---

become inefficient or perish. For the world cannot and dare not dispense with it" (*Secular Authority: To What Extent It Should Be Obeyed*, in *Martin Luther: Selections from His Writings*, 374–75). The contrast between Lutheran and Calvinist positions about such matters is frequently overdrawn. See, for example, Quentin Skinner, *The Foundations of Modern Political Thought*, II (Cambridge, England: Cambridge University Press, 1978), 189–238.

15. John Calvin, *Institutes of the Christian Religion*, ed. John MacNeill, trans. Ford Lewis Battles (Philadelphia: Westminster Press, 1960), chap. 3, 1.

knowledge of the diversity of moral convictions, modern people think of themselves as haunted by the problem of relativism. If our "ethics" are relative to time and place, what if anything prevents our moral opinions from being "conventional"? And if they are conventional, some assume they must also be "arbitrary." But if our morality is conventional, how can we ever expect to secure agreements between people who disagree? Is it our fate to be perpetually at war with one another? "Ethics" becomes that quest to secure a rational basis for morality so we can be confident that our moral convictions are not arbitrary.

The great name associated with this quest is Immanuel Kant. Kant sought to secure knowledge and morality from the skepticism that the Enlightenment, by its attempt to free all thought from its indebtedness to the past, had produced. Kant also wanted thought to be free from the past; thus his famous declaration: "Enlightenment is man's release from his self-incurred tutelage. Tutelage is man's inability to make use of his understanding without direction from another. Self-incurred is this tutelage when its cause lies not in lack of reason but in lack of resolution and courage to use it without direction from another."[16]

Kant's commitment to this Enlightenment ideal was his response to the breakdown of the Christian world. If ethics depended on or was derived from religious belief, then there seemed to be no way to avoid the continuing conflict, as heirs of the Reformation,[17] between Catholics and Protestants. Accordingly, Kant sought to ground ethics in reason itself, since, in Kant's words, "It is there I discover that what I do can only be unconditionally good to the extent I can will what I have done as a universal law."[18] Kant called this principle the "Categorical Imperative" because it has the form "Act only ac-

16. Immanuel Kant, *Foundations of the Metaphysics of Morals and What Is Enlightenment?*, trans. Lewis White Beck (New York: Liberal Arts Press, 1959), 85. The quote comes from the first paragraph of "What Is Enlightenment?"

17. It should never be forgotten that one of Kant's last projects was his *On Perpetual Peace* in which he sought to provide an account for how nations determined by republican principles based in his ethics had a better chance of maintaining a world free of war. The oft-made claim that liberalism, and in particular the liberal nation-state, arose in response to the wars between Catholics and Protestants is simply wrong. William Cavanaugh notes: "The rise of a centralized bureaucratic state preceded these wars and was based on the fifteenth-century assertion of civil dominance of the church in France." See his "A Fire Strong Enough to Consume the House: The Wars of Religion and the Rise of the State," *Modern Theology* 11, no. 4 (October 1995): 397–420.

18. Kant, *Foundations*, 18.

cording to that maxim by which you can at the same time will that it should become a universal law."[19]

Only an ethics based on such an imperative can be autonomous, that is, free of all religious and anthropological presuppositions. Only by acting on the basis of such an imperative can an agent be free. Such an ethic is based on reason alone and can therefore be distinguished from religion, politics, and etiquette. Yet Kant did not understand his attempt to make ethics independent of religion to be an antireligious project but rather one that made faith possible. Indeed, in many ways Kant becomes the greatest representative of Protestant liberalism; that is, Protestant liberal theology after Kant is but a series of footnotes to his work.[20]

For example, Protestant theologians, no longer sure of the metaphysical status of Christian claims, sought to secure the ongoing meaningfulness of Christian convictions by anchoring them in anthropological generalizations and/or turning them into ethics. No longer convinced that Jesus is the resurrected Messiah, his significance is now said to be found in his proclamation of the Kingdom of God. The Kingdom is the outworking in human history of the fatherhood of God and the brotherhood of man.[21] Theology, at least Protestant liberal theology, became ethics, but the ethics it became was distinctively Kant's ethics dressed in religious language.

Such a generalization must be qualified in the light of Friedrich Schleiermacher's theology and philosophy. Schleiermacher was part of the romantic revolt against the rationalism of Kant, but it was a revolt that sought to stay within the presuppositions of the Enlightenment. Schleiermacher's great work, *The Christian Faith*, has no section devoted to ethics.[22] Yet Karl Barth rightly argues that Schleiermacher's work was motivated by the ethical project of drawing people into the movement of education, the exaltation of life, which

---

19. Ibid., 39.

20. The liberal presuppositions that shape Kant's religious views are nicely exemplified in his observation that "in the appearance of the God-Man (on earth), it is not that in him which strikes the sense and can be known through experience, but rather the archetype, lying in our reason, that we attribute to him (since, so far as his example can be known, he is found to conform thereto), which is really the object of saving faith, and such a faith does not differ from the principle of a course of life well-pleasing to God" (Immanuel Kant, *Religion within the Limits of Reason Alone*, trans. with an introduction by Theodore Green [New York: Harper Torchbooks, 1960], 109–10).

21. Though this position is associated with Ritschl and Harnack, it perhaps found its most powerful expression in the American social gospel movement.

22. Friedrich Schleiermacher, *The Christian Faith*, trans. H. R. Macintosh and J. S. Stewart (Edinburgh: T and T Clark, 1960).

he understood at bottom to be religious and, thus, Christian. Barth goes so far as to suggest that "Schleiermacher's entire philosophy of religion, and therefore his entire teaching of the nature of religion and Christianity was something secondary, auxiliary to the consolidation of this true concern of his, the ethical one. The fact that, in academic theory, he ranked theology below ethics, is but an expression of this state of affairs."[23]

Schleiermacher sought to support Christian theology through the development of a philosophical theology that could demonstrate that the existence of the church was necessary for the development of humanity. This philosophical project was ethical just to the extent that ethics is understood to express those principles of history by which reason permeates nature and gives it form. In short, ethics is the study of how nature comes to consciousness. The most determinative form of such consciousness Schleiermacher identifies with the "feeling of absolute dependence." Thus he begins *The Christian Faith* with a long prolegomenon to establish the proposition that "the totality of finite being exists only in dependence upon the Infinite is the complete description of that basis of every religious feeling which is here to be set forth."[24]

Christian theology and ethics for Schleiermacher are descriptive disciplines inasmuch as their task is to set forth the ideas and behavior of Christian communities in different times and places. Though Schleiermacher often lectured on philosophical and Christian ethics, unfortunately he never published his ethics. From his lectures and posthumous writings we know that Schleiermacher was critical of what he considered the formalism and legalism of Kant's ethics. As a great Plato scholar, he reintroduced the language of virtue and the highest good, though he identified the latter with the rational content of life as a whole. His account of the Christian life was that of "a continuum between the beginnings of one's desire for communion with God and the culmination of that desire in absolute blessedness."[25]

More important, however, than Schleiermacher's explicit view about ethics was his conception of the dogmatic task as a civilizing and thus ethical task. The crucial institution for such a task in civilizing for Schleiermacher was the university, and in particular, the University of Berlin.[26] Theology could be part

23. Karl Barth, *Protestant Thought: From Rousseau to Ritschl*, trans. Brian Cozens (New York: Harper and Bros, 1959), 317.

24. Schleiermacher, *The Christian Faith*, 142.

25. Friedrich Schleiermacher, *Introduction to Christian Ethics*, trans. and with introduction by John Shelley (Nashville, TN: Abingdon Press, 1989), 27 of Shelley's introduction.

26. For a wonderful account of the significance of the University of Berlin as well as Schleier-

of the university, according to Schleiermacher, insofar as it meets, like medicine and the law, human needs indispensable for the state.[27] Since the state needs religion, theology is justified for the training of clergy who are thus seen as servants of the state. The theology that is so justified is now the name of a cluster of disciplines (scripture, church history, dogmatics, and practical theology) that are understood to be descriptive in character. Accordingly, theology is no longer understood to be practical knowledge necessary for the acquisition of wisdom, but a "science" for the training of semipublic officials.

This reconstrual of the tasks of theology shaped and continues to shape the curricula not only in Germany but in universities and seminaries around the world and, in particular, in the United States. Of course the division of the curriculum into scripture, church history, dogmatics, and practical disciplines in these different contexts does not mean that theology was or is necessarily understood in Schleiermacher's terms. But the curriculum so structured did and continues to create the "problem" of what relation there might be between theology and ethics. In other words, it is unclear exactly where "ethics" should be located. Is its proper place in "dogmatics" or in the "practical disciplines"? The rise and importance of Christian ethics as a discipline in the United States (associated with such people as Reinhold and H. Richard Niebuhr, Paul Ramsey, and James Gustafson) has not resolved this fundamental issue. If anything, it has only deepened and further obscured the issue. Indeed, the institutional shape of the theological curriculum, particularly in Protestant seminaries and increasingly in Catholic institutions that, at least in America, have imitated the Protestants, has resulted in intellectual developments that distort the character of theological discourse. The assumption, for example, that students should take "systematic theology" before they take ethics invites the presumption that theology is in some sense more basic than ethics. In such a context theology begins to look like a "metaphysics" on which one must get straight before one can turn to questions of ethics. Yet as I have indicated above, through most of Christian history Christians have not thought it possible to distinguish so easily between what they believe and what

---

macher's decisive role in its shaping, see Hans Frei's *Types of Christian Theology*, ed. George Hunsinger and William Placher (New Haven: Yale University Press, 1992), 95–132.

27. Edward Farley provides an extremely helpful account of the importance of Schleiermacher's views on these matters in *Theologia: The Fragmentation and Unity of Theological Education* (Philadelphia: Fortress Press, 1983), 73–98. Schleiermacher's position concerning the university was quite similar to Kant's. Schleiermacher, in spite of his criticism of Kant, continued to presuppose the basic structure of Kant's position.

they do. At stake is the question of whether theology is first and foremost a discipline of the church or of the university.

Thus the significance of Karl Barth's challenge to Schleiermacher and the tradition of Protestant theological liberalism. For Barth, indisputably the greatest Protestant theologian of this century, there can be no ethics that is not from beginning to end theological. Indeed, ethics is theological through and through because for Barth theology is more than simply one discipline among others. Theology rather is the exposition of how God's Word as found in Jesus Christ provides not only its own ground but the ground for all that we know and do. Barth, therefore, rejects Schleiermacher's attempt to make theology part of a "larger essential context, of a larger scientific problem-context," by returning theology to its proper role as servant to the church's proclamation of Jesus Christ.[28] For Barth dogmatics cannot have access to a higher or better source of knowledge than that which is found in the church's proclamation that the God Christians worship is Triune.

Barth thus begins his *Church Dogmatics* with the doctrine of the Trinity since it is from that doctrine "we actually gather who the God is who reveals Himself and therefore we let it find expression as the interpretation of revelation."[29] For Barth "ethics" is but an integral part of the dogmatic task and, therefore, cannot be treated as an independent subject. Barth's explicit reflections on ethics occur in several places in his multivolume *Church Dogmatics*,[30] but it would be a mistake to assume that Barth's ethics is to be found only in those sections explicitly devoted to ethics. As John Webster argues, Barth's *Church Dogmatics* is

> a moral ontology—an extensive account of the situation in which human agents act. Barth's ethics has, therefore, a very particular character, both

28. Karl Barth, *Church Dogmatics* I/1, trans. G. T. Thomson (Edinburgh: T and T Clark, 1960), 39.

29. Ibid., I/1, 358.

30. Barth's first treatment of ethics is to be found in *Church Dogmatics* II/1 as part of his exposition of the doctrine of election. His special ethics is in *Church Dogmatics* III/4, that is, the last volume in his doctrine of creation. The ethics volume that was meant to climax his account of the doctrine of reconciliation was not completed but in it Barth was explicating the Christian life in terms of baptism with the Holy Spirit and water. See *Church Dogmatics* IV/4, trans. G. W. Bromiley (Edinburgh: T and T Clark, 1969). Further lecture fragments of Barth's last reflections about the Christian life can be found in his *The Christian Life*, trans. Geoffrey Bromiley (Grand Rapids, MI: Eerdmans, 1981). In this last volume Barth builds his reflections around the Lord's Prayer.

materially and formally. It is primarily devoted to the task of describing the "space" which agents occupy, and gives only low priority to the description of their character and to the analysis of quandary situations in which they find themselves. Barth's ethics tends to assume that moral problems are resolvable by correct theological description of moral space. And such description in-volves much more than describing the moral consciousness of agents. A Christianly successful moral ontology must be a depiction of the world of human action as it is enclosed and governed by the creative, redemptive, and sanctifying work of God in Christ, present in the power of the Holy Spirit.[31]

The "ethics" that animates Barth's project is thus quite different from that of Schleiermacher. Barth does not seek to make the church a servant of a civilizing project and thus a supplement for what is a prior conception of ethics. Rather, just as Israel "annexed" the land of Palestine, so Christians must appropriate "ethics" as a secular, Enlightenment subject matter.[32] For example, notions such as "the good" or the "Categorical Imperative" are far too abstract to give the guidance that can come only from the concreteness of God's command as found in Jesus Christ.[33]

Barth provides extensive discussions of such matters as suicide, euthanasia, marriage and singleness, the ethics of war, the Christian calling to serve the neighbor, but denies that casuistry can ever predetermine "God's concrete specific command here and now in this particular way, of making a corre-sponding decision in this particular way, and of summoning others to such a concrete and specific decision."[34] Accordingly Barth's ethics is often criticized for being too "occasionalistic," since he denies that we can ever predetermine what we should do prior to God's command. While Barth may be vulnerable to such criticism, what should not be lost is that Barth in his *Dogmatics* has sought to do nothing less than displace human self-consciousness as the legitimating notion for the creation of ethics independent of God's revelation in Christ. By doing so he has returned theology to the presumption that there can be no "ethics" separate from theology, particularly when theology is understood as an activity of the church.

31. John Webster, *Barth's Ethics of Reconciliation* (Cambridge, England: Cambridge University Press, 1995), 1–2. For another excellent secondary source on Barth's ethics, see Nigel Biggar, *The Hastening That Waits: Karl Barth's Ethics* (Oxford: Clarendon Press, 1993).
32. Barth, *Church Dogmatics* II/2, 518.
33. Ibid., II/2, 665–69.
34. Ibid., IV/4, 9.

Further Reading

"On Keeping Theological Ethics Theological" (1983), essay 2 in this volume

"The Church as God's New Language" (1986), essay 7 in this volume

"Casuistry in Context: The Need for Tradition" (1995), essay 13 in this volume

"Reconciling the Practice of Reason: Casuistry in a Christian Context" (1986), in CET

"The Truth about God: The Decalogue As Condition for Truthful Speech" (1998), in STT

Gifford Lectures on Barth (2001), in WGU; see chapters 1, 6–8

2. On Keeping Theological Ethics Theological (1983)

A distinctive programmatic history of the development of "Christian ethics" in the United States in the twentieth century, this evaluation of Rauschenbusch, Reinhold and H. Richard Niebuhr, Ramsey, and Gustafson attempts to answer the following question: How did Christian ethics go from "Christianizing the Social Order" (a Rauschenbusch book title) to "Can Ethics Be Christian?" (a Gustafson book title)? Against tendencies of Protestant liberalism, Hauerwas advocates a more confessional approach to theological ethics, one centered on the life, death, and resurrection of Jesus Christ as witnessed to in the church. Principal influences are Barth and Yoder. Although the history offered is "Protestant," Hauerwas sees analogous developments in recent Catholic moral theology.

I. The Ethical Significance of Saying Something Theological

"Say something theological" is a request, as Gustafson notes, theologians frequently hear.[1] Such a request, often made in a more oblique manner, may be entirely friendly, as the inquirer—possessed by an archaeological curiosity in still living antiquities—simply wants an example of a religious relic. More likely, however, the request is really a challenge: "Say something theological in a way that convinces me that you are not talking nonsense." Such a challenge thus assumes that anyone who wants theological language to be taken seriously—that it is essential for telling us about how things are or ought to be—bears the burden of proof.

This is particularly the case in matters having to do with ethics. For even though at a popular level many continue to assume there must be a close

[From *Revisions: Changing Perspectives in Moral Philosophy*, ed. Stanley Hauerwas and Alasdair MacIntyre. © 1983 by University of Notre Dame Press. Used by permission. This essay was reprinted in AN. It has been edited for length and clarity.]
1. James Gustafson, "Say Something Theological," *1981 Nora and Edward Ryerson Lecture* (Chicago: University of Chicago Press, 1981), 3. Gustafson notes that he has the presence of mind to say "God."

connection between religion and morality, this is not the dominant philosophical view. Indeed, the persistence of this popular assumption only testifies how hard it is to kill certain habits of thought. For the assumption that there is a strong interdependence between religion and morality is but the remains of the now lost hegemony of Christianity over Western culture. That many still assume religion is essential to motivate us to do the good is an indication, however, that no satisfactory alternative has been found to replace Christianity, as worldview and cult, in sustaining the *ethos* of our civilization. We find ourselves in the odd situation in which many of our society's moral attitudes and practices are based on Jewish and Christian beliefs that are widely thought by many to be irrelevant or false. This situation does not provide an argument for the continued viability of religious practices, but only an indication that as a culture we still have not fully faced the implications of generating a genuine secular morality.

Our culture's persistent failure to find an adequate substitute for Christianity has presented theologians with a temptation almost impossible to resist. Even if they cannot demonstrate the truth of theological claims, they can at least show the continued necessity of religious attitudes for the maintenance of our culture. Of course these theologians think it unwise to continue to use the explicit beliefs derived from the particular historic claims associated with Christianity (and Judaism) as the basis of a secular morality. Such beliefs bear the marks of being historically relative and contingent. If religion is to deserve our allegiance, so the thinking goes, it must be based on what can be agreed upon universally. Thus, theologians have sought, at least since the Enlightenment, to demonstrate that theological language can be translated into terms that are meaningful and compelling for those who do not share Christianity's more particularistic beliefs about Jesus of Nazareth. In short, theologians have tried to show that we do not need to speak theologically in order to "say something theological," as other forms of speech are really implicitly religious. After all, hasn't talk of God always really been but a way to talk about being human?[2]

Even though this understanding of the theological task is relatively recent,

2. This development is as true of Roman Catholic as of Protestant theology. See, for example, Thomas Sheehan's review of Karl Rahner's *Foundations of Christian Faith*, in which he applauds Rahner's attempt to carry out Feuerbach's program of transforming theology into anthropology. Of course, the odd thing about Sheehan's enthusiasm for this move is that Feuerbach assumed that to do so was the agenda of atheism, not theism. "The Drama of Karl Rahner," *New York Review of Books*, 4 February 1981, 13–14.

there is ample precedent for this endeavor in Christian tradition. As early as the second century, Christians felt their faith contained enough in common with the nonbeliever to legitimate an apologetic strategy. Moreover, such a strategy seems required by a faith that claims a strong continuity between the God who redeems and the God who creates. Thus Christians should not be surprised to find their specific religious beliefs confirmed by the best humanistic alternatives.

Without denying some continuity between recent theological strategies and some modes of past Christian theology, it is equally important that we see the fundamental differences. The apologist of the past stood in the church and its tradition and sought relationship with those outside. Apologetic theology was a secondary endeavor because the premodern apologist would never allow questions of unbelief to order the theological agenda. But now the theologian stands outside the tradition and seeks to show that selected aspects of that tradition can no longer pass muster from the perspective of the outsider. Such theologians try to locate the "essence" of religion in a manner that frees religion from its most embarrassing particularistic aspects.

Ironically, the success of this strategy has only served to underwrite the assumption that anything said in a theological framework cannot be of much interest. For if what is said theologically is but a confirmation of what can be known on other grounds or can be said more clearly in nontheological language, then why bother saying it theologically? Of course, it may still be useful to keep theologians around to remind us of what people used to believe, or to act as a check against the inevitable perversities of those in our culture who persist in the more traditional forms of religious practices and belief, but theology as such can no longer be considered a constructive or even serious intellectual endeavor. Furthermore, while contemporary theologians may have important insights concerning general human and moral issues, that is but a testimony to their individual intelligence and insight rather than to the significance of their particular theological convictions or training.

For example, much of the recent work in "medical ethics" has been done by theologians, but their prominence in that area has been purchased largely by demonstrating that they can do "medical ethics" just as well as anyone who is not burdened by a theological agenda. As a result it is very hard to distinguish between articles in medical ethics written by theologians and those written by nontheologians except that often the latter are better argued.[3]

3. That is not to say that much of the work done by philosophers in medical ethics is free from

The fact that it has become hard to distinguish work done by theologians in ethics from that of philosophers has only reinforced the impression that theologians have nothing interesting to say as theologians. Theologians and religious ethicists avidly read philosophers; the compliment is seldom returned. There are signs, however, that philosophers are beginning to turn their attention to matters traditionally the province of theologians.

For example, many philosophers writing about ethics are beginning to challenge the assumption that ethics is best understood on analogy with law. For centuries Christian theologians discussed that question and at no time more intensely than the Reformation. That discussion had rich results, with Christian thinkers consistently maintaining that law is not sufficient to depict the Christian moral life.[4] In a related manner many philosophers now challenge overly optimistic assumptions about humanity and moral rationality. Nowhere in modern literature have such assumptions been more decisively challenged than by Reinhold Niebuhr.[5] Furthermore, some philosophers are now suggesting that ethicists must free themselves from their fascination with quandaries and rules, and pay more attention to the virtues and character. Again religious traditions provide rich resources for such an analysis, and some theologians, for example, James Gustafson, have developed well-argued accounts of ethics so understood.[6] Yet each of these significant developments in theology has largely been ignored outside the theological community. Why is that the case?

Undoubtedly, one of the reasons is the sheer prejudice of many secular thinkers. They are simply ignorant of the disciplined nature of theological reflection and assume any reflection informed by religious claims cannot possibly be intelligible. But I suspect that there is a further reason, not so easily addressed, that is internal to how theological reflection about ethics has been done in our time: the lack of attention to the inability of Christian theologians to find a sufficient medium to articulate their own best insights for those who do not share their convictions. In order to understand why that is the case, it

---

difficulty. By "better argued" I mean it is more adept at working within the set paradigms of philosophical analysis. However I am by no means happy with those paradigms. For example, see my SP.

4. See, for example, Edward Long's fine article, "Soteriological Implications of Norm and Context," in Norm and Context in Christian Ethics, ed. Eugene Outka and Paul Ramsey (New York: Scribner's, 1968), 265–96.

5. In particular, see Reinhold Niebuhr, The Self and the Dramas of History (New York: Scribner's, 1955).

6. James Gustafson, Can Ethics Be Christian? (Chicago: University of Chicago Press, 1975).

will be necessary to describe the development of Christian ethics during this century. For it is only against this historical background that we can understand the failure of Christian ethics to command attention, and furthermore, why that failure should not be perpetuated, since those convictions still offer a powerful resource for ethical reflection, even for those who find they are unable to envision and construe the world through them.

II. The Difficulty of Keeping Christian Ethics Christian: The Heritage of Protestant Liberalism

The very idea of Christian ethics as a distinct discipline is a relatively recent development.[7] Of course, Christians have always had a lot to say about moral matters, but neither in their practical discourse nor their more systematic reflection did they try to make ethics a subject separable from their beliefs and convictions. The Church fathers did not write ethics per se; rather, their understanding of theology shaped their view of the moral life. Prior to the Enlightenment, the notion that there might be an independent realm called "morality" to which one must try to determine one's relation religiously and theologically simply did not exist.

The story of the development of "Christian ethics" as a distinct field, at least in the Protestant context, has two different strands, one philosophical and the other more pastoral. The first begins in Europe, especially in Germany, where Protestant liberalism tried to save theology by isolating its essence, that is, the fatherhood of God and the brotherhood of man. Immanuel Kant, the great exponent of this solution, maintained with his characteristically admirable clarity that "since the sacred narrative, which is employed solely on behalf of ecclesiastical faith, can have and, taken by itself, ought to have absolutely no influence upon the adoption of moral maxims, and since it is given to ecclesiastical faith only for the vivid presentation of its true object (virtue striving toward holiness), it follows that this narrative must at all times be taught and expounded in the interests of morality; and yet (because the

---

7. I am keenly aware of the inadequacy of the brief overview of the development of Christian ethics over the past century. Not only do I leave out of the account many of the main actors, even those I treat are not analyzed with the nuance they deserve. I hope soon to write a more adequate, book-length account that will do justice to this complex story. However, for present purposes I thought it worthwhile to tell the history in a somewhat contentious manner, since my interests are more systematic than historical. Moreover, I am certainly ready to defend the interpretive features of my account, even though I have not taken the time here to document them adequately.

common man especially has an enduring propensity within him to sink into passive belief) it must be inculcated painstakingly and repeatedly that true religion is to consist not in the knowing or considering of what God does or has done for our salvation, but in what we must do to become worthy of it."[8] For Kant, morality becomes the "essence" of religion, but ironically it is understood in a manner that makes positive religious convictions secondary.

1. Rauschenbusch and the Social Gospel

The other part of our story does not begin with such an explicit intellectual agenda, but involves a group of Protestant pastors in the late nineteenth and early twentieth centuries and their attempt to respond to the economic crisis of their people.[9] Taking their bearings from the prophetic traditions of the Hebrew Scripture, these men challenged the widespread assumption that poverty was the fault of the poor. They preached against political and economic structures that they believed were the roots of poverty. They thought they had rediscovered an old truth—lost through centuries of Christian accommodation with the status quo—that the essential characteristic of the Christian religion is its insistence on organic unity between religion and morality, theology and ethics.[10] For Walter Rauschenbusch, salvation consists in nothing less than "an attitude of love in which we would freely coordinate our life with the life of our fellows in obedience to the loving impulses of the spirit of God, thus taking our part in a divine organism of mutual service. God is the all-embracing source and exponent of the common life and good of mankind. When we submit to God, we submit to the supremacy of the common good. Salvation is the voluntary socializing of the soul."[11]

The "social gospel," as we learned to call this movement, cared little for the development of Christian ethics as a reflective mode of discourse. The purpose of "Christian ethics" was to mobilize the energy and power of the church for social renewal.[12] Adamant in their opposition to all eschatologies that

8. Immanuel Kant, *Religion Within the Limits of Reason Alone,* trans. with an introduction by Theodore Greene and Hoyt Hudson (New York: Harper, 1960), 123.

9. C. H. Hopkins, *The Rise of the Social Gospel in American Protestantism, 1865–1915* (New Haven: Yale University Press, 1940).

10. Walter Rauschenbusch, *A Theology for the Social Gospel* (Nashville, TN: Abingdon Press, 1945), 140.

11. Ibid., 98–99.

12. Ibid., 210. That does not mean that advocates of "the social gospel" were unsophisticated, for they were deeply influenced by Protestant liberalism, particularly the Kantianism of Albrecht Ritschl.

might justify passive Christian response to societal injustice, advocates of the social gospel sought "to develop the vision of the Church toward the future and to cooperate with the will of God which is shaping the destinies of humanity."[13]

In the wake of the social gospel movement, serious courses began to be taught in American Protestant seminaries in Christian ethics—though they were often called "Christian sociology." These courses tended to be primarily concerned with why Christians should be committed to social justice and this required analysis of the economic and social strategies that furthered that end. As a result, one of the central agendas of Christian ethics, still very much present, was a concern to make use of the social sciences for social analysis and action.[14] As a result, many Christian ethicists became social scientists with a religious interest. Furthermore, this concern for social analysis meant that the primary conversation partners for most Christian ethicists were not philosophers but social scientists.

It was not long, however, before some of the more naïve theological and social assumptions of the social gospel began to be questioned, especially by historical criticism in biblical studies and post–World War I cultural pessimism. Regarding the former, the social gospel's conviction that "the first step in the salvation of mankind was the achievement of the personality of Jesus"[15] was rendered problematic by historical-critical claims that the Gospels do not portray Jesus "the way he really was."[16] Regarding the latter, the social strategy of the social gospel was called into question by the intractability of many social problems that resisted unambiguous solutions. In spite of their trenchant criticism of American capitalism, the social gospelers were committed to progressivist ideology and policies. They never doubted the uniqueness of the American experience or entertained any critical doubt about the achieve-

13. Ibid., 224.

14. For example, in his fine article on one of the early social gospelers, Francis Greenwood Peabody, David Little observes that "like many of his contemporaries, Peabody recommended wide exposure to the methods of social science as the basis for sound moral action. Since the ethical aims of true religion and manifest patterns of social development were believed to be rooted in one and the same phenomenon, inductive empirical investigation of social life could only complement and enrich the moral task. He is very clear about this: 'Ethics is finally social science and social science is ethics. *Ethics is* the end of sociology' " ("Francis Greenwood Peabody," *Harvard Library Bulletin* 15, no. 3 [July 1967]: 287–300).

15. Rauschenbusch, *Theology,* 151.

16. Thus the attempt of liberal Protestantism to free Jesus from past "schemes of redemption," to base his divine quality not in metaphysical questions but on the free and ethical acts of his personality, ironically failed to meet the challenges of a critical approach to Scripture.

ment of the American ideal, which they saw as nothing less than the realization of the Kingdom of God. The only question was how to bring the economic institutions of American life under the same spirit of cooperation that American political institutions had already achieved. The primary difference between "saved and unsaved organizations" for the social gospel is that the former are democratic and the latter are autocratic and competitive. Their attempt to turn American business into worker cooperatives was but the continuing attempt to create the secure "saved institutions."[17]

Though often more realistic and theologically profound than these aims suggest, it was clear that the movement started by the social gospel required not only a new social strategy, but also a new theological rationale.[18] "Christian ethics" became the discipline pledged to find just that. The great figure representing this project was Reinhold Niebuhr, who began his long career as a social gospel advocate, became its most powerful critic, and was quite possibly the last publicly accessible and influential theologian in America. Niebuhr seemed to be saying something theological that was compelling to a wide range of people, including people in government, but, as we shall see, his accomplishment was fraught with ambiguity.

2. Reinhold Niebuhr's "Neo-Orthodox" Criticism of the Social Gospel
Niebuhr's criticism of the social gospel originally centered on his increasing dissatisfaction with its optimistic view of social institutions and change. His own experience as a pastor in Detroit during the great labor struggles taught him to distrust any idea that institutions qua institutions are capable of moral transformation, much less salvation.[19] Influenced by Marx, he came to see the exercise of power and coercion as essential for achieving, not a "saved" society, but one that might be more relatively just.

Niebuhr's theological transformation was at least partly the result of wrestling with the implications of this changed perspective on social action. Theologically, how can we come to terms with living in a world that might well require us to kill for a relative political good, and with the full knowledge that

17. Rauschenbusch, *Theology*, 112–13.
18. For a particularly able defense of Rauschenbusch, see Max Stackhouse's, "The Continuing Importance of Walter Rauschenbusch" (Nashville, TN: Abingdon Press, 1968), 13–59, which introduces Rauschenbusch's *The Righteousness of the Kingdom.*
19. Niebuhr's reflections on his change of mind can be found in his *Leaves from the Notebook of a Tamed Cynic* (New York: Living Age Books, 1957). See also Niebuhr's "Intellectual Autobiography," in *Reinhold Niebuhr: His Religious, Social, and Political Thought,* ed. Charles Kegley and Robert Bretall (New York: Macmillan, 1956), 1–24.

any achievement of some justice necessarily results in some injustice. Thus Niebuhr came to conclude that "the tragedy of human history consists precisely in the fact that human life cannot be creative without being destructive, that biological urges are enhanced and sublimated by demonic spirit and that this spirit cannot express itself without committing the sin of pride."[20]

Though by education a theological liberal, Niebuhr found the liberal progressivism with its optimistic understanding of humanity insufficient to sustain his social vision. He turned to that line of Christian theology represented by Augustine, Luther, and Kierkegaard, who emphasized humanity's fallenness and the need for a redemption not of human making. What is needed to sustain the struggle for social justice is not, as the social gospel presumed, a grand idealistic vision, but the possibility of forgiveness which is necessarily a "moral achievement which is possible only when morality is transcended in religion."[21] Thus, for Niebuhr, Jesus' cross represents the ultimate sacrificial love that will always call into question every social and political order. Such a cross is necessary to sustain moral action in an inherently unjust world, for only as it stands on the edge of history do we have the basis for a hope that does not result in either despair or utopianism.[22]

Under Niebuhr's influence, the task of Christian ethics came to be understood by many as the attempt to develop those theological, moral, and social insights necessary to sustain the ambiguous task of achieving more relatively just societies. Though Niebuhr understood himself to be making a decisive break with his social gospel forebears, in fact Niebuhr continued to accept the social gospel's most important theological and social presuppositions. Like them he assumed that the task of Christian ethics was to formulate the means for Christians to serve their societies, particularly American society. His understanding and justification of democracy was more sophisticated, but like

20. Reinhold Niebuhr, *The Nature and Destiny of Man* (New York: Scribner's, 1941), 1:10–11.

21. Reinhold Niebuhr, *An Interpretation of Christian Ethics* (New York: Living Age Books, 1956), 201. It is interesting that Niebuhr's stress on forgiveness as the hallmark of Christian ethics is not carried forward in his later work. Rather, his emphasis is almost entirely on self-sacrificial love. It is my hunch that Niebuhr was much closer to being right by focusing on forgiveness than love as more important for the systematic display of Christian ethics.

22. In his *Christian Realism and Liberation Theology* (Maryknoll, NY: Orbis Books, 1981), Dennis McCann suggests that rather than providing a strategy for social action Niebuhr is best interpreted as trying to form a "spirituality" necessary to sustain political activity. That seems to me to be a particularly fruitful way to read Niebuhr, as it helps account for the lack of any conceptually clear connections between Niebuhr's theological views and his strategic judgments.

the social gospelers he never questioned that Christianity has a peculiar relationship to democracy. For Niebuhr and the social gospelers the subject of
Christian ethics was America.[23] They differed only on how nearly just such a
society could be and the theological presuppositions necessary to sustain
social involvement.

Niebuhr, far more than was seen at the time, continued to be essentially a
liberal theologian. His emphasis on the sinfulness of humankind in his magisterial *The Nature and Destiny of Man* led many to associate him with the
"neo-orthodox" movement of Bultmann, Brunner, and Barth. Yet Niebuhr
never shared Barth's theological rejection of liberalism as a basic theological
strategy; he, like Bultmann, continued liberal theology's presumption that
theology must be grounded in anthropology. Thus, his compelling portrayal
of our sinfulness, which seemed to function as a critique of liberal optimism,
was in fact a continuation of the liberal attempt to demonstrate the intelligibility of theological language through its power to illuminate the human
condition. In spite of Niebuhr's personally profound theological convictions,
many secular thinkers accepted his anthropology and social theory without
accepting his theological presuppositions.[24] And it is not clear that in doing so
they were making a mistake, as the relationships between Niebuhr's theological and ethical positions were never clearly demonstrated.

It was becoming increasingly apparent that Christian ethics must be written in a manner that allowed, and perhaps even encouraged, the separation of
ethics from its religious roots. Perhaps this seems an odd result for a move-

23. See, for example, Niebuhr's *The Children of Light and the Children of Darkness* (New York:
Scribner's, 1944) and *The Irony of American History* (New York: Scribner's, 1962). This perhaps
helps explain the oft-made observation that Niebuhr paid almost no attention to the social
significance of the church—for finally, in spite of all the trenchant criticism he directed at
America, America was his church. Thus the criticism that failed to sustain his trenchant
perspective in the last years of his life in some ways is misplaced, since it fails to note that
Niebuhr from beginning to end was involved in a stormy love affair with America. In some
ways the social gospelers were less accommodationist than Niebuhr in this respect; Rauschenbusch, in particular, assumed the necessity of the church to stand as a critic against American
society.

The importance of America as the subject of Christian ethics can also be seen in the
tendency of many Christian ethicists to think of ethics as a form of "American studies." H. R.
Niebuhr's *The Kingdom of God in America* (New York: Harper, 1937) remains the classical text
for this genre.

24. Niebuhr profoundly influenced such people as Hans Morgenthau, George Kennan,
Arthur Schlesinger Jr., and many others. It is, perhaps, a mark of the instability of Niebuhr's
position that often both sides of a political issue, particularly in foreign affairs, can claim with
some justice to be Niebuhrians.

ment that began by asserting the "organic unity" between religion and ethics, but it was a development that was a necessary outgrowth of the social gospel commitments. The social gospelers were able to make direct appeals to their religious convictions to justify their social involvement, because in the late nineteenth century they could continue to presuppose that America was a "religious" or even a "Christian civilization and country." Niebuhr, more aware of our religious pluralism as well as the secular presuppositions underlying the American experience, attempted to provide a theological rationale for why Christians should not seek to make their theological commitments directly relevant for social policy and strategy. Though extremely critical of the Lutheran law–Gospel distinction, Niebuhr also drew extensively on the resources of that tradition, now reinterpreted in existential categories, to justify an understanding of justice and its social attainment that did not require any direct theological rationale.

Niebuhr's views prevailed for no other reason than that they were more in accord with the changing social and religious situation in America. American society was increasingly becoming a pluralist and secular society.[25] As a result, Christian social ethicists felt it necessary to find ways in which their ethical conclusions could be separated from any theological framework. In the hope of securing societal good, the task of Christian ethics thus became the attempt to develop social strategies that people of goodwill could adopt even though they differed religiously and morally.

Though Niebuhr criticized the Catholic natural law tradition for "absolutizing the relative," he nonetheless was a natural law thinker. Albeit Niebuhr's understanding of natural law, through which justice was defined, involved "not so much fixed standards of reason as they are rational efforts to apply the moral obligation, implied in the love commandment, to the complexities of life and the fact of sin, that is, to the situation created by the inclination of men to take advantage of each other."[26] In fact, Niebuhr's understanding of the "law of love" as an unavoidable aspect of the human

25. Arthur Schlesinger documents this well in "The Political Philosophy of Reinhold Niebuhr," in *Reinhold Niebuhr: His Religious, Social, and Political Thought*, 125–50. Schlesinger rightly notes that Niebuhr, the penetrating critic of the social gospel and pragmatism, ended up "the powerful reinterpreter and champion of both. It was the triumph of his own remarkable analysis that it took what was valuable in each, rescued each by defining for each the limits of validity, and, in the end, gave the essential purposes of both new power and vitality. No man has had as much influence as a preacher in this generation; no preacher has had as much influence in the secular world" (149).

26. Reinhold Niebuhr, *Faith and History* (New York: Scribner's, 1951), 188–89.

condition was in many ways a powerful attempt to provide a natural theology that could make the cross intelligible as a symbol of human existence.[27]

3. H. Richard Niebuhr's Theological Critique of the Social Gospel

If Reinhold Niebuhr's work resulted in an ambiguous account of Christian ethics, in many ways his brother's work proved to be a more decisive challenge for that task. While Reinhold Niebuhr's critique of the social gospel arose primarily from difficulties with its way of sustaining the social imperative, H. Richard Niebuhr was preoccupied with the theological difficulties that the social gospel had occasioned. Deeply influenced by Ernst Troeltsch, he was acutely aware that the social gospelers' attempt to move directly from their theological convictions to social strategies was fraught not only with social ambiguities but with theological difficulties. Moreover, he was increasingly doubtful of any position that assumed that God could be used to underwrite humanity's interests, even if those interests were most impressive.

Under H. Richard Niebuhr's influence it became the business of many Christian ethicists to find the most adequate conceptual means to explicate what kind of moral implications might follow from Christian convictions.[28] Thus, Christian theologians began to give more serious attention to what philosophers were doing, hoping they would supply just such conceptual tools. But the kind of philosophical ethics to which Niebuhr's students turned had exactly the opposite effect. They learned from those philosophical sources that there was an inherent problem in trying to move from theological claims to normative recommendations, for in doing so one commits the "super-naturalistic fallacy."[29] As a result, theological ethicists began to pay even less attention to positive theological claims and instead attempted to show that, formally, a theological basis for ethics was not inherently incoherent and, in

27. Niebuhr's stress on the sinfulness of man leads some to forget that for Niebuhr theology is still primarily anthropology. As a result Niebuhr never answered satisfactorily how the cross of Jesus is necessary for our adequately understanding why the cross is the necessary symbol of "the perfection of *agape* which transcends all particular norms of justice and mutuality in history" (*The Nature and Destiny of Man*, 2:74).

28. For the best short introduction to H. R. Niebuhr's work, see James Gustafson, introduction to *The Responsible Self: An Essay in Christian Moral Philosophy*, by H. R. Niebuhr (New York: Harper and Row, 1963), 6–41.

29. H. R. Niebuhr was not himself very taken with ethics done out of the analytical tradition, but instead was influenced more by the pragmatist tradition of Royce and Perry. However, a later generation of students, trained by Gustafson, turned increasingly to Moore, Ross, and Hare in attempts to think through the problems they had inherited from Niebuhr.

particular, that theological claims could underwrite antirelativist and objectivist concerns.[30] In the hands of some, Christian ethics became but another form of metaethics. In the process, it became just as ahistorical as its philosophical counterpart.

That was certainly not a result that would have made H. Richard Niebuhr happy. Even though in his work Christian ethics was less an aid to action than an aid to understanding, he did not want Christian ethics to lose its theological rationale. On the contrary, his focus on the question "What is going on?" rather than "What should we do?" was an attempt to keep theological questions primary for ethical reflection. It was H. R. Niebuhr's task to show that the former question could only be answered adequately in theological terms. Thus, in *The Responsible Self,* he maintained that the central Christian claim is "God is acting in all actions upon you. So respond to all actions upon you as to respond to his action."[31]

For H. R. Niebuhr the problem was not how to secure justice in an unjust world, but rather how to account for moral activity amid the relativities of history. His theological project was to provide a theological interpretation of the relativity of our existence so that the knowledge of our finitude was relativized by our relation to a God who alone deserves our complete loyalty. While the task of Christian ethics for H. R. Niebuhr was theological, the ironic result was that his own theology made it difficult to keep Christian ethics Christian. For the very idea of "Christian ethics" suggested a far too narrow conception of God to do justice to the relativities of our existence.[32]

While Karl Barth was certainly influential on H. R. Niebuhr, Friedrich Schleiermacher was even more influential. Niebuhr reacted strongly against the christocentrism of Barth and—equally importantly—shared with his brother Reinhold a faith in the liberal project of securing the intelligibility of theological discourse by demonstrating how it reflects as well as describes the human condition. Therefore, while differing deeply with his brother on particular theological issues, he remained essentially in the tradition of Calvin-

---

30. Arthur Dyck's enthusiasm for and theological justification of the "ideal observer" theory is a good example of this tendency. See his *On Human Care: An Introduction to Ethics* (Nashville, TN: Abingdon, 1977).

31. H. R. Niebuhr, *The Responsible Self,* 126.

32. For H. R. Niebuhr, Jesus is normative only as he "represents the incarnation of radical faith," which is faith that "Being is God, or better, that the principle of being, the source of all things and the power by which they exist, is good, as good for them and good to them" (*Radical Monotheism and Western Culture* [New York: Harper and Row, 1960], 38).

ism, as opposed to Reinhold's Lutheranism, but in many ways the structure of their theologies was similar. H. Richard Niebuhr's *The Responsible Self* was an attempt to analyze the inherent relatedness of human to human, human to nature, human and nature to God, who enters a covenant with his creation.[33]

4. Recent Developments in Christian Ethics: 1960–1980

The recent history of the discipline called "Christian ethics" in the American context has largely been the story of the attempt to work out the set of problems bequeathed to us by the social gospel and the Niebuhrs. Since Vatican II, the other significant figure in the drama has been Roman Catholic moral theology. Roman Catholic moral theologians have increasingly made contact with their Protestant counterparts, hoping to learn how to put their natural law commitments in a more compelling theological framework. For their part, Protestant thinkers, struggling with the failure of their own tradition to develop nuanced arguments about particular issues, looked to the Catholic tradition of casuistry for help in thinking about such issues as marriage, abortion, and war. This tendency among Protestant thinkers was best represented by Paul Ramsey. For Ramsey continued to assume that the task of Christian ethics is to address the American body politic. But by Ramsey's time, there was no longer the hope of transforming the polity (as was hoped by the social gospelers), but merely the hope of sustaining that polity against the increasing onslaught of relativistic and consequentialist moral theories. While an heir of both Niebuhrs, Ramsey could not find an adequate framework for disciplined ethical argument in either the work of the brothers Niebuhr or in Protestant thought generally. To find arguments that, at least in principle, would be publicly acceptable, Ramsey looked to the Catholic tradition. Still, the influence of the Niebuhrs meant that Ramsey could not accept Roman

---

33. Thus he says,

> Man responsive and responsible before nature, fitting his actions into those of nature; man responsive in political or economic or cultural society as responsible citizen; responsible businessman, responsible educator, responsible scientist, responsible parent, responsible churchman—such men we know and understand. But what ties all these responsivities and responsibilities together and where is the responsible *self* among all these roles played by the individual being? Can it be located within the self, as though by some mighty act of self-making it brought itself into being as one "I" among these many systems of interpretation and response? The self as one self among all the systematized reactions in which it engages seems to be the counterpart of a unity that lies beyond, yet expresses itself in, all the manifold systems of actions upon it. In religious language, the soul and God belong together; or otherwise stated, I am one within myself as I encounter the One in all that acts upon me. (*The Responsible Self*, 122)

Catholic assumptions about the relative autonomy of natural law and morality. As a result, his work clearly manifested the tension inherent in the development of Christian ethics: namely, a concern to provide a theological account of the moral life while at the same time underplaying the significance of theology for purposes of public discussion.[34]

A major context for Ramsey's perspective was the situation ethics debate of the 1950s and 1960s. Against Joseph Fletcher's advocacy of "act-agapeism" (a Christianized form of act-utilitarianism) as the most appropriate expression of Christian love, Ramsey insisted that Christian love must be "in-principled." Moreover, the principles he thought best expressed or embodied Christian love were very much like the traditional Roman Catholic prohibitions against unjust life-taking, lying, sexual misconduct, and so on. Thus Ramsey maintained that Christian ethics was best expressed in terms of deontological normative theories and should reject all forms of consequentialism.[35]

While on one level it is hard to see any relationship between this agenda and that of the social gospelers, in many ways Ramsey continued that project. Though Ramsey did not promote the social activism that the social gospelers thought required by the "organic unity between religion and ethics," he did share their assumption that the primary subject of Christian ethics was to support and sustain the moral resources of American society.[36]

---

34. The theological side of Ramsey's work was more apparent in his early work where he was emphatic that "natural law" must be transformed by love. See in particular his *War and the Christian Conscience* (Durham, NC: Duke University Press, 1961). Ramsey's shift to the motif of covenant fidelity as the central metaphor for Christian reflection also seems to have been accompanied with a greater appreciation for the continuity between the "natural" covenants we find in our lives and that which God has made with us. As a result he is able to proceed with much less direct appeal to theological warrants. See, for example, *The Patient as Person* (New Haven: Yale University Press, 1970).

35. Thus Ramsey argues that "Protestant Christian ethics is often too profoundly personal to be ethically relevant, if in this is included even a minimum of concern for the social habits and customs of a people. Ordinarily, we do not take Christian ethics with enough seriousness to illumine the path that men, women, and *society* should follow today. This suggests that only some form of rule-agapism and not act-agapism, can be consistent with the elaboration of a Christian's social responsibilities. No social morality ever was founded, or ever will be founded, upon a situational ethic" (*Deeds and Rules in Christian Ethics* [New York: Scribner's, 1967], 20).

36. Moreover, like Reinhold Niebuhr he assumes that this project requires an account sufficient to underwrite a politics of realism in which we see that we may well have to kill in the name of a lesser evil; but unlike Niebuhr, Ramsey sought to provide, through a theological reinterpretation of the just war tradition, a control on realism's tendency to consequentialism. Ramsey's profound debt to Niebuhr can be most clearly seen in *The Just War: Force and*

As for what makes ethics Christian, Ramsey believed that the deontological commitments of our culture required theological convictions to be sustained. Therefore, in Ramsey's work in such areas as medical ethics, most of the theology can be done in the preface of his books. As a result, even many of those who are sympathetic with Ramsey's construal of the ethos of medicine in deontological terms see no reason why those deontological commitments require Ramsey's peculiar theological views about the significance of covenant love to sustain that ethos. Or again, many may well side with Ramsey against the act-utilitarianism of Fletcher, but see no reason why that debate involves theological questions, since it is simply a straightforward philosophical matter involving whether a coherent deontological or teleological normative theory can be defended. All the talk about love by both Fletcher and Ramsey is but an obfuscation of the issue.

Therefore, contemporary theologians found themselves in a peculiar situation. Having increasingly turned to philosophical sources to help them illumine the logic of their ethical commitments, they wound up finding it increasingly difficult to articulate what, if anything, Christian ethics had to contribute to discussions in ethics. What they failed to see was that the very philosophical sources from which they drew to clarify the nature of their normative claims made it difficult to suggest how religious convictions might challenge just those philosophical frameworks. Thus theologians assumed, along with their philosophical colleagues, that ethics must basically be about dealing with quandaries, the only question being whether Christian convictions are more basically deontological or teleological or some as yet unspecified combination of the two.

Thus, the distinctive nature of much of theological ethics in the 1970s continued to be shown not by the expression of any distinctive convictions, but rather in the sets of issues theologians addressed. By continuing to draw on the inspiration of the social gospel, theologians continued to be concerned about questions of social and economic justice, marriage and the family, the

---

Political Responsibility (New York: Scribner's, 1968). There Ramsey, like Niebuhr, argues that the failure of all peace movements is that they presume the illusion that force can be avoided in politics and as a result only increase the likelihood of war. In contrast the just war tradition influenced by the theological insights of Augustine rightly sees that war can never be fought for peace, but only for more relative just ends. Thus Ramsey argues the ethos necessary to control violence through just war principles must ultimately draw on religious presuppositions. For only if you think death is not ultimate power over life can you be willing to expose yourself to death and to kill others for the limited moral goods of political community.

status of the nation-state, that hitherto had tended to be ignored by the philosopher. Yet, with the work of John Rawls and the rise of journals such as *Philosophy and Public Affairs* (founded in 1971) the theologian could no longer claim even that mark of distinction. The only alternatives left seemed to be to retreat to working in a confessional stance or analyzing the methodological issues and alternatives for understanding how theological ethics has been or should be done.

Much of the latter work has been done by James Gustafson, a student of H. R. Niebuhr, who has sought through careful analysis of historical and current options within theological ethics to keep the discourse alive.[37] Though much of Gustafson's work is descriptive, his concerns are primarily constructive. It is, therefore, not accidental that Gustafson began to direct attention to the importance for ethics of the "sort of persons we are," of character and virtue, as the appropriate context for assessing the significance of theological language for ethical behavior.[38]

Above all, Gustafson's work is centered on the question "Can ethics be Christian?" For him the Christian theologian's ethical task is done for the sake of a community that shares a set of common experiences and beliefs about God and his particular revelation in Jesus Christ.

> The Christian community is not, however, the exclusive audience. Since the intention of the divine power for human wellbeing is universal in its scope, the historically particular medium through which that power is clarified for Christians also has universal significance. The theologian engaged in the task of "prescriptive" ethics formulates principles and values that can guide the actions of persons who do not belong to the Christian community. They will be persuasive to others, however, on the basis of supporting reasons different from those that Christians might respond to. In effect, the theologian moves from the particular Christian belief to a statement of their moral import in a more universal language. These statements will be persuasive to nonreligious persons only by the cogency of the argument that is made to show that the

---

37. See, for example, Gustafson's *Christian Ethics and the Community* (Philadelphia: Pilgrim Press, 1971) and *Theology and Christian Ethics* (Philadelphia: Pilgrim Press, 1974), both of which are collections of his essays that attempt to bring some intellectual clarity to the activity of other Christian ethicists.

38. This emphasis, of course, is but an indication of Gustafson's indebtedness to H. R. Niebuhr's attempt to identify the central issue of Christian ethics as that of the "self." Unfortunately many of the interpreters of H. R. Niebuhr tend to stress more his account of "responsibility" and, as a result, fail to see that Niebuhr's primary concern was the "self."

"historical particularity" sheds light on principles and values that other serious moral persons also perceive and also ought to adhere to. Indeed, since
the Christian theologian shares in the general moral experience of secular
people, and since one facet of this work that is theologically warranted is the
inferring of principles and values from common experience, he or she need
not in every practical circumstance make a particular theological case for
what is formulated. The theologian ought, however, to be able to make a
Christian theological case if challenged to do so.[39]

Gustafson's reasoning is based on his theological belief that God's purposes
are for "the well-being of man and creation," and thus on most occasions the
reasons that justify any moral act would justify the moral acts of Christians.
The only case he can give that might be an exception to this is some Christians'
commitment to nonviolent resistance to evil, since the justification of such a
response clearly must rely on appeal to certain "religious" reasons that go
beyond what we mean by morality.[40]

5. Summary

If this is all that is to be gained by speaking theologically about morality, then
one may well question if it is worth the effort. In this brief history of the
development of the "discipline" of Christian ethics, I have tried to show how
the primary subject theologically became how to keep Christian ethics Christian. This situation is no doubt partly the result of the changing historical and
sociological stance of the churches vis-à-vis American society. As American
society becomes increasingly secular, Christian ethicists come to think that, if
they wish to remain political actors, they must translate their convictions into
a nontheological idiom. But once such a translation is accomplished, why is
the theological idiom needed at all?

The difficulty of making and keeping Christian ethics Christian, however,
derives not only from social strategies, but, as we have seen, also from theological difficulties. For the recovery of the ethical significance of theological
discourse was part of a theological movement within Protestantism that in
large measure sought to avoid the more traditional particularistic claims of

---

39. Gustafson, *Can Ethics Be Christian?*, 163.

40. It is telling, I think, that in his recent constructive work, *Ethics from a Theocentric
Perspective* (Chicago: University of Chicago Press, 1981), Gustafson thinks John Howard
Yoder's "sectarian" stance to be the most intelligible alternative to his own position.

Christianity. Ironically, just to the extent that the development of Christian ethics as a field was a success, it reinforced the assumption that more positive theological convictions had little purchase on the way things are or should be. It is no wonder, therefore, that the dominant modes of philosophical ethics received little challenge from the theological community. Indeed, exactly to the contrary, theologians and religious thinkers have largely sought to show that the modes of argument and conclusions reached by philosophical ethicists are no different from those reached by ethicists with more explicit religious presuppositions. The task of Christian ethics, both socially and philosophically, was not revision but accommodation.

III. A Revision of Theological Ethics

I have tried to suggest why the development of Christian ethics during this century provided no significant alternative to the dominant modes of ethical reflection done by philosophers. While aspects of the work of Rauschenbusch, the Niebuhrs, Ramsey, and Gustafson certainly stand in sharp contrast with the accepted mode of doing philosophical ethics, it is simply the case that their work has failed to influence or even to be taken very seriously by ethicists working in a nontheological context.

Of course part of the reason for that is more sociological than intellectual. Religion has increasingly become marginal in our culture, both politically and intellectually. Attempts to assert the relevance of religion in the social and political realm are often done with a crudeness that serves to underwrite the general assumption that our society will do better to continue to relegate religious concerns to the private and subjective realm. This same kind of relegation has occurred in the intellectual realm, often with much less good reason. Few modern intellectuals feel the obligation to read the better work done in theology, because they prejudicially assume that theology must inherently be a form of special pleading.

As I suggested at the beginning, attempts to address this prejudice on its own terms are doomed to failure. The more theologians seek to find the means to translate theological convictions into terms acceptable to the nonbeliever, the more they substantiate the view that theology has little of importance to say in the area of ethics. It seems that the theologian is in a classical "no-win" situation.

Yet in important ways this is not the case. It may be that theology can make a virtue of necessity. In many ways the social and intellectual marginality of the church in our culture is an intellectual resource that can provide the opportunity to recover some of the more important aspects of Christian reflection, particularly concerning morality. As I have tried to suggest, the very development of "Christian ethics" as a branch of theology was inspired by an attempt to reawaken Christian social responsibility. But the very terms of that reawakening and its underlying theology had already accommodated itself far too much to the secular ethos. Therefore, in spite of the significant advances in Christian reflection represented by the development of Christian ethics, in many ways it failed to represent adequately the resources for ethical reflection within the Christian tradition. Thus one of the ironies is that many of the challenges made by philosophers against the reigning paradigm could have been made, and perhaps made even more forcefully, from a theological perspective. But they were not, and they were not because Christians in general and theologians in particular continued to assume that they had built a home within Western civilization that they had a stake in continuing. As a result, Christian ethicists accepted an account of the social good that failed to manifest the struggle and the transformation of the self necessary for any adequate account of the moral life.

It is odd that Christians, of all people, could have made that mistake, since who could know better than they that the moral good is not an achievement easily accomplished by the many, but a demanding task that only a few master. Christians are not called merely to do what is right, or merely to observe the law, though doing the right and observing the law are not irrelevant to being good. Rather, for Christians the moral life is to be seen as a journey through life sustained by fidelity to the cross of Christ, which brings a fulfillment no law can ever embody. Thus Aquinas says:

> There is a twofold element in the Law of the Gospel. There is the chief element, namely, the grace of the Holy Ghost bestowed inwardly. And as to this, the New Law justifies. Hence Augustine says: "There (that is, in the Old Testament) the Law was set forth in an outward fashion, that the ungodly might be afraid; here (that is, in the New Testament) it is given in an inward manner, that they might be justified." The other element of the Evangelical Law is secondary; namely, the teachings of faith, and those commandments which direct human affections and human actions. And as to this, the New Law does not justify. Hence the Apostle says: "The letter killeth, but the spirit quickeneth" (II Cor. 3:6), and Augustine explains this by saying that the letter

denotes any writing that is external to man, even that of the moral precepts such as are contained in the Gospel. Therefore the letter, even of the Gospel, would kill, unless there were the inward presence of the healing grace of faith.[41]

From such a perspective Christian thinkers, above all, should have been among the first to criticize the attempt to model the moral life primarily on the analogy of the law. Instead, fearing moral anarchy, like our philosophical colleagues, Christian ethicists assumed that questions of the "right" were prior to questions of the "good," that moral principles were more fundamental than virtues, that a coherent morality required a single primary principle from which all others could be derived or tested, and that the central task of morality was to help us resolve difficult moral quandaries.

Ironically, Christian theology attempted to deny the inherent historical and community-dependent nature of our moral convictions in the hopes that our "ethics" might be universal. But as Schneewind reminds us, the justification of our moral principles and assertions cannot be done from the point of view of anyone, but rather requires a tradition of moral wisdom.[42] Such a tradition is not a "deposit" of unchanging moral "truth," but is made up of the lives of men and women who are constantly testing and developing that tradition through their own struggle to live it. The maintenance of such a tradition requires a community across time sufficient to sustain the journey from one generation to the next. The Christian word for such a community is church.[43]

It is my suspicion that if theologians are going to contribute to reflection on the moral life in our particular situation, they will do so exactly to the extent they can capture the significance of the church for determining the nature and content of Christian ethical reflection. This may seem an odd suggestion, for it seems such a move would only make the theologian that much further removed from being a serious conversation partner. It is as-

41. Thomas Aquinas, *Summa Theologica*, I–II.106.2, trans. Fathers of the English Dominican Province (New York: Benziger Brothers, 1946). Many others besides Aquinas could be quoted to substantiate this point. I purposely chose Aquinas, since many who defend a natural law approach to Christian ethics appeal to him as their primary authority. Yet as the quotation makes clear, Aquinas assumed that an adequate theological ethics could not be limited to or based on an analogy with law.

42. J. B. Schneewind, "Moral Knowledge and Moral Principles," in *Revisions: Changing Perspectives in Moral Philosophy,* ed. Stanley Hauerwas and Alasdair MacIntyre (Notre Dame, IN: University of Notre Dame Press, 1983), 113–26.

43. For a fuller account of this perspective, see CC.

sumed, by theologian and philosopher alike, that any distinctive contribution of theological ethics must begin with beliefs about God, Jesus, sin, and the like, and the moral implications of those beliefs. And of course there is much truth to that. Yet the problem with putting the matter in that way is that such "beliefs" look like descriptions of existence, some kind of primitive metaphysics, that one must then try to analyze for their moral implications. To force Christian moral reflection into such a pattern is to make it appear but another philosophical account of the moral life.

But that is exactly what it is not. For Christian beliefs about God, Jesus, sin, the nature of human existence, and salvation are intelligible only if they are seen against the background of the church—that is, a body of people who stand apart from the "world" because of the peculiar task of worshiping a God whom the world knows not. This is a point as much forgotten by Christian theologians as by secular philosophers, the temptation being to simply make Christianity another "system of belief." Yet what was most original about the first Christians was not the peculiarity of their beliefs, even beliefs about Jesus, but their social inventiveness in creating a community whose like had not been seen before. To say they believed in God is true but uninteresting. What is interesting is that their very understanding that the God they encountered in Jesus required the formation of a community distinct from the world exactly because of the kind of God he was. From a Christian perspective, the atheist cannot understand the kind of God he or she does not believe in apart from understanding the kind of community necessary across time to faithfully worship such a God. The flabbiness and banality of contemporary atheism is, thus, a judgment on the church's unwillingness to be a distinctive people.

Therefore, when as Christians we are asked to say something theological, especially when the questioner is seeking to understand the ethical significance of religious convictions, perhaps we should not say "God" (as does Gustafson) but "Church." For my criticism of the emphasis in contemporary ethics on law, on rights, on principles, on quandaries, on facts distinguished from values, is fundamentally a criticism of what becomes central when one tries to write ethics for anyone, as if ethics can be done in abstraction from any concrete community. It is not surprising that the law becomes the primary analogue for such an ethic as law is often seen as that set of minimum principles needed to secure order between people who share little in common. Ethics, like law, thus becomes the procedural means to settle disputes and resolve problems while leaving our individual "preferences" and desires to our own choice. To say more about morality requires not simply a conception of the good, but a tradition that carries the virtues necessary for training in movement toward the good.

Many philosophers and theologians are calling for a fuller account of the moral life. They rightly criticize the "thinness" of much of contemporary ethical theory; yet they offer no persuasive alternative. They point to the need for revision, but the social and political practices necessary for that revision to be institutionalized are missing. Moreover, any attempts to create them appear utopian or totalitarian. Of course, appeals can be made to particular individuals as paradigms of the kind of moral life desired, but moral geniuses are never sufficient to sustain our best moral convictions. For such sustenance we need a community to direct attention toward, and sustain the insights of, those who have become more nearly good.

Christians believe that to live well, we need not only a community, but a community of a particular kind. We need a community of people who are capable of being faithful to a way of life, even when that way of life may be in conflict with what passes as "morality" in the larger society. Christians are a people who have learned that belief in God requires that we learn to look upon ourselves as creatures rather than as creators. This necessarily creates a division between ourselves and others who persist in the pretentious assumption that we can and should be morally autonomous. Of course Christians are as prone to such pretensions as non-Christians. What distinguishes them is their willingness to belong to a community that embodies the stories and the rituals of the faith, to belong to other people committed to worshiping God truthfully. Such a community must challenge our prideful pretensions as well as provide the skills for the humility necessary for becoming not just good, but holy.

Theologians, therefore, have something significant to say about ethics, but they will not say it significantly if they try to disguise the fact that they think, write, and speak out of and to a distinctive community. Their first task is not—as has been assumed by many Christian ethicists who continue to write under the spell of Christendom—to write as though Christian commitments make no difference in the sense that they only underwrite what everyone already in principle can know, but rather to show the difference those commitments make. At least by doing that, philosophers may have some idea how the attempt to avoid presuming any tradition or community may distort their account of the moral life. Our task as theologians remains what it has always been: namely, to exploit the considerable resources embodied in particular Christian convictions which sustain our ability to be a community faithful to our belief that we are creatures of a graceful God. If we do that we may well discover that we are speaking to more than just our fellow Christians, for others as a result may well find we have something interesting to say.

Further Reading

"How Christian Ethics Came to Be," essay 1 in this volume

"The Non-Resistant Church: The Theological Ethics of John Howard Yoder" (1972), in *vv*

"Why the 'Sectarian Temptation' Is a Misrepresentation: A Response to James Gustafson" (1988), essay 4 in this volume

"God as Participant: Time and History in the Work of James Gustafson" (1985), in *ww*

"Tragedy and Joy: The Spirituality of Peaceableness" (1983), in *PK*

"History as Fate: How Justification by Faith Became Anthropology and History in America" (1997), in *ww*

"The Irony of Reinhold Niebuhr: The Ideological Character of Christian Realism," with Mikael Broadway (1992), in *ww*

"How Christian Ethics Became Medical Ethics: The Case of Paul Ramsey" (1995), in *ww*

"Communitarians and Medical Ethicists: Why I Am None of the Above" (1993), in *DF*

3. A Retrospective Assessment of an "Ethics of Character": The Development of Hauerwas's Theological Project (1985, 2001)

In this adapted excerpt from the preface to the second edition of Character and the Christian Life *(a revised version of Hauerwas's doctoral dissertation), Hauerwas discusses how his earliest work on the "ethics of character" was a "door, that once opened, forced [him] to see things [he] had no idea existed when [he] started the work." In this self-critical piece, Hauerwas charts the way in which he came to see notions of "vision" and "narrative" and the community of the church as necessary companions to virtue and character. In this "midcareer" analysis of this project, he both points out the errors of his early work in theological ethics and lays out future directions.*

On Beginning with an Ending

Back in the days when I made an honest living laying brick I learned a great deal from the colorful ways bricklayers and laborers described their work. For example, when laying the last brick, tile, or stone in a particularly difficult job a bricklayer often says, "Man, I wish I had started with that one." In some ways now, ten years down the road from when *Character and the Christian Life* was first published, I feel that way: namely, I wish I could have started then with what I know now. Yet I am not so sure I believe that. I have tried to be candid about where I think I could have improved this book, but unless I had done the work here I do not think I would ever have seen why and where such improvement was needed. I am not stating the obvious point that until you do something you cannot know where you made the mistakes. Rather I am suggesting that on the whole I think the book was enough on the right track that its mistakes have proved fruitful. For finally I think this is the best most of us can do: make interesting mistakes.

[This essay is based on an excerpt from the introduction to the 2d edition of CCL, xiii–xxxiii. It has been revised, reorganized, and updated with the approval of the author.]

Looking Back at Character and the Christian Life

Ten years ago, when *Character and the Christian Life* was first published, it was a shot in the dark. Character and/or the virtues were seldom discussed, much less considered central for understanding the moral life. There were glimmers here and there that suggested these might be fruitful themes to develop, but little sustained work was being done in that direction. For example, in philosophy, G. E. M. Anscombe and Stuart Hampshire were calling for renewed attention to moral psychology; in theology, H. Richard Niebuhr's concentration on the nature of the self and James M. Gustafson's sense of the importance of the dispositions at least suggested character and the virtues might be fruitful categories for investigation. But on the whole the matters with which the book dealt were thought worthy at best of mention in footnotes in serious works in ethics and theology.

Now it seems everything has changed. Not only are character and virtue no longer ignored, they have even begun to be regarded with some suspicion. Thus Gilbert Meilaender in his recent book, *The Theory and Practice of Virtue*, suggests, "before Christian ethicists latch too quickly onto an ethic of virtue, it is important to remember that an emphasis on character may sit uneasily with some strands of Christian belief."[1] Quite apart from the substance of Meilaender's claim, what is striking is that not only is it now assumed that something called "an ethic of virtue" exists, but it can also be seen as a threat.

What has happened is that what only ten years ago was a side issue in ethics now seems to command widespread attention. I must admit I fear such attention. I fear it because I do not assume that an "ethics of virtue or character" is, as it is often characterized, an alternative to an "ethic of obligation." Too often I find many theological ethicists, with the best will in the world, assume that

---

1. Gilbert Meilaender, *The Theory and Practice of Virtue* (Notre Dame, IN: University of Notre Dame Press, 1984), x. Later Meilaender expands this theme, quoting Josef Pieper to the effect that "'Acquiring an excellence, be it a skill or a virtue, is not only acquiring a capacity or tendency to act in a certain way; it is also a matter of acquiring merit.' These words suggest a difficulty for anyone wishing to write about the virtues within a framework of Christian belief. Concentration upon the gradual development of one's character and an effort to cultivate the virtues within one's life may, from a Christian perspective, appear suspect. The entire effort may seem too self-centered, a failure to focus one's attention upon God and the neighbor. And the very fact that virtues are habits of behavior engrained in one's character may suggest that they become our possession and that the moral life is not continually in need of grace" (36). Though Meilaender and I sometimes disagree about the theological status of the virtues, I hope it is apparent how much I have learned from him.

the meaning and validity of an ethics of virtue has been established. As a result, they do not think they need to return to basic issues in moral psychology and theology that the emphasis on virtue requires. If *Character and the Christian Life* does nothing else, it should be a reminder that most of the work for understanding the moral life in terms of virtue and character is still to be done.

Yet the question still remains how to understand the renewed interest in character and the virtues. In some ways I suspect a Thomas S. Kuhnian-like explanation may be appropriate. For in effect the paradigm of ethics inherited from Kant has been burdened by so many anomalies, has died the death of so many qualifications, that a new alternative simply needed to be suggested. Thus some may well have been attracted to the emphasis on virtue and character because it offered a relief from boredom. Such reasons are not to be gainsaid if you believe, as I do, that at least one of the tests of validity in ethical reflection is whether it is interesting and even entertaining.

Of course, Alasdair C. MacIntyre's *After Virtue* happened.[2] A book composed of such bold, erudite, contentious, and global insights and claims could not be ignored. With his virtuoso performance MacIntyre has changed the agenda of contemporary philosophers and theologians by an almost violent redirection of their attention. At least for philosophers the virtues can no longer be ignored because MacIntyre cannot be ignored. I am sure MacIntyre would be the first to acknowledge that such is the case because he has had many colleagues to help him along the way. MacIntyre's great achievement is to have told the story of recent philosophy that makes intelligible why so little attention has been paid to virtue and character and why it is now imperative that they no longer be ignored.

MacIntyre's book helps explain the renewed interest in the virtues among philosophers and theologians, but this is not sufficient to understand the general interest in character and virtue among those less philosophically schooled. I suspect it involves many of the complex historical and sociological factors that MacIntyre traced in *After Virtue*. In an increasingly fragmented world one would expect a renewed appreciation for the virtues and the correlative sense of community. Yet such interest can also distort the renewed

2. Alasdair C. MacIntyre, *After Virtue: A Study in Moral Theory,* 2d ed. (Notre Dame, IN: University of Notre Dame Press, 1984). Though he does not often appear in the footnotes of *Character and the Christian Life,* MacIntyre's occasional essays on explanation in history and the social sciences were very important for helping set the general perspective from which I worked in this book.

emphasis on character as our subsequent accounts can more be shaped by than shape the individualism that has occasioned the new interest in character and virtue in the first place. There are and should be no easy victories.

This is a reminder that in spite of the recent interest in virtue and character those who emphasize these notions remain and are likely to remain in the clear minority of scholars doing philosophical and theological ethics. Most, concerned by the alleged subjectivistic and relativistic implications of an emphasis on character, continue to develop ethics of principles capable of resolving moral conflicts on a nonarbitrary basis.

I have always seen this book as part of a conversation that hopefully would prove fruitful for others besides myself. I think, moreover, this has been the case, as *Character and the Christian Life* has been the occasion for others to enter into the conversation not only in terms of what I have done but in criticism for what I failed to do. I am thinking particularly of those who have criticized me for failing to include in any satisfactory account of the virtues a more substantive discussion of the passions.[3]

I think it is important in this context, however, to note that this project was not the beginning of a conversation but rather the continuation of one already begun. I suspect I overemphasized, as young authors often do, the "original-

---

3. For example, see Patricia B. Jung, "Sanctification: An Interpretation in Light of Embodiment," *Journal of Religious Ethics* 11 (1983): 75–95. This was a condensation of her dissertation at Vanderbilt University. Jozef Van Gerwen, in his dissertation, *The Church in the Theological Ethics of Stanley Hauerwas* (Ph.D. diss., Graduate Theological Union, 1984), has developed some extremely interesting criticisms from a sociological perspective. Paul Nelson, in his dissertation, *Narrative and Morality: A Theological Inquiry* (Ph.D. diss., Yale University, 1984), criticizes my arguments concerning the narrative dependency of any ethic.

For the most telling critique of as well as the most constructive response to my notion of character, see Richard Bondi, "The Elements of Character," *Journal of Religious Ethics* 12 (1984): 201–18. Bondi notes that there has been a shift in my work from the self as agent to the self as story that requires a fuller phenomenology than I have developed. In particular he argues: "The proper subject matter of the language of character is the self in relation. There is no need to look for a self behind character which character somehow represents, projects, or qualifies, for there is none there, at least none that can be spoken of either cognitively or affectively except in relational terms. When I talk about my character, I am talking about more than the history of my reasonable choices or the degree to which the direction of those choices conforms to a truthful story. I must also speak of my existence as one of much less control and far more ambiguity. In this sense character can force us to see our failures and limitations as it enables us to foresee our transformations" (204). Bondi's subsequent account of the four elements of character—(1) the capacity for intentional action, (2) involvement with the affections and passions, (3) subjection to the accidents of history, and (4) the capacity of the heart—strikes me as particularly suggestive.

ity" of the notion of character for ethics. As I briefly suggested above, the seeds for that were already present in some of Niebuhr's work, and Gustafson had begun to develop those suggestions in depth.[4] Less noticeable, but no less significant, was the work of Paul Ramsey and George Thomas. It is too easy to forget that Ramsey devoted a chapter in *Basic Christian Ethics*[5] to an analysis of the virtues as did George Thomas in his *Christian Ethics and Moral Philosophy*.[6] This is a reminder that often what we think is our peculiar insight is but our forgetting where we read it.

The conversation that *Character and the Christian Life* involves, however, is also a conversation with myself. For some a book like this one is a room in which they can stay for the rest of their life. For me the book was more like a door that, once opened, forced me to see things I had no idea existed when I first began the work. My emphasis on the importance of vision and the centrality of narrative, together with the stress on the methodological significance of the church, are all the result of trying to work out the loose ends and implications involved in this book. It is my hope, therefore, that others may continue to find this book fruitful, namely by critically engaging it to discover what I still have failed to see or understand.

Philosophical Issues

Given the nature of my subsequent work, I think it is apparent my primary agenda was and always has been theological. Indeed, I resist calling myself an "ethicist" since so often this is meant to distinguish one from those who are "real" theologians. It may be presumptuous but I prefer to think my work is theology pure and simple. Yet some have suggested that the philosophical issues were given far too much space in *Character and the Christian Life* so that the philosophical questions determined, if not distorted, the theological perspective of the book. I think there is something to that observation, but it needs to be very carefully stated.

First of all I do not think in terms of clearly delineated disciplines, one called "philosophy," the other "theology." I did not write *Character and the Christian Life* thinking that a certain amount of space should be given to what philoso-

4. Frederick S. Carney had also already begun to develop the importance of virtue for Christian ethics.
5. Paul Ramsey, *Basic Christian Ethics* (New York: Scribner's, 1950), 191–233.
6. George F. Thomas, *Christian Ethics and Moral Philosophy* (New York: Scribner's, 1955), 485–521.

phers might have had or have to say about these issues. I simply do not think that clear lines can be drawn between what philosophers and theologians do. Too often it seems we are concerned with the same set of issues and require quite similar conceptual skills to explore how and what we should think. Both philosophy and theology are activities that come in many shapes and sizes. As such each may well lead its practitioners into areas they had not anticipated. I, therefore, was drawn into issues such as the nature of agency, the primacy of the agent's perspective, intentionality, and causality because I found I could not avoid them if I was to develop an adequate account of character.

However, I now think that I was insufficiently critical of some of the presuppositions involved in the "action theory" to which I was drawn in my attempt to develop an account of agency. I was attracted to the discussion of action because it promised to provide the means to develop an account of the self that avoided both dualistic and behavioristic accounts.[7] Yet I think there is a fundamental problem with the attempt to defend a concept of agency in terms of an analysis of action in and of itself. Such an analysis presupposes that "action" or "an action" is a coherent and conceptually primitive notion, but this is simply wrong. As MacIntyre has argued, "The concept of an intelligible action is a more fundamental concept than that of an action as such. Unintelligible actions are failed candidates for the status of intelligible action; and to lump unintelligible actions and intelligible actions together in a single class of actions and then to characterize action in terms of what items of both sets have in common is to make the mistake of ignoring this. It is also to neglect the central importance of the concept of intelligibility."[8]

I think that MacIntyre is exactly right about this. When I wrote *Character and the Christian Life* I simply failed to appreciate the significance of the point. I think the discussion concerning the agent-dependent character of action descriptions was partly an attempt to move in the direction suggested by MacIntyre but it was not sufficient to qualify my assumption that an abstract account of action, and thus agency, made sense. To say that "character is the

---

7. Thomas F. Tracy, in *God, Action, and Embodiment* (Grand Rapids, MI: Eerdmans, 1984), has developed the notion of agency in an extremely fruitful and compelling manner. He has, moreover, defended in a way I did not the metaphysical presuppositions necessary to sustain such an account. Seriously argued books such as Tracy's can be lost amid the sloganeering of contemporary theology. His book is too important to be so lost, and I hope it will be widely read.

8. MacIntyre, *After Virtue*, 209. This issue obviously relates to the kind of criticisms developed by Bondi.

qualification of our self-agency" still suggests a kind of dualism insofar as a "self" seems to stand behind our character. If I had better understood the significance of MacIntyre's conceptual point, I would have been able to argue more forcefully that character is not so much the qualification but the form of our agency.

Worrying about this issue was the reason I was increasingly drawn, if not forced, to see the importance of narrative for developing the significance of character. I say "forced" because it was not a notion I wanted to make part of my intellectual agenda. I simply became convinced that I could not avoid it; the very analysis I had developed in this book begged for a treatment of how narrative may help us understand moral continuity and discontinuity. For again, as MacIntyre has suggested, "in successfully identifying and understanding what someone else is doing we always move towards placing a particular episode in the context of a set of narrative histories, histories both of the individuals concerned and of the settings in which they act and suffer. It is now becoming clear that we render the actions of others intelligible in this way because action itself has a basically historical character. It is because we all live out narratives in our lives and because we understand our own lives in terms of the narratives that we live out that the form of narrative is appropriate for understanding the actions of others. Stories are lived before they are told— except in the case of fiction."[9] To this I would only add that narrative is no less important for understanding our own actions.

I certainly do not mean to deny that people of character may possess extraordinary self-awareness. What I want to deny, however, is that such self-awareness is a necessary correlative to having character. For example, it may be quite sufficient for persons to claim their action as their own by saying simply "I am a Jew" or "I am a Christian." The primacy of "intelligible action" reinforces this point as it helps us see that consciousness is not so much an awareness as it is a skill, that is, the ability to place our action within an intelligible narrative. Indeed it may well be that the dominance of the "introspective self" as our paradigm of consciousness is an indication of our failure to appreciate the nature and significance of character.

In this respect I think the emphasis on character in our cultural situation may have connotations with which I am very unsympathetic. Character tends to suggest to us a heroic conception of the moral life that presupposes just the kind of explicit self-awareness I have just criticized. Thus it is people who are

9. Ibid., 211–12.

able to stand against the "crowd," who go their own way, who are often seen as persons of character. While certainly such people may be persons of character, it is important that they not be taken as paradigmatic examples of character. The Mennonite farmer in central Indiana may be quite happy in his community and strikingly "unaware" of himself, but that in no way disqualifies him from being a person of character. This example helps remind us that "consciousness" is not a quality inherent to the individual, but rather is a skill made possible by our participation in a substantive community with an equally substantive history.

I am sure that part of the fault lies in the highly abstract account of the relation between agency and action I provided. If I had seen the significance of the notion of "intelligible action" I would have been able to argue better than I did against possible subjectivistic distortions implied by the primacy of the agent's perspective. In particular I would have been able to suggest that the necessity of giving reasons for our behavior as well as justifying our actions entails our ability to place what we have done within an ongoing narrative.[10] Such an account, moreover, would have provided me with the means to note how certain types of moral notions serve in communities to remind us of the kind of people, the kind of characters, we ought to be.

This particular emphasis requires a much more extended discussion of the nature of moral description than I provided in this book. I have returned to the issue of description on a rather haphazard basis, but I have never devoted the sustained analysis required.[11] Yet I regard as correct the general conceptual point that our moral notions and/or descriptions not only are means to "describe" a set of circumstances but presuppose that we are, or are meant to make us, persons capable of using such descriptions. As a result there can finally be no hard and fast distinction between an action and an agent though communities may fasten on the former for educative and legal purposes. Therefore I continue to resist the view that this book, while rightly reminding us of an overlooked aspect of morality, fails to deal with the really hard moral

---

10. The relationship between explanation and justification, however, is one I think is often distorted in modern moral philosophy. As MacIntyre observes, "From an Aristotelian standpoint to identify certain actions as manifesting or failing to manifest a virtue or virtues is never only to evaluate; it is also to take the first step towards explaining why those actions rather than some others were performed" (*After Virtue*, 199).

11. However, see Charles R. Pinches's dissertation, *Describing Morally: An Inquiry Concerning the Role of Description in Christian Ethics* (Ph.D. diss., University of Notre Dame, 1984), for a much more extended discussion of this issue.

questions that involve "decisions." I do so because such a view entails a moral psychology that cannot be justified on descriptive or normative grounds.

Aristotle and Aquinas

Another set of issues revolves around my use of Aristotle and Aquinas. The question is not so much whether I misinterpreted them, which I may well have, but whether I failed to make adequate use of the full range of the analysis they provided. For example, I have been rightly criticized for failing to provide sufficient account of the passions. As a result my analysis of character is insufficiently "bodily." If I had attended to Aquinas's account of the passions I might well have avoided the rather one-sided account I provided.[12] Related to this issue is my attempt to develop an account of character without at the same time suggesting a fuller account of the virtues and their interrelation. I tended to concentrate on the more formal aspects of Aristotle's and Aquinas's accounts of virtue and as a result my account of character in this book is abstract. I do not deny the justice of criticisms at this point, but I simply felt that these issues would so overburden the book I would never be able to develop my central argument. Had I tried to provide an account either of the passions or of the passions and virtues, I would have had to deal with the question of how the virtues are individuated as well as their interrelation—both questions on which Aristotle and Aquinas are uncharacteristically not very helpful.

More serious, however, is my ignoring entirely the importance of happiness and friendship in Aristotle and Aquinas. Again I can plead lack of time and space, but I am not sure this is really defensible. I am increasingly convinced that happiness, virtue, and friendship are crucially interrelated in a manner necessary for any adequate account of character. All I can say is that my attention has steadily turned to those subjects.[13]

I think the most serious issue concerning these matters, however, is whether *Character and the Christian Life* has a sufficient account of the *telos* of the Christian life. In part I think I tended to make my philosophical analysis in this

---

12. Paul Wadell's dissertation, *An Interpretation of Aquinas' Treatise on the Passions, the Virtues, and the Gifts from the Perspective of Charity as Friendship with God* (Ph.D. diss., University of Notre Dame, 1985) will soon be published. There he helps us see why no account of Aquinas's ethics can be complete without close attention to the passions. [See Wadell's book *Friends of God: Virtues and Gifts on Aquinas* (New York: Peter Lang, 1991).]

13. [In fact, Hauerwas's reflections on the topics of happiness and friendship resulted in a series of three essays entitled "Theological Reflections on Aristotelian Themes" with Charles Pinches (1997) in CAV. See the annotated bibliography for more information.]

book rather formal because I assumed the material content, that is the teleological presuppositions, would be supplied by the theological perspective. While I think this was done to some extent, I am equally sure it was not sufficient. The development of such a theme *should* have affected the structure of the book, and it did not do so. These issues, however, are best discussed in terms of the theological issues raised by the book, and it is to them we must turn.

Theological Issues

The beginning of *Character and the Christian Life* contains an outright mistake: namely, that virtue or character was the metaphor that determined the perspective of this book in contrast to the traditional Protestant emphasis on the metaphor of "command." I remember at the time that I was uncomfortable with the claim, but thinking it not all that important, I let the matter stand. In retrospect, I think this was a decisive mistake and involves one of the major weaknesses of the book.

At the most obvious level it is clear that virtue and character are not metaphors. I realize that some theories of metaphor are so generous as perhaps to construe them as such, but I certainly do not wish to underwrite such theories in order to save my claim. Nor do I think it appropriate, though it may be more probable, to think of command as a metaphor. It is certainly a concept that determines an ethic such as Karl Barth's, but I think even in Barth command is not a metaphor.

The Lutheran theologian Gilbert Meilaender is much closer to the truth when he suggests that two of the most basic metaphors determining how the Christian life is to be understood are those of journey and dialogue. The latter basically sees the Christian life as going nowhere. Rather, as Meilaender puts it, the Christian life is a "going back and forth, back and forth, back and forth. That is to say, the Christian is simply caught within the dialogue between the two voices with which God speaks: the accusing voice of the law and the accepting voice of gospel. Hearing the law, he flees to the gospel. Hearing the gospel, he is freed to hear what the law requires. But hearing what the law requires, he must again flee to the gospel. Life is experienced as a dialogue between these two divine verdicts, and within human history one cannot escape that dialogue or progress beyond it."[14]

14. Gilbert Meilaender, "The Place of Ethics in the Theological Task," *Currents in Theology and Mission* 6 (1979), 199.

In contrast, when the Christian life is conceived as a journey, a process is implied through which people are gradually and graciously transformed by the very pilgrimage to which they have been called. "Righteousness here is substantive rather than relational. It consists not in right relation with God but in becoming (throughout the whole of one's character) the sort of person God wills us to be and commits himself to making of us. Picturing the Christian life as such a journey, we can confess our sin without thinking that the standard of which we fall short, in its accusation of us, must lead us to doubt the gracious acceptance by which God empowers us to journey toward his goal for our lives."[15]

It now seems obvious to me that what I was trying to suggest by claiming that character and command were metaphors is put much better in Meilaender's terms of journey and dialogue. The language of command is nicely correlated with the metaphor of dialogue since the "back and forth" character of life can be seen as the response or failure of response to individual commands. Character is correlative to the image of journey as not only is one on a journey but one's very life is conceived as a journey. Although dialogue is dominant in Barth's work, his Christology forces him to conceive of existence as a journey in a way that qualifies his constant use of the language of command. For example, I think it is not accidental that one of Barth's most important Christological sections is subtitled "The Way of the Son of God into the Far Country."[16] In fact, his whole Christology is determined by the image of God's journey and the corresponding invitation for us to be part of this journey.

More significant for the constructive intent of *Character and the Christian Life*, the use of the metaphor of journey would have provided the means for me to develop an alternative to my emphasis on justification and sanctification.[17] For I am no longer convinced that justification and sanctification provide the best means to spell out the theological significance of the emphasis on character for the moral life. As I suggest in *The Peaceable Kingdom*,

15. Ibid., 200.

16. Karl Barth, *Church Dogmatics,* IV/1, trans. G. W. Bromiley, ed. G. W. Bromiley and T. F. Torrance (New York: Scribner's, 1956), 157–210. Barth's ethics, I think, exemplifies a position whose substantive insights are constantly in tension with the conceptual categories used to express those insights.

17. [Hauerwas discussed issues of justification and sanctification in chapter 5 of CCL, where he presented his constructive proposal for "an ethics of Character" in relation to the theological proposals of John Wesley, John Calvin, Jonathan Edwards, and Karl Barth.]

justification and sanctification are secondary theological notions;[18] they are rules intended to remind us how the self is to be situated in order to hear and live the story of God as revealed through the life and death of Jesus of Nazareth.[19] If I had attended to the metaphor of journey, I suspect I would have been able to display the nature of the Christian life more concretely and with greater attention to the richness of the biblical witness than the notions of justification and sanctification provide.

This is not to say that I think what I have to say about justification and sanctification is wrong. The problem is not what I said but what was left unsaid. By focusing primarily on the issue of the systematic relation of justification and sanctification, I did not explicate what it means for Christians to *be*—as well as how they should live as Christians. In contrast to my view of sanctification, Meilaender suggests that there is an inevitable tension between the pictures of the Christian life as a dialogue and as a journey that cannot and should not be overcome.[20] This strikes me as what a good Lutheran should say—namely, that it is crucial to keep the two metaphors in dialectical tension so that the full range of Christian existence *coram deo* is before us.[21] But I am

18. Stanley Hauerwas, *PK*, 94–95. For a more extended reflection on the place of sanctification, see my "Characterizing Perfection: Second Thoughts on Character and the Christian Life," in *STT*.

19. For this sense of rule, see George A. Lindbeck, *The Nature of Doctrine: Religion and Theology in a Postliberal Age* (Philadelphia: Westminster Press, 1984).

20. Meilaender, "The Place of Ethics in the Theological Task," 210. Meilaender notes that each way of picturing the Christian life has its particular strength and weakness:

> The image of the Christian life as journey makes place for the *truth about reality*—the truth that God intends to turn us into people who (gladly and without contrary inclination) do his will. Yet, by encouraging the pilgrim to concentrate on his own progress toward the goal, it also makes possible the twin dangers of presumption and despair. We may forget that the entire journey, empowered by grace, leaves no room for self-confidence or boasting. Or, seeing little progress, we may begin to doubt whether God really intends to do this for us. The image of the Christian life as dialogue stays close to a central truth about experience—that we are often unable to experience our lives as accepted by God and are, therefore, in constant need of hearing the renewing word of the gospel. Yet precisely by adhering so steadfastly to this central insight about Christian experience, it may blur or ignore the distinction between God-pleasing service to the neighbor and activity which harms the neighbor. (210)

21. However, in his *Theory and Practice of Virtue* Meilaender rightly notes that Luther did not think in terms of acts but in terms of character. Yet this aspect of Luther's thought was balanced by his view, according to Meilaender, that one's being is first and last one of sin. Therefore, for Luther "life is not the gradual development of a virtuous self; it is a constant return to the promise of grace. The examined life, if honestly examined, will reveal only that the best of our works are sin" (106–7).

not a good Lutheran, and I want to argue that the metaphor of the journey is and surely should be the primary one for articulating the shape of Christian existence and living.[22]

Put in philosophical terms, the underlying contention of this book is that the moral life, and in particular the Christian moral life, requires a teleological conception of human existence that gets somewhere rather than forever being a movement between the "back and forth." As MacIntyre has contended, "Unless there is a *telos* which transcends the limited goods of practices by constituting the good of a whole human life, the good of a human life conceived as a unity, it will *both* be the case that a certain subversive arbitrariness will invade the moral life *and* that we shall be unable to specify the context of certain virtues adequately. These two considerations are reinforced by a *third:* that there is at least one virtue recognized by the tradition which cannot be specified at all except with reference to the wholeness of a human life—the virtue of integrity or constancy. 'Purity of heart,' said Kierkegaard, 'is to will one thing.' This notion of singleness of purpose in a whole life can have no application unless that of a whole life does."[23]

This seems to me to be exactly right. My emphasis on character was an attempt to give an account of "singleness," the singleness that Aristotle and Aquinas both sensed was essential for the development as well as the possession of all the other virtues, yet I failed to spell out the contours of the journey inherent to Christian convictions that makes such singleness possible. This is basically another way of saying why it is so important not to divorce the discussion of character from questions of happiness and friendship. I suspect that the necessary interrelation of these themes is one of the more promising ways we have to display the nature of the journey to which Christians have been called. Moreover such a display should provide the means to specify each of the virtues as well as their complex interrelation.[24]

---

22. The argument necessary to sustain this contention is complex and many-sided. Theologically it means that the eschatological presuppositions of Jesus' preaching must be seen as intrinsic to Christology; or put in terms I was using in *Character and the Christian Life,* it means that sanctification is a more determinative category than justification, or, in Meilaender's terms, it means that the metaphor of dialogue only makes sense as a necessary and continuing part of the journey.

23. MacIntyre, *After Virtue,* 203. For a development of this notion of constancy, see my "Constancy and Forgiveness: The Novel as a School for Virtue," in *DF,* 31–57.

24. The absence of this fuller account of the teleological character of the Christian life accounts for the rather curious Kantian flavor that is still present in *Character and the Christian Life.* For there is a sense that my account of character at times appears like that of

I am aware that my claim for the priority of the journey metaphor for the display of the Christian life can only reinforce the suspicion of some that I have abandoned the central Christian contention of the priority of God's grace. I know of no way in principle to calm such fears. Moreover I am aware it is not sufficient to claim, as I have here and elsewhere, that I have no intention of qualifying the necessity of God's grace for the beginning, living, and end of the Christian life. What I hope is now clear, however, is that I refuse to think the only or best way to depict the priority of God's grace is in terms of the dialogue metaphor. This has certainly been the dominant mode among Protestants, but exactly because it has been so, we have had difficulty articulating our sense of the reality of and growth in the Christian life. In this respect I think that *Character and the Christian Life* remains an exercise to help Protestants reconceive our own best insights by offering a new set of linguistic skills gleaned from a rereading of Aristotle's *Ethics* and the *Summa Theologica* of St. Thomas Aquinas.

One final difficulty with my use of the themes of justification and sanctification was the absence of any reference to the nature and significance of the church as crucial for sustaining the Christian journey. Though I had stressed the relational character of the self, this is not sufficient to indicate the centrality of a particular community called the church for the development of the kind of character required of Christians. Systematic relations, even those dealing with such matters as justification and sanctification, are no substitute for spelling out the nature and practice of the church Christians believe God has made possible through the life, death, and resurrection of Jesus Christ.[25]

Kant—namely, the attempt to secure a unity to our lives not because we know where we are going but because we do not. The power of Kant's account of morality is not easily broken, and I would not pretend that I did so successfully in this book. Just to the extent that this book's claims remain at an abstract or formal level, some are convinced that I failed to provide a compelling alternative to Kant's account of the self that is immune to the flux of history.

25. Systematics is often where theologians retreat, however, when they forget that the intelligibility of their work depends on people who actually believe and live the life which God has made possible. As Patrick Sherry has observed, "If Christians were never changed by the practice of their religion, this would count against, if not decisively refute, certain important Christian doctrines: in particular, it would tell against those of grace and of the sending of the Holy Spirit, and thereby call into question our view of divine activity. Hence a failure to continue to produce saints would count against the truth of Christianity, because certain of its crucial doctrines require men be changed by God. The common objection to Christianity that Christians are not better than they are (as Nietzsche said, 'they don't look redeemed') can be regarded as an implicit appeal to falsification" (*Spirits, Saints, and Immortality* [Albany: State University of New York Press, 1984], 47). Sherry's observation expresses what I have always

This specifically ecclesiological agenda is now the focus of my constructive work as a theologian. Ten years later, I now realize that the church as Christ's body is a conceptual cornerstone of my constructive project. As the bricklayer says, "Man, I wish I had started with that one."[26]

Further Reading
"Toward an Ethics of Character" (1972), in *VV*
"Aristotle and Thomas Aquinas on the Ethics of Character" (1975), in *CCL*
"A Critique of the Concept of Character in Theological Ethics" (1975), in *CCL*
"The Virtues and Our Communities: Human Nature as History" (1981), in *CC*
"On Being Historic: Agency, Character, and Sin" (1983), in *PK*
"Agency: Going Forward by Looking Back" (1996), in *STT*
"Characterizing Perfection: Second Thoughts on Character and Sanctification" (1985), in *STT*
"Character, Narrative, and Growth in the Christian Life" (1980), essay 11 in this volume
"The Testament of Friends: How My Mind has Changed" (1990) in *The Christian Century* 107, no. 7 (28 February 1990): 212–216

---

considered to be the wider context for *Character and the Christian Life* as well as my subsequent work. Sanctification is not simply a concept that plays a part in relation to other theological concepts, but rather is crucial for helping us understand as well as argue what it might mean to say our convictions are true.

26. I thank Harmon L. Smith, Dennis M. Campbell, John H. Westerhoff III, and L. Gregory Jones for reading, editing, and criticism. The closing sentences of this paragraph were written by Michael G. Cartwright and John Berkman and approved by Stanley Hauerwas.

4. Why the "Sectarian Temptation" Is a Misrepresentation: A Response to James Gustafson (1988)

In books such as A Community of Character *(1981) and* The Peaceable Kingdom *(1983), Hauerwas had forcefully pressed his claim of the epistemological
priority of the church. Under the influence of John Howard Yoder, this emphasis
was interpreted by James Gustafson (among others) as a form of sectarian retreat
that leads to a civic irresponsibility. Here Hauerwas responds to Gustafson's
published charge of sectarianism, probably the most persistent negative characterization of Hauerwas's position. Hauerwas's response calls attention to the fact
that the charge is based on certain presumptions of the role of religion in liberal
political orders (i.e., conceptions of "public theology"), and he challenges his
critics to defend their charges on more thoroughly theological grounds.*

1. On Representing "Something New"

One of the theologian's tasks is to understand how Christian convictions can
be said to be true or false. As a result, my work appears to many as a strange
mix of philosophy, literature, a few historical asides, theology, and ethics.
However, I do not see how any genuine investigation can avoid doing so.
When I began my work I had no idea I would believe the church to be as
important as I now think it is for understanding the nature and truth of
Christian convictions. Even less did I think that Christian nonviolence might
be crucial for the epistemological status of Christian belief. Writing and thinking, which are often the same thing, are a conversation with an ongoing
community. Those who disagree with me are as precious as those who are
supportive (though I prefer the latter), for without disagreements I would
have little sense of what I really think. For example, I am sure my views on the

[An excerpt from the introduction to *CET*, 1–19. The editors have deleted those portions of the
introduction that introduce the essays in the volume, but have retained Hauerwas's response
to Gustafson's critique of Hauerwas's work.]

significance of the church as a social ethic would lack critical edge if I did not always have Reinhold Niebuhr in mind.

Furthermore, I suspect James Gustafson's critique of my work gives voice to the disquiet many feel about the "newness" of my perspective. By responding to Gustafson I hope to help some readers understand better what I am about. I think many interpret me as having reminded us of the importance of virtue or the church for ethics in a manner that leaves everything else as is. But that simply is not the case. One cannot understand what I am about if one continues to presuppose the dominant philosophical and theological intellectual habits of the past hundred years. For example, though I have learned much from both Niebuhrs, the way I think cannot be easily joined with their work. As a result, I do not pretend that coming to understand me is easy or without risk but only that such a rethinking is required. I do not expect that those who make the effort will necessarily agree with me, but I do hope that having made the effort they will have learned something.

2. James Gustafson's Thesis Regarding "Sectarian" Ecclesiology

James Gustafson began his critique by reporting that he discovered at the 1984 meeting of the British Society for the Study of Christian Ethics some enthusiasm for my work among theologians from the Church of Scotland and the Church of England, as well as the Roman Catholic Church.[1] Gustafson described this enthusiasm as a "seduction" and advised that anyone tempted to follow me give some consideration to the incongruities between the "sectarian ecclesiology" I represent and the ecclesiology represented by their more traditional churches. Moreover, he suggested that some thought be given to the tension between the adherence to the classic creeds on the Incarnation and the Trinity made by these churches and my historicist portrayal of Jesus. In short, Gustafson found it surprising that theologians who should know better are accepting a position that would require them to abandon their most cherished commitments. I find all this a little odd, since Gustafson's most recent work argues that Christians should abandon their traditional understanding of Christ as an unwarranted form of anthropocentric theology.

Though I am of course pleased that my work has had some influence, even in England, I cannot be happy that Gustafson sees that influence in such a

1. James Gustafson, "The Sectarian Temptation: Reflections on Theology, the Church and the University," *Proceedings of the Catholic Theological Society* 40 (1985): 83–94. Further citations are in the text.

negative light. I understand myself neither to represent the kind of sectarianism he describes nor to deny the doctrines of the Incarnation and Trinity. It is my hope that this book will help make clear that such charges are oversimplifications. Contrary to Gustafson's characterization, I stand in the catholic tradition that both affirms the universality of the church and confesses God's trinitarian nature. Yet, how then am I to explain the vast difference between how Gustafson and I understand my work? By exploring that question through an analysis of Gustafson's critique, I hope to suggest the main lines of the position developed in this book.

Gustafson reported that the strange influence I have had in Britain was explained to him a few days later by a Scottish theologian at a conference on Reinhold Niebuhr. It was suggested that my "sectarianism" was attractive "because it made clear a historic confessional basis on which Christian morality could be distinguished from the culture, and how Christians could stand prophetically as Christians on matters of nuclear armaments and the like" (85). That such a stance might be attractive in England, where the churches have lost so much influence that they have nothing more to lose, is not surprising to Gustafson. From his perspective the situation of the churches in England is but a dramatic example of the contemporary state of Christianity in general. As he says,

> Christianity is a beleaguered religion. In the secularization of Western culture we have many alternative interpretations of how things really and ultimately are—that is, functional equivalents to theology. We have, even in the West, a variety of moralities, many of which are defended by modern ways of interpreting the nature of persons and the nature of morality itself . . . Religious pluralism is an inexorable fact. In this situation every *aggiornamento* in the Christian community poses threats to its historic uniqueness and identity, every such move stimulates a conservative reaction. Pastors engaged in care of their parishioners are informed by theories of psychotherapy and begin to wonder what distinguishes them as Christians from their competitors down the street. Moralists become engaged in practical problems and social policy questions and wonder whether they are being faithful to their Christian commitments. Theologians take account of the learning provided by various non-theological disciplines in the university and are criticized for too much revisionism in their writing. (83–84)

Therefore, Gustafson understands why a "sectarian withdrawal" is a temptation, but that is what it is—a temptation—for to give into it, Gustafson argues, is to betray the church and the theologians' task. According to Gustafson, a theology formed by this temptation cannot but result in a fideistic stance that legitimates a tribalistic understanding of Christianity. While such sectarianism may provide Christians with a clear identity and ensures distinctiveness of belief, it has the unfortunate effect of "isolating Christianity from taking seriously the wider world of science and culture and limits the participation of Christians in the ambiguities of moral and social life in the patterns of interdependence in the world" (84).

Gustafson develops this broadside by suggesting that my sectarianism reflects the position of certain "Wittgensteinian fideists," such as Paul Holmer and George Lindbeck, who allegedly hold that the language of science and the language of religion are totally incommensurable. They do so, Gustafson argues, in the interest of making theological claims incorrigible, such that persons are socialized into a particular form of life so thoroughly that they are not open to other ways of viewing the world that might challenge their religious categories. Drawing on hermeneutical theory, this position simply adopts a text, namely the Bible, without justifying that text as worthy of interpretation (87). From such a position it is hard to see what prevents doctrine from becoming ideology, since it is not clear how one can criticize the tradition so construed, either internally or externally.

In opposition to this view, Gustafson argues that insofar as religion and science are rational activities, it must be possible in principle to subject theological claims to correction and revision in terms of what we have learned from the social and physical sciences. Any attempt to maintain that knowing religiously and theologically is radically distinct from other ways of knowing can only result in making Christianity unintelligible in a world in which fewer and fewer people are formed by the "Christian language." The alternative is for theologians to relativize the Christian tradition by drawing on other sources of knowledge so that we can construe God's relation to the world in the light of our modern knowledge.

Gustafson, moreover, argues that my "theological fideism" is correlative to a "sociological tribalism," resulting in a truncated ethic unable to deal adequately with contemporary challenges. In particular, the emphasis on "narrative theology" and sectarianism go hand in hand. Thus, he characterizes my emphasis on narrative in the following manner:

> We grow up in communities in which we share narratives, the stories of the
> community. This, I would agree, is partly true in a descriptive sense. The nar-

ratives and our participating in the community, in [Hauerwas's] case the "Church" (very abstractly), gives shape to our characters. Our characters are expressed in our deeds and actions. Further, the narratives of the community give shape to the way in which we interpret life in the world. So far this is a description. A turn to the normative takes place. Since we belong to the Christian community its narratives ought to shape the lives of its members. In Hauerwas' case, for example, this means that Christian morality is not based on a concern to be responsible participants in the ambiguities of public choices. It is based on its fidelity of the biblical narratives, and particularly of the Gospel narratives. Thus the principal criterion for judging Christian behavior is its conformity to the stories of Jesus. For Hauerwas this means, for example, that Christian morality must be pacifist because he reads the Gospel narratives as pacifist. In this example, we have wedded a way of doing theology—narratives—to an ecclesiology—classical sectarian—and to an ethic which is also classically sectarian. (88)

Gustafson argues that by succumbing to this sectarian temptation I assume wrongly that the church is socially and culturally isolable from the wider society and culture. As a result Christians are turned into a kind of tribe living in a ghetto, unable to participate in universities or to be called to serve in the professions and making no contribution to "critical ambiguous choices" necessary in political and public life (91). Such a tribalism, however, is based on a false sociological assumption that cannot help but lead to failure. "Because of the power that other institutions in society and culture have to furnish symbols and constructs that interpret the same reality that Christian faith and theology does, the parish and congregational life of churches necessarily have to take these matters into account as it seeks to educate and form persons in Christian faith and life" (91). In short, Christians are never just members of the church but must rightly live in the world. As long as people have to make a living, there is no way to withdraw.

But for Gustafson the unrealistic sociology of my tribalizing is not nearly as serious an error as the theological presuppositions that underlie it. For my sectarian tendencies are based on the theological assumption

that God is known only in and through history, and particularly the history of the Biblical people culminating in the events of Christ and their effects. Insofar as this describes an assumption it ignores a great deal of the Biblical witness itself. In Christian sectarian form God becomes a Christian God for Christian people: to put it most pejoratively, God is assumed to be the tribal

God of a minority of the earth's population. Or, if God is not a tribal God there is only one community in the world that has access to knowledge of God because God has revealed himself only in the life of that community. Or still another possible assumption, and worse from my perspective than the other two, Christian theology and ethics really are not concerned so much about God as they are about maintaining fidelity to the Biblical narratives about Jesus, or about maintaining the "Biblical view" as a historical vocation that demands fidelity without further external justification, or idolatrously maintaining a historic social identity. (93)

Gustafson seems to suggest that I have fallen into the last mistake because I have argued that any attempt to move beyond the "particularistic historical tradition" (as defined, in the end, by him), either to justify it or to criticize and possibly alter it, is to move to what he calls "universalism" (89). But since I supply neither a doctrine of revelation (as Barth does) nor a way that the revelatory power of the biblical material can be confirmed in human experience (as the Niebuhrs do), my position can only be a defensive effort "to sustain the historical identity of the Christian tradition virtually for its own sake" (89).

In particular, Gustafson faults me for omitting any doctrine of creation as a basis for ethics, for only on the basis of creation can contemporary ways of knowing nature be appropriated. Moreover, it is only on the basis of such knowledge that an ethic adequate for our times can be mounted. "Faithful witness to Jesus is not a sufficient theological and moral basis for addressing the moral and social problems of the twentieth century. The theologian addressing many issues—nuclear, social justice, ecology, and so forth—must do so as an outcome of a theology that develops God's relation to all aspects of life in the world, and develops those relations in terms which are not exclusively Christian in a sectarian form. Jesus is not God" (93).

3. Responding to Gustafson's Charges

Because of the story Christians tell about our first parents and their run-in with a subtle serpent, we tend to think temptations are necessarily to be resisted. Yet if I represent a temptation, even to the British, I hope they will give in to it. I equally hope neither they nor others will accept Gustafson's characterization of that temptation, as I certainly do not recognize in his depiction of my work a position I defend. I have taken the time, however, to spell out his criticism, not only because his views will have added weight due to his well-deserved stature in the field but also because they bring together often-made characterizations and criticisms of my position.

Consider first the allegation that I am a "sectarian." What I find disconcerting about that claim is the assumption that the one making the charge has the argumentative high ground, so that the burden of proof is on me. But where is the generally agreed criterion for the use of this term, "sectarian"? Too often those making the charge assume epistemological (as well as sociological) positions that are question begging. Has it not been long recognized that Ernst Troeltsch's typology *presumed* the normative status of the "church type"?[2]

That I have been critical of the moral limits of liberalism is certainly true, but I do not understand why that makes me a ready candidate for being a sectarian. Insofar as the church can reclaim its integrity as a community of virtue, it can be of great service in liberal societies.[3] Moreover, the fact that I have written about why and how Christians should support as well as serve the medical and legal professions,[4] Christian relations with Judaism,[5] how we might think about justice,[6] as well as an analysis of the moral debate concerning nuclear war[7] seems to have no effect on those who are convinced I am a "withdrawn" sectarian. To be sure, I have made no secret of my indebtedness to the Mennonite theologian John Howard Yoder, but Gustafson has no more demonstrated that Yoder is a sectarian than that am I, unless one assumes

2. For Troeltsch's account, see *The Social Teachings of the Christian Churches* (New York: Macmillan, 1931). Troeltsch says a "sect is a voluntary society, composed of strict and definite Christian believers bound to each other by the fact that all have experienced 'the new birth.' These 'believers' live apart from the world, are limited to small groups, emphasize the law instead of grace, and in varying degrees within their own circle, set up the Christian order, based on love; all this is done in preparation for the expectation of the coming Kingdom of God" (11:993). For a judicious criticism of Troeltsch, see Duane Friesen, "Normative Factors in Troeltsch's Typology of Religious Association," *Journal of Religious Ethics* 3, no. 2 (fall 1975): 271–83.

3. *VV*, 222–60. See also *CC*.

4. Stanley Hauerwas, *SP*.

5. See "Remembering as a Moral Task: The Challenge of the Holocaust" (1981), essay 17 in this volume.

6. Stanley Hauerwas, "Should Christians Talk So Much about Justice?", *Books and Religion* 14, no. 6 (May–June 1986): 5ff, as well as "On the Right to Be Tribal," *Christian Scholars Review* 16, no. 3 (March 1987): 238–41. Though these essays are more recent, they expand themes I was developing as early as "The Politics of Charity" (1979) in *TT*.

7. See "Should War Be Eliminated? A Thought Experiment" (1984), essay 20 in this volume, as well as "On Surviving Justly: Ethics and Nuclear Disarmament" (1983) and "An Eschatological Perspective on Nuclear Disarmament" (1982), both in *AN*.

uncritically that a Mennonite must be a sectarian. At the very least those making that charge should attend to Yoder's arguments concerning the Christian's positive duties to wider society and the state.[8]

I am certainly aware that the position I have developed is not in the recent mainstream of Christian ethical reflection. To be candid, I often am a bit surprised by some of the implications that arise as I continue to try to think through the course on which I am set. So I do not blame anyone for approaching my work (or Yoder's) with a good deal of caution and skepticism. What I find unfair, however, is the assumption that my critic has a hold on my task by calling me "sectarian." Show me where I am wrong about God, Jesus, the limits of liberalism, the nature of the virtues, or the doctrine of the church—but do not shortcut that task by calling me a sectarian.

Gustafson's criticisms must still be addressed, if for no other reason than that they have the virtue of interrelating the theological, epistemological, and ecclesiological (sociological) themes in my work. Gustafson is surely right to suggest that these themes are interrelated, for I have never tried to maintain neat distinctions among theology, philosophy, and ethics. That does not mean I have any ambition to develop a grandiose system. I simply do not think so systematically, as is clear from the unsystematic and occasional nature of my work. Rather, I try to respond, for example, to epistemological questions only as is necessary in terms of the argument I am making at the time. That I do so, of course, reflects my conviction that there is no way to deal with the question of "truth as such" but only with the question of the truth of this or that claim.

That said, however, I will now try to respond as directly as I can to Gustafson's claims: (1) that I am a fideist, (2) that I justify an irresponsible attitude of Christians toward worldly involvement, and (3) that I either lack a theological doctrine of creation or that I am an idolator.

3.1 On Questions of Truth vs. "Fideism"

Gustafson suggests that those representing the "sectarian temptation" are responding to the "beleaguered" state of contemporary Christianity in a secu-

8. John Howard Yoder, *Christian Witness to the State* (Newton, KS: Faith and Life Press, 1964). It is not clear to me why Gustafson did not criticize Yoder in his article since Yoder has argued about these matters more extensively and conclusively than I. Moreover, in his *Ethics from a Theocentric Perspective, I* (Chicago: University of Chicago Press, 1981), Gustafson avows that Yoder represents the most compelling alternative to his position (74–76). Gustafson's suggestion that I can offer no internal critique of the Christian tradition is surely odd in the light of my defense of nonviolence. From such a perspective the mainstream of the Christian tradition has been at odds with itself.

lar world. In the name of narrative we make a virtue of our inability to free ourselves from our parochial starting points by underwriting the assumption that every position is ultimately parochial. While this may be an effective survival tactic, Gustafson charges that such a strategy necessarily gives up on the central Christian claim setting all things relative to God.

I suspect few of us are able to know or account for all the presuppositions with which we work, but I have never thought myself working out the agenda Gustafson attributes to me. Though I am convinced that Christianity has wrongly tried to underwrite foundationalist epistemologies, at times perhaps in the interest of justifying the imperialistic political strategies of the West, I have not argued in the manner I have because I think the culture of the West is beginning to fail. Nor have I tried to justify Christian belief by making Christian convictions immune from challenge from other modes of knowledge, particularly science.

Indeed, as I have argued elsewhere[9] as well as here, theological convictions inextricably involve truth-claims that are in principle open to challenge. The claim that our existence has a teleological character that requires narrative display is a "metaphysical" claim. I take it that such claims might well be challenged, but I cannot predict what all such challenges will look like. Thus, while I certainly believe that Christian convictions make claims about our existence, I do not believe that the veridical status of those claims can be or should be based on the questionable assumption that all possible challenges have been anticipated and taken into account or defeated.

Indeed, I have avoided all appeals to a Kuhnian-like position (with which Kuhn may unfairly be identified) designed to protect theological convictions from possible scientific challenge. But rather than asserting that material theological convictions must be revised in the light of science, should not Gustafson indicate which scientific conclusions should be considered and why? Certainly I see no reason why the central affirmations of the Christian faith need to be surrendered or denaturalized in terms of the mere activity of science, and I am unaware of any scientific conclusion that would now require such revision—particularly those about the ultimate end of human life or even the world that so impress Gustafson. The history of modern theology is littered with the wrecks of such revision done on the basis of a science that no longer has any credence; which is but a way of saying that while I have eminent

9. See "Christian Ethics in a Fragmented and Violent World" and "A Qualified Ethic: The Narrative Character of Christian Ethics," both in PK.

respect for scientific work, I am less confident than is Gustafson that it is meaningful to assign to science qua science an overriding veridical status. Certain kinds of science, and particularly the presuppositions of some scientific research agendas, may present theological challenges—for example, that humans are completely explicable in terms of mechanistic chemical reactions—and nothing I have said is meant to protect theology or Christians from such challenges. Of course, I do not assume that such confrontations will necessarily result in victory for the challenger.

I cannot hope to address here the many questions involved in assessing the truthfulness of theological claims. Indeed, I do not believe that all theological language works at the same level or takes out similar drafts about the way the world is. Suffice it to say that, as I try to suggest in several of the essays in this book, I assume that Christian theology has a stake in a qualified epistemological realism.[10] I certainly do not believe, nor did Wittgenstein, that religious convictions are or should be treated as an internally consistent language game that is self-validating. What Wittgenstein has taught me, however, is that if we attend to the diversity of our language we learn to appreciate what a marvelously diverse world we inhabit and how complex claims about the way the world is will inevitably be.

There is, however, one characteristic of Christian convictions that, while not unique to Christians, is nonetheless a stumbling block to many who

---

10. Sabina Lovibond, in her *Realism and Imagination in Ethics* (Minneapolis: University of Minnesota Press, 1983), developed with philosophical rigor the kind of epistemological realism I have only asserted. See also Alasdair MacIntyre, "Objectivity in Morality and Objectivity in Science," in *Morals, Science, and Society,* ed. Tris Engelhardt and Dan C. Callahan (New York: Hastings Center, 1978), 21–47. As MacIntyre puts it, "History has primacy over semantics and the continuities of history are moral continuities, continuities of tasks and projects which cannot be defined except with reference to the internal goods which specify the goals of such tasks and projects. Those tasks and projects are embodied in practices, and practices are in turn embodied in institutions and in communities. The scientific community is one among the moral communities of mankind and its unity is unintelligible apart from commitment to realism. . . . To be objective is to understand oneself as part of a community and one's work as part of a project and of a history. The authority of this history and this project derives from the goods internal to the practice. Objectivity is a moral concept before it is a methodological concept, and the activities of natural science turn out to be a species of moral activity" (36–37). For a decisive critique of those who would seek to use Wittgenstein's reference to "language games" or "forms of life" to avoid testing religious language, see Joseph Incandela, "The Appropriation of Wittgenstein's Work by Philosophers of Religion: Towards a Re-Evaluation and an End," *Religious Studies* 21 (1986): 457–74. For a defense of Lindbeck against the charge of relativism, see Michael Root, "Truth, Relativism, and Postliberal Theology," *Dialog* 25, no. 3 (1987): 175–80.

would assess whether Christian convictions are true. Moreover, it is an aspect that I have repeatedly emphasized; it may be the ultimate issue troubling Gustafson. For I have argued that the very content of Christian convictions requires that the self be transformed if we are adequately to see the truth of the convictions—for example, that I am a creature of a good creator yet in rebellion against my status as such. Talk of our sin, therefore, is a claim about the way we are, but our very ability to know we are that way requires that we have already begun a new way of life. That is why the Christian doctrine of sanctification is central for assessing the epistemological status of Christian convictions. Assessing the truthfulness of religious convictions cannot be separated from the truthfulness of the persons who make those claims.

Therefore, the most important knowledge Christian convictions involve, and there is much worth knowing for which Christians have no special claim, requires a transformation of the self. Christianity is no "worldview," not a form of primitive metaphysics, that can be assessed in comparison to alternative "worldviews." Rather, Christians are people who remain convinced that the truthfulness of their beliefs must be demonstrated in their lives. There is a sense in which Christian convictions are self-referential, but the reference is not to propositions but to lives. While such a view has similarities to some pragmatic theories of truth, I suspect that the Christian sense of "fruitfulness" involves a "realism" that might make some advocates of those theories uneasy.

Putting the matter this way, however, is still too formal, for it may appear that Christians are left with nothing to say other than "Try it—you will like it." As a result, Christians are epistemologically in the same position as Nazis or Moonies. Yet such a conclusion is false because the content of the convictions of those communities cannot stand challenge scientifically, metaphysically, or morally. However, that does not mean that disputes between all communities can be resolved by applying such tests. For example, I do not think the differences among Jews, Christians, and Muslims can be settled in terms of what we know here and now.[11] To realize that is to begin to appreciate what it means to live eschatologically.

11. That does not mean that all discussion is useless. For example, see David Burrell's *Knowing the Unknowable God: Ibn-Sina, Maimonides, Aquinas* (Notre Dame, IN: University of Notre Dame Press, 1986). One simply cannot deny, however, that questions about God transform, or better, challenge our epistemological paradigms. As Nicholas Lash suggests:

We are gravely mistaken if, in our attempts to sustain our awareness of the difference between "God" and "the world," we construe the quest for God or one particular quest

Yet this objection is a crucial reminder that the subject of transformation for Christians is not the isolated individual, but a community living through time. For the convictions that Christians hold about the way things are entail the existence of a people, since what we know can be known only through witness. Moreover, contrary to Gustafson's claim that such a community lacks any means to criticize its tradition, its worship of God requires it be open to continual "reality checks." God comes to this community in the form of a stranger, challenging its smugness, exposing its temptations to false "knowledge," denying its spurious claims to have domesticated God's grace. Thus, one of the tests of the truthfulness of Christian convictions cannot help being the *faithfulness* of the church.

3.2 On the Christian Social Engagement vs. "Irresponsibility"

I hope I have made clear that the acceptance of my epistemology, morally and theologically speaking, does not prevent someone from participating in the cultural, intellectual, and political life of society. Indeed, I share with Gustafson his concern about the overspecialization of disciplinary fields legitimized by the modern university. I do, after all, continue to teach in a university that while not unfriendly to religion certainly gives it no special status. Such a position seems appropriate for theological work, since as theologians we are put in a position of engaging critically other perspectives as well as remaining open to the challenge of other perspectives without the outcome of those challenges being predetermined by legal or social power. It may be that some

---

upon which we may be sometimes engaged alongside the quest for domestic happiness, unified field theory, social justice, a cure for cancer, or whatever. All attempts to construe the difference between God and the world fall into the trap of supposing "God" to be one of a number of actual or possible objects of experience, expectation and discourse. But *such* a "God" would be merely a "feature" of reality, a part of the world, not the incomprehensible mystery of its origin, significance and destiny. If God were one of a number of actual or possible objects of experience and discourse, then the concept of God would have immeasurably more restricted range than the concept of "truth." If however, the God whom we seek, the God whose truth sustains and infinitely transcends all projects and all imaginings is, in fact, the incomprehensible ground and goal of all reality and all significance, the creator and redeemer of nature and history, then each and every aspect of the human quest—in all of its bewildering, uncontrollable and often conflictual diversity—is an aspect of the quest for God, even when it is not so named or characterized. There is no truth, no reality, "outside" the truth and reality of God and his grace. (*Theology on the Way to Emmaus* [London: S.C.M. Press, 1986], 13–14)

universities at present or in the future may for political reasons find it difficult to support the teaching of Christian theology as a university subject, but I know of no reasons intrinsic to the canons of scholarship and thought of the university why such an excommunication would be necessary.

In that respect I find Gustafson's attitude odd, as he seems to assume that the only option for Christians is either *complete* involvement in culture or *complete* withdrawal. I see no reason why such stark alternatives are necessary. The issue is how the church can provide the interpretative categories to help Christians better understand the positive and negative aspects of their societies and guide their subsequent selective participation. Moreover, such categories cannot be developed in the abstract, since they depend on the actual societies in which Christians find themselves. The gospel does not simply contain a theory of society and/or legitimate government. All we know as Christians is that government will exist—not what form it will or must take.

That does not mean that Christians, along with others, will not try, through the study of history and social and political thought, to gain wisdom about how societies, the law, and government best work. Such knowledge, however, lacks the status of "gospel truth," as we are too much the product of accidents of geography, climate, and history to speak with certainty about what society ought to look like. Every society has its strengths and weaknesses which change through time. How Christians relate to those strengths and weaknesses will and should also change through time.

It is certainly true that I have been critical of liberal social and political presuppositions, particularly as these are played out in American society. Indeed, part of my concern has been with liberalism's presumption, linked to the peculiarity of its origin in America, that people can create a society and government de novo. The ahistorical character of liberal social and political theory strikes me as particularly pernicious, as in the name of freedom manipulative social relations are legitimated. Moreover, I have emphasized the importance of a recovery of the integrity of the church as an alternative political community. That I have done so, however, does not commit me to a sectarian ecclesiology, unless it is assumed that the secular state has the right to determine what will and will not count as political. Unless the church and Christians are trained first to understand their community's language, they will lack resources to notice times when the language of the state is not their own. To be sure, there may also be continuities among those languages, but those continuities cannot be recognized unless Christians first know that their community's language is determined by what Walter Brueggemann has called the "singular holiness of God."[12]

Drawing on the wonderful exchange at the city wall between the Assyrian ambassador, Hezekiah, and Isaiah in II Kings 18–19, Brueggemann notes that without Israel having a language behind the wall there would have been no way to resist the seduction of the language at the wall with its claim that Israel's God had been defeated. As Brueggemann puts it,

> The Assyrian negotiators at the wall are not offering a policy in the general interest, but under such a guise are pursuing Assyrian policy at the expense of all those behind the wall. Then the dominant conversation partner acts and speaks only from a narrow interest that is sectarian. We are not accustomed to thinking of the voice of the empire as a sectarian voice. But so it is when it serves only a narrow interest. *Empire as sect* is a theme worth pursuing in our own situation because it may be suggested that the voice of American power, for example, claims to be the voice of general well-being and may in a number of cases be only the voice of a narrow range of economic and political interest. The ideological guise is effective if large numbers of people can be kept from noticing the narrow base of real interest. That narrow base will not be noticed unless there is another conversation behind the wall which gives critical distance and standing ground for an alternative assessment. In ancient Israel, the prophets are the ones who regularly expose the voice of the empire as a sectarian voice not to be heard as a comprehensive, disinterested voice.[13]

To this I can only add that the church is a prophet only when it is capable of remembering it has a history that is neither that of nations nor empires—and is in its own way finite.

Such a position does not commit me to believing we live socially and politically in a night when all cats are gray. For example, Richard Neuhaus chides me for suggesting in "A Christian Critique of Christian America" that we are lucky if we live in regimes that justify themselves in the name of consent of the governed. He argues that such a view is inconsistent, since I also maintain that democracy is not different in kind from other forms of states.[14]

---

12. Walter Brueggemann, "II Kings 18–19: The Legitimacy of a Sectarian Hermeneutic," *Horizons in Biblical Theology* 7 (1985): 15.
13. Ibid., 22–23.
14. Richard Neuhaus, "Democratic Morality: A Possibility," unpublished paper delivered at University of Indiana, March 1986, p. 11. [A response to essay 22 in this volume.]

Drawing on the latter claim he attributes to me the view that it makes no difference to Christians whether rulers are just or unjust. I certainly do not believe that nor do I think the views I have defended require me to believe it.

My call for Christians to recover the integrity of the church as integral to our political witness does not entail that Christians must withdraw from the economic, cultural, legal, and political life of our societies. It does mean, however, that the *form* of our participation will vary given the nature of the societies in which we find ourselves. For example, I support a Mennonite attempt to avoid using law courts to sue, but that does not entail that Christians are to avoid all contact with the law or are in principle prevented from practicing law. Rather, I understand the kind of restraint shown in not suing to be the condition necessary to help us find the means to be a more cooperative, virtuous, and peaceful polity.

In that respect I am sympathetic with what Robert Rodes calls a jurisprudence of aspiration. He understands the law to be an expression of what we aspire to as a community,

> which is not necessarily what we can realistically hope to accomplish. If as a community we aspire to live virtuously, to deal virtuously with one another, to encourage and support one another in leading virtuous lives, then the law must bear an effective witness to the whole of that aspiration rather than merely coerce or manipulate a measure of compliance with some part. It was no sentimentalist or visionary, but the ever-practical Justice Holmes who said that "The law is the witness and external deposit of our moral life. Its history is the history of the moral development of the race. The practice of it, in spite of popular jests, tends to make good citizens and good men." If we concern ourselves only with what can or should be enforced, we overlook this function of our law, and, as a consequence, badly attenuate the moral life of our society.[15]

Ironically, exactly because liberal societies have tended to undercut the moral aspirations of the law in the name of individual freedom, the law has become increasingly coercive in the interest of maintaining order. As a result, the

15. Robert Rodes, "On Law and Virtue," in *Virtue: Public and Private,* ed. Richard Neuhaus (Grand Rapids, MI: Eerdmans, 1986), 35. I should say on the same grounds that I assume the church necessarily must develop a law internal to herself. See, for example, Rodes's "The Church as a Liberating Judicial Presence," in *Law and Liberation* (Notre Dame, IN: University of Notre Dame Press, 1986), 16–18.

Christians who presently serve as lawyers may find themselves in greater tension with their profession.

There is one final issue that must be addressed if I am to meet Gustafson's criticism fairly. In a paper written for *Theology Today* Michael Quirk perceptively observes that though I have drawn on as well as aligned myself with critics of liberalism such as Alasdair MacIntyre, Michael Sandel, Charles Taylor, and Michael Walzer, I am not of them.[16] For, as Professor Quirk notes, even if we were able to move to some form of civic republicanism in America, I would still consider that society but a form of humanism. According to Professor Quirk, my position on the church commits me to holding that "Christianity entails allegiance to a story which is inevitably alien to all forms of secular political institutions however 'humanistic' they may be."[17]

That is accurate but I do not believe it entails an indiscriminate rejection of the secular order. Rather, I maintain that Christians must withdraw their support from a "civic republicanism" only when that form (as well as any other form) of government and society resorts to violence in order to maintain internal order and external security. At that point and that point alone Christians must withhold their involvement with the state. Such an admission, however, hardly commits me to a sectarian stance, unless one assumes, as some do, that every function of the state depends on its penchant for violence. Indeed, I believe it to be the responsibility of Christians to work to make their societies less prone to resort to violence. Surely one of the ways they can do that is by using the law as a means to settle disagreements short of violence.

I am aware that such a response will not satisfy those who believe a disavowal of violence requires a withdrawal from politics. In contrast, it is my contention that politics only begins with such a disavowal, for only then are we forced genuinely to listen to the other, thus beginning conversations necessary for discovering goods in common. From my perspective, far from requiring a withdrawal from the political arena, pacifism demands strenuous political engagement, because such a commitment forces us to expand our social and political imaginations. Christians therefore stand ready to be citizens, even if we finally must remain in Rowan Greer's memorable phrase "alien

---

16. Michael Quirk, "Stanley Hauerwas' *Against the Nations:* Beyond Sectarianism," *Theology Today* 44, no. 1 (April 1987): 78–86. See also my response in the same issue, "Will the Real Sectarian Stand Up?", 87–94.

17. Quirk, "Stanley Hauerwas' *Against the Nations,*" 79.

citizens."[18] If my work appears sectarian in our time I suspect it is because in the name of being responsible too many Christians are under the illusion that we live in societies in which we can be at home because the societies are our creations. To reclaim alien status in contexts which were once thought home requires transformation of social and intellectual habits that cannot help but be a wrenching process.

Because I have been intent to help Christians rediscover our alien status I may have left the impression that the only community in which Christians can or should live is the church. No such view is either descriptively or normatively defensible. Christians rightly find themselves members of many communities. Thus I am not only a Christian but a university teacher, a Texan, a U.S. citizen, and a devoted fan of the Durham Bulls. Neither the general position I have developed nor my stance as a pacifist requires a general withdrawal from these communities. The essays on virtue and politics as well as those on the university should help make this point. What is required for Christians is not withdrawal but a sense of selective service and the ability to set priorities. This means that at times and in some circumstances Christians will find it impossible to participate in government, in aspects of the economy, or in the educational system. Yet such determinations can be made only by developing the skills of discrimination fostered in and through the church.

3.3 On a Theology of Creation and Redemption vs. Atheological "Tribalism"

I am sure these last remarks only reinforce Gustafson's conviction that I lack an adequate doctrine of creation. Such a charge actually involves two separable issues: (1) whether I have a doctrine of creation, and (2) whether my purported lack of a doctrine of creation and my corresponding emphasis on Jesus result in my failure to have an adequate theological and moral basis for addressing the moral and social problems of the twentieth century—that is, nuclear weapons, social justice, ecology. I note that these are separable criticisms because Gustafson does not indicate what is wrong with what I have written about nuclear war or show that the problem results from my Christocentric perspective. Moreover, he does not say why a doctrine of creation in and of itself is superior for dealing with these issues.

I suspect the assumption underlying his criticism is that without a doctrine of creation we have no way to underwrite the natural orders, and in particular

18. Rowan Greer, *Broken Lights and Mended Lives: Theology and Common Life in the Early Church* (University Park: Pennsylvania State University Press, 1986), 141–61.

the givenness of our social and political orders, as self-validating. Yet I have not denied the place of the state—even the coercive state—as part of God's "order." Rather, what I have refused in the name of an autonomous created order is to legitimate the state as an end in and of itself.

Admittedly, these are murky matters, but I think Gustafson exhibits a rather doubtful theological alternative by suggesting we need an independent doctrine of creation as a basis for ethics. Why doesn't Gustafson simply say that what is needed is a morality on which all people can agree? To appeal to doctrines of creation is only to make such agreement less likely. That is especially the case if we recognize, as Gustafson seems not to do, that Christian affirmation of God as creator is, because of God's trinitarian nature, a Christological claim.

Gustafson's call for a doctrine of creation, I suspect, involves a method not unlike that of H. Richard Niebuhr in *Christ and Culture*. In that book Niebuhr judges each of the various types, except "Christ the transformer," by how well it maintains the proper relation between creation and redemption.[19] Yet creation and redemption are treated in such an abstract manner that they almost become ciphers, especially since no reference is made to Israel and/or Jesus to explicate their content. Yet by appealing to some unspecified relation that should be maintained between these concepts, Niebuhr is able to make criticisms of every position without revealing his own material theological convictions; or put more argumentatively, in the name of creation Niebuhr in effect accepts "culture" as an independent norm that determines the significance of the work of Christ.[20]

This is but a way of saying that I doubt whether the issue is really a question of the doctrine of creation at all. I certainly have never denied the Christian affirmation of God as creator; rather, I have refused to use that affirmation to

19. [In his extremely influential book *Christ and Culture,* H. Richard Niebuhr delineated five different idealized "types" as to how Christians have historically responded to the problem of the relationship between Christ and culture. The five types were "Christ against culture," "Christ above culture," "Christ as culture," "Christ and culture in paradox," and "Christ transforming culture." Hauerwas's reading of H. Richard Niebuhr's *Christ and Culture* was influenced by J. H. Yoder's "How H. Richard Niebuhr Reasons: A Critique of *Christ and Culture,*" published in J. Howard Yoder, Diane Yeager, and Glen Stassen, *Authentic Transformation: A New Vision of Christ and Culture* (Nashville, TN: Abingdon, 1994).]

20. I owe this way of putting the matter to John Howard Yoder, who has developed it at length in his still unpublished paper, "How Richard Niebuhr Reasons: A Critique of Christ and Culture." [This essay has since been published in a revised form in *Authentic Transformation: A New Vision of Christ and Culture,* ed. Glen Stassen, Diane Yeager, and John H. Yoder (Nashville, TN: Abingdon Press, 1997), 31–89.]

underwrite an autonomous realm of morality separate from Christ's lordship. The issue is not creation, but the kind of creation Jews and Christians continue to affirm as integral to God's being. What allows us to look expectantly for agreement among those who do not worship God is not that we have a common morality based on autonomous knowledge of autonomous nature, but that God's kingdom is wider than the church.

Gustafson suggests that I believe that God is known only through history and in particular through that small tribe we call the church. Certainly I believe that God as savior is known in Israel and Jesus in a way not available anywhere else. But I see no other basis for affirming God as creator if we mean anything more by that claim, as I assume we must theologically, than the hypothesis or hunch that something must have started it all. For creation in Christian theology is an eschatological act that binds nature and history together by placing them in a teleological order. Indeed, from a theological perspective nature and history are both abstractions when considered in the light of God's redemption. In Christ's bodily resurrection nature and history are made forever inseparable.[21] I certainly would not deny the natural order as a manifestation of God's kingdom.

I am aware that this response will hardly allay Gustafson's concern but instead will only reinforce his views that I represent a form of Jesus idolatry. Hence, Christology is the issue, though not in the way that Gustafson seems to think. To assert as Gustafson does that "Jesus is not God" is simply not a very interesting claim. It is not interesting because we have no context or

21. Oliver O'Donovan, *Resurrection and Moral Order* (Grand Rapids, MI: Eerdmans, 1986). O'Donovan notes:

> The sign that God has stood by his created order implies that this order, with mankind in its proper place within it, is to be totally restored at the last. This invites a comment on a debate which has occupied too much attention, the debate between the so-called "ethics of the kingdom" and the "ethics of creation." This way of posing the alternatives is not acceptable, for the very act of God which ushers in his kingdom is the resurrection of Christ from the dead, the reaffirmation of creation. A kingdom ethics which was set up in opposition to creation could not possibly be interested in the same eschatological kingdom as that which the New Testament proclaims. At its root there would have to be a hidden dualism which interpreted the progress of history to its completion not as a fulfillment, but as a denial of its beginnings. A creation ethics, on the other hand, which was set up in opposition to the kingdom, could not possibly be evangelical ethics, since it would fail to take note of the good news that God had acted to bring all that he had made to fulfillment. In the resurrection of Christ creation is restored and the kingdom of God dawns. Ethics which start from this point may sometimes emphasize the newness, sometimes the primitiveness of the order that is there affirmed. But it will not be tempted to overthrow or deny either in the name of the other. (15)

speaker to know what is being denied and so lack any way to know what the denial means.

Classical Christian theologians have never, in fact, made so blunt a statement as Gustafson seems to think worth denying. Of course Jesus is not God if you mean, for example, God is no longer eternal by being identified with Jesus. It is just such worries that have made the Christian people careful about how they say God is present to us in the life, death, and resurrection of Jesus. That God was peculiarly at work in Jesus there is, for us, no doubt. How that work is to be explained is quite another matter—Jesus, "very God and very man,"[22] is not a bad place to start.

One issue that can be overlooked in Gustafson's jeremiad against my "tribalism" is that the criticism he makes against me applies equally against the Jews. After all, affirmations of God's redemption through Jesus are not different in kind from the claim that "Israel is God's promised people." Yet Jews as well as Christians believe that insofar as we are faithful to God's call the world has an opportunity to be freed from such tribes as "the West" or "Europe" or "oppressed people of the world." So rather than being a justification for tribalism, my emphasis on Jesus as the first form of the new age is, I believe, our best hope to stand against contemporary tribalism. I suspect that behind Gustafson's use of "tribalism" is the Enlightenment presumption that tribes are regressive since they do not represent "open and tolerant communities"—that is, they fail to acknowledge universal rights. Of course, it was exactly such an ideology that justified American treatment of the Indians as well as European policies in Africa. Christians do not have a stake in the denial of tribal identity as such, but rather for us "tribalism" is only a problem if it threatens the new unity of creation in Christ Jesus which we believe is most nearly embodied in the church.

Further Reading

"The Nonresistant Church: The Theological Ethics of John Howard Yoder" (1971), in *vv*

"The Church as God's New Language" (1986), essay 7 in this volume

"Introduction: The Scope of this book" (1985), in *AN*

"Remembering as a Moral Task: The Challenge of the Holocaust" (1985), essay 17 in this volume

"The Church in a Divided World" (1980), in *CC*

22. The phrase "very God and very man" is, of course, an allusion to the Nicene Creed.

"The Servant Community: Christian Social Ethics" (1983), essay 19 in this volume

"The Modern World: On Learning to Ask the Right Questions" (1989), in RA

"On Keeping Theological Ethics Theological" (1983), essay 2 in this volume

"The Politics of Salvation: Why There Is No Salvation Outside the Church" (1991), in AC

"Why *Resident Aliens* Struck a Chord" (1991), in IGC

"Christianity: It's not a Religion, It's an Adventure" (1991), essay 26 in this volume.

"The Importance of Being Catholic: Unsolicited Advice from a Protestant By-stander" (1990), in IGC

"No Enemy, No Christianity: Preaching Between 'Worlds'" (1998), in STT

"Virtue in Public" (1986), in CET

5. Reforming Christian Social Ethics:
Ten Theses (1981)

These theses are meant as a challenge to the way mainline Protestants and Catholics in the United States understood and did "social ethics" in the 1970s. The social ethicists that Hauerwas has in mind in one or more of these theses include such luminaries in the field as Reinhold Niebuhr, H. Richard Niebuhr, James Gustafson, and Paul Ramsey. The theses serve to encapsulate the key presuppositions of Hauerwas's alternative to what was at that time the dominant account in Christian ethics. The key thesis is that the Christian community is formed by the conviction that the story of Christ is a truthful account of our existence, and thus the central task of Christ's church is to witness to the kind of social life possible for those formed by that story. This leads to Hauerwas's famous and oft-repeated programmatic statement that "the church does not have a social ethic; the church is a social ethic."

1. The social significance of the Gospel requires the recognition of the narrative structure of Christian convictions for the life of the church.[1]

Christian social ethics too often takes the form of principles and policies that are not clearly based on or warranted by the central convictions of the faith. Yet the basis of any Christian social ethic should be the affirmation that God has decisively called and formed a people to serve him through Israel and the work of Christ. The appropriation of the critical significance of the latter depends on the recognition of narrative as a basic category for social ethics.

[From CC © 1981 by University of Notre Dame Press. Used by permission. Originally the first part of "A Story-Formed Community: Reflections on *Watership Down*" in CC. See essay 9 of this volume. With the new title, the theses being argued stand on their own.]
1. [Since the writing of these ten theses, Hauerwas has developed each in various contexts. Thus, we are providing salient examples of publications where these programmatic statements are further developed. For further explication of thesis 1, see "A Qualified Ethic: The Narrative Character of Christian Ethics," chapter 2 of PK.]

2. *Every social ethic involves a narrative, whether it is concerned with the for-mulation of basic principles of social organization and/or with concrete policy alternatives.*[2]

The loss of narrative as a central category for social ethics has resulted in a failure to see that the ways the issues of social ethics are identified—that is, the relation of personal and social ethics, the meaning and status of the individual in relation to the community, freedom versus equality, the interrelation of love and justice—are more a reflection of a political philosophy than they are crucial categories for the analysis of a community's social ethics. The form and substance of a community is narrative-dependent, and therefore what counts as "social ethics" is a correlative of the content of that narrative.

3. *The ability to provide an adequate account of our existence is the primary test of the truthfulness of a social ethic.*[3]

No society can be just or good that is built on falsehood. The first task of Christian social ethics, therefore, is not to make the "world" better or more just, but to help Christian people form their community consistent with their conviction that the story of Christ is a truthful account of our existence. For as H. R. Niebuhr argued, only when we know "what is going on," do we know "what we should do," and Christians believe that we learn most decisively "what is going on" in the cross and resurrection of Christ.

4. *Communities formed by a truthful narrative must provide the skills to trans-form fate into destiny so that the unexpected, especially as it comes in the form of strangers, can be welcomed as gift.*[4]

We live in a world of powers that are not our creation and we become determined by them when we lack the ability to recognize and name them. The Christian story teaches us to regard truthfulness more as a gift than a possession and thus requires that we be willing to face both the possibilities

2. [For further explication of thesis 2, see "The Politics of Salvation: Why There Is No Salvation Outside the Church," chapter 1 in *AC*, and "A Christian Critique of Christian America," 22 in this volume.]

3. [For further explication of thesis 3, see "The Kingship of Christ: Why Freedom of Belief Is Not Enough," chapter 13 of *IGC*, and "Why the 'Sectarian Temptation' Is a Misrepresentation," 4 in this volume.]

4. [For further explication of thesis 4, see "Timeful Friends: Living with the Handicapped," chapter 7 of *STT*; "The Servant Community: Christian Social Ethics," 19 in this volume; and "Having and Learning to Care for Retarded Children," chapter 10 of *TT*.]

and threats a stranger represents. Such a commitment is the necessary condition for preventing our history from becoming our fate.

5. The primary social task of the church is to be itself—that is, a people who have been formed by a story that provides them with the skills for negotiating the danger of this existence, trusting in God's promise of redemption.[5]

The church is a people on a journey who insist on living consistent with the conviction that God is the lord of history. They thus refuse to resort to violence in order to secure their survival. The fact that the first task of the church is to be itself is not a rejection of the world or a withdrawal ethic, but a reminder that Christians must serve the world on their own terms; otherwise the world would have no means to know itself as the world.

6. Christian social ethics can only be done from the perspective of those who do not seek to control national or world history but who are content to live "out of control."[6]

To do ethics from the perspective of those "out of control" means Christians must find the means to make clear to both the oppressed and the oppressor that the cross determines the meaning of history.[7] Christians should thus provide imaginative alternatives for social policy as they are released from the "necessities" of those that would control the world in the name of security. For to be out of control means Christians can risk trusting in gifts, so they have no reason to deny the contingent character of our existence.

7. Christian social ethics depends on the development of leadership in the church that can trust and depend on the diversity of gifts in the community.[8]

5. [For further explication of thesis 5, see "What Could It Mean for the Church to Be Christ's Body: A Question without a Clear Answer," chapter 1 of *IGC;* "The Non-Violent Terrorist: In Defense of Christian Fanaticism," chapter 10 of *STT;* and "The Radical Hope in the Annunciation: Why Both Single and Married Christians Welcome Children" (2001), essay 24 in this volume.
6. [For further explication of thesis 6, see "Creation, Contingency, and Truthful Nonviolence: A Milbankian Reflection," chapter 12 of *WW*.]
7. Thus John Howard Yoder argues that "the triumph of the right is assured not by the might that comes to the aid of the right, which is of course the justification of the use of violence and other kinds of power in every human conflict; the triumph of the right, although it is assured, is sure because of the power of the resurrection and not because of the inherently greater strength of the good guys. The relationship between the obedience of God's people and the triumph of God's cause is not a relationship of cause and effect but one of cross and resurrection." See *The Politics of Jesus* (Grand Rapids, MI: Eerdmans, 1972), 238.
8. [For further explication of thesis 7, see "The Politics of Church: How We Lay Bricks and

The authority necessary for leadership in the church should derive from the willingness of Christians to risk speaking the truth to and hearing the truth from those in charge. In societies that fear the truth, leadership depends on the ability to provide security rather than the ability to let the diversity of the community serve as the means to live truthfully. Only the latter form of community can afford to have their leaders' mistakes acknowledged without their ceasing to exercise authority.

8. For the church to be, rather than to have, a social ethic means we must recapture the social significance of common behavior, such as acts of kindness, friendship, and the formation of families.[9]

Trust is impossible in communities that always regard the other as a challenge and threat to their existence. One of the most profound commitments of a community, therefore, is providing a context that encourages us to trust and depend on one another. Particularly significant is a community's determination to be open to new life that is destined to challenge as well as carry on the story.

9. In our attempt to control our society Christians in America have too readily accepted liberalism as a social strategy appropriate to the Christian story.[10]

Liberalism, in its many forms and versions, presupposes that society can be organized without any narrative that is commonly held to be true. As a result it tempts us to believe that freedom and rationality are independent of narrative—that is, we are free to the extent that we have no story. Liberalism is, therefore, particularly pernicious to the extent it prevents us from understanding how deeply we are captured by its account of existence.

10. The church does not exist to provide an ethos for democracy or any other form of social organization, but stands as a political alternative to every nation, wit-

---

Make Disciples," chapter 4 of *AC;* "Clerical Character," chapter 7 of *CET;* "Authority in the Profession of Medicine," chapter 2 of *SP;* and "The Moral Authority of Scripture: The Politics and Ethics of Remembering," chapter 3 of *CC.*]

9. [For further explication of thesis 8, see "Tragedy and Joy: The Spirituality of Peaceableness," chapter 8 of *PK;* "The Radical Hope of the Annunciation," 24 in this volume; and "The Moral Significance of the Family" in *CC.*]

10. [For further explication of thesis 9, see "The Politics of Freedom: Why Freedom of Religion Is a Subtle Temptation," in *AC* and "The Church and Liberal Democracy: The Moral Limits of a Secular Polity," chapter 4 of *CC.*]

nessing to the kind of social life possible for those that have been formed by the story of Christ.[11]

The church's first task is to help us gain a critical perspective on those narratives that have captivated our vision and lives. By doing so, the church may well help provide a paradigm of social relations otherwise thought impossible.[12]

Further Reading

"Taking Time for Peace: The Ethical Significance of the Trivial" (1986), in CET

"Peacemaking: The Virtue of the Church" (1985), essay 16 in this volume

"Whose Church? Which Future? Whither the Anabaptist Vision?" (1994), in IGC

"The Church's One Foundation Is Jesus Christ Her Lord, or In a World without Foundations All We Have Is the Church" (1994), in IGC

"Salvation Even in Sin: Learning to Speak Truthfully about Ourselves" (1998), in STT

"Positioning: In the Church and University but Not of Either" (1994), in DF

11. [For further explication of thesis 10, see "The Servant Community: Christian Social Ethics," 19 in this volume, and "The Politics of Justice: Why Justice Is a Bad Idea for Christians," chapter 2 in AC.]

12. Readers who would like to see a narrative exposition of these theses should read the original essay [essay 9 in this volume].

6. Jesus and the Social Embodiment of
the Peaceable Kingdom (1983)

In this pivotal chapter of Hauerwas's most well-known book, Hauerwas is reasserting what now may appear obvious to many, namely, the centrality of Jesus' life, death, and resurrection for reflection in Christian ethics. What may not be obvious is why the reassertion of the ethical significance of Jesus was necessary. Influenced by Karl Barth's Church Dogmatics *IV,1 and IV,2 and by John Howard Yoder's work, especially* The Politics of Jesus, *Hauerwas responds to a number of highly influential works in Protestant Christian ethics (Reinhold Niebuhr's* Interpretation of Christian Ethics, *H. Richard Niebuhr's* Radical Monotheism and Western Culture, *James Gustafson's* Christ and the Moral Life, *and Joseph Fletcher's* Situation Ethics) *and in Catholic moral theology (Timothy O'Connell's* Principles for a Catholic Morality *and antecedent articles by Joseph Fuchs, Richard McCormick, and Charles Curran), which have for a variety of reasons largely ignored the life of Jesus of Nazareth.*

In this essay Hauerwas displays Christian discipleship in the context of Israel and the coming reign of God. Such a context requires one to see both the world and the kingdom in terms of a story, with a beginning, a continuing drama, and an end. To live this story is to live as those who do not need to control history and thus as those who need not resort to violence. Toward the conclusion of the essay, Hauerwas imaginatively refigures soteriology in narrative terms—faith, sanctification, and justification become descriptions of the journey by which Christians make the story of Christ their own.

1. Why Beginning with Jesus Is Not the Same as Beginning with Christology

Christian ethics has tended to make "Christology" rather than Jesus its starting point. His relevance is seen as resting in broader claims about the incarna-

[From PK © 1983 by University of Notre Dame Press. Used by permission. Originally entitled "Jesus: The Presence of the Peaceable Kingdom." It has been extensively edited for clarity. All substantive changes have been approved by the author.]

tion. Christian ethics then often begins with some broadly drawn theological claims about the significance of God becoming man, but the life of the man whom God made his representative is ignored or used selectively. Some have placed such great emphasis on Jesus' death and resurrection as the source of salvation that there is almost no recognition of him as the teacher of righteousness. Others subordinate even Jesus' death and resurrection to claims concerning Jesus as very God and very man—for it is God taking on himself our nature that saves, rather than the life of this man Jesus.

This emphasis on Jesus' ontological significance strikes many as absolutely essential, especially in light of modern historical criticism on the Gospels. For it has become obvious that the writers of the Gospels were not trying to write "objective history" but rather told the story of Jesus in terms of the needs and concerns of their communities. Some even argue that there is no possibility of knowing the "historical Jesus." On this view, we only know the Jesus given to us by the early church, which had its own particular axes to grind. This approach concludes that there is no alternative but to provide a "hermeneutical principle" prior to the Gospels that can establish Jesus' nature and significance.

Yet there is a deep difficulty with the strategy that attempts to avoid dealing with Jesus as he is portrayed in the Gospels. Christologies that emphasize the cosmic and ontological Christ tend to make Jesus' life almost incidental to what is assumed to be a more profound theological point. In particular the eschatological aspects of Jesus' message are downplayed. Yet there is widespread agreement that one of the most significant "discoveries" of recent scholarship is that Jesus' teaching was not first of all focused on his own status but on the proclamation of the kingdom of God.[1] Jesus, it seems, did not direct attention to himself, but through his teaching, healings, and miracles tried to indicate the nature and immediacy of God's kingdom.[2] It may be

---

1. For just one example, see A. E. Harvey, *Jesus and the Constraints of History* (Philadelphia: Westminster, 1982), 84.
2. Jesus' emphasis on the Kingdom in itself was not unique. As Sean Freyne suggests, "According to Acts 5:33–39 such an influential Pharisaic scribe as Gamaliel I, Paul's teacher, was prepared to let the new movement take its course and attempt to authenticate its claims that it was from God. At Qumran the teacher of righteousness and his followers clearly experienced the presence of the new age in their own community which they can describe as 'the covenant which God established with Israel forever in the land of Damascus.' Throughout the whole first century a series of Zealot leaders presented themselves as messianic figures who were about to launch the final holy war against evil . . . In itself then, there was nothing startlingly new in the proclamation of God's kingly rule, even in its final phase, as present and operative" (*The World of the New Testament* [Wilmington, DE: Michael Glazier, 1980], 139).

objected that even this conclusion about him seems to presuppose exactly what we just said could not be assumed—namely, that we are able to isolate the real Jesus from the Jesus created by the early churches. Yet we can at least say that Jesus as depicted in Mark, Matthew, and Luke does not call attention to himself, but to the kingdom that the early Christians felt had been made present and yet was still to come.

2. To Know Jesus Is to Follow Jesus

It is not my intention to settle to what extent we can know the "real Jesus." I am quite content to assume that the Jesus we have in Scripture is the Jesus of the early church. Even more important, I want to maintain that it cannot or should not be otherwise, since the very demands Jesus placed on his followers means he cannot be known abstracted from the disciples' response. The historical fact that we learn who Jesus is only as he is reflected through the eyes of his followers, a fact that has driven many to despair because it seems they cannot know the real Jesus, in fact is a theological necessity. For the "real Jesus" did not come to leave us unchanged, but rather to transform us to be worthy members of the community of the new age.

It is a startling fact, so obvious that its significance is missed time and time again, that when the early Christians began to witness the significance of Jesus for their lives they necessarily resorted to a telling of his life. Their "Christology" did not consist first in claims about Jesus' ontological status, though such claims were made; their Christology was not limited to assessing the significance of Jesus' death and resurrection, though certainly these were attributed great significance; rather, their "Christology," if it can be called that,[3] showed the story of Jesus as absolutely essential for depicting the kind of kingdom they now thought possible through his life, death, and resurrection. Therefore, though Jesus did not call attention to himself, the early Christians rightly saw that what Jesus came to proclaim, the kingdom of God as a present and future reality, could be grasped only by recognizing how Jesus exemplified in his life the standards of that kingdom.

3. See Gerza Vermes's caution about the language of Christology for analysis of the Gospels: "The Gospels without Christology," in *God Incarnate: Story and Belief*, ed. A. E. Harvey (London: SPCK, 1981), 55–68. It may be objected that the Pauline writings stand as clear evidence against the claim made here. However, I would argue that though Paul's letters do not provide the details about Jesus' life as do the Gospels, they in fact presuppose those details. Moreover, Paul's scheme of redemption, his eschatology, is nothing less than the story of God that makes Jesus' life from birth to the resurrection essential for that scheme's coherence.

But the situation is even more complex. The form of the Gospels as stories of a life are meant not only to display that life, but to train us to situate our lives in relation to that life. For it was assumed by the churches that gave us the Gospels that we cannot know who Jesus is and what he stands for without learning to be his followers. Hence the ironic form of Mark, which begins by announcing to the reader this is the "good news about Jesus, the anointed one, the son of God," but in depicting the disciples shows how difficult it is to understand the significance of that news. You cannot know who Jesus is after the resurrection unless you have learned to follow Jesus during his life. His life and crucifixion are necessary to purge us of false notions about what kind of kingdom Jesus brings. In the same way his disciples and adversaries also had to be purged. Only by learning to follow him to Jerusalem, where he becomes subject to the powers of this world, do we learn what the kingdom entails, as well as what kind of messiah this Jesus is.

Like Mark, my own emphasis on the ethical significance of Jesus' life and the necessity of attending to the narrative portrait of that life is different from that usually given in Christian ethics. Indeed, that very way of putting it—that is, the ethical significance of Jesus—is misleading. For it is not as though we can know Jesus or understand him apart from his ethical significance. To locate our lives in relation to his is already to be involved with the basic issues of Christian ethics. Jesus is the one who comes to initiate and make present the kingdom of God through healing of those possessed by demons, by calling disciples, telling parables, teaching the law, challenging the authorities of his day, and by being crucified at the hands of Roman and Jewish elites and raised from the grave. Insisting that Jesus is the initiator and presence of the kingdom, of course, does not mean he was not the Christ, or that he is not God incarnate, or that his death and resurrection have nothing to do with the forgiveness of sin, but it does mean that each of these claims are subsequent to the whole life of this man whom God has claimed as decisive to his own for the presence of his kingdom in this world.

Indeed, it is interesting to note that when the fathers wish to explicate the word "incarnation" in speaking of Jesus, the word they use is "economy," which simply means how God manages the world. So for Athanasius the incarnation notes how God's economy—that is, God's Word—appropriated a human body so that he might die and be raised.[4] Thus incarnation is not a doctrine that places all significance on the birth of Jesus, nor is it a doctrine

---

4. Athanasius, *The Incarnation of the Word of God* (New York: Macmillan, 1946), 34.

about Jesus' person or nature, but it is a reminder that we cannot assess God's claim of Jesus' significance short of seeing how his whole life manifests God's kingdom.[5]

My emphasis on Jesus' life as depicted by the early church is not, therefore, an example of a "low Christology."[6] Indeed, it is my contention that by attending to the narrative form of the Gospels we will see all the more clearly what it means for Jesus to be God's anointed. By learning to be followers of Jesus we learn to locate our lives within God's life, within the journey that comprises his kingdom. I will try to show how the very heart of following the way of God's kingdom involves nothing less than learning to be like God. We learn to be like God by following the teachings of Jesus and thus learning to be his disciples.

For we have been told:

> "You have heard that it was said, 'An eye for an eye and a tooth for a tooth.' But I say to you, Do not resist one who is evil. But if any one strikes you on the right cheek, turn to him the other also; and if any one would sue you and take your coat, let him have your cloak as well; and if any one forces you to go one mile, go with him two miles. Give to him who begs from you, and do not refuse him who would borrow from you.
>
> "You have heard that it was said, 'You shall love your neighbor and hate your enemy.' But I say to you, 'Love your enemies and pray for those who persecute you, so that you may be sons of your father who is in heaven; for he makes his sun rise on the evil and on the good, and sends rain on the just and the unjust. For if you love those who love you what reward have you? Do not even the tax collectors do the same? And if you salute only your brethren, what more are you doing than others? Do not even the Gentiles do the same?

---

5. I am indebted to Dr. Rowan Greer for this interpretation of the Patristic understanding of the incarnation.

6. [Hauerwas is here making reference to and challenging the adequacy of the terms of particular Christological debates that emerged in European Protestant and Catholic theology in the 1960s and 1970s. See, for instance, Wolfhart Pannenberg, *Jesus: God and Man* (Philadelphia: Westminster, 1968); Walter Kasper, *The God of Jesus Christ* (London: SCM Press, 1984); and Jurgen Moltmann, *The Way of Jesus Christ* (San Francisco: HarperCollins, 1990). For a helpful interpretive essay on this debate, see Nicholas Lash, "Up and Down in Christology," in *New Studies in Theology, I*, ed. S. W. Sykes and J. D. Holmes (London: Duckwork, 1979). For a helpful explication of Hauerwas's Christology and the distinctive significance of his "theological politics," see Arne Rasmusson, *The Church as Polis: From Political Theology to Theological Politics as Exemplified by Juergen Moltmann and Stanley Hauerwas* (Notre Dame, IN: University of Notre Dame Press, 1995).]

You, therefore, must be perfect, as your heavenly Father is perfect.' " (Matt. 5:38–48)

We are called to be like God: perfect as God is perfect. It is a perfection that comes by learning to follow and be like this man whom God has sent to be our forerunner in the kingdom. That is why Christian ethics is not first of all an ethics of principles, laws, or values, but an ethic that demands we attend to the life of a particular individual: Jesus of Nazareth. It is only from him that we can learn perfection—which is at the very least nothing less than forgiving our enemies.

3. Jesus, Israel, and the Imitation of God

The theme of "imitation" is subject, however, to much misunderstanding. In particular, it carries with it individualist presuppositions that are antithetical to the social nature of the Christian life. For there is no way to learn to "imitate" God by trying to copy in an external manner the actions of Jesus. No one can become virtuous merely by doing what virtuous people do. We can only be virtuous by doing what virtuous people do in the manner that they do it. Therefore one can only learn how to be virtuous, to be like Jesus, by learning from others how that is done. To be like Jesus requires that I become part of a community that practices virtues, not that I copy his life point by point.

There is a deeper reason that I cannot and should not mimic Jesus. We are not called on to be the initiators of the kingdom, we are not called on to be God's anointed. We are called on to be *like* Jesus, not to *be* Jesus. As I will try to show, that likeness is of a very specific nature. It involves seeing in his cross the summary of his whole life. Thus to be like Jesus is to join him in the journey through which we are trained to be a people capable of claiming citizenship in God's kingdom of nonviolent love—a love that would overcome the powers of this world, not through coercion and force, but through the power of this one man's death.

A proper appreciation of the centrality of the theme of imitation must begin, however, not with Jesus but with Israel. For Jesus brought no new insights about the law or God's nature that had not already been revealed to Israel. The command to be perfect as God is perfect is not some new command, nor is the content of that command to love our enemies new. Both the structure and the content of the command draw from the long habits of thought developed in Israel through her experience with the Lord. Jesus' activity as presented in the Gospels makes no sense without assuming what Israel had long known, that any story worth telling about the way things are requires an account of God's activity as the necessary framework for that story.

It was Israel's conviction, as displayed in the Hebrew Scriptures, that a series of events in her history was decisive for God's relation to humankind. In these events God had spoken, and Israel constantly returned to them to guide her future relations with God. For the interpretation that came to be put on the journey of Moses from Egypt was such that the Exodus, "the law-giving at Sinai, the crossing of Jordan, the temple on Zion were seen as the formative phases in God's creation of his people Israel. . . . The life of the people of God had necessarily to retain (through 'remembering' and 'meditation') an intimate organic relation to this vital formative period of their history, because in it the essential shape of life had been clearly indicated by God himself. In this sequence of history God had shown that he is always *prevenient:* life is a journey where he goes before men as guide and as example; and that he is always *provident:* he accompanies them as their companion and instructor, and, as it turns out in the end, he is himself the route."[7]

Therefore, the task for Israel, indeed the very thing that makes Israel Israel, is to walk in the way of the Lord, that is, to imitate God through the means of the prophet (Torah), the king (Sonship), and the priest (Knowledge).[8] To walk in the way of God meant that Israel must be obedient to the commands (Deut. 8:6), to fear the Lord (Deut. 10:12), to love the Lord (Deut. 11:22), and thus to be perfect in the way (Gen. 17:1). But the way of obedience is also the way of intimacy, for Israel is nothing less than God's "first-born son" (Ex. 4:22). Moreover, Israel has the knowledge of the Lord as a just and compassionate God and so Israel too must act justly and with compassion (Jer. 22:16).

Israel is Israel, therefore, just to the extent that she "remembers" the "way of the Lord," for by that remembering she in fact imitates God. Such a remembering was no simple mental recollection; rather, the image remembered formed the soul and determined future direction. "To remember the works of Yahweh and to seek him, i.e., to let one's acts be determined by his will, is in reality the same. Consequently, to 'remember' the 'Way' from the Reed Sea onwards is to act *now* on the basis of the relationship between God and Israel there revealed, and in so doing to appropriate it, and know it to be most real."[9]

7. E. J. Tinsley, *The Imitation of God in Christ* (London: s.c.m. Press, 1960), 31.
8. Ibid., 35.
9. Ibid., 55.

Thus the call of the prophets to Israel was always a summons to return to the vocation of an *imitator Dei:* God "asks of men that they shall reflect his own character, so far as it can be reflected within the limitations of human life. . . . When the prophets denounced harshness and oppression and called for compassion for the unfortunate, they were calling men to reflect the character which was uniquely expressed in God's deliverance of his people."[10] For Israel, therefore, to love God meant to learn to love as God loved and loves: "The Lord set his heart upon your fathers and chose their descendants after them, you above all peoples, as at this day. . . . For Yahweh your God is God of gods and Lord of lords, the great, the mighty, and the terrible God, who is partial and takes no bribe. He executes justice for the fatherless and the widow, and loves the sojourner, giving him food and clothing. Love the sojourner therefore; for you were sojourners in the land of Egypt. You shall fear the Lord your God; you shall serve him and cleave to him, and by his name you shall swear. . . . You shall therefore love the Lord your God, and keep his charge, his statutes, his ordinances, and his commandments always" (Deut. 10:15, 17–20; 11:1).

Each of the major offices in Israel—king, priest, and prophet—also drew its substance from the need for Israel to have a visible exemplar to show how to follow the Lord.[11] What was needed were people who embodied in their lives and work the vocation of Israel to "walk" in the "way" of the Lord. The king, the prophet, and the priest were judged by how well they dedicated their lives to being suitable models for the people to imitate. As a result there was a clear tendency in Israel for the three functions to coalesce in one figure—for example, Moses or the servant in the "Servant" songs of Isaiah. For, like the prophet, the servant is predestined (Isa. 49:1) and called by God for a special task. But the servant is also commissioned to be a king, to walk in the way of the Torah of the Lord. Even more, the servant becomes the priestly sacrifice, giving himself for the people. By enacting in his life these offices, the servant displays to Israel not only their task, but the very life of God.

It is against this background that the early Christians came to understand and believe in Jesus' life, death, and resurrection. They had found a continuation of Israel's vocation to imitate God. In so doing, they depicted God's kingdom for the world in a decisive way. Jesus' life was seen as the recapitulation of the life of Israel and thus presented the very life of God in the world. By

10. Here, Tinsley is quoting from H. H. Rowley's *The Unity of the Bible* (Philadelphia, Pa.: Westminster Press, 1953), 25.
11. Ibid., 61.

learning to imitate Jesus, to follow in his way, the early Christians believed they were learning to imitate God, who would have them be heirs of the kingdom.

How Jesus' life was seen as the recapitulation of God's way with Israel is perhaps nowhere better presented than in the temptation narratives. For in the wilderness Jesus, like Israel, discovers his vocation through being tempted to pervert God's gifts to Israel. In the first temptation we see Jesus so identified with Israel that he experiences Israel's perennial desire for certainty of her own choosing. Is he to be like Moses and turn stone to bread? Surely it would be a good thing to turn stone to bread, to be a ready resource to feed the hungry and the poor. But Jesus rejects that means of proving how God reigns with his people, knowing that the life offered Israel is more than bread can supply (Luke 4:4).

Again the devil tempts him, this time with dominion, with kingship even greater than that of the great David. It is a dominion that can bring peace to the nations, since one powerful king can force all to his will. But again Jesus rejects such dominion. God's kingdom, it seems, will not have peace through coercion. Peace will come only through the worship of the one God who chooses to rule the world through the power of love, which the world can perceive only as weakness. Jesus thus decisively rejects Israel's temptation to an idolatry that necessarily results in violence between peoples and nations. For our violence is correlative to the falseness of the objects we worship, and the more false they are, the greater our stake in maintaining loyalty to them and protecting them through coercion. Only the one true God can take the risk of ruling by relying entirely on the power of humility and love.

Finally, Jesus is tempted to act as the priest of priests, to force God's hand by being the sacrifice that God cannot refuse. In short, Jesus is tempted to play the hero, to take his life in his hands, to be in control of his destiny, and thus to force God's kingdom to be present because of his sacrifice. But such a heroic role contrasts starkly with the man who died on the cross, subject to others' will. For by being so subject we see that finally it is not his will but God's that is worked out through his life and death. The resurrection, therefore, is not an extraordinary event added to this man's life, but a confirmation by God that the character of Jesus' life prior to the resurrection is perfectly faithful to his vocation to proclaim and make present God's kingdom. Without the resurrection our concentration on Jesus would be idolatry, but without Jesus' life we would not know what kind of God it is who has raised him from the dead.

The temptation narratives are but a particularly concentrated example of how the early church understood Jesus' life as recapitulating the life of the Lord with Israel. The baptism, the turning to Jerusalem, the cleansing of the temple, the last supper, the crucifixion, and the resurrection were equally understood to be the deliberate representing of Jesus as Israel's king-messiah. But also the calling of the twelve, the necessity of wandering throughout Israel, the signs on the sabbath, the desert feedings, and the special attention to the poor and the outcast are understood to be at once recapitulation and innovation of the life of Israel and her relationship to God.[12] Thus it is not surprising that the early Christians assumed that by imitating the "Way" of Jesus they were imitating the "Way" of God himself. For the content of the kingdom, the means of citizenship, turns out to be nothing more or less than learning to imitate Jesus' life through taking on the task of being his disciple.

And one becomes a disciple by following the way of God, which is the way of renunciation: "If any man would come after me let him deny himself and take up his cross and follow me" (Mark 8:34). Moreover, such a renunciation is not merely an existential giving up of the self, but the surrender of family life and affection (Matt. 10:37), and perhaps even the giving up of life itself (Mark 10:45).[13] But it is also a life of humility: "You know that those who are sup-

12. Ibid., 86–87. The strong emphasis on the continuity between Jesus and Israel may be felt to be misleading exactly in terms of the central theme of this book—namely, nonviolence. For the depiction of war and violence in the Hebrew Scriptures continues to underwrite the crude, but still powerful picture held by many, that the God of the Old Testament is one of wrath and vengeance compared to the New Testament God of mercy and love. Yet those who hold this picture often, ironically, appeal to the Hebrew Scriptures to justify Christian approval of war. It is beyond the scope of this book to attempt to challenge this understanding of war in the Hebrew Scripture. However, see Millard Lind, *Yahweh Is a Warrior: The Theology of Warfare in Ancient Israel* (Scottsdale, PA: Herald Press, 1980), for a carefully developed argument that makes views such as the above exegetically doubtful. Lind argues that "Yahweh the warrior fought by means of miracle, not through the armies of his people; 'it was not by your sword or by your bow' (Josh. 24:12). By miracle we mean an act of deliverance that was outside of Israel's control, beyond the manipulation of any human agency. This conviction was so emphatic that Israel's fighting, while at times a sequel to the act of Yahweh, was regarded ineffective; faith meant that Israel should rely upon Yahweh's miracle for her defense, rather than upon soldiers and weapons. The human agent in the work of Yahweh was not so much the warrior as the prophet" (23).

13. John Howard Yoder, *The Original Revolution* (Scottsdale, PA: Herald Press, 1971), 1–32. Thus Yoder argues, "To repent is not to feel bad but to think differently. Protestantism, and perhaps especially evangelical Protestantism, in its concern for helping every individual to make his own authentic choice in full awareness and sincerity, is in constant danger of confusing the kingdom itself with the benefits of the kingdom. If anyone repents, if anyone turns around to follow Jesus in his new way of life, this will do something for the aimlessness of his life. It will do something for his loneliness by giving him fellowship . . . So the

posed to rule over the Gentiles lord it over them and their great men exercise authority over them. But it shall not be so among you; but whoever would be great among you must be your servant, and whoever would be first among you must be slave of all. For the Son of man also came not to be served but to serve, and to give his life as a ransom for many" (Mark 10:42–45).

In this way of service we learn of the kind of God we are to love and to whom we are called to obedience. For Jesus' life is the life of God insofar as he serves others as God serves us: "His first allegiance is to God; then he loves the neighbor as himself. So he has no need to lord over out of fear or to get others to serve him; and his commitment to serve is courageous, for he loses his life by so doing. So Jesus' idea of service does not become a matter of doing what others want him to do except insofar as it remains consonant with his understanding of God's will. He will heal others who request it, like Bartimaeus, but he will not grant the request of James and John who want power and glory. Strong-willed and independent, Jesus has a clear sense of his own mission, and neither traditions nor laws nor public pressure nor fear of indictment prevent him from speaking or acting."[14]

Thus Jesus' whole life, as narratively depicted in the Gospels, is a life of noncoercive power. Jesus' noncoercive power does not serve by forcing itself on others. Thus he "calls" the disciples and teaches them to be faithful, but he does not try to control their responses. We can only be dispossessed of the powers currently holding our lives if we give up those things and goods that possess us. But we do not dispossess ourselves just by our willing, but by taking up the offer of selfless power. Thus Jesus finally goes to his death not knowing what the future behavior of the disciples might be or their ultimate fate. He dies out of obedience and entrusts the future to God.

In like manner Jesus serves those he would help and those he must confront. In response to people's faith he heals, crediting not his own authority but the person's faith and God's power as the source of healing. He does not seek out those to heal, for he came out to preach, but he heals those who come to him. Moreover, he serves the authorities by confronting them. "Jesus confronts the authorities with the nature of God's rule and with the seriousness of

---

Bultmanns and the Grahams whose 'evangelism' is to proclaim the offer of restored selfhood, liberation from anxiety and guilt, are not wrong . . . But *all of this is not the Gospel.* This is just the bonus, the wrapping paper thrown in when you buy the meat, the 'everything' which will be added, without our taking thought for it, if we seek first the Kingdom of God and His righteousness."

14. Donald Mickie and David Rhoads, *Mark As Story* (Philadelphia: Fortress Press, 1982), 109.

their offenses against it, but he does not impose his authority on them. After each confrontation, he moves on, leaving the authorities to choose their responses. He is not a military messiah who uses a sword or manipulates the crowds to impose his authority. He does not even fight to defend himself, and he endures the consequences of his opponent's scorn."[15]

In Jesus' life we cannot help but see God's way with Israel and Israel's subsequent understanding of what it means to be God's beloved. For God does not impose God's will upon Israel. Rather, God calls Israel time and time again to be faithful to the covenant, but always gives Israel the possibility of disobedience. It is thus in the cross that Christians see the climax of God's way with the world. In the cross of Jesus we see decisively the one who, being all-powerful, becomes vulnerable even to being a victim of our refusal to accept his Lordship. For in this cross we find the very passion of God. Through that cross God renews the covenant with Israel; only now the covenant is with the "many." Through this one man's life, death, and resurrection, all are called to be his disciples. We are therefore invited to drink this drink, and to be baptized with this baptism (Mark 10:39), and in doing so we believe that we become participants in God's very life. In short, we begin to know what it means to imitate God.[16]

4. Jesus and the Kingdom of God

But we must remember that for Israel to imitate God or for Christians to imitate Jesus is not an end in itself. Such an imitation is to put one in the position of being part of a kingdom. As we have already noted, Jesus as portrayed in the synoptic Gospels does not call attention to himself. He comes to announce the kingdom as a present reality. To what extent he understood then how his life would be chosen by God to be the means by which that kingdom would be made a reality to all people, we have no way of knowing. What is significant is not what Jesus may or may not have thought about

15. Ibid., 111.

16. [In addition to the references to Tinsley and Yoder's *The Original Revolution*, we would also call attention to the consonance of Hauerwas's Christological argumentation with chapters 11–13 of John Howard Yoder's *Preface to Theology: Christology and Theological Method*, forthcoming from Brazos Press, 2002 (edited with a foreword by Stanley Hauerwas), where Yoder invokes the threefold office of Jesus as prophet, priest, and king as the heart of any Christian theology. In effect, this approach repositions the Christological issues by focusing more attention on the biblical narratives of Jesus of Nazareth in relation to the announcement of the kingdom of God.]

himself, though he certainly acted as one having authority (Matt. 12:28), but that he was obedient to his calling and therefore is the sign and form of the reality of God's kingship then and now.

To begin to understand Jesus' announcement of the kingdom we must first rid ourselves of the notion that the world we experience will exist indefinitely.[17] We must learn to see the world as Israel had learned to understand it—that is, eschatologically. Though it sounds powerful and intimidating, in fact it is quite simple, for to view the world eschatologically is to see it in terms of a story, with a beginning, a continuing drama, and an end. And "a story needs an ending. A point must be reached at which one can feel that certain issues are resolved, a certain finality has been achieved. In this respect a story departs from real life. In reality there never is an end. . . . But the story-teller cannot accept this. . . . The story-teller needs finality, a closed sequence of events such that a judgment can be passed."[18] It is against this background that Jesus' announcement of the kingdom must be seen, for he came to announce an end that, while not yet final, nonetheless provided a necessary perspective for our continuing life in the world.

It has long been noted that in the Gospels we have texts that indicate variously that the kingdom is coming, that it is present, and that it is still to come. Several theories have been proposed as to how these statements might be reconciled. Some suggest that one or another tense cannot have been Jesus' own words. They either identify him with the more immediate apocalyptic expectation or suggest that he saw the kingdom to come in the future. I would agree, however, with A. E. Harvey that the whole question is irresolvable in the terms in which it is raised.[19] Not only do we lack the means to know what is Jesus'

---

17. The current concern about nuclear war as a threat to end all life in some ways makes our situation similar to that of the early Christians. For example, see my "Eschatology and Nuclear Disarmament," *NICM Journal* 8, no. 1 (winter 1983): 7–16.

18. Harvey, *Jesus and the Constraints of History,* 71–72.

19. Ibid., 91. Harvey argues, "New Testament scholars, who seem agreed at last that Jesus' Kingdom-sayings contain statements that are both irreducibly future and irreducibly present, tend to speak at this point of a tension between the 'already' and the 'not yet'; and indeed some tension of this kind is inevitable whenever the phrase 'the Kingdom of God' is used. For it is in reality nothing more than the abstract noun corresponding to the factual statement that God is king, which itself carries the same tension between present and future. That God is king, here and now, no believer would dream of denying. But if asked whether God is yet fully king, whether the world as we know it now is the perfect paradigm of his kingship, the believer who stands in the tradition of the Bible would be bound to say there is a sense in which God is not yet king. His kingdom is not yet universally acknowledged by his creatures. . . . The tension between the already and the not-yet is an academic tension to which nothing real corresponds, either in the experience of life or in the teaching of Jesus."

view and that of the early church, but it by no means follows that Jesus had a rigorously consistent view. Moreover, by letting the issue be dominated by the question of "when" we miss the more important question of the "what."

The kingdom is not simply some cipher that we can fill in with our ideas about what a good society ought to look like. Nor is it merely a way of reemphasizing the eternal sovereignty of God, though this is certainly part of what the proclamation of the kingdom entails. Rather, the proclamation of the coming kingdom of God, its presence, and its future coming is a claim about how God rules and the establishment of that rule through the life, death, and resurrection of Jesus. Thus the Gospels portray Jesus not only offering the possibility of achieving what were heretofore thought to be impossible ethical ideals. He actually proclaims and embodies a way of life that God has made possible here and now.

Jesus directs our attention to the kingdom, but the early followers rightly recognized that to see what that kingdom entailed they must attend to his life, death, and resurrection, for his life reveals to us how God would be sovereign. Therefore, to learn to see the world eschatologically requires that we learn to see the life of Jesus as decisive for the world's status as part of God's kingdom.

Just as we cannot understand what it means to learn to follow Jesus without understanding what it means for Israel to be on a journey with the Lord, so we cannot understand the kingdom without understanding its role in Israel. The kingdom ideal that Jesus proclaimed is no new idea nor does he seem to have given it some startling new meaning. Rather, he proclaims that the kingdom is present insofar as his life reveals the effective power of God to create a transformed people capable of living peaceably in a violent world.

Israel as God's chosen, as I have already suggested, had been schooled to look on the world eschatologically. That she could do so depended on her knowing who it was that gave her the destiny to be the people of God. That is, she knew who her true king was: the Lord of Abraham, Isaac, and Jacob. It was this Lord who established the covenant with her, who gave her the law, who gave her the land, who fought to secure the land. It was this Lord who appointed a king, who sent the prophets, and who provided the means to worship and holiness. Thus what made Israel Israel was her steadfast devotion to the true Master of the universe.

Yet there were in Israel differences about what acknowledgment of God's sovereignty entailed—differences that were still being debated and acted on during Jesus' lifetime. For some, to worship God as king meant the refusal to call any man master, even if that man was Caesar. Thus some, in the name of

Yahweh's sovereignty, thought such allegiance entailed the obligation to try to free Israel, if necessary by violent means, from her masters. Judas the Galilean revolted against Rome and a Roman census on the grounds that submitting to Roman rule amounted to a denial of the Lord. Drawing on the holy war tradition, he believed that God is the God of battles, who will help his people overthrow and destroy their enemies.[20]

An alternative understanding of God's sovereignty was that created by piety. In this view, to affirm God as King does not entail violent overthrow of those who currently hold the power of the state, but the creation of a sphere of life through the law where God's will dominates: "Thus the affirmation of God's sole kingship implies not military revolt but the submission of one's whole life to the regulations of the Torah, notably to its ritual prescriptions. It means severing oneself from all that is outside the realm of God's rule, viz., from all who do not 'take the yoke upon themselves'. . . . Taking the yoke of the kingdom upon oneself is associated with the necessity of daily set prayers and of following a complex set of ritual prescriptions. We may reasonably conjecture that the God who is addressed as King in such prayers is conceived of as a God of holiness and purity such that he will not tolerate the presence of that which is ungodly, impure, polluted."[21]

There were many variations of these alternatives alive in Israel prior to and during Jesus' life. Some, rejecting both alternatives, tended in a more apocalyptic direction. "If the time was short and judgment strictly by the Law, then the appropriate course was to withdraw as far as possible from the contamination of the world and prepare oneself by asceticism, study and discipline."[22] Thus the sects rejected both the gradualism of the Pharisees and the self-initiated violence of the revolutionaries.

No doubt Jesus' and the early church's understanding of the kingdom bore similarities to each of these alternatives. It seems likely, however, that Jesus' understanding was most similar to that represented by the Pharisees. "Like them, he offered a way of life in which religion would seem relevant to every activity; like them, he based his teaching on the will of God as revealed in the law; like them, he addressed much of his teaching to a public far wider than his immediate followers. But at the same time the differences are striking. On

---

20. John Riches, *Jesus and the Transformation of Judaism* (London: Darton, Longman and Todd, 1980), 93–94. See Lind's *Yahweh Is a Warrior: The Theology of Warfare in Ancient Israel* for a fuller account of this understanding of the holy war tradition.

21. Riches, *Jesus and the Transformation of Judaism*, 95.

22. Harvey, *Jesus and the Constraints of History*, 86.

three matters which were of central importance to the Pharisees—a detailed code of observances, a careful selectiveness in the company they kept, and a concern for the authority of the tradition in which they stood—Jesus adopted a radically different stance."[23]

Jesus' openness to the "unclean," for example, is but one of the ways we see how his understanding of God's sovereignty was a challenge to that of the Pharisees. Such openness denotes that the community created by that kingdom cannot shield itself from the outsider. It must have confidence that God is present even in the unclean—a confidence made possible only because the community itself was formed by the presence of the ultimate stranger, Jesus Christ.

Through Jesus' life and teachings we see how the church came to understand that God's kingship and power consists not in coercion but in God's willingness to forgive and have mercy on us. God wills nothing less than that men and women should love their enemies and forgive one another; thus we will be perfect as God is perfect. Jesus challenged both the militaristic and ritualistic notions of what God's kingdom required—the former by denying the right of violence even if attacked, and the latter by his steadfast refusal to be separated from those "outside."[24]

Jesus issued this challenge not only through his teaching, but through his life. Indeed, the very announcement of the reality of the kingdom, its presence here and now, is embodied in his life. In him we see that living a life of forgiveness and peace is not an impossible ideal but an opportunity now present. Thus Jesus' life is integral to the meaning, content, and possibility of

---

23. Ibid., 51.

24. The question of Jesus' continuity and discontinuity with the various forms of Judaism of his day is not easily resolved. Certainly most of Jesus' message was in continuity with what Israel had already discovered about her relation with God. The decisive difference was that now that relation turned on the life of this man Jesus, and that put him in quite different ways in conflict with the various groups of his day. As Sean Freyne notes, "By claiming that the divine presence, defined both as God's kingly rule and as Father, was accessible to people in his own life and person, Jesus undercut the various systems that had been devised within Judaism to control that presence and people's access to it. Therein lay the source of power within actual Palestinian life for parties like the Pharisees and Sadducees, and the aspirations to power of other groups like the Essenes and Zealots. Insofar as Jesus' claims suggested alternative means of access to God, or better, of God's coming to people, outside and independently of all the groups and their programmes, and to the extent that this had been found attractive, he was clearly striking at the very reasons for existence of each of the groups and their philosophies. To do so in the name of God's final and irrevocable promises to his people was intolerable" (*The World of the New Testament*, 140).

the kingdom. For the announcement of the reality of this kingdom, of the possibility of living a life of forgiveness and peace with one's enemies, is based on our confidence that that kingdom has become a reality through the life and work of this man, Jesus of Nazareth. His life is the life of the end—this is the way the world is meant to be—and thus those who follow him become a people of the last times, the people of the new age.

The nature and reality of the kingdom is manifest throughout Jesus' life and ministry. Like the prophets he called Israel back to obedience to the law— a law that appeared strenuous. But there is no indication that the rigorous demands of the Sermon on the Mount were meant only as some unrealizable ideal. To believe so is to lose the eschatological context of Jesus' teaching. To be sure, Jesus' demand that we forgive our enemies challenges our normal assumptions about what is possible, but that is exactly what it is meant to do. We are not to accept the world with its hate and resentment as a given, but to recognize that we live in a new age that makes possible a new way of life.

The reality of that new age, moreover, is manifest through Jesus' healings and exorcism, where Jesus comes face to face with the demons that rule our lives and this world and decisively defeats them. Thus in Mark Jesus comes preaching "The time is fulfilled, and the kingdom of God is at hand; repent, and believe in the gospel" (1:15), but it is the demons and unclean spirits that recognize him as a threat (1:23, 1:34). Jesus' healing is not an end in itself, or simply a sign of compassion, but an indication of the power of the kingdom. He makes no attempt to cure all; rather, he must go to the next towns to preach, "for that is why I came out" (1:38).

The kind of kingdom that is present is also revealed in Jesus' relations with others. He makes no attempt to keep himself "pure," but enjoys meals with the poor and the outcast. Moreover his meals are not tied to one time or place, but are spontaneous occasions of fellowship denoting the hospitality of God's kingdom. The celebration of such meals while Israel was under foreign rule with the (albeit indirect) agents of that rule also indicates the inherent political nature of the kingdom. For God's "Kingdom is not established only where other rulers have been overthrown; rather God's power erupts in the midst of oppression, forgiving and healing, and wherever that power is, there is cause for rejoicing. The world is not, that is to say, given over to Satan, or to Caesar, until God will restore his rule over it by destroying the alien rulers. On the contrary, God is already present in this 'evil age,' overcoming it by mercy."[25]

---

25. Riches, *Jesus and the Transformation of Judaism*, 106.

Finally, the nature of God's kingdom is found also, and perhaps most particularly, in the calling of the disciples. Jesus calls his disciples to follow him, to leave all that they have, leaving dead to bury dead, in a manner not dissimilar to what is required of those called to fight a holy war. They are to make a radical break with security and possessions, with the customs and habits of everyday life, for no other purpose than to share in his ministry of preaching the repentance needed to become part of the kingdom (Mark 3:13; Matt. 10:5ff). Discipleship is quite simply extended training in being dispossessed. To become followers of Jesus means that we must, like him, be dispossessed of all that we think gives us power over our own lives and the lives of others. Unless we learn to relinquish our presumption that we can ensure the significance of our lives, we are not capable of the peace of God's kingdom.

For our possessions are the source of our violence. Fearing that others desire what we have, or stung by the seldom acknowledged sense that what we have we do not deserve, we seek self-deceptive justifications that mire us in patterns of injustice that can be sustained only through coercion. And of course we believe our most precious possession to be the self we have created, that we have chosen. Such a possession we do not lose—as we see clearly in the character of the disciples in the Gospels—simply by willing to give up all that we have. What Jesus offers is a journey, an adventure. Once undertaken, we discover that what we once held valuable, even the self, we no longer count as anything.

Jesus' cross, however, is not merely a general symbol of the moral significance of self-sacrifice. The cross is not the confirmation of the facile assumption that it is better to give than receive. Rather, the cross is Jesus' ultimate dispossession through which God has conquered the powers of this world. The cross is not just a symbol of God's kingdom; it is that kingdom come. It is only by God's grace that we are enabled to accept the invitation to be part of that kingdom. Because we have confidence that God has raised this crucified man, we believe that forgiveness and love are alternatives to the coercion the world thinks necessary for existence. Thus, our true nature, our true end, is revealed in the story of this man in whose life, we believe, is to be found the truth.

5. The Resurrection: The Establishment of a Kingdom of Forgiveness and Peace

Jesus' death was not a mistake but what was to be expected of a violent world that does not believe that this is God's world. In effect Jesus is nothing less than the embodiment of God's sabbath as a reality for all people. Jesus proclaims peace as a real alternative, because he has made it possible to rest, to have the confidence that our lives are in God's hands. No longer is the sabbath one day, but the form of life of a people on the move. God's kingdom, God's peace, is a movement of those who have found the confidence through the life of Jesus to make their lives a constant worship of God. We can rest in God because we are no longer driven by the assumption that we must be in control of history, that it is up to us to make things come out right.

Such a peace is not just that among people, but between people and our world. For it is a genuine eschatological peace that renews the peace of the beginning, where humans and animals do not depend on one another's destruction for their own survival (Gen. 29). Thus it is a time when

> The wolf shall dwell with the lamb, and the leopard shall lie down with the kid, and the calf and the lion and the fatling together, and a little child shall lead them.
>
> The cow and the bear shall feed; their young shall lie down together; and the lion shall eat straw like the ox.
>
> The suckling child shall play over the hole of the asp, and the weaned child shall put his hand on the adder's den.
>
> They shall not hurt or destroy in all my holy mountain; for the earth shall be full of the knowledge of the Lord as the waters cover the sea. (Isa. 11:6–9)

As members and citizens of such a kingdom, moreover, we are pledged to extend God's peace through the care and protection of his creation. We resist one who is evil, not because life is inherently sacred, but simply because life belongs to God. As Yoder reminds us, "The idea that human life is intrinsically sacred is not a specifically Christian thought. But the gospel itself, the message that Christ died for His enemies, is *our* reason for being ultimately responsible for the neighbor's—and especially the enemy's—life. We can only say this [to another] if we say to ourselves that we cannot dispose of him according to our own will."[26]

Therefore the Christian commitment to the protection of life is an eschatological commitment. Our concern to protect and enhance life is a sign of our confidence that in fact we live in a new age in which it is possible to see the other as God's creation. We do not value life as an end in itself—there is much worth dying for; rather, all life is valued, even the lives of our enemies, because God has valued them.

26. Yoder, *The Original Revolution,* 42.

The risk of so valuing life can be taken only on the basis of the resurrection of Jesus as God's decisive eschatological act. For through Jesus' resurrection we see God's peace as a present reality. Though we continue to live in a time when the world does not dwell in peace, when the wolf cannot dwell with the lamb and a child cannot play over the hole of the asp, we believe nonetheless that peace has been made possible by the resurrection. Through this crucified but resurrected savior we see that God offers to all the possibility of living in peace by the power of forgiveness.

It is crucial that we understand that such a peaceableness is possible only if we are also a forgiven people. We must remember that our first task is not to forgive, but to learn to be the forgiven. Too often to be ready to forgive is a way of exerting control over another. We fear accepting forgiveness from another because such a gift makes us powerless—and we fear the loss of control involved. Yet we continue to pray "Forgive our debts." Only by learning to accept God's forgiveness as we see it in the life and death of Jesus can we acquire the power that comes from learning to give up that control. Freed from our need to coerce, we learn " 'not to be anxious about your life, what you shall eat or what you shall drink, nor about your body, what you shall put on. Is not life more than food, and the body more than clothing? Look at the birds of the air: they neither sow nor reap nor gather into barns, and yet your heavenly Father feeds them. Are you not of more value than they? And which of you by being anxious can add one cubit to his span of life?' " (Matt. 6:25–27).

It is true, of course, that in a sense to be a "forgiven people" makes us lose control. To be forgiven means that I must face the fact that my life actually lies in the hands of others. I must learn to trust them as I have learned to trust God. Thus it is not accidental that Jesus teaches us to pray for our daily bread. We cannot live to ensure our ultimate security, but must learn to live on a day-to-day basis. Or, perhaps better, we must be a people who have learned not to fear surprises as a necessary means to sustain our lives. For, ironically, when we try to exclude surprise from our life, we are only more subject to the demonic. We become subject to those "necessities" that we are anxious about because without them we fear we lack the power to control our lives.

But because we have learned to live as a forgiven people, as a people no longer in control, we also find we can become a whole people. Indeed, the demand that we be holy is possible only because we find that we can rest within ourselves. When we exist as a forgiven people we are able to be at peace with our histories, so that now God's life determines our whole way of being— our character. We no longer need to deny our past, or tell ourselves false stories, as now we can accept what we have been without the knowledge of our sin destroying us.

Here we see the essential links among learning to live as a forgiven people, accepting our historicity, and being at peace with ourselves and with one another, for we are able to have a past only to the extent that we are able to accept forgiveness for what we have done and have not done but that we must claim as our own if we are to have a worthy history.[27] My sin is inexorably part of me, but I now no longer need to deny it. As I learn to locate my life within the kingdom of forgiveness found in Jesus' life, death, and resurrection, I acquire those virtues of humility and courage that are necessary to make my life my own.

That we are only able to have a history, a self, through the forgiveness wrought by God means that the resurrection of Jesus is the absolute center of history. It is on the basis of the resurrection that we can have the confidence to remember the history of our sin. Through the resurrection, by being invited to recognize our victim as our hope, we are gifted with the power to break the hold of our most determined oppressor: ourselves. As Rowan Williams has suggested, "The Christian proclamation of the resurrection of the crucified just man, his return to his unfaithful friends and his empowering of them to forgive in his name offers a narrative structure in which we can locate our recovery of identity and human possibility, a paradigm of the 'saving' process; yet not only a paradigm. It is a story which is itself an indispensable agent in the completion of this process, because it witnesses to the one personal agent in whose presence we may have full courage to 'own' ourselves as sinners and full hope for a humanity whose identity is grounded in a recognition and affirmation by nothing less than God. It is a story which makes possible the comprehensive act of trust without which growth is impossible."[28]

Only if our Lord is a risen Lord, therefore, can we have the confidence and the power to be a community of forgiveness. For on the basis of the resurrection we have the presumption to believe that God has made us agents in the history of the kingdom. The resurrection is not a symbol or myth through which we can interpret our individual and collective dyings and risings. Rather, the resurrection of Jesus is the ultimate sign that our salvation comes

27. For an often overlooked but classic account of the relation between forgiveness and our ability to recount our history, see H. R. Niebuhr, *The Meaning of Revelation* (New York: Macmillan, 1960), 82–90.
28. Rowan Williams, *Resurrection* (London: Darton, Longman and Todd, 1982), 49.

only when we cease trying to interpret Jesus' story in the light of our history, and instead we interpret ourselves in the light of his.[29] For this is no dead Lord we follow but the living God, who, having dwelt among us as an individual, is now eternally present to us, making possible our living as forgiven agents of God's new creation.

Because we Christians believe we worship a resurrected Lord, we can take the risk of love. Thus we are told in 1 John 4:13–21:

> By this we know that we abide in him and he in us, because he has given us of his own spirit. And we have seen and testify that the Father has sent his son as the Savior of the world. Whoever confesses that Jesus is the Son of God, God abides in him, and he in God. So we know and believe the love God has for us. God is love, and he who abides in love abides in God, and God abides in him. In this is love perfected with us, that we may have confidence for the day of judgment, because as he is so are we in this world. There is no fear in love, but perfect love casts out fear. For fear has to do with punishment, and he who fears is not perfected in love. We love, because he first loved us. If any one says, "I love God," and hates his brother, he is a liar; for he who does not love the brother whom he has seen, cannot love God whom he has not seen. And this commandment we have from him, that he who loves God should love his brother also.

This love that is characteristic of God's kingdom is possible only for a forgiven people—a people who have learned not to fear one another. For love is the nonviolent apprehension of the other as other. But to see the other as other is frightening, because to the extent others are other they challenge my way of being. Only when my self—my character—has been formed by God's love, do I know I have no reason to fear the other.

The kingdom of peace initiated by Jesus is also the kingdom of love that is most clearly embodied in the Christian obligation to be hospitable. We are a community standing ready to share our meal with the stranger. Moreover we must be a people who have hospitable selves—we must be ready to be stretched by what we know not. Friendship becomes our way of life as we learn to rejoice in the presence of others. Thus Jesus' kingdom is one that requires commitment to friends, for without them the journey that is the kingdom is impossible. We can only know where we walk as we walk with others.

29. Ibid., 85.

6. An Ethics of Salvation and Faith

It may well be asked, What has happened to the traditional Christian affirmations of salvation and faith in all this talk of the kingdom? Has not the talk of peace and the necessity of our becoming peaceful members of God's kingdom come perilously close to turning the gospel into a moral ideal rather than the good news of salvation? For example, what are we to make of such a classical text as Romans 3:21–26: "But now the righteousness of God has been manifested apart from law, although the law and the prophets bear witness to it, the righteousness of God through faith in Jesus Christ for all who believe. For there is no distinction; since all have sinned and fall short of the glory of God, they are justified by his grace as a gift, through the redemption which is in Christ Jesus, whom God put forward as an expiation by his blood, to be received by faith. This was to show God's righteousness, because in his divine forbearance he has passed over former sins; it was to prove at the present time that he himself is righteous and that he justified him who has faith in Jesus."

This Pauline emphasis on justification has sometimes been interpreted in a manner that amounts to a denial of the ethical. What is important is not that we are good or bad, that we do the right or wrong thing, but that we have faith. Of course, that does not mean that Paul is recommending that we sin, or that what Christians are and do have no relation to their "faith," but it is not at all clear from such a perspective how the "indicatives" of the faith—God has done X and Y for you—provide the rationale or justify the imperatives: Do this X or Y. To put it concretely, there seems to be a problem about how the admonitions Paul delivers in Romans 12 follow from and/or are integral to the claim of justification in Romans 3: "Let your love be genuine; hate what is evil, hold fast to what is good; love one another with brotherly affection; outdo one another in showing honor. Never lag in zeal, be aglow with the Spirit, serve the Lord. Rejoice in your hope, be patient in tribulation, be constant in prayer. Contribute to the needs of the saints, practice hospitality. Bless those who persecute you; bless and do not curse them. Rejoice with those who rejoice, weep with those who weep. Live in harmony with one another; do not be haughty, but associate with the lowly, never be conceited. Repay no one evil for evil, but take thought for what is noble in the sight of all. If possible, so far as it depends upon you, live peaceably with all. Beloved, never avenge yourselves, but leave it to the wrath of God; for it is written, 'Vengeance is mine, I will repay, says the Lord.'"

What does our having "faith" have to do with this way of life? Quite simply, faith is our appropriate response to salvation, and it is fundamentally a moral response and transformation. Faith for Paul is not some mystical transformation of the individual; rather, it is to be initiated into a kingdom. Faith is not belief in certain propositions, though it involves the attitude and passion of trust. Faith is not so much a combination of belief and trust, as simply fidelity to Jesus, the initiator of God's kingdom of peace. "Therefore, since we are justified by faith, we have peace with God through our Lord Jesus Christ. Through him we have obtained access to this grace in which we stand, and we rejoice in our hope of sharing the glory of God. More than that, we rejoice in our sufferings, knowing that suffering produces endurance, and endurance produces character, and character produces hope, and hope does not disappoint us, because God's love has been poured into our hearts through the Holy Spirit which has been given to us" (Rom. 5:1–5).

Faith is, in effect, finding our true life within the life of Christ. Thus in baptism we are literally initiated into his life. "For if we have been united with him in death like his, we shall certainly be united in a resurrection like his. We know that our old self was crucified with him so that the sinful body might be destroyed, and we might no longer be enslaved to sin. For he who has died is freed from sin. But if we have died with Christ, we believe that we shall also live with him. For we know that Christ being raised from the dead will never die again; death no longer has dominion over him. The death he died he died to sin, once for all, but the life he lives he lives to God. So you also must consider yourselves dead to sin and alive to God in Christ Jesus" (Rom. 6:5–11).

But notice that this life is fundamentally a social life. We are "in Christ" insofar as we are part of that community pledged to be faithful to this life as the initiator of the kingdom of peace.

It is not that we have a prior definition of peace and then think of Christ as the great exemplar of that peace. Rather, what Jesus has done enables us to know and embody God's peace in our lives by finding peace with God, with ourselves, and with one another. We have been justified because, as always, we find that our God has gone before, preparing the way for us to follow. But justification is only another way of talking about sanctification, since it requires our transformation by initiation into the new community made possible by Jesus' death and resurrection.

Of course, it may be objected that all this language about being a new people—a sanctified people—is a bit overblown. After all, Christians oftentimes do not look very new; nor do we feel very new. We may claim that we are among the redeemed, but basically we feel pretty much the way we always do.

The very idea that we are a holy people therefore seems overdrawn. Moreover, such language has the inevitable result of tempting us to self-righteousness. Perhaps it is better to face up to the fact that we are not the holy people, only more of the moderately good.

But this kind of thinking merely indicates that we have failed to let the challenge of the kingdom form our lives. For the language of "sanctification" and "justification" is not meant to be descriptive of a status. Indeed, part of the problem with those terms is that they are abstractions. When they are separated from Jesus' life and death, they distort Christian life. "Sanctification" is but a way of reminding us of the kind of journey we must undertake if we are to make the story of Jesus our story. "Justification" is but a reminder of the character of that story—namely, what God has done for us by providing us with a path to follow.[30]

That I can and should grow into that story is not a claim about my moral purity, but denotes a wholeness of self that depends on how far I have gone along that journey. My wholeness, my integrity, is made possible by the truthfulness of the story. Through the story of Jesus I can increasingly learn to be what I have become, a participant in God's community of peace and justice. Only by growing into that story do I learn how much violence I have stored in my soul, a violence that is not about to vanish overnight, but that I must continually work to recognize and lay down.

To do that I need skills; that is, I need to learn how to make my own the peace that comes from the knowledge that I am a creature of a gracious God. Such skills are not the sanctification of discrete actions, but the sanctification of the self as nonviolent. Sanctification is the formation of our lives in truth, since only such lives have the capacity for peace. Violence results from our attempting to live our lives without recognizing our falsehoods. Violence derives from the self-deceptive story that we are in control—that we are our own creators—and that only we can bestow meaning on our lives, since there is no one else to do so.

We mightily fear giving up our illusions; they are as dear to us as our selves. We fear that if we learn to make the story of God our story we may have no self, no individuality left. Or that we will lose our autonomy. But the blessing

---

30. [Here Hauerwas's reinterpretation of traditional Protestant ways of thinking about justification and sanctification opens the way for a constructive account of salvation and faith that cannot be separated from the kinds of moral skills needed to embody the inauguration of the kingdom in the Christian community. This account suggests that new possibilities for overcoming traditional Protestant/Catholic divisions on these issues should also be apparent.]

lies in the irony that the more we learn to make the story of Jesus our story, the more unique, the more individual, we become—thus, the example of the saints.

Substantive stories cannot easily be made one's own. They challenge some of our most cherished illusions—for example, the illusion that we really want to know the truth about ourselves. True stories thus require extensive training in skills commensurate with that story. The Christian claim that life is a pilgrimage is a way of indicating the necessary and never-ending growth of the self in learning to live into the story of Christ. He is our master and from him we learn the skills to live faithfully to the fact that this is God's world and we are God's creatures.

Though it is often tried, such skills can never be reduced to techniques. For example, learning to live in such a way that I need not fear death means coming to a real understanding that Jesus has for all times defeated death. The skill does not come easily, yet it is the truth. The challenge is in making it true for myself. But the good news is I cannot learn it by myself. We learn such a truth only by being initiated into it by others. That is why the question of the nature and form of the church is the center of any attempt to develop Christian ethics.

Further Reading
"Jesus: The Story of the Kingdom" (1981) in cc
"On Being a Church Capable of Addressing a World at War" (1988), essay 21 in this
    volume
"A Story-Formed Community: Reflections on *Watership Down*" (1981), essay 9 in
    this volume
"The Nonresistant Church: The Theological Ethics of John Howard Yoder" (1972),
    in vv
"Messianic Pacifism" (1973), in *Worldview* 16, no. 6: 19–23
"What Could It Mean for the Church to Be Christ's Body" (1998), in stt

7. The Church as God's New Language (1986)

Although rarely cited, this essay is extremely important for understanding Hauerwas's larger project. It signals a significant shift for Hauerwas in the mid-1980s, distancing him from formal appeals to the notion of narrative (or, for that matter, character) and emphasizing the material specification of the Christian narrative in the lived experience of the church. Hauerwas reminds us that, philosophically speaking, narrative does not refer, people do. Deliberately beginning within an ecclesial context—the essay begins with a sermon for Pentecost—Hauerwas displays the narrative interrelation among the primeval Genesis history, the life, death, and resurrection of Jesus, and the birth of the church. Noting Hans Frei's appeal to the church as the subject as well as the agent of the narrative, Hauerwas demonstrates that the "where, how, and who tells the story" of Jesus is crucial for specifying the nature of the truth claims being made on behalf of the Christian community.

It is a bit unusual to begin a putatively scholarly essay with a sermon—particularly when one is writing in honor of a theologian as scholarly as Hans Frei. I have, however, begun with a sermon partly because I did not think the world needed from me yet another formal and methodologically oriented essay about the significance of narrative theology for theology and ethics.[1] Too often

[Originally published in *Scriptural Authority and Narrative Interpretation*, ed. Garrett Green, © 1987 Fortress Press. Reprinted by permission of Augsburg Fortress. The volume was a Festschrift for Hans Frei, a theologian and teacher of Hauerwas at Yale University. The essay was reprinted in CET.]
1. Even a book as rich as Robert Alter's *The Art of Biblical Narrative* (New York: Basic Books, 1981) remains formal insofar as he seems to assume that the examination of the form (or art) of narrative will reveal the meaning of the text. It is unfair, however, to accuse Alter of formalism without attending to his claim that the narrative art of the Bible is tied to the monotheistic convictions and the correlative understanding of human nature. See, for example, pages 25, 91, 115, and 126 of *The Art of Biblical Narrative*. That said, it is still the case that

many of us who have written about narrative end up using that emphasis to talk about how we should do theology if we ever get around to doing any. So I thought I would try to do a little by writing a sermon. Of course, since I was trained at Yale I am too insecure to let the sermon stand on its own, so it is followed by methodological commentary. Yet I believe if I have anything of value to say on these matters it is said in the sermon. In particular, I hope the sermon suggests why questions of the veridical character of Christian convictions cannot be abstracted from their ecclesial and moral context.

1. A Pentecost Sermon

> Genesis 11:1–9
> Acts 2:1–21
> John 15:26–16:11

At Pentecost we celebrate the birth of the church by the Holy Spirit. Pentecost is the climax of the Christian year, as only now are we able liturgically to tell the whole story of God's redemption of his creation. All is finally summed up through God's new creation of the church. By creating this timeful people God has storied the world, as now we have everything necessary to know the time in which we live. For God saves by making possible the existence of a people who are formed by God's time so that the world can know that we are creatures of a good creator, formed by God's time.

The grand sweep of the texts for today reminds us that the salvation wrought by God in the death and resurrection of Jesus of Nazareth is cosmic

---

Alter owes us a more thorough account of the relation between form and content than he provides in his book. I am grateful to Michael Cartwright for pointing out the formal nature of Alter's analysis.

In his *Sinai and Zion* (Minneapolis: Winston-Seabury, 1985), Jon Levenson provides an extremely interesting discussion of Israel's "monotheism" (56–70). Levenson's analysis provides nuances to Alter's account by noting that it was not "monotheism" in and of itself that provided Israel's historical consciousness but the actual confrontation of Israel with YHWH. As he says, "Israel began to infer and to affirm her identity by telling a story. To be sure, the story has implications that can be stated as propositions . . . But Israel does not begin with the statement that YHWH is faithful; she infers it from a *story.* And unlike the statement, the story is not universal. It is Israel's story, with all the particularities of time, place, and *dramatic personae* one associates with a story and avoids in a statement that aims at universal applicability. In other words, if there is a universal truth of the sort philosophers and even some religions aim to state, Israel seems to have thought such truth will come through the medium of history, through the structures of public knowledge, through time, and not in spite of these" (39–40).

in scope. All nature has now been renewed—returned to its ordered relation to God. The mighty wind that gave birth to the church involves the affairs of nations and empires. That wind created a new nation that was no longer subject to the constraints of the past. Salvation cannot be limited to changed self-understanding or to ensuring meaningful existence for the individual. Salvation is God's creation of a new society that invites each person to become part of a time that the nations cannot provide.

For we believe that at Pentecost God has undone what was done at Babel. In Genesis we are told that originally the whole earth had one language, though few words. That such was the case allowed for unusual cooperativeness as people migrated together seeking a good place to live. Finding the land of Shinar they discovered how to make bricks and became builders. As the son of a bricklayer I think I have a deep appreciation for that achievement. Making bricks, while simple enough, makes possible shelter, the home, and that wonderful, complex phenomenon we call the city. Please note that God does not object to people using their creative energies to embellish creation—he wants us to make bricks. We are invited to plant vineyards and cultivate the soil that our lives might be less subject to chance. Equally important is our capacity for concerted effort through which community is formed in the effort to discover the goods we share in common.

The problem at Babel is not human inventiveness; it is when our forebears used their creative gifts to live as if they need not acknowledge that their existence depends on gifts. Thus the people said, "Come, let us build ourselves a city, and a tower with its top in the heavens, and let us make a name for ourselves, lest we be scattered abroad on the face of the earth." It is not technology that is the problem but the assumption that God's creatures can name themselves—ensuring that all who come after will have to acknowledge their existence. They thus erect a tower, an unmistakable edifice, so they will never have to fear being lost in this vast world. God acknowledges our extraordinary power, as seeing the accomplishments of this united people he feared they would think that now nothing they proposed would be impossible. Such is the power of human cooperativeness.

So, God confused their language such that people could no longer understand one another. So confused they were scattered across the earth, abandoning all attempts to build the one city of humanity. Condemned to live as separate peoples isolated into homes, lands, and histories and no longer able to cooperate, people lost their ability for the concerted action so necessary for the grand project of "making a name for themselves."

God's confusing the people's language as well as his scattering of them was meant as a gift. For by being so divided, by having to face the otherness created by separateness of language and place, people were given the resources necessary to recognize their status as creatures. God's punishment was the grace necessary to relearn the humility that ennobles.

But our parents refused to accept this gift as gift and instead used their separateness as a club, hoping to force all peoples to speak their tribe's language. Thus, at Babel war was born, as the fear of the other became the overriding passion that motivated each group to force others into their story or to face annihilation. The killing begun in Cain was now magnified as humankind's cooperative ability unleashed a destructiveness that is as terrible as it is irrational. Humans became committed to a strategy of destroying the other even if it meant their own death. Better to die than to let the other exist. To this day we thus find ourselves condemned to live in tribes, each bent on the destruction of the other tribes so that we might deny our tribal limits. Our histories become the history of war as we count our days by the battles of the past.

Babel is the climax of the primeval history, as after scattering humankind over the face of the earth God no longer acts toward humankind as a unity. Rather, he calls Abraham out of his tribe and makes a covenant with him to be a great people. In calling Abraham, God creates a rainbow people so that the world might know that in spite of our sinfulness God has not abandoned us. The history of Abraham's people is, of course, one of unfaithfulness as well as faithfulness, yet they remained faithful enough so that they might be truthful about their unfaithfulness.

The faithfulness of Israel is manifest in her unwavering conviction that the main character of the story they tell of the world is not Israel herself but God. As Robert Alter has reminded us, the very narrative art of Israel involves the ability to destabilize any monolithic system of causation in favor of a narrative account of the world. Such an art reflects the profound belief that God, not humanity, is the ultimate determiner of human history. Israel develops that means to be a faithful storyteller just to the extent she resists the temptation to resolve the tension between the divine promise and its failure to be fulfilled and/or the tension between God's will and human freedom.

Thus the call of Abraham foreshadows God's care for all creation through the existence of a people who can stand as a light to the nations. For again we are reminded that God's salvation is not simply knowledge, even the knowledge captured by a story, but rather salvation is the creation of a people who have the capacity to be timeful. To be timeful means to be capable of rest, of worship, in a world bent on its own destruction.

It is only against the background of Babel, therefore, that we can understand the extraordinary event of Pentecost. The sound that was like the rush of a mighty wind signaled a new creation. The fire of the Holy Spirit burned clean, making possible a new understanding. The Jews of diaspora heard these Galilean followers of Jesus telling of the mighty works of God in their own language. The promised people themselves, who had been scattered among the tribes, learning their languages, were now reunited in common understanding. The wound of Babel began to be healed first among the very people God had called into the world as a pledge of God's presence.

The joy of that healing surely must have made them ecstatic. It is literally a joy not possible except by God's creation. It is a joy that comes from recognizing we have been freed from our endless cycle of injury and revenge. It is the joy of unity that we experience all too briefly in moments of self-forgetfulness. It is no wonder, therefore, that some onlookers simply attributed this strange behavior to the consumption of potent wine.

Peter denies such is the case by pointing out that they can hardly be drunk, since this is only the third hour of the day. Yet what has happened is a matter of time, as this reconstitution of our unity portends the last times. Thus, Peter reminds his hearers that this extraordinary creation is what is to be expected at the end time:

> And in the last days it shall be,
>   God declares,
> that I will pour out my Spirit upon
>   all flesh,
> and your sons and your daughters
>   shall prophesy,
> and your young men shall see
>   visions,
> and your old men shall dream
>   dreams,
> yea, and on my menservants and
>   my maidservants in those days
> I will pour out my Spirit; and they
>   shall prophesy.
> And I will show wonders in the
>   heaven above

and signs on the earth beneath,
blood, and fire, and vapor of
        smoke;
and the sun shall be turned into darkness
and the moon into blood,
before the day of the Lord comes,
the great and manifest day.
And it shall be that whoever calls
        on the name of the Lord shall be saved. (Acts 2:1–21, citing Joel 2:23–28)

This is a strong apocalyptic language, but it is necessary if we are to appreciate the significance of this new creation at Pentecost. Creations are, after all, not everyday affairs. They are dramatic in their power to make and consume time. For this new creation aborning through the power of the Spirit does not make irrelevant all that has gone before nor make indifferent all that comes after. Rather, this apocalyptic time places all history in a new time—the time made possible by the life, death, and resurrection of Jesus of Nazareth.

Some have suggested that the so-called delay of the parousia, that is, the sheer continuation of history after Pentecost, creates an impossible problem for Christians, for it seems that the end did not come. Such a reading, however, fails to remember that the apocalyptic expectations created in the early Christian community draw on the conviction that in Jesus of Nazareth Israel's cosmic desires were being fulfilled. Apocalyptic does not deny the continuation of the history of creation but rather reminds us it is historical exactly because it has an end. The end Peter proclaimed is now present at Pentecost.

That Peter proclaimed the presence of the end time to better his ability to recognize that the fiery Spirit was so timeful was because he knew it as the same Spirit that rested on Jesus of Nazareth. Thus, following Peter's appeal to Joel's prophecy of the last days he said, "Men of Israel, hear these words: Jesus of Nazareth, a man attested to you by God with mighty works and wonders and signs which God did through him in your midst, as you yourselves know—this Jesus, delivered up according to the definite plan and foreknowledge of God, you crucified and killed by the hands of lawless men. But God raised him up, having loosed the pangs of death, because it was not possible for him to be held by it."

The Spirit, to be sure, is a wild and powerful presence creating a new people where there was no people, but it is a spirit that they and we know. For the work it is doing is not different from the work that was done in Jesus of Nazareth. Therefore, in John Jesus tells his disciples that he must go so that the

Counselor, the Spirit of truth, might be present to bear witness to him. Moreover, that same witness that the Spirit makes to Jesus transforms the witness of the disciples, as they are now able to see what they have seen from the beginning but not seen at all.

In this transformation of the disciples we see the central theme of the Gospel. To be a disciple of Jesus it is not enough to know the basic "facts" of his life. It is not enough to know his story. Rather, to be a disciple of Jesus means that our lives must literally be taken up into the drama of God's redemption of this creation. That is the work of the Spirit as we are made part of God's new time through the life and work of this man, Jesus of Nazareth.

That is why the Trinity is such a central affirmation to sustain the Christian life. The Trinity is not metaphysical speculation about God's nature in and of itself but rather is our affirmation that God has chosen to include us in his salvific work. Thus, the Spirit proceeds from the Father so that Jesus might continue to be present with us. It is this Spirit that was received at Pentecost that made possible the affirmation that in Jesus of Nazareth we have seen time renewed by the end time having come.

After Pentecost we can better understand how Jesus' life was from the beginning integral to God's life. For creation itself heralds the presence of this Jesus. From the beginning God's being as Trinity, rather than being a denial of time, is an affirmation of God's timefulness. Thus, even at Babel God says "Let us go down," prefiguring even then the necessary sacrifice of his Son so that the world might be judged, and if judged, redeemed. For in that sacrifice we are given the grace to know our sin, and judgment is made on the rulers of this world who rule by fraud and fear.

It is no wonder, therefore, that being made part of that judgment by the Spirit at Pentecost we may well be thrown out of synagogues and even killed. Moreover, those who do the killing will think they are serving God, not knowing or acknowledging that we now know that God is the Father because we have beheld his Son. Jesus tells us such hard truths even before we have experienced them because we can learn such truths well only by remembering them in the light of our living faithful to the Spirit's call. Such a faithfulness no doubt will challenge the powers of this world who continue to believe that we lack an alternative to war and violence. The unity of humankind prefigured at Pentecost is not just any unity but that made possible by the apocalyptic work of Jesus of Nazareth. It is a unity of renewed understanding, but the kind of understanding is not that created by some artificial Esperanto that denies the reality of other languages. Attempts to secure unity through the creation of a single language are attempts to make us forget our histories and differences rather than find the unity made possible by the Spirit through which we understand the other as other. At Pentecost God created a new language, but it was a language that is more than words. It is instead a community whose memory of its savior creates the miracle of being a people whose very differences contribute to their unity.

We call this new creation *church*. It is constituted by word and sacrament, as the story we tell, the story we embody, must not only be told but enacted. In the telling we are challenged to be a people capable of hearing God's good news such that we can be a witness to others. In the enactment, in Baptism and Eucharist, we are made part of a common history that requires continuous celebration to be rightly remembered. It is through Baptism and Eucharist that our lives are engrafted onto the life of the one that makes our unity possible. Through this telling and enactment we, like Israel, become a people who live by distinctively remembering the history of God's redemption of the world.

The creation of such a people is indeed dangerous, as we know from Babel. For the very strength that comes from our unity has too often led the church to believe that it can build the tower of unity through our own efforts. Not content to wait, in time we try to make God's unity a reality for all people through coercion rather than witness. The church's relation to the Jews is particularly painful to remember in this respect. Such a history of unfaithfulness has led many to downplay the peculiar mission of the church to witness to the world the reconstitution of humankind through the life, death, and resurrection of Jesus of Nazareth.

Pretension and presumptuousness, however, cannot be defeated by false humility. Rather, our task is to be what we were made to be at Pentecost: a people so formed by the Spirit that our humility is but a reflection of our confidence in God's sure work. Without such confidence no doubt the church is constantly tempted to self-righteousness and self-aggrandizement. But we have a sure check against such temptations by the very Savior who has made us what we are. For how can we be prideful when the very God we worship is most fully manifest on a cross?

There is no way, if we are to be faithful to God's gift at Pentecost, that the church can avoid calling attention to itself. To be sure, like Israel, the church has a story to tell in which God is the main character. But the church cannot tell that story without becoming part of the tale. The church as witness to God's work for us in Israel and Jesus of Nazareth means that here the teller and the tale are one. For this is not just another possible story about the way the world is, it is the story of the world as created and redeemed by God. That story, the story of the world, cannot be told rightly unless it includes the story of the church as God's creation to heal our separateness.

After all, as Christians we confess, WE believe in one holy catholic and apostolic Church. That surely seems an odd thing to do, even given the eschatological nature of such a claim, since why do we need to confess belief in something we can to some extent see and experience? That we do so is a recognition that the church, catholic and apostolic, is not our but God's creation. Moreover, it is not a creation that God did at one point in time and does not need to do again. Rather, it is our belief that what God did at Pentecost he continues to do to renew and to sustain the presence of the church so that the world might know there is an alternative to Babel.

So as we celebrate Pentecost, may our joy be so manifest some may even mistake our behavior as that produced by "new wine." For we are a people of God's time, and we rejoice in the knowledge that we are not condemned to repeat the past. That means that we really do have an alternative to Babel, to fear of one another, and finally then to war. Even more happily, it means that insofar as we are the church, we do not just have an alternative, we are the alternative. We do not have a story to tell but in the telling we *are* the story being told. So, as we move once again to the feast of the new age, let us praise God for the creation of his church.

2. The "End" of "Narrative Theology"

I would not want questions about the possibilities and limits of narrative for theological reflection to be determined or judged by whether it translates into good sermon practice and even less in terms of my sermon in particular. I am not even sure how good or bad a sermon it may be—it is certainly short on contemporary examples. However, I did try to write the sermon drawing on what I have learned about the narrative character of theological convictions from Professor Frei, as well as David Kelsey, George Lindbeck, Ron Thiemann, James McClendon, and many others.[2] Though the sermon itself does not tell a

2. For Frei's work, see *The Identity of Jesus Christ* (Philadelphia: Fortress Press, 1975); *The Eclipse of Biblical Narrative* (New Haven: Yale University Press, 1974); and "The 'Literal Reading' of Biblical Narrative in the Christian Tradition: Does It Stretch or Will It Break?" in *The Bible and the Narrative Tradition,* ed. Frank McConnell (New York: Oxford University Press,

story, in it I boldly interrelate the birth of the church, the primeval history in Genesis, and the life, death, and resurrection of Jesus in a way that presumes they are narratively interrelated.

Yet why should I have chosen those particular texts? The answer is quite simple: I did not choose them. They were the lectionary texts given me by my church for Pentecost. I was therefore authorized by the church to hold them up authoritatively for the whole church. But why choose the form of a sermon in the first place?[3] Could you not as easily make a case in a Barth-like fashion

---

1986), 36–77. See also David Kelsey, *The Uses of Scripture in Recent Theology* (Philadelphia: Fortress Press, 1975); Ronald Thiemann, *Revelation and Theology* (Notre Dame, IN: University of Notre Dame Press, 1985); and James McClendon, *Systematic Theology: Ethics* (Nashville, TN: Abingdon Press, 1986). By listing these together I do not mean to imply that they are in agreement or even constitute a common position in general. However, they share enough that they can generate a good argument, for which we should be grateful.

3. I had intended originally to develop a more general thesis concerning the relation of liturgy and ethics as a way to exhibit the centrality of the church for situating claims about the significance of narrative for theological reflection. Such a project turned out to be too unwieldy for one essay. [Hauerwas would later take up this task in, e.g., "Worship, Evangelism, Ethics: On Eliminating the 'And'" (1998), in BH.] I mention it, however, to remind the reader that the sermon cannot be isolated from the liturgical actions of prayer, praise, and Eucharist. The whole liturgy enacted over the whole Christian year developed over a lifetime is the presumption necessary to enable one sermon to concentrate on a few texts and specifiable topics. The traditional issue of the relation of word and sacrament becomes even more pressing once the narrative character of Christian convictions is acknowledged.

In *The Identity of Christianity* (Philadelphia: Fortress Press, 1984), Stephen Sykes has rightly directed attention to the centrality of worship not only for the identity of Christianity but for better knowing what it might mean to claim that our convictions are true. He suggests that without distracting from the doctrinal aspect of Christianity, "the phenomenon of Christian worship makes a vital difference to the conditions under which vigorous argument of a radical kind may be regarded as a constructive contribution, not a destructive irrelevance, to the performance of Christian identity in the modern world" (265). Moreover, he notes that three vital conditions are incorporated into worship: "In the first place, the condition for the Christian character of what is done is satisfied by the necessary reference to the achievement of Jesus, which is recalled. *Anamnesis* in worship is of the deeds of Jesus set in the context of God. But secondly, the *anamnesis* is a prayer and praise. Finally, the worship is corporate; it is an arrangement so devised as to take place at a time and place known to be convenient for those who desire to assemble" (265). My use of "sermon" is but a shorthand for this sense of worship.

Finally, some may wonder if any church exists where such a sermon could be preached— that is, it's too "theological," "long," and so on. This is not just an issue of style, for if the argument of the sermon is valid, it means there has to be a people capable of demanding as well as responding to such a sermon. I have no doubt such a people exist, but I am aware some will see the general argument of this essay as but an attempt to avoid the really hard question

by doing systematic reflection on scriptural texts? Of course the answer is yes, except I lack Barth's knowledge of Scripture as well as his genius.[4]

But there is a still more significant reason I have used a sermon, which the sermon itself, I hope, exhibits. Part of the difficulty with the rediscovery of the significance of narrative for theological reflection has been a too concentrated attention on texts qua texts. It is no doubt significant to rediscover the literary and narrative character of the texts of the Bible. That is particularly the case if one is interested in redirecting the attention and method of those engaged in the scholarly study of the Bible.[5] But the emphasis on narrative can only result in scholarly narcissism if narrative texts are abstracted from the concrete people who acknowledge the authority of the Bible. Thus, I wrote a sermon in the hopes of reminding us that the emphasis on narrative is unintelligible abstracted from an ecclesial context. Indeed, I suspect the project to develop general hermeneutical theories by some theologians is an attempt to substitute a theory of interpretation for the church.

I do not mean, thereby, to imply that Professor Frei or others who have reminded us of the significance of narrative would approve of this sermon in whole or in any of its parts. Yet I have written a sermon to try to illumine some of the unease Professor Frei has begun to express about the great upsurge of interest in narrative in theology. Having been one of the prime movers behind

---

confronting narrative theology, that is, to tell us we should trust the church as a truthful community is no more helpful than to direct our attention to the narrative character of Scripture. Both are equally arbitrary. This essay is an attempt to show why that is not the case if the church, in fact, provides an alternative to Babel.

4. David Ford's *Barth and God's Story* (Frankfurt am Main: Verlag Peter Lang, 1985) is an extremely enlightening treatment of Barth from this perspective. Ford notes that "Barth's comprehensive alternative world of meaning is an overarching story which is not the traditional one from creation to parousia but is the lifetime of Jesus Christ. A doctrine of time based on an interpretation of the resurrection supports the inclusiveness of that stretch of time, and the Old Testament history and all world history are 'figured' into it" (165). Such "figuring" depends on an account of the church that Barth largely fails to develop.

5. This issue is complex, as it is often not easy to separate claims about the Scripture as canon from the narrative character of Scripture. As Charles Wood suggests, "When one regards the biblical canon as a whole, the centrality to it of a narrative element is difficult to overlook: not only the chronological sweep of the whole, from creation to new creation, including the various events and developments of what has sometimes been called 'salvation history,' but also the way the large narrative portions interweave and provide a context for the remaining materials so that they, too, have a place in the ongoing story, while these other materials— parables, hymns, prayers, summaries, theological expositions—serve in different ways to enable readers to get hold of the story and to live their way into it" (*The Formation of Christian Understanding* [Philadelphia: Westminster Press, 1981], 100).

that development, Professor Frei seems to be ready to declare an end to the story of "narrative theology." Moreover, given the extraordinarily diverse claims made on behalf of the importance of story, one cannot help but be sympathetic with Frei's attempt to distance himself from the groundswell for narrative.

Elie Wiesel's story of the great Israel Baal Shem Tov and his subsequent followers is certainly a good story, but one can be told one too many times that "God made man because he loves stories."[6] After the initial enthusiasm for the rediscovery of the significance of stories, one begins to feel the need for some good old-fashioned arguments that are scholastic-like in form. Those satisfied with Wiesel's claim would do well to read his later book, *Souls on Fire*, where he tells the same story of how it fell to Israel of Rizhim to avert disaster when all he could do was tell the story of what the Baal Shem had done. Following the story, with its optimistic claim of the sufficiency of stories, Wiesel notes that such stories are no longer sufficient because "the threat has not been averted. Perhaps we are no longer able to tell the story. Could all of us be guilty? Even the survivors? Especially the survivors?"[7] Of course, Wiesel is not thereby retreating from his earlier claim of the significance of stories, but his later gloss is a sobering reminder that when we have said "story" we have just begun, not ended, the project.

Frei has a deeper concern with the enthusiasm for narrative as the key to all theological work than the confusing and contradictory claims made in the name of narrative. Frei rightly fears that the theological construal of Scripture as a narrative of God's work on behalf of his creation might be qualified by claims of the narrative quality of existence and/or the self. When narrative becomes a general category prior to the theological claim, Frei suspects that such a position threatens to become but a masked form of another kind of foundationalism and/or is susceptible to the deconstructionist critique. He makes this point well by observing that the "irony of New Criticism (and it is not the first instance of this kind) is to have taken this specific case and rule and to have turned them instead into a general theory of meaning, literature, and even culture, in their own right. Detached from the original that is the actual, indispensable ground and subject matter of its meaning, the specific rule is turned about instead into its very opposite, a scheme embracing a whole class of general meaning constructs, from a Christian culture (in the

---

6. Elie Wiesel, *The Gates of the Forest* (New York: Holt, Rinehart, and Winston, 1966), xii.
7. Elie Wiesel, *Souls on Fire* (New York: Vintage Books, 1972), 168.

religiously imperialistic and more than mildly fantasizing visions of T. S. Eliot's cultural-theological writings) to genres of literature. They are all understood 'incarnationally' or 'sacramentally.' As a result, the original of this process of derivation, the doctrine of the Word of God in the person and destiny of Jesus of Nazareth, has now become an optional member within the general class, in which those who subscribe to the class may or may not wish to believe."[8]

The point Frei is making is very similar to his earlier argument that because a Christ figure must be constituted by universal redemptive scope (that is, an unsubstitutable personal identity in which the scope is enacted, and a pattern wholly different from that of Jesus' story), any Christ figure's identity is already preempted by the one who is the Christ of Scripture. "In short, there can be no Christ figure because Jesus is the Christ, unless an author depicts the figure in terms of a particular identity and pattern wholly different from that of Jesus' story. But in that case it would not make any sense to talk of a Christ figure at all. To speak of Christ involves an enormous claim—a claim so large that it is made exclusively of whomever it is made. The claim is that in *one unique case* identity and presence are so completely one that to know who he is is to confront his presence. In him and in him alone, so the claim goes on, are also to be found these three elements by which the 'Christ figure' is identified."[9]

This stress on the irreducibility or, if you prefer, unsubstitutability of Jesus is similar to the reason Frei qualifies some of the claims for "realistic narrative" made in the *Eclipse of Biblical Narrative*. Even though his primary thesis concerning the narrative character of the Scripture has been fruitful for recent biblical scholarship,[10] Frei argues that "theories of realistic narrative are not likely to be highly plausible except in tandem with an informal cultural con-

8. Frei, "The 'Literal Reading' of Biblical Narrative in Christian Tradition," 66. Frei continues, "There may or may not be a class called 'realistic narrative,' but to take it as a general category of which the synoptic Gospel narratives and their partial second-order redescription in the doctrine of the Incarnation are a dependent instance is first to put the cart before the horse and then cut the lines and claim that the vehicle is self-propelled."

9. Frei, *The Identity of Jesus Christ*, 65.

10. For example, see R. Alan Culpepper, *Anatomy of the Fourth Gospel* (Philadelphia: Fortress Press, 1983); David Rhoads and Donald Michie, *Mark as Story* (Philadelphia: Fortress Press, 1982); Jack Dean Kingsbury, *Matthew as Story* (Philadelphia: Fortress Press, 1986); and Dan O. Via, *The Ethics of Mark's Gospel in the Middle of Time* (Philadelphia: Fortress Press, 1985). I suspect Frei would be less sympathetic with Via's approach, since he tends to assume that a general hermeneutical theory is needed in order to translate the biblical claims into existential truths.

sensus that certain texts have the quasi-sacred and objective literary status of 'classics,' which form the core of a broader 'canon.' The plausibility structure in this case is a literary imitation of a religious community's authority structure; it rests on a tradition, reinforced by communal, usually professional, agencies authorized to articulate the consensus about what is to be included with the canon and what is to be especially exalted within the privileged group as 'classic.' "[11]

Thus, narrative as a category does not precede the content of the Christian witness. Jesus is prior to story, though Jesus' life and resurrection can be displayed only narratively. Yet the "reason why the intratextual universe of this Christian symbol system is a narrative one is that a specific set of texts, which happen to be narrative, has become primary, even within Scripture, and has been assigned a literal reading as their primary or 'plain' sense. They have become the paradigm for the construal not only of what is inside that system but for all that is outside. They provide the interpretive pattern in terms of which all of reality is experienced and read in the religion. Only in a secondary or derivative sense have they become ingredient in a general and literary narrative tradition."[12]

Frei's position in this respect seems quite similar to his interpretation of

11. Frei, "The 'Literal Reading' of Biblical Narrative in Christian Tradition," 68. The general argument by Charles Wood is obviously along these lines. What is frustrating about Frei's (and Wood's) position is the failure to specify the liturgical context through which such consensus is formed. This is not just a genetic point, as without the liturgy the text of Scripture remains just that: text. It is important to remember that before the church had the New Testament it nonetheless worshiped and prayed to God in the name of Jesus of Nazareth. In effect, the worship of the church created Scripture, though once formed Scripture governs the church's worship. For a fascinating account of the development of the Christian interpretation of the Bible, see James Kugel and Rowan Greer, *Early Biblical Interpretation* (Philadelphia: Westminster Press, 1986). In particular, see Greer's discussion of Irenaeus' method that at least in principle requires Scripture to be interpreted in a temporal way (168–76). Greer notes that Irenaeus tended to qualify this emphasis by using "type" to refer to an earthly representation of a heavenly reality. While I think typological interpretation is unavoidable, the crucial question is what controls the types. Originally, I had written the sermon using first person in relation to the story of Babel (e.g., "So God confused our language"). While I certainly think we continue to live out Babel's history, I am equally convinced that we also indicate that is a time theologically in our past. Thus, I tried to relate the texts temporally rather than contemporaneously.

12. Frei, "The 'Literal Reading' of Biblical Narrative in Christian Tradition," 72. While Frei is certainly right to emphasize the "plain sense" as primary, I think that he does not sufficiently note that the "plain sense" is that determined through the corporate life of the Christian community.

Karl Barth's theological project as one of conceptual description. He notes that Barth took the classical themes of "communal Christian language molded by the Bible, tradition and constant usage in worship, practice, instruction and controversy, and he restated or redescribed them, rather than involving arguments on their behalf."[13] Therefore, the style of Barth's *Church Dogmatics* is integral to Barth's theological position. For by his lengthy and leisurely unfolding of Christian language Barth was attempting to "recreate a universe of discourse, and he had to put the reader in the middle of that world, instructing him in the use of that language by showing him how—extensively, and not only by stating the rules or principles of the discourse."[14]

Of course, by associating Frei's basic intent with that of Barth I may only be confirming some of Frei's critics' deepest suspicions. For it would then appear that all the talk about the importance of narrative, particularly in the form of a denial of any foundational starting point, is in fact a cover for a confessional starting point that results in a fideistic theology. Narrative, therefore, becomes but a way for Barthians reinforced by Wittgensteinian "language-game" analysis to avoid dealing with the veridical status of theological claims.

It is not my place to defend Frei (or Barth) from this charge, as he is more than capable of defending himself. But I believe the sermon with which I began, both in its form and content, at least helps throw a different light on Frei's position. By reminding us that narrative works within a timeful community, the alternative that Ronald Thiemann notes between narrative as a transcendental quality of experience, on the one hand, or a literary form that demands appropriate interpretative approaches for proper reading, on the other, turns out to be a false choice. According to Thiemann, when the former predominates, narrative is seen as useful for theology primarily by

> providing a deep structure which captures the essential temporality of human being and understanding. Narrative provides the key for a revised philosophical understanding of human selfhood which is applicable to specifically Christian tasks. Narrative as a literary category becomes important for theology because "stories" are the most appropriate form of expression for an essentially temporal self. When the latter conception of narrative predominates, the category is most useful as a tool for the interpretation of *biblical* narrative. While speculation about the transcendental temporality of the self

13. Hans Frei, "An Afterword: Eberhard Busch's Biography of Karl Barth," in *Karl Barth in Review,* ed. Martin Romscheidt (Pittsburgh: Pickwick Press, 1981), 100.
14. Ibid., 111.

may be interesting and occasionally even helpful, they are not directly or primarily relevant for the task of theology. Theology on this view is the description or redescription of biblical narrative into a coherent language which displays the logic of Christian belief. Narrative highlights both a predominant literary category for interpreting the canon within the Bible and an appropriate theological category for interpreting the canon as a whole. Theology is primarily concerned with the interpretation of text and tradition and only secondarily, if at all, with speculations about the true nature of the self and the deep structures of human understanding.[15]

Thiemann rightly thinks Frei's project is the latter alternative, but if I am right about the significance of the sermon, then I think such an interpretation of Frei (an interpretation Frei may himself share) limits the significance of Frei's achievement. Why that is the case I must try to explain.

3. The Significance of Where, How, and Who Tells the Story

As I indicated above, the difficulty with the suggestion that narrative is primarily a proposal about theology's task being largely one of conceptual redescription is that one is unsure how questions of truth can ever be asked. As long as one remains in the "language-game" it may seem intelligible and even significant,[16] but it seems that by the very nature of the "game" one is not permitted to ask questions external to the narrative. So the narrative, particularly the biblical narrative, threatens to create a world that "overcomes our

---

15. Thiemann, 83.

16. Much silliness has been written for and against the theological use of Wittgenstein's "language-games." For an insightful and careful account of Wittgenstein on this matter, see James Edwards, *Ethics without Philosophy: Wittgenstein and the Moral Life* (Tampa: University of South Florida Press, 1985), 123–42. Edwards argues that "Language-games can neither be heuristic devices used to illustrate substantive philosophical theses arguable on other grounds, nor can they be the final philosophical standard of sense; both these conceptions fail because they presuppose a 'scientific' model of philosophical reasoning. If language-games are heuristic devices, there must actually be philosophical truths to be argued and illustrated; but the whole tenor of Wittgenstein's later work is to disavow such a 'scientific' (metaphysical) conception of philosophy. And language-games cannot be the final standards of sense, most obviously because language-games can be invented as well as discovered: they can be fantastic as well as realistic" (142). Because Wittgenstein meant his analysis of "language-game" to help us attend to the diversity of ways we use language to help us learn about the way things are, I have always avoided appeal to "language-game" in itself. What is important is not whether this or that is a language-game but what is actually being said.

reality."[17] But the very power of the narrative to engulf us makes us doubt its veracity, since we have no means to check its truthfulness. It may be true that the biblical accounts are only "historylike," but does not that history finally have to refer in a way that makes it liable to standard forms of reference?

Frei's position might be liable to such a critique if he assumed that narrative, and in particular the biblical narrative(s), in and of itself was intelligible. But in fact he has never done that, reminding us that "when Christians speak of the Spirit as the indirect presence now of Jesus Christ and of the God who is one with him, they refer to the church. The church is both the witness to that presence and the public and communal form the indirect presence of Christ now takes, in contrast to his direct presence in his earthly days. In the instance of the church, reference to the Spirit means affirmation of the spatial, temporal basis of Christ's indirect presence in unity with his presence in and to the shape of public events of the world and of human history."[18]

In philosophical terms Frei's appeal to the church as the subject of the narrative as well as the agent of the narrative is a reminder that the narrative does not refer but rather people do. To isolate the biblical narratives in and of themselves would be equivalent to considering the truth and falsity of sentences separate from their context of utterance.[19] Once this is understood, Frei's proposal cannot be seen as an attempt to avoid realist claims but rather as an attempt to situate the context of those claims. It is to remind us, as Janet Soskice has argued, that "the notion of reference is not a useful notion in a theory of meaning, if we mean by reference some freestanding relation supposed to obtain between individual proper names and what they name, complex singular terms and what they denote, and predicates and that of which

17. Frei, *Eclipse of Biblical Narrative,* 3. How the Gospel "engulfs" the world is not by denying the reality of our diverse narratives but by providing an invitation to be part of a new people. The imperial character of the story that the church embodies requires witness, not coercion. Exactly because the content of the story requires us to recognize our fallibility means we cannot anticipate how God will use our witness in relation to the diverse stories of the world. Indeed, the story we believe entrusted to the church does not displace all other stories, as it does not pretend to tell us all that is worth knowing about our existence—it only tells us what we need to know about God's saving work.

18. Frei, *The Identity of Jesus Christ,* 157. John Milbank has put this forcefully in "An Essay against Secular Order," *Journal of Religious Ethics* 15, no. 2 (fall 1987), as he says, "If we are to say 'salvation is a fact,' 'salvation has appeared on the historical stage,' then we have to enunciate, not just an ecclesiology, but also an ecclesiology which recounts and resumes the church's *actual concrete* intervention in the human social order, where the rules of 'non-interference' have not really applied" (207).

19. Janet Martin Soskice, *Metaphor and Religious Language* (Oxford: Clarendon Press, 1985), 86.

they are true. When dealing with meaning, we must see that 'Words have no function save as they play a role in sentences . . .'; and so, too, words make no reference beyond that which speakers employ them to make in sentences. It is the fact that it is not strictly words which refer but speakers using words, which makes metaphor possible, and enables us to speak about one thing in terms which are seen as suggestive of another."[20]

As Soskice notes, one of the attractive features of such an account of reference is that it has a significant social aspect, since the notion of membership in a linguistic community is a crucial feature of such a theory of reference—whether that community be one of science or the church. It is not words or narratives that refer, but "speakers using words who refer. So Hilary Putnam says, 'The realist explanation, in a nutshell, is not that language mirrors the world but that *speakers* mirror the world; i.e., their environment—in the sense of constructing a symbolic representation of that environment."[21]

There is no way such a theory can avoid the importance of experience on which reference is grounded, but each speaker in that community need not have had the particular experience necessarily embodied by different aspects of the language. For good communities depend on "what Putnam has called a 'division of linguistic labour,' that is, we rely on authoritative members of our community to ground referring expression. We refer to Columbus when we mention his name, because we have heard the name from others, who heard it from others, etc., going back to Columbus himself."[22] Thus, each speaker of a particular linguistic community is connected through the members of that community, living and dead, to a range of experience exceeding his own.

And so the necessity of the sermon as the communal action whereby Christians are formed to use their language rightly. For it must be remembered that it is not the preacher who makes the sermon efficacious. To think that would be but the form of *ex operator operans* applied to the preached word. Rather, for the preached word to be God's word the Holy Spirit must make us a body of people capable of hearing that word rightly. Put differently, the preached word's power is its capacity to create a people receptive to being formed by that word.

The sermon is a churchly event, even when it is used to witness to those not

20. Ibid., 135–36.
21. Ibid., 136.
22. Ibid., 145. Such is the reason that questions of authority are unavoidable in any community. In the church it is the responsibility of those we invest with authority to direct our attention to those without whom we could not exist as church: that is, the saints.

Christian, as it proclaims the power of God to create a new people by being made part of God's continuing story. Yet Christians confess that any continuation of that story that is valid must take its form from the story of Jesus Christ. As Frei observes, in this respect the "relation between the church and Jesus Christ is somewhat like that between Israel and Jesus. To describe the people of Israel is to narrate its history. And to identify that people with the identity of Jesus Christ is to narrate the history of Jesus in such a way that it is seen as the individual and climactic summing up, incorporation, and identification of the whole people, by which the people receive their identification. The church likewise moves toward an as yet undisclosed historical summing up that must be narrated, though it cannot yet be because the story is unfinished and the new Israel's Kingdom of God not yet climaxed or visible in our midst."[23]

The emphasis on narrative, therefore, is not first a claim about the narrative quality of experience from some unspecified standpoint, but rather is an attempt to draw our attention to *where the story is told,* namely, in the church; *how the story is told,* namely, in faithfulness to Scripture; and *who tells the story,* namely, the whole church through the office of the preacher. For as we see from the sermon above, the story is not self-referential but rather creates a people capable of being the continuation of the narrative by witnessing to the world that all creation is ordered to God's good end. The church is the necessary context of inquiry for the testing of that narrative, as it must always remain open to revision since the subject of its narrative is easily domesticated.

Thus, we do not have to choose between narrative as a transcendental category of experience or a literary form illuminative of Scripture, once we recognize that the church is crucial for the intelligibility of the story that Christians have to tell.[24] For example, it is obviously true that not all of

---

23. Frei, *The Identity of Jesus Christ,* 159. Again as John Milbank says, "The church is not primarily a *means* of salvation, but rather a *goal* of salvation insofar as it is nothing other than the community of the reconciled. Our way back to God is through our incorporation into the historical body of the redeemed" ("An Essay against Secular Order," 8).

24. As L. Gregory Jones argues, "It is certainly true that there is a narrative quality to human life that is morally significant. But that is not the primary claim Christians are concerned to make. It is rather that the biblical *narrative* seeks to incorporate all people into God's narrative. Thus there is a strong sense in which the narrative of a single human life does not begin with birth and end with death: for by being incorporated into the life of Christ the narrative of a single human life begins at creation and ends with the consummation of the Kingdom. It is by being incorporated into the Church that it is possible to develop the virtues necessary to live truthfully and morally. (Therefore) the narrative of the Christian tradition is a way of

Scripture is narrative in form, but the issue is not which "form" is predominant but how the content of the Scripture is properly displayed. I have suggested that the church is the community that is at once the storyteller as well as a character in the story that is required by Christian affirmation of God's redemption of the world through the people of Israel and the cross and resurrection of Jesus of Nazareth.

Moreover, the church is crucial for sustaining claims of the narratability of the world. Our experience, of the world as well as of ourselves, is open to narrative construal, but experience in and of itself does not entail the form of narrative and/or the kind of story Christians learn to tell about the world and our place in it. The church is, therefore, an ontological necessity if we are to know rightly that our world is capable of narrative construal. Without the church the world would have no history. Such a claim is not just a "confessional" stance but the most determinative *realist* claim Christians can possibly make.

Which brings us back to Babel. If I have been right, we are in a position to appreciate why the faithfulness of the church is crucial for the destiny of the world. To be sure, God's kingdom is more determinative than the church, yet at Pentecost God storied a people with gifts so that they might be capable of witnessing to the world the renewal of our unity made possible in Jesus of Nazareth. The church's theological witness cannot help, therefore, be anything less than a challenge to the conventional wisdom of the world. For the church is involved in nothing less than offering an alternative to war by providing the world with a history by our willingness as Christians to go making "disciples of all nations, baptizing them in the name of the Father, and of the Son, and of the Holy Spirit, teaching them to observe all that I have commanded you; and lo, I am with you always to the close of the ages" (Matthew 28:19–20).[25]

Further Reading

"The Insufficiency of Scripture: Why Discipleship Is Needed" (1993), essay 12 in this volume

---

displaying two claims: on the one hand it displays the continuing embodiment of the community through the ages (thus showing that the claim is not a utopian fantasy), and on the other hand it displays the claim that each person's salvation is indispensable to the salvation of everyone else, even the dead" ("Alasdair MacIntyre on Narrative, Community, and the Moral Life," *Modern Theology* 4, no. 1 [October 1987], 67).

25. I am indebted to Michael Cartwright, L. Gregory Jones, Richard Lischer, and Dennis Campbell for their criticisms and suggestions.

"On Being a Church Capable of Addressing a World at War" (1987), essay 21 in this
  volume
"Sex in Public: How Adventurous Christians Are Doing It" (1978), essay 23 in this
  volume
"Abortion, Theologically Understood" (1991), essay 31 in this volume
"The Church's One Foundation Is Jesus Christ Her Lord, or In a World without
  Foundations All We Have Is the Church" (1994), in *IGC*
"The Liturgical Shape of the Christian Life: Teaching Christian Ethics as Worship"
  (1995), in *IGC*
"Why the 'Sectarian Temptation' Is a Misrepresentation" (1998), essay 4 in this
  volume
"Politics, Vision, and the Common Good" (1970), in *VV*
"Worship, Evangelism, Ethics: On Eliminating the 'And'" (1998), in *BH*

What Are Christians to Be? Christian Discipleship

8. Vision, Stories, and Character (1973, 2001)

This is Hauerwas's earliest attempt to show the necessity of narrative for constru-
ing the self. Drawing explicitly on the work of Iris Murdoch, Donald Evans, and
James McClendon and implicitly on that of Wittgenstein, Hauerwas argues that
an adequate construal of the self requires a moral vision that always involves the
emplotment of our lives through metaphors and stories. Moral principles are
inadequate for such a task because the moral task involves describing the world
not merely as it is, but also how it ought to be seen and intended. It is on this
level—the practice of describing the world in a way that our lives have coherence
and unity—that the "specificity of theological ethics" becomes clear. Thus moral-
ity for Christians is not the same as for other persons, though there may be great
areas of agreement. While resisting those who argue that this view leads to
relativism, Hauerwas believes this approach takes much more seriously the vari-
ety of the moral life.

For purposes of analysis moral philosophy should remain at the level of the differences, taking the forms of life as a given, and not try to get behind them to a single
form. There is perhaps in the end no peace between those who think that morality is
complex and various, and those who think it is simple and unitary, or between those
who think that other people are usually hard to understand and those who think they
are usually easy to understand.—IRIS MURDOCH[1]

This essay, while informed by theological commitments, is a philosophical
exercise to expand the arbitrary limits embodied in the religion-morality

[From vv © 1974 by University of Notre Dame Press. Used by permission. This selection is an
abbreviated and edited version of the essay "The Self as Story: A Reconsideration of the
Relation of Religion and Morality from the Agent's Perspective" in vv.]
1. Iris Murdoch, "Vision and Choice in Morality," in *Christian Ethics and Contemporary
Philosophy*, ed. Ian Ramsey (New York: Macmillan, 1966), 195–218.

discussion. Often implicit in the arguments of those who deny any specificity to Christian moral behavior is the assumption that there is one form of the moral life, that underneath the variety of human activity there is one moral way of life, one form of moral justification that is the same for all. It is my contention that it is possible to appreciate the variety of the moral without falling into the vicious relativism that those who take the unitary view so fear. It should be clear that the significance of this argument is not limited to Christian ethics. I assume that Jewish, Muslim, Hindu, and other religious ethicists will also wish to claim some specificity for their own position.

Contemporary ethics has paid little attention to character, vision, stories, and metaphors as part of our moral experience. I want to argue that the particularity of the Christian moral life cannot be accounted for apart from these notions.[2] Metaphors and stories suggest how we should see and describe the world—that is, how we should "look-on" ourselves, others, and the world—in ways that rules and principles taken in themselves do not.[3] They do this by providing the narrative accounts of our lives that give them coherence.[4]

Contrary to the assumption of many philosophers, moral principles do not serve as the "essence" of stories, as if they might be abstracted from the story and still convey the same meaning. Rather, our principles are but shorthand reminders necessary for moral education and explanation; their moral significance is contained in stories. Though principles (or policy statements) such as "I have decided to live an agapeistic life"[5] appear to be story-neutral, they are nothing of the sort. For our principles "are intelligible at all only if their implicit 'stories' are explicated. The need for stories then lies precisely in the fact that policy statements are about intentions to act in certain ways, and action is inconceivable apart from stories. . . . The precise meaning of and

2. In what follows I am purposefully leaving vague the meaning of story and metaphor. Any attempt to provide a conceptually responsible definition of either in the bounds of this paper would be insufficient to account for the variety of the different kinds and uses of stories. Any attempt to develop this position beyond the methodological point I am concerned with would necessarily entail a more critical use and analysis of these aspects of our moral experience.

3. For this sense of "look-on" and for many other things, I am dependent on Donald Evans, *The Logic of Self-Involvement* (London: S.C.M. Press, 1963).

4. James Olney, *Metaphors of Self: The Meaning of Autobiography* (Princeton, NJ: Princeton University Press, 1972), 30–31.

5. [Hauerwas is referring to discussions of "love monism" that were addressed by Joseph Fletcher, Paul Ramsey, Donald Evans, and Gene Outka in *Norm and Context in Christian Ethics*, ed. Gene Outka and Paul Ramsey (New York: Scribner's, 1968), and Gene Outka, *Agape: An Ethical Analysis* (New Haven: Yale University Press, 1972).]

hence the differences between Confucian policy statements and Christian policy statements are entirely a function of their differing stories."[6]

A commonplace example can illustrate the irreducibility and significance of metaphors and stories for learning to see the world in which we must act.[7] Suppose a woman is trying on a hat she thinks she likes but remains somewhat doubtful that it is right for her. A friend observing her indecision observes, "My dear, it's the Taj Mahal," and suddenly her indecision is resolved. It is of course possible to say that the friend has simply employed a colorful way to suggest that the hat is too ostentatious, but such a suggestion fails to convey the sense of the metaphor. One can no more translate the metaphor into "literal" language than poetry can be translated into prose, for in a certain correct and straightforward way the hat is the Taj Mahal. Poetry and literature do not just bolster our moral intentions; they affect how we perceive the world and hence what the moral life is about. For poetry does not just describe the known; it reveals dimensions of the unknown that make the known seem unfamiliar.

Perhaps an ethical example would make this point more persuasively. This woman may exemplify in her every action what we consider to be the application of the rule to treat others fairly. She not only always treats others justly, but she even goes out of her way to serve their needs. In other words, she seems to be the perfect example of one who actually lives and orders her behavior so as to love others as she loves herself. She might claim that her behavior is not determined by any such maxim of fairness, for she is but "loving and treating others as if they are her brothers and sisters in Christ." While it is undeniable that her behavior embodies basic moral rules, her understanding of "all people as brothers and sisters in Christ" can no more be translated into rules of fairness than the Taj Mahal can be understood simply as a synonym for "ostentatious." For her, human beings are not just to be treated fairly, they are literally brothers and sisters in Christ. This will at times entail concrete behavior that is not envisaged in the rule to treat everyone fairly and benevolently. It is this irreducible aspect of their religious beliefs and commitments that makes religious people so uncomfortable with any attempt to abstract a "moral core" from their religious convictions.

6. William Poteat, "Myths, Stories, History, Eschatology, and Action: Some Polanyian Meditations," in *Intellect and Hope,* ed. Thomas Langford and William Poteat (Durham, NC: Duke University Press, 1968), 216–17.

7. I borrow this example from James McClendon as he borrowed from John Wisdom. See McClendon, "Biography as Theology," *Cross Currents* 21, no. 4 (fall): 415–31.

It would be a mistake to limit this formal claim to religious or metaphorical language. Rather, these are but paradigm instances that make clear an essential aspect of all language used ethically. For our moral language does not just describe what is; it describes how we ought to see and intend the world. The truth that is at least partly captured in the naturalistic fallacy is that moral language necessarily must presuppose a world that is not but should be. Our metaphors and stories entice us to find a way to bring into existence the reality that at once should be but will not be except as we act as if it is. Morally the world is always wanting to be created in correspondence to what it is but is not yet.

This does not mean we morally intend the world "as if" our basic commitments were true or that we can transform our existence to make them true even though they are empirically false. Our religious stories and metaphors embody the normative commitments we need to make if we desire to live our lives in a morally appropriate way. The association of religious morality with fundamental metaphors and stories does not mean it is logically different from other moral language; or that it can be dismissed as dealing with the "irrational" aspects of our moral existence.

Because ethicists have concentrated on moral justification of principles associated with specific actions and practices, they have tended to overlook the importance of stories for the moral life. The prevalent model of the moral life has tended to support the assumption that there is only one way to be moral.[8] To be sure, in specific situations there may be no specifiable difference discernible between the woman who embodies the ethics of fairness and the woman who acts toward others as her brothers and sisters in Christ. Rules and principles appear to be sufficient because they are typically associated with rather common moral problems and situations.

But our moral lives are not simply made up of the addition of our separate responses to particular situations. Rather, we exhibit an orientation that gives our life a theme through which the variety of what we do and do not do can be scored. To be agents at all requires a directionality that involves the development of character and virtue. Our character is the result of our sustained attention to the world that gives a coherence to our intentionality. Such attention is formed and given content by the stories through which we have learned

---

8. For example, see Iris Murdoch's devastating characterization of the liberal and optimistic view of the self and moral choice she thinks is assumed by contemporary philosophical ethicists in "Vision and Choice in Morality," 197–98.

to form the story of our lives. To be moral persons is to allow stories to be told through us so that our manifold activities gain a coherence that allows us to claim them for our own. Stories and character are interdependent in the sense that the moral life, if it is to be coherent, always has beginnings and endings.[9]

Our character is constituted by the rules, metaphors, and stories that are combined to give a design or unity to the variety of things we must and must not do in our lives. If our lives are to be reflective and coherent our vision must be ordered around dominant metaphors or stories. Therefore it is crucial to our moral life to allow the metaphors that make up our vision to check and balance each other in terms of their appropriateness for the various demands of our life and the overall "life plan" that we live.[10] From this perspective, it makes sense to suggest that the woman who serves others as her brothers and sisters in Christ may well engage in activities the woman who acts according to principles of fairness does not.

The metaphors and stories we use to organize our life plan are inherited from our culture and our particular biographical situation. Christianity can be understood as but one set of coherent metaphors and stories that constitute an understanding of the nature of the world and a possible life plan.[11] Christianity involves a claim about how our lives must be centered to correspond to the truth of human existence. It is certainly not my intention to argue that Christianity is the only religion to provide humankind with such accounts of the moral life. But I do defend the position that Christian ethics must not be reduced to a conception of the moral life that does not share its stories and metaphors. It cannot be assumed that moral behavior for Christians is the same as for other persons, though there may be great areas of agreement.

In summary, I have suggested that a claim for the specificity of theological ethics is defensible once we realize that to be "moral" involves learning to see

9. Steven Crites, "The Narrative Quality of Experience," *Journal of the American Academy of Religion* 39, no. 3 (September 1971): 291–311. For some very useful suggestions about how autobiographies can be more or less true, see Roy Pascal, *Design and Truth in Autobiography* (Cambridge, MA: Harvard University Press, 1960).

10. For an analysis of the idea of "life plan," see Charles Fried, *An Anatomy of Values* (Cambridge, MA: Harvard University Press, 1970), 97–101. Fried uses this phrase to indicate "that persons must and do exhibit some order, some consistency in their ensemble of ends, that their ends as a whole comprise a system."

11. Austin Farrer has done the most disciplined reflection on how images and metaphors work and their relation to history. For the images and stories at the heart of the Christian life are formed and informed by the person of Jesus. The significance of this for how Christian ethics is to be understood is crucial, for in a certain sense it is probably incorrect to think of Christ as a story. See Austin Farrer, *The Glass of Vision* (London: Dacre Press, 1958).

the world in a way that our lives have coherence and unity. It should now be clear that my concentration on the importance of stories and metaphors for the moral life avoids any implication of a vicious relativism. Even though moral principles are not sufficient in themselves for our moral existence, neither are stories sufficient if they do not generate principles that are morally significant. Principles without stories are subject to perverse interpretation (i.e., they can be used in immoral stories), but stories without principles will have no way of concretely specifying the actions and practices consistent with the general orientation expressed by the story.

Further Reading

"The Significance of Vision: Toward an Aesthetic Ethic" (1972), in vv

"Situation Ethics, Moral Notions, and Moral Theology" (1971), in vv

"From System to Story: An Alternative Pattern for Rationality in Ethics" (1977), in TT

"Character, Narrative, and Growth in the Christian Life" (1980), essay 11 in this volume

"Why Truthfulness Requires Forgiveness: A Commencement Address for Graduates of a College of the Church of the Second Chance" (1992), essay 15 in this volume

"Must a Patient Be a Person to Be a Patient? Or, My Uncle Charlie Is Not Much of a Person, But He Is Still My Uncle Charlie" (1975), essay 30 in this volume

"Practicing Patience: How Christians Should Be Sick" (1997), essay 18 in this volume

"On Learning to See Red Wheelbarrows: On Vision and Relativism" (1977), *Journal of the American Academy of Religion* 45, no. 2:225, 644–655

"The Church in a Divided World: The Interpretive Power of the Christian Story" (1980), in cc

9. A Story-Formed Community:
Reflections on *Watership Down* (1981)

Richard Adams's novel Watership Down, *a best-selling novel in the late 1970s about a warren of rabbits, inspired what is probably Hauerwas's best exemplification of his claim about the moral significance of narrative for construing the Christian life. It is certainly his most extensive reading of a piece of fiction directed toward constructive reflection on the Christian life. Like the rabbits of* Watership Down, *Christians depend on a narrative to be guided and rely on a power of which the world knows not against those who would rule the world with violence. Furthermore, while Christians also often fail to be faithful to their guiding stories, this does not entail that the Christian story makes unrealistic demands. It does show the difficulty of being the kind of community where such a story can be told and embodied by a people formed in accordance with it and the challenge of developing skills to combat the tendency to self-deception that marks social life.*

1. Reforming Christian Social Ethics

Each of the ten theses I have proposed for the reformation of Christian social ethics obviously involves highly controversial claims that require disciplined philosophical and theological argument.[1] However, I do not intend to supply that kind of discursive argument here, as I am more interested in trying to illuminate what the theses mean and how they are interrelated. To do that I am going to tell a story about some very special rabbits that inhabit the world of

[From CC © 1981 by University of Notre Dame Press. Used by permission. Originally the second part of "A Story-Formed Community: Reflections on *Watership Down*." Most of the material in the first section is found in "Reforming Christian Social Ethics: Ten Theses" as essay 5 in this volume.]
1. [See essay 5, "Reforming Christian Social Ethics: Ten Theses."] For at least a beginning defense of the significance of narrative for moral rationality, see my TT.

Richard Adams's book *Watership Down.*[2] I cannot hope to convince you of the correctness of my theses by proceeding in this way, but I do hope at least to help you understand what they might mean. Moreover, it seems appropriate for someone who is arguing for the significance of narrative to use a story to make his point.

2. The Narrative Context of Social Ethics

It would be misleading if I were to give the impression that I am using *Watership Down* only because it offers an entertaining way to explain my theses. The very structure of the book provides an account of the narrative nature of social ethics that is seldom noticed or accounted for by most political and social theory. Adams's depiction of the various communities in *Watership Down* suggests that they are to be judged primarily by their ability to sustain the narratives that define the very nature of man, or in this case, rabbits. Thus *Watership Down* is meant to teach us the importance of stories for social and political life. But even more important, by paying close attention to *Watership Down* we will see that the best way to learn the significance of stories is by having our attention drawn to stories through a story.

Watership Down is at once a first-class political novel and a marvelous adventure story. It is extremely important for my theses that neither aspect of the novel can be separated from the other. Too often politics is treated solely as a matter of power, interests, or technique. We thus forget that the most basic task of any polity is to offer its people a sense of participation in an adventure. For finally what we seek is not power, or security, or equality, or even dignity, but a sense of worth gained from participation and contribution to a common adventure. Indeed, our "dignity" derives exactly from our sense of having played a part in such a story.

The essential tie between politics and adventure not only requires recognition of the narrative nature of politics, but it also reminds us that good politics requires the development of courage and hope as central virtues for its citizens. As we will see, *Watership Down* is primarily a novel about the various forms of courage and hope necessary for the formation of a good community. Adventure requires courage to keep us faithful to the struggle, since by its very nature adventure means that the future is always in doubt. And just to the

2. Richard Adams, *Watership Down* (New York: Avon Books, 1972). All page references to *Watership Down* are in the text.

extent that the future is in doubt, hope is required, as there can be no adventure if we despair of our goal. Such hope does not necessarily take the form of excessive confidence; rather, it involves the simple willingness to take the next step.

Watership Down begins with the exodus of a group of rabbits from a well-established warren on the slim basis that one rabbit with the gifts of a seer thinks that warren is threatened with destruction. As a result the group is forced to undergo a hazardous journey in search of a new home, ultimately Watership Down, as well as the dangerous undertaking of securing does from the militaristic warren of Efrafa. It is important to note that the rabbits of *Watership Down* do not leave their old warren as a people (or a rabbithood). They leave only as a group of individuals joined together by their separate reasons for leaving the warren. All they share in common is the stories of the prince of the rabbits, El-ahrairah. They become a people only as they acquire a history through the adventures they share as interpreted through the traditions of El-ahrairah.

For this reason *Watership Down* is fundamentally a political novel. It is concerned with exploring what conditions are necessary for a community to be a viable polity. Thus much of the novel depicts contrasting political communities that bear striking similarities to past and present polities. Sandleford, the warren they must leave, is a traditional class society whose government is determined by loyalty to a strong and competent leader. On their journey they encounter a warren that has no name but bears a striking resemblance to the modern welfare state in which the freedom of the individual is primary. And the third warren, Efrafa, from which they try to secure some does, is a highly organized and regimented totalitarian society. Each of these societies is characterized by a virtue that embodies its ideal form—that is, loyalty, tolerance, and obedience.[3]

Even though none of these communities perfectly represents actual societies, they provide imaginative paradigms for tendencies in every polity, whether it be a state, a corporation, or a church. Issues fundamental to political theory, such as the relation of individual to community, the primacy of freedom and its relation to justice, and the legitimation of power, are obviously present in each of the communities described. It is extremely tempting, therefore, to interpret *Watership Down* as a commentary on current

---

3. Robert Paul Wolff has pointed out how each form of society has a corresponding virtue in *The Poverty of Liberalism* (Boston: Beacon Press, 1968), 123.

actual and theoretical political options. Only Watership Down itself seems to be an exception, as it is presented as an ideal society for which there is no ready analogue.

Without denying that *Watership Down* is a ready source of standard forms of political reflection, the book has a deeper insight to offer for social ethics. Although each society can be characterized by traditional political opinions and theory, Adams's intention is to show how such discussions are subordinate to the ability of a community to live and tell its stories. As we shall see, the crux of the viability of any society in *Watership Down* is whether it is organized so as to provide for authentic retelling of the stories of the founder and prince of rabbit history, El-ahrairah.

Adams is trying to help us understand politics not only as it organizes people for particular ends, but also as it forms them to be inheritors and exemplifications of a tradition. In other words, Adams suggests that society can best be understood as an extended argument, since living traditions presuppose rival interpretations. Good societies enable the argument to continue so that the possibilities and limits of the tradition can be exposed. The great danger, however, is that the success of a tradition will stop its growth and in reaction some may deny the necessity of tradition for their lives. The truthfulness of a tradition is tested in its ability to form people who are ready to put the tradition into question, or at least to recognize when it is being put into question by a rival tradition. Of course, as we shall see, some traditions lapse into complete incoherence and can be recovered only by revolutionary reconstitution.[4]

2.1 The Story-Shaped World of Rabbits

This is all very abstract, but I can make it concrete by calling your attention to the way stories function for the rabbits of *Watership Down*. First, there are several things about rabbits that we need to know. A rabbit is constantly in danger. Mr. Lockley, a famous expert on rabbits, suggests that rabbits are as strong as the grass (167). That is certainly not very strong, for the strength of grass consists primarily in being able to grow back after it has been stepped on, cut, or burned. And just as grass grows back, so rabbits depend on their

---

4. Alasdair MacIntyre, "Epistemological Crisis, Dramatic Narrative, and the Philosophy of Science," *Monist* 60, no. 4 (October 1977): 460–61. The general debt this paper owes to MacIntyre's work will be obvious to those familiar with his position. I have relied on MacIntyre's occasional essays; however, his *After Virtue* (Notre Dame, IN: University of Notre Dame Press, 1981) will soon be published. There MacIntyre systematically develops his position in a powerful and compelling manner.

stubborn will to survive against all odds. And they are able to survive because they are fast, constantly vigilant, and have the wit to cooperate with one another.

Another thing we need to know about rabbits, at least the rabbits of *Watership Down*, is that they are lovers of stories. There is a saying among them that a rabbit "can no more refuse to tell a story than an Irishman can refuse to fight" (99). Rabbits are, to be sure, creatures of nature, but their "nature" is the result of the interaction of their biology with their stories. Their stories serve to define who they are and to give them skills to survive the dangers of their world in a manner appropriate to being a rabbit.

The first story told in *Watership Down* is the story of the "Blessing of El-ahrairah." I suspect it is not accidental that this is the first story told by the rabbits who left Sandleford, as all new communities must remind themselves of their origin. A people are formed by a story that places their history in the texture of the world. Such stories make the world our home by providing us with the skills to negotiate the dangers in our environment in a manner appropriate to our nature.

The "Blessing of El-ahrairah" is the account of Frith, the god of the rabbits, allocating gifts to each of the species. In the beginning all animals were friends and El-ahrairah was among the happiest of animals, as he had more wives than he could count and his children covered the earth. They became so numerous that Frith told El-ahrairah he must control his people, since there was not enough grass for everyone. Rabbits, however, are intent on living day by day, so El-ahrairah refused to heed Frith's warning.

Frith, therefore, called a meeting at which he gave a gift to all animals and birds. El-ahrairah, busy dancing, eating, and mating, was late to the meeting. As a result he heard too late that Frith had given the fox and the weasel cunning hearts and sharp teeth, the cat silent feet and eyes to see in the dark. El-ahrairah, realizing that Frith was too clever for him, tried to hide by digging a hole. But he had only dug halfway when Frith came by, finding El-ahrairah with only his back legs and tail above ground. El-ahrairah responded to Frith's greeting by denying he was El-ahrairah, but Frith, feeling a kinship with this mischievous creature, blessed El-ahrairah's bottom and legs, giving them strength and speed. El-ahrairah's tail grew shining and his legs long and powerful, and he came running out of his hole. And Frith called after him, "El-ahrairah, your people cannot rule the world, for I will not have it so. All the world will be your enemy, Prince with a Thousand Enemies, and whenever they catch you they will kill you. But first they must catch you, digger, listener, runner, prince with the swift warning. Be cunning and full of tricks and your people shall never be destroyed" (37).

It is tempting to reduce this story to its obvious etiological elements: why rabbits have white tails and strong legs. But this would distort the importance of the story as the source of skills for rabbits to negotiate their world. The rabbit's task is not to try to make the world safe, but rather to learn to live in a dangerous world by trusting in stories, speed, wit, and each other's gifts. Rabbit existence in the world is contingent on the utilization of the lessons learned from the story of their origin and the gifts provided by Frith. These gifts determine their very character as wild creatures of the world. When they try to exist without relying on their gifts they pervert their nature and become tame, subject to even more tyrannical powers.

2.2 The Substitution of Security for Narrative

Only against this background can we understand the events at Sandleford that resulted in the escape of some of the rabbits. Not that Sandleford was an extraordinarily unjust society, but it was no longer sensitive to the dangers that always threaten. In effect, the destruction of Sandleford was the result of its success.

In many ways Sandleford was a typical rabbit community. At the top of the social order was the chief rabbit, named Threarah but usually referred to as "*the* Threarah." "He had won his position not only by strength in his prime, but also by level-headedness and a certain self-contained detachment, quite unlike the impulsive behavior of most rabbits. It was well known that he never let himself become excited by rumor or danger. He had coolly—some even said coldly—stood firm during the terrible onslaught of the myxomatosis, ruthlessly driving out every rabbit who seemed to be sickening. He had re-sisted all ideas of mass emigration and enforced complete isolation in the warren, thereby almost certainly saving it from extinction" (19). As a result the rabbits at Sandleford assumed that their security rested in their loyalty to the Threarah.

Directly under the chief rabbit were the owsla, "a group of strong or clever rabbits—second year or older—surrounding the chief rabbit and his doe and exercising authority" (14). The character of the owsla varies from one warren to another, but at Sandleford the owsla had a rather military character; their chief duties were seeing that no one tried to leave the warren and protecting the Threarah. The rest of the warren were rank-and-file ordinary rabbits or "outskirters." Basically, at Sandleford warren the higher one's status, the more favorable one's share in the distribution of goods. A member of the owsla, for instance, had the advantage over the outskirter in silflay (feeding), mating, and choice of burrows. The primary occupation of the rabbits at Sandleford had become competition for the higher-status positions. The rule of the warren thus became "These are my claws, so this is my cowslip [a particular delicacy among rabbits]. These are my teeth, so this is my burrow" (14).

Stories of El-ahrairah still seem to have been told at Sandleford, but primarily as a means of entertainment, for it was assumed that the warren had weathered the worst. Into this warren were born Hazel, destined to become the chief rabbit of Watership Down, and Fiver, his strange brother who had the ability to sense the future. It was because Hazel had learned to trust his brother's gift that he paid attention to Fiver's premonition that Sandleford must be abandoned because it was soon to be destroyed. The basis for Fiver's concern was nothing but a piece of wood nailed to a post with the unintelligible script: "THIS IDEALLY SITUATED ESTATE, COMPRISING SIX ACRES OF EXCELLENT BUILDING LAND, IS TO BE DEVELOPED WITH HIGH CLASS MODERN RESIDENCES BY SUTCH AND MARTIN, LIMITED, OF NEWBURY, BERKS" (16).

Hazel convinced one of the lesser members of the owsla, Bigwig, to obtain an audience with the Threarah so Fiver might deliver his prediction of destruction of Sandleford and the recommendation that they leave the warren. The Threarah, however, said in an extremely understanding voice:

"Well, I never did! That's rather a tall order, isn't it? What do you think yourself?"

"Well, Sir," said Hazel, "my brother doesn't really think about these feelings he gets. He just has the feelings, if you see what I mean. I'm sure you're the right person to decide what we ought to do."

"Well, that's very nice of you to say that. I hope I am. But now, my dear fellows, let's just think about this a moment, shall we? It's May, isn't it? Everyone's busy and most of the rabbits are enjoying themselves. No elil [enemies] for miles, or so they tell me. No illness, good weather. And you want me to tell the warren that young-er—young-er—your brother here has got a hunch and we must all go traipsing across country to goodness knows where and risk the consequences, eh? What do you think they'll say? All delighted, eh!"

"They'd take it from you," said Fiver suddenly.

"That's very nice of you," said the Threarah again. "Well, perhaps they would, perhaps they would. But I should have to consider it very carefully indeed. A most serious step, of course. And then—" (20–21)

Suddenly Fiver went into a trance, which gave the Threarah the excuse to dismiss them and to reprimand Bigwig for letting such unstable characters into his presence. That very stability provided by the Threarah for his warren made it impossible to be open to the seer. The stories of El-ahrairah had been domesticated in the interest of security and Sandleford thus became victimized by its own history. In fact its history had become its fate; it was no longer able to use tradition to remain open to the gifts and dangers of rabbit existence.

2.3 The Loss of Narrative as the Loss of Community

It might be expected that this would have happened at Sandleford; a key purpose of most societies is to provide a sense of security. For example, though we are constantly reminded of the violent and accidental deaths occurring around us every day, most of us live as if we assume our social order is secure and we are safe. We can do this because we assume death happens only to other people. We are even sometimes vaguely comforted by reports of others' deaths, as such reports confirm our own presumption that we are protected by a magical invulnerability. Absorption into most societies is training in self-deception as we conspire with one another to keep death at bay. Ironically, the more our societies confirm this self-deception, the more dangerous our life becomes. We lose the skill of recognizing what danger is and where it lies. Deception becomes the breeding ground for injustice, since the necessity to hide the dangers of our world make it impossible to confront those aspects of our social order that impose unequal burdens on others.[5] Our conspiracy for safety forces us to see our neighbor as a stranger.

Good and just societies require a narrative, therefore, that helps them know the truth about existence and fight the constant temptation to self-deception. Lack of such a narrative is most vividly depicted in *Watership Down* by the encounter of Hazel and his friends with a warren that, because it lacks a name, I call Cowslip's warren, after the rabbit who invited them to rest there. The primary characteristic of this warren was that it allowed each rabbit to do as he pleased. The story that formed them was that they were no longer

---

5. See, for example, Simone Weil's powerful reflections on this theme in *The Iliad or The Poems of Force* (Wallingford, PA: Pendle Hill Pamphlet, 1964).

dependent on tradition. They assumed the way to stop history from becoming their fate, as it had for Sandleford, was to have no history at all.[6]

Before I can describe Hazel and his friends' encounter with Cowslip's warren I need to introduce two other characters crucial to the story. In addition to Fiver and Bigwig (who had left with them because he obviously had no future at Sandleford), there was Pipkin and Blackberry. Pipkin, like Fiver, was small; unlike Fiver, he had no gift or skill. Though weak and constantly in need of help, in some ways he is the most crucial rabbit for the determination of the character of Watership Down warren. By endangering themselves in order to care for Pipkin, they develop an openness to the stranger.[7]

Blackberry, who was as rational as Fiver was insightful, also joined the band. It was he who helped them escape from Sandleford without having to leave the completely exhausted Pipkin behind by suggesting the extraordinary idea of floating Pipkin across a stream on a board. It should be noted that Blackberry's gift, like those of all the other rabbits, is a manifestation of the virtue of courage. For Blackberry's intelligence is more than brightness; it stems from his willingness to consider all aspects and alternatives of a problem, even when they are extremely threatening or unpleasant.

It is therefore to Blackberry that Hazel turns for advice on whether they should accept Cowslip's invitation to rest at his warren. It is a very tempting invitation, since they are tired after their escape from Sandleford, they are out in the open, and a storm is soon to break. Blackberry argues,

> There's no way of finding out whether he's to be trusted except to try it. He seemed friendly. But then, if a lot of rabbits were afraid of some newcomers and wanted to deceive them—get them down a hole and attack them—they'd start—wouldn't they?—by sending someone who was plausible. They might

6. Langdon Gilkey provides an insightful analysis of fate in *Reaping the Whirlwind* (New York: Seabury Press, 1976), 49–50.

7. Our culture has unfortunately confused the moral significance of gift giving by assuming that what is important is giving rather than receiving. As a result we have failed to pay adequate attention to the difficulty of knowing how to receive a gift. For nothing is harder than knowing how to simply accept a gift and be thankful for it. We fear the power of the gift-giver and want to do something in return so we will not be in debt. Pipkin's gift was the ability to accept gifts without assuming that he owed anyone anything in return, and also not to feel resentment that he was the one that had to receive the gifts. Of course, Pipkin's ability to receive gifts depended on his community sense that they would not have it otherwise.

For further reflections on this theme, particularly as it challenges how the commitment to equality can too easily be used to deny the importance of diversity for a good polity, see my "Community and Diversity: The Tyranny of Normality," in SP.

want to kill us. But then again, as he said, there's plenty of grass and as for turning them out or taking their does, if they're all up to his size and weight they've nothing to fear from a crowd like us. They must have seen us come. We were tired. Surely that was the time to attack us? Or while we were separated, before we began digging? But they didn't. I reckon they're more likely to be friendly than otherwise. There's only one thing that beats me. What do they stand to get from asking us to join their warren? (75)

Blackberry's logic is perfect, of course, but we shall see it leads to exactly the wrong conclusion. Fiver is convinced that they should not enter the warren, but as usual he is unable to give any reason and thus Hazel decides to follow Blackberry's advice. On entering they discover that there are some very "unnatural" aspects to the warren. It is roomy and well made with a large central room, but very few rabbits inhabit it. Those that do live there are big, but they are not, as Bigwig observes, very strong—nor do they have any fighting skill.

Even stranger is the absence of a chief rabbit, as everyone is allowed to do as he pleases.[8] Cowslip's invitation to them, for example, was made on his own initiative. They need no chief rabbit, because there is no need to worry about foxes or other enemies (elil). It seems that there is a man who kills all the rabbits' enemies and provides the rabbits with the best kind of food. They no

---

8. One of the most persistent problems with the liberal understanding of society is how to account for and legitimate authority. According to John Rawls, the primary purpose of liberalism is to make "society a cooperative venture for mutual advantage" (*A Theory of Justice* [Cambridge, MA: Harvard University Press, 1971], 4). In other words, it is the intention to supplant the need for leadership with procedural rules of fair play. The continued phenomenon of leadership in society thus can appear to the liberal only as due to the incomplete institutionalization of liberal principles. Robert Nozick is, perhaps, a clearer example of the tendency of liberalism to assume that some kind of invisible-hand explanation of state power and authority is possible. See his *Anarchy, State, and Utopia* (New York: Basic Books, 1968), 10–25.

A correlate of the liberal attempt to avoid providing an account of legitimate authority is their assumption that society can be construed as a voluntary venture. It is the function of liberal theory to convince us that we can choose our own story, that we are free from the past, that our participation in society is "voluntary." There is perhaps no better metaphor for this than Rawls's utilization of the "original position," where we are explicitly stripped of all history in an effort to have us assume the "moral point of view." Even though one can appreciate the powerful moral motivation behind Rawls's method, he fails to give an adequate account of how our social order is as much our fate as it is our destiny. As a result, liberalism can become self-deceptive, as it gives us the illusion that freedom is more a status than a task. See, for example, Richard Sennett's insightful analysis of the deceptions involved when "autonomy" is claimed to replace "authority" in *Authority* (New York: Knopf, 1980), 84–121.

longer need to hunt for their food, and they have even begun the unheard of practice of storing food underground.

Stranger yet is that stories are no longer told. To repay them for their hospitality, Hazel suggests that Dandelion, a fellow escapee from Sandleford who has a gift for telling stories, entertain everyone by telling the story of the king's lettuce.[9] It is a story of how El-ahrairah bet Prince Rainbow not only that he could steal King Darzin's lettuce, which was guarded night and day, but that he could even get the king to deliver the lettuce to Rainbow's warren. If he won the bet Prince Rainbow must let the rabbits out of the marshes to breed and make homes everywhere.

El-ahrairah's plan was to have Rabscuttle, his close friend and commander of his owsla, gain entrance to the palace by playing with some children and then being taken inside with them. Once admitted to the palace, Rabscuttle found his way to the royal storeroom and made some of the lettuce bad, so that King Darzin would fall ill after eating it. At that moment El-ahrairah arrived disguised as a physician and examined the king. He told the king that the lettuce was infected by the dreaded virus Lusepedoodle, and because the infected lettuce is particularly deadly to rabbits he advised the king to send the lettuce to his worst enemy, El-ahrairah. The king thought this was a splendid idea, so El-ahrairah had the lettuce delivered and thus freed his people from the marshes.

Now this is obviously a story to delight any rabbit, for it is a story of wit, cunning, and humor that reinforces the point that the rabbits must survive using the gifts provided to El-ahrairah by Frith. After hearing the story, however, the rabbits of the warren of freedom were less than enthusiastic.

> "Very nice," said Cowslip. He seemed to be searching for something more to say, but then repeated, "Yes, very nice. An unusual tale."
>
> "But he must know it, surely?" muttered Blackberry to Hazel.
>
> "I always think these traditional stories retain a lot of charm," said another of the rabbits, "especially when they're told in the real old-fashioned spirit."
>
> "Yes," said Strawberry [another rabbit of Cowslip's warren]. "Conviction,

---

9. The stories of El-ahrairah are not only told, but told at the right time. Thus, the story of the "Trial of El-ahrairah," which involves El-ahrairah's use of other animals, is told as they are beginning to develop Watership Down, that is, just before Hazel's care of Kehaar, the wounded gull. Adams seems to be suggesting that good communities not only know how to tell truthful stories truthfully, but also when to tell them.

that's what it needs. You really have to *believe* in El-ahrairah and Prince Rainbow, don't you? Then all the rest follows."

"Don't say anything, Bigwig," whispered Hazel: for Bigwig was scuffling his paws indignantly. "You can't force them to like it if they don't. Let's wait and see what they can do themselves." Aloud, he said, "Our stories haven't changed in generations, you know. After all, we haven't changed ourselves. Our lives have been the same as our fathers' and their fathers' before them. Things are different here. We realize that, and we think your new ideas and ways are very exciting. We're all wondering what kind of things you tell stories about."

"Well, we don't tell the old stories very much," said Cowslip. "Our stories and poems are mostly about our own lives here. . . . El-ahrairah doesn't really mean much to us. Not that your friend's story wasn't very charming," he added hastily.

"El-ahrairah is a trickster," said Buckthorn, "and rabbits will always need tricks."

"No," said a new voice from the further end of the hall, beyond Cowslip. "Rabbits need dignity and, above all, the will to accept their fate." (108)

The speaker was Silverweed, the poet of this strange warren, who recited a poem that ended as follows: "I am here, Lord Frith, I am running through the long grass. O take me with you, dropping behind the woods, Far away, to the heart of light, and the silence. For I am ready to give you my breath, my life, The shining circle of the sun, the sun and the rabbit" (110). As Silverweed recited his poem, Fiver became increasingly nervous and finally caused a stir by bolting out of the warren. Hazel joined him and Fiver again emphasized that they must leave because Silverweed spoke the truth for this warren—that rabbits in such a warren must learn to accept death. Hazel and Bigwig ignored this warning, however, since they continued to think that the warren might make a good permanent home.

Their hopes were quickly dashed when the next morning Bigwig was caught in a snare prepared by the farmer who protected the rabbits. Only by an extraordinary effort were they able to chew through the stake holding the snare and free Bigwig. Even that would not have been possible if Pipkin's small size had not allowed him to get down to where the peg was narrower. Though in bad shape, Bigwig immediately wanted to turn on Cowslip and the others for leading them into such a warren. Fiver restrained him, however, by constructing the story of this strange warren.

He suggested that the warren was the result of the farmer's realization that he did not have to keep rabbits in hutches if he fed and looked after some wild ones. He would snare a few from time to time, but not enough to frighten them away. As a result of the farmer's plan, the rabbits grew big and forgot the ways of wild rabbits. They also forgot El-ahrairah, for they had no use for tricks and cunning. Moreover, they had no need for a chief rabbit:

> For a Chief Rabbit must be El-ahrairah to his warren and keep them from death: and here there was no death but one, and what Chief Rabbit could have an answer to that? Instead, Frith sent them strange singers, beautiful and sick like oak apples, like robins' pincushions on the wild rose. And since they could not bear the truth, these singers, who might in some other place have been wise, were squeezed under the terrible weight of the warren's secret until they gulped out fine folly—about dignity and acquiescence, and anything else that could make believe that the rabbit loved the shining wire. But one strict rule they had; oh, yes, the strictest. No one must ever ask where another rabbit was and anyone who asked "Where?"—except in song or a poem— must be silenced. To say "Where?" was bad enough, but to speak openly of the wires—that was intolerable. For that they would scratch and kill. (123–24)

Because they could not ask where anyone was, they also lost the most precious skills rabbits needed to survive: cooperation and friendship. One could not risk getting too close to another rabbit, for that one might be the next to die. Friendship implies mutual giving of aid, but these rabbits had accepted a social system that required them to look after themselves first.[10] Cowslip had extended invitations to strangers only because that increased the odds that he himself would not be caught in the wire. Deception thus became the rule for this society, since the truth would require a concern for and trust in one another that these "free" rabbits were no longer able to give. It was no wonder that such rabbits were not interested in hearing about the adventures of Hazel and his friends or even those of El-ahrairah, for who "wants to hear about brave deeds when he's ashamed of his own, and who likes an open, honest tale from someone he's deceiving" (124).

Finally taking Fiver's advice, Hazel and the others decided to leave immediately. However, just as they were leaving, Strawberry, whose doe had recently

---

10. Contemporary political and ethical theory seems to ignore entirely the nature and social significance of friendship and other special relations such as the family. As a result we are left devoid of any language that can help articulate the significance of friendship and the family for our personal and political existence.

been snared, asked to be allowed to join their company. Just as the others were about to say no, Hazel simply said, "You can come with us" (126). Thus, still homeless but in the beginnings of community, they accept a stranger even though he was a former enemy. As we shall see, their willingness to take the stranger into their midst becomes the very means of their survival.

3. Gifts, Strangers, and Community

By attending to the stories in *Watership Down* I have tried to illuminate the relation between narrative and social ethics. For whatever else can be said about Sandleford and Cowslip's warren, their inability to maintain the traditions of El-ahrairah resulted in the corruption of rabbit community and nature.[11] There is, in addition, a close connection between the ability to tell the stories of El-ahrairah and the capacity to recognize and use gifts that often come in the form of friends. To better appreciate this connection we need to pay closer attention to the character of Hazel's warren, Watership Down.

The scraggly band of rabbits who escaped from Sandleford were changed by their journey. The demands of their journey gave them not only renewed appreciation for the significance of El-ahrairah for their lives, but they learned to trust and depend on one another. They had become tenacious in their struggle for survival, and now understood one another and worked together:

11. Alasdair MacIntyre has argued that our culture lacks a moral scheme that might provide "a vision" of man's true end, of the relation of his empirical nature to his essential nature. "It is a tacit assumption of secular, liberal, pluralist culture, of the culture of modernity, that to a rational man no such vision is now available, because we can have no rationally defensible concept of man's true end or of an essential human nature. Consequently, what we inherit from the varied and different strands of our past is a collection of fragments, of moral premises detached from the contexts in which they were once at home, survivals now available for independent moral assertion from a variety of moral points of view. It is this that makes moral argument appear to consist merely of the clash of bare assertion and counterassertion, marked by what is only the appearance of argument, so that nonrational persuasion seems to be the only way for an agent to resolve the issues in his own mind" ("How Virtues Become Vices," in *Evaluation and Explanation in the Biomedical Sciences,* ed. H. T. Engelhardt and Stuart Spicker [Boston: Reidel Publishing, 1974], 100). See also MacIntyre's "An Essay Prepared for the National Commission for the Protection of Human Subjects of Biomedical and Behavior Research on the Subject of How to Identify Ethical Principles," *The Belmont Report* (Washington, DC: DHEW Publications, 1978), article 10, pp. 1–20, 41. From this perspective the commitment of liberal political and ethical theory to the autonomy of the individual is not so much a rational necessity as it is the only practical alternative. The problem with such a strategy, however, is that it only leads us further away from confronting our situation, as we fail to see the narratives that in fact constitute our "autonomy."

"The truth about the warren had been a grim shock. They had come closer together, relying on and valuing each other's capacities. They knew now that it was on these and nothing else that their lives depended, and they were not going to waste anything they possessed between them. In spite of Hazel's efforts beside the snare, there was not one of them who had not turned sick at heart to think that Bigwig was dead and wondered, like Blackberry, what would become of them now. Without Hazel, Blackberry, Buckthorn, and Pipkin, Bigwig would have died. Without himself he would have died, for which else, of them all, would not have stopped running after such punishment? There was no more questioning of Bigwig's strength, Fiver's insight, Blackberry's wits or Hazel's authority" (129).

Such a community depends on the ability to trust in the gifts each brings to the group's shared existence. They must in a certain sense "be out of control," often dependent on luck to help them over their difficulties. "Luck" can be a very misleading term; more properly, it is fate put to good use by the imaginative skills acquired through a truthful tradition.[12] This is perhaps best exemplified in the story of the "Black Rabbit of Inlé."

3.1 How Gifts Make Us Safe

The story of the Black Rabbit of Inlé is told at the most dangerous moment in the lives of the rabbits who constitute the Watership warren. It is a time when their lives hang in the balance, a time when they will be called on to take chances that few rabbits are willing to take. For they must secure does from Efrafa if their warren is to have a future. Bigwig insists that the story of the Black Rabbit be told, even though he will soon enter Efrafa itself in hopes of convincing some does to escape.

The story begins with King Darzin, tired of being constantly tricked and outwitted by El-ahrairah, finding an effective way to stop the rabbits from

---

12. For one of the few attempts to provide a philosophically adequate account of luck, see Bernard Williams, "Moral Luck," *Aristotelian Society Supplementary* 50 (1976): 114–35. Williams makes an important distinction between luck that is intrinsic to my project and luck that is extrinsic, but points out that knowing how to make such a distinction in respect to our own lives is extremely difficult. He also rightly criticizes Rawls's claim that the guiding principle of a rational individual is to act so that he need never blame himself for how things turn out. For such a view "implicitly ignores the obvious fact that what one does and the sort of life one leads condition one's later desires and judgments: the standpoint of that retrospective judge who will be my later self will be the product of my earlier choices" (130–31). In other words, Rawls fails to see that my "autonomy" depends exactly on my being able to accept responsibility for what I have not, strictly speaking, "done."

leaving their warrens. The rabbits are beginning to die of starvation and disease because they can silflay only with the greatest difficulty. El-ahrairah concludes that his only hope is to journey far away to the cold and lifeless world of the Black Rabbit of Inlé. It is his plan to bargain with the Black Rabbit to free his people.

We cannot take the time to speculate about the ontological status of the Black Rabbit, but we should know that he is fear and everlasting darkness. Though a rabbit himself, the Black Rabbit hates the rabbits and wants their destruction. Even in his darkness he serves Lord Frith by doing his appointed task, which is "to bring about what must be" (274). As it is said, "We come into the world and we have to go: but we do not go merely to serve the turn of one enemy or another. If that were so, we would all be destroyed in a day. We go by the will of Black Rabbit of Inlé and only by his will. And though that will seems hard and bitter to us all, yet in his way he is our protector, for he knows Frith's promise to the rabbits and he will avenge any rabbit who may chance to be destroyed without the consent of himself. Anyone who has seen a game-keeper's gibbet knows what the Black Rabbit can bring down on elil [foxes] who think they will do what they will" (274–75).

El-ahrairah, with Rabscuttle, undertakes the arduous journey to the warren of the Black Rabbit so that he can offer his life in return for the lives of the rabbits. But the Black Rabbit points out that El-ahrairah's life is his already so he has nothing with which to bargain. El-ahrairah tries to trick the Black Rabbit into taking his life by enticing him into several contests, but El-ahrairah succeeds only in losing his whiskers, tail, and ears; finally he even tries to contract the dreaded white blindness. The Black Rabbit, although still completely unmoved by El-ahrairah's suffering, suddenly declares that "this is a cold warren: a bad place for the living and no place at all for warm hearts and brave spirits. You are a nuisance to me. Go home. I myself will save your people. Do not have the impertinence to ask me when. There is no time here. They are already saved" (283).

Because of El-ahrairah's weakened condition it took many months for him and Rabscuttle to find their way home. Their wits were confused, and they survived only by other animals giving them direction and shelter. After finding their way back to the warren at last, they discover that all their old companions have been replaced by their children. Rabscuttle, inquiring about the whereabouts of Loosestrife, one of the captains of owsla during the fighting, was asked:

"What fighting?"

"The fighting against King Darzin," replied Rabscuttle.

"Here, do me a favor, old fellow, will you?" said the buck. "That fighting—I wasn't born when it finished."

"But surely you know the owsla captains who were?" said Rabscuttle.

"I wouldn't be seen dead with them," said the buck. "What, that white-whiskered old bunch? What do we want to know about them?"

"What they did," said Rabscuttle.

"That war lark, old fellow?" said the first buck. "That's all finished now. That's got nothing to do with us."

"If this Loosestrife fought King What's-His-Name, that's his business," said one of the does. "It's not our business, is it?"

"It was all a very wicked thing," said another doe. "Shameful, really. If nobody fought in wars, there wouldn't be any, would there? But you can't get old rabbits to see that." (284–85)

El-ahrairah did not try to respond to this conversation, but rather found a place under a nut bush to watch the sun sink into the horizon. In the failing light he suddenly realized that Lord Frith was close beside him.

> "Are you angry, El-ahrairah?" asked Lord Frith.
>
> "No, my lord," replied El-ahrairah, "I am not angry. But I have learned that with creatures one loves, suffering is not the only thing for which one may pity them. A rabbit who does not know when a gift has made him safe is poorer than a slug, even though he may think otherwise himself." (285)

Lord Frith then gave El-ahrairah a new tail and whiskers and some new ears that had a little starlight in them, but not enough to give away a clever thief like El-ahrairah.

Hazel's warren is Adams's attempt to show what kind of community might result in a group of rabbits that have learned that a gift has made them safe. But the recognition that their lives depend on luck causes them to work all the harder to make the necessities of their lives their destiny. Thus after a long journey they come to a particularly lonely and well-protected down that Fiver feels is the right place for their home. " 'O Frith on the hills!' cried Dandelion. 'He must have made it, for us!' 'He may have made it, but Fiver thought of it for us,' answered Hazel" (133).

Any community that has a story such as the "Black Rabbit of Inlé" in its tradition can never assume that it "has control" of its existence.[13] As much as Hazel and his companions desire a warren they can call home, they know also that they can never cease being on a journey. When rabbits yearn for and try to secure complete safety, their nature is perverted. They can only continue to rely on their wit and their courage and each other. Bigwig is particularly interesting in this respect, since we see him learn to trust not only in his strength and bravery but in his wit and the aid of others—particularly those who seem to have little to contribute.

3.2 Tradition, Nature, and Strangers

Often, claims that tradition is central for political and social theory are meant to have a primarily conservative effect. We are supposed to be convinced that we must do as our fathers did if we are to preserve those values we hold dear, or that society is too complex for planned change because such change always has effects that we have not anticipated. Those who would change society too often feel the only alternative to the conservative option is to find a rational basis for social organization that is tradition-free. As a result they become captured by a tradition that is more tyrannical because it has the pretense of absolute rationality. In contrast, I am suggesting that substantive traditions are not at odds with reason but are the bearers of rationality and innovation. The establishment of the warren at Watership Down is particularly interesting in this regard, because here we see tradition opening up new ways to distinguish the "natural from the unnatural" and to turn the stranger into a friend.

For example, among rabbits it has always been assumed that digging warrens is does' work. The rabbits that established Watership Down, however, were all bucks. Hazel argued that in the warren of "freedom" many things the rabbits did were "unnatural," but "they'd altered what rabbits do naturally because they thought they could do better. And if they altered their ways, so

---

13. It may be that the popularity of *Watership Down* denotes a change of consciousness in our culture. For it was just a few years ago that the Kennedy administration represented the "can do" mentality of our society. If we have a problem, then it is bound to be solvable by well-trained people using the amazing technology developed by our scientists. However, since then we have found ourselves brought to a halt by our lack of oil. Our solutions seem to cause as many problems as they solve. Ecologically we are damned if we do and damned if we do not. In other words, it may be that we identify with rabbits because we suddenly feel that like them we do not have control of our world. But even more disturbing we do not know how to get control of our world, nor are we sure how to live in such a world.

can we if we like" (138). Blackberry, following the example of how the warren of the snares was dug around tree roots to allow for the large common room, began to dig amid some birch trees. Soon all the bucks followed his example.

It is important to note, however, that Hazel does not assume that rabbit nature is infinitely malleable. As we will see later, Efrafa is condemned because it is an "unnatural society" led by a fierce leader, General Woundwort, who is so unrabbitlike he will even fight a dog. In Efrafa, Woundwort has attempted to organize his rabbits so that they will feed at a certain time, rest at a certain time, breed at a certain time, and so on. Nature has its revenge, and rabbits in this strange warren actually die of old age, and overpopulation causes does to reabsorb their litters. For long ago El-ahrairah made a bargain with Frith that rabbits should not be born dead or unwanted; thus if there was little chance of a decent life it was a doe's privilege to take them back into her body unborn.[14]

The other crucial aspect of Watership Down is that this community continues to remain open to the stranger. Soon after finishing some of the runs they find a bloodied rabbit near death. As they tend to him they realize that it is Captain Holly of the Sandleford owsla. He tells them that Sandleford has indeed been razed by men and that only a few, like himself, were able to escape. Such destruction is almost impossible for rabbits to comprehend, "for all other elil do what they have to do and Frith moves them as he moves us. They live on the earth and they need food. Men will never rest till they've spoiled the earth and destroyed the animals" (157). Holly, even though he is a sign of this terrible and incomprehensible evil, is allowed to join Watership Down. In doing so he apologizes to Bigwig for attacking him as he tried to leave Sandleford: "It wasn't I who tried to arrest you—that was another rabbit, long, long ago" (166). He has been changed through his suffering, and as such becomes a crucial member of Hazel's warren.

---

14. I suspect the continual return of natural law is best explained as an indication that our "nature" seldom tells us what we ought to do but often tells us what we are doing is inappropriate. Thus natural law is primarily a test, as the "principles" of natural law are means to sensitize us to ways our nature can and may be distorted. The traditional claim that the Christian life is in harmony with natural law is a promissory note that Christian existence stands ready to be challenged by "nature." It has been a mistake, however, to assume that Christian ethics can therefore begin on the basis of clearly articulated "principles" of natural law. For the "principles" of natural law are known only through the articulation of a positive tradition. [For Hauerwas's constructive understanding of the role of the natural law, see "Natural Law, Tragedy and Theological Ethics" (1975) in *TT*, and "The Truth about God: The Decalogue as Condition for Truthful Speech" (1998) in *STT*.]

It is one thing to accept an enemy who is like yourself, but it is quite another to help those with whom you share no kinship at all. But that is what Hazel does, for just as El-ahrairah had been helped by other animals, so he helps a mouse escape a kestrel by letting him hide in one of the warren's runs. Hazel's friends are offended by this, but Hazel explains that in their situation they cannot "afford to waste anything that might do us good. We're in a strange place we don't know much about and we need friends. Now, elil can't do us good, obviously, but there are many creatures that aren't elil—birds, mice, yonil [hedgehogs] and so on. Rabbits don't usually have much to do with them, but their enemies are our enemies, for the most part. I think we ought to do all we can to make these creatures friendly. It might turn out to be well worth the trouble" (169). And soon another mouse tells them where to find the grass rabbits favor most.

Even more astounding is Hazel's rescue of Kehaar, a gull that had been injured by a cat so it could not fly. Condemned to the ground, he faced certain death, but Hazel offers him hospitality in the warren. The rabbits even undertake an activity degrading to rabbits to ensure his survival: digging for worms so that Kehaar might eat. Soon, however, Kehaar and Bigwig become fast friends, because it is apparent they share the same aggressive spirit toward life. Moreover, as we shall see, Kehaar proves invaluable in helping them secure the does from Efrafa.

For Hazel knew that as soon as they became reasonably safe the bucks would become lonely for does. While rabbits tend not to be romantic in matters of love, they have a strong will to perpetuate their own kind. Without does, no matter how good a life they established for themselves at Watership Down, nothing would matter. Rabbits survive by their dogged refusal to let the dangers of their life stop them from carrying on—which is nowhere more centrally embodied than in their insistence on having and rearing kittens. For it is only through their children that the tradition can be carried on. To fail to have kittens would be tantamount to rejecting the tradition and would symbolize a loss of confidence in their ability to live out that tradition.

As soon as Kehaar is well Hazel asks him to act as their air force and search the countryside for does. He finds two groups of does: some hutch rabbits at the nearby Nuthanger Farm and at the huge warren of Efrafa some distance away. Hazel chooses Holly to lead a group to Efrafa to see if they might be willing, because of overcrowding, to allow some does to leave. However, they find that not only is that not possible, but that Efrafa represents an even more frightening political alternative than either Sandleford or the warren of freedom.

4. Leadership, Community, and the Unexpected

Though the differences among the communities in *Watership Down* are pronounced, the most dramatic contrast is certainly between Efrafa and Cowslip's warren, the former being completely organized with each rabbit belonging to a "Mark" with a captain who controlled every movement, and the latter being characterized by almost complete freedom. The former was led by a fierce and dominant rabbit, and the latter had no chief rabbit at all. But in spite of their differences, in neither were the stories of El-ahrairah told. In Efrafa, Bigwig discovers that does recite poetry, such as:

Long ago The Yellowhammer sang, high on the thorn.
He sang near a litter that the doe brought out to play,
He sang in the wind and the kittens played below.
Their time slipped by all under the elder bloom.
But the bird flew away and now my heart is dark
And time will never play in the fields again. . . .

The frost is falling, the frost falls into my body.
My nostrils, my ears are torpid under the frost.
The swift will come in the spring, crying "News! News!
Does, dig new holes and flow with milk for your litters."
I shall not hear. The embryos return
Into my dulled body. Across my sleep
There runs a wire fence to imprison the wind
I shall never feel the wind blowing again. (323)

The loss of the narratives of El-ahrairah at Efrafa has also resulted in a transformation of the position of chief rabbit. For General Woundwort is unlike any rabbit ever seen. As Holly described him, "He was a fighting animal—fierce as a rat or a dog. He fought because he actually felt safer fighting than running. He was brave, all right. But it wasn't natural; and that's why it was bound to finish him in the end. He was trying to do something that Frith never meant any rabbit to do" (467).

As a kitten Woundwort had seen his father killed by a man and his mother wounded and as a result eaten by a fox. He was rescued by a man who fed him so well he grew huge and strong. At the first opportunity he escaped, took over a small warren by killing any that would challenge his rule, and then united by force his warren with others close by to form Efrafa. In order to secure Efrafa he would not allow any further runs to be dug or the warren extended in any way: to do so might attract elil.

Though Woundwort had immense personal power, his only object seems to have been to create a warren that would be free from the tragedy of his parents. He not only organized the warren into Marks, but he gathered around him the bravest and most ferocious rabbits and made each of them live only to gain his special favor. These rabbits were sent out on periodic patrols so that any elil in the area could be reported and that strange rabbits, who might unwittingly attract elil, could be killed or captured. For Efrafa's safety depended on seeing that the unexpected did not upset their defenses. The primary rule for the owsla had become "Anything out of the ordinary is a possible source of danger" and must thus be reported immediately (338).

It would be a mistake, therefore, to think Woundwort an evil tyrant, for he was more like Dostoyevski's Grand Inquisitor. Nor is there any doubt that his leadership produced results, for Efrafa was remarkably safe. The only difficulty was that his followers lost the ability to think and make decisions for themselves. As a result, they increasingly had to bring every matter for judgment to Woundwort himself.

The kind of leadership that Hazel provides is obviously in marked contrast to Woundwort. Although he cares no less than Woundwort for his warren, he is prepared to take the risk of depending on others for the governance of the warren. In fact, Hazel was never formally installed as chief rabbit, he just became chief rabbit because he seemed to know how to make the decisions that made best use of everyone's talents and he made everyone face up to the necessities of their situation. As they left Sandleford, for example, they became hopelessly lost and some wanted to simply quit or go back. It was Hazel, as lost as the rest, who said,

> "Look, I know there's been some trouble, but the best thing will be to try to forget it. This is a bad place, but we'll soon get out of it."
>
> "Do you really think we will?" asked Dandelion.
>
> "If you'll follow me now," replied Hazel desperately, "I'll have you out of it by sunrise." (62)

Note that Hazel's primary gift is his willingness to accept responsibility for making the decision when it is not clear what it is that should be done. Moreover, he is willing to pay the price for such decisions; thus it is he who refuses to leave Pipkin behind at the stream on the grounds that "I got Pipkin into this and I'm going to get him out" (44). Other than this he lacks any characteristic that should make him the chief rabbit: he is not as strong as Bigwig, lacks Fiver's insight, and is not as clever as Blackberry. All he is able to do is say "Let's do this," and then live with the consequences. After finally making it through the night they reach some hills and Blackberry says, "Oh, Hazel, I was so tired and confused, I actually began to wonder whether you knew where you were going. I could hear you in the heather, saying 'Not far now' and it was annoying me. . . . I should know better. Frithrah, you're what I call a chief rabbit" (64).

Of course, as a leader Hazel does have one advantage as he is the rare leader who has the courage to listen to the seer. Listening to seers is tricky business and is safely done only in a community on which the seer's insight depends. At one point, when Hazel decides against Fiver's advice to be as heroic as Bigwig and raid the Nuthanger Farm for the hutch does, the whole affair almost ends in disaster. He was simply not cut out to be a hero. His leadership and his use of Fiver's insight depends on his willingness to rely on the other's strength. A leader like Woundwort simply cannot understand this kind of leadership. Thus in the final confrontation between Efrafa and Watership Down he is shocked to discover that Bigwig is not the chief rabbit.

Note that Hazel is not only an exceptional chief rabbit, but that it takes an exceptional community to have a chief rabbit like Hazel. This is nowhere better exemplified than in the decision to raid Efrafa to get the does. After Holly's failed attempt to secure the does peacefully from Efrafa it was clear to Hazel that their only hope was to get the does by a raid. His plan was to have Bigwig join Efrafa as a stray rabbit and then with the help of Kehaar to escape with some willing does during a silflay. Hazel's problem was that he did not know how to get the group back to Watership Down without Woundwort's patrols overtaking them. But the incompleteness of the plan did not prevent them from following Hazel; they would simply have to trust in luck.

To make a very complicated story short, Bigwig was able to successfully join Efrafa and secure the cooperation of some does in an escape attempt. However, the escape was complicated by an unexpected thunderstorm, which they were nonetheless able to turn to their advantage, and they were aided by an attack by Kehaar. Their escape, however, was successful only because Blackberry discovered a boat and saw how to use it.

During their march back to Watership Down an event occurred that graphically highlights the difference between Efrafa and Watership Down. In spite of the difficulty that escape from Efrafa involved, Bigwig took the time to also rescue Blackavar, a rabbit who had been severely beaten by Woundwort's guards for trying to escape earlier. As they proceeded home Blackavar warned them that they needed to be particularly careful of fox in a certain area, since he had learned that fox were often there through his patrols with General Woundwort. However, Hazel decided that, because of the risk of General Woundwort catching them, they needed to go through the area, and as a result a fox got one of the does that had come with them from Efrafa. Later when Bigwig suggested to Blackavar that they should have taken his advice, he was shocked to discover that Blackavar had forgotten he had ever given the warning. Hyzenthlay, a doe from Efrafa, was able to explain why:

> "In Efrafa if a rabbit gave advice and the advice wasn't accepted, he immediately forgot it and so did everyone else. Blackavar thought what Hazel decided; and whether it turned out later to be right or wrong was all the same. His own advice had never been given."
>
> "I can't believe that," said Bigwig. "Efrafa! Ants led by a dog! But we're not in Efrafa now. Has he really forgotten that he warned us?"
>
> "Probably he really has. But whether or not, you'd never get him to admit that he warned you or to listen while you told him he'd been right. He could no more do that than pass hraka underground."
>
> "But you're an Efrafan. Do you think like that, too?"
>
> "I'm a doe," said Hyzenthlay. (390)[15]

It was thus that the rabbits of Watership Down learned how extraordinary the form of leadership was that they had evolved. Hazel was remarkable for his willingness to learn from all the others and for his ability to see that Watership Down depended on all their gifts. But even more remarkable was the character of their community manifested in their ability to sustain a leader who could make mistakes and yet remain chief rabbit. Security could not be bought by placing absolute faith in any chief rabbit, no matter how talented or brave. Rather, their security depended on their willingness to trust one an-

---

15. *Watership Down* is obviously not a book that contemporary feminists will find very satisfactory. However, it is at least worth observing that Hyzenthlay's affirmation of being a doe made her the freest of the rabbits at Efrafa. For every society corrupts us by tempting us to identify with the ends of the society in order to do good as a means for personal aggrandizement. Those who are the "outs" in a society often have the best perspective to appreciate the coercive aspects of a social order, since they are not easily tempted to accept the stated idealizations of their society.

other with their lives. For only then could their various talents be coordinated in service for the community.

4.1 The Insufficiency of Power as Coercion

It is well-known that Stalin responded to Pius XII's condemnation with the taunting question about how many divisions had the pope. Most assume that Stalin's point is well taken, for without divisions the power of the church counts for nothing. Yet in spite of all appearances to the contrary, Stalin's response masks the fundamental weakness of his position. A leadership that cannot stand the force of truth must always rely on armies. But a leadership so constituted must always respond to the slightest provocation that might reveal its essential weakness.

So Woundwort could not afford to let the successful escape of the does go unnoticed. His power depended on never being embarrassed, and the rabbits of Watership Down had done just that.

> "And fools we look now," said Woundwort. "Make no mistake about that. Vervain will tell you what the Marks are saying—that Campion was chased into the ditch by the white bird and Thlayli [Bigwig's alias while in Efrafal] called down lightning from the sky and Frith knows what besides."
>
> "The best thing," said old Snowdrop, "will be to say as little about it as possible. Let it blow over. They've got short memories." (416)

But Woundwort could not settle for that, and he made plans to send out patrols to find Watership Down. As he said, "I told Thlayli I'd kill him myself. He may have forgotten that but I haven't."

Hazel, confronting Woundwort on such a patrol, tried to make peace.

> "You're General Woundwort, aren't you? I've come to talk to you."
>
> "Did Thlayli send you?" asked Woundwort.
>
> "I'm a friend of Thlayli," replied the rabbit. "I've come to ask why you're here and what it is you want."
>
> "Were you on the riverbank in the rain?" said Woundwort.
>
> "Yes, I was."
>
> "What was left unfinished there will be finished now," said Woundwort. "We are going to destroy you."
>
> "You won't find it easy," replied the other. "You'll take fewer rabbits home than you brought. We should both do better to come to terms."
>
> "Very well," said Woundwort. "These are the terms. You will give back all

the does who ran from Efrafa and you will hand over the deserters Thlayli and Blackavar to my owsla."

"No, we can't agree to that. I've come to suggest something altogether different and better for us both. A rabbit has two ears; a rabbit has two eyes, two nostrils. Our two warrens ought to be like that. They ought to be together—not fighting. We ought to make other warrens between us—start one between here and Efrafa, with rabbits from both sides. You wouldn't lose by that, you'd gain. We both would. A lot of your rabbits are unhappy now and it's all you can do to control them, but with this plan you'd soon see a difference. Rabbits have enough enemies as it is. They ought not to make more among themselves. A mating between free, independent warrens—what do you say?"

At that moment, in the sunset on Watership Down, there was offered to General Woundwort the opportunity to show whether he was really the leader of vision and genius which he believed himself to be, or whether he was no more than a tyrant with the courage and cunning of a pirate. For one beat of his pulse the lame rabbit's idea shone clearly before him. He grasped it and realized what it meant. The next, he had pushed it away from him. . . .

"I haven't time to sit here talking nonsense," said Woundwort. "You're in no position to bargain with us. There's nothing more to be said. Thistle, go back and tell Captain Vervain I want everyone up here at once."

"And this rabbit, sir," asked Campion. "Shall I kill him?"

"No," replied Woundwort. "Since they've sent him to ask our terms, he'd better take them back.—Go and tell Thlayli that if the does aren't waiting outside your warren, with him and Blackavar, by the time I get down there, I'll tear the throat out of every buck in the place by ni-Frith tomorrow." (421–22)

I cannot take the time to provide the details of Woundwort's attack, but Hazel and the rabbits of Watership Down were able to defeat him. They were able to do it because Bigwig used cunning as well as his strength and was able to fight Woundwort in a place where he could not make full use of his bulk; Hazel, taking a cue from Dandelion's telling of "Rowsby Woof and the Fairy Wogdog" (a story of El-ahrairah's tricking a dog into letting him steal the cabbage he was supposed to guard for his master), unleashed a dog from Nuthanger Farm that drove off Woundwort for the last time. (We are later told, however, that his body was never found. As a result he was said to live alone as a killer of elil. To this day does threaten their kittens by saying that if they do not behave the General will get them.)

4.2 Peace

Peace, as has often been pointed out, is not the absence of disorder and cannot be built on injustice. Peace is built on truth, for order that is built on lies must resort ultimately to coercion. It is, therefore, remarkable that peace seems to have come to Watership Down. Campion, one of Woundwort's former Mark captains, has now become chief rabbit of Efrafa. Hazel's original peace proposal is put into effect and a new warren made up of Efrafans and Downers is established between the two warrens. Hazel, never one to overlook a good thing, even incorporates some of the advantages of Efrafa, such as hiding run openings.

Perhaps even more significant is a suggestion that someday there might be peace between humans and rabbits. In the process of releasing the dog, Hazel was attacked by a cat and saved by a little girl at the farm. She saw that his wounds were cared for by a veterinarian, who released Hazel not far from Watership Down. It is not much, but it is something.

A yet more profound peace awaits Hazel, because a few springs later, as Hazel is dozing in his burrow, a stranger with ears shining with strange silver light comes and invites Hazel to join his owsla. Thus Hazel's part in the story ends, but his life has contributed to the further telling of the story. One lovely spring day shortly before his death, he and Silver come across one of the does of the warren telling her litter a story:

> "So after they had swum the river, El-ahrairah led his people on in the dark, through a wild, lonely place. Some of them were afraid, but he knew the way and in the morning he brought them safely to some green fields, very beautiful, with good, sweet grass. And here they found a warren; a warren that was bewitched. All the rabbits in this warren were in the power of a wicked spell. They wore shining collars round their necks and sang like the birds and some of them could fly. But for all they looked so fine, their hearts were dark and tharn [forlorn]. So then El-ahrairah's people said, 'Ah, see, these are the wonderful rabbits of Prince Rainbow. They are like princes themselves. We will live with them and become princes, too.'
>
> "But Frith came to Rabscuttle in a dream and warned him that the warren was enchanted. And he dug into the ground to find where the spell was buried. Deep he dug, and hard was the search, but at last he found that wicked spell and dragged it out. So they all fled from it, but it turned into a great rat and flew at El-ahrairah. Then El-ahrairah fought the rat, up and

down, and at last he held it, pinned under his claws, and it turned into a great white bird which spoke to him and blessed him."

"I seem to know this story," whispered Hazel. "But I can't remember where I've heard it." (470–71)

But at least as long as the story was told, his children would know that a gift had made them safe.

5. Are Rabbits Relevant to Christian Social Ethics?

I have reached the end of my tale (no pun intended) and some may feel that I have failed to make my case. But remember I have told the story of the rabbits only to illustrate and illuminate my ten theses for the reform of Christian social ethics. The story was not meant to demonstrate that the theses must be accepted. That must await more direct theological and philosophical arguments.

Even allowing such a qualification, you may feel that the story is less than illuminating, because the life of rabbits is so discontinuous with our life. After all, rabbits, even the extraordinary rabbits of *Watership Down,* have no complex economic interaction, they do not form political parties, they do not invent complex forms of technology or machinery. They are simply too unlike us even to illustrate my case.

Without trying to claim a strong continuity between rabbits and us, I think at least the suggestion that we, no less than rabbits, depend on narratives to guide us has been made. And this is particularly important to Christians, because they also claim that their lives are formed by the story of a prince. Like El-ahrairah, our prince was defenseless against those who would rule the world with violence. He had a power, however, that the world knew not. For he insisted that we could form our lives together by trusting in truth and love to banish the fears that create enmity and discord. To be sure, we have often been unfaithful to his story, but that is no reason for us to think it is an unrealistic demand. Rather, it means we must challenge ourselves to be the kind of community where such a story can be told and manifested by a people formed in accordance with it—for if you believe that Jesus is the messiah of Israel, then "everything else follows, doesn't it?"

Further Reading
"Jesus and the Social Embodiment of the Peaceable Kingdom" (1983), essay 6 in
    this volume

"Self-Deception and Autobiography" (1974), essay 10 in this volume

"Vision, Stories, and Character" (1973, 2001), essay 8 in this volume

"From System to Story" (1977), in *TT*

"The Gesture of a Truthful Story" (1985), in *CET*

"A Tale of Two Stories: On Being a Christian and a Texan" (1981), in *CET*

"A Child's Dying" (1990), in *NS*

"Courage Exemplified" (1993), essay 14 in this volume

10. Self-Deception and Autobiography: Reflections on Speer's *Inside the Third Reich* (1974) *with David B. Burrell*

This early essay emphasizes the importance of moral skills for combating self-deception. Using the life of Albert Speer as an exemplar of the problem of self-deception, Hauerwas argues for the importance of developing skills of truthfulness. One reason Speer cannot see what he has done in a truthful manner is the poverty of the narrative account he gives of his actions. Inadequate stories cannot help but foster self-deception, whereas true stories are those with power adequate to check the endemic tendency toward self-deception. The saving narrative of the Christian gospel trains us to accept the limits of our own abilities to be truthful, and thus it must be a story that is continually discomforting. It is a hard and painful discipline, but it cannot be avoided if Christians wish to live lives free of self-deception.

1. Introduction

This essay brings together two interests: the relationship of philosophy of mind to ethics and the challenge of Auschwitz for persons who intend to be Christian. Any analysis of Speer's autobiography necessarily joins these interests, for *Inside the Third Reich* offers a paradigm illustration of the connection between self-deception and cooperation with murder. The argument structuring this essay shows how our ability to know what we are up to and live authentically depends on our capacity to avoid self-deception. We cannot hope to avoid an inveterate tendency to self-deception, however, unless we work at developing the skills required to articulate the shape of our individual and social engagements, or forms of life. At the heart of such skills lies a practiced eye and ear for the basic images and stories that provide our actions with direction and our lives with a sense.

[From *TT* © 1977 by University of Notre Dame Press. Used by permission. This essay was coauthored with David Burrell.]

Contrary to our dominant presumptions, we are seldom conscious of what we are doing or who we are. We choose to stay ignorant of certain engagements with the world, for to put them all together often asks too much of us and sometimes threatens the more enjoyable engagements. We profess sincerity and normally try to abide by that profession, yet we neglect to acquire the very skills that will test that profession of sincerity against our current performance. On the contrary, we deliberately allow certain engagements to go unexamined, quite aware that areas left unaccountable tend to cater to self-interest. As a result of that inertial policy, the condition of self-deception becomes the rule rather than the exception in our lives, and often in the measure that we are trying to be honest and sincere. Sobering as this fact is, however, it does not license a wholesale charge of hypocrisy. Self-deception remains more subtle.

Some of our self-deceptions, moreover, have more destructive results than others. Auschwitz stands as a symbol of one extreme to which our self-deception can lead. For the complicity of Christians with Auschwitz did not begin with their failure to object to the first slightly anti-Semitic laws and actions. It rather began when Christians assumed that they could be the heirs and carriers of the symbols of the faith without sacrifice and suffering. It began when the very language of revelation became an expression of status rather than an instrument for bringing our lives gradually under the sway of "the love that moves the sun and the other stars." Persons had come to call themselves Christians and yet lived as though they could avoid suffering and death. So Christians allowed their language to idle without turning the engines of the soul, and in recompense, their lives were seized by powers that they no longer had the ability to know, much less to combat.

It is not likely that anyone reading this actually cooperated with Auschwitz, but the conditions of self-deception that created Auschwitz still prevail in our souls. We prefer to believe that the powers of darkness that reigned at Auschwitz have left the scene of combat, overcome by the sheer horror of what happened there. But we cannot afford to ignore Auschwitz, for to overlook it sets the stage for yet further self-deception. Moreover, by forgetting Auschwitz we neglect the grammar of the language we have learned from the cross of Christ.

This essay is divided into three sections: the first offers a preliminary philosophical analysis of self-deception; the second examines Speer's claim of self-deception in *Inside the Third Reich;* the third attempts to delineate some conditions necessary to live our lives more truthfully. The specific convictions about ethical life and reflection that shape this essay are not made explicit here. We cannot do better, however, as a way of summarizing the general position than to endorse David Harned's claim:

> Seeing is never simply a reaction to what passes before our eyes; it is a matter of how well the eye is trained and provisioned to discern the richness and the terror, beauty and banality of the worlds outside and within the self. Decisions are shaped by vision, and the ways that we see are a function of our "character," of the history and habits of the self, and ultimately of the stories that we have heard and with which we identify ourselves. More precisely seeing is determined by the constellation of images of man and the world that resides within the household of the self. Sometimes they inhibit and corrupt a person as much as they sustain him, but their common source is always faith, the tangle of loyalties that the self has developed in the course of time. . . . The real problem, however, is not the variety of faiths we entertain or images of man by which we are all beset, not their partiality, nor even the conflicts among them, but our need for a master image of the self that can reconcile the lesser ones that draw a person first one way and then another toward conflicting goals, each of them claiming greater authority than it deserves, promising greater rewards than it can provide.[1]

This essay is an attempt to illustrate these claims by showing the inadequacy of one man's master image. While we write as Christians and believe that Speer's case bears peculiarly upon Christians, we do not believe our analysis and reflections are confined in their import to Christians.

2. Self-Deception: A Theoretical Account

As familiar as we are with self-deception, we find it elusive to get hold of analytically. We tend to think of self-deception as a case of self-lying, but lying to oneself turns out to be a paradoxical enterprise. A mother may maintain that her son is a good boy when all the evidence indicates he is not, but we assume that she really knows differently. Confidence in her son may be a strategy to straighten him out by creating certain expectations or an attempt to ward off the shame she thinks she should feel for rearing such a son. Many other explanations could be offered for her state of self-deception, but explanations of this type all conspire to deny that the mother is genuinely self-

---

1. David Harned, *Faith and Virtue* (Philadelphia: Pilgrim Press, 1973), 29–30. See also vv.

deceived. She would not be deceived if she merely told herself that he was a good boy; she must be convinced that he is.

Self-deception must stem from a purpose strong enough that our position cannot be interpreted as a sham. The model of self-lying overlooks intentional or purposive origins of self-deception and leaves us in a paradoxical situation. To be sure, self-deception often seems to involve the coexistence in one person of two incompatible beliefs, but when individual cases are so analyzed they turn out to be something other than self-deception. For the agent must be assumed to be aware of both beliefs while playing like he or she does not hold one of them. We know, however, that we do not just play at self-deception. For we have often come to realize how deceived we have been, yet quite unsuspectingly all the while.

2.1 Consciousness as Knowing How

Our rudimentary view of consciousness as awareness will not suffice to offer a plausible account of self-deception. We presume that we are conscious of our activity since we seem to be aware of what we are doing most of the time. But this is hardly the case. I can be conscious of what I am doing without perceiving myself doing it, and I can be aware of what I am up to yet fail to take it into account. Furthermore, to think of being conscious as "taking a look" is not only misleading but leads to an analytical regress, since every intentional act (including looking) is deemed to be conscious.[2] Consciousness is more like an ability to say than the power to see. Our native powers of consciousness are susceptible of progressive training. It would not be amiss to insist that we must be trained to be conscious.

Herbert Fingarette offers the model of an operating skill to replace the more passive image of awareness, and shows how the skill model can elaborate our sense of being explicitly conscious. "To become explicitly conscious of something is to be exercising a certain skill. Skills, of course, are learned but need not be routinized. We are born with certain general capacities which we shape, by learning, into specific skills, some of them being quite sensitive and artful. The specific skill I particularly have in mind as a model for becoming explicitly conscious of something is the skill of saying what we are doing or experiencing. I propose, then, that we do not characterize consciousness as a

2. Bernard J. F. Lonergan anticipated this systematic shift in his *Insight* (New York: Philosophical Library, 1957). For an interpretation of Lonergan in this connection, see David Burrell, "Method and Sensibility: Novak's Debt to Lonergan," *Journal of American Academy of Religion* 40 (1972): 349–67.

kind of mental mirror, but as the exercise of the (learned) skill of 'spelling out' some feature of the world we are engaged in."[3]

To become explicitly conscious of one's situation, then, demands that one rehearse what one is doing. We seldom feel it necessary to spell out our engagements in any detail, however. Conventional descriptions of our actions are readily available, and they normally dispense us from spelling things out any further. There are many things we do every day—dressing, eating, playing with our children, or talking with our spouses—that can be carried on without bothering to delineate how they may contribute to an overall life plan. We seldom "spell out" what we are doing unless we are prodded to do so: "Rather than taking explicit consciousness for granted; we must see explicit consciousness as the further exercise of a specific skill for special reasons."[4]

Furthermore, at times we sense it to be a more reasonable policy *not* to spell out some of our engagements. By adopting such a policy, however, we not only avoid becoming explicitly conscious. We also set up a situation that allows us to avoid becoming explicitly conscious that we are avoiding it. It is this very reduplication, of course, that ensures self-deception. By suggesting that we regard explicit consciousness as perfecting a native ability to spell things out, Fingarette renders the curiously reflexive maneuver a bit more plausible. The mother who insists her son is good when he is engaged in doubtful activities not only refuses to apply her ordinary criteria for right and wrong in this case. She also avoids recognizing that she is not employing these criteria as she normally does. To bring certain things to consciousness requires the moral stamina to endure the pain that such explicit knowledge cannot help but bring. The mother's self-deception plays a supportive role by staving off the pain that would inevitably accompany her spelling out what her son's behavior entails.

2.2 An Avoidance Policy

We can now offer a preliminary account of what self-deception involves. A self-deceived person is one of whom "it is a patent characteristic that even when normally appropriate he *persistently* avoids spelling out some feature of his engagement with the world."[5] A state of self-deception cannot issue from a single decision, then, but represents a policy not to spell out certain activities in which the agent is involved. Moreover, once such a policy has been adopted,

---

3. Herbert Fingarette, *Self-Deception* (New York: Humanities Press, 1969), 38–39.
4. Ibid., 42.
5. Ibid., 47.

there is even more reason to continue it, so that a process of self-deception has been initiated. Our overall posture of sincerity demands that we make this particular policy consistent with the whole range of our engagements. In this way, a specific policy leads to a pervasive condition called self-deception. Curiously enough, it is our prevailing desire to be consistent that escalates a policy into an enveloping condition. Thus the mother in our example may begin to believe that there is a conspiracy by school officials to discredit her son. Our protective deceits become destructive when they begin to serve our need to shape a world consistent with our illusions. The power of fabrication makes it that much harder to uncover our deceptions by masking them with sufficient plausibility to render them acceptable. Occasionally we are fortunate enough to be forced to face our deceptions, but ironically the very same imaginative and intellectual skills that lead us to discriminate falsity from truth also empower us to create those webs of illusion that lend plausibility to our original deceptive policy.

We may even feel that the commitments we have made require us to keep up an ongoing policy of avoidance. We may feel compelled to maintain our web of illusion because we have drawn others into it. We can quiet any misgivings we may have for fear of the injury that spelling things out could inflict upon those who love us. Jules Henry's *Pathways in Madness*,[6] an account of families of psychotic children, offers a tragic commentary on the avoidance strategies some families have elaborated, ostensibly to preserve the love they have achieved. It so happens, however, that one of their members must pay the toll for a policy that tries to preserve a love story by overlooking certain disharmonious subplots.

Our lives are replete with illusions for they constitute an essential part of our coping equipment. Henry points out how professors can continue to act as if they were effective teachers when they are not, because they must feel effective to earn a living to support their family. There are often moral reasons to sustain the illusions of our lives. Consider the many conversations with others that appear to be congenial but that may bore or otherwise annoy both parties, "yet each person harbors the necessary illusion that he is pulling the wool over the other person's eyes. The illusions must be maintained in order for people to carry on. The illusions of concealment, of safety, of deceiving the

6. Jules Henry, *Pathways to Madness* (New York: Vintage Press, 1973).

other are part of the absolutely necessary structure of consciousness. The illusion keeps us sane."[7]

The complexity and extent of our self-deception explains why we avoid spelling out our engagements. Each of us needs to establish some sense of identity and unity in order to give coherence to the multifariousness of our history as uniquely ours and as constitutive of the self.[8] Self-deception can accompany this need for unity, as we systematically delude ourselves in order to maintain the story that has hitherto assured our identity. We hesitate to spell out certain engagements when spelling them out would jeopardize the set of avowals we have made about ourselves.

Societal roles provide a ready vehicle for self-deception, since we can easily identify with them without any need to spell out what we are doing. The role is accepted into our identity. It may define our identity in the measure that we feel committed to live out and defend our identification with it. In the narrow confines of a job and of corporate loyalty, such an individual can easily be caricatured as a "company man" and come under a simple censure of establishment myopia. Where the description is more exalted and vocational however, the opportunity for deceiving oneself increases. A man may think of himself as a public servant concerned with the public good. Even though he may be party to decisions that compromise the public good, he has a great deal invested in continuing to describe them as contributing to the public good. To call certain decisions he makes by their proper name would require too painful a readjustment in his primary identification of himself as a public servant. Thus our deceit can be a function of wanting to think of ourselves as honest persons.

The irony of self-deception is that a cynic is less vulnerable to self-deception than a conscientious person. "The less integrity, the less there is motive to enter into self-deception. The greater the integrity of the person, and the more powerful the contrary inclination, the greater is the temptation to self-deception (the nearer to saintliness, the more a powerful personality suffers). It is because the movement into self-deception is rooted in a concern for the integrity of spirit that we temper our condemnation of the self-deceiver. We feel he is not a *mere* cheat. We are moved to a certain comparison in which there is awareness of the self-deceiver's authentic inner dignity as the motive of his self-betrayal."[9]

7. Ibid., xviii.
8. On the question of the constitution of the self, see CCL.
9. Fingarette, 140.

What the self-deceiver lacks is not integrity or sincerity but the courage and skill to confront the reality of his or her situation. Self-deception is correlative with trying to exist in this life without a story sufficiently substantive and rich to sustain us in the unavoidable challenges that confront the self. It may be possible to "function effectively" without such a story, but to do so we necessarily reduce our rightful expectations and interests. To live bravely is to be willing to risk our present lives in pursuing the consequences of the commitments we have made. A policy of fidelity cannot help but challenge the story we currently hold about ourselves. We can afford to let go of our current story, however, only to the extent that we are convinced that it does not hold the key to our individual identity. So we will remain subject to those propensities that lead to a state of self-deception as long as we feel ourselves to be constituted either by the conventional roles we have assumed or by the level of awareness we have been able to articulate. Alternatively, we will have some leverage on these powers in the measure that we believe ourself to be constituted by a story given to us by a power beyond our will or imagination.

2.3 Discriminating Stories

In summary, self-deception results from an expedient policy of refusing to spell out our engagements in order to preserve the particular identity we have achieved. The extent of our self-deception correlates with the type of story we hold about who and what we are. If it is to counter our propensity to self-deception, the story that sustains our life must give us the ability to spell out in advance the limits of the various roles we will undertake in our lives. The story must enable us to discriminate within those roles the behavior that can easily entrap and blind us. The more noble and caring the role, the more discriminating the story must be. To lack such a story, as we shall see in the case of Speer, is to be deprived of the skills necessary to recognize or challenge the demonic. And to be bereft of those skills is to fall prey to these powers. That much we can now say, after Auschwitz.

3. Albert Speer: The Life of an Architect

Speer's autobiography can be read as one long confession of self-deception. As he says of himself, "I have always thought it was a most valuable trait to recognize reality and not to pursue delusions. But when I now think over my life up to and including the years of imprisonment, there was no period in which I was free of delusory notions."[10] Rather than try to use his self-deceit as an excuse for participation in Hitler's government, Speer explicitly states that he accepts and should accept full responsibility for all the crimes committed by Hitler—including the murder of six million Jews.

We cannot help but ask, however, whether Speer's admission is not an extremely clever way of reclaiming his place in decent society. For is not claiming responsibility for the murder of the Jews an empty gesture? What could anyone do to render such a claim credible? Even the theme of self-deception seems to give Speer a kind of legitimacy and integrity that excuses his active participation in Hitler's government. How are we to connect, in other words, the admissions of the autobiography with the life Speer led as a Nazi?[11]

3.1 The Account

Speer's account rings true. He recognizes how impossible it is to claim responsibility for the murder of the Jews. Only when we again see the pictures of the bodies and the ovens filled with bones can we even begin to imagine that reign of death. It is not the murder of the six million that we comprehend, but the murder of the one person or family that we see in a picture. Speer does not claim to see all six million but says he is haunted by the "account of a Jewish family going to their deaths: the husband with his wife and children on the way to die are before my eyes to this day" (25). It is less agonizing to claim responsibility for the murder of six million, as their very number makes them an abstraction, but Speer recognizes that such a claim means that he helped murder this family.

Speer's account of his activities as a Nazi is corroborated by other investigations. Trevor-Roper criticizes Speer severely, but acknowledges that his conclusions about the war and his involvement in it "are never naive, never parochial; they seem always honest; they are often profound. If he seems sometimes to have fallen too deeply under the spell of the tyrant whom he served, at least he is the only servant whose judgment was not corrupted by attendance on that dreadful master; at least he retained the capacity to exam-

10. Albert Speer, *Inside the Third Reich* (New York: Avon Books, 1970), 379. Hereafter, all page references to this work are in the text.

11. For a good analysis of the way truth functions in autobiography, see Roy Pascal, *Design and Truth in Autobiography* (Cambridge, MA: Harvard University Press, 1960), 61–83. He argues that "too scrupulous adherence to the factual truth may injure an autobiography," for the "truth remembered is the only truth that matters—A person's life illusion ought to be as sacred as his skin."

ine himself, and the honesty to declare both his errors and his convictions. In the last days of Nazism he was not afraid to tell Hitler of his own acts of defiance; and in Allied captivity he was not afraid to admit, after his searching analysis of Hitler's character and history, the residue of loyalty which he could not altogether shed."[12] Ironically enough, testimonies like these to Speer's personal integrity undermine our trust in his account. For we fail to see how a man of integrity and substance could have served Hitler so well. What staggers us is not what Arendt in describing Eichmann called the banality of evil, but the reality of a good man serving such masters.[13] It would be easier if we could think of Speer as a dedicated and committed Nazi, for then his actions would be intelligible. Perhaps Speer's confession of self-deception carries us beyond an attempt to clear his own name. He is reminding us that integrity and sincerity in themselves are not sufficient safeguards against the seduction of evil.[14]

But how could a man like Speer become involved in so monstrous a self-deception? He was a man who could make realistic assessments. He was among the first to realize that the war could not be won because Allied bombing made it impossible for Germany to match the Allies' technological capacity (445). He was also a keen observer of the faults and pettiness of the men around Hitler. Notwithstanding his strong personal attachment to Hitler, Speer almost singlehandedly, and with great courage, stayed the execution of Hitler's scorched-earth policy against Germany (565).[15]

12. H. R. Trevor-Roper, *The Last Days of Hitler* (New York: Macmillan, 1947), 75.

13. Hannah Arendt, in *Eichmann in Jerusalem: A Report on the Banality of Evil* (New York: Viking, 1963), says, "The trouble with Eichmann was precisely that so many were like him, and that many were neither perverted nor sadistic, that they were, and still are, terribly and terrifyingly normal. From the viewpoint of our legal institutions and of our moral standards of judgments, this normality was much more terrifying than all the atrocities put together, for it implied—as had been said at Nuremberg over and over again by the defendants and their counsel—that this new type of criminal, who is in actual fact *hostis generis humani*, commits his crimes under circumstances that make it well-nigh impossible for him to know or to feel that he is doing wrong" (253).

14. Stuart Hampshire, in *Freedom of the Mind* (Princeton, NJ: Princeton University Press, 1971), says, "If sincerity is interpreted as undividedness of mind, and if to be sincere in regretting, or to be sincere in one's whole mind, then 'watching oneself live' may be, not an obstacle, but rather a necessary condition of sincerity" (246). Interpreted in this sense, Speer did not have a story from which he could "watch himself live" that was sufficient for the kind of engagement he had begun.

15. In spite of his work against Hitler in these matters, and even with his somewhat halfhearted attempts to kill Hitler, the personal attraction and loyalty Speer felt for Hitler lasted right until the end. For example, see his account of his decision to fly to Berlin for one last meeting with

Nothing in Speer's background would seem to have led him into the company of Nazis. He came from a prosperous and professional family and he enjoyed a happy childhood. Even though politics was seldom discussed at home, his father was a liberal committed to social reform. Speer received an excellent education and admits himself that as an intellectual he should have been repulsed by Hitler's crude propaganda. That aspect of Nazism he simply ignored, however, as politics and not to be taken seriously (48). At his father's urging he continued the family tradition by becoming an architect, studying under one of the finest architects in Germany, and even becoming his assistant. He fell in love, married, and seems to have been a humane and loving father.

Yet this same man served as Hitler's Minister of Armaments. Many estimate that his accomplishments lengthened the war by at least two years. For some time Speer was the second most powerful man in Germany as he organized Germany's industry to provide the military hardware for Hitler's armies. In that capacity he also approved of and willingly accepted the use of slave labor in Germany's factories and mines. It was this policy that earned him twenty years in prison at Nuremberg.

He not only knew slave labor was being used; he saw the inhumane conditions under which these men lived and worked. He did try to assure them at least minimal living conditions, but he was forced to admit that he really did not see these men at all: "What preys on my mind nowadays has little to do with the standards of Nuremberg nor the figures on lives I saved or might have saved. For in either case I was moving within the system. What disturbs me more is that I failed to read the physiognomy of the regime mirrored in the faces of those prisoners—the regime whose existence I was so obsessively trying to prolong during those weeks and months. I did not see any moral ground outside the system where I should have taken my stand. And sometimes I ask myself who this young man really was, this young man who has now become so alien to me, who walked through the workshops of the Linz steelworks or descended into the caverns of the Central Works twenty-five years ago" (480).

Even though Speer never thought of himself as anti-Semitic and took no part in the destruction of the Jews, he also admits that he deliberately made himself blind to what was happening to the Jews. Because he felt no hatred

---

Hitler (606). Speer and Hitler's mutual enthusiasm for architecture formed a bond between them not broken to the end.

toward the Jews, he assumed that he had no involvement in their harassment. He saw the burned-out synagogues but reacted quite indifferently. For as he says, "I felt myself to be Hitler's architect. Political events did not concern me" (162). Later he was warned by his friend, Gauleiter Karl Hanke, never to go to Auschwitz. Speer admits he purposely refused to ask him why. Nor did he ask Himmler or Hitler or anyone else from whom he could have easily found out the truth.

> For I did not want to know what was happening there. During those few seconds, while Hanke was warning me, the whole responsibility had become a reality again. Those seconds were uppermost in my mind when I stated to the international court at the Nuremberg Trial that as an important member of the leadership of the Reich, I had to share the total responsibility for all that had happened. For from that moment on, I was inescapably contaminated morally; from fear of discovering something which might have made me turn from my course I had closed my eyes. This deliberate blindness outweighs whatever good I may have done or tried to do in the last period of the war. Those activities shrink to nothing in the face of it. Because I failed at that time, I still feel to this day responsible for Auschwitz in the wholly personal sense. (481)

3.2 His Story

But how did Speer get to the point that there was "no moral ground outside the system"? Why would any man make himself "deliberately blind"? Speer knew that the knowledge of Auschwitz—if articulated—would destroy his very being. He had no skill to explain such a horror and still know how to go on as the young man he had become. His original commitment to Hitler offered him a ready reason for refusing to spell out the consequences of his present involvements. His self-deception was correlative to his identity as he clung to the story of being Hitler's apolitical architect. As Speer says, "My new political interests played a subsidiary part in my thinking. I was above all an architect" (51).[16]

16. In response to his daughter's letter asking how an intelligent man like her father could go along with Hitler, Speer says:
> Let me begin my answer by a confession which is most difficult to make: in my case there is no excuse. The fault is mine, and expiation there must be. . . . Sometimes in the life of a people collective suggestion shows its effect. Man is full of bad instincts which he tries to suppress. But if the barriers once give way, then something dreadful is unleashed. Some few

But he was an architect born and trained in a defeated country. He aspired to erect monuments to the human spirit, but he lived in a country ready only to build garages. Hitler offered Speer hope, he offered him a vision, a story of a country that would again ask its architects to raise up public buildings. What Hitler offered Speer is what every professional dreams of: the opportunity to make his wildest ambitions come true. The long chapters describing the architectural plans he worked on with Hitler display the extent of these ambitions.

Speer cared nothing for politics in itself. He thought National Socialism was a better alternative than communism, but such considerations were not what led him to join the party. He joined the party and was increasingly drawn into its activities because, as he says, "My position as Hitler's architect had soon become indispensable to me. Not yet thirty, I saw before me the most exciting prospects an architect can dream of" (64).

Hitler gave Speer the opportunity to lose himself in his work: assured identity with the equal security of serving a high ideal. Everything else would have to give way, of course, and Speer gave up "the real center of my life: my family. Completely under the sway of Hitler, I was henceforth possessed by my work" (64). As one architectural assignment followed another, Speer had less and less reason to spell out the engagement he had begun. He knew what he was doing: he was an architect. No more was needed.

---

individuals escape the common folly, but when it is all over, and one regains awareness, the world takes its head in its hands and asks: "How did I come to do it?" Then for me personally there was one factor making for the exclusion of all criticism, if I had wished to express any. You must realize that at the age of thirty-two, in my capacity as architect, I had the most splendid assignments of which I could dream. Hitler said to your mother one day that her husband could design buildings the like of which had not been seen for two thousand years. One would have had to be morally very stoical to reject the prospect. But I was not at all like that. As I have already told you, I did not believe in any God, and that would have been the only possible counterbalance. There was one enormous fault, one which I shared with others. It had become a habit to do one's job without occupying oneself with what the neighbors were doing. By that I wish to say that I did not think it had anything to do with me when somebody else said that all the Jews ought to be wiped out. Clearly I said nothing of this kind, neither did I think like that. I never showed any Anti-Semitism myself, and stayed calm. The fact that I helped many Jews is no excuse. On the contrary, it aggravates the moral fault. More than once I have put myself the question what I would have done if I had felt myself responsible for what Hitler did in other spheres of activity. Unfortunately, if I am to stay sincere, the answer would be negative. My position as an architect and the magnificent projects on which I was engaged became indispensable to me. I swallowed all the rest, never giving it a thought. (Quoted in William Hamsher, *Albert Speer: Victim of Nuremberg* [London: Leslie Frewin, 1970], 65–66)

Even when he became Minister of Armaments Speer continued to think of himself primarily as an architect. The reorganization of German industry to serve the ends of war was a creative technological task with which he could readily identify. This new position was a natural extension of the skills learned from his architectural training; he brought form in a different medium through technological manipulation. In this highly political task he could continue to disdain politics as perverting the ends of efficiency and good order. So Speer's new position did not require him to rethink the master image of his life: he continued to be above all an architect.

What he failed to appreciate, of course, was how seductive and destructive it was to be "Hitler's architect" (64). Seductive because it put him on intimate terms with power, as the picture he draws of himself arriving for lunch at his new chancellery betrays so candidly: "The policeman at the entrance to the front garden knew my car and opened the gate without making inquiries. . . . the SS member of Hitler's escort squad greeted me familiarly" (168). Destructive even of his architectural sense, as a chance auto trip through Castile in 1941 warned him. Remarking on the Escorial of Philip II, he recaptures his sentiments at that time: "What a contrast with Hitler's architectural ideas: in the one case, remarkable conciseness and clarity, magnificent interior rooms, their forms perfectly controlled; in the other case, pomp and disproportionate ostentation. . . . In hours of solitary contemplation it began to dawn on me for the first time that my recent architectural ideals were on the wrong track" (251). Yet the insight proved inoperable. The architect in him had become Hitler's architect.

It was later when he began to write his autobiography that Speer realized how "before 1944 I so rarely—in fact almost never—found the time to reflect about myself or my own activities, that I never gave my own existence a thought. Today, in retrospect, I often have the feeling that something swept me up off the ground at the time, wrenched me from all roots, and beamed a host of alien forces upon me" (64). Toward the end of the war Speer was able to distance himself from Hitler's will to realize that the future of Germany over-reached that of Hitler (574). Yet that very patriotism had drawn him to Hitler originally. He had no effective way to step back from himself, no place to stand. His self-deception began when he assumed that "being above all an architect" was a story sufficient to constitute his self. He had to experience the solitude of prison to realize that becoming a human being requires stories and images a good deal richer than professional ones, if we are to be equipped to deal with the powers of this world.

3.3 The Lesson Presented

As a justification for writing his story Speer says he intends the book to be a warning to the future (659). But it is not clear exactly what that warning is. A ready candidate for "a lesson for the future" seems to be Speer's final speech at Nuremberg, as he warned of the potential tyrannical use of technology: "Hitler's dictatorship was the first dictatorship of an industrial state in this age of modern technology. A dictatorship which employed to perfection the instruments of technology to dominate its own people. . . . Dictatorship of the past needed assistants of high quality in the lower ranks of the leadership also— men who could think and act independently. The authoritarian system in the age of technology can do without such men. The means of communication alone enable it to mechanize the work of the lower leadership. Thus the type of uncritical receiver of orders is created" (654).

We suspect, however, that the writing lies closer to Speer's own life than his direct remarks can say. The British newspaper article from *The Observer* (April 9, 1944) that Speer showed Hitler to prevent Bormann from using it against him is closer to the truth. It suggested that even though Speer was not one of the flamboyant and picturesque Nazis, he was more important to Germany than Hitler, Himmler, Goering, or the generals. For Speer

> is very much the successful average man, well-dressed, civil, noncorrupt, very middle class in his style of life, with a wife and six children. Much less than any of the other German leaders does he stand for anything particularly German or particularly Nazi. He rather symbolizes a type which is becoming increasingly important in all belligerent countries: the pure technician, the classless bright young man without background, with no other original aim than to make his way in the world and no other means than his technical and managerial ability. It is the lack of psychological and spiritual ballast, and the ease with which he handles the terrifying technical and organizational machinery of our age, which makes this slight type go extremely far nowadays. . . . This is their age; the Hitlers, the Himmlers we may get rid of, but the Speers, whatever happens to this particular special man, will long be with us. (443)

Speer's reflections reach beyond the potential dangers of technology to warn us about people who think they need no story or skills beyond their profession. Such people are open to manipulation by anyone who offers them a compelling vision of how that skill can be used. We all require a sense of worth, a sense of place in the human enterprise, and the person with no story beyond his or her role yearns to be so placed by another. We yearn for a cause in which we can lose ourselves. Persons with no politics become political pawns, lacking as they do the skills to grasp the shape of their involvements. Speer was a man who began his engagement with life with a story inadequate to articulate the engagements he would be called upon to undertake. He shared the German distrust of things political and turned instead to his profession, where he had the satisfaction (along with the illusion) of "knowing what he was doing." Trevor-Roper argues that from this perspective Speer is the most culpable of the Nazis, for

> it is quite clear that in Hitler's court Albert Speer was morally and intellectually alone. He had the capacity to understand the forces of politics, and the courage to resist the master whom all others have declared irresistible. As an administrator, he was undoubtedly a genius. He regarded the rest of the court with dignified contempt. His ambitions were peaceful and constructive: he wished to rebuild Berlin and Nuremberg, and had planned to make them the greatest cities in the world. Nevertheless, in a political sense, Speer is the real criminal of Nazi Germany, for he more than any other represented the fatal philosophy which has made havoc of Germany and nearly shipwrecked the world. For ten years he sat at the very center of political power; his keen intelligence diagnosed the nature, and observed the mutations of Nazi government and policy; he saw and despised personalities around him; he heard the outrageous orders and understood their fantastic ambitions; but he did nothing. Supposing politics to be irrelevant, he turned aside, and built roads and bridges and factories, while the logical consequences of government by madmen emerged. Ultimately, when their emergence involved the ruin of all his work, Speer accepted the consequences and acted. Then it was too late; Germany had been destroyed.[17]

Speer's life warns us, certainly, of possible misuses of technology, but the warning is directed more accurately against those who feel they need no images and symbols beyond those offered by conventional roles to give coherence to their lives. We have thought that the way to drive out the evil gods was to deny the existence of all gods. In fact, however, we have found ourselves serving a false god that is all the more powerful because we fail to recognize it

17. Trevor-Roper, 240–41.

as a god.[18] Yet the gods, it seems, will have their due. Any story that overlooks the powers must pretend that the self can be constituted by the roles one has assumed or by the current story a person has been able to compose. Yet neither of these will suffice, as we have seen, for each of them is susceptible of confirming us in a state of self-deception.

A true story could only be one powerful enough to check the endemic tendency toward self-deception—a tendency that inadequate stories cannot help but foster. Correlatively, if the true God were to provide us with a saving story, it would have to be one that we found continually discomforting. For it would be a saving story only as it empowered us to combat the inertial drift into self-deception.

4. Story, Skill, and the Knowledge of Evil

To be is to be rooted in self-deception. The moral task involves a constant vigilance: to note those areas where the tendency has taken root. This task is made more difficult by the illusions of the past that we have unsuspectingly inherited. Even the wisdom of the last generation fails to serve us as it did our fathers, since we have received it without a struggle. Principles, too, that have served to guide one part of our lives can countenance destructive activity if we unwittingly press them into service in other areas. Love of country that once inspired noble deeds can lead us to commit the worst crimes when we have lost the skills to recognize how other loyalties must qualify that of patriotism.

Rather than demand whether it was possible to avoid self-deception, we should try to assess how effectively deceived we have become. Our ability to "step-back"[19] from our deceptions is dependent on the dominant story, the master image, that we have embodied in our character.[20] Through our experi-

---

18. Carl Jung, *Civilization in Transition: The Collected Work of C. G. Jung* (Princeton, NJ: Princeton University Press, 1964), 10:179–93.

19. Hauerwas, *CCL*, 124 and 153 n. 82.

20. Every significant narrative contains images many and various, of course, but among them there are never many that can serve as master images enabling us to grasp concretely and practically what the story means. A master image provides a distillation of a story; among several options, the best is the one that enshrines the most possibilities for articulation of the entire narrative. . . . Obviously enough, if master images are not themselves qualified and enriched by all the other metaphors in the story, they are not master images at all. The more numerous are the images of the self as moral agent that a narrative provides, the more numerous will be the possibilities for individual life, because we do not intend what we cannot see and imagine ourselves accomplishing. Even so, there still must be a master

ence we constantly learn new lessons, we gain new insights, about the limit of our life story. But "insights are a dime a dozen"[21] and even more useless unless we have the skills—the images and the stories—that can empower those insights to shape our lives. It is not enough to see nor is it enough to know; we must know how to say and give expression to what we come to see and know. "Understanding what something is demands more than insight or vision—it requires appropriate discipline."[22]

Like Columbus, we all have encounters that we do not know how to describe. Our basic stories and images determine what we discover, but often, like Columbus, we insist on describing our engagements with an image that misleads us. To the extent that we cannot make anything of what we are doing, we fail to make our lives into anything. Columbus could not understand what he had done because he did not have the skills to get it right. Fortunately, we can keep sending out our ships to explore the coastlines of our engagements and learn the limits of our past descriptions; and on the strength of previous failures, we can develop more adequate skills to say what we have done. Too often, however, we adopt the first coherent description of what we have done and it leads to greater self-deception. Our endemic need for order—the same demand we experience to make a story of our lives—also presses us to forge a unity before we have discovered one adequate to our situation. Hence the inertial tendency to a state of self-deception.

4. 1 Art of Articulation

The art of autobiography offers the best illustration of how to recheck and test the adequacy of the central story and image we have of our lives. The constraints and requirements of autobiography parallel those of a life well lived. Like the moral person, the autobiographer cannot simply recount the events of his or her life. He or she must write from the dominant perspective and image of his or her present time. If this effort is successful, these images and metaphors will provide the skills to articulate the limits of past images and show how they have led to the autobiographer's current perspective. Autobiography is the literary form that mirrors the moral necessity to free our-

---

image that expresses the unity within the variety and that condenses the sprawl and prosody of the narrative into a concrete and powerful metaphor which is able to acquaint the self with the core of whatever the story means. (Harned, 160)

21. Bernard Lonergan, *Method in Theology* (New York: Herder and Herder, 1972).

22. David Burrell, "Reading *The Confessions* of Augustine: An Exercise in Theological Understanding," *Journal of Religion* 50 (October 1970): 331.

selves from the hold of our illusions by exercising the skills that more demanding stories provide. Autobiography is the literary act that rehearses our
liberation from illusory goals by showing how to bring specific skills of understanding to bear on our desires and aversions, so that an intelligible pattern
emerges. An autobiographer, like a moral person, needs to find a story that
gives a life coherence without distorting the quality of his or her actual engagements with others and with the world.

This requirement means that skill cannot be confused with technique, for
the skills required to ferret out the truth cannot be separated from the images
that sustain the skill. We need a story that allows us to recognize the evil we do
and enables us to accept responsibility for it in a nondestructive way. We sense
far too accurately the suffering that the knowledge of evil can cause, and we
comfort ourselves with deceptions that excuse. We live out stories that attempt
to free us from the terrible knowledge that our sins are real. We fear such
knowledge because we sense how it can destroy whatever we have managed to
become and paralyze our ability to act. How can we know the truth about
ourselves and still know how to go on?

Malcolm X came to realize that he could not avoid becoming a "white
man's nigger." Yet he could hardly afford to admit the self-hate symbolized by
straightening his hair, for such knowledge would have destroyed him completely. Instead, he swallowed his dignity and survived by learning the small
hustles that white men allowed blacks to perpetrate on one another. There was
no story readily available that could give him the skill to recognize the truth
about himself without destroying everything. For how do you recognize that
you have been a "white man's nigger" and know how to go on?

The story of the Black Muslims that Malcolm learned in prison provided
the precise skill necessary for him to face up to his situation.[23] The story
offered an explanation of why blacks in America necessarily became the
"white man's nigger," and that interpretation gave him the skills to know how
to go on. This story intended to create a new people, to prepare for a new
exodus, in effect to bestow a new name. The story also gave institutional skills
that could be embodied in ritual and gestures: cease eating pork, participate in
the temple, and accept the disciplined life that frees from the white man's ways
and stereotypes. Any story that fails to provide institutional forms is power-

---

23. Malcolm later found that the story he learned from the Black Muslims also led to illusion
because of its inability to countenance men and women of other colors as potential brothers
and sisters. His involvement in normative Islam represented another development of his story
in his quest for truth.

less, for it is not enough merely to offer the story. One must know how to tell it in such a way that persons can become the story.

Malcolm's story cannot be ours, however—if we are white, Christian, and American or even European—for the evil he had to recognize is not the same as ours. Malcolm had to learn to live as the victim and the ravaged; we must learn to live as the victor and the ravager. For we are people who not only have the suppression of the blacks to our name, but the reality of Auschwitz as part of our history. Like slavery, Auschwitz was not an accidental sideshow to the main events of Western Christendom. We cannot ask the Jew, any more than we can ask the black, to forget that these things have been done by Christians. No reconciliation is possible between white and black, Jew and Christian, unless we can learn to carry the burden of these past crimes.

5. Concluding Reflections

Our problem is not unlike Speer's, for we too must find a place and perspective from which we can write our story without distortion. We must learn how to hold the guilt that such a story brings without trying to rid ourselves of it by morbid self-denunciation or false gestures of identifying with our victim. Speer reveals little of the perspective from which he now writes his life. Perhaps he is wise enough to know that his past deceptions would make any explicit statement of his current convictions problematic. Whatever wisdom he has gained is better shown than said. Beyond that, silence would appear a more truthful policy.

But wisdom needs more than silence, for understanding comes only through images. Christians claim to find the skill to confess the evil that we do in the history of Jesus Christ.[24] It is a history of suffering and death that must be made our own if we are to mine its significance. The saints formed by this story testify to its efficacy in purging the self of all deception as it forces the acceptance of a new self mirrored in the cross. Moreover, this story has given

---

24. This story allows them even to confess to God sins that they cannot fully understand. Thus one confession reads, "O God, our heavenly Father, I confess unto thee that I have grievously sinned against thee in many ways; not only by outward transgressions, but also by secret thoughts and desires which I cannot fully understand, but which are all known to thee. I do earnestly repent, and am heartily sorry for these my offences, and I beseech thee of thy great goodness to have mercy upon me, for the sake of thy dear Son, Jesus Christ Our Lord, to forgive my sin and graciously to help my infirmities."

the saints a way to go on as they become disciples of the way—the way of learning to deal with evil without paying back in kind.

The stories that produce truthful lives are those that provide the skills to step back and survey the limits of our engagements. Nations, no less than individuals, require such stories. These stories will help us to recognize and acknowledge the evil we perpetrate and to confront ourselves without illusion and deceit. Our urge to be good, to have a coherent and unified self, and our need to have a sense of worth are strong. We will do almost anything to avoid recognizing the limits on our claims to righteousness.[25] In fact, we seem to be able to acknowledge those limits only when life has brought us to the point where we can do nothing else. To accept the Gospel is to receive training in accepting the limits on our claims to righteousness before we are forced to. It is a hard and painful discipline but it cannot be avoided, we suspect, if we wish to have a place to stand free of self deception.

Further Reading

"The Gesture of a Truthful Story" (1985), in CET

"Why Truthfulness Requires Forgiveness" (1992), essay 15 in this volume

"A Story-Formed Community: Reflections on *Watership Down*" (1981), essay 9 in this volume

"On Taking Religion Seriously: The Challenge of Jonestown" (1985), in AN

"Situation Ethics, Moral Notions, and Moral Theology" (1971), in VV

"Aslan and the New Morality" (1973), in VV

---

25. "Man loves himself inordinately. Since his determinate existence does not deserve the devotion lavished upon it, it is obviously necessary to practice some deception in order to justify such excessive devotion. While such deception is constantly directed against competing wills, seeking to secure their acceptance and validation of the self's too generous opinion of itself, its primary purpose is to deceive, not others, but the self. The self must at any rate deceive itself first. Its deception of others is partly an effort to convince itself against itself. The fact that this necessity exists is an important indication of the vestige of truth which abides with the self in all its confusion and which it must placate before it can act. The dishonesty of man is thus an interesting refutation of the doctrine of man's total depravity" (Reinhold Niebuhr, *The Nature and Destiny of Man*, I [New York: Scribner's, 1949], 203).

11. Character, Narrative, and Growth
in the Christian Life (1980)

In this essay, Hauerwas argues that theories of moral and spiritual development (e.g., Kohlberg and Fowler) are inadequate insofar as they rely on a Kantian description of the autonomous (i.e., un-storied and in-dependent) self. In contrast, Hauerwas gives an account of moral formation based on Aristotle's and Aquinas's discussions of virtue and character. Taking an example from his own life—receiving a gift from his father—Hauerwas argues that the appropriate response to such an offering is inextricably bound up with morally significant contingencies in his own life, and no universal set of principles can give him the skills necessary to respond properly. But these very skills of integrating one's past with one's present are necessary to provide a coherent sense of self—that is, one's character, or one's narrative. This places Christian ethics in deep conflict with the Kantian ethic, which often, and self-deceptively, is taken to imply that our primary story is that we have no story, whereas "the kind of character the Christian seeks to develop is a correlative of a narrative that trains the self to be sufficient to negotiate existence without illusion or deception. For our character is not the result of any one narrative; the self is constituted by many different roles and stories. Moral growth involves a constant conversation between our stories that allows us to live appropriate to the character of our existence. By learning to make their lives conform to God's way, Christians claim that they are provided with a self that is a story that enables the conversation to continue in a truthful manner."

1. Moral Development and the Christian Life

Recent attention to the nature and process of development occasioned by the work of Jean Piaget and Lawrence Kohlberg is a welcome occurrence. Philosophers and theologians have for too long left the analysis of moral development

[From *Toward Moral and Religious Maturity* (Morristown, NJ: Silver Burdett, 1980). Reprinted in cc.]

to educators and psychologists. Yet it is important that we not forget that the experience and necessity of moral growth has always been the subject of philosophical reflection and theological inquiry, and of course has been embodied in actual religious practices and disciplines. Every community has to provide some account and means to initiate their young into their moral traditions and activities, and it seems every community finds some way to encourage its members to move from the less good to the better, and from the good to the excellent.

The fact that some sense of moral development is implicit in any account of morality is not, however, sufficient to allow us to make generalizations about what moral development means and how it must take place.[1] It may be that there are certain biological and social aspects of human nature that allows us to draw some generalizations about moral development,[2] but I remain skeptical that these are sufficient to provide an account of moral development that is independent of content.

The phrase "moral development" is seductive, as it seems to imply that we know what we mean by "moral." Since the Enlightenment, moreover, powerful philosophical accounts have attempted to provide a foundation for sustaining the assumption that "moral" is a univocal concept. In contrast, I assume that the notion of morality has no one meaning and any attempt to talk in general about morality will require analogical control. Correlatively, this means that one community's sense of moral development may be quite different from another's.

This is particularly important for trying to understand how and why Christians have been concerned with moral development. While it is certainly true that Christians have emphasized the necessity of moral development, it is equally interesting to note that they have seldom used phrases such as "moral development" to talk about it. Rather, they have talked about the necessity of

1. It is not clear what a theory of "moral development" is meant to do. Is it an attempt to describe how moral development *does* occur? Or is the object to indicate how moral development *should* occur? In much of the recent literature these two issues are confused. The assumption seems to be that if you can learn how development occurs you will be better able to suggest how it ought to occur, but that by no means follows. Descriptive "stages" do not in themselves indicate what *ought* to be the case.

2. I have no doubt that there must be some correlation between cognitive development and moral development. But I am less sure what is sufficient to describe this relationship, since what is meant by "moral" will necessarily differ among cultural contexts. Empirical cross-cultural correlations cannot resolve the issue, for they presuppose exactly the conceptual point at issue: namely, the assumption that "moral" is a univocal term.

spiritual growth, growth in holiness, the pilgrimage of the self, being faithful to the way, and the quaint, but still significant, notion of perfection. It is quite legitimate, of course, to suggest that these are simply more colorful ways to talk about moral development, but such a suggestion fails to do justice to the kind of life Christians have been concerned to promote. For the language of spiritual growth, holiness, and perfection directs attention to the development of the moral self in a manner quite different from the contemporary concern with moral development.[3]

It is equally true that Christians have failed to develop the conceptual categories necessary to illuminate the kind of morality appropriate to their language.[4] Because of their lack of conceptual paradigms, in recent years Christians have eagerly adopted the language of moral development as their own. The translation of the language of perfection into the language of development, however, involves a transformation that robs the language of its religious import.

There are a number of ways such a contention might be stated, but here are only three: (1) The Christian thinks it important to live in recognition that life is a gift rather than to live autonomously; (2) Christian ethics involves learning to imitate another before it involves acting on principles (though principles are not excluded); and (3) the Christian moral life is finally not one of "development" but of conversion. We can examine each of these only briefly.

It is often assumed that Christians cannot be wholly satisfied with the language of moral development because they are also concerned with a dimension beyond the moral which is suggested by the term "faith." So con-

3. James Fowler argues that Kohlberg and his colleagues have "not attended to the differences between constitutive-knowing in which the identity or worth of the person is not directly at stake and constitutive-knowing in which it is. This has meant that Kohlberg has avoided developing a theory of the moral conscience. Strictly speaking, his stages describe a succession of integrated structures of moral logic. He has given very little attention to the fact that we 'build' our selves through choices and moral (self-defining) commitments. His theory, for understandable theoretical and historical-practical reasons, has not explicated the dynamics of the inner dialogue in moral choice between actual and possible selves" ("Faith and the Structuring of Meaning," in *Toward Moral and Religious Maturity*, ed. James Fowler [New York: Silver Burdett, 1980], 60–61). Even though I think Fowler is right about this, Kohlberg, like Kant, can and does give an account of moral character. The difficulty is that such accounts lack what we think is crucial for having character: our personal history. Later I will try to show why this is the case.

4. It must not be forgotten, however, that Christians have developed spiritual writings and disciplines that provide means to make their lives conform more perfectly with their language. Their practice was often better than they knew how to say.

strued, faith does not change or add anything, but denotes something beyond the moral or provides a different perspective.[5] Not only is this a misunderstanding of faith; more significantly, it fails to see that the kind of life Christians describe as faithful is substantively at odds with any account of morality that makes autonomy the necessary condition and/or goal of moral behavior. For the Christian seeks neither autonomy nor independence, but rather to be faithful to the way that manifests the conviction that we belong to another. Thus Christians learn to describe their lives as a gift rather than an achievement.

From the perspective of those who assume that morality is an autonomous institution, the idea that life is a gift can only appear heteronomous. For it is supposed that autonomy entails freeing oneself from all relations except those freely chosen, while the language of gift continues to encourage dependence.[6] Yet, for the Christian, autonomous freedom can only mean slavery to the self and the self's desires. In contrast, it is the Christian belief that true freedom comes by learning to be appropriately dependent, that is, to trust the one who wills to have us as his own and who wills the final good of all. In more traditional language, for the Christian, to be perfectly free means to be perfectly obedient. True freedom is perfect service.

Yet it may be objected that the contrast between gift and autonomy is

5. Kohlberg simply assumes, for example, that faith denotes our most general attitude toward the world: it is how we answer the question of "the meaning of life." "Faith" is thus understood to be a general epistemological category that categorizes a necessary stance anyone must take vis-à-vis the world. In fairness to Kohlberg it must be admitted that modern theology has often described faith in this manner, but such an understanding of faith can do little to advance our understanding of how Christian convictions work and require moral growth. For what Christians are concerned with is not that all people need to assume an ultimate stance toward the universe, but that Christians learn to be faithful to the way of God revealed in the death and resurrection of Christ. Faith is not an epistemological category, but a way of talking about the kind of faithfulness required of worshipers of the God of Israel. For Kohlberg's understanding of faith, see his "Education, Moral Development and Faith," *Journal of Moral Education* 4, no. 1 (1974): 5–16.

6. For a critique of the concept of autonomy, see Gerald Dworkin, "Moral Autonomy," in *Morals, Science and Sociality,* ed. H. Tristram Engelhardt and Daniel Callahan (Hastings on Hudson, NY: Hastings Center, 1978), 156–70. Dworkin rightly argues that "it is only through a more adequate understanding of notions such as tradition, authority, commitment, and loyalty, and of the forms of human community in which these have their roots, that we shall be able to develop a conception of autonomy free from paradox and worthy of admiration" (170). But the whole force of the modern concept of autonomy has been to make the individual "a law unto himself" and thus free from history. See Kant, *Foundations of the Metaphysics of Morals* (New York: Liberal Arts Press, 1959), 65.

overdrawn. For Kant also argued that autonomy consists of doing our duty in accordance with the universal law of our being. Such an objection, however, fails to appreciate that for Christians freedom is literally a gift. We do not become free by conforming our actions to the categorical imperative but by being accepted as disciples and thus learning to imitate a master. Such discipleship can only appear heteronomous from the moral point of view, since the paradigm cannot be reduced to, or determined by, principles known prior to imitation.[7] For the Christian, morality is not chosen and then confirmed by the example of others; instead, we learn what the moral life entails by imitating another. This is intrinsic to the nature of Christian convictions, for the Christian life requires a transformation of the self that can be accomplished only through direction from a master. The problem lies not in knowing *what*

---

7. For an exposition of this point, see James McClendon, *Biography as Theology* (Nashville, TN: Abingdon Press, 1974). In stark contrast to McClendon, Kant argued that imitation of another, even God or Jesus, would be pathological except as the other is a representative of the moral law known through reason. Thus Kant says:

> The living faith in the archetype of humanity well-pleasing to God (in the Son of God) is bound up, in itself, with a moral idea of reason so far as this serves us not only as a guideline but also as an incentive; hence, it matters not whether I start with it as a rational faith, or with the principle of a good course of life. In contrast, the faith in the self-same archetype in its (phenomenal) appearance (faith in the God-Man), as an empirical (historical) faith, is not interchangeable with the principle of the good course of life (which must be wholly rational), and it would be quite a different matter to wish to start with such a faith (which must base the existence of such a person on historical evidence) and to deduce the good course of life from it. To this extent, there would be a contradiction between the two propositions above. And yet, in the appearance of the God-Man (on earth), it is not that in him which strikes the senses and can be known through experience, but rather the archetype, lying in our reason, that we attribute to him (since, so far as his example can be known, he is found to conform thereto), which is really the object of saving faith, and such a faith does not differ from the principle of a course of life well-pleasing to God. (*Religion Within the Limits of Reason Alone*, trans. Theodore Green [New York: Harper Torchbooks, 1960], 109–10)

Of course, it was Kant's hope that "in the end religion will gradually be freed from all empirical determining grounds and from all statutes which rest on history and which through the agency of ecclesiastical faith provisionally unite men for the requirements of the good; and thus at last the pure religion of reason will rule over all, 'so that God may be all in all'" (112).

It is extremely instructive to note the contrast in style between Kant's way of doing ethics and works dealing with the spiritual life. For the latter, the use of examples is crucial, as they invite the reader to imaginatively take the stance of another as the necessary condition for the examination of their own life. Thus, for example, in William Law's 1728 *A Serious Call to a Devout and Holy Life* (New York: Paulist Press, 1978), characters are created and discussed with almost the same detail as a novelist. Indeed, it may be for that reason that the novel remains our most distinctive and powerful form of moral instruction.

we must do, but *how* we are to do it. And the how is learned only by watching and following.[8]

Finally, to be holy or perfect suggests more radical transformation and continued growth in the Christian life than can be captured by the idea of development. The convictions that form the background for Christian growth take the form of a narrative that requires conversion, since the narrative never treats the formation of the self as completed. Thus the story that forms Christian identity trains the self to regard itself under the category of sin,[9] which means we must do more than just develop. Christians are called to a new way of life that requires nothing less than a transvaluation of their past reality-repentance.

Moreover, because of the nature of the reality to which they have been converted, conversion is something never merely accomplished but remains also always in front of them. Thus growth in the Christian life is not required only because we are morally deficient, but also because the God who has called us is infinitely rich. Therefore, conversion denotes the necessity of a turning of the self that is so fundamental that the self is placed on a path of growth for which there is no end.

1.1 Character, Narrative, and the Christian Life

Nevertheless, Christian reflection has largely failed to provide conceptual categories for understanding and articulating the kind of moral development appropriate to these Christian convictions. As a result, claims about the Chris-

---

8. I suspect that there are extremely significant theoretical reasons why this is the case which reach to the very heart of what morality is about. For if Aristotle is right that ethics deals with those matters that can be otherwise (*Nicomachean Ethics,* trans. Martin Ostwald [Indianapolis: Bobbs-Merrill, 1962], 1094b10–1095a10), then ethics must deal with particular and contingent events and relations. Because Aristotle posited a "final good," it is often overlooked that he maintained that "the good cannot be something universal, common to all cases, and single, for if it were, it would not be applicable in all categories but only in one" (1096a26). Or again: "The problem of the good, too, presents a similar kind of irregularity, because in many cases good things bring harmful results. There are instances of men ruined by wealth, and others by courage" (1094b16). To learn to be "moral," therefore, necessarily requires a guide, since there are no universal standards that are sufficient to ensure our morality.

9. At least one curiosity concerning the current enthusiasm among Christians for "moral development" is the complete lack of any sense of sin associated with the process of moral development. From the Christian perspective, growth necessarily entails a heightened sense of sinfulness. For only as we are more nearly faithful do we learn the extent of our unfaithfulness. Put differently, "sin" is not a natural category, that is, another way of talking about a failure of "moral development" or immoral behavior, but rather a theological claim about the depth of the self's estrangement from God. That is why we are not just "found" to be sinners, but that we must be "made" to be sinners.

tian life have too often appeared to be assertions that certain kinds of behavior or actions were to be done simply because "that is the way Christians do things"—the relationship between behavior and belief was assumed rather than analyzed.[10] This has had many unfortunate consequences, as it has often created the context for and even encouraged the growth of legalism, self-righteousness, and a refusal to analyze the rationality of Christians' moral convictions. On a more theoretical level, the Christian life was divided into internal matters dealing with the spiritual life and external concerns about morality. Indeed, in some traditions distinct disciplines developed to deal with each aspect of the Christian life: thus moral theology dealt with matters of right and wrong abstracted from concern with the agent's moral growth, while ascetical or spiritual theology dealt with the spiritual growth of the inner man.[11]

The Protestant condemnation of moral theology did not help, as Protestants did little more than assert that good works "flow" from faith. Concern for moral development from the Protestant perspective was thus seen as a form of works righteousness. And in the absence of any way to talk about and form the behavior of Christians, Protestants were left vulnerable to whatever moralities happened to pertain in their cultures. Thus, being Christian often simply became a way to indicate what the society generally regarded as decent.

Because of the lack of conceptual categories, attempts to deal with moral development in the Christian life always seem to call forth irresoluble issues, such as the relation between faith and works and so on. I will try to avoid these issues by providing conceptual categories that may help us see that such alternatives fail to do justice to the nature of the Christian life. In particular I will argue that the language of virtue and character is especially fruitful in providing moral expressions appropriate to Christian convictions.[12] More-

10. That such is the case is not surprising, as most communities are not called on to articulate the conceptual linkages between what they "believe" and what they do. Such linkages are forged through the traditions and customs of a people developed from the interaction of their convictions and experiences. Once such a linkage is broken, no amount of "conceptual clarification" can restore the "naturalness" of the relationship. Indeed, the development of "ethics" as a distinct discipline that takes as its task the establishment of the "foundation" of morality may in fact denote that something decisive has happened to a community's moral convictions that no "foundation" can rectify.

11. For a fuller discussion of this distinction, see my "Ethics and Ascetical Theology," *Anglican Theological Review* 61, no. 1 (January 1979): 87–98.

12. For a more complex analysis of the idea of character, see my CCL. There I describe "character" as "the qualification or determination of our self-agency, formed by our having

over, I hope to show how the concepts of virtue and character help account for the kind of moral development required of those who have undertaken to live faithful to the Christian story. It is my view that language of virtue or character might well be useful to *most* accounts of moral development, but I am content here merely to make the case that they are conceptually crucial for articulating the kind of growth commensurate with Christian convictions.

Even though the concepts of virtue and character help situate the appropriate locus for Christian growth, they do not in themselves provide a sufficient account of the kind of growth required. "Character" is but a reminder that it is the self that is the subject of growth. But the kind of character the Christian seeks to develop is a correlative of a narrative that trains the self to be sufficient to negotiate existence without illusion or deception.[13] For our character is not the result of any one narrative; the self is constituted by many different roles and stories. Moral growth involves a constant conversation—between our stories—that allows us to live in a way appropriate to the character of our existence. By learning to make their lives conform to God's way, Christians claim that they are provided with a self that is a story that enables the conversation to continue in a truthful manner.

1.2 Puzzles of Moral Growth and the Ethics of Character

I am acutely aware that the concepts of character and narrative have received scant attention in recent moral theory.[14] In this essay I cannot hope to provide

---

certain intentions rather than others" (115). However, no one-sentence description can do justice to the complexity of a concept such as character. Indeed, it is my hope that this essay, through the development of the idea of narrative, will supplement the insufficiency of my analysis in CCL of how character is acquired and the necessary condition for us to be able to "step back" from our engagements.

13. For an analysis of the relation of narrative and self-deception as well as a more general account of the nature of narrative, see "Self-Deception and Autobiography," essay 10 in this volume, and "From System to Story: An Alternative Pattern for Rationality in Ethics" with David Burrell (1976) in TT.

14. For more detailed critiques of moral philosophy from this perspective, see VV and TT. In particular, I criticize recent moral philosophy's assumption that the primary moral question is What should I do? rather than What should I be? From my perspective the former question masks a deep despair about the possibility of moral growth, as it accepts us as we are. The only sign of hope such a view entertains is that we can free ourselves from who we are by making moral decisions from "the moral point of view." Yet the material content of the "moral point of view" assumes that the description of the "situation" does not require reference to the self for how the description should be made. In contrast, the question What should I be? demands

an analysis of character and narrative sufficient to defend the significance I have claimed for them. However, I can show how the ideas of character and narrative provide natural or useful ways to think about moral growth by analyzing some of the puzzles that bedevil most theories of moral development, that is, (1) growth as a threat to moral integrity; (2) how someone can be held responsible for acting in a manner that requires moral skills that he has not yet developed; and (3) how moral growth increases our capacity for moral degeneracy. By providing a brief discussion of each of these puzzles I hope not only to demonstrate how the concepts of narrative and character may help explicate moral growth, but also to introduce themes necessary for the development of the more constructive aspect of this essay.

The general assumption that it is a good thing for anyone to grow morally involves a paradox that is seldom noticed—for how can we grow and yet at the same time remain faithful to ourselves? We have little respect for people who constantly seem to be "changing," as we are not sure we can trust them to be true to themselves. Or even more troubling, we sometimes find ourselves unable to grow as we think we should, because such growth requires a betrayal of a relationship dependent on my being "true to my past self." Marriage often provides a particularly intense example of this kind of problem.

I suspect this to be the underlying reason why moral philosophy generally has been so disinclined to analyze the different "stages" of moral growth. Modern moral philosophy has been written from the perspective of some last stage, as if everyone were already at that stage or at least should have it in sight and should be working to achieve it.[15] The problem of moral development is

---

we live hopeful lives, as it holds out the possibility that we are never "captured" by our history, because a truer account of our self, that is, a truer narrative, can provide the means to grow so that we are not determined by past descriptions of "situations." Our freedom comes not in choice but through interpretation.

Interestingly, almost all ethical theory since Kant assumes that the moral life is lived primarily prospectively; that is, our freedom comes only as each new "choice" gives us a new possibility. But as we look back on our "choices," they seldom seem to be something we "chose," for we often feel we would have done differently had we "known what we now know." In contrast, I assume that ethics must be concerned with retrospective judgments, as we seek the means to make what we have "done" and what has happened to us our own. Moral "principles" cannot do that; what is required is a narrative that gives us the ability to be what we are and yet go on.

15. Kohlberg's Kantian commitments are commendably explicit, and like most Kantians he seems to assume that there really exist no other moral alternatives. He thus argues that morality must be "autonomous," that is, independent of any community or tradition, and

then taken to be how to reach the last stage of morality where moral growth ceases. Childhood is largely ignored because it is taken to represent a pre- or nonmoral stage of development.[16]

To proceed in this manner seems to assume that there is no way to account for present moral integrity *and* moral growth. Theories of morality are thus

---

"formal." Yet, like many Kantians he wants to claim that this "formal" understanding of morality provides substantive and material implications for actual moral behavior—that is, his concern for justice. Yet in fact, it remains to be shown that purely formal accounts of morality can generate the kind of commitment to justice Kohlberg desires. In particular, see Kohlberg's "From Is to Ought: How to Commit the Naturalistic Fallacy and Get Away With It in the Study of Moral Development," in *Cognitive Development and Epistemology*, ed. T. Mischel (New York: Academic Press, 1971), 215–18. For a perspective on Kant very similar to mine, see Alasdair MacIntyre, *A Short History of Ethics* (New York: Macmillan, 1966), 190–99. MacIntyre helps make clear that the Kantian program is not as free from history as it claims but rather is a moral philosophy written to meet the needs of liberal societies. In other words, we should not be surprised to get the kind of theory of moral development we find in Kohlberg, as it is an attempt to secure "moral" behavior in a society of strangers. It is questionable, however, whether such a "morality" is sufficient to produce good people. Martin Luther King, whom Kohlberg admires, would never have been produced nor would he have been effective if all we had was Kohlberg's sense of "justice." Rather, Martin Luther King's vision was formed by the language of black Christianity, which gave him the power to seek a "justice" that can come only through the means of "nonresistance." See, for example, Mc-Clendon's account of King in *Biography as Theology*, 65–86.

Ralph Potter has documented Kohlberg's impoverished sense of justice in his "Justice and Beyond in Moral Education," *Andover Newton Quarterly* 19, no. 3 (January 1979): 145–55. He suggests that Kohlberg's difficulty involves an attempt to define a program of moral education which can be undertaken within what are assumed to be constitutionally defined limitations of the content suitably treated in public schools. Thus he quotes Kohlberg's claim that the "moral development approach restricts value education to that which is moral or, more specifically, to justice. This is for two reasons. First, it is not clear that the whole realm of personal, political, and religious values is a realm which is non-relative, i.e., in which there are universals and a direction of development. Second, it is not clear that the public school has a right or mandate to develop values in general. In our view, value education in the public schools should be restricted to that which the public school has the right and mandate to develop: an awareness of justice, or of the rights of others in our Constitutional system" (149). That seems to be a nice confirmation of MacIntyre's argument and also explains the current enthusiasm for Kohlberg's work among educators, for it allows them to discuss "moral issues" in the classroom, seemingly without substantive moral commitments. The ideological bias of the assumption that a "formal" account of morality is "neutral" vis-à-vis actual moral convictions is overlooked, as it is exactly the ideology necessary to sustain a society that shares no goods in common.

16. For an extremely interesting account that treats "childhood" as an integral moral project, see David Norton, *Personal Destinies: A Philosophy of Ethical Individualism* (Princeton, NJ: Princeton University Press, 1976), 170–78. Kohlberg, unfortunately, never analyzes or defends

constructed to ensure grounds for integrity by supplying monistic moral principles that might render coherent all our activities. The two dominant contemporary moral theories, utilitarianism and formalism, share a common presumption that in the absence of any one moral principle our lives cannot help but be chaotic. They assume the possibility of integrity or moral identity depends on a single moral principle sufficient to determine every moral situation. The moral self results from or is the product of discrete decisions that have been justified from the moral point of view. The integrity of the self, in terms of these accounts, ironically results from always acting as if we are a moral judge of our own actions. For we can claim our actions morally as our own only if they were done from the point of view of anyone.[17]

The concepts of character and narrative provide a means, however, to express the moral significance of integrity without assuming that any one moral principle is available, or that moral development requires that there be a final stage. Indeed, the necessity of character for the morally coherent life is a recognition that morally our existence is constituted by a plenitude of values and virtues, not all of which can be perfectly embodied in any one life. Integrity, therefore, need not be connected with one final end or one basic

---

his assumption that the metaphor of stages is appropriate to describe the process of moral development. One of the reasons for this, I suspect, is that he has not noticed that it is, in fact, a "metaphor."

One of the anomalies of Kohlberg's commitment to Kant is that Kant was very clear that the development of virtue could not be learned or come through "stages." Thus, in *Religion Within the Limits of Reason Alone,* Kant says:

The ancient moral philosophers, who pretty well exhausted all that can be said about virtue, have not left untouched the two questions mentioned above. The first they expressed thus: Must virtue be learned? (Is man by nature indifferent as regards virtue and vice?) The second they put thus: Is there more than one virtue (so that man might be virtuous in some respects, in others vicious)? Both questions were answered by them, with rigoristic precision, in the negative, and rightly so; for they were considering virtue *as such,* as it is in the idea of reason (that which man ought to be). If, however, we wish to pass moral judgment on this moral being, man *as he appears,* i.e., such as experience reveals him to us, we can answer both questions in the affirmative; for in this case we judge him not according to the standard of pure reason (at a divine tribunal) but by an empirical standard (before a human judge). (20)

From Kant's perspective, Kohlberg's attempt to provide a naturalistic account of "autonomy" is a category mistake, since autonomy must be free from all "natural" causes. Kohlberg's interests are, oddly enough, Aristotelian in inspiration, but I think his attempt to express them through Kantian categories has prevented him from having the conceptual tools for a fuller account of moral development.

17. For a more detailed argument concerning this point, "From System to Story" (1976) in TT.

moral principle, but is more usefully linked with a narrative sufficient to guide us through the many valid and often incompatible duties and virtues that form our selves. From such a perspective growth cannot be antithetical to integrity, but essential to it; our character, like the narrative of a good novel, is forged to give a coherence to our activities by claiming them as "our own."

But if our character is always in process, how can we ever attribute responsibility to anyone? The reason deontological theories seem to have such explanatory power is that they seem to allow us to be held responsible for our behavior even though we were personally not able to avoid what we did or did not do. Thus, children grow by being held responsible, not by becoming responsible. But there are the more troubling cases, like that of Patty Hearst, where we hold a person responsible though we are not sure she was herself, but we think she should have been. Thus Patty Hearst, it is alleged, may not have known how to deal with the SLA, but anyone her age and with her experience should have known how. As a result, we hold her morally and legally responsible for bank robbery.

Such a judgment, though harsh, seems unavoidable. If responsibility were to be relative to each agent's character, public morality would be undermined. But to attribute responsibility to the agent from the perspective of public morality often seems unjust. Recent moral theories have tried to solve this tension by writing moral philosophy from the perspective of the moral observer. To become moral thus entails that each person learn to describe and judge his or her own behavior "from the perspective of anyone." As a result, the subject of moral development—the agent—ironically seems to be lost.

By contrast, I assume that no moral theory is capable in principle of closing the gap between what I should do (my public responsibility) and what I can or have to do (my own responsibility). What is needed is not a theory that will ensure correspondence between public and agent responsibility, but an account of how my way of appropriating the convictions of my community contributes to the story of that people. I am suggesting that it is useful to think of such an account as a narrative that is more basic than either the agent's or observer's standpoint. To claim responsibility for (or to attribute responsibility to) the agent is to call for an agent to be true to the narrative that provides the conditions for the agent to be uniquely that agent.

Finally, there is the problem of moral degeneracy. From the perspective of moral development, the possibility of degeneracy simply should not exist. For why would anyone backslide if he or she had reached a higher stage of morality? And yet empirically there simply seems to be the stubborn fact that we do backslide. The only explanation offered by advocates of "the moral point of view" is that backsliders had yet to form every aspect of their life according to the supreme moral principle; that is, it was not really backsliding.

But such an explanation fails to do justice to the struggle we all feel in learning to lead decent lives. What we need is an account that will help us deal with the "war that is in our members," that requires constant vigilance if growth is to occur. For as soon as we feel we have "made it," we discover that we have lost the skills necessary to sustain the endeavor. Ironically, the demand for moral growth requires an account of morality that allows us to understand that with every advance comes a new possibility of higher-level degeneracy.[18] The greater the integrity of our character, the more we are liable to self-deception and fault.[19] Moral growth thus requires a narrative that offers the skills to recognize the ambiguity of our moral achievements and the necessity of continued growth.

2. Moral Virtues and the Unity of the Self

So far I have tried to suggest that the categories of character and narrative offer a promising way to discuss the moral formation of the self: how Christian convictions may or should function to form lives. I have also hinted that the self can be held to have sufficient coherence to deal with the diversity of our moral existence only if that self is formed by a narrative that helps us understand that morally we are not our own creation, but rather our life is fundamentally a gift. In order to supply a more disciplined discussion of this latter contention, I am going to analyze some of the interesting suggestions and problems found in Aristotle's and Aquinas's ethics.

Aristotle and Aquinas, more than any other philosophers, were concerned with how the self, through its activity, acquires character. It is obviously not possible, nor is it necessary, to provide here a complete account of their extremely complex and often quite different accounts of moral virtue. Rather, it is my intention to explore certain unresolved problems in their accounts so

18. For example, Aquinas maintains that the more excellent a man is, the graver his sin (*Summa Theologica*, [New York: Benziger Bros., 1947], I–II, 73, 10). Subsequent references to the *Summa* appear in the text.
19. See, for example, Herbert Fingarette's analysis in *Self-Deception* (New York: Humanities Press, 1969), 140. See also "Self-Deception and Autobiography," essay 10 in this volume.

as to illuminate the meaning and necessity of character and the importance of narrative.

I will call particular attention to Aristotle's and Aquinas's insistence that only behavior that issues from a "firm and unchangeable character," that is, those actions I am able to claim as mine, can constitute moral virtue. Such a contention appears circular, since those capable of claiming their action as their own must already possess "perfect virtue." This is further complicated by Aristotle's and Aquinas's view that to be virtuous requires that one possess all the virtues, since they assumed that the virtues formed a unity. A perspective like theirs seems to pose insoluble problems for moral development, since one must already be morally virtuous to act in a manner that contributes to moral growth.

I shall try to show that Aristotle and Aquinas are right to think that moral growth is dependent on the development of character sufficient to claim one's behavior as one's own. But they were incorrect to assume that the development of such a self is but the reflection of the prior unity of the virtues. What is required for our moral behavior to contribute to a coherent sense of the self is neither a single moral principle nor a harmony of the virtues but, as I have already said, the formation of character by a narrative that provides a sufficiently truthful account of our existence. If I can show this to be the case, then at least I will have found a way to make intelligible the Christian claim that understanding the story of God as found in Israel and Jesus is the necessary basis for any moral development that is Christianly significant.

2.1 Acting as a Virtuous Man

There are certainly aspects of Aristotle's account of the moral life that might lead one to think that for him "moral character consists of a bag of virtues and vices."[20] If that is Aristotle's view, he seems to have no way to avoid the difficulty that "everyone has his own bag." The problem is not only that a virtue such as honesty may not be high in everyone's bag, but that my definition of honesty

---

20. Kohlberg, "Education for Justice: A Modern Statement of the Platonic View," in *Moral Education*, ed. Nancy Sizer and Theodore Sizer (Cambridge, MA: Harvard University Press, 1970), 59. In an interesting manner Kohlberg rightly seems to see that there is a deep connection between Plato and Kant, as each in quite different ways tries to provide a "foundation" for "morality" that makes the acquisition of "habits" secondary. Aristotle's insistence that "morality" must begin with habits simply assumes that there is no "foundation" for "morality" abstracted from historic communities.

may not be yours. The objection of the psychologist to the bag of virtues should be that virtues and vices are labels by which people award praise or blame to others, but the ways people use praise and blame toward others are not the ways in which they think when making moral decisions themselves.[21] The issue thus seems to be that the language of virtue reinforces an unreflective habituation to do the moral thing while ignoring the morally central issue—namely, that we not only do the right thing but do it for the right reason as well.

It is certainly true that Aristotle's resort to the mean fails to give an adequate explanation for the individuation of the various virtues.[22] Nor does he seem to appreciate the theoretical significance of the fact that the meanings of individual virtues are relative to different cultural and societal contexts. In the language I used above, he fails to see that the virtues are narrative-dependent.

Moreover, Aristotle at times seems to claim that becoming virtuous is simply a matter of training. Thus "moral excellence is concerned with pleasure and pain; it is pleasure that makes us do base actions and pain that prevents us from doing noble actions. For that reason, as Plato says, men must be brought up from childhood to feel pleasure and pain at the proper things;

---

21. Kohlberg, "From Is to Ought," 226–27. Kohlberg's criticism in this respect seems a bit odd, since his own commitment to a formal account of morality entails that a moral theory is not required to adjudicate among various accounts of "honesty." Kohlberg assumes far too easily that the "individuation" of "moral" situations is unproblematic. If he delved more deeply into this kind of issue he might be less sure that he holds a "nonrelative" moral theory. Moreover, in this criticism he fails to distinguish or confuses the issue of the individuation of the virtues with the suggestion that virtues and vices are arbitrary categories of public praise or blame.

22. Indeed, the whole problem of how the various virtues are individuated remains still largely unexamined. It seems that there is a general agreement that honesty, justice, courage, and temperance should be recognized as essential, but the fact that such "agreement" exists tends to mask the fact that there is little consensus about what "honesty" should entail. For an extremely interesting analysis of this kind of problem, see Alasdair MacIntyre, "How Virtues Become Vices: Medicine and Social Context," in *Evaluation and Explanation in the Biomedical Sciences,* ed. H. Tristram Engelhardt and Stuart F. Spicker (Boston: Reidel, 1975), 97–121. MacIntyre argues that truthfulness, justice, and courage are virtues that are necessary parts of any social structure, but that these "central invariant virtues" are never adequate to constitute "a morality." He holds that "to constitute a morality adequate to guide a human life we need a scheme of the virtues which depends in part on further beliefs, beliefs about the true nature of man and this true end" (104). In the absence of such a "scheme" MacIntyre argues that once the traditional virtues are no longer pursued for themselves they in effect become vices.

For an interesting example of the different transformations of meaning of one virtue, see Helen North's analysis of temperance in Greek and Roman society, "Temperance and the Canon of the Cardinal Virtues," in *Dictionary of the History of Ideas,* IV (New York: Scribner's, 1973), 365–78.

for this is correct education" (*Ethics*, 1104b10–12).[23] Aristotle thinks it does little good, therefore, to argue with people who have not been "well brought up," for they

> do not even have a notion of what is noble and truly pleasant, since they have never tasted it. What argument indeed can transform people like that? To change by argument what has long been ingrained in a character is impossible or, at least, not easy. Argument and teaching, I am afraid, are not effective in all cases: the soul of the listener must first have been conditioned by habits to the right kind of likes and dislikes, just as land must be cultivated before it is able to foster seed. For a man whose life is guided by emotion will not listen to an argument that dissuades him, nor will he understand it. And in general it seems that emotion does not yield to argument but only to force. Therefore, there must first be a character that somehow has an affinity for excellence or virtue, a character that loves what is noble and feels disgust at what is base. (1179b15–30)

Of course, Aristotle does not mean to imply that someone can become virtuous simply by being taught to be virtuous. The virtues must be acquired by putting them into action.

> For the things which we have to learn before we can do them we learn by doing: men become builders by building houses, and harpists by playing the harp. Similarly, we become just by the practice of just actions, self-controlled by exercising self-control, and courageous by performing acts of courage. . . . In a word, characteristics develop from corresponding activities. For that reason, we must see to it that our activities are of a certain kind, since any variations in them will be reflected in our characteristics. Hence, it is no small matter whether one habit or another is inculcated in us from early childhood; on the contrary it makes a considerable difference, or rather, all the difference. (1103a30–1103b25)[24]

---

23. All references to Aristotle's *Ethics* appear in the text.

24. It is well-known that Aristotle thought "ethics" to be primarily a branch of politics, since "becoming good" ultimately depended on the existence of good politics. Yet Aristotle was by no means ready to despair at the possibility of producing morally decent people if such a polity did not exist. Thus he says, "With a few exceptions, Sparta is the only state in which the lawgiver seems to have paid attention to upbringing and pursuits. In most states such matters are utterly neglected, and each man lives as he pleases, 'dealing out law to his children and his wife' as the Cyclopes do. Now, the best thing would be to make the correct care of these matters a common concern. But if the community neglects them, it would seem to be

The behavioristic overtones of these passages have led some to misinterpret Aristotle as an early Skinnerian. Yet he was acutely aware that people do not become just simply by doing just acts. Though some people do what is laid down in the laws, he knows that if they do so involuntarily, or through ignorance, or for an ulterior motive, they do not become just. They cannot be just "despite the fact that they act the way they should, and perform all the actions which a morally good man ought to perform" (1144a15–17).

Aristotle was no less concerned than Kant (or Kohlberg) that the morally right thing be done for the right reason. Where he differs from Kant is in his characterization of the kind of reason that forms our agency so that we are capable, not just of acting, but of becoming moral through our activity. A formal principle of rationality could not be sufficient, as the self must be formed to desire and act as a man of virtue desires and acts. Even though, as Kohlberg observes, Aristotle distinguishes between the intellectual and moral virtues,[25] the latter are formed rightly only when they are the result of practical wisdom.

2.2 The Circularity Involved in the Acquisition of Virtue
Aristotle notes that we are capable of performing just actions without becoming just, yet "it is possible for a man to be of such a character that he performs

---

incumbent upon every man to help his children and friends attain virtue. This he will be capable of doing, or at least intend to do" (*Ethics* 1180a26–31). Friendship thus becomes the crucial relationship for Aristotle, since, in the absence of good polities, it provides the context necessary for the training of virtue. It is certainly not too farfetched to suggest that Aristotle's description of his social situation is not that different from our own. The ethics of "autonomy" is an attempt to secure the objectivity of "morality" by basing "morality" in "rationality" abstracted from primary relations. Perhaps a more fruitful strategy is for us to try to recover the centrality of friendship for the moral life.

25. Kohlberg, "Education for Justice," 59. For Aristotle, practical wisdom is not necessary just to know the good, but to "become just, noble, and good" (*Ethics,* 1143b29). For a more complete account of Aristotle's understanding of practical wisdom and choice, see my *Character and the Christian Life,* 56–61. R. S. Peters has argued in a very similar fashion in his critique of Kohlberg, "Moral Development: A Plea for Pluralism," in *Cognitive Development and Epistemology* (New York: Academic Press, 1971).

Needless to say, I am in agreement with Peters's critique. In particular, I think Peters is right that Kohlberg has failed to appreciate the "rational" character of Aristotelian "habits." Moreover, as he suggests, Kohlberg's failure to deal with the class of virtues involving "self-control" is a serious deficiency. I suspect, however, that Kohlberg has not felt compelled to respond to Peters's criticism because he thinks "virtues of self-control" remains too vague. In a sense, he is correct about that, as obviously more is needed than "virtues of self-control"—namely, the self requires a narrative that suggests what kind of and how self-control is to function within our project.

each particular act in such a way as to make him a good man—I mean that his acts are due to choice and are performed for the sake of acts themselves" (*Ethics*, 1144a17–20). Or again: "In the case of the virtues an act is not performed justly or with self-control if the act itself is of a certain kind, but only if in addition the agent has certain characteristics as he performs it: first of all, he must know what he is doing; secondly, he must choose to act the way he does, and he must choose it for its own sake; and in the third place, the act must spring from a firm and unchangeable character. In other words, acts are called just and self-controlled when they are the kind of acts which a just or self-controlled man would perform; but the just and self-controlled man is not he who performs these acts, but he who also performs them in the way just and self-controlled men do" (1105a30–1105b8).

Note that this seems clearly to be circular.[26] I cannot be virtuous except as I act as a virtuous man would act, but the only way I can become a virtuous man is by acting virtuously. Aristotle seems to have thought that there was something about the very exercise of practical reason itself that, if rightly used, made us virtuous.[27] Yet, even if there is some truth to that, it cannot be sufficient, since he also argues that without virtue rational choice can at best be cleverness. A man can have practical wisdom only if he is good, for only the good man can know and judge his true end (1144a25–36).

26. There are actually two circles in Aristotle: (1) that only by acting justly can we become just, but to act justly seems to require that we be just, and (2) that in order for practical reason to desire and choose the right things rightly it must first be formed by the virtues, but the latter require the right use of right reason to be formed well. The two circles are obviously interrelated, but it is not easy to say how. Aristotle seems to have felt that the first circle, which he was quite aware of, was not vicious, since if people were taught to do the right things and to think about what they were doing, they would simply become people of character. The circularity of Aristotle's account of the virtues is but an indication that he rightly understood that morality needs no "foundations." Rather, he assumed that we are already morally engaged—the task of ethics being to help us understand and refine our engagement. Ethics for Aristotle is, therefore, an activity that is meant to remind us and draw out the implications that our nature is an activity.

27. I cannot develop it here, but I suspect it is no accident that Aristotle treats the virtue of courage immediately after his analysis of voluntary activity. For to act "voluntarily" is but a way of indicating that a man of practical wisdom must act in a manner that he is "in possession of himself." To act in such a manner requires more than "knowledge," for we must have the "courage" to face the world as it is, not as we want it to be. Courage and self-control involve more than restraining the passions, for they require the kind of self-knowledge that enables man to face reality and renounce delusion. Because he may have been assuming something like this, Aristotle may have thought that the exercise of practical reason in certain aspects of our lives necessarily would have an effect on the self, so that the other virtues would be formed accordingly.

The obvious circularity of the arguments did not bother Aristotle. He assumed that if people were started off right they would naturally over time become people of character capable of moral development.[28] At least one of the reasons he felt no need to explore the issue further was that he assumed we are capable of acting voluntarily—so that we can claim our actions as our own. In Aristotle's language we are capable of choice, that is, "deliberate desire for things within our power" (1113a10). Therefore, the acquisition of virtue is possible, since we are capable of acting in such a manner that the "initiative lies in ourselves" (1113b20).[29]

2.3 On Being Responsible for Our Character

Indeed, Aristotle even goes so far as to suggest that we must finally be responsible for our character. He notes, for example, that some may object that carelessness is simply part of a man's character. "We counter, however, by asserting that a man is himself responsible for becoming careless, because he lives in a loose and carefree manner; he is likewise responsible for being unjust or self-indulgent, if he keeps on doing mischief or spending his time in drinking and the like. For a given kind of activity produces a corresponding character. This is shown by the way in which people train themselves for any kind of contest or performance: they keep on practicing for it. Thus, only a man who is utterly insensitive can be ignorant of the fact that moral characteristics are formed by actively engaging in particular actions" (*Ethics*, 1114a4–10). Aristotle is prepared to admit, however, that once an unjust or self-indulgent man has acquired these traits voluntarily, "then it is no longer possible for him not to be what he is" (1114a20).

Finally, Aristotle asks what we are to make of the theory put forward by some that the end is not determined by choice of the individual himself, but is

28. Aristotle's claim that all men have a "natural" desire for happiness can easily be misleading for interpreting his thought. For the "end" of happiness is not simply given, but rather the "happy life is a life in conformity with virtue" (*Ethics*, 1099b27). Moreover, it must be the kind of "happiness" that encompasses a complete span of life (1177b25). Therefore, the "end" is not simply given, but correlative of the kind of persons we ought to be as people of virtue or character.

29. Of course, what is tricky about this is that how much the "initiative" resides in us is a correlative of the kind of "character" we have. So "freedom" for Aristotle is not a status prior to our acquisition of character, but is exactly dependent on our having become virtuous. It was Kant's great project to make morality dependent on freedom, in order that we might be held responsible for our "morality." In contrast, Aristotle (and I) assumed that our ability to hold ourselves responsible for our "character" is context-dependent on the kind of narratives into which we have been initiated.

a natural gift of vision that enables him to make correct judgments and to choose what is truly good. In contrast, he argues that such a theory cannot be true, for how then can

> virtue be any more voluntary than vice? Thus whether the end that appears (to be good) to a particular person, whatever it may be, is not simply given to him by nature but is to some extent due to himself; or whether, though the end is given by nature, virtue is voluntary in the sense that a man of high moral standards performs the actions that lead up to that end voluntarily: in either case vice, too, is bound to be no less voluntary than virtue. For, like the good man, the bad man has the requisite *ability to perform actions through his own agency,* even if not to formulate his own ends. If, then, our assertion is correct, viz., that the virtues are voluntary because we share *in some way* the responsibility for our own characteristics and because the ends we set up for ourselves are determined by the kind of person we are, it follows that the vices, too, are voluntary; for the same is true of them. (1114b14–25; italics mine)

But obviously everything depends on the ambiguous phrase "in some way." Aristotle has suggested we can become virtuous because we have the ability to make our actions our own—that is, to do them in a manner appropriate to our character. Yet our ability to act so seems to depend on our having become a person of virtue. Indeed, that is why Aristotle (and Aquinas) are doubtful that a morally weak person can be said to be acting at all, since such a person lacks the strength of character to make his actions his own.[30]

From within Aristotle's position I think there is no satisfactory way to deal with the circularity of his position. Yet for our purposes, the circularity is extremely instructive, since it suggests that the ability to act and to claim my action as my own depends on my "having" a self through which I am able to give an intelligibility to that which I do and to that which happens to me. But Aristotle simply lacked the conceptual means to articulate the nature of such a self, and as a result he finally has no alternative but to assume that the conventions of Greek society will be sufficient to provide the conditions necessary for us to be morally virtuous.

---

30. To try to analyze Aristotle's theory of moral weakness would simply take us too far afield of this point. However, it would provide a fascinating way to attack the issue of "moral development."

2.4 Aquinas on Acquiring the Virtues

I suspect that some circularity will bedevil my account of moral development. For we must all begin somewhere, and Aristotle cannot be faulted for insisting that we must develop certain sorts of habits early if we are to learn how to be moral in a more refined and nuanced sense.[31] The question is not whether such habits are necessary, but what kind would encourage the development of truthful character. Aristotle, and Aquinas, however, too easily assumed that "character" would result if we rightly embodied all the virtues.

This is perhaps more evident in Aquinas than in Aristotle. For Aquinas argued explicitly that all the virtues are united in the virtue of prudence; indeed, every virtue "is a kind of prudence" (*Summa Theologica* I–II, 58, 4 and 2). Like Aristotle, Aquinas emphasized the centrality of practical wisdom, since the doing of good deeds is not sufficient to make a man virtuous: "It matters not only what a man does but also how he does it" (I–II, 57, 5). And the "how" is always determined by prudence.

As a result, we find the same kind of circularity in Aquinas that we saw in Aristotle: The practice of any virtue requires prudence, yet prudence cannot be developed without moral virtue. The reason for this, according to Aquinas, is

> prudence is right reason about things to be done, and this not merely in general but also in particular. Now right reason demands principles from which reason proceeds. And when reason argues about particular cases, it needs not only universal but also particular principles. Consequently, just as one is rightly disposed in regard to the universal principles of action by the natural understanding or by the habit of science, one needs to be perfected by certain habits by which it becomes connatural, as it were, to judge rightly particular ends. This is done by moral virtue; for the virtuous man judges rightly of the end of virtue because such as a man is, such does the end seem to him (Aristotle, *Ethics,* 1114a32). Consequently the right reason about things to be done, namely prudence, requires man to have moral virtue. (I–II, 58, 5)

2.5 The Unity of the Virtues

Unlike Aristotle, however, Aquinas tried to provide a rational scheme to suggest why certain virtues are more prominent than others; thus, prudence is the perfection of the practical intellect, temperance perfects the concupiscible passions, courage perfects the irascible passions, and justice perfects all opera-

---

31. Peters's account of different kinds of habits and virtues strikes me as very promising in this respect (257–62).

tions. These are, of course, the classical cardinal virtues that Aquinas claims are called such because they "not only confer the power of doing well, but also cause the exercise of the good deed" (*Summa Theologica* I–II, 61, 1).

Even though Aquinas defends the view that each of the virtues is distinct, he also maintains that they

> qualify one another by a kind of overflow. For the qualities of prudence overflow on to the other virtues insofar as they are directed by prudence. And each of the others overflows onto the rest, for the reason that whoever can do what is harder, can do what is less difficult. Therefore, whoever can curb his desires for the pleasures of touch, so that they keep within bounds, which is a very hard thing to do, for this very reason is more able to check his daring in dangers of death, so as not to go too far, which is much easier; and in this sense fortitude is said to be temperate. Again, temperance is said to be brave, by reason of fortitude overflowing into temperance, insofar, namely, as he whose soul is strengthened by fortitude against dangers of death, which is a matter of great difficulty, is more able to stand firm against the onslaught of pleasures. (I–II, 61, 4)[32]

Aquinas, therefore, maintains that if anyone has "perfect moral virtue"— that is, a "habit that inclines us to do a good deed well"—then he or she has all the virtues. He thus assumes that perfect moral virtue necessarily provides a unity to the self, since there is no possibility of the virtues conflicting. However, he is able to make such an assumption only because he asserts that all men have a single last end that orders the various virtues appropriately. Aquinas's claim that "charity is but the form of the virtues" (I–II, 24, 8) is but a theological restatement of his assumption that the unity of the virtues (and the self) is a correlative of men having a single "last end."

Before criticizing Aquinas's (and Aristotle's) views on the unity of the virtues, I think it is well to call attention to the strength of their analysis. For by calling attention to the virtues they at least make the question of the self central to ethical reflection: "The form of an act always follows from a form of

32. It is interesting that though Aquinas argues that the virtues must be connected, sins cannot be. Thus, the "goods, to which the sinner's intention is directed when departing from reason, are of various kinds, having no mutual connection; in fact, they are sometimes contrary to one another. Since, therefore, vices and sins take their species from that to which they turn, it is evident that, in respect of that which completes a sin's species, sins are not connected with one another. For sin does not consist in passing from the many to the one, as is the case with virtues, which are connected, but rather in forsaking the one for the many" (*Summa Theologica* I–II, 73, 1).

the agent" (I–II, 24, 2). Moreover, they do not assume that there is any one external or neutral standpoint from which

> the various conditioned moralities can be judged. Precisely the force of the Aristotelian good for man is that it does single out, in necessarily vague terms, the perfect life of a man, taking account of his unconditioned powers of mind; and that this abstract ideal constitutes the permanent standard or norm to which the historically conditioned moralities can be referred when they are to be rationally assessed. In fact, the historically conditioned moralities do converge upon a common core and are not so diverse as the relativists claim. Courage, justice, friendship, the power of thought and the exercise of intelligence, are the essential Aristotelian virtues, although the concrete forms that they take greatly vary in the different socially conditioned moralities. The virtues of splendid aristocratic warriors are not the same as the virtues of a Christian monk; but they are not merely different. Each of the two ways of life demands courage, fairness or justice, loyalty, love and friendship, intelligence and skill, and self control.[33]

2.6 The Disunity of the Virtues and the Unity of the Self

But Aristotle and Aquinas were unable to conceive that we live in a world in which we must choose among ways of life that are inherently incompatible. No positing of a single end or good for man is sufficient to provide a solution for that fact. As Stuart Hampshire has observed:

> The ways of life which men aspire to and admire and wish to enjoy are normally a balance between, and combination of, disparate elements; and this is so, partly because human beings are not so constructed that they have just one overriding concern or end, or even a few overriding desires or interests. They find themselves trying to reconcile, and to assign priorities to widely different and diverging and changing concerns and interests, both within the single life of an individual, and within a single society. They also admire, and pursue, virtues which could not be combined without abridgement in any possible world: for instance, literal honesty and constructive gift of fantasy, spontaneity and scrupulous care, integrity and political skill in manoeuvre. Serious moral problems typically take the form of balancing strict but conflicting requirements, which Plato dramatized in the *Republic* by representing the man educated to be just as educated to combine and

33. Stuart Hampshire, *Two Theories of Morality* (Oxford: Oxford University Press, 1977), 44.

balance gentleness and firmness. As there must be conflicts in society, so there must be conflict in the soul, and it is the same virtue that strikes the right balance in situations of conflict.[34]

Aristotle and Aquinas seemed to assume that no self could bear such conflict. It was necessary, therefore, to assert that there could be no inherent incompatibility among the virtues. Rather, the right balance among the virtues could be exercised within a single complete life. As a result, they failed to see that we often find ourselves involved in ways of life that require that certain virtues go undeveloped or be essentially transformed. We cannot depend on "the virtues" to provide us with a self sufficient to give us the ability to claim our actions as our own. Rather, virtues finally depend on our character for direction, not vice versa.

2.7 The Narrative Unity of the Self

Aristotle's and Aquinas's difficulty in accounting for the unity of the self helps one to appreciate the way Kohlberg has approached the problem of moral development. Like Aristotle and Aquinas, he is concerned to articulate, or perhaps better, discover, the structure of our moral existence that enables us to make our actions and our life our own. But, unlike them, he feels it is hopeless to confuse the issue of "ego development" with moral development. "For the requirements for consistency in logic and morals are much tighter than those for consistency in personality, which is a psychological, not a logical, unity. Furthermore, there are relatively clear criteria of increased adequacy in logical and moral hierarchies, but not in ego levels."[35]

This does not mean that Kohlberg is uninterested in "ego development," or character; rather, his assumption seems to be that "consistency" of self depends on our willingness to guide our lives from the perspective of a universal moral standpoint: "A more differentiated and integrated moral structure handles more moral problems, conflicts, or points of view in a more stable or self-consistent way. Because conventional morality is not fully universal and prescriptive, it leads to continual self-contradictions, to definitions of right which are different for Republicans and Democrats, for Americans and Vietnamese,

---

34. Ibid., 17–18.

35. Kohlberg, "Moral Stages and Moralization," in *Moral Development and Behavior*, ed. Thomas Lickona (New York: Holt, Rinehart and Winston, 1976), 52. At least part of the difference between my position and Kohlberg's involves my attempt to show through the idea of character that "personality" can be more than a "psychological" category.

for fathers and sons. In contrast, principled morality is directed to resolving conflicts in a stable self-consistent fashion."[36]

Kohlberg is looking for something equivalent to Aristotle's and Aquinas's last end, but no moral principle (not even the most universal) or last end is sufficient to provide the self with the kind of unity he seeks. For even if such a principle existed, any attempt to guide our lives by it would necessarily require the moral confinement of the self. What we need is not a principle or end but a narrative that charts a way for us to live coherently amid the diversity and conflicts that circumscribe and shape our moral existence.

In summary, I am suggesting that descriptively the self is best understood as a narrative, and normatively we require a narrative that will provide the skills appropriate to the conflicting loyalties and roles we necessarily confront in our existence. The unity of the self is therefore more like the unity that is exhibited in a good novel—namely, with many subplots and characters that we at times do not closely relate to the primary dramatic action of the novel. But ironically, without such subplots we cannot achieve the kind of unity necessary to claim our actions as our own.

Yet a narrative that provides the skill to let us claim our actions as our own is not the sort that I can simply "make mine" through a decision. Substantive narratives that promise me a way to make my self my own requires me to grow into the narrative by constantly challenging my past achievements. That is what I mean by saying that the narrative must provide skills of discernment and distancing. For it is certainly a skill to be able to describe my behavior appropriately and to know how to "step back" from myself so that I might better understand what I am doing. The ability to step back cannot come by trying to discover a moral perspective abstracted from all my endeavors, but rather comes through having a narrative that gives me critical purchase on my own projects.

3. Growth in the Christian Life: A Story

As a way of trying to bring the disparate parts of my argument together I am going to tell a story. It is not a complicated story, but I think it suggests nicely

---

36. Kohlberg, "From Is to Ought," 185. I suspect that there is much to be said for Kohlberg's contention that moral growth occurs through the cognitive dissonance occasioned through our role conflicts. Exercises that help us to anticipate and rehearse such conflicts, moreover, may well help us to moral maturity. But such "growth" cannot simply be a question of being better able to justify our decisions from a "universal" perspective. For the subject of growth is the self, which is obviously more than the sum of principles to which we adhere.

how character and narrative can help us understand how the self can and should be capable of moral growth. Moreover, I hope this story will serve to suggest how the convictions peculiar to the Christian story require the development of certain kinds of skills. The story relates an incident between me and my father that occurred in an instant but has stayed with me for many years. In order to make it intelligible, I need to supply a little background.

My father is a good but simple man. He was born on the frontier and grew up herding cows. Living with a gun was and is as natural to him as living with an automobile is for me. He made his living, as his father and five brothers did, by laying brick. He spent his whole life working hard at honest labor. It would have simply been unthinkable for him to have done a job halfway. He is, after all, a craftsman.

I have no doubt that my father loves me deeply, but such love, as is often the case among Westerners, was seldom verbally or physically expressed. It was simply assumed in the day-to-day care involved in surviving. Love meant working hard enough to give me the opportunity to go to college so that I might have more opportunity than my parents had.

And go on I did in abstruse subjects like philosophy and theology. And the further I went the more unlike my parents I became. I gradually learned to recognize that blacks had been unfairly treated and that the word "nigger" could no longer pass my lips. I also learned that Christianity involved more than a general admonition to live a decent life, which made belief in God at once more difficult and easy. And I learned to appreciate art and music that simply did not exist for my parents.

Married to a woman my parents would always have difficulty understanding, I then made my way to Yale Divinity School, not to study for the ministry, but to study theology. During my second year in divinity school, every time we called home the primary news was about the gun on which my father was working. During the off months of the winter my father had undertaken to build a deer rifle. That meant everything from boring the barrel and setting the sight, to hand-carving the stock. I thought that was fine, since it certainly had nothing to do with me.

However, that summer my wife and I made our usual trip home and we had hardly entered the door when my father thrust the now completed gun into my hands. It was indeed a beautiful piece of craftsmanship. And I immediately allowed as such, but I was not content to stop there. Flush with theories about the importance of truthfulness and the irrationality of our society's gun policy, I said, "Of course, you realize that it will not be long before we as a society are going to have to take all these things away from you people."

Morally, what I said still seems to me to be exactly right as a social policy. But that I made such a statement in that context surely is one of the lowest points of my "moral development." To be sure, there are ready explanations supplied by the Freudians to account for my behavior, but they fail to do justice to the moral failure my response involved. For I was simply not morally mature enough or skillful enough to know how to respond properly when a precious gift was being made.

For what my father was saying, of course, was "Someday this will be yours and it will be a sign of how much I cared about you." But all I could see was a gun, and in the name of moral righteousness, I callously rejected it. One hopes that now I would be able to say, "I recognize what this gun means and I admire the workmanship that has gone into it. I want you to know that I will always value it for that and I will see that it is cared for in such a manner that others can appreciate its value."

I have not told the story to give an insight into my family history or because I get some pleasure from revealing my moral shortcomings. Rather, I have told it because I have found it illuminating for reflecting generally about moral growth. For the insensitivity of my response to my father did not reflect my failure to grasp some moral principle, or to keep the maxim of my action from being universalized, but showed that I did not yet have sufficient character to provide me with the moral skills to know that I had been given a gift and how to respond appropriately. On the surface my response was morally exemplary: I was straightforwardly honest and my position was amply justified. But in fact what I did was deeply dishonest, as it revealed a lack of self, the absence of a sustaining narrative sufficient to bind my past with my future.[37]

37. Of course, it is equally true that every "binding" requires a "loosing," as we cannot and should not be bound to everything in our past. It may even be true that some of us inherit a history so destructive we may rightly wonder how we could ever be bound to it. Yet my freedom from such a history cannot come by having "no history" but by acquiring a narrative that helps me have a stance toward my past without resentment. For resentment would continue to bind me to the destructive, since the self would still be essentially defined by my assumption that I am primarily a creature of injustice. I suspect that one of the reasons growth in the Christian life is described as conversion is that it requires us to learn to live without resentment. And to be able to live in that manner requires us to learn that our life, including the destructive past, is nothing less than a gift. I wish to thank Michael Duffy for helping me formulate this point.

For my response was meant only to increase further the alienation between my father and myself in the interest of reinforcing what I took to be a more "universal" and objective morality. I discovered that the person who responded so insensitively to my father was not "who I was" or at least not what "I wanted to be." I was and am destined to be different from my parents, but not in a manner that means I no longer carry their story with me. But my own self, my story, was not sufficient to know how that might be done.

And I am struck by how little I would have been helped by becoming more sophisticated in ethical theory or even by conforming my life more completely to the best ethical theory of our day. My problem was not that I lacked skill in moral argument and justification, but that I lacked character sufficient to acknowledge all that I owed my parents while seeing that I am and was independent of them. Indeed, it has taken me years to understand that their great gift to me was the permission to go on, even though they sensed my "going on" could not help but create a distance between me and them that love itself would be unable to bridge.

Equally interesting to me has been the attempt to explain to myself how I could have been so unbelievably self-righteous. My temptation has always been to think that what I said was not "the real me." Moreover, there is some good reason to accept that kind of explanation, since I certainly would not have said what I did had I "known better." Therefore, I was not responsible for what I did, though I clearly did it at the time.

But such an explanation is a "temptation," as it is equally clear to me that my moral growth depends on taking responsibility for what I said as something done by me. Not to take responsibility for my response is to remain the person who made that kind of response. Philosophically that seems to be a puzzle, for how am I to explain that I must take responsibility for what "I did 'unknowingly' " in order that I can now claim responsibility for what I am and have become? As puzzling as the philosophical problem is, the moral intelligibility of claiming such an action as mine is just as sure. For retrospectively all my actions tend to appear more like what "happened to me" than what I did. Yet to claim them as mine is a necessary condition for making my current actions my own. Our ability to make our actions our own—that is, to claim them as crucial to our history—even those we regret, turns out to be a necessary condition for having a coherent sense of self: that is, our character. But such a coherence requires a narrative that gives us the skill to see that our freedom is as much a gift as it is something we do.

For our freedom is dependent on our having a narrative that gives us skills of interpretation sufficient to allow us to make our past our own through incorporation into our ongoing history. Our ability to so interpret our past often may seem to require nothing less than conversion as we are forced to give up false accounts of ourselves. Because of the pain such conversions often entail, the language of discontinuity tends to predominate in our accounts of our moral development. But the freedom acquired through our reinterpretations is dependent on our having a narrative sufficient to "make sense" of our lives by recognizing the continuity between our past and present and our intended future. In order to see that, we need a story that not only provides the means to acknowledge the blunders as part of our own story, but to see ourselves in a story where even our blunders are part of an ongoing grace, that is, are forgiven and transformed for "our good and the good of all the church."[38]

3.1 Gifts, Sociality, and Growth

These last claims obviously require a defense more elaborate than I can hope to develop here. Indeed, I am unsure I even know how to defend such a claim or know what defense would or should look like. In fact, I have suggested two related but different points: (1) that the self is a gift and (2) that we need a story that helps us accept it as a gift. It is from the story that we gain the skills to recognize the gift on which our life depends, as well as ways of acting appropriate to such a gift. For the language of gift, without an appropriate account of the gift itself, can be just as destructive as the claim that we are our own possession.

Yet the language of gift at least offers us a way to deal with Aristotle's claim that we are responsible for having a careless character. Even though we may intuitively think that to be correct, it remains quite unclear how we can be said to be responsible for our character. For the very condition required to claim responsibility seems to be character itself. Therefore, Aristotle seems right in suggesting that it does not just make considerable difference how we are brought up, it makes "all the difference."

And it is certainly true that we need to be trained to acquire certain habits. But it is equally important to be introduced to stories that provide a way to locate ourselves in relation to others, our society, and the universe. Stories capable of doing that may be thought of as adventures, for there can be no self devoid of adventure. What we crave is not dignity as an end in itself, but the

---

38. I am particularly grateful to James McClendon for suggesting this way of putting the matter.

participation in a struggle that is dignifying. Without self-respect, integrity is impossible. And self-respect comes from a sense of the possession of a self correlative to our participation in a worthy adventure. Yet my very ability to take on a role in the adventure is dependent on my understanding that there are other roles I am not called on to play or cannot play. But the very existence of these other roles gives me the ability to step back and test my own involvement in the adventure. They provide a standpoint that helps me see the limits and possibilities of my own role. Moral growth comes exactly through the testing of my role amid the other possibilities in the adventure.

Moreover, through initiation into such a story I learn to regard others and their difference from me as a gift. Only through their existence do I learn what I am, can, or should be.[39] To be sure, the other's very existence necessarily is a threat to me, reminding me that I could have been different than I am. The truthfulness of the adventure tale is thus partly tested by how it helps me negotiate the existence of the other both as a threat and as a gift for the existence of my own story.

The necessary existence of the other for my own self is but a reminder that the self is not something we create, but is a gift. Thus, we become who we are through the embodiment of the story in the communities in which we are born. What is crucial is not that we find some way to free ourselves from such stories or community, but that the story that grasps us through our community is true. And at least one indication of the truthfulness of a community's story is how it forces me to live in it in a manner that gives me the skill to take responsibility for my character. That does not mean that there will ever be a point at which I can say "I am now what I have made myself," for the story must help me see that claiming myself as my own is not the same as claiming that I have made or chosen what I am. Rather, it means I am able to recognize myself in the story that I have learned to make my own.

This is a particularly foreign perspective for most of us today. For our primary story is that we have no story, or that the stories that we have must be overcome if we are to be free. Thus, we demand a universal standpoint so that the self may reach a point from which it can judge and choose objectively among competing particularistic stories; in short, we seek a story that frees us from the adventure. Ironically, the story that we have no story is one that

39. For example, see Enda McDonagh's suggestion that "threat" is always the necessary other side of a "gift," *Gift and Call* (St. Meinrad, IN: Abbey Press, 1975), 36–39. That such is the case makes Aristotle's understanding of the centrality of courage for moral wisdom all the more compelling.

prevents moral growth. For it provides us with a self-deceptive story that fails to adequately account for the moral necessity of having a story and of being a self in the first place.

What we require is not no story, but a true story. Such a story is one that provides a pilgrimage with appropriate exercises and disciplines of self-examination. Christians believe Scripture offers such a story. There we find many accounts of a struggle of God with his creation. The story of God does not offer a resolution of life's difficulties, but it offers us something better than adventure and struggle, for we are possessors of the happy news that God has called people together to live faithfully to the reality that he is the Lord of this world. All men have been promised that through the struggle of this people to live faithful to that promise God will reclaim the world for his Kingdom. By learning their part in this story, Christians claim to have a narrative that can provide the basis for a self appropriate to the unresolved, and often tragic, conflicts of this existence. The unity of the self is not gained by attaining a universal point of view, but by living faithful to a narrative that does not betray the diversity of our existence. No matter how hard such a people work to stay faithful to such convictions, they never can forget that it is only through a gift that they are what they are.

To argue that what we need is a true story if we are to grow in a morally appropriate way is not to deny the importance of the "universal." But the test of the truthfulness of any story does not reside in its conforming to or embodying a prior universal norm, but rather in how we and others find their lives illuminated and compelled by the accuracy and truthfulness of its particular vision. There is no "story of stories," but only particular stories that more or less adequately enable us to know and face the truth of our existence. Thus, there is no universal point of view, a point of view that does not bear the marks of a particular history. The recognition of that is one of the first indications that we are dealing with a story that should demand our attention for its power to reveal the truth.

3.2 How Can We Be Taught and Grow into the Story?
Every account of moral development must necessarily have educational implications. We must be given some exercises appropriate to the kinds of moral growth desired. That is an incontrovertible risk. The various sets of exercises through which Christians learn to understand and live appropriate to the story of God's dealing with them in Israel and Jesus may be called tradition. The Christian life requires the development of certain kinds of habits, but

those very habits require us to face ambiguities and conflicts through which our virtues are refined. Therefore, there is every reason to think that Christians have always been prescribing a form of moral development for training in their own community.

Growth in the Christian life may well involve encouraging a greater conflict between the self and wider society than is generally approved. Thus, Christians train or should train their children to resist the authority of the state, not in the name of their "rights" as individuals, but because the "justice" of the state is to be judged against God's justice. Such training is "risky," as it separates the young of the Christian community from powerful support necessary to being "a self." To be trained to resist the state, therefore, requires nothing less than an alternative story and society in which the self can find a home.

Such a society can never be satisfied with external compliance with the story. For the story itself demands that only those who are willing to be the story are capable of following it. That is why it has been the brunt of Christian spirituality through the ages to provide exercises and examples through which Christians might better be what they are. What is crucial is not that Christians know the truth, but that they be the truth. "For if the doctrines of Christianity were practiced, they would make a man as different from other people as to all worldly tempers, sensual pleasures, and the pride of life as a wise man is different from a natural; it would be as easy a thing to know a Christian by his outward course of life as it is now difficult to find anybody that lives it."[40]

I suspect that the insistence on learning to live as you are and be as you live is part of the reason that Christians have maintained that the Christian life finally requires attention to masters of that life. For it is from the masters that we learn skills necessary to have lives appropriate to the claim that we are nothing less than God's people. For the most central of Christian convictions is the assumption that no statement or principle of morality can be sufficient to make us moral. Rather, to be moral requires constant training, for the story that forms our lives requires nothing less than perfection—that is, full participation in an adequate story.

---

40. Law, *A Serious Call to a Devout and Holy Life*, 55. There is an unjustified intellectualistic bias in much of the literature dealing with moral development. The assumption seems to be that the more "self-conscious" we are of our "values" and principles, the better chance we have for moral growth. While I suspect any significant tradition must develop some who are "self-conscious," it is by no means clear that all need to be such. We must remember that the Gospel does not require us to be self-conscious as our first order of business. Rather, it requires us to be faithful.

4. Conclusion

I am acutely aware that the twisting and turnings in this chapter are enough to test the patience of even the most sympathetic reader. Therefore, some attempt at summing up seems called for. I began with the claim that Christians have always been concerned with moral development, but that the kind of moral growth they wish to promote is not equivalent with current theories of moral development. For Christian convictions require that the self be transformed in a manner that befits their conviction that the world is under the lordship of Jesus Christ—that is, that the fundamental character of our life is that of a gift. By exploring some of the puzzles endemic to accounts of moral growth, I suggested that the concepts of character and narrative are particularly important for understanding moral growth and in particular the kind of growth appropriate to Christians.

The exploration of these puzzles also allowed me to suggest some of the difficulties of theories of moral development inspired by Kant. By analyzing the strength and weakness of Aristotle's and Aquinas's understanding of the acquisition of virtue, I tried to suggest how the growth of the character, and the corresponding ability to claim our actions as our own, is a correlative of our being initiated into a determinative story. For it is only through a narrative that we learn to "live into" that we acquire a character sufficient to make our history our own.

By telling and analyzing a story from my own experience, I sought to suggest in a more concrete manner the rather abstract analysis of Aristotle and Aquinas. The development of character involves more than adherence to principles for their own sake; rather, it demands that we acquire a narrative that gives us the skill to fit what we do and do not do into a coherent account sufficient to claim our life as our own. Such narratives may of course be false and as a result produce false character. Indeed, an indication of a truthful narrative is one that remains open to challenge from new experience. That is why a truthful narrative necessarily must be one that can provide integrity in a manner that does not deny the diversity of our lives and the necessity to claim as mine what I wish I had not done, as well as what I have done well.

By suggesting how the story Christians tell offers them a place in an adventure, I have tried to indicate how such a theory provides a pattern for moral growth. But this suggestion remains enigmatic, apart from my few suggestions concerning learning to trust in our existence as a gift. A more detailed account would require showing how that claim is spelled out through the story of

God's dealing with his people and how the struggle that always goes with learning is necessary to make that story ours. For internal to the story itself is the claim that we cannot know the story simply by hearing it, but only by learning to imitate those who now are the continuation of the story.

Further Reading

"Sanctification and the Ethics of Character" (1975, 1985), in CCL

"Self-Deception and Autobiography" (1974), essay 10 in this volume

"A Tale of Two Stories: On Being A Christian and a Texan" (1981), in CET

"Characterizing Perfection: Second Thoughts on Character and Sanctification" (1985), in STT

"Theological Reflections on Aristotelian Themes" (1997), with Charles Pinches in CAV

"The Sanctified Body: Why Perfection Does Not Require a 'Self'" (1998), in STT

12. The Interpretation of Scripture:
Why Discipleship Is Required (1993)

This popular piece is a homily on Christian discipleship, one of many that Hauerwas has preached at the Divinity School of Duke University, where he has taught since 1984. The tendency of many North American Christians to assume that we merely have to pick up the Scriptures to understand them is compared to the view that if Jesus had joined us on the Emmaus road, we necessarily would have recognized him. However, rightly seeing the Lord, or rightly reading the Scriptures, is not a given, but requires the hard discipline of existing as a people constituted by the practices of the risen Lord.

A Sermonic Exhibit

Isaiah 25:6–9

Luke 24:13–35

My family loves to tell the story of my cousin Billy Dick. The very name, Billy Dick, indicates that we are Texans. One Easter, when Billy Dick was six, he was in Sunday School at Lakewood Methodist Church in Dallas, Texas. He was listening to the story of the crucifixion. He suddenly realized that the crucifixion was a very unhappy affair. He waved his hand in a desperate attempt to attract the teacher's attention. The teacher finally acknowledged him. He stood up and blurted out, "If Roy Rogers had been there, those dirty s.o.b.s would not have been able to do it."

My family loves this story even though the language is a bit embarrassing. The language after all is familiar, coming, as we do, from the world of bricklaying. We like the story also because it underwrites a sense of who we are. We do

[From *us*. Used by permission. This essay was published as one of many "sermonic exhibits" in *us*. For Hauerwas's commentary on the significance of sermons, see "The Church as God's New Language," essay 7 in this volume.]

not think of ourselves as among the makers and breakers of a society but rather as the kind of simple people who do the right thing year in and year out. Such modesty, however, can hide very strong moral idealism. For we believe that if we had been at the crucifixion we certainly would not have let it happen. We are not the kind of people that let innocent people be killed.

Yet my family tends to miss the irony of Billy Dick's story. For that story presumes that we would rescue a savior who dies rather than using force with the blazing six-guns of Roy Rogers. We assume that there is no inherent incompatibility between our use of violence and what Jesus was about.

I think my family in that regard is no different from most Christians today. We believe that on the whole we should be nonviolent except when there is a real crisis. I often ask my students, for example, whether it might be a good idea to keep a gun in church. After all, many of them serve in Western Carolina, in the mountains, and you never know when a motorcycle gang might break into the church threatening to rape the women and make the men watch. So the idea that we ought to keep a gun rack under the Cross, preferably with a submachine gun in it, seems quite sensible. They are rather taken aback at that suggestion, but I suspect that most of us nevertheless harbor the assumption that there must be guns in our lives if for no other reason than because we never know when we might be asked to defend the innocent.

Not only my family but most of us like Billy Dick's appeal to Roy Rogers. We might say it differently, with much more sophistication, but we do not believe that we would have let Jesus be unjustly crucified. Part of the appeal of Billy Dick's reaction to the crucifixion is, of course, the general American penchant for siding with the underdog. We entertain imaginatively heroic roles assuming when the time comes that we would be ready to rise to the occasion. We assume that if we had just been there with Jesus, if we had just been able to follow him day in and day out, to witness his miracles, to hear his teachings, to observe his confrontations with the leaders of the society, we would have been faithful. We would not have abandoned him at the Cross. We are even more confident that we would have recognized him if Jesus had joined us on the road to Emmaus.

That we think we would have stood with Jesus against the crucifixion, that we think we would recognize him after the resurrection, is an extraordinary presumption. Just to the extent that we find our lives embedded in the Gospel makes clear that most of us, even if we had known all there was to know about Jesus, would have at worst been in the crowd shouting "Crucify him, Crucify him!" At best we would have returned to Galilee thinking it was good while it lasted, but we had better get back to the "real world." If I had missed being there to shout "Crucify him, Crucify him," I am sure it would not have been because I sided with Jesus but rather because of my dislike of crowds.

To claim that if Jesus had joined us on the Emmaus road we would have recognized him is not unlike claiming that in order to understand the Scripture all we have to do is pick it up and read it. Both claims assume that "the facts are just there" and reasonable persons are able to see the facts if their minds are not clouded. Yet, as we shall see, the story of the Emmaus road makes clear that knowing the Scripture does little good unless we know it as part of a people constituted by the practices of a resurrected Lord. So Scripture will not be self-interpreting or plain in its meaning unless we have been transformed in order to be capable of reading it.

The story of the Emmaus road neatly challenges our presumption that a resurrected Lord would be readily recognizable. We are simply told that "two of them" were leaving Jerusalem, walking toward Emmaus, discussing what had happened over the past few days. It seems that they must have seen, for example, a cleansing of the temple or perhaps observed the examination of Jesus before the Sanhedrin. Perhaps these people may well have been following Jesus for some time, having heard the Sermon on the Mount or having observed his miracles. They seem to be close associates of Jesus, not perhaps among the apostles, but nonetheless people deeply attracted to what Jesus was about.

I tend to think of these two as admirers. I do so because they remind me of a story that Jim McClendon reports about Clarence Jordan. Clarence Jordan was the founder of the Koinonia Farm near Americus, Georgia. It was set up to be an interracial community before anyone knew what civil rights were all about. Jordan himself was a pacifist as well as an integrationist and thus was not a popular figure in Georgia, even though he came from a prominent family.

The Koinonia Farm, by its very nature, was controversial and, of course, it was in trouble. McClendon reports that in the early fifties Clarence approached his brother Robert Jordan (later a state senator and justice of the Georgia Supreme Court) to ask him to represent legally the Koinonia Farm. They were having trouble getting LP gas delivered for heating during the winter even though it was against the law not to deliver gas. Clarence thought Robert could do much through a phone call. However, Robert responded to Clarence's request:

"Clarence, I can't do that. You know my political aspirations. Why, if I represented you, I might lose my job, my house, everything I've got."

"We might lose everything too, Bob."

"It's different for you."

"Why is it different? I remember, it seems to me, that you and I joined the church on the same Sunday, as boys. I expect when we came forward the preacher asked me about the same question he did you. He asked me, 'Do you accept Jesus as your Lord and Savior.' And I said, 'Yes.' What did you say?"

"I follow Jesus, Clarence, up to a point."

"Could that point by any chance be—the cross?"

"That's right. I follow him to the cross, but not *on* the cross. I'm not getting myself crucified."

"Then I don't believe you're a disciple. You're an admirer of Jesus, but not a disciple of his. I think you ought to go back to the church you belong to, and tell them you're an admirer, not a disciple."

"Well now, if everyone who felt like I do did that, we wouldn't *have* a church, would we?"

"The question," Clarence said, "is, 'Do you have a church?' "[1]

That we find these two on the way to Emmaus, walking away from Jerusalem, gives us some basis for thinking that they were admirers not unlike Robert Jordan. They clearly understood that what had been taking place in Jerusalem around this man Jesus concerned very serious matters indeed. In fact, they were continuing to discuss it in an effort to understand what had taken place. Maybe they were not admirers. Perhaps they were intellectuals or even theologians. One can almost hear them say "That was really an interesting set of suggestions Jesus had to make about the kingdom. Damned insightful, though a bit overstated, I must say. Though he is quite provocative, he really lacks the characteristics of a carefully trained mind."

Because they are so enthralled with the events in Jerusalem around Jesus, they are astounded that this stranger who joins them on the way to Emmaus seems to know nothing about those events. He was coming from Jerusalem, and surely he must have known the front page news of the day. Yet he has to ask them what they are talking about. It surely seems that this stranger is at a disadvantage.

However, as they proceed on their way to Emmaus, instructing Jesus along

1. James Wm. McClendon Jr., *Biography as Theology* (Nashville, TN: Abingdon Press, 1974), 127–28.

the way, it is remarkable that they do not recognize who he is. We tend to blame them for this, but perhaps we are far too quick. We are not talking "regular stuff" here. We are talking about the resurrection. That we expect these two on the way to Emmaus to recognize Jesus shows us how difficult it is for any of us to comprehend the resurrection. No matter how hard we try, it is difficult to shake the picture that the resurrection is the resuscitation of a corpse that we would recognize if confronted by it.

Of course, that is exactly what the resurrection is not. It is not the resuscitation of a corpse but rather the final eschatological act by God through which the Kingdom stamp is put on this man Jesus as the decisive life for the inauguration of a new age. Resurrection is the reconfiguration of all we know, have known, and will know. It is that which forces a redescription of all history as well as the movement of the planets. Resurrection is Kingdom come in the person and work of this man Jesus. It is, in the wonderful title of Allen Verhey's book, *The Great Reversal.*

That Jesus has been marked by such a stamp must surely make us think twice about our claim that we would be able to easily spot him—this man, this crucified messiah—just as he is also the power that moves the sun and the stars. We do not readily comprehend that here in this cross and resurrection the very destiny of the cosmos is determined. It is surely presumptuous on our part that we would easily recognize him. We should be much more sympathetic to our companions on the way to Emmaus than we were initially.

But if their failure to recognize Jesus is a reminder that the resurrection is not the resuscitation of a corpse, it also renders problematic all subjectivistic theories of the resurrection. Those theories suggest that Jesus' resurrection is merely a poetic, symbolic, or mythological way of describing the disciples' sense of the continuing presence of Jesus. Such accounts of the resurrection are compared to memories of outstanding figures such as Gandhi, or Martin Luther King Jr., or Dorothy Day. We tend to imagine the resurrection in these terms as if we were friends sharing a meal, discussing all that Jesus had done, and suddenly thinking that the very experience of discussing Jesus made Jesus still alive. Such theories assume that the experience we have is itself the resurrection; we fail to understand that insofar as we are capable of remembering well, it is because God's resurrection of Jesus is sure regardless of what we may or may not experience.

One of the problems with such subjectivistic accounts of the resurrection is that they make the resurrected Jesus far too familiar, far too subject to our needs and wants. Indeed, it makes us lose the eschatological character of the resurrection entirely, as we force Jesus into the limits of our lives. In fact, the resurrection forces our lives to conform to God's Kingdom. The early Christians' discovery that they could pray to Jesus, that they could worship Jesus, is intelligible only if this Jesus is the resurrected Lord of all creation.

Therefore, that these two admirers of Jesus did not recognize him is a reminder to us that Jesus, after the resurrection, is a stranger. We cannot recognize him by looking, but we have to be instructed through the lives of others. We must learn that, resurrected though he may be, it is the crucified Jesus that is so resurrected. Jesus is not the exemplification of savior stories that we have learned elsewhere, but he is the defining figure for what salvation means. That is why Hans Frei, in his *Identity of Jesus Christ,* rightly reminds us that Jesus is no Christ figure since he was the Christ. He was not a "man for others," for there have been many such people. Rather, this Jesus is the eschatological Messiah of the God of Israel who makes possible the calling of the Church into existence so that the world might know that our destiny is determined by a kingdom that the world cannot know separate from this man. Therefore, in order to recognize this Messiah, this crucified but risen Jesus, we need training and instruction. We do not possess in ourselves what we need to recognize Jesus as the resurrected Lord, because such recognition depends upon training by that very Lord. That such training is required is clear from the way Jesus' companions try to explain why they are leaving Jerusalem. In their explanations it is clear that they do not recognize this companion as the resurrected Jesus for the simple reason that they have not understood the Jesus of Golgotha.

They had thought that in this man Jesus they had found the long-expected Messiah. They acknowledge that Jesus was no doubt a powerful prophet in word and deed. In fact, they thought he had the potential to set Israel free: "But we had hoped that he was the one to redeem Israel." The redemption of Israel is after all the political freeing of the people of Israel from perpetual control of others. It is the rebirth of the land of Palestine. They were sure that this Jesus had the power to effect this.

Yet they say that the leaders conspired to kill him, and they accomplished their task well. They had seen the crucifixion, it seems. Even more, they had now heard that the tomb was empty. The women say it is empty. The women and others even saw an angel who said that Jesus was alive. They acknowledged that some have verified all this. Jesus is not in the grave. He is not there. Where he is, is not clear.

Now, you must wonder about our companions on the way to Emmaus at this point. If the tomb is empty and this has been verified, why are they leaving Jerusalem? You would think that they might want to stay and find out what has happened. While there have certainly been people raised from the dead in the past, you would think that it is a fairly extraordinary event and that they would have wanted to stay to find out what had happened. But no, they leave Jerusalem thinking that they had seen all that they had needed to see. They start to Emmaus.

How can we explain this strange behavior? Surely even if Jesus is alive, even if Jesus is resurrected, they wanted a different outcome. He is not, it seems, the Messiah who was to liberate Israel. What does resurrection have to do with the liberation of Israel? Resurrection is not the politics for which they had looked. So they could not see the resurrected Jesus exactly because the resurrected Jesus embodied the politics of a kingdom for which they were unprepared.

Jesus therefore has to begin to explain to them what they had seen in Jerusalem. He points out to them that they had missed the very meaning of the prophets who had taught them that "the Messiah had to undergo much to enter into his Glory." And Jesus must begin with Moses to show them the kind of Messiah that was among them. Namely, it was a Messiah whose politics required that he be killed in order that the world might know the character of God's Kingdom. This is not a death that is sacrificial in and of itself; rather, it is a death required by the very politics of the Kingdom. For Jesus has come that some of us might be called from the world, in order to live in a manner different from the violence of the world.

As Jesus explained the Scripture, we have what might be called a hermeneutical moment. But it is not just explaining the text and what it meant that Jesus is about, for these people on the way to Emmaus clearly seemed to have known the text. Their problem is that they did not know how to find Jesus in it. They had not received the training that would put them in a whole set of practices that would give the text a whole different reading. In effect, Jesus had to deconstruct their narratives so that they might see, for example, why a text such as Isaiah 52 and 53 is about Jesus:

> [13] See, my servant shall prosper; he shall be exalted and lifted up, and shall be very high.
>
> [14] Just as there were many who were astonished at him—so marred was his appearance, beyond human semblance, and his form beyond that of mortals—
>
> [15] So he shall startle many nations; kings shall shut their mouths because of

him; for that which had not been told them they shall see, and that which they had not heard they shall contemplate. . . .

[3] He was despised and rejected by others; a man of suffering and acquainted with infirmity; and as one from whom others hide their faces he was despised, and we held him of no account. . . .

[5] But he was wounded for our transgressions, crushed for our iniquities; upon him was the punishment that made us whole, and by his bruises we are healed. . . .

[8] By a perversion of justice he was taken away. Who could have imagined his future? For he was cut off from the land of the living, stricken for the transgression of my people.

[9] They made his grave with the wicked and his tomb with the rich, although he had done no violence, and there was no deceit in his mouth.

[10] Yet it was the will of the LORD to crush him with pain. When you make his life and offering for sin, he shall see his offspring, and shall prolong his days; through him the will of the LORD shall prosper.

[11] Out of his anguish he shall see light; he shall find satisfaction through his knowledge. The righteous one, my servant, shall make many righteous, and he shall bear their iniquities.

[12] Therefore I will allot him a portion with the great, and he shall divide the spoil with the strong; because he poured out himself to death, and was numbered with the transgressors; yet he bore the sin of many, and made intercession for the transgressors.

We assume under the authority of the Church that when we hear these texts from Isaiah they are about Jesus. We can assume that because we are on this side of Emmaus. We have become trained in this kind of rereading, but our companions on the way to Emmaus did not assume that these texts were about Jesus. They had to be taught that such a text is about Jesus by Jesus. I am sure, moreover, that as their companions we must continue to relearn this over and over again.

We never learn this lesson well because we and our companions on the way to Emmaus assume that Messiahs are people of power, not suffering servants such as we find in Isaiah. Søren Kierkegaard tells a story, which I retell, that exemplifies our presumptions about these matters. It is a story about a prince and a beautiful peasant maiden. The prince spots this beautiful young woman one day when he is riding in his fields. She is gathering wheat. Watching her work he falls deeply in love, but vows to win her without using his power as prince. So he returns to his castle, puts on peasant clothes over the purple, and goes to work beside her.

Kierkegaard observes that our attention is held in this story not by whether this beautiful young peasant woman will come to love the prince. He is, after all, a noble and handsome prince. They are both young, and there is no doubt that they will love one another. Rather, our attention is grabbed in such a story by predicting: When will he tell her he is the Prince? Will it be perhaps at a break in their work after she has come to know him over weeks and months? During that break, will he declare his love and will she, perhaps demurely respond positively? With that response, will he rip back the coarse cloth of the peasant and reveal the purple underneath?

Storytellers, of course, are wonderful in how they build our suspense. Perhaps he will wait until the wedding. After she pledges her troth and he does likewise he will rip back the peasant clothes and reveal the purple. Perhaps he will even wait until after the wedding, when he will say, "You have not only become my wife, but indeed you are the princess of the land." Such a story is romantic, and it rightly holds our attention. Kierkegaard notes that ironically such stories also determine how we think of Jesus. For we tend to think that Jesus is like a prince pretending to have coarse cloth of the human, of crucifixion, of death, of powerlessness, that covers the purple. There really is the kind of power here that the world knows is just. We must wait for him to rip it away so the purple will be revealed. That rip we think to be the resurrection. There is the purple that makes it possible for Christians to acquire the power to rule the world. That is the politics we want through this Jesus.

Yet in Jesus there is no purple other than the crucifixion—the purple is the crimson of the Cross. There is no hidden power here. For our savior comes not as the world knows powerful figures. Rather, our savior comes offering us the practice of reconciliation necessary for us to be a people able to live in the world without violence and envy. Like our companions on the way to Emmaus, we expected a politics of power from this Messiah and instead we get crucifixion and resurrection. Like our companions on the way to Emmaus, we want the certainty and power of a text, but instead we get the call to discipleship. So, like those on the way to Emmaus, who now have the disadvantage of enjoying an account of Christianity that we believe puts us in control of history, we continue to fail to recognize this One who comes to call those able to live out of control.

Yet after Jesus' explication of the Scriptures, we see that our companions on the road to Emmaus still cannot see who it is that has joined them. Nonetheless, in general they have found him pleasant to be with. So, even though he seems bent on going further, they suggest he spend the night with them. As they sit together, as he breaks the bread, their eyes are opened and they recognize him. The guest had become the host, reconstituting the very meaning of hospitality.

But upon recognition he disappears. Their eyes have been opened. Adam's and Eve's eyes were opened, and they were blind. Now through the sharing of Christ's presence in the meal, our blindness is reversed and we see. The effects of sin are turned back, and we are made new creatures capable of being in communion with one another through Christ.

What are we to make of this strange occurrence? Certainly it at least means that Jesus is present to our companions on the way to Emmaus and to us most powerfully in the fellowship meal of the new age in which he has made it possible for us to share. Surely this must mean that the presence we have with Christ at Eucharist is even more determinative than an appearance on the way to Emmaus. Once you have such a presence, you no longer need an appearance.

Indeed, one suspects that part of the felt need for something as absurd as "the search for the historical Jesus" may have some connection with the fact that these guests tend to originate in those traditions where Eucharist is celebrated not as presence but rather as absence. The search for the historical Jesus is a substitute for the willingness to share the life of Christ. It presumes that if we could just get the facts right, we could really make up our minds about whether our life could be fully shaped by the Kingdom that is determined by this man's life. Yet, the "real historical Jesus" and/or the "objective text of Scripture" cannot be substituted for the reality of Christ that is found through the sharing of this meal.

In receiving food from Jesus after Easter we receive the gift of his life, God's life, through which we are made part of the adventure called Kingdom. Through the sharing of God's very life as Trinity we are made part of a community that can live by forgiveness rather than hate, envy, and resentment. It is a community that is the creation of a new time and a new age. That is why all readings from the past must be transformed by the habits of this community. In this meal we learn of God's unfailing hospitality, of God's unrelenting character to be reconciled to us, thus making it possible for us to be a community of peace in a violent world.

Jesus' Cross and resurrection is not just some exchange between himself and God, it is not God playing games with himself; rather, Jesus' resurrection makes us agents in God's history of reconciliation by transforming us into a community of the reconciled. The good news is that we were once no people but now we are a people of peace that stand as a sign that resurrection is the end of the new beginning for the world. The reality of the resurrection is thus manifest in the fact that we exist. We exist as a people who testify in the resurrection of this man that God has, as was promised in Isaiah 25, "swallowed up that veil that shrouds all the people; the pall thrown over all the nations—he has swallowed up death forever." Christ has become our temple through which all are now directed to worship in order that all creation may be made at one with and at peace with God.

So as we again and again are welcomed by this host at his meal of the kingdom of peace, we become people of peace and reconciliation. Only such a people are capable of recognizing and witnessing to others concerning this stranger who is the heart of our existence. Only such a people will be capable of rightly reading the Scripture. Only such a people are capable of in fact performing the Scripture.

In *Christianity Rediscovered*, Vincent Donovan tells of his mission work with the Masai. One of the most significant gestures for the Masai is to offer one another a handful of grass as a sign of peace, happiness, and well-being. During arguments that might arise, a tuft of grass offered by one Masai and accepted by another is an assurance that no violence will erupt because of the argument. As Donovan says, "No Masai would violate that sacred sign of peace offered, because it was not only a sign of peace; it was peace."[2]

Donovan describes how the Mass begins among the Masai as soon as the priest enters the village. Dancing begins as well as praying for the sick. This can last for a whole day before the climax in eucharistic celebration. Yet he says he never knew if Eucharist would in fact emerge from all this. For the leaders of the village would be the ones to decide yes or no if the Eucharist was to be performed. For if the life in the village had been less than holy, then there was no Mass. If there had been selfishness and forgetfulness and hatefulness and lack of forgiveness in the work that had been done, in the life that had been led there, they would not make a sacrilege out of the Eucharist by calling it the Body of Christ. Donovan says that from time to time leaders did decide, despite the prayers and readings and discussions, if the grass had stopped, if someone or some group in the village had refused to accept the grass as a sign of the peace of Christ, there would be no Eucharist.

2. Vincent J. Donovan, *Christianity Rediscovered* (Maryknoll, NY: Orbis Books, 1982), 127.

So when we pass the grass by wishing for each other the peace of Christ, let us remember it is in that we are able to recognize the presence of this stranger, our resurrected Lord, and how in that recognition lies our salvation. The resurrected Lord is a stranger, but he is also the host that invites us to become his friend and thus become friends with ourselves and others; so let us keep the feast of peace and reconciliation made possible because our Lord has risen from the grave. Perhaps even the world will see that we are a "biblical people."

Further Reading
"The Moral Authority of Scripture" (1981), in cc
"The Church as God's New Language" (1986), essay 7 in this volume
"Jesus and the Social Embodiment of the Peaceable Kingdom" (1983), essay 6 in this volume
"Stanley Fish, the Pope and the Bible" (1993), in us
"The Bible and America" (1993), in us
"A Sermon on the Sermon on the Mount" (1993), in us
"Practice Preaching" (1997), in stt

13. Casuistry in Context: The Need for Tradition (1995)

As one who had written on issues of casuistry since the mid-1970s, Hauerwas appreciated casuistry's attention to the particulars of the description of moral situations and to what can be learned from attention to these particulars. The publication of Albert Jonsen and Stephen Toulmin's The Abuse of Casuistry *in 1987 signaled an attempt to reintroduce the practice of casuistry ("case-based reasoning") into theological ethics. Hauerwas argues that Jonsen and Toulmin's approach to casuistry is still too determinatively formed by Enlightenment assumptions, namely, that casuistry can be done as autonomous reflection outside of any particular authoritative tradition of inquiry. Contrary to the assumption that such "liberal" casuistry is truly free and open to innovation, Hauerwas thinks that in the end such casuistry cannot but be rather conservative, captured by the status quo.*

I. Why Casuistry Is Not Applied Ethics

I was raised a Methodist. That means before I was twelve I had already had all the experience I could take. That is the reason I sometimes suggest that there are some words that certain religious traditions should never be allowed to use. Anglicans should never be allowed to say "Incarnation" because they usually mean by that "God became human and said, 'Say, this is not too bad.'" In like manner, Methodists should not be allowed to use the word "experience" because they usually mean that salvation consists in having the right feelings at the right time and in the right place. Rather than our confrontation with God being an occasion for challenging our endemic narcissism, the emphasis on experience thus only underwrites our fatal narcissism.

[From *IGC* © 1995 by University of Notre Dame Press. Used by permission. The version reprinted here includes material from the original lecture not included in the version published in *IGC*.]

All of which is to say that I am not all that happy with an emphasis on experience as an end in and of itself for moral reflection. I feel about experience as I do about talk about values; namely, I do not want to know what you value—tell me what you want. So do not tell me about the importance of experience, but rather name the experience you think is important. What is important is not that we attend to experience, but whose experience, where they had it, and how they understand it. More important than having had an experience is whether we know how to describe it or name it.

I think the same is true about casuistry. I am completely convinced that Albert Jonsen (and Stephen Toulmin) are right to remind us of the significance of casuistry.[1] Moreover, I think Jonsen is right to suggest that modern moral philosophy has tended to ignore the importance of casuistry in its attempt to secure the foundation of morality qua morality; or perhaps more accurately, modern moral philosophy has tended to distort the nature of casuistrical reasoning with a model of basic principles applied to particular cases. The "cases" discussed turned out to be cases amenable to our theories. For instance, what do you do about the fat person stuck in the mouth of the cave with the water rising on the inside threatening to drown the four companions left in the cave? Can you use the dynamite that has been conveniently found to blow the fat one out of the hole in order to save the four inside?

It is instructive that this kind of case is assumed to be crucial for almost all varieties of contemporary ethical theory—for example, Kantian, utilitarian, contractarian, and all the various ways they can be combined. Such cases are made for such theories because, as Alasdair MacIntyre has observed, these various theories share the presumption that the role of ethics is

> to specify universally binding principles or rules whose universality has the scope of humanity itself. Detachment from and disinterestedness towards all social particularity and positivity is thus a defining mark of morality. It follows that morality can be formulated and understood independently of any considerations which arise from highly specific forms of social structure.

1. [This essay originated as a response to a conference presentation by the biomedical ethicist Albert Jonsen on the relation of casuistry and experience. Both essays were presented at an international conference on the importance of experience for medical ethics, organized by Warren Reich of Georgetown University. In the essay, Hauerwas responds not only to Jonsen's essay, but also to his then recently published book, that is, Albert Jonsen and Stephen Toulmin, *The Abuse of Casuistry: A History of Moral Reasoning* (Berkeley: University of California Press, 1988). Jonsen's conference presentation was revised (see n. 4 below), but never published.]

Ignorance of sociology and history will not be a defect in the student of morality as such. But what then of those areas of human life in which the regulation of conduct requires the framing of rules which specify how institutionalized relationships of physician, nurse and patient, of lawyer, client and judge, of elected public officials to civil servants and to the public? The answer, according to the dominant standpoint, is that the rules of morality as such have to be applied to this kind of socially and institutionally specific rules. The academic discipline of ethics as such, which enquires into the nature of morality as such, has to be supplemented by the discipline of applied ethics.[2]

Examples like that of the cave above become standard cases for such a conception of "applied ethics." For what it seems needed is but the statement of ethical principle (e.g., "Never do evil that good may come" or "Always act for the greatest good for the greatest number") and the testing of its implications in such "cases." It is to be noted that such "cases" are ideal for such ethical theories since the variables of the cases are interchangeable with other cases. Therefore, all that is needed to make such theories relevant to medicine, for example, is to change the situation to the problem of scarce medical resources such as dialysis machines and how patient selection is to be done fairly. When those captured by this understanding of ethics, and in particular "applied ethics," turned their attention to medicine, they were not challenged to change their conception of ethics but instead simply changed the examples so that their theories seemed relevant to issues raised in medicine.

MacIntyre argues that this understanding of "applied ethics" is incoherent in its very conception because it cannot be the case that we can first comprehend the rules of morality in the abstract and then ask how they are applied: "For, were this to be the case, the rules of morality as such would be effectively contentless. On the dominant view, for example, we are first and independently to frame a rule or rules about truth-telling and honesty in general and then only secondly need to enquire how they are to be applied in such relationships as those of physician to patient or lawyer in respect to his or her client's affairs and so on. But no rule exists apart from its applications, and if, as we approach the question of whether a physician on a particular type of occasion ought to answer a question by a patient, truthfully or not, it must be

2. Alasdair MacIntyre, "Does Applied Ethics Rest on a Mistake?", *The Monist* 67, no. 4 (October 1984): 499. See also my "Reconciling the Practice of Reason: Casuistry in a Christian Context" (1986), in *CET*.

in the light of previous applications of the rule. But these applications will have been to situations and relationships quite as socially specific as is the physician-patient relationship."[3]

MacIntyre's analysis of the incoherence of the very notion of "applied ethics" at first seems to share much with Jonsen's criticism of ethical theory since Sedgwick. Yet I hope to show that Jonsen (and Toulmin) are actually much closer to Sedgwick than to MacIntyre. For the problem is not, as Jonsen would have it, that philosophers have tried to do ethics on the model of scientific detachment, but rather, they have tried to do ethics free from any concrete traditional and corresponding moral practices. In order to accomplish this they have sought to reduce morality to a few basic moral principles that are allegedly constitutive of rationality qua rationality. Unless ethics could be so grounded, it was assumed that there could be no defense against relativism, subjectivism, and arbitrary starting points. Though Jonsen's defense of casuistry is an attempt to critique or at least supplement this kind of moral theory, I find that his account of casuistry still assumes the fundamental correctness of the account of ethics sponsored by the heirs of Sedgwick.

II. Casuistic Reasoning

In this respect it is interesting how modern accounts of Christian ethics has attempted to model the philosophical project of modernity. Thus theologians stress love, justice, or some other monistic principle as all-determining for ethical rationality and judgment. I say it is interesting because we might have expected that those from religious traditions would have resisted such monistic reductions because they would have noticed that they were working from within an ongoing tradition. I suspect, however, that because the social and political context we occupy makes the particularity of traditions something to be overcome, we perpetuate this kind of ethical reductionism. We try to use our theories to supply for reason and the self a unity that can only be forthcoming from our communities and their practices.

Against this background the call for us to attend to "experience" and/or casuistry makes great sense. For I take it that "experience" is meant to name those aspects of our moral existence that are simply ignored or distorted by our longing for the certainty and unity that our theories promise but fail to supply. Therefore, by calling our attention to a method of casuistry that is not

3. MacIntyre, "Does Applied Ethics Rest on a Mistake?", 502.

the application of theory but rather the ongoing reflection about cases, Jonsen is trying to help us recover what anthropologists call a "thick description" of our moral existence. In that respect I think we are in his and Toulmin's debt, not only for trying to rescue casuistry but for providing us with the rich history of casuistry. In particular, I am sure they are right to direct our attention to rhetoric as a crucial component for understanding moral reflection.

But just as I suggested that I am suspicious of any appeal to experience in itself, so I am suspicious of appeals to casuistry as a good in and of itself. Put as succinctly as I can, what bothers me about Jonsen's account of casuistry, both in his paper and in his book, is the failure to acknowledge that casuistry is only intelligible in an ongoing tradition.[4] I am well aware that with the introduction of the term "tradition," most will anticipate that I am going to begin a MacIntyrian critique of Jonsen. Such suspicion is not wrong, but I do not think it would be all that useful for our purposes for me to spell out MacIntyre's arguments in *Whose Justice? Which Rationality?*[5] Rather, I find the leverage needed to carry out this critique within Jonsen's description of casuistry. In *The Abuse of Casuistry* Jonsen and Toulmin point out that classical casuistry was not closely associated with any ethical theory,[6] but as a result

4. In the revision of his original paper (unpublished), Jonsen acknowledges that casuistry presupposes "a relatively coherent social and cultural community." However, I continue to think he wants to have the "universal morality" and the concreteness of casuistry at the same time. In other words, I am suggesting that casuistry still looks too much like "applied ethics" rather than how in a tradition rules are extended, limited, or reformulated.

5. Alasdair MacIntyre, *Whose Justice? Which Rationality?* (Notre Dame, IN: University of Notre Dame Press, 1988).

6. In his essay Jonsen notes that in their book, he and Toulmin argued that classical casuistry was not closely associated with any ethical theory even though the practitioners worked within the framework of "natural law." Yet he maintains that the methods of reasoning and principles of casuistry were equally compatible with any "modern ethical theory." But that simply cannot be the case if, as MacIntyre argues, no rule exists apart from its application—exists, that is, as a working rule in a moral tradition. It would be unfair to attribute Jonsen and Toulmin's account of casuistry entirely to their experience on the National Commission for the Protection of Human Subjects of Biomedical and Behavioral Research, but one cannot help but think, as they testify in their book (16–19), that their appreciation as well as understanding of casuistry derives at least in part from that experience. For as Toulmin reports, as a staff member for that commission, the commissioners found it relatively easy to reach agreement on particular concrete issues raised by difficult types of cases, even though they continued to disagree about matters of moral principles or about what the basic rules of morality actually were (Stephen Toulmin, "The Tyranny of Principles," *Hastings Center Report* 11, no. 6 [December 1981]: 31–32). Their experience on this commission seems to have left Jonsen and Toulmin to conclude that concentrating on "cases" while leaving behind "theory" might be a way to "do" ethics—that is, a way to get on with the task of building consensus about the good

I think they fail to note how the intelligibility of casuistry depends on a tradition-formed community constituted and sustained by particular sets of virtues. So, rather than rehearsing MacIntyre, I will try to suggest what I hope is a compatible account of casuistry by exposing some of the tensions in the account Jonsen provides.

---

in and for our society. Yet MacIntyre argues, and I think correctly, that Toulmin fails to appreciate that such agreements are not a testimony to rational and moral achievement, but rather a "nonrational social transaction" ("Does Applied Ethics Rest on a Mistake?", 501). According to MacIntyre, that agreement is reached in situations celebrated by Toulmin is but an indication of the ideological function of the very idea of "applied ethics." For even though the liberal presumption that morality is constituted by a set of principles to which any rational agent would assent has proved to be unfounded, that does not mean this conception of morality is without social influence:

> What it tends to provide are a set of standards by means of which each contending party in fundamental disputes is able to discredit the rational pretensions of its opponents. And this is one more source of the systematically inconclusive character of debate over fundamental issues in our contemporary culture. But the ongoing necessities of social life require that these fundamental rifts and conflicts be kept out of view so far as possible, hence the everyday practical life of our social institutions has to be insulated so far as possible from fundamental debate. The phenomenon, which Toulmin noted in the members of the National Commission, of an ability to combine disagreement on moral issues at theoretically fundamental levels with agreement at the level of immediate practicality is in fact and has to be pervasive in our social lives. One central way in which this is achieved is by conferring a high degree of indeterminacy upon our actual shared moral principles. . . . and no finite number of applications will remove that indeterminacy. . . . Why is this? It is first of all because characteristically and generally what renders the relevant type of situation problematic is that adducing of a number of rival and incompatible considerations and hence in arriving at a decision how to act the idiom of "a balancing of considerations" is often and appositely used; only—there are no scales—and so the metaphor of balancing, if thought of as rational process, is a misleading and disguising fiction. . . . We do not bind our successors and we are not bound by our predecessors. Nor indeed could we, if this account of our shared principles and rules is true, for the indeterminacy of our principles or rules is such that they do not in any substantial sense at all bind us. This is why these are not genuinely moral principles or rules. ("Does Applied Ethics Rest on a Mistake?", 510–11)

Yet as MacIntyre points out, there are important areas of our life where there has to be shared public agreement (i.e., medicine, law, accountancy, engineering, and the military), and we should not be surprised that it is exactly in those areas that the idea of applied ethics has flourished. This dominant conception of applied ethics can in such circumstances mask transactions in which professional power is asserted so that professional autonomy can be protected from general moral scrutiny. But in other areas the very notion of applied ethics conceals a rediscovery of morality as such. "When physicians or nurses for instance discuss truth-telling, honesty, trust, and allied subjects it is almost always the case that they are doing nothing other than reopening that general discussion of truth-telling in which Aristotle, Maimonides, Aquinas, Kant and Mill are among their predecessors. Their questions concern what the rules are and whether they need to be extended or reformulated, questions perhaps

Jonsen rightly emphasizes that crucial to casuistry is a "procedure of reasoning based on paradigms and analogies, leading to the formulation of expert opinion about the existence and stringency of particular moral obligations framed in terms of rules and maxims that are general but not universal or invariable" (n.p.). There can be no question that analogical reasoning is central for casuistral reflection. But I think it is a mistake to use the phrase "reasoning based on paradigms and analogies," because it implies that paradigms and analogies have the same status or function. That surely cannot be the case, as I illustrate by putting the matter in Kantian fashion: Analogy without paradigms is empty.

Since Jonsen might well respond that he certainly understands that analogical reasoning depends in a crucial way on examples, it may be thought that this is surely an insubstantial quibble. Yet I think the issue cannot so easily be resolved because of the very way he goes on to display the nature of casuistrical reflection—namely, in terms of morphology, taxonomy, and kinetics. As he notes, the primary work of casuistry so construed "is to determine which maxim should rule the case and to what extent" (n.p.). I am tempted to make something of the fact that maxim is Kantian language—indeed, I believe everything Jonsen wants could be accounted for from within a Kantian-construed moral theory—but it would be uncharitable to attribute a philosophical position to him on the basis of a word. Rather, the problem is his assumption that it is the interplay of "circumstances and maxims that give structure to the case" (n.p.).

For example, Jonsen says, "The work of casuistry is to determine which maxim should rule the case and to what extent." That sounds, however, very much like MacIntyre's account of "applied ethics": namely, one assumes the existence of a rule or several rules or maxims and then sees if and how they fit certain kinds of cases. Thus it is assumed that the rules—"Competent persons have a right to determine their own fate," "The physician should respect the wishes of the patient," "Relieve pain," "Thou shalt not kill," "Give no deadly

---

occasioned for them by peculiarly medical issues and questions peculiarly urgent for physicians and nurses, but not at all peculiarly medical questions. The rubric of 'applied ethics' is thus in both areas a barrier to understanding what is actually going on" ("Does Applied Ethics Rest on a Mistake?", 512). Of course, Jonsen most certainly would object that his (and Toulmin's) attempt to help us recover the importance of casuistry is not "applied ethics" in MacIntyre's sense. There are certainly important differences, but Jonsen's very disavowal of "theory" is exactly the kind of move that you would expect from someone under the influence of the kind of theory of morality that MacIntyre is critiquing.

poison, even if requested"—exist separate from their application. Maxims are not, as Jonsen would have it, the "moral" of the story, for the story is the moral of the story.

My difficulty with Jonsen's way of putting the matter is that it overlooks the prior question of how paradigms are located in the first place, what interests determine the reason they are seen as crucial, and what determines our description of them. Paradigms do not spring from the head of Zeus unmediated, but are located within an ongoing tradition in which the telling of stories suggests why certain examples are crucial. Thus, for some cultures the eating of meat is a paradigmatic issue for informing and shaping moral rationality as well as living.

I am, in this respect, particularly suspicious of Jonsen's suggestion that necessary assumptions about causality grant an invariant character to practical reasoning. Indeed, I am suspicious of the distinction between physical and moral causality when dealing with descriptions of human significance. Causality is a term that is secondary to the narrative display necessary for arriving at the appropriate description. Jonsen, in this respect, is quite right to direct our attention to detective stories, but not because detectives display "invariant patterns" of reasoning, but because by watching them we see how "solutions" depend on retrospective judgments that consistently reconfigure relations between contingent events through narrative construals.

In this respect I think no text explores these issues in a more troubling fashion than Eco's *The Name of the Rose.*[7] Eco's detective, a Franciscan nominalist theologian who does not believe in necessary causation, must discover who the murderer is by painstaking narrative reasoning. The dark side of such a project seems suggested by Eco as he has his detective discover the right murderer based on a false narrative—thus suggesting that all narratives are illusory constructs we impose on a random world. Of course, the only way we come to understand the irony of the detective's narrative is through Eco's narrative; that is, the only way to discover a false or inadequate narrative is by a true one.

I want to be very careful not to attribute to Jonsen a theory about casuistry he may not hold, but I find some of his language at least troubling. For example, he suggests that the "morphology of a case reveals the invariant structure of the particular case, whatever its contingent features, and also the invariant forms of argument relevant to any case of this sort. The first task of the casuist

---

7. Umberto Eco, *The Name of the Rose* (Hollywood, CA: Script City, 1984).

is to discern the structure. To modify the metaphor, the casuist must 'parse' the case, getting below the surface of the story to the grammatical structure of argument from grounds to claim through warrant and to the deeper grammar of the topics that underlie that argument" (n.p.). I am suggesting that such language as "invariant structure" and "getting below the surface of the story" leads us away from the very nature of casuistry. For we do not reason analogically by "getting below the surface" but rather by comparing and contrasting similarities and differences between paradigmatic examples.

Jonsen tells us that we get our cases from the "moral experience of mankind," though he notes that such a simple answer sheds little light (n.p.). Yet he seems to suggest that it is at least important in order to inform us why we are all drawn to cases as the heart blood of ethical reflection. I think that appeals to the "moral experience of mankind" not only fail to shed much light on the issue, but are furthermore positively misleading. They suggest that there is some universal perspective that can help us locate the "cases" of "examples" or "paradigms" that shape our reasoning.

Jonsen acknowledges that casuistry succeeds only when it is employed in a relatively coherent social and cultural community in which certain paradigms are "enshrined." While I worry a bit about the qualifier "coherent," since in our social context that word too often suggests a society without conflict rather than a community capable of having significant moral disagreement, I am still happy to see Jonsen acknowledge this point. Yet I think he has still not accepted the full implications of such an acknowledgment.

He rightly says that casuistry can only be done within a moral community but then denies that such a community can be identified with any specific "sociocultural continuities in time and space" (n.p.). I must admit I simply do not know what Jonsen means by a community that is free from actual determination in time and space. He calls for the development of a "comparative casuistry" but fails to tell us from what possible perspective such "comparisons" might be made. Presumed in the call for such comparisons is the assumption that "we" stand in a community that has somehow freed itself from its particularity.

The same arguments MacIntyre makes in *Whose Justice? Which Rationality?* against the idea of translation based on the assumed internationalized languages of modernity render Jonsen's "comparison" problematic. Only when it is recognized that a language is used in and by a particular community at a particular time and place with particular shared beliefs and practices can we appreciate the impossibility of thinking that we can translate Irish-as-such into

English-as-such. There simply are no such languages, but rather only Irish-as-written-and-spoken-in-sixteenth-century-Ulster.[8] Thus, the Irish Doire Columcille can never be the English Londonderry. Just as the pseudolanguages of modernity carry imperialistic presumptions that any language can be translated into English, so Jonsen assumes "casuistry" to be a common practice subject to common comparison. Such a "casuistry" would be so abstracted from the practices of any community that it could not pretend to do any serious work.

I am aware that this criticism may seem deeply unfair as Jonsen is struggling to help us recover the concreteness of moral discourse. Yet I think his machinery—morphology, taxonomy, and kinetics—gives the impression that casuistry has an invariable pattern in and of itself. I think the point of contention between us becomes clearer by attending to the quotation Jonsen uses from Aristotle's *Nichomachean Ethics*: "Prudence apprehends the ultimate particular, which cannot be apprehended by scientific knowledge, but only by perception—not the perception of objects peculiar to one sense, but the sort by which we perceive that the ultimate figure in mathematics is a triangle; because there too there will be a halt. But this is perception rather than prudence, although it is another kind of perception" (*EN* 1142aff).

This is one of my favorite passages in Aristotle's *Ethics* because it seems as right as it is obscure.[9] Aristotle I think rightly sees that the crucial issue is one of perception: "This is a murder" or "This was a suicide." But is "murder" or "suicide" the same as "triangle"? I think there can be no in-principled answer to this since the ability to answer it depends on the tradition in which one has been trained. As a Christian, I want to say that "murder" or "suicide" marks when our perception should come to a halt. As Philip Devine pointed out long ago, the word "murder" means neither "wrongful homicide" nor "killing of the innocent" but rather a homicide that is neither justified nor excused nor mitigated.[10] It is therefore a philosophical mistake to ask what is wrong with murder. If we rightly understand the grammar of the word murder, we understand that the only issue is whether this or that killing is a case of murder.

8. MacIntyre, *Whose Justice? Which Rationality?* 370–78.

9. For extensive discussions of Aristotle's account of practical reason, see ibid., 124–45; Norman Dahl, *Practical Reason, Aristotle, and Weakness of Will* (Minneapolis: University of Minnesota Press, 1984); and Troels Engberg-Pedersen, *Aristotle's Theory of Moral Insight* (Oxford: Clarendon Press, 1983).

10. Philip Devine, *The Ethics of Homicide* (Ithaca, NY: Cornell University Press, 1978), 44–45; rpt. Notre Dame, IN: University of Notre Dame Press, 1990.

But, of course, the attempt to explain or to give a further reason why murder is wrong has been one of the besetting temptations of modern moral philosophy. Fearing that if morality is based on the "intuition" that murder is wrong then such judgments are arbitrary, it became the philosophical task to find a single principle that could "ground" such "intuitions." That is the reason, moreover, that modern moral philosophy has tended to corrupt our morality through the attempt to give reasons when no reason is required and has the effect of undercutting our true judgments.

Jonsen rightly sees that a renewed appreciation of casuistry might be a check against the endemic tendency of theory to undercut our moral perceptions and judgments. For the casuist does not seek to get "behind" our moral perceptions, but rather to aid us through the analogical comparison of cases. Yet that process only works in the context of a community's practices that are materially embodied in space and time. Just to the extent that Jonsen wants casuistry to create moral community "where it has ceased to exist or not yet come into being" (n.p.), he is coming dangerously close to assimilating casuistry to the very forms of moral "theory" for which he is trying to provide an alternative. Jonsen simply cannot commend casuistry to us, but he must commend the casuistry of Catholics or Southern Baptists, very different casuistrical traditions to be sure, if we are rightly to understand his proposal.

If we are to take seriously the quote about "ultimate particulars" from Aristotle, it has to be recognized that casuistry, at least the kind of casuistry in the Catholic tradition, is not about making decisions but rather about getting descriptions right. Moreover, if descriptions are at the heart of the casuistrical enterprise they will be found only as part of practices that give our discourse life in the first place. For example, until we know why we use the description "abortion" rather than "termination of pregnancy," or why "suicide" is central for our moral description rather than "self–life taking," we cannot know what we are doing when we reason analogically. What must be recognized is that the description "abortion" intelligibly derives from a whole set of practices and beliefs of a community, practices and beliefs about the place of children that can only be characterized as a tradition. Those who use the language of abortion and/or suicide dwell in a different world from those who use the language of termination of pregnancy and/or self–life taking.

That does not mean that those who use the language of abortion and those who talk of termination of pregnancy may not share some practices in common, but it does mean they may well find that their differences on such a significant issue create gulfs they had not anticipated. I suspect that behind antiabortion advocates' appeal to "slippery slopes" lies an intuition about the relation of practices to description that is not stated candidly. The problem is not whether justification for abortions may lead to infanticide, though they may; rather, the question is, Once the description "abortion" is no longer working, how do you sustain the ability to be open to children at all?

It would be a mistake for us to get into this nest of problems. I raise them only to suggest that analogical reasoning about cases (e.g., what difference, if any, does it make that conception occurred in a rape) depends on the prior description. That description, moreover, is dependent on a tradition that sustains the practices necessary for that description to make sense. As a result, casuistry does not end with the problem of the "perception of the ultimate particular"—it begins there.

III. On Casuistry in a Christian Context

That Jonsen does not begin there may be due to a certain understanding of his (and Toulmin's) project. Faced with our interminable inability to resolve differences in ethical theory, they are attempting to remind us that in spite of our theories people go on living fairly decent, if not morally admirable, lives. This is, perhaps, manifested particularly in times of crisis that so often are associated with medical practice. Confronted with our own difficulties or the crisis of someone for whom we care we discover moral resources and limits we did not know we had. By drawing our attention to the actual discourse and casuistrical reflection present in such contexts, we can find ways to get on with our lives. Jonsen and Toulmin are not suggesting we forget theory but are trying to find a way not to let our theories corrupt our lives.

I am sympathetic with this project, but I think it does not adequately account for the complexity of our situation, because their analysis accepts an account of the relation of theory to practice that is theory determined. It is an account that has been spanned by what MacIntyre calls the liberal tradition. Liberal presuppositions have encouraged us in the first place to associate theory with the formal presuppositions or principles that allegedly underlie our moral experience. This way of construing our experience fails to see that we cannot step back from our moral traditions into theory; rather, our ability to have critical purchase on our moral practices depends on the substantive presuppositions of our traditions. The penchant for theory derived from liberal presuppositions cannot be cured by appeal to the importance of casuistry; rather, we must be willing to reason about our moral lives with the confidence that we are possessed by a truth-finding tradition.

I think Jonsen is right to direct our attention to the importance of rhetoric in this respect, but I wish he had carried his analysis further. I am sure he is right that rhetoric is crucial to moral reflection not simply because moral language is persuasive but because rhetoric only makes sense in particular communities and contexts. Rhetoric, as Jonsen points out, is the study of appropriate speech by the right person, at the right time, in the right manner. But crucial to rhetoric are assumptions of audience. Unless the rhetorician and his or her audience share fundamental assumptions, appeals to rhetoric will be of no more help than appeals to casuistry.[11]

All of which is to say that the community in which we do casuistry makes all the difference. In that respect I think casuistry in the Christian community is different from that done in other communities. As Jonsen and Toulmin document, casuistry in the Christian community arose against the background that it was a new community of holiness, a background that forced reflection on moral behavior that had not been anticipated.[12] Casuistry makes no sense for Christians unless it presupposes the practice of baptism. Only in view of baptism are questions about serving in the military, cooperation with pagans, observance of vows, or behavior during persecution questions at all.

Indeed, baptism provides the background for the understanding of the penitential practices that spawned the development of formal casuistrical methods. The necessity of confession and repentance was the church's way of maintaining communal corrections necessary to be the kind of community capable of receiving the Eucharist. Confession, which required people to learn to name their sins, was necessary for the church to deal with sin after baptisms. Though private penitential practice developed, interestingly enough initiating monastic forms of spiritual direction, it was never "private" in the sense that penitents could think of themselves as individuals. Their confession was necessary for the good of the church so that the whole church could come to the table as a reconciled community.

No doubt casuistry could degenerate into minimalistic ethics that were

11. Rhetorically, rhetoric is making a comeback in many intellectual disciplines. There can be no question that this is good, as hopefully it will help us recover the political dimension of all accounts of rationality. For a rhetorically strong defense of rhetoric, see Stanley Fish, *Doing What Comes Naturally* (Durham, NC: Duke University Press, 1990), 471–502.

12. Jonsen and Toulmin, 91–136.

concerned primarily with avoiding evil rather than doing good, but to so characterize casuistry in this way would be a distortion. For the whole enterprise for Christians only made sense against the background of the Christian presumption that it was not sufficient to avoid evil since Christians were called to be holy. Jonsen and Toulmin's treatment of usury, equivocation, and insult witnesses to the church's attempt to understand the implications of Christian practices of sharing goods, saying the truth, and avoiding killing.[13] This does not mean I would agree with how such matters were always worked out, but one cannot help but admire the seriousness with which moral theologians addressed questions occasioned by Christians' positive commitments.

As Jonsen and Toulmin rightly argue, casuistry was not, as it is often depicted, an attempt to help Christians evade the imperatives of the Gospel in the name of worldly power. For they note, "Even today Christian moral theologians are troubled by the problems of linking a faith that includes moral imperatives of paradoxical sublimity with the incessant demands of a rough and mean world."[14] This statement is but a confirmation of my claim that casuistry in a Christian context makes sense only against the background of a determined set of practices shaped by a commitment to be imitators of God.

13. These are the examples Jonsen and Toulmin treat in chapters 9, 10, and 11 of their book. We are in their debt for their discussion of these extremely interesting issues. I do find it odd, however, that in their discussion of pride they state that Augustine incorporated into his just war doctrine a reluctant acceptance of self-defense. They may be right about this, but Paul Ramsey spent a lifetime arguing that Augustine's defense of just war derived entirely from Augustine's understanding of the Christian's responsibility to defend the innocent.

I think it also worth mentioning the following interesting question, though admittedly not immediately relevant to the subject of this paper. What is the relationship between Jonsen and Toulmin's historical account of casuistry and their theoretical argument? I am not sure how the first and last chapters of their book are related to the history they relate. Jonsen and Toulmin tell the story of casuistry with the hope of rescuing it from the reputation Pascal gave it in *The Provincial Letters*, and thus casuistry is identified as informal moral reasoning. As a result, their history appears a little too coherent as casuistry; as they present it, it has more continuity across the centuries than in fact it had. For other accounts of the history of moral theology, see John Mahoney, *The Making of Moral Theology* (Oxford: Clarendon Press, 1987), and John Gallagher, *Time Past, Time Future: A Historical Study of Catholic Moral Theology* (New York: Paulist Press, 1990). For a good critique of these histories, see John Berkman, "The Politics of Moral Theology: Historicizing Neo-Thomist Moral Theology, with Special Reference to the Work of Germain Grisez" (Ph.D. diss., Duke University, 1994).

14. Jonsen and Toulmin, 23. However, I think this claim is put in a far too negative fashion. Casuistry was not in the Christian tradition required to help Christians avoid the hard sayings of the Gospel but rather was an imaginative attempt to help Christians intend the world on that basis. No doubt casuistry could become a means of compromise, but that was a clear perversion.

In this respect, however, I think Jonsen and Toulmin do not adequately account for the close interrelation between the flourishing of the virtues and casuistry. They note that casuistry had never been intended as a substitute for ethical theory or moral theology. It was not, in itself, a doctrine about what is the best life for man, what virtues characterize the good person, or what ideals humans should strive for. It did not even offer a general or fully elaborated doctrine about what sort of acts are right or about how principles and rules are to be justified. It was a simple, practical exercise directed at attempting a satisfactory resolution of particular moral problems. In this respect it resembled philosophy or theology less than it did present-day "counseling," or, as it would have been called, "cure of souls."[15]

I think this is a bit of an overstatement. First, many of the confessional books were written for the laity with the clear intent that they should not only do the good but do it in a way that in the doing they became good.[16] But even more important, the development of casuistry presupposed that such reflection was necessary not because people were devoid of the virtues but because having the virtues forced the community to think about matters that might otherwise have been avoided. People consider questions of sexual immorality only if they first presume that those in their community are pledged to live lives of fidelity. So casuistry and virtue necessarily presuppose one another.[17]

---

15. Jonsen and Toulmin, 242.

16. For example, David Steinmetz observes: "Roughly speaking, there were two penitential traditions which lived side by side in the later middle ages, sometimes in harmony, more often in a fragile and uneasy truce. The first tradition stressed the importance of the disposition of the penitent in the confession, the sincerity and completeness of the penitent's confession, and the necessity for finding a competent and sensitive spiritual advisor. The other tradition stressed the authority of the Church and its sacraments, the power of priestly absolution, and the consolation which the faithful can find when they turn their attention away from themselves and focus on the efficacious rites and ceremonies of the Church. It was not impossible to want to stress both the necessity of a proper disposition and the power of priestly absolution, but almost all theologies of penance tended to tilt in one direction or the other" (*Luther in Context* [Bloomington: Indiana University Press, 1986], 2–3). Steinmetz points out that Dietrich Kolde's *Mirror for Christians*, which was written in 1480, went through forty-six editions—a book that was written for laity to help them be genuinely contrite. It can hardly be thought that the confessional practice and casuistrical reflection is easily characterized as "legalistic" if by that is meant a slavish following of rules with no concern for how the rules are obeyed.

17. I find it odd that Jonsen says so little about the virtues and their relation to casuistry in the light of his appreciation of Aristotle's account of prudence and its perception of the ultimate particular. For the person of practical reason in Aristotle is such only as he or she possesses all the virtues. Admittedly this creates some interesting puzzles about the circularity of Aristotle's

From this perspective, casuistry is less an attempt to find the minimal requirements for the Christian life than it is the imaginative mode for the Christian community to locate the innovative aspects of our convictions. No one can anticipate what being formed virtuously may require. I may well discover that if I am to be courageous in one aspect of my life I am required to confront matters in other areas I had not even anticipated. Casuistry is the mode of wisdom developed by a community to test past innovations as well as anticipate future challenges.

Put differently, the ultimate test of casuistry in the Christian community is how well our reasoning embodies as well as witnesses to the lives of the saints. Casuistry rightly done is meant to call Christians to attend to the innovative lives that we believe help us know better what our convictions entail. That does not mean we are called to slavishly imitate the saints; rather, they provide the paradigms to help us know better what we are to reason about.

Of course, the innovative aspect of casuistry is also occasioned because our lives confront new developments we had not anticipated. For example, when monied economies developed, Christian thinking about usury had to be re-thought; I might add I am not at all sure it was rethought well. However, new developments do not necessarily mean adjustment, but it might well mean refusal to adapt and thus occasion new duties.

But what, if anything, do these broad claims about how casuistry worked in the Christian tradition have to do with the attempt to recover the importance of experience for rethinking medical ethics and, in particular, the importance of casuistry? I fear the implications are largely negative. For I think what is missing from most discussions of "case studies" in medical ethics is exactly the kind of tradition necessary to make the discussion of cases useful. Rather than being an exercise in casuistrical reasoning, too often the cases become the testing ground of ethical theories and their fundamental principles. So the "cases" are the means that students and doctors decide if they are more or less consequentialist or deontological in their approach to ethics.

Jonsen's appeal to casuistry is, of course, an attempt to avoid this mode of presentation of "case." But in fact, I fear, his very way of presenting casuistry will result only in legitimating the practice of medical ethics as we currently have it. If medical ethicists heeded Jonsen's argument they might attend more to the "structure" of the cases, but to what end? For what is missing is the

account, but I think it is clear that Aristotle never thought it possible to see rightly without being rightly formed by the virtues.

tradition and institutional means to make the comparison of cases serve for moral illumination.

One of the ways we might think of our current situation is an analogy with past Roman Catholic practice. "Medical ethicists" have now become the institutional figures that help the liberal tradition think through the issues raised by medical practice. Just as Roman Catholicism produced moral theologians who were charged with the task of knowing the cases from the past in order to test new developments, "medical ethicists" have become the keepers of the moral quandaries raised by trying to practice medicine in a liberal culture. The only difficulty is that these new "moral theologians" lack sufficient shared practices that can give their enterprise moral coherence. In short, "medical ethicists" lack authority and as a result they must become "experts."

The situation, however, is more complicated. I think it is no accident that "ethicists" have been drawn to medicine as a particularly rich area for moral reflection. For medicine is a moral practice with a rich casuistrical tradition, though it was not recognized as such. The casuistry that medicine embodied was based on the everyday practice of physicians through which wisdom was acquired about how to care for this patient with this particular problem.[18] Medicine has been a rich storehouse of paradigmatic examples that have been subsequently extended and qualified in the light of new challenges.

That is why the "case-study" method in medicine works so differently from that in business schools. In business schools, cases are presented only as "problems" to be solved. It is assumed that what one learns from one case may not carry over to another except as one learns certain management skills in "problem solving." In this respect, medical education is much closer to legal education, as the medical student is introduced to a narrative of a particular illness and given a sense of the various responses. Of course, this does not preclude the possibility of radical innovation and change—not only new illnesses but reconfigurations of past descriptions of illness and therapeutic alternatives.

So by all means let us attend to the experience of illness and those who attempt to provide care for the ill. For it is surely the case that such care represents one of the last set of practices we have left that can be characterized as a tradition. It is, of course, a tradition that is constantly threatened by institutional perversion, but in fact the actual commitment of physicians to their patients remains a moral resource that stands as impressive testimony

18. Eric Cassell, *Talking with Patients*, vols. 1 and 2 (Cambridge, MA: MIT Press, 1985).

that our culture still possesses substantive moral convictions. In a world like ours we ought to pay particular notice to that kind of "experience."

Further Reading

"Reconciling the Practice of Reason: Casuistry in a Christian Context" (1986), in
    CET

"Casuistry as a Narrative Art" (1983), in PK

"Can a Pacifist Think about War?" (1994), in DF

"Memory, Community, and the Reasons for Living: Reflections on Suicide and
    Euthanasia" (1976), essay 29 in this volume

"The Radical Hope of the Annunciation: Why Both Single and Married Christians
    Welcome Children" (1998), essay 24 in this volume

"Is Obedience a Virtue?" (1997), in CAV

"How 'Christian Ethics' Came to Be" (1997), essay 1 in this volume

"Authority and the Profession of Medicine" (1982), in SP

How Are Christians to Live? Discipleship Exemplified

14. Courage Exemplified (1993)
with Charles Pinches

Hauerwas writes this essay at a time when he is attempting to distance himself from the increasing popularity of an ethical theory known as "virtue ethics." For by the early 1990s "virtue theory" was simply taking its place as an alternative to "deontological," "teleological," and "responsibility" ethics as another ethical methodology that could be employed to shore up the cultural ethos of late modernity. With broader civic virtue advocates such as William Bennett and theological virtue advocates such as Jean Porter and James Keenan in mind, Hauerwas here shows why it is that "virtue ethics" is not enough—that virtues can only be adequately inculcated and displayed within traditions of moral inquiry. Taking courage as an example, Hauerwas shows how Aristotle's "courage" differs from Aquinas's, and then goes on to show how virtues "Christianly conceived" will at times be in significant tension with those aimed at upholding contemporary social orders.

1. The Arming of Virtue

The newfound enthusiasm for a recovery of an ethic of virtue which has concerned us in this book [CAV] might be thought to be a "good thing" for religious communities in the United States. Widespread enthusiasm for virtue may provide the churches, who have become increasingly irrelevant to the public discussion of the issues before the American polity, a way to contribute to that polity by producing people of virtue. Or so some hope. In this essay we want to suggest that, even if enticing, this is a false hope, one Christians must eschew.

[From CAV © 1997 by University of Notre Dame Press. Used by permission. This essay was coauthored with Charles Pinches. An earlier version was published by Hauerwas under the title "The Difference of Virtue and the Difference it Makes," *Modern Theology* 9, no. 3 (July 1993).]

To be clear, we do not mean to deny that issues concerning virtue are important for political practice and/or theory. Indeed, we have argued against the predominant forms of moral theory produced by liberal society precisely because they have been based on a lawlike paradigm that ignores the significance of the virtues. In short, it has been the project of liberal political and ethical theory to create just societies without just people, primarily by attempting to set in place social institutions and/or discover moral principles that ensure cooperation among people who share no common goods or virtues. Examples of this project are legion, although none is better than John Rawls's *A Theory of Justice*,[1] where the art of argument is elegantly displayed. Mind you, Rawls does not exclude considerations of virtue, but he follows the standard theories we have already investigated in assuming that any account of virtue is secondary to "principles of justice" and institutions based upon them.

Without systematically engaging Rawls at this point,[2] we hope it is sufficiently plain that we think the liberal project he represents has failed, as it was bound to. But now, one might interject, with this failure behind us, isn't the public recovery of virtue all the more pressing? And isn't it irresponsible not to work to further it? For if liberalism cannot create a just society without just people, must we not return with renewed vigor to creating just people so a just society can remain within our sights?

While not unfamiliar in the more distant past, this is a new and interesting challenge for our age, one we must take seriously. To begin to respond, we would like to draw attention to a series of comments made by Jean Bethke Elshtain written in answer to the call for a return to civic virtue made by the authors of *Habits of the Heart*. As she notes, "The problem with the tradition of civic virtue can be stated succinctly: that virtue is *armed*."[3] As we emphasized in chapter 4 [of CAV], "virtue" is of Greek origin, and not accidentally so. As Elshtain observes, for the Greeks war was a natural state of affairs and the basis of society. Moreover, the presumption of war was continued by the great civil republicans such as Machiavelli and Rousseau. Thus, the first duty of

1. John Rawls, *A Theory of Justice* (Cambridge, MA: Harvard University Press, 1971).

2. For a more thorough critique of Rawls's project, see Michael Sandel, *Liberalism and the Limits of Justice* (Cambridge, England: Cambridge University Press, 1982), and George Parkin Grant, *English-Speaking Justice* (Notre Dame, IN: University of Notre Dame Press, 1985).

3. Jean Bethke Elshtain, "Citizenship and Armed Civic Virtue: Some Questions on the Commitment to Public Life," in *Community in America: The Challenge of Habits of the Heart*, ed. Charles H. Reynolds and Ralph Norman (Berkeley: University of California Press, 1988), 50.

Machiavelli's prince is to be a soldier and create an army of citizens, that is, not simply to create an army to protect citizens, but to make citizens an army. Napoleon in this respect is but the full realization of Machiavelli, and democratic order itself is based on the idea that all citizens should be armed.[4]

In fact, according to Elshtain, Rousseau is the great prophet of armed civic virtue, because he saw most clearly that for modern societies a vision of total civic virtue is required. The chief process that draws people out of their provincial loyalties and makes them conscious of belonging to a wider community—a national community—is military conscription. Elshtain comments, "[The] *national* identity that we assume, or yearn for, is historically inseparable from war. The nation-state, including our own, rests on mounds of bodies."[5] Indeed, the United States is a society that is especially constituted by war. As Elshtain observes, a nation-state can exist on paper long before it exists in fact. Accordingly, "a *united* United States is a historical construction that most visibly comes into being as cause and consequence of American involvement in the Great War. Prior to the nationalistic enthusiasm of that era, America was a loosely united federation with strong and regional identities."[6]

Within this context the virtue of courage assumes great importance, for at root courage is a virtue of war that is best exemplified by soldiers facing death in battle. This fits well with the common notion that courage involves a disposition toward death that pervades many aspects of our life, but for all of these aspects the courage of soldiers in battle is the paradigm. However, we want to suggest that for Christians "courage" cannot start with these assumptions nor this paradigm. In fact, from a Christian point of view such "courage" is not courage at all but only its semblance, which when wrongly used can turn demonic.[7]

4. Hegel perhaps best understood this as he saw that without war bourgeois life would be a "bog" in which the citizens of the liberal state would lack the means to rise above their own self-interest. For Hegel, without war the state cannot become the embodiment of the universal. For a good exposition of Hegel's views, see Michael Gillespie, "Death and Desire: War and Bourgeoisification in the Thought of Hegel," in *Understanding the Political Spirit: Philosophical Investigations from Socrates to Nietzsche* (New Haven: Yale University Press, 1988), 153–79.
5. Elshtain, 51.
6. Ibid.
7. By placing "courage" in quotation marks we mean to suggest that all "courages" are not created equal, nor, for that matter, are any of the virtues. Investigation of the full implications of such a claim is complex, and we have not anywhere in this book [CAV] treated the question with the rigor it deserves. At the least such an investigation would require inquiry concerning how the virtues are individuated or if and how they are unified. As usual, MacIntyre makes some fascinating suggestions about these matters in *After Virtue*. He criticizes Aquinas for

If, then, the trumpeted return to civic virtue involves the arming of virtue with the courage of the soldier (as Elshtain has suggested) and if Christians are committed to another sort of courage not formed on war, there is good reason to think that the Christian churches cannot and should not underwrite a program of return to civic virtue, at least not in all of its aspects.

2. Aristotle on Courage

To see how accounts of courage might differ, we propose to look, once again, to the two great proponents of virtue around whom much of this book has revolved: Aristotle and Aquinas. The latter, of course, depends significantly on the former, yet with great insight deviates on an especially important point: for Aquinas it is the martyr and not the soldier who exemplifies true courage.

To see the significance of this difference, we must begin with Aristotle's account of courage. It is offered in book 3 of the *Nicomachean Ethics*,[8] where it

---

trying to provide an exhaustive and consistent classificatory scheme of the virtues because such a scheme betrays the empirical character of much of the knowledge of the virtues. "We learn what kind of quality truthfulness or courage is, what its practice amounts to, what obstacles it creates and what it avoids and so on, only in key part by observing its practice in others and in ourselves. And since we have to be educated into the virtues and most of us are incompletely and unevenly educated in them for a good part of our lives, there is necessarily a kind of empirical untidiness in the way that our knowledge of the virtues is ordered, more particularly in respect of how the practice of each relates to the practice of all the others" (178). This problem bedevils not only Aquinas, but also Aristotle, who continued the Platonic assumption of the unity of the virtues, thus committing himself to the corollary that the virtuous person must have all the virtues at once. There certainly seems something right about the insistence on the interrelation of the virtues, since, for example, courage depends to some degree on temperance. Yet as MacIntyre suggests, strong accounts of the unity of the virtues have difficulty accounting for their acquisition over time.

MacIntyre notes that, because of his insistence on the unity of the virtues, P. T. Geach is led to deny that a devoted Nazi can possess the virtue of courage. MacIntyre resists this because the moral reeducation of the Nazi would not require relearning everything, since he already knows what cowardice in the face of harm amounts to, even if his notion of what harm or danger might involve, and why it should be borne, would need to be transformed by humility and charity.

MacIntyre also rightly notes, however, that an account of the virtues cannot be generated from practices alone. The virtues, both for their identification and their relation, require a narrative that displays what a concrete human life looks like in a community of such lives. Thus we can see the importance of the paradigms through which courage is exemplified. [See Alasdair MacIntyre, *After Virtue*, 2d ed. (South Bend, IN: University of Notre Dame Press, 1984).]

8. We are using the translation of the *Nichomachean Ethics* by Martin Ostwald (Indianapolis: Bobbs-Merrill, 1962). Subsequent references appear in the text.

is coupled with an analysis of temperance. Although Aristotle says little about this explicitly, we may suppose that he followed others in believing that this pair of virtues, courage and temperance, controls our desires, rendering us capable of the habits that make possible the lifelong process of formation of our characters to the good.

For Aristotle, and Aquinas as well, any account of the virtues requires that they be exemplified in concrete lives; after all, we become virtuous people by copying the deeds of virtuous people. Here, to "copy" is not to imitate mechanically, though that may not be a bad way to start, but it involves having the same feelings, emotions, desires, and so on that the virtuous person has when he acts. As Aristotle observes, it is a hard task to be good, and it requires growth in knowledge: "Not everyone can find the middle of a circle, but only a man who has the proper knowledge. Similarly, anyone can get angry—that is easy—or can give away money or spend it; but to do all this to the right person, to the right extent, at the right time, for the right reason, and in the right way is no longer something easy that anyone can do. It is for this reason that good conduct is rare, praiseworthy, and noble" (1109a25–30).

The point, then, is that being virtuous involves not only having dispositions for appropriate action, but also a right "attitude" that includes having the appropriate emotions and desires. This is one of the reasons virtue requires such training, for we become what we are only through the gradual buildup of the appropriate characteristics. It also helps us see why and how courage needs to be carefully distinguished from its counterfeit: recklessness.

Courage and temperance are the virtues that form what Aristotle assumed were our most basic appetites: fear and pleasure. Their purpose is not to repress these appetites but to form them to function rightly. Hence courage does not eliminate fear—that would be recklessness. Rather, courage forms us to have fear in the right amount, at the right time, about the right things, and so on. Granted, a reckless person may appear to do just what a courageous person does, but he is not acting courageously as he does, for he is not being properly affected by fear.[9]

---

9. It is important to see how Aristotle, and later Aquinas, assumes that the descriptions of actions are separable from the character of the agent. That certain actions are always wrong is but a way of saying that no virtuous person could ever envision so acting. Accounts of the virtues do not exclude rules of prohibited actions, but they may very well insist as well that rules (laws) against such actions injure the practices of the community necessary for sustaining virtuous people. (See MacIntyre's comments in *After Virtue*, 149–52.) For an important discussion of the relation of these matters to Roman Catholic moral disputes, see Martin

It follows that courage is not only difficult to practice, it is difficult to recognize. To decipher it we must consider the various possible objects of fear, and which of these is most fearful. So Aristotle comments:

> It is true that we fear all evils, e.g., disrepute, poverty, disease, friendlessness, death. But it does not seem that a courageous man is concerned with all of these. There are some evils, such as disrepute, which are proper and right for him to fear and wrong not to fear: a man who fears disrepute is decent and has a sense of shame, a man who does not fear it is shameless. Still, some people describe a man who fears no disrepute as courageous in a metaphorical sense, for he resembles a courageous man in that a courageous man, too, is fearless. Perhaps one should not fear poverty or disease or generally any evil that does not spring from vice or is not due to oneself. However, it is not the man who has no fear of these things who is courageous. But we call him so because of his resemblance to the courageous man. For some people who are cowards on the battlefield are generous and face the loss of money cheerfully. On the other hand, a man is not a coward if he fears insult to his wife and children, or if he fears envy or the like; nor is he courageous if he is of good cheer when he is about to be flogged. (1115a10–24)

The great variety of circumstances in which we are faced with fear calls for a paradigm case. What fears put courage to the test? What circumstances plainly distinguish the truly courageous person from those who display its counterfeits, such as recklessness, or even from those who display courage, but only now and then? The paradigm must involve death, for it is the most fearful thing. Yet not all deaths allow for the display of courage.

> For example, death by drowning or by disease does not. What kind of death, then, does bring out courage? Doubtless the noblest kind, and that is death in battle, for in battle a man is faced by the greatest and most noble of dangers. This is corroborated by the honors which states as well as monarchs bestow upon courage. Properly speaking, therefore, we might define as courageous a man who fearlessly faces a noble death and in situations that bring a sudden death. Such eventualities are usually brought about by war. But of course a courageous man is also fearless at sea and in illness, though not in the same way as sailors are. Because of their experience, the sailors are optimistic, while the courageous man has given up hope of saving his life but finds the thought

Rhonheimer, " 'Intrinsically Evil Acts' and the Moral Viewpoint: Clarifying a Central Teaching of *Veritatis Splendor*," *Thomist* 58, no. 1 (1994): 1–39.

of such an (inglorious) death revolting. Furthermore, circumstances which bring out courage are those in which a man can show his prowess or where he can die a noble death, neither of which is true of death by drowning or illness. (1115a28–1115b5)

It should not surprise us that the paradigm for courage for Aristotle is facing death in battle, for we know that his ethics is but the preface to his politics.[10] All virtues are in a sense political virtues, since they reflect the common good as well as provide it with specific content. They are, therefore, inescapably conventional, as they depend on practices that are generally agreed to be good. To call them conventional is not to call them into question but rather to indicate that any account of the virtues for any community requires the display of behavior that is commonly held to be good.

It is important to see that this behavior is more than an example of virtue in the way chess is an example of a board game, for the virtues have no sense unless there are practices that hold them in place in the arena of everyday human exchange. To take an example from another culture than our own, Lee Yearley has noted that propriety was a virtue central to Chinese culture in the time of Mencius. It covered such activities as solemn religious activities, such as funerals, as well as what we call etiquette, including not just which fork to use when but also common rituals such as saying "Excuse me" after a sneeze. Mencius links the solemn activities with the more mundane because he assumes they both foster a behavior that manifests distinctly human activities rather than instinctive reasons. As Yearley comments:

> Mencius believes these emotional reactions require conventional rules for their expression; they can find expression only through the ritual forms a society possesses. The rules or forms, in fact, are what allows people to

10. Aristotle's reflections on Sparta are especially interesting, given his account of courage and its relation to war in the *Ethics*. He observed that the Spartans, because of their skill and training for war, "remained secure as long as they were at war; but they collapsed as soon as they acquired an empire. They did not know how to use the leisure which peace brought; and they had never accustomed themselves to any discipline other and better than that of war" (*The Politics of Aristotle,* trans. Ernest Barker [New York: Oxford University Press, 1958], 29 [1271b2–61]). See also Steven White's *Sovereign Virtue: Aristotle on the Relation between Happiness and Prosperity* (Stanford, CA: Stanford University Press, 1992), 219–46. We are indebted to White for helping us see the significance of Aristotle's criticism of Sparta for understanding courage. Had Aristotle pressed these criticisms systematically, letting them inform their account more deeply, we suspect he could have escaped many of the criticisms we attempt to articulate in this chapter.

achieve the good found in expressing and cultivating these reactions. For example, I cannot easily, or even adequately, show my respect for a cook, a host, or an elderly person unless social forms exist that allow me to express such attitudes. Furthermore, both I and others must know what those forms are and what they express. I need to know, for instance, that a slight bow and somewhat servile smile express respect, not irony or rancor. The attitude of respect toward others, Mencius thinks, must express itself in a disposition to follow the conventional rules of propriety. A person observes these rules as an expression of reverence for people, their roles, and even the social-organism that they embody and help preserve.[11]

The point we can derive from this is that virtues such as "respect"—or courage—are more than the attitudes a person might hold within himself, bringing them to expression now and then in some activity. No doubt respect or courage include certain attitudes, as we have noted, but they require display as well. Indeed, we cannot know their shape unless we see them in particular behaviors that we together identify as good. As the central paradigm of courage, facing death in battle is like this for Aristotle. It is not merely an example of courage, it is rather the rightful *exemplification* of what true courage entails. It follows that without war courage could not be fully known.

All this is not to say that Aristotle thinks the courageous person is by necessity warlike. Courage cannot stand on its own; at the very least it requires the guidance of prudence regarding how much fear to have, about what, and so on. Soldiers may lack fear in battle, but that does not by itself mean they are courageous. For example, Aquinas notes that some soldiers, "through skill and practice in the use of arms, think little of the dangers of battle, as they reckon themselves capable of defending themselves against them; thus Vegetius says 'no man fears to do what he is confident of having learned to do well.' "[12]

Likely this is true of a certain General Skobeleff, whose comments are reproduced by Yearley, although there is something more than mere familiarity with danger or with arms at work in his self-appraisal. Says he: "I believe that my bravery is simply the passion for and at the same time the contempt of danger. The risk of life fills me with an exaggerated rapture. The fewer there

---

11. Lee Yearley, *Mencius and Aquinas: Theories of Virtue and Conceptions of Courage* (Albany: State University of New York Press, 1990), 37.

12. Aquinas, *Summa Theologica* (New York: Benziger Bros., 1947), II–II, 123, 1, 2. Subsequent references are in the text.

are to share it, the more I like it. The participation of my body in the event is required to furnish me an adequate excitement. Everything intellectual appears to me to be reflex; but a meeting of man to man, a duel, a danger into which I can throw myself headforemost, attracts me, moves me, intoxicates me. I am crazy for it, I love it, I adore it. I run after danger as one runs after women; I wish it never to stop."[13]

From Aristotle's perspective, General Skobeleff is not a courageous man, not only because he is untouched by appropriate fear, but also because he lacks the wisdom to subject his daring to the appropriate purposes. Nevertheless, who would doubt that Skobeleff is in one sense an excellent soldier, perhaps even better because he lacks true courage? Indeed, at one point Aristotle muses that the very best soldiers are not courageous but rather those who are ready to face danger because "they have no other good" (1117b–17).

The General Skobeleffs of the world notwithstanding, the battlefield is still the true test of courage for Aristotle. As opposed to men like Skobeleff, the courageous person, because he has the other virtues (he is "happy"), knows that his life is a true good, rightly prized, and its loss is rightly feared. Nevertheless, this man stands and fights knowing full well what this might bring: "Death and wounds will be painful for a courageous man, and he will suffer them unwillingly, but he will endure them because it is noble to do so or base to do otherwise. And the closer a man is to having virtue or excellence in its entirety and the happier he is, the more pain will death bring to him. Life is more worth living for such a man than for anyone else, and he stands to lose the greatest goods, and realizes that fact, and it is painful. But he is no less courageous for that and perhaps rather more so, since he chooses noble deeds in war in return for suffering pain. Accordingly, only insofar as it attains its end is it true to say of every virtue that it is pleasant when practiced" (1117b7–15).

Death on the battlefield, therefore, stands as the paradigm of courage for Aristotle precisely because it gives the genuinely courageous person the chance to offer the one great good that unifies all other particular goods, that is, his life, for an even higher good: namely, the common good of the state. Moreover, he can do this in a noble manner—in what Aristotle calls the "noble deeds of war"—with full knowledge of what is at stake. This is the height of courage, by which all other acts of courage take their bearing.

13. Quoted in Yearley, 18.

3. Aquinas on Courage

Many of us are prone to a certain suspicion of Aquinas's intellectual originality when we discover how frequently he borrows from Aristotle.[14] This suspicion can arise particularly when Aquinas moves from the natural to the theological virtues, for at first glance the latter appear as no more than a fluffy topping spread over the natural virtues—which virtues depend substantially on Aristotle for their clearest articulation. Yet this perspective cannot jibe with the role Aquinas ascribes to the theological virtues, and particularly to charity. As he says, "In morals the form of an act is taken chiefly from the end. The reason for this is that the principle of moral acts is the will, whose object and form, so to speak, are the end. Now the form of an act always follows from a form of the agent. Now it is evident that it is charity which directs the acts of all other virtues to the last end, and which, consequently, also gives the form to all other acts of virtue; and it is precisely in this sense that charity is called the form of the virtues, for these are called virtues in relation to 'formed' acts" (II–II, 23, 8).

If we take Aquinas at his word, no true virtue is possible without charity. Yet, as he specifies, apart from the true virtues formed by charity, there exist semblances of the virtues that have their particular orderings, generally corresponding to the ordering of the true virtues. Indeed, as Yearley points out, these semblances themselves have semblances according as we move closer or further from a given true virtue: "For instance, acquired virtues are semblances of virtue if we use infused virtues as the standard of measurement. But any specific, acquired virtue will resemble more or less closely the integral

---

14. MacIntyre rightly observes that Aquinas's appropriation of Aristotle involves fitting together the inheritance from heroic cultures with a Christianized culture but also with specifically biblical virtues:

> Aquinas in his treatise on the virtues treats them in terms of what had become the conventional scheme of the cardinal virtues (prudence, justice, temperance, courage) and the trio of theological virtues. But what then of, for example, patience? Aquinas quotes the Epistle of St. James: "Patience has its perfect work" (S. Th., qu. LXI art. 3) and considers whether patience should not therefore be listed as a principal virtue. But then Cicero is quoted against St. James, and it is argued that all the other virtues are contained within the four cardinal virtues. Yet if this is so Aquinas cannot of course mean by the Latin names of the cardinal virtues entirely what Aristotle meant by their Greek equivalents, since one or more of the cardinal virtues must contain within itself both patience and another biblical virtue which Aquinas explicitly acknowledges, namely humility. Yet in the only place in Aristotle's account of the virtues where anything resembling humility is mentioned, it is a vice, and patience is not mentioned at all by Aristotle. (After Virtue, 177)

form of that virtue. Acquired courage always is a semblance of infused courage and yet a particular instance of acquired courage will be only a semblance of real acquired courage. Indeed, he [Aquinas] can identify the 'same' phenomenon (e.g., giving up one's life for one's country) both as a semblance and as a standard. That identification depends on which criteria of value or sort of explanation he uses and thus on which hierarchies he employs."[15]

This complex pattern helps us begin to see how Aquinas's account of courage can be at once very similar and yet significantly different from Aristotle's. Like Aristotle, Aquinas assumes that courage (or fortitude) is a mean between inordinate fear and daring: "It belongs to the virtue of fortitude to remove any obstacle that withdraws the will from following the reason. Now to be withdrawn from something difficult belongs to the notion of fear, which denotes withdrawal from an evil that entails difficulty. Hence fortitude is chiefly about fear of difficult things, which can withdraw the will from following the reason. And it behooves one not only firmly to bear the assault of these difficulties by restraining fear, but also moderately to withstand them, when, to wit, it is necessary to dispel them altogether in order to free oneself therefrom for the future, which seems under the notion of daring. Therefore fortitude is about fear and daring, as curbing fear and moderating daring" (II–II, 123, 3).

Having already considered the complexities of Aristotle's account of courage, we should not be surprised by this structural similarity. For the meaning of daring and of excessive fear cannot be clear until the practices that correspond to each—or to fortitude itself—have been specified. If Aquinas is good to his word, we should expect that what we should fear and in what we should place our confidence will depend in some way upon charity, which ultimately determines the mean of courage. This turns out to be the case. For according to Aquinas, it is spiritual goods that are truly virtuous people's first concern. Thus hope in God, who promises these goods, cannot but modify our fears about loss of temporal goods. So Yearley comments: "Aquinas never claims that Christ teaches that temporal goods will appear if spiritual goods are sought. He does claim, however, that spiritual goods should be people's major concern, and they should hope (not presume) that temporal goods will appear. The higher perspective of 'a view to the final good for the whole of life' allows people to understand the crucial issue of what really ought to be feared. The major fear courage ultimately should deal with is the fear of not possess-

15. Yearley, 33.

ing fully the spiritual goods virtuous people pursue and manifest, as Christ's teachings on providence both underline and illuminate."[16]

Of course, the pursuit of spiritual goods as well as the pursuit of temporal goods depends upon our having life. Hence death is rightly to be feared as well as avoided: "It belongs to the notion of virtue that it should regard something extreme: and the most fearful of all bodily evils is death, since it does away with all bodily goods. Wherefore Augustine says (De Morib. Eccl. XXII) that 'the soul is shaken by its fellow body, with fear of toil and pain, lest the body be stricken and harassed with fear of death lest it be done away and destroyed.' Therefore the virtue of fortitude is about the fear of dangers of death" (II–II, 123, 4).

So Aristotle and Aquinas are in agreement that a key locus of courage is our fear of death. Yet we must go on to ask what *kind* of death each thinks we should fear if we are to draw nearer to the thing Aquinas calls fortitude. We might recall, for instance, that Aristotle thought certain deaths (e.g., by drowning) could not be undertaken courageously.[17] And of course, for him it is death on the battlefield while fighting for a noble end that best displays courage.

What does Aquinas think? He follows Aristotle's assumption that fortitude has something to do with death in battle, but adds that "a brave man behaves well in face of danger of any other kind of death; especially since man may be in danger of any kind of death on account of virtue: thus may a man not fail to attend on a sick friend through fear of deadly infection, or not refuse to undertake a journey with some godly object in view through fear of shipwreck or robbers" (II–II, 123, 5).

Quite simply, with these additions and in the texts surrounding them, Aquinas treats fortitude in such a way that its ends are transformed by charity,

16. Ibid., 129.
17. That Aristotle uses the example of drowning is in itself interesting. One can easily imagine a case in which the courageous person dies in battle by drowning. For example, he is storming the deck of an enemy's ship, slips and falls to his watery grave. Is this a courageous death? Aristotle provides no analysis, but we could imagine it. In such a death the cause is not the battle itself but rather the water; it is not the thrust of the opponent's sword that finishes the man off but rather the vast and indifferent sea. He therefore does not die fighting but is swallowed by a sea against which his struggling is petty and hopeless. Of course, with some imagination we can construct a case where a man drowns while fighting, perhaps with his rival in a chokehold. If there is a casuistry of the "noble acts of war," it would be interestingly applied here. (For example, how did the two of them happen to get into the water?) If a problem arose it would likely center on the question of whether the man died while displaying his prowess, for, again, who can display prowess against the sea?

so that death in battle no longer stands as its paradigm. In this particular text, Aquinas considers death in battle, but he then adds as *equivalents* death while tending to the sick or while undertaking a journey with some godly object. To consider the first, one might ask, what is the noble end of this? and why is it noble? But plainly charity tells us, for charity demands care for the sick and dying, and the risk of one's life in it is courageous, no less than the risk for the common good in battle.

With regard to the second, a "journey with a godly end," where we might face "shipwreck or robbers," Aquinas appears to mean this literally; no doubt the missionary journeys of Paul or the man who journeys from Jerusalem to Jericho in the parable of the good Samaritan echo in the back of his mind as he writes. Yet it is possible, as we have earlier stated, to take the notion of journey in a more metaphorical way such that it connects to the journey of the Christian life, which is not only difficult but extended through time. In any case, in a journey (as well as in the tending of the sick) the immediacy and excitement of a pitched battle disappears, and the courage required is quieted. Indeed, Aquinas's "fortitude," while used synonymously with "courage," suggests that what is demanded is a kind of endurance in the face of difficulty, danger, or oppression, a steadfastness of purpose and vision that will not be swayed even by threat of death. Hence, for Aquinas, patience and perseverance are integral to the very meaning of courage. To return to the metaphor, this emphasis connects to Aquinas's settled view that the moral life is a journey to God during which we must learn to endure much.[18] In this, patience and perseverance are key. Again Yearley provides a concise account of Aquinas's position: "Perseverance, with its opposed vices of obstinacy and softness (a too easy yielding to pleasure), concerns the need to adhere to the good sought. Patience concerns the need to overcome the sorrow brought by the inevitable loss of some goods."[19]

Wittgenstein was right: the world of the courageous person is different from that of the coward. This is borne out in Aristotle's account when one considers the vision of the soldier who faces death with indifference since he sees no other good. But it is also true that the world of the courageous

18. MacIntyre argues that medieval thinkers did not have the modern conception of history as discontinuous discovery and rediscovery of what history is, but that is in part because medieval thinkers took the basic historical scheme of the Bible to be one within which they could rest assured. On this kind of medieval view the virtues are therefore those qualities that enable human beings to survive evils on their historical journey. See *After Virtue*, 176.

19. Yearley, 130.

Christian is different from the world of the courageous pagan. This is so because of their differing visions of the good that exceeds the good of life itself. These differing visions come to bear, ultimately, on the differing paradigms for courage. For Aristotle, as we have seen, this is death in battle. Yet Aquinas has already introduced additional cases as equivalents, which serves to demote death in battle to one of a number of possible ways to die courageously. As for a new paradigm for Aquinas, it is *martyrdom*. He speaks of it, still, as a kind of death in battle. But of course the battle—and the person fighting it—has been transformed as is shown by the weapons required in it, such as patience and faith.[20] So Christians are required patiently to persevere in the face of persecution, since they have the confidence that enduring wrong is a gift of charity: "Now it is evident that in martyrdom man is firmly strengthened in the good of virtue, since he cleaves to faith and justice notwithstanding the threatening danger of death, the imminence of which is moreover due to a kind of particular contest with his persecutors. Hence Cyprian says in a sermon: 'The crowd of onlookers wondered to see an unearthly battle, and Christ's servants fighting erect, undaunted in speech, with souls unmoved, and strength divine.' Wherefore it is evident that martyrdom is an act of fortitude; for which reason the Church reads in the office of Martyrs: They 'became valiant in battle'" (II–II, 124, 2).

The prominence of martyrdom in Aquinas's account of courage confirms that true courage, as opposed to its semblances, is a gift of the Holy Spirit. Thus the patience of Christians is that which displays the joy of being of service to God (II–II, 136, 3). Such joy is possible because patience is formed by charity. In like manner, courage as a gift of the Spirit protects the martyr from the "dread of dangers" in a distinctive manner: "The Holy Spirit moves the human mind further (than the steadfastness of normal courage), in order that one may reach the end of any work begun and avoid threatening dangers of any kind. This transcends human nature, for sometimes it does not lie within human power to attain the end of one's work, or to escape evils or

20. The use of military imagery within the arena of the Christian life is, of course, hardly of Aquinas's invention; it infuses the Bible. Unfortunately this has been frequently narrowed to refer to "the defense of the faith," which allows for a transference of militarism rather than its transformation. This is plainly refuted in Ephesians 6, where Christians are urged to "take up the whole armor of God," which includes the shoes that "will make you ready to proclaim the gospel of peace." Moreover, Isaiah's oft repeated hope for a day when the nations "shall beat their swords into plowshares, their spears into pruning hooks" (Isaiah 2:4) suggests not so much the utter ceasing of a certain kind of activity, but rather its transformation, as evidenced by its changed weaponry, and so too the purposes of those who wield it.

dangers, since these sometimes press in upon us to the point of death. But the Holy Spirit achieves this in us when he leads us to eternal life, which is the end of all good works and the escape from all dangers. And he pours into our mind a certain confidence that this will be, refusing to admit the opposing fear."[21]

Put another way, the work of our lives transcends our capacities, since it demands that we love and serve God. Yet we receive of the Spirit the strength and courage to persevere in it precisely because we have been given confidence that God will complete God's work in us even if our lives are taken by our enemies.

It follows that the fear of death, around which both Aristotle's and Aquinas's courage take shape, will actually be a different sort of fear for Christians and pagans. Both fear the loss of the possibility of the various goods that give our lives form and texture. Yet the good that life is for, and therefore the good for which it can be courageously sacrificed, is not for Aquinas the common good of the nation but rather friendship with God. This good, interestingly, is beyond the power of human beings to effect; they must learn to accept it as a gift. Yet this is also the source of their strength, for they trust that God will bring to completion the work He has begun in them even in the face of death itself.

It follows that Christians are freed from the anxiety of having to secure the meaning of their lives in the mode of their death. Indeed, there is considerable anxiety in death in the battlefield, since the courageous warrior must see himself as carrying the life of his nation on his shoulders. He dies for its continued life, but if all die like him, all die in vain. The martyr dies with the hope that her death will strengthen the church, but it is not quite right to say she dies for the church. Rather, in her death, she imitates Christ.

This is why the martyr can *receive* her death in a way a warrior cannot. As the warrior dies in the midst of the frenzied whir of battle, he is active as he dies; as Aristotle would have it, he dies displaying his prowess in the "noble deeds of war." The martyr dies precisely because she refuses to act as others have specified. Moreover, precisely as she is able to receive death as a consequence of her life's commitments, her martyrdom, while extraordinary, is not different in kind from the other things she has done or suffered throughout her life. In fact, this is an important final difference between the two paradigms of courage. Courage based on martyrdom is no easier than courage

---

21. Aquinas, II–II, 139, 1, as quoted in Yearley, 141.

based on heroics in battle; it is, however, more accessible.[22] Heroics in battle require not only extraordinary talents but also extraordinary luck at death; indeed, most of those even who serve in war will die, not in this service, but at home or in hospitals, like most of us. For Aristotle, such deaths cannot be courageous, since, as he implies (1115a37), like the water that surrounds the drowning man, their illness has made a mockery of their prowess and they cannot display it at death.

By contrast, the martyr's acceptance of her death as a continuing part of her service to God demonstrates how fortitude can infuse our lives and remain even as we die in our weakness. Martyrs, in effect, have to be ready to lose to their persecutors, dying ingloriously. They can do so only because they recognize that neither their life nor their death carries its own (or anyone else's) weight of meaning; rather, that is carried by the God who supplies it. Unlike the great heroes of war, martyrs can be followed in daily life, for their courage is none other than an extension of the daily courage we need to carry on as faithful servants of God, which courage we receive as a daily gift of the Spirit. Yearley rightly notes that courageous Christians have confidence that God will secure their ultimate future. But, as he goes on to say, this "confidence includes more than just an assurance about what will happen in the future. They [the courageous] also feel assurance about the meaning of those signs that ensure them that the Holy Spirit moves them and that they are participating in the relationship of friendship with God that characterizes charity."[23]

4. Courage: Christian or American?

One matter remains unresolved. Earlier in this essay we noted, with the help of Jean Bethke Elshtain, that civic virtue comes armed. For those of us living

22. Peter Geach resists R. M. Hare's view that courage is largely a thing of the past on the ground that Hare has assumed, with Plato and Aristotle, that courage had mainly to do with conduct on the battlefield. Quite to the contrary, as Geach asserts, the "ordinary course of the world, even in times of peace, is so ordered that men regularly need some courage; courage to endure, courage to face the worst." As we are alleging in the text, Geach takes the courage of the martyrs to be accessible to us all, and castigates those who would use the term "heroic virtue" as applied traditionally by the church to the martyrs as a reason to suppose "it is not to be expected of ordinary folk." (Understanding "heroic virtue" in this way is, he thinks, a "cunning snare of Hell's Philological Arm.") Accordingly, in an ironic twist, he urges that "to the plea 'I'm no hero' the reply may be made: 'You are a hero, in the Greek sense of the word: a son not just of mortal parents, but of God.'" See The Virtues (New York: Cambridge University Press, 1977), 153–54.

23. Yearley, 141.

in America this is especially true, since we have little common history that is not also a history of war. Moreover, as we in our daily lives become ever more distant from the spiritual goods for which we might live, we begin to hunger for the meaning war can bestow or perhaps even for a shot at dying coura-geously in battle rather than wasting away in an aging body as we lose control over the physical pleasures that have heretofore diverted us from facing our mortality.

But some will say that is just the point. We in America have lost our moral vision precisely as we have lost our courage to fight for what is right and good. A return to virtue may indeed require a new call to arms, but there is no other way to save the soul of our nation. Moreover, as some Christians might add, not only Aristotle but Aquinas (and many other thoughtful Christians) recog-nized the duty we all have to fight for the common good. Enthusiastic pacifists may wish to gloss it over, but the fact remains that although Aquinas added to Aristotle's list of courageous deaths some of those that occur elsewhere than on the battlefield, he yet retained it as a genuinely courageous act.

It is no part of our purpose to turn Aquinas into a pacifist. Aquinas was not a pacifist, he was a just warrior.[24] Yet Aristotle was not a just warrior. The relevant consideration, then, is not that both Aristotle and Aquinas thought war was permissible, but rather what sort of view each carried about war and therefore about what kind of behavior within it could be called courageous. In this way we would suggest that for Aquinas the transformation of courage worked by charity cannot but change the meaning of a death on the battlefield.

To return briefly to the relevant passage in Aquinas, he remarks that "the dangers of death which occur in battle come to man directly on account of some good, because, to wit, he is defending the common good by a *just fight*" (II–II, 123, 5; emphasis added). This is the first important qualification. The noble good that courage necessarily serves (else it is not courage) is not made noble by the fight itself or by the party involved in the fight (i.e., my city or my

---

24. While we think just warriors are wrong, they might not be—another way of saying that we think the just war position as articulated by an Augustine or a Paul Ramsey is a significant challenge to our own Christian pacifism and is theological to its core. Just warriors and pacifists within the Christian church must be committed to continued engagements that teach them not only to recognize their differences but also their similarities, similarities that make them far more like one another than the standard realists' accounts of war that rule our contemporary culture and that have taken a firm hold in the church. For a concrete display of how this engagement might go, see Paul Ramsey's *Speak Up for Just War or Pacifism* (Univer-sity Park: Pennsylvania State University Press, 1988). [Hauerwas wrote a long epilogue to this volume, which is reprinted here as essay 21.]

country), but rather by the justice of the fight. There is, for Aquinas, no such freestanding category as the "noble acts of war," even though this evidently figures strongly in Aristotle's articulation of the paradigm of courage. For Aquinas, the nobility of the cause in war must be judged independently of our allegiance to one of the parties; consequently, glamorous deaths in battle fighting for an unjust cause cannot be for him acts of courage. There is no hint of this in Aristotle.

Furthermore, Aquinas goes on in this same passage to speak of a "just fight" as falling into two types, each with an illustration. First, there is courage as displayed in battle within a just war, and second, there is the courage displayed in "private combat," as when a judge rules justly even when this places his life or person in considerable peril. By supposing that both of these "just fights" are equally capable of displaying courage, Aquinas places the violent combat of war in relation to other sorts of (nonviolent) combat. In so doing he effectively reorients the courage displayed in war on the new paradigm, namely, martyrdom. Courage in war is not courage because it is particularly glamorous or valiant, nor because it involves the "noble acts of war," nor because it is highly honored in city-states, nor because it provides the warrior a unique chance to display his prowess as he dies—all possible reasons suggested by Aristotle's account which assumes its paradigmatic status. Rather, courage in battle is courage because in the face of great peril the soldier has persevered in doing what is just—according to a justice now formed by charity.

To sum up the point in a différent light, Aquinas offers Christians a courage that will make us patient enough to fight a just war. Indeed, Aristotle's remark that it is unlikely that the truly courageous man will make the very best soldier applies all the more to Aquinas's just warrior, for not only will he know what is at stake in his own death, he will be dogged by the concern that he not kill unjustly. He will not follow the command of his superiors or his country without giving this thought—which means, we think, that precisely as he is courageous according to the courage formed by charity he will be the more likely to subvert the political order as he seeks to serve it by fighting for it.[25]

---

25. Tertullian counsels new believers to abandon military service, not just because of the bloodshed or idolatry that so frequently accompanied it but also because staying in the service as a Christian will mean that "all sorts of quibbling will have to be resorted to in order to avoid offending God, and this is not allowed [for Christians] even outside of military service." *On the Crown*, 11. The Tertullian text can be found online at http://www.tertullian.org/anf/index.htm.

Put ironically, Christian courage will subvert any political order based on courage, that is, upon the courage that derives its intelligibility from the practice of war. That is why Rousseau was right to think that the Christians should be suppressed. Their "acts of courage," even when allegedly in service of the social order, do not sustain it but rather threaten its very foundations.

In reply to his line of argument, it might be suggested that the subversion has already occurred and we are now reaping its benefits with the coming of age of modern representative democracy. The great difference with democracy is that it is a social order that thrives on difference and dissent, and so the peculiar courage of Christians can be tolerated, or even welcomed. Yet this response will not work, for inherent in such an account of the church's relation to democracy is the distinction between the public and private, which—as we have tried to detail in our conversation with John Casey[26]—cannot but marginalize courage of any sort. Indeed, that distinction is itself the principal agent of the destruction of any coherent account of civic virtue in liberal societies.

Here we return once again to Elshtain's armed civic virtue and so to a form of the earlier suggestion that any virtue is better than none, even if it arms us. For a nonliberal Christian (such as Richard John Neuhaus), while the revival of civic virtue may bring only a semblance of courage (and of the other virtues) to social orders such as America, a semblance of virtue, as Aquinas himself saw, can teach true virtue. Hence, those formed by the courage necessary to face death well will be more easily led to the fuller account of courage offered by Christians.

This is a powerful suggestion and one reason why we are initially disposed to take those who have fought in war with great seriousness. However, there is no reason—in fact, there is reason to the contrary—to think that it is the job of the Christian churches to shore up virtue's semblances for the sake of the wider society in which they live.[27] They may articulate the connections, but this will remain possible only as they speak clearly of, and clearly live, the true virtues that are formed by charity. This is not just a matter of the division of labor, but of truth, for without true courage the semblance of courage cannot be known as it truly is, namely, a semblance. Moreover, at no time can Chris-

26. [See chap. 6 of CAV.]

27. MacIntyre explores how the semblance of virtue can distort and even render impossible living virtuously in his "How to Seem Virtuous without Actually Being So," *Committee of the Centre for the Study of Cultural Values, Occasional Papers,* Lancaster University, England, 1991, 1–20.

tians assume that their articulation of true courage will be received as such in the wider society. Besides showing us the shape of true courage, this is another thing the martyrs have taught us. The martyrs must yet stand as a reminder to us all, and particularly to those American Christians who would revive it, that the spirit of civic virtue can and has killed many Christians, and more Jews, all in the name of the common good.

Further Reading

"Pagan Virtue and Christian Prudence" (1997), with Charles Pinches, in CAV

"The Renewal of Virtue and the Peace of Christ" (1997), with Charles Pinches, in CAV

"Hope Faces Power: Thomas More and the King of England" (1978), in CET

"Practicing Patience: How Christians Should Be Sick" (1997), essay 18 in this volume

"A Story-Formed Community: Reflections on *Watership Down*" (1981), essay 9 in this volume

"Practice Discipleship: Embodiment" (1996) (esp. 73–76), with William H. Willimon, in WRAL

15. Why Truthfulness Requires Forgiveness:

A Commencement Address for Graduates of a College

of the Church of the Second Chance (1992)

This is an essay about what it is for a Christian to live successfully. Originally delivered as the 1992 Commencement Address for Graduates of a Mennonite college in Indiana, Hauerwas draws on Anne Tyler's novel Saint Maybe *to display some radical implications of a Christian's commitment to seek forgiveness and reconciliation and to live truthfully in the light of that. As shown here, such a commitment does not require any "withdrawal," but may lead to a very different life than one imagined for one who seeks to be a success in American culture. Hauerwas thinks that the graduates of this Mennonite college are sent out with a greater chance than most to live successfully, because their college has well educated them to be watchful of certain kinds of lies so prevalent in our culture.*

[From *DF* © 1994 by Duke University Press.]
As will become clear, the college in this title is Goshen College. I was honored by being asked to give the commencement address on April 18, 1992. Goshen is a college sponsored and supported by the Mennonite Church, though non-Mennonites are also faculty and students. The address was obviously written presupposing some knowledge of Mennonite life and churchly practice. I have tried not to change that for the non-Mennonite reader, though I have added a few explanatory notes that make references clearer. I have not tried to "translate" what I say here to a non-Mennonite audience, preferring to let what seems puzzling remain puzzling.

I should make clear to the non-Mennonite reader, however, that though the Mennonites are perhaps most widely identified by their commitment to pacifism, that commitment is but part of their practice of reconciliation based on Matthew 18. So "pacifism" does not simply name their refusal to go to war, but rather is an aspect of their practice of resolving disputes and conflicts through confrontation, forgiveness, and reconciliation. Put in a somewhat misleading fashion, the Mennonites made the Catholic practice of penance the character of their relation with one another and the world. See, for example, Walter Klaassen's *Anabaptism: Neither Catholic nor Protestant* (Waterloo, Canada: Conrad Grebel Press, 1973). For a wonderful account of "The Rule of Christ" for Mennonite ecclesiology, see Michael Cartwright, "Practices, Politics, and Performance: Toward a Communal Hermeneutic for Christian Ethics" (Ph.D. diss., Duke University, 1988), 298–434.

Ian Bedloe, the hero of Anne Tyler's novel *Saint Maybe,* had not meant to say anything. He had only gone into the storefront church, whose plate glass window bore the name The Church of the Second Chance, because he had been attracted by the hymns sung by the fifteen or so people he found inside. Yet he felt he just had to say something after he had uncontrollably laughed when a "sister," Lula, had asked the church to pray for her. It seems that Chuckie, her paratrooper son, had just died in Vietnam because he forgot to put on his parachute before he jumped. Ian had done shameless things before but to laugh out loud at a mother's bereavement was perhaps one of the most shameless. Tyler continues her narrative:

> He wished he could disappear. He wanted to perform some violent and decisive act, like leaping into space himself.
> "No prayer is unworthy in the eyes of our Creator."
> He stood up.
> Heads swiveled once again.
> "I used to be—" he said.
> Frog in his throat. He gave a dry, fake-sounding cough.
> "I used to be good," he said. "Or I used to be not bad, at least. Not evil. I just *assumed* I wasn't evil, but lately, I don't know what's happened. Everything I touch goes wrong. I didn't mean to laugh just now. I'm sorry I laughed, Mrs. . . ."
> He looked over at the woman. Her face was lowered and she seemed unaware of him. But the others were watching closely. He had the sense they were weighing his words; they were taking him seriously.

Ian's confession of sin, or at least of "wrong," derived from the recent death, a possible suicide, of his brother. His brother had married a young woman who had two children from a previous marriage. Ian often baby-sat for her and had come to suspect, even though she was pregnant, that she may be unfaithful to his brother. One night when Ian was sitting, she failed to return at the appointed time. As a result Ian was not able to keep a date with his girlfriend, which meant he probably missed his first sexual opportunity. Asked by the awkward but intense Reverend Emmett if he had gotten a response to his prayer, Ian confesses:

> "Response."
> "Did you get a reply?"
> "Well, not exactly."

"I see," Reverend Emmett said. He watched an aged couple assist each other through the door—the very last to leave. Then he said, "What was it that you needed forgiven?"

Ian couldn't believe his ears. Was this even legal, inquiring into a person's private prayers? He ought to spin on his heel and walk out. But instead his heart began hammering as if he were about to do something brave. In a voice not quite his own, he said, "I caused my brother to, um, kill himself."

Reverend Emmett gazed at him thoughtfully.

"I told him his wife was cheating on him," Ian said in a rush, "and now I'm not even sure she was. I mean I'm pretty sure she did in the past, I know I wasn't *totally* wrong, but . . . So he drove into a wall. And then his wife died of sleeping pills and I guess you could say I caused that too, more or less . . ."

He paused, because Reverend Emmett might want to disagree here. (Really Lucy's death was just indirectly caused by Ian, and maybe not even that. It might have been accidental.) But Reverend Emmett only rocked from heel to toe.

"So it looks as if my parents are going to have to raise the children," Ian said. Had he mentioned there were children? "Everything's been dumped on my mom and I don't think she's up to it—her or my dad, either one. I don't think they'll ever be the same, after this. And my sister's busy with her own kids and I'm away at college most of the time . . ."

In the light of Reverend Emmett's blue eyes—which had the clean transparency of those marbles that Ian used to call gingerales—he began to relax. "So anyhow," he said, "that's why I asked for that prayer. And I honestly believe it might have worked. Oh, it's not like I got an answer in plain English, of course, but . . . don't you think? Don't you think I'm forgiven?"

"Goodness, no," Reverend Emmett said briskly.

Ian could not believe his ears. To be told he was not forgiven seemed to contradict everything he assumed about Christianity—"I thought God forgives everything." Reverend Emmett, agreeing, pointed out, "You can't just say, 'I'm sorry, God.' Why anyone could do that much! You have to offer reparation—concrete, practical reparation, according to the rules of our church." "Rules of our church," of course, was just the problem, for it was clear that this was no ordinary church filled as it seemed to be with outcasts and misfits. For example they only used first names in church because as Reverend Emmett told him, "Last names remind us of the superficial—the world of wealth and connections and who came over on the *Mayflower*."

Ian reasonably countered the suggestion that he had not been forgiven by observing, "But what if there isn't any reparation? What if it's something nothing will fix?" Reverend Emmett responded, using that "itchy" word, Jesus. Jesus "helps us do what you can't undo. But only after you've tried to undo it." Ian could not imagine what such an undoing would take. Reverend Emmett, however, was more than ready to tell Ian what he must do: he would have to begin by "seeing to the children."

"Okay. But . . . see to them in what way, exactly?"

"Why, raise them, I suppose."

"Huh?" Ian said. "But I'm only a freshman!"

Reverend Emmett turned to face him, hugging the stack of hymnals against his concave shirt front.

"I'm away in Pennsylvania most of the time!" Ian told him.

"Then maybe you should drop out."

"Drop out?"

"Right."

"Drop out of college?"

"Right."

Ian stared at him.

"This is some kind of test, isn't it?" he said finally.

Reverend Emmett nodded, smiling. Ian sagged with relief.

"It's God's test," Reverend Emmett told him.

"So . . ."

"God wants to know how far you'll go to undo the harm you've done."

"But He wouldn't really make me follow through with it," Ian said.

"How else would He know, then?"

"Wait," Ian said. "You're saying God would want me to give up my education. Change all my parents' plans for me and give up my education?"

"Yes, if that's what's required," Reverend Emmett said.

"But that's crazy! I'd have to be crazy!"

"Let us not love in word, neither in tongue," Reverend Emmett said, " 'but in deed and truth.' First John three, eighteen."

"I can't take on a bunch of kids! Who do you think I am? I'm nineteen years old!" Ian said. "What kind of a cockeyed religion is this?"

"It's the religion of atonement and complete forgiveness," Reverend Emmett said. "It's the religion of the Second Chance."

Then he set the hymnals on the counter and turned to offer Ian a beatific smile. Ian thought he had never seen anyone so absolutely at peace.

This scene from Tyler's novel should help you capture what it means to graduate from Goshen College, a school of the Mennonite church. For graduations can be and often are a symbol of legitimation. You have finally made it. You have gotten your college degree and now you are on the path to success in America.

You just have one big problem: you are graduating from Goshen College, a college sponsored by the Mennonite church. That means to the world you are about as odd as the Church of the Second Chance. From the world's perspective it is something of a disability that your degree is from a strange little college in Goshen, Indiana, sponsored by the Mennonite church. If you want to make it in the world you made a big mistake when you applied to Goshen College and you may be making an even bigger mistake to graduate here. You are graduating from a storefront college.

Of course, you have earned your reputation for oddness for exactly the same reason that Reverend Emmett told Ian he was not forgiven. For Mennonites, after all, refuse to buy the idea that forgiveness is simply a matter of being told that God had forgiven us. Mennonites have been about reminding other Christians that forgiveness is a community process that makes discipleship possible. Indeed, the nature of discipleship as the hallmark of Mennonite life was determined by people who had learned that forgiveness was a practice of a community committed to the truthful worship of God.[1]

Anne Tyler helps us capture these complex relations between forgiveness and reconciliation by telling Ian's story. For it is only in doing what Reverend Emmett said he must do (i.e., leave school and raise those children for the next twenty years) that Ian comes to understand his "sin." In the process he learns that forgiveness is the gifts that these children bring to him through making him more than he otherwise could have possibly been. He learns he must forgive as well as be forgiven and by so doing he is able to claim the life he has been given as his own.

Of course, the name you Mennonites have come to give this complex rela-

---

1. It is only in the context of the reconciliation as a practice that the use of the Mennonite "ban" is intelligible. For rightly understood, the ban is an act of love by the community to help erring members discover that they in fact are not living in unity with the body. See, for example, Marlin Jeschke, *Discipling the Brother* (Scottdale, PA: Herald Press, 1972).

tionship among forgiveness, reconciliation, discipleship, and truth is peace. For your pacifism is not based on some abstract principle that all violence, whatever that is, is wrong in and of itself, but rather peace names those practices and processes of your community necessary to be a people of truth. It seems harsh, and even violent, to be told that no matter how sorry we are for what we have done we still are not forgiven. Yet Mennonites know the truth of that because they know they are seldom in a position to know the truth about their sin until they have made their lives available to others in a manner that they might be taught the truth about themselves—particularly in matters where the wrong done cannot be made right—which in fact is the character of most matters that matter. That is why reconciliation is so painful: it requires us to be ready to confront one another with the truth so that we will be better able to name and confront those powers that feed on our inability to make our wrongs right.

As Ian discovers, when you become a member of the Church of the Second Chance, it means that certain options simply are no longer options for you. He is going to be a cabinetmaker, not a college graduate.[2] He is going to do that because being a cabinetmaker will give him time to raise the children. When he tells his parents what he intends to do they are incredulous. They are not reassured when he reports that the members of the Church of the Second Chance are going to help raise the kids.

> "Ian, have you fallen into the hands of some sect?" his father asked.
>
> "No, I haven't," Ian said. "I have merely discovered a church that makes sense to me, the same as Dober Street Presbyterian makes sense to you and Mom."
>
> "Dober Street didn't ask us to abandon our educations," his mother told him. "Of course we have nothing against religion; we raised all of you children to be Christians. But our church never asked us to abandon our entire way of life."
>
> "Well, maybe it should have," Ian said.
>
> His parents looked at each other.
>
> His mother said, "I don't believe this. I do not believe it. No matter how

---

2. I think it is not accidental that Ian makes his living by becoming an apprentice to a master cabinetmaker, becoming in the process a master craftsman himself. Reconciliation is no less a craft than making cabinets, as each requires a transformation of habits and vision if they are to be acquired happily. For the development of this point, see my AC, 93–111.

long I've been a mother, it seems my children can still come up with something new and unexpected to do to me."

"I'm not doing this to you! Why does everything have to relate to you all
the time? It's for me, can't you get that into your head? It's something I have to
do for myself, to be forgiven."

"Forgiven for what, Ian?" his father said.

Ian swallowed.

"You're nineteen years old, son. You're a fine, considerate, upstanding
human being. What sin could you possibly be guilty of that would require
you to uproot your whole existence?"

Reverend Emmett had said Ian would have to tell them. He'd said that was
the only way. Ian had tried to explain how much it would hurt them, but
Reverend Emmett had held firm. Sometimes a wound must be scraped out
before it can heal, he had said.

Ian said, "I'm the one who caused Danny to die. He drove into that wall on
purpose."

Nobody spoke. His mother's face was white, almost flinty.

"I told him Lucy was, um, not faithful," he said.

He had thought there would be questions. He had assumed they would
ask for details, pull the single strand he'd handed them till the whole ugly
story came tumbling out. But they just sat silent, staring at him.

"I'm sorry!" he cried. "I'm really sorry!"

His mother moved her lips, which seemed unusually wrinkled. No sound
emerged.

After a while, he rose awkwardly and left the table. He paused in the
dining room doorway, just in case they wanted to call him back. But they
didn't. He crossed the hall and started up the stairs.

For the first time it occurred to him that there was something steely and
inhuman to this religious business. Had Reverend Emmett taken fully into
account the lonely thud of his sneakers on the steps, the shattered, splintered
air he left behind him?

Ian had begun the process of being freed from the powers. Those powers
can often come in the form of the love of parents who want their children to
be successes. Of course, you and your parents have already had that conversation. They wanted you to come, or at least they let you come, to Goshen
College. They knew you were going to be odd because they wanted you to be

part of that continuing tradition of discipleship as reconciliation so that the world might know that we were intended to live peaceably with one another.

I know it is hard to remember on occasions like this how odd you are. But just think about it. First of all you have a theologian—who, to put it kindly, has a controversial reputation—giving your commencement address. If Goshen College had any sense they would have invited, like the University of Notre Dame, George Bush—or at least the Governor of Indiana—to give this commencement address. Administrators of Goshen College are obviously not politically savvy. Second, just think what I am talking about. I am talking about forgiveness and reconciliation and you are graduating from college. What does that have to do with graduating from college? From most colleges not much, but I hope it has everything to do with your graduating from this college.

The education you have received at Goshen College has been different. I teach in a university that is at the heart of the so-called PC controversy. Some fear that people will be forced to think what is only politically correct—that is, that they cannot say certain kinds of things about women, blacks, or gays. There is the fear that the curriculum will have introduced into it literature that does meet the standard of the "classics" of something called "Western culture." The "PC debate" cannot help but appear in universities like Duke as a clash for power between interest groups. For without the narratives and practices of forgiveness and reconciliation we are devoid of the resources to tell our diverse histories in a manner that contributes to a common purpose that we Christians call love.

Because you are a college of the Church of the Second Chance you have such resources. After all, you have never been a college of the "mainstream," so the stories that many find so oppressive have never been your story. You are descendants of a people who knew that the only thing that Catholics and mainstream Protestants could agree about is that it was a very good thing to kill the anabaptists. You are a people who have been formed by a strange book called *Martyrs Mirror*.[3] You are a people who knew that (in spite of this

---

3. *Martyrs Mirror*, whose full title is *The Bloody Theater of Martyrs Mirror of Defenseless Christians Who Baptized Only Upon Confession of Faith, and Who Suffered and Died for the Testimony of Jesus, Their Savior, from the Time of Christ to the Year A.D. 1660*, was compiled in 1660 by the Dutch Mennonite Thielerman J. van Braght. It is currently published by Herald Press of Scottdale, Pennsylvania (1950). As the title indicates, the book is composed of the stories of Christian martyrs from the beginning to 1660. The book has been used since its inception as a way to give Mennonites a sense of what makes them Mennonites. Hermeneu-

country's celebration of something called "freedom of religion"), as non-violent followers of Jesus Christ, you were tolerated because at best you were an ethnically quaint people. All that made a difference for the education that you received here. For political science is not taught at Goshen College the way it is taught at Duke, since political science at Goshen College is not at the service of nation/state ideologies. The history you learn is different because you know you are members of a community more determinative than that power called the United States of America. You have learned to distrust abstract claims about objectivity because you are part of the people of the Second Chance that learned long ago that such claims are used to silence the voices of dissent.

I knew, for example, that when I spoke at this assembly there would not be an American flag present.[4] You must remember, however, that this is a hard-won absence. The powers embodied in that flag are hard to resist. That you are able to resist them is due to the sacrifices made by your mothers and fathers in the faith. But those accomplishments require equal, but perhaps, different sacrifices from you as you must learn how to live as a people constituted by the practice of forgiveness.

For the power of the flag is, by necessity, violent.[5] It cannot be the non-violent power of truthfulness that comes from the practice of reconciliation and forgiveness. Because there is no flag here, Goshen College is potentially a more truthful, and thus academically interesting, educational institution than those that serve such flags. It is so because it is a college made possible and

---

tically, the book at least suggests Mennonite insistence that they stand in continuity with the church through the ages, not so much on the basis of "doctrine," which is not unimportant, but on the basis of witness. For an excellent account of the background as well as the continued diverse use of *Martyrs Mirror,* see John D. Roth, "The Significance of the Martyr Story for Contemporary Anabaptists," *Brethren Life and Thought,* 37 (spring 1992): 97–106.

4. I was told by the Egyptian Orthodox student who picked me up at the airport in South Bend that there had been no pro-war sentiment for the Gulf War at Goshen College. That is the kind of political correctness I admire.

5. The violence of the flag also embodies the moral significance of sacrifice. I am acutely aware that when many honor the flag they honor those that died in war as well as those who sacrificed their general unwillingness to kill. As a Christian pacifist those sacrifices are a constant reminder of how profoundly we have failed to help Christians be an alternative to war. Thus good German Lutherans and Catholics made Hitler's war possible. Any compelling account of nonviolence as an ongoing practice requires explaining how those who have fought in war remain part of God's kingdom. For further reflections along these lines, see my "Pacifism: A Form of Politics," in *Peace Betrayed: Essays on Pacifism and Politics,* ed. Michael Cromartie (Washington, DC: Ethics and Public Policy Center Publication, 1989), 133–41.

sustained by a people who know that God has made you odd. That is why you know there is no such thing as a "liberal arts education" in which knowledge is an end in itself. Rather, you know that you have been educated in an institution that constantly reminds you that any truth that is neither based on nor serves the practice of reconciliation, and thus "peace," cannot be anything other than demonic.

As graduates of the college of the Church of the Second Chance you must remember, however, that the people that have made you possible do not understand Second Chance to be only about their own lives. For the Church of the Second Chance is the second chance for all the world. For the One that has made you a people of the second chance has done so that we might be a witness for the second chance that God has made possible for all people. As graduates of Goshen College you have been given skills, cabinetmaking skills, that make you particular kinds of witnesses for the world.

As graduates of Goshen College the church calls you to be agents of truth in a world of mendacity. Therefore you must be the most political of people, reminding this society of what a politics of truth might look like. For example, when George Bush nominated Justice Thomas for the Supreme Court he had to say that Judge Thomas was the most qualified justice he could find. We know that is the politics of the lie. Someone like Justice Thomas should have been nominated for the Supreme Court because America is and continues to be a racist society. George Bush could not tell Americans that we need Afro-Americans in such offices so they might use their power to protect their people in this racist society. He could not say that because Americans do not want to acknowledge that this is a racist society. We have not the skill to know how to live truthfully with such sin. That is a truth we lack the power to acknowledge because we do not want to pay the price that forgiveness requires, a forgiveness that would make reconciliation possible.

As graduates of the college of the Second Chance you have been trained to have the power to call those in power to truth. Just to the extent you do that you make it possible for all of us to be able, as Vaclav Havel puts it, to live in truth—thus to live nonviolently. For unless we are able to tell one another the truth through the practice of reconciliation and forgiveness, we are condemned to live in a world of violence and destruction. As people of the Second Chance we know we in fact live in a violent world—a world that may be all the more violent when confronted by you who refuse to call that order built on lies, peace. Yet as people of the Second Chance we know that we can live with hope, even in that world, because we have been constituted by the practices of reconciliation and forgiveness that has made truth, and thus peace, possible. Go therefore into the world to be disciples of our savior Jesus of Nazareth who has made us second chance people. May God bless you as you so live.

Further Reading

"Peacemaking: The Virtue of the Church" (1985), essay 16 in this volume

"Constancy and Forgiveness: The Novel as a School for Virtue" (1994), in DF

"The Christian Difference, or Surviving Postmodernism" (1999), in BH

"Why Time Cannot and Should Not Heal the Wounds of History, But Time Is and Can Be Redeemed" (1999), in BH

"Whose Church? Which Future? Whither the Anabaptist Vision?" (1994), in IGC

"For Dappled Things: Commencement Address for Duke University Ph.D. Ceremony" (1996), in STT

16. Peacemaking: The Virtue of the Church (1985)

In this more pastoral essay Hauerwas attempts to overcome some misperceptions about what it is for Christians to seek peace. First of all, peace is not the avoidance of conflict. Rather, Christians must necessarily be involved in disagreement to overcome the temptation to invoke violence to win peace. Second, because peacemaking is more characteristic of communities than individuals, peacemaking is often not seen as a virtue. Third, peacemaking must not be seen as an isolated activity, but one that enables all forms of moral excellence in the Church. In various ways, Hauerwas attempts to show how the Christian virtue of peace is distinctive and requires communities of forgiveness and reconciliation. This piece develops and expands themes found in the previous selection.

> If your brother sins against you, go and tell him his fault, between you and him alone. If he listens to you, you have gained a brother. But if he does not listen, take one or two others along with you, that every word may be confirmed by the evidence of two or three witnesses. If he refuses to listen to them, tell it to the church; and if he refuses to listen even to the church, let him be to you as a Gentile and a tax collector. Truly, I say to you whatever you bind on earth shall be bound in heaven, and whatever you loose on earth shall be loosed in heaven. Again I say to you, if two of you agree on earth about anything they ask, it will be done for them by my Father in heaven. For where two or three are gathered in my name, there am I in the midst of them. Then Peter came up and said to him, "Lord how often shall my brother sin against me, and I forgive him? As many as seven times?" Jesus said to him, "I do not say to you seven times, but seventy times seven." (Matthew 18:15–22)

This is surely a strange text to begin an article on peacemaking as a virtue. The text does not seem to be about peacemaking but about conflict making. It

[Originally published in *The Furrow* 36 (October 1985): 605–614. Used by permission. Subsequently reprinted in CET.]

does not say if you have a grievance you might think about confronting the one you believe has wronged you. The text is much stronger than that. It says if you have a grievance you must, you are obligated to, confront the one you believe has sinned against you. You cannot overlook a fault on the presumption that it is better not to disturb the peace. Rather, you must risk stirring the waters, causing disorder, rather than overlook the sin.

But on what possible grounds could Christians, people supposedly of peace, be urged actively to confront one another? It seems out of character for Jesus to urge us to do so, and out of character for the Christian community to follow such an admonition. Yet I want to suggest that we will understand peacemaking as a virtue only when we see that such confrontation is at the heart of what it means to be a peacemaker. Even more important, however, I think that by attending to this passage we will be able to see how peacemaking, as well as any virtue, is correlative to a community's practices.

This is a crucial issue if we are to appreciate peacemaking as a virtue. It is interesting to note how seldom peacemaking is treated as a virtue. Courage, temperance, and even humility are usually acknowledged as virtues much more readily than is peacemaking. For many, peacemaking may sound like a "good thing," but they would be hesitant to call it a virtue. Peacemaking is usually seen more as a matter of political strategy than a disposition forming the self. Some people may even be peaceful, but that hardly seems a virtue.

Why do we seem reticent to think of peacemaking as a virtue? I suspect it is because we think of virtue as personal characteristics that everyone should possess irrespective of their membership in any specific community. But, as I hope to show, such an understanding of virtue is far too limited, if not an outright mistake. For as Aristotle argues, some virtues, such as justice and friendship, are correlative to certain kinds of relations and cannot exist without those relations being valued by a community.[1] Peacemaking is that sort of virtue insofar as the church believes that peace (and a very particular kind of peace at that) is an essential characteristic of its nature.

As important as understanding why we rightly consider peacemaking a virtue is how we understand what kind of activity it is. It is in this context that

---

1. Aristotle, in truth, is a bit unsure if friendship is a virtue. He says it either is a virtue or at least "involves virtue." The reason he is hesitant is that he has no conceptual means to say how a virtue can be a quality of a relation. This remains a difficult issue worth considerable reflection, but I have refrained from pursuing it in this essay. [For more on friendship and Aristotle, see "Theological Reflections on Aristotelian Themes" with Charles Pinches (1997) in CAV.]

the passage from Matthew is so important for helping us understand peace-making as a virtue. Normally we tend to think of peacemaking as the resolution of conflict rather than the encouragement of conflict. That such is the case, I suspect, is also one of the reasons that peacemaking, even if it is understood as a virtue, is not really all that appealing. Have you ever known anyone, yourself included, who would rush out to see a movie or play about peace?

We say we want peace, but in fact we know we love conflict and even war. Indeed, I suspect that one of the deepest challenges for those of us who call ourselves pacifists is that on the whole peace just does not seem very interesting to most people. We may all say that we want peace, but I suspect that most of us would be deeply upset if we got it. We want to work for peace, we like the struggle for peace, but the idea that peace might actually be achieved would actually scare us to death. For we associate peace with rest, but we fear that rest without conflict is but another name for death. We thus pray like Augustine, but we pray "give us peace—but not yet."

We simply have to admit that for most of us peace is boring. Of course, in the midst of terrible turmoil we may well think we could stand a bit of boredom, but it is interesting how often people look back on past "troubles" nostalgically. Life needs movement, which most of us believe, rightly or wrongly, entails conflict. Therefore, peacemaking for most of us appears a bit like Bernard Shaw's views of heaven—namely, that on reflection he thought he preferred hell, since at least hell promised to contain some interesting people.

But this text from Matthew puts the issue of peacemaking in quite a different light. As I noted above, Jesus does not suggest that if you have a grievance against someone in the community it might be a good idea for you to "try to work it out." Rather, he says that you must go and speak to the one whom you believe has sinned against you. Such a speaking, of course, may well involve nothing less than confrontation. You must do it first alone, but if reconciliation does not take place then you must "go public," taking witnesses with you. If that still is not sufficient, you must take the matter before the whole church.

Our first reaction to this text is to think that surely this procedure is far too extreme for most of our petty conflicts. I may get angry at someone, but if I wait I discover that I will get over it. Moreover, who wants to appear like someone who is too easily offended? No one likes people who tend to make mountains out of molehills, especially when they claim to be doing so only because of the "principle involved." Even more important, most of us learn

that time heals all wounds, and thus we are better off waiting for some conflicts to die through the passage of time.

Yet Jesus seems to have been working with a completely different set of
presuppositions about what is necessary to be a community of peace and
peacemaking. It seems that peace is not the name of the absence of conflict,
but rather, peacemaking is that quality of life and practices engendered by a
community that knows it lives as a forgiven people. Such a community cannot
afford to "overlook" one another's sins because they have learned that such
sins are a threat to being a community of peace.

The essential presupposition of peacemaking as an activity among Christians is our common belief that we have been made part of a community in
which people no longer regard their lives as their own. We are not permitted
to harbor our grievances as "ours." When we think our brother or sister has
sinned against us, such an affront is not just against us but against the whole
community. A community established as peaceful cannot afford to let us relish
our sense of being wronged without exposing that wrong in the hopes of
reconciliation. We must learn to see wrongs as "personal" because we are part
of a community where the "personal" is crucial to the common good.

It is an unpleasant fact, however, that most of our lives are governed more
by our hates and dislikes than by our loves. I seldom know what I really want,
but I know what or whom I deeply dislike and even hate. It may be painful to
be wronged, but at least such wrongs give me a history of resentments that, in
fact, constitute who I am. How would I know who I am if I did not have my
enemies?

It seems our enemies are exactly who Jesus is forcing us to confront. For he
tells us that we cannot cherish our wrongs. Rather, we are commanded to
engage in the difficult task of confronting those whom we believe have sinned
against us. Such confrontation is indeed hard because it makes us as vulnerable as the one we confront. The process of confrontation means that we may
well discover that we have been mistaken about our being wronged. Still more
troubling, it means that even if we have been wronged, by confronting our
brother or sister we will have to envision the possibility that, like Jonah, he or
she may repent and we will therefore have to be reconciled. We will be forced
to lose the subject of our hatred.

From this perspective peacemaking is anything but boring. Rather, it is the
most demanding of tasks. One of the interesting aspects of this passage in
Matthew is it assumes that the Christian community will involve conflict and
wrongs. The question is not whether such conflict can be eliminated but

rather how we are to deal with the conflict. Conflict is not to be ignored or denied, but rather conflict, which may involve sins, is to be forced into the open. That we are to do so must surely be because the peace that Jesus brings is not a peace of rest but rather a peace of truth. Just as love without truth cannot help but be accursed, so peace without truthfulness cannot help but be deadly. In short, peacekeeping is that virtue of the Christian community that is required if the church is to be a community of people at peace with one another in truth.

The truth seems to be about the last thing we want to know about ourselves. We may say that the truth saves, but in fact we know that any truth worth knowing is as disturbing as it is fulfilling. Surely that is why Jesus is so insistent that those who would follow him cannot simply let sins go unchallenged. For when we fail to challenge sinners, we in fact abandon them to their sin. We show we care little for them by our unwillingness to engage in the hard work of establishing a truthful peace.

That the church is such a community of truthful peace depends on its being a community of the forgiven. As the text from Matthew notes, Peter realized that Jesus' command that we confront the sinner is not an easy one. For such confrontation is based on the presupposition that forgiveness is also to be offered. But how often, Peter asks, can forgiveness be offered—seven times? We cannot help but be sympathetic with Peter's question, for it just seems to be against good sense to be ready to offer forgiveness. What kind of community would ever be sustained on the presupposition that forgiveness is always available?

Yet there seems to be no limit to forgiveness, as Jesus elaborates his response to Peter by telling the story of the servant who, having been forgiven his debt, refuses to forgive a fellow servant his debt. The lord of the unforgiving servant, on being told of his servant's behavior, threw him in jail until he paid his debt. And so, we are told, our "heavenly Father will do to every one of you, if you do not forgive your brother from your heart" (Matthew 18:35). What it seems we must remember, if we are to be peacemakers capable of confronting one another with our sins, is that we are forgiven and we are part of a community of the forgiven. Our ability to be truthful peacemakers depends on our learning that we owe our lives to God's unrelenting forgiveness.

The forgiveness that makes peacemaking possible, moreover, does not mean that judgment is withheld. The question is not whether we should hold one another accountable but what is the basis for doing so and how is it to be done. To be sinned against or to know we have sinned requires that we have a language and correlative habit that makes it possible to know what it is to be a sinner. Only on such a basis do we have the capacity to avoid arbitrariness of judgment as we learn to see our relations with one another as part of a continuing tradition of discourse that helps us serve a common good. That good, at least among Christians, is to be a community of the forgiven empowered to witness to God's kingdom of peace wrought through Jesus of Nazareth.

We therefore do not confront one another from a position of self-righteousness; we must come to the other as one who has been forgiven. Such a perspective, I think, throws quite a different light on this passage from that which is often given it. Too often it is assumed that this text legitimates our confrontation with the brother or sister on the assumption that we have power over the other because we have been wronged and thus can decide to forgive. Forgiveness from such a position is but another form of power, since it assumes that one is in a superior position. But the whole point of this text is that we confront one another not as forgivers, not as those who use forgiveness as power, but first and foremost as people who have learned the truth about ourselves—namely, that we are all people who need to be and have been forgiven.

That is why we must and can confront one another as sinners, because we understand ourselves to share with the other our having been forgiven. We thus share a common history of forgiveness and repentance that makes our willingness to confront one another a process of peace rather than simply another way to continue conflict. That is why those who refuse to listen must be treated as a Gentile or tax collector, for they are acting like those who have not learned that they have been forgiven. To act like one not needing forgiveness is to act against the very basis of this community as a community of peacemaking. That is why they must be excluded: they must learn that they are not peacemakers insofar as they refuse to live as the forgiven. From such a perspective there is no more violent act than the unwillingness to accept reconciliation freely and honestly offered. But the truth is that few of us are willing to be so reconciled.

From this perspective, we should not be surprised if peacemakers and peacemaking appear anything but peaceful. Moreover, if the church is to be a community of peace in a world at war, it cannot help but be a community that confronts the world in uncompromising manner. The task of peacemaking cannot ignore real wrongs, past or present. The peace that the world knows too often is but order built on forgetfulness, but that is not the peace of the church, which is built on forgiveness. No genuine peace can come from simply forgetting past wrongs, but rather must come by encompassing those wrongs in a history of forgiveness. Those peacemakers, however, who insist on reminding us of our past sins cannot help but often appear as troublemakers.

This is particularly true when so often the wrongs that we must remember are those that no amount of effort or goodwill can make right. No matter how hard Christians work against anti-Semitism, there is finally nothing that can be done to make "right" the terror of the Holocaust. If there is to be a reconciliation between Christians and Jews, it cannot come through forgetting such a terrible wrong but by learning to face that history as a forgiven people.

This is but to remind us that peacemaking as a virtue has a peculiar stake in the temporal. Peace, as well as forgiveness, must take place in time. Disembodied beings cannot know peace; only beings who know themselves as timeful are capable of being at peace. As we are told in Ephesians, the relation between Israel and the Gentiles has not been resolved by some temporal decree, but rather, "now in Christ Jesus you who once were far off have been brought near in the blood of Christ. For he is our peace, who has made us both one, and has broken down the dividing wall of hostility, by abolishing in his flesh the law of commandments and ordinances, that he might create in himself one new man in the place of the two, so making peace, and might reconcile us both to God in one body through the cross, thereby bringing the hostility to an end. And he came and preached peace to you who were far off and peace to those who were near; for through him we both have access in one Spirit to the Father" (Ephesians 2:13–18).

Peacemaking among Christians, therefore, is not simply one activity among others but rather is the very form of the church insofar as the church is the form of the one who "is our peace." Peacemaking is the form of our relations in the church as we seek to be in unity with one another, which at least means that we begin to share a common history. Such unity is not that built on shallow optimism that we can get along if we respect one another's differences. Rather, it is a unity that profoundly acknowledges our differences because we have learned that those differences are not accidental to our being a truthful people—even when they require us to confront one another as those who have wronged us.

If peacemaking as a virtue is intrinsic to the nature of the church, what are we to say about those without the church? First, I think we must say that it is the task of the church to confront and challenge the false peace of the world which is too often built more on power than truth. To challenge the world's sense of peace may well be dangerous, because often when sham peace is exposed it threatens to become violent. The church, however, cannot be less truthful with the world than it is expected to be with itself. If we are less truthful we have no peace to offer to the world.

Second, Christians are prohibited from ever despairing of the peace possible in the world. We know that as God's creatures we are not naturally violent nor are our institutions unavoidably violent. As God's people we have been created for peace. Rather, what we must do is to help the world find the habits of peace whose absence so often makes violence seem like the only alternative. Peacemaking as a virtue is an act of imagination built on long habits of the resolution of differences. The great problem in the world is that our imagination has been stilled, since it has not made a practice of confronting wrongs so that violence might be avoided. In truth, we must say that the church has too often failed the world by its failure to witness in our own life the kind of conflict necessary to be a community of peace. Without an example of a peacemaking community, the world has no alternative but to use violence as the means to settle disputes.

I have tried to show how peacekeeping as a virtue is community-specific—that is, how it is an activity intrinsic to the nature of the church. Yet the fact that peacekeeping is community-specific does not mean it ought to be community-restrictive.[2] The "brother" referred to in Matthew is no doubt a member of the Christian community, but the Matthean community is also one that understood it was to go among the nations to witness to God's peace. Therefore, the habits of peacekeeping acquired in the church are no less relevant when the church confronts those not part of our community and who may even threaten or wrong our community. For it is our belief that God is no less present in our enemy calling us to find the means of reconciliation.

If the tack I have taken is close to being right, then it puts pacifism in singular perspective. For pacifism is often associated with being passive in the face of wrong. As a result, some even suggest that pacifism is immoral insofar as the pacifist suffers wrong and as a result fails to fulfill the obligation to the brother by resisting his injustice. But peacemaking is not a passive response;

2. I am indebted to Gregory Jones for this helpful way of putting the matter. I also owe Dr. Harmon Smith much for his painful but truthful critique of an earlier draft of this essay.

rather, it is an active way to resist injustice by confronting the wrongdoer with the offer of reconciliation. Such reconciliation is not cheap, however, since no reconciliation is possible unless the wrong is confronted and acknowledged.

Contrary to usual stereotypes, this means that peacekeepers, rather than withdraw from politics, must be the most political of animals. Peacekeeping requires the development of the processes and institutions that make possible confrontation and resolution of differences so that violence can be avoided. The problem with politics, at least as politics is currently understood, is not that it involves compromises but that it so little believes in truth. As a result, it becomes but a form of coercion without due acknowledgment that it is so. In such a situation the church can be a peacemaker by being the most political of institutions.

No doubt peacemaking, as I have tried to depict it, is a demanding business. I think it is impossible to sustain it if it is thought to be a virtue of heroic individuals. Rather, peacemaking must be a virtue of a whole community, so that the kind of support and care necessary to sustain peacemaking as an ongoing task will be forthcoming. As Christians, however, we cannot help but rejoice that God has called us to be peacemakers, for what could possibly be a more joyful and exciting task than to be a part of God's peace.

Further Reading

"A Story-Formed Community: Reflections on Watership Down" (1981), essay 9 in this volume

"Taking Time for Peace: The Ethical Significance of the Trivial" (1988), in CET

"Pacifism: Some Philosophical Considerations," *Faith and Philosophy* 2, no. 2 (April 1985): 99–104

"Companions on the Way: The Necessity of Friendship" (1997), in CAV

"The Radical Hope in the Annunciation: Why Both Single and Married Christians Welcome Children" (1998), essay 24 in this volume

"A Trinitarian Theology of the Chief End of All Flesh" (1992), with John Berkman, in IGC

"Is Obedience a Virtue?" (1997), in CAV

17. Remembering as a Moral Task: The Challenge of the Holocaust (1981)

Hauerwas here engages the Jewish debate about how to properly locate the significance of the Holocaust within Jewish self-understanding. Critiquing the view put forward by Berkovits that the liberal state provides the most hospitable environment for Jewish survival or flourishing, Hauerwas argues that within the liberal political order Jewish particularism cannot in fact be accommodated. Without a theological perspective, therefore, the uniqueness of the Holocaust cannot be sustained in liberal political orders. Drawing on the work of Michael Wyschogrod and Rosemary Radford Ruether, Hauerwas notes that in order for Jews to remember their past rightly, they must remember their historical particularity as an elect people. Too often, Christians have underwritten various forms of imperialism in the name of one or another version of "universalism," and in the process have lost their sense of the eschatological character of both Jewish and Christian existence as peoples. Contra Kant's conception of religion within the limits of reason alone, Hauerwas argues that, like Jews, Christians must be the kind of "community of remembrance" that resists abstract universalistic accounts of humankind.

Consider the following two statements by Rosemary Radford Ruether and Immanuel Kant about the place of the Jewish people in the era of the secular nation-state:

> Emancipation (of the Jews) did not depend on who won the arguments, but on the process of secularization that shaped the modern state and which could not tolerate self-governing groups apart from the monolithic organizations of the nation-state. It was on these grounds that the Jews had to either be drawn into a secular definition of citizenship, based on nationalism, or

[Originally published in *Cross Currents* (spring 1981). Used by permission. Subsequently reprinted in AN.]

else be regarded as incapable of assimilating into this national identity and eliminated by expulsion (or extermination). It was here that liberal philosophy and theology played an ambivalent role. Their definition of religion, either as universal, national religion of reason, or else as profound inwardness, made Judaism the antithesis of the concept of "religion." Since Judaism was not a religion, according to either Christian rationalist or Christian romantic theories, Judaism came to be defined in this tradition of thought in nationalist, quasi-racial terms. Judaism was said to be, not a religion, but the laws of a nation. Jews were not a religious group, but a foreign nation. The antithesis of Judaism and Christianity was translated into an antithesis between Jews and Europeans, or Jews and Germans.[1]

 Rosemary Radford Ruether

We can deal only with the history of that church which contained within itself, from its first beginning, the seed and the principles of the objective unity of the true and *universal* religious faith, to which it is gradually brought nearer. . . . The *Jewish faith* was, in its original form, a collection of mere statutory laws upon which was established a political organization; for whatever moral additions were then or later appended to it in no way whatever belong to Judaism as such. Judaism is really not a religion at all but merely a union of a number of people who, since they belonged to a particular stock, formed themselves not into a church; nay, it was *intended* to be merely an earthly state so that, were it possible to be dismembered through adverse circumstances, there would still remain to it the political faith in its eventual reestablishment.[2]

 Immanuel Kant

1. The Holocaust: The Methodological Challenge

"In what ways has the Holocaust had an impact on the way Jewish and Christian thinkers make judgments and decisions about modern moral and political problems? What implications does the Holocaust have for the interaction between Jewish thinkers and Christian theologians as they confront

---

1. Rosemary Ruether, *Faith and Fratricide: The Theological Roots of Anti-Semitism* (New York: Seabury Press, 1979), 220.
2. Immanuel Kant, *Religion Within the Limits of Reason Alone,* trans. Theodore Green and Hoyt Hudson (New York: Harper and Brothers, 1960), 116.

contemporary moral and political problems? What are the implications of the Holocaust for the Jewish and Christian assessment of Liberalism and the ideals of liberal democracies?"[3]

These questions presuppose that one already has an understanding of the reality, causes, and meaning of the Holocaust—issues that most agree continue to require further critical investigation. Therefore, it seems that we who address the ethical significance of the Holocaust must shed our "scholarly detachment" and say what we think should be said about its relevance. In particular, it seems I should address the relevance of the Holocaust for religious ethics and the social strategy of Jews and Christians in a liberal society. For in spite of the various issues surrounding the causes and meaning of the Holocaust, few would deny its significance for how we understand ourselves and act today. If it fails to have such significance, then the deaths that occurred there are even more meaningless and Hitler will seem to have his victory.

Yet, as important as the task is, I feel completely unequal to it. I have read and thought about the Holocaust since I was a seminarian and I still feel I have almost nothing to say about it. For me it simply continues to stand there starkly as sheer horror. The horror lies not just in the massive numbers of those murdered, but in the systematic and effective attempt of the Nazis to rob those deaths of all meaning. As Emil Fackenheim suggests, "Auschwitz was the supreme, most diabolical attempt ever made to murder martyrdom itself and, failing that, to deprive all death, martyrdom included, of its dignity."[4]

Moreover, I remain unsure how, if at all, the Holocaust was unique in Jewish or world history. I am not even sure if the question of uniqueness is the right question, though I will suggest why it seems so unavoidable for us. Nor am I even sure which theological issues are raised by Auschwitz or how to answer those that are asked. It may even be that the fundamental rethinking about Christianity in the face of the continuing existence of the Jews is misdirected when the Holocaust is made the central issue. I certainly do not know

---

3. These are the questions I was asked to address at the International Scholars Conference, "Thinking about the Holocaust," at Indiana University, November 3–5, 1980. Previous sessions had dealt with historical and theological issues. Because my interests are primarily constructive I have dealt very little with the first question. However, it ought to be noted that the Holocaust has not commanded the attention of most Christian ethicists or affected the way they work.

4. Emil Fackenheim, *God's Presence in History: Jewish Affirmations and Philosophical Reflections* (New York: Harper and Row, 1970), 74.

what should be said about God and his relationship to us in light of the Holocaust. One part of me tends to favor those who counsel silence as the only appropriate theological response simply because they know of no alternative.[5]

Yet we rightly feel that we cannot or should not, especially when it involves questions of ethics and social policy, let silence be our only response. Therefore, it seems we must say something about what the implications of the Holocaust are or should be. But what? I have no adequate answer that I can unhesitatingly put forward for anyone. Therefore I will try to suggest how the Holocaust has influenced the way I attempt to do Christian ethics as well as how the Church should be related to liberal society. For even though I have not been able to develop any position or "theory" about the Holocaust, I have always assumed that the Holocaust, and Christian complicity in the Holocaust, is a decisive test case for anyone attempting to think ethically as a Christian.

That may seem an odd claim since I have seldom directly discussed the Holocaust. But it seems odder still since I have been one of the few persons working in contemporary religious ethics who has called for Christian ethics to be unapologetically and particularistically Christian. I have emphasized those aspects of the moral life—character, narrative, the separateness of the church—that make Christian convictions about Jesus morally intelligible and significant. But from the perspective of many, and especially those concerned with Auschwitz, this reassertion of the particularity of Christian ethics cannot but appear as a dangerous new tribalism. It may even be an indication that Christians, realizing that their theological claims cannot pass modern evidential muster, are retreating into self-protective enclaves. As a result they lack moral resources to prevent another Holocaust just as they were devoid of a universal ethic to challenge the narrow loyalties that led to the Holocaust.[6]

5. For an excellent account of various theological options for interpreting the Holocaust, see Pinchas Peli, "In Search of Religious Language for the Holocaust," *Conservative Judaism* 32, no. 2 (winter 1979): 3–24. Peli ends by suggesting that silence is required as a response, but it must be the silence that is "part of conversation, silence that incorporates a relationship to a 'thou' ('for Thee')—but not silence that ends all communication and removes all possibility of discovering meaning." For what I take to be a similar point, see Alvin Rosenfeld's insightful analysis of Wiesel's use of silence, "The Problematics of Holocaust Literature," in *Confronting the Holocaust: The Impact of Elie Wiesel* (Bloomington: Indiana University Press, 1978), 1–30. Rosenfeld rightly suggests that it is no accident that Wiesel has increasingly turned toward Midrashic literature as a model of how silence can be made to speak without being domesticated by conventionalities.

6. In this respect it is interesting to note Richard Rubenstein's comment that he was able to

Therefore, it would seem that if Christians, as I am encouraging them to do, took seriously the particularity of their convictions as primary for forming their morality, they would lack the means to challenge the subtle and implicit anti-Semitism that constantly threatens to reawaken in our society and the church. What then of my claim that the challenge of the Holocaust should be a decisive test case for Christian ethics? The claim still stands, for it is my conviction that Christian anti-Semitism, without which the Holocaust would not have been possible, is rooted in an account of Christian existence that ignores the particularity of our convictions. Moreover, it is my contention that the failure to appreciate the particular nature of our convictions was fueled by a social policy and ethic that, often with the best intentions and idealism, perversely attempted to make the "ethic of Jesus" an ethos sufficient to sustain a civilization. In the process, Christians lost exactly those convictions concerning God's judgment on all nations that should have prevented them from identifying with as well as cooperating with those powers that perpetrated Auschwitz.

The methodological significance of the Holocaust first confronted me in the context of studying modern German theology. I approached that study assuming that those theologians who represented Protestant liberalism would have been the first to stand against the Nazis and their anti-Semitic program. Much to my surprise, I discovered that it was not the liberals but Barth who had the resources to recognize and challenge the Nazis at their deadly game.[7]

---

encounter the Christian world "without anger or resentment" because "we could only be angry or resentful if we expected some standard of conduct from the Christian world which it failed to observe. But, if Auschwitz has taught us anything, it is that in times of stress rights and dignity are operative only within one's primary or kinship group, if indeed they are operative at all" (quoted in Robert E. Willis, "Christian Theology after Auschwitz," *Journal of Ecumenical Studies* 12, no. 4 [fall 1975]: 494). Rubenstein's own fuller view is worked out in his *After Auschwitz: Radical Theology and Contemporary Judaism* (Indianapolis: Bobbs-Merrill, 1966). Rubenstein's point is a bit different from mine but he seems to assume that the only check against tribalism is some form of universalistic ethic and community standard. That is exactly what I am suggesting we do not have, but that does not mean that the kind of behavior he notes is any less morally reprehensible. It was reprehensible for Christians, not because they violated "rights and dignity" but because they betrayed the very God they claim to worship.

7. For an account of Barth's role, see Arthur Cochrane, *The Church's Confession under Hitler* (Philadelphia: Westminster Press, 1962). I am aware that there were, of course, many kinds of "liberalism" that resulted in diverse forms of political expression. It is certainly, therefore, not my intention to "blame" the Holocaust on "theological liberalism," but I am suggesting that liberalism in its many modes lacked the resources that might have rightly acted as a check against the nationalism that underwrote Auschwitz.

Just as Barth's own mind was changed in the face of his theological mentor's capitulation to earlier German war aims, so I began to understand that the relationship between theological convictions and their social expression was not as simple as I assumed. For it seemed to me that the liberal attempt to make Christianity a "reasonable" set of beliefs turned out to be an ideology for theological and social imperialism.[8] Of course, I am not accusing the liberals of being anti-Semites, though some were; nor am I suggesting that Barth's own challenge to the rise of the German Christians was as sharp as it should have been, especially on the question of the persecution of the Jews.

Liberal theologians were right to force the issue of the truthfulness of Christian convictions. But too often they failed to see that the question of the truthfulness of those convictions did not lie in their "universality," but in their practical force that was dependent on their particularity. And it is in this context that the Holocaust stands as a challenge to Christian convictions. For certainly one of the basic tests of the truthfulness of any significant set of convictions lies in the kind of lives in which they are embodied. If it can be shown that the Holocaust lies at the heart of Christian claims about the kind of life required to be a disciple of Jesus, it would surely provide strong evidence that Christianity is a false and perverse faith.

Only by recovering the particularity of Christian convictions and their

---

8. As Ruether points out:

Even the liberalism with which Jews allied themselves in their struggle for emancipation harbored fundamental ambivalences toward Jews. The price of emancipation was also seen as one of cultural assimilation. Most liberals actually thought of this as paving the way for Jewish conversion to Christianity. All liberals took it for granted that ghetto Judaism represented a bad moral, spiritual, and intellectual condition. The price of emancipation was the destruction of Jewish self-government and autonomous corporate identity, possible in the medieval corporate state, which had allowed the Jews to keep a sense of peoplehood within Christian society. It was this sense of autonomous corporate identity and peoplehood which the modern nationalist state could not tolerate and which became the basis of modern anti-Semitism. Now Jewish identity in an ethnic sense was seen as intrinsically evil. It must be dissolved as the Jew could become a "German" or else it was seen as indissolvable, and so the Jew must be expelled. In any case, the Jew must pay for emancipation by ceasing to be a Jew in a corporate sense. (*Faith and Fratricide*, 217–18)

This process appears more benign in America, as here the Enlightenment was qualified for a period by the Puritan and Republican political traditions. However, it has become increasingly the case that America has become the best example of Enlightenment political thought and as a result Judaism has been interpreted, by Jew and non-Jew alike, to be a matter of "personal conviction." Ironically, in spite of claims about the pragmatic nature of American society and government, no society and state has ever been more the product of a theory than America.

correlative ethical implications can we gain a perspective by which the Holocaust can be seen as perversion of the Gospel and gain a better sense of how
Christians should relate to the world. This does not mean to deny or excuse
the centuries of Christian anti-Semitism that prepared the way for countless
injustices against the Jews, culminating in the Holocaust. Christians have
much for which to be guilty, but we cannot let our guilt guide what we must
now say.[9] I am not suggesting that the particularity of our claims about Jesus
must be recovered in order to prevent another Auschwitz, but rather that a
renewed appreciation of the particularity of Jesus helps us to understand more
truthfully Christian failure in the Holocaust. For it is my contention that the
church lost the means to challenge the Nazis exactly to the extent it tried to
base its "ethics" on grounds other than those made possible by the faithful life
of Jesus of Nazareth. In doing so it necessarily attributed to culture and the
state a hegemony they cannot and should not have.

From a Jewish point of view, my position may entail some deep losses. For
if the political significance of the Gospel lies exactly in its power of forming a
people who are able to maintain a separated existence among the nations, that
means we cannot promise "Never again." Put more strongly, those who continue to do Christian social ethics from the perspective of forming a culture
that will ensure "Never again" are but continuing to be caught in the same
logic that resulted in Christian complicity with the Holocaust.

2. Jew and Christian in a Secular Society

Many will find this an odd claim, since the dominant assumption is that
liberal and secular cultures—social systems that seek to free politics from
religious presuppositions and involvement—are the best strategy to prevent
another Auschwitz. Liberalism, in the many different forms it has assumed
since the Enlightenment, stands as the uncompromising challenge to those
who would seek to control any society and state by religious presuppositions.

Yet the presumption of the moral advantage of liberalism for Jewish and
Christian existence must be challenged. By issuing such a challenge, I do not
mean to suggest that liberalism, especially in its social form, is worse than

9. See, for example, my "The Holocaust and the Duty to Forgive," *Sh'ma* 10, no. 198 (October 3, 1980): 137–39; and my "Forgiveness and Forgetting," *Sh'ma* 11, no. 202 (November 28,
1980): 15–16. Interestingly enough, forgiveness turns out to be essential for historical objectivity, since only by forgiveness can we avoid denying our past wrongs or perpetrating an
ideology that only continues to underwrite our assumed righteousness.

other social systems, but only to remind Christians and Jews that it involves peculiar challenges for each of us. To be sure, liberalism offers moral opportunities that should be exploited, but it also involves subtle temptations that can rob Jewish and Christian communities of their substance.

2.1 Eliezer Berkovits's Secular Universalism

As a way to explore this contention, I want to call our attention to Eliezer Berkovits's account of the implications of the Holocaust.[10] Berkovits is attractive in that he has little use for ecumenical etiquette. He deeply distrusts, and I suspect dislikes, Christianity, and thus is not impressed by the recent attempts of Christians to take a more positive attitude toward Judaism. Moreover, he also sees with great clarity that relations between Jews and Christians have entered a new period, not because of the Holocaust, but because Christianity can no longer dominate Western culture or states. The crucial question for Berkovits, therefore, is what the proper social strategy for Jews should be in a post-Christian era.

Berkovits argues that the Christian era did not begin with the birth of Jesus, but dates from the first half of the fourth century, when Constantine made Christianity the state religion. "The characteristic mark of that era was militancy. This was inherent in its beginnings: Christianity did not capture the Roman Empire by the power of a religious idea but by the sword of the emperor. As soon as Christianity was established, Judaism was declared an odious heretic sect whose propagation was forbidden under the penalty of death. Even the vast missionary activities in Asia and Africa were possible only because the Western colonizing powers which opened up these new lands were Christian. The preachers of the gospel marched in the wake of the swift and terrible sword of Constantine" (38).

But according to Berkovits, this era has come to an end. The sword of Constantine has been passed to numerous other hands: the Soviets, the Chinese, Moslems, and many developing nations, where Christianity has no decisive role. Berkovits suggests that this is what accounts for the new Christian ecumenism and tolerance. After centuries of resisting the principle of tolerance and freedom of religion, Christians now have seized those slogans as their own simply because "Christianity is no longer supreme in the world. When the Church leaders speak of freedom of religion, they mean first of all

---

10. Eliezer Berkovits, *Faith after the Holocaust* (New York: KTAV Publishing, 1973). Subsequent references to Berkovits are in the text.

freedom for Christians to adhere to their faith in Communist lands. Christianity is now on the side of tolerance because this is the post-Christian age of world history, because in this post-Christian era the old policies of intolerance are no longer viable" (39–40).

This change in our social situation means that for the first time since the fourth century the confrontation between Jews and Christians can take place in freedom. In such a time it is the responsibility of the Jew to confront Christianity with the meaning of the Christian—which is nothing less than the accusation of the moral and spiritual bankruptcy of Christian civilization and religion. "After nineteen centuries of Christianity, the extermination of six million Jews, among them one and a half million children, carried out in cold blood in the very heart of Christian Europe, encouraged by the criminal silence of virtually all Christendom including that of an infallible Holy Father in Rome, was the natural culmination of this bankruptcy. A straight line leads from the first act of oppression against the Jews and Judaism in the fourth century to the holocaust in the twentieth" (41).

Berkovits is therefore little interested in entering a "fraternal dialogue" with Christians. Indeed, there is no reason why Jews should be interested in it. Unlike Christianity, "it is not Judaism's ambition to save mankind, because it never maintained that mankind was lost without it. Judaism is the only possible way of life for Jews. Judaism is free from missionary zeal" (46). Jews, therefore, are not interested in whether Christians are now willing to acknowledge the "fragmentary truths of Judaism." Rather, all they desire from Christians is to "keep their hands off us and our children! Human beings ought to treat each other with respect and hold each other dear, independently of theological dialogues, Biblical studies, and independently of what they believe about each other's religion. . . . It is not interreligious understanding that mankind needs but interhuman understanding—and understanding based on our common humanity and wholly independent of any need for common religious beliefs and theological principles" (46).

Berkovits does not deny the possibility of Jewish and Christian cooperation in some areas of endeavor: "A common front is useful and necessary in the struggle for freedom of conscience and worship, for peace and social justice; our interests are identical in these fields of human striving. In the post-Christian era, however, these goals of freedom, peace, and social justice have universal validity. It would be extremely foolish to seek their realization by means of a narrowly Jewish-Christian front" (48). Indeed, Berkovits suggests that even in the field of ethics the Jew should be very cautious about Jewish-

Christian endeavors. Because Christianity has been so compromised by its involvement in Western imperialism, it is not easy to determine what is humanitarian-ethical idea and what is Christian propaganda. On the whole, therefore, Berkovits thinks it better for Judaism simply to go its own way.

I have no interest in trying to qualify or answer the Berkovits argument. For I think the main lines of his case are correct: Christians and Jews do now live in a different world, where the sword of Constantine has passed to new hands. But I question whether Berkovits has rightly read the implications of this transition to the "post-Christian age" and whether his acceptance of the values of "universal validity" constitute the most appropriate framework to think about the relation of Christianity and Judaism with each other in the kind of world in which we both must now live. In particular I question whether his claim of Judaism's lack of "missionary zeal" is not due more to his adherence to those values than to an accurate reading of Judaism's task to be a "light to the nations." But even more I doubt whether Berkovits has provided an analysis of what it means to live in a "post-Christian" world that alerts us adequately to the challenge such a world presents for Judaism as well as Christianity. For Berkovits fails to understand that societies putatively founded on values of "universal validity" cannot help but interpret the par-ticularistic commitments of the Jewish people as morally retrogressive.

In this respect I think it is interesting to compare Berkovits's commitment to those values—freedom, justice, and peace—to that of liberal Christianity. From Berkovits's perspective such values and their institutionalization repre-sent an advance because they now provide the means to keep the Christian foot off the Jewish neck. Indeed, elsewhere in his book Berkovits suggests he has little sympathy with the idealism of secular societies with their illusions of our "common humanity."[11] Therefore, Berkovits's adherence to and support of liberal societies is but a continuation of the classical Jewish defense strategy. Insofar as these values help Jews survive they will use them, but not place their trust in them.

---

11. But Berkovits believes that Judaism does underwrite the ideal of "common humanity." For "mankind is not a group; it is not a historical entity. Mankind is an idea, an ideal. The comprehensive group to be created to suit the comprehensive deed as a historical reality is a people in sovereign control of the major areas of its life. The faith of Judaism requires such a comprehensive deed. Realization through and within the all-comprehensive collective, man-kind, is the ideal; the instrument of its realization in history is the people. Since our concern is with the comprehensive need of Judaism, the people of Israel, of necessity, the covenant had to create the people with which the covenant was concluded" (149).

But from certain Christian perspectives these values are not just strategy for survival—they are the continuation of the divine mission of the church to make the world more nearly God's kingdom. Christian advocates of these values can and do share Berkovits's condemnation of the shameful history of Christian coercion through the state, but they have not given up the assumption that Christians have a stake in forming the ethos of societies that embody the "universal" values of the Gospel. Thus "Constantinianism" is shifted to a new key. No longer able to control the governmental apparatus itself, Christians seek to form societies that embody their values on the assumption that those values are universal.

This presumption has dominated the strategy of Christian social ethics for the past century and could easily be documented from the writing of Christian social ethicists. It is equally true of the liberal and conservative, Catholic or Protestant, social ethic. It continues to be found in recent debates about whether America has a civil religion as well as in discussions regarding the theological meaning of secularity. Such debates are but an indication that, contrary to Berkovits's assumption, Christians are anything but ready to let go of our civilization.

Moreover, if Rosemary Ruether is right, Berkovits has failed to read correctly the implications of the transference of power from the Christian era to more secular governments. For the universal values appealed to in order to justify emancipation of the Jews exacted a price as it revivified anti-Judaism in new forms, "translating the basis for contempt from theological to nationalist and then racial grounds. Where the Middle Ages was intolerant of the religious alien, the modern state was intolerant of the person of alien national identity. The Jew in the modern state became the representative of the 'outsider' to nationalist identity. But the same stereotypes, the same set of psychological attitudes were preserved in this change of theoretical grounds. Philosophical liberalism provided the theoretical basis for emancipation, but at the same time suggested the basis for this transition from religious to nationalist anti-Semitism. Protestant theology and biblical studies absorbed and deepened this cultural anti-Semitism."[12]

It may be objected that this "nationalistic anti-Semitism" was a perversion of the liberal values that provided for emancipation. The test case should not be

---

12. Ruether, *Faith and Fratricide*, 215. For documentation of Ruether's last point, see Charlotte Klein, *Anti-Judaism in Christian Theology*, trans. Edward Quinn (Philadelphia: Fortress Press, 1978).

Europe, and in particular Germany, with its centuries of religious anti-Semitism, but America. It is here, in America, that the Jew has benefited from the liberal faith in the common brotherhood of man. It is in America that Judaism rightly supports the development of a secular society not only as the means of the survival of Judaism but also as a more nearly just society for all people.

None of us is in a position to assess whether such a claim is true or not.[13] For in effect, the Jew in America has until recently been affected by the disadvantages and advantages of diverse forms of an anti-Semitism that is still far from absent. Rather than trying to judge the success of the American experiment for Judaism (which is surely a task best left to the Jews), I simply want to call attention to the problem such a society as America presents for a proper assessment of the Holocaust.

I think it fair to say that for American Jewry the Holocaust has become nothing less than an obsession in the past ten years. There has been much of value that has resulted from this heightened awareness, but at the same time religiously much remains ambiguous. For many secular Jews in America the Holocaust has become the means to reassert Jewish identity—an identity often downplayed in the interest of being just another good American.[14] But when the Holocaust becomes the basis for being Jewish, then the very reason why the Holocaust is such a serious challenge for Jews and Christians is lost.

---

13. I suspect that in many ways America does present both a kind of opportunity and a challenge for Judaism different from those offered by Europe. For example, Lucy Dawidowicz suggests that "The 'Christian' state had once been meant to serve 'Christian' purposes, that is, the expansion of Christianity. The Volkist state appropriated that purpose. The Jew, by definition an outsider in the 'Christian' state, remained an outsider in the Volkist conception of the state" (*The War against the Jews, 1933–1945* [New York: Bantam Books, 1979], 36). America's lack of "history" and the necessity to deal with pluralism seem to avoid some of the most explicit forms of anti-Semitism that still plague Europe. However, I think it would be extremely unwise to underestimate the depth of anti-Semitism that is often embodied in American commitments to "tolerance." Too often tolerance becomes a formula for condemning anyone who demands that his or her differences be taken morally and politically seriously. Moreover, the justification of American "secularism" as a nonideological solution to the problem of religious pluralism and totalitarianism has beguiled too many Christians to overlook the fact that we live not in a "Christian society" but in the time of a new paganism—a paganism made all the more destructive and potent because it uses the symbols of Christian civilization.

14. See, for example, Eugene Borowitz's criticism of this tendency in "Liberal Jews in Search of an 'Absolute,'" *Cross Currents* 29 (spring 1979): 9–14. An article in the *New York Times Magazine* documents how many are concerned that the popularization of the Holocaust may lead to trivialization. See Paula E. Hyman, "New Debate on the Holocaust," *New York Times Magazine*, September 14, 1980, 65–67, 78–82, 86, 109.

2.2 Michael Wyschogrod's Jewish Particularism

Michael Wyschogrod has pointed out:

> It is necessary to admit that we are fixated on the Holocaust to an extent quite unacceptable in a universalistic framework. The moral force of those who cannot share this fixation must be recognized. It is, I believe, necessary to abandon the attempt to find "objective" criteria in accordance with which such a fixation on the Holocaust will be made plausible, simply because any and all such criteria bestow uniqueness on the Holocaust at the expense of diminishing the other occasions of human suffering. To argue that one is asserting only the uniqueness of the Holocaust and not that it is a greater or more tragic crime than all others, simply won't do because the uniqueness which is asserted ("groundless, infinite hate indiscriminately directed against adults and children, saints and sinners, and so relentlessly expressed in action") turns out to be morally decisive and not just an attribution of abstract uniqueness. It is necessary to recognize that, from any universally humanistic framework, the destruction of European Jewry is one notable chapter in the long record of man's inhumanity against man, a record which compels the Holocaust to resign itself to being, at most, a first among equals.[15]

Wyschogrod goes on, however, to argue that he and Fackenheim are right to have a fixation on the Holocaust, but such a fixation is only justified theologically. The uniqueness of the Holocaust lies in the claim of Israel to being God's chosen people: "The fate of Israel is of central concern because Israel is the elect people of God through whom God's redemptive work is done in the world. However tragic human suffering is on the human plane, what happens to Israel is directly tied to its role as that nation to which God attaches His name and through which He will redeem man. He who strikes Israel, therefore, engages himself in battle with God and it is for this reason that the history of Israel is the fulcrum of human history. The suffering of others must, therefore, be seen in the light of Israel's suffering. The travail of man is not abandoned, precisely because Israel suffers and, thereby, God's presence is drawn into human history and redemption enters the horizon of human existence" (293).[16]

15. Michael Wyschogrod, "Faith and the Holocaust," *Judaism* 29, no. 3 (summer 1971): 299. Subsequent references are in the text.
16. I do not mean to suggest that Wyschogrod and Fackenheim are thus in agreement on the Holocaust. Indeed, Wyschogrod's position stands as a challenge to Fackenheim's view that the Holocaust must be the starting point for Jewish theological reflection. While it is perhaps

Wyschogrod admits this must appear as a scandal in the eyes of the nonbeliever. For how can the nonbeliever be expected to concede that the fate of Israel is more central than the fate of any other people? Wyschogrod thinks the Jew cannot and must not expect this, and therefore the Jew must neither be surprised nor outraged when the Holocaust, as it inevitably will, fades from general consciousness. But Jews must remember the Holocaust because only a believing "community can transcend time, can fixate on events of very limited 'historic' significance (how 'significant' was the Exodus to the ancient world whose records never mention it?) and find in them the significance of a redemption history apparent only to the eyes of faith. For believing Israel, the Holocaust is not just another mass murder but, perhaps, the final circumcision of the people of God. But how else, except by the power of God, can anyone believe that?" (293).[17]

A people who are determined to remember in this way will never rest easy in a culture that pretentiously believes it represents universal values. Such a people are especially offensive when those values are thought to represent mankind's control of our own lives. For the faith that God, not humankind, rules and determines the value of our lives is antithetical to the very presumption of modernity. Berkovits is surely right to underwrite those values that freed the Jew from feeling the direct power of Christian anti-Semitism at the hands of the power of the state, but it is not clear that those values do not result in a more subtle but no less destructive form of anti-Semitism. It is more subtle because now the Jew is tempted to remember the Holocaust for the wrong reasons.

It is not my place to try to work out social strategy for Jews vis-à-vis

---

wrong for a Christian theologian to take sides on this issue, it should be clear that my sympathies are with Wyschogrod. From this perspective Richard Rubenstein's position seems to me to involve a deep pathos. For he argues that Auschwitz means nothing less than for Jews to reject the "myth" of their special destiny, yet he provides little or no alternative other than vague appeals to the necessity of "true dialogue" (*After Auschwitz*, 74–75). Yet at the same time, Rubenstein has no faith in the attempt to build a completely secular society, for such a society lacks a sense of the tragic (79). Thus we seem left with two people ready to talk but who have nothing to say to one another since they have been denied any appeal to any sense of their own history.

17. It would be interesting to contrast Wyschogrod's sense of the Holocaust to that of the Eckardts in terms of the theological presumptions of both. I suspect that the Eckardts' claim of "transcending uniqueness" betrays a commitment to liberal Protestant theology for which Wyschogrod would have little sympathy. See, for example, Alice Eckardt and A. Roy Eckardt, "The Holocaust and the Enigma of Uniqueness: A Philosophical Effort at Practical Clarification," *The Annals* 450 (July 1980): 165–78.

liberalism. Rather, my concern must be with what the implications of this may be for how Christian ethics is conceived and executed. Earlier I suggested that the Holocaust made me more convinced that Christian ethics must begin not with the assumption that our liberal society is grounded on universal values, but on the basis of the particular convictions of the Church. I think I can now explain more clearly why I think this, and what implications this has for Christian social ethics done in a liberal social order.

3. A Community of Remembrance: The Social Implications

Like the Jews, Christians are called to be a community and a people capable of remembering; indeed, this is their first social task. The social significance of being such a community is often ignored today since "social ethics" is primarily identified with issues set by our wider social order. But the "social ethics" of the church is not first of all what the church can or should do to make the societies in which it exists more just. The church does not *have* a social ethic in that sense, but rather the church is a social ethic as it serves this or any society by first being the kind of community capable of nourishing its life by the memory of God's presence in Jesus Christ.[18]

But if that is the case, the great social challenge for Christians is learning how to remember the history of the Jews, as part of and as essential to our history.[19] Such remembering cannot be based on feeling guilty about the Holocaust, since guilt soon fades or becomes a substitute for honest appraisal. Rather, we must learn to remember with the Jews a history that certainly includes the Holocaust because we are learning that the Jews are our partners in discerning God's way in the world.[20] To learn to remember in this manner is a radical political act in that it must of necessity change our understanding of the Christian community and its relationship to our world.[21]

18. For a fuller elaboration of these themes, see CC.

19. The remembering of such a history depends on a story as much as it does historical "fact," though of course the story cannot be without fact. For an account of the complex interrelation of "story" and "history," see Julian Hartt's chapter "Story as the Art of Historical Truth," in his *Theological Method and the Imagination* (New York: Seabury, 1977), 219–54.

20. Paul Van Buren is surely on the right path in this respect as he has formed his recent attempt at "systematic theology" around the metaphor of being on a journey—that Jews and Christians must necessarily walk together. See his *Discerning the Way* (New York: Seabury, 1980).

21. See, for example, Robert E. Willis, "Auschwitz and the Nurturing of Conscience," *Religion in Life* (winter 1975): 432–48.

As Rosemary Ruether points out:

> Learning history is never really an act of "detached" scholarship, as academicians like to think. Learning history is, first of all, a rite of collective identity. Christians learn who they are by learning the story of Jesus, and through Jesus, carrying down a history created by the Christian Church and society. The history of the Jews disappears at the time of Jesus. This testifies to the Christian claim that it is the true Israel which alone carries on the biblical legacy. This Christian way of learning history negates ongoing Jewish existence. If we learned not only New Testament, but rabbinic Midrash; if we viewed the period of the Second Temple, not merely through the eyes of early Christianity, but through the eyes of the disciples of Rabban Yohanan ben Zakkai; if we read Talmud side by side with the Church Fathers; if we read the Jewish experience of Christendom side by side with Christian self-interpretation, this Christian view of history would fall into jeopardy. For this reason, Jewish history "after Christ" is not merely unknown but repressed. Its repression is essential for the maintenance of Christian identity. For Christians to incorporate the Jewish tradition after Jesus into their theological and historical education would involve ultimately the dismantling of the Christian concept of history and the demythologizing of the myth of the Christian era.[22]

And it would, I am suggesting, mean a radical change in the political form of the church. For to be a people of remembering is nothing less than a prophetic call for the church to respond to the God who has called them to be a new people amid the nations. It would mean that the church would have to give up the security of having its ethos enforced or at least reinforced by wider social structures, trusting rather in the power of the Holy Spirit to be its sustainer and guide.

Some may think this would require Christians to qualify our commitment to Jesus as the source of our life and the object of our worship. I think that is not the case. Certainly it would require a challenge to some Christological formulations, but Christology after all is not the object of our faith. God is the object of our faith, and as Christians we must affirm that it is in the presence of this Jesus that we have been most decisively drawn into fellowship with God.[23] Nor can we qualify our obligation to witness to others the joy of the

22. Ruether, *Faith and Fratricide*, 257.
23. In his unfortunately ignored book, *Jesus and the Nonviolent Revolution* (Scottdale, PA:

fellowship and our wish for them to share it. However, the obligation to witness does not mean that we are in possession of a universal truth that can compel assent or serve as the basis for an ethic of wider society.

Christianity may be a "universalistic" religion in a way that Judaism is not, though I doubt it.[24] However, what is certainly the case is that the nature of our universalism has been deeply misunderstood and subject to ideological perversion. Again, as Ruether points out:

> Catholic Christianity regarded itself as the universal messianic fulfillment of the election of the Jews. Some of the verisimilitude for this perspective on the Church, as the fulfilled messianic in-gathering of the nations of Zion, rested on its later fusion with the ecumenical empire. After Christianity became the

---

Herald Press, 1973), André Trocmé contends, "If the New Testament should be demythologized, it should not be done with the help of our modern myths but with the assistance of the Old Testament. The more the strict monotheistic faith in the God of Israel is exalted, the more visible becomes the thought of Jesus Christ. Let us never forget that the God of Jesus Christ was the God of Israel. The Christian faith dissolves into mythology as soon as it no longer leans upon Judaism. Nothing can be lost by rejudaizing Christianity. Judaism is the point of departure for all research destined to rediscover the Jesus of history. We need not hesitate to examine those ideas which the authors of the New Testament borrowed from sources other than the Old Testament in order to explain Jesus to their Jewish and Greek contemporaries. But let us not sacrifice the Old Testament" (2).

24. Fackenheim maintains, for example:

> Jewish Messianism always requires the particularity of Jewish existence. Its God is universal; but, because His presence is in history and does not (or not yet) transfigure history, it can only be a particularized presence, and for this if for no other reason, it is a fragmentary presence. The saving divine Presence at the Red Sea had revealed its fragmentariness, if only because the Egyptians were drowning; the divine commanding Presence at Mount Sinai had been fragmentary, if only because it could be rejected as well as accepted; the law has not yet put in the inward parts (Jer. 31:33). For the Jew to experience or reenact such a fragmentary divine presence is, on the one hand, to be singled out by it and, on the other, to be made to hope for wholeness; that is, to be made witness to the Messianic future and to remain stubbornly at this post until all has been accomplished. This Jewish particularity, however, has been a scandal, first, to ancient pagans (who denied that history stood in need of redemption) and, subsequently, to Christians (to the degree to which they hold that the redemption affirmed by the Jewish testimony has already arrived). (*God's Presence in History*, 52–53)

Like the Jew's, however, Christian universalistic claims must always be eschatological.

Interestingly, Jews and Christians are communities of memory exactly because their existence is necessarily historical. If they were founded as a "truth" that could be known without remembering, then they would be no more than philosophical alternatives. That they are fundamentally communities of memory—that is, they depend on scripture, ritual, and holy people—denotes that the character of their understanding of the truth is particular and historical.

established religion of this empire, Christian theologians came to imagine that the religion of the biblical God had literally captured all peoples and all lands. Christianity took the universalism of the messianic hope and fused it with the ideological universalism of the ecumenical empire. The result was a doctrine of the Church as the one Catholic faith for all people which could no longer tolerate the concessions to particularism possible for a polytheistic empire. One God, one faith, and one Church, founded on this revelation, the cultural and political vehicle for which became the Roman Empire.[25]

What often goes unnoticed about such "universalism" is that it not only results in cultural and social imperialism, but it also distorts the nature of faith itself. For too often in order to sustain the presumed universality of our convictions, the convictions are transformed into general truths about "being human" for which "Christ" becomes a handy symbol. Our universalism is not based on assumed commonalities about mankind; rather, it is based on the belief that the God who has made us his own through Jesus Christ is the God of all people. Christian universality is too often based on a high view of the human, rather than a high view of Jesus.[26]

25. Ruether, *Faith and Fratricide*, 233–34.

26. Philip Hallie provides an interesting example of this in *Lest Innocent Blood Be Shed: The Story of the Village of Le Chambon and How Goodness Happened There* (New York: Harper and Row, 1979). In this highly praised book, Hallie tells the story of André Trocmé, the pastor of the village of Le Chambon in France, who led his people to provide shelter for Jewish children during the war. Hallie tells well how they did this and indicates that the Huguenot background of the village no doubt helped prepare the people to assume a position of resistance. But what Hallie is completely unable to do is explain Trocmé's own commitments that led him to take such a courageous stand. Hallie suggests several times that Trocmé's commitment was based in his belief about Jesus (34, 161), but he is never able to tell us what in fact those beliefs were. Instead, he constantly reiterates throughout the book that Trocmé's action was based on his belief in the preciousness of all human life (42, 48, 53, 54, 274). That Trocmé believed in the preciousness of all human life is certainly true and that such a conviction was related to his belief in Jesus was also true. For example, see his *Jesus and the Nonviolent Revolution*, 145–46. But what is not true is that Trocmé's belief in nonviolence was grounded in a general humanistic concern about each individual's life. Rather, his nonviolence was based on his deep belief that Jesus had inaugurated a social revolution based on the jubilee year that necessarily entailed the church to be a counterculture to all social orders with their humanistic pretensions. As Trocmé says, "Christian nonviolence is not a part of the fabric of the universe, as in Hindi nonviolence. Rather, it has a temporary character. It is tied to the delay God grants men because of the voluntary sacrifice of the messianic King. By deriving nonviolence not from a philosophy of the universe (which may be utopian) but from His sacrifice on the cross, Jesus gives it historical precision and a much greater impact. Through redemption, nonviolence thrusts itself upon all Jesus' disciples. It becomes an article of faith, a mark of obedience, a sign of the kingdom to come as it was for Jesus Himself" (*Jesus and the*

When the universality of humanity is substituted for our faith in the God of Abraham, Isaac, and Jacob, the eschatological dimension of our faith is lost.[27] Christian social ethics then becomes the attempt to do ethics for all people rather than being first of all an ethic for God's eschatological people who must learn to wait between the times. Our conviction that the God whom we worship is in fact the God of all creation does not give us the warrant to assume that others *must* already share our faith and/or moral presumption, but only to hope that if we manifest in our own social life some of the marks of

Nonviolent Revolution, 66). That Hallie was able to explain this kind of conviction only in the pieties of general humanistic rhetoric is understandable, but such an account misses entirely the force of Trocmé's position. I should note in passing that the kind of social ethic I am attempting to develop is closer to Trocmé's views than that of mainstream Christianity.

27. For a defense of the necessity of Christianity to "spiritualize" eschatology, see John Pawlikowski's "The Historicizing of the Eschatological: The Spiritualizing of the Eschatological: Some Reflections," in *Antisemitism and the Foundations of Christianity,* ed. Alan Davies (New York: Paulist Press, 1979), 151–66. Pawlikowski writes in criticism of Ruether's "historicizing of the eschatological" and defends the view that Jesus' primary importance is that in him people came to see clearly for the first time that humanity is an integral part of God. This means that each person is divine, that he or she somehow shares in the constitutive nature of God. As we learn from the later strata of the New Testament materials, this humanity has existed in the Godhead from the beginning. So in a very real sense God did not explain why, if this is the case, it is only in Jesus that it was first seen. In this respect I think Ruether is exactly right to suggest that Pawlikowski is not "spiritualizing eschatology," but "spiritualizing the messianic." Moreover, she is correct to argue that such a spiritualization is basically a denial of the messianic as it robs the category of messianism of the Jewish hope in a historical fulfillment. She does not deny that one may well "solve" the problem of Christ that way, "but do not call it christology; just call it by its right name, Platonic soteriology" (Rosemary Ruether, "The *Faith and Fratricide* Discussion: Old Problems and New Dimensions," in *Antisemitism and the Foundation of Christianity,* 224–45).

In substantiation of Ruether's point, Pawlikowski goes on to suggest that in one sense the final version of the Church's Christology is the culmination of the Jewish tradition not in terms of "the fulfillment of the messianic prophecies, but the fulfillment of the growing sense of the dignity and uniqueness of the human person" (162). Judaism retains a "unique and distinctive role" in the sense that it has maintained a sense of peoplehood and the belief that no individual person can achieve salvation without the whole human family having attained salvation. But that surely is a "truth" separable from the "existence" of the Jews and hardly makes intelligible the persistence and suffering the Jews have experienced over the centuries. Moreover, Pawlikowski thinks Christians' contact with Judaism is necessary if the Church is to correct its long-standing tendency to overcome a false "privatization of religion," but that is exactly the social implication written into his Christology. Even more troubling is his suggestion that his Christology recaptures the sense of the "human person as Co-creator, as responsible for history and for the world God has created" (163). It is hard for me to understand how anyone can use such language in light of the Holocaust. If any event has taught us that we are not cocreators, it is that. What we require is not a god that underwrites our pretensions, but one who is capable of calling us from our false notions of power and control.

what it means to be a new people, others will be converted to the reality of his kingdom. Otherwise, what does it mean for the church to be an eschatological community whose primary task is not to make the world the kingdom, but rather to witness to the power of God to transform our lives more nearly appropriate to service in that kingdom?[28] To be sure, as Christians we do believe that the unity of all peoples has been established in principle, but this unity is not an accomplished fact nor can it be presumed to be the basis of a universal ethic. Rather, it can only be manifested in the kind of community made possible by a people who have learned to remember and thus tell rightly the story of God's choosing and caring for his people—both Jews and Christians.

The mainstream of Christian social ethics continues to be written as if Christians share the primary values of their culture and/or that Christians should seek to be the primary political and social actors in that culture. Rosemary Ruether has suggested that the end of Christendom means Christianity now must think of itself as a Diaspora religion.[29] I am trying to suggest that Christianity, whether it is forced to or not by the end of Christendom, *must always be* a Diaspora religion. But we have hardly begun to think through the social implications of that claim.

---

28. The criticisms above of Pawlikowski may appear too harsh, especially in light of his work on the relation of Jews and Christians. His intention has been to "liberalize" Roman Catholic attitudes by emphasizing those "universalizing" tendencies in Catholicism. Thus, for example, he points out that Pius XII was primarily concerned to keep the Church alive, no matter what the cost in non-Catholic lives, because he thought the Church was the institution through which "the principal components for human salvation—the Eucharist and the other sacraments—were made available to the Human community" ("Method in Catholic Social Ethics: Some Observations in Light of the Jewish Tradition," in *Formation of Social Policy in the Catholic and Jewish Tradition,* ed. Eugene Fisher and Daniel Polish [Notre Dame, IN: University of Notre Dame Press, 1980], 172–73). Pawlikowski points out that this ecclesiology was not intentionally indifferent or hostile to the rights and very existence of non-Catholics: "Rather it so envisioned the Church and its purpose for existence that in moments of crises, when hard decisions were required concerning the institution's survival, non-Catholics occupied no central role in the definition" (173). I have no doubt that Pawlikowski sees his emphasis on a more universalistic Christology as a corrective for this, but as a result he fails to challenge the most decisive failure of Catholic ecclesiology: the idea that the primary task of the Church is to survive. The task of the Church is not to survive, but to be faithful to its eschatological mission. The "success" of that mission is not measured by whether the Church survives or not, but whether her survival or nonsurvival serves the ends of that kingdom. Any time Christians presume that the "success" of God's kingdom depends on the "success" of the Church they have already betrayed their belief in God's lordship of history.

29. Ruether, *Faith and Fratricide,* 226–27.

As long as that strategy is simply assumed I think there is little chance that Christians can make the Holocaust part of their own existence, integral to their own identity. Under the spell of liberal assumptions, we lack the means to recognize the significance that indeed the sword of Constantine has passed to many other hands. As such, we continue to be captured by the illusion that Christians, unlike the Jews, are not simply a people who must find the means to survive among the nations. We will thus continue to lack the means to help the world see how deeply divided it is and why in fact it needs redemption.

From the world's perspective, being a community capable of remembering the Holocaust cannot appear politically significant. But from the perspective of the Gospel, there can be no more potent political task.

Further Reading
"Peacemaking: The Virtue of the Church" (1985), essay 16 in this volume
"A Christian Critique of Christian America" (1986), essay 22 in this volume
"The Democratic Policing of Christianity" (1993), in DF
"The Holocaust and the Duty to Forgive," *Sh'ma* 10, no. 198 (October 3, 1980): 137–39
"Forgiveness and Forgetting," *Sh'ma* 11, no. 202 (November 28, 1980): 15–16
"Why Time Cannot and Should Not Heal the Wounds of History, But Time Is and Can Be Redeemed" (1999), in BH.
"Jews and the Eucharist," *Perspectives* 9, no. 3 (March 1994): 14–15
"Christian Ethics in Jewish Terms: A Response to David Novak," *Modern Theology* 16, no. 3 (July 2000): 293–99

18. Practicing Patience:
How Christians Should Be Sick (1997)
with Charles Pinches

Hauerwas begins this essay by calling attention to the moral significance of the retention of the term "patients" in the contemporary practice of medicine and why "the continued practice of patience by patients is key to the good practice of medicine." In the first half of the essay, Hauerwas draws on the theological reflections of Cyprian, Tertullian, Augustine, and Saint Thomas Aquinas to reintroduce the Christian virtue of patience into contemporary medical ethics. In the second half, he extends this discussion of patience with respect to what it means for Christians to practice patience when they are sick. He specifically argues that Christian patience is rooted in the theological virtues of faith, hope, and love, which are made possible through our friendship with God. He concludes that the practice of patience by Christian patients, then, can serve as "a witness to the non-Christian neighbor of the truth of the story of God's patient care of God's creatures." This witness by Christians also has significant implications for the practice of medicine by those Christians who, serving as physicians and nurses, care patiently for their patients.

1. The Terms of Our Professions

In our current setting there is something of a rush to call any and every line of work a profession. A number of interesting consequences have followed from this, including that the term "professional" has broken free of older ties in our language to the originating idea of a calling for a special service to the common good. This is not to say, however, that the term "professional" has lost its moral power. If anything it has gained more, albeit a different kind. For there is now no more stinging charge against an aspiring inductee into any

[From CAV © 1997 by University of Notre Dame Press. Used by permission. This essay was coauthored with Charles Pinches.]

one of a legion of careers we call professions than that he or she has acted "unprofessionally."

What counts as unprofessional varies, of course, but in all cases it has some connection with how the professional has treated his "client." Indeed, it is this term that has seized the day, becoming a virtual pair with the ubiquitous "professional." Their intertwining is not, however, entirely complete, a fact that gives us our subject for this essay. For in the practice of medicine, even though some physicians may treat their patients as clients, or, worse, customers, they yet call them "patients." Indeed, as we shall attempt to show, the retention of "patients" in medicine and the continued practice of patience by patients is key to the good practice of medicine.

When we fix on the connection between patience and patients we cannot but feel some discomfort. It is an empirical fact that often patients are extremely impatient. As a society, nothing upsets us more than having to wait for our bodies. Indeed, our bodies are like our cars: they are to serve as we direct without calling attention to themselves (although we may use them to call attention to us). If they do call for our attention, we are quick to anger, with both our bodies and cars, and with those whose job it is to repair them.

This impatience is of interest to us. At the least, and as we shall briefly try to show, it dooms the practice of medicine. More important, however, is the shape of the patience it lacks. Christians are called to be a patient people, in health and in sickness. Indeed, impatience is a crucial sin that carries us into other sins. The shape of Christian patience, then, will be our chief concern in this chapter, although we mean to describe it concretely as it relates to the practice of medicine. If Christians are faithful, they will be, we think, the most patient of patients. As such they will embody the skills necessary for the sustenance of the practice of medicine.

2. The God That Failed: The Pathos of Medicine in Modernity

The title *The God That Failed* originally was used for a book of essays by former communists describing how they became communists and why and how they lost their faith in communism.[1] Arthur Koestler, one of the essayists, notes that communism, like all true faiths, "involves a revolt against the believer's social environment, and the projection into the futures of an ideal

1. *The God That Failed,* ed. with an introduction by Richard Crossman (New York: Harper and Row, 1963). The book was first published in 1949. It contains essays by Arthur Koestler, Ignazio Silone, Richard Wright, Andre Gide, Louis Fisher, and Stephen Spender.

derived from the remote past. All utopias are fed from the sources of mythology; the social engineer's blueprints are merely revised editions of the ancient text."[2] For many today, medicine is to be viewed analogously. As they suggest, modern medicine is fueled by the utopian presumption that illness can be cured or tamed by skill and science. As such, medicine represents another utopia, another god that has failed.

According to its critics, as a failed god medicine is not the mode of liberation it professes to be but rather a legitimating ideology that allows some people to control others in the name of liberation. Moreover, like most effective forms of control, the power that medicine exercises is covert, since it stems from and is secured by its invisibility. As such, medicine is but another of the supervisory strategies so prevalent in modern political regimes.[3] Insofar as we desire what medicine teaches us to desire, we willingly shape our lives to become pliant medical subjects. The very understanding of our bodies, our "biology," produces and reproduces us to be good servants of the medical regime.[4]

As for the rise of medical ethics in the past twenty-five years, say the critics, it is but icing on the ideological cake.[5] Just as princes once surrounded themselves with priests whose function it was to legitimate their power to rule, so physicians now employ "ethicists" for structurally similar purposes. A strange creature that only modernity could produce, the "ethicist" may imagine himself to be the patient's advocate against the power of the physician when he champions—as he is doing with increasing frequency—the "autonomy" of the patient. Ironically, however, the stress on autonomy turns out to produce just the kind of ahistorical account of moral agency that so effectively disguises medicine's power over us. Indeed, it is the job of the "ethicist" to devise rules

---

2. Ibid., 16.

3. See Michel Foucault, *The Birth of the Clinic* (New York: Vintage Books, 1973).

4. For a wonderful set of essays that question the understanding of the body prevalent in modern medicine, see Paul Komersaroff, ed., *Troubled Bodies: Critical Perspective on Postmodernism, Medical Ethics, and the Body* (Durham, NC: Duke University Press, 1995). In his introduction Komersaroff observes, "The infiltration of the categories of medicine into the way we think about pregnancy and childbirth, the menopause, sexual relationships and caring for a sick relative, for example—or, for that matter, merely eating, exercising or just lying in the sun—may profoundly transform the quality of these experiences. In these cases, medical modes of thought introduce into previously unproblematic life experiences evaluative criteria that are formulated in purposive-rational terms. That is, they are presented as purely technical values" (3).

5. [On the rise of medical ethics and the role of theology, see Hauerwas's "How Christian Ethics Became Medical Ethics: The Case of Paul Ramsey" (1995) in ww.]

and guidelines that, while ostensively helping us to resolve hard decisions about life and death, in the end convince us that our lives are nothing without such "decisions."[6]

One device we have found effective in teaching students something of the power the church once held over people's lives is to ask them to reflect on how it feels to experience the amazingly technical, administrative, and bureaucratic complexity of a major medical center. Those of us unfortunate enough to have found ourselves patients in such centers recognize deep feelings of powerlessness in the fact of such a faceless giant, feelings that more often than not are followed by an overwhelming sense that we must please those "caring" for us or else they will hurt us. Indeed, the hierarchical politics of such medical centers are enough to make the description "Byzantine" inadequate. Medicine, in fact, has become more powerful and pervasive in our lives than the church ever was and surely far more powerful than it is today. This may explain why the current attack against medicine appears ready to exceed the furor of the revolt against the church. It is perhaps the only sort of revolt that makes sense in modernity now that the church is far too weak as an institution to make revolt against it worthwhile.

Despite our deep sympathies with the shape of this revolt against medicine, however, we cannot entirely credit its story. Those currently in revolt against medicine in our society overestimate the intensity of public antipathy toward medicine and its servant, medical ethics. In fact, the revolt has had to this point very little effect, since the questions it has raised can easily be dismissed as extreme moralistic nonsense.

That the revolt is so effortlessly deflated, absorbed, or repudiated may be, as the rebels allege, another sign of medicine's iron grip on our minds. We think, however, that it is a sign of the insufficiency of the moral resources the

---

6. For an extraordinary account of how "ethics" has served to legitimate the presumptions of modern medicine, see Gerald McKenny, *To Relieve the Human Condition: Bioethic and the Technological Utopianism of Modern Medicine* (Albany: State University of New York Press, 1996). McKenny observes, "A moral discourse which related the health of the body as well as its mortality and its susceptibility to illness and suffering to broader conceptions of a morally worthy life was succeeded by a moral discourse characterized by efforts to eliminate suffering and expand human choice and thereby overcome the human subjections to natural necessity or fate. The result is that standard bioethics moves within the orbit of the technological utopianism of what I call the Baconian project, and its agenda and content are designed to resolve certain issues and problems that arise within that project." McKenny identifies the "Baconian project" with the attempt to eliminate suffering and to expand the realm of human choice through technology.

rebels have brought to bear on medicine as an institution. Modern medicine is not quite a god that failed. It is, rather, a failed substitute for God when God was failed by us. For *modern* medicine was formed by a modern culture that forced upon medicine the impossible role of bandaging the wounds of societies that are built upon the premise that God does not matter.[7] Such social orders, which we rightly call liberal, take as their central problem how to secure cooperation among self-interested individuals who have nothing in common other than their desire to survive. Cooperation is secured by bar-

7. Colin Gunton is to be commended for his attempt to read modernity in this fashion. See his *The One, the Three, and the Many: God, Creation, and the Culture of Modernity* (Cambridge, England: Cambridge University Press, 1993). We are sympathetic to Gunton's account, though we may have a different reading of who have been and currently are friends and enemies. John Milbank's *Theology and Social Theory,* which we have drawn on extensively in "The Renewal of Virtue and the Peace of Christ" (1997) in cav, provides an important contrast to Gunton. Gunton suggests that Milbank is insufficiently trinitarian and, as a result, fails to see that "modernity" did not begin with nominalism and the Reformation but is rooted earlier (55). We lack the learning to enter into such debates, but it is clear to us that the hard problem with which both Gunton and Milbank are struggling is how to narrate the "secular" theologically. Secular modes of discourse are now so powerful that theological claims no longer seem to do any work; thus we fail to supply what MacIntyre says we must, that is, a *theological* critique of secular culture and morality.

Few have accomplished this task better than Cardinal John Henry Newman. According to Robert Pattison, Newman regarded what most people take as the character of liberalism—that is, a movement for individual rights, free markets, and material progress—as only the trappings of liberalism. For Newman, liberalism's political program was but a symptom of the heretical belief that shaped its basic principles. Liberalism was only a modern version of the Socinianism of the Reformation and that was but a version of the Arian heresy of the fourth century. According to Newman, what offended the Arians about Nicaea and Constantinople was not that the church declared the Son to be "the same in nature" as the Father, but that anything at all was declared about God. The Arians denied our knowledge of God in Christ and as a result became the first liberals!

In the face of the limits of language and our inability to express the truth fully within its parameters, truth must finally be constructed as a contest of wills. Pattison, a liberal, admires Newman because "he was the last good mind in which the dogmatic principle still excited all the ideological excitement of seventeenth-century controversy. As a result, he denominated ancient theological errors and modern social theories indifferently by the interchangeable names Arianism, Socinianism, Hoadlyism, and liberalism. Newman is the missing link between the belief of the old world and the ideology of the new. As he seemed absurd to his brother, so must he to us; his absurdity is inseparable from his message, which is that those things that the worldly mind of the modern era considers ridiculous—namely the orthodox assertion that belief has a real object, that truth is abiding, and that words can dogmatically state truth—are in fact sublime realities" (Pattison, *The Great Dissent: John Henry Newman and the Liberal Heresy* [Oxford: Oxford University Press, 1991], 143).

gains being struck that will presumably secure the best outcomes possible for each individual.[8]

"Liberalism" names those societies wherein it is presupposed that the only thing people have in common is their fear of death, despite that fact that they share no common understanding of death. So liberalism is that cluster of theories about society that are based on the presumption that we must finally each die alone. Our fear of such a death becomes the resource for cooperation as we conspire to create social practices that embody the presumption that holds so many moderns in its grip, namely, that there is nothing quite important enough in our lives to risk dying for.[9] Yet, at the same time, we all know we must die. Even more telling, we know that the way we die is the result of the very forms of cooperation (often taking the form of competition) that are created to hide our own deaths from ourselves and from one another. In such social orders, medicine becomes an insurance policy to give us a sense that none of us will have to come to terms with the reality of our death.

Nowhere is this better seen than in the abandonment of the traditional medical imperative "Do no harm" in its correlating form: "When in doubt do not act." If there is a cardinal rule now in medicine it is that in any and every state of uncertainty, physicians must nonetheless find something to do. If a physician does not act, her patient will quickly either lose hope in medicine, or, more likely, come to believe her incompetent. Moreover, the imperative to

8. Obviously the account of such bargains varies from Hobbes to Locke to Rousseau, and in our own day, to Rawls and Nozick. Such differences matter, but we are concerned with how to articulate how medicine works in social orders so conceived. The current enthusiasm for rational choice methodologies in the social sciences is a wonderful confirmation of bargaining as the central metaphor for social organization today. For a good critique of the inability of rational choice methods to deliver what they promise, at least in political science, see Donald P. Green and Ian Shapiro, *The Pathologies of Rational Choice Theory: A Critique of Applications in Political Science* (New Haven: Yale University Press, 1994).

9. This paragraph is a slight rewording of a footnote from Hauerwas's *NS*, 123. I (Hauerwas) think it the heart of the argument of that book, though few have recognized the importance I attribute to this point. That is, of course, not the fault of my readers, since I was in truth trying to disguise the main argument of that book. *Naming the Silences* is allegedly a book about the suffering and death of children, and I hope it is at least that. But I also wanted to make the case that medicine has become the theodical project of modernity, part of whose task is to save liberalism. That is why I claimed that the book was really an exercise in political theory. We are here simply trying to articulate in a straightforward fashion what I attempted to do indirectly in that book. *Naming the Silences* has recently [1993] been reprinted by Eerdmans under the title *God, Medicine, and Suffering*. Eerdmans thought my original title was hurting the sales of the book. So much for being subtle.

act has driven medical research to discover ever newer and more fantastic modes of intervention, which, while temporarily increasing confidence in a medicine of technological miracles, may in the long run undercut it more deeply. For the risk of error is all the greater and the fall to death all the more jolting since the technological miracles have schooled us in the false hope that death might be avoided altogether. To avoid error, physicians have become increasingly specialized, hoping that by knowing more and more about less and less they will be prone to fewer mistakes, a strategy that ironically results in more mistakes, since, as a matter of fact, the patient happens to be more than the sum of his parts. Unfortunately, he is increasingly cared for by a medicine that is something less than the sum of its specializations.

To position ourselves clearly, we are not distant from the rebels against modern medicine in our diagnosis of its problems. Where we differ profoundly, however, is in the ascription of blame to the institution of medicine for our present state of ill health. No one can or should be blamed. The simple fact is that we are getting precisely the kind of medicine we deserve. Modern medicine exemplifies a secular social order shaped by mechanistic economic and political arrangements, arrangements that are in turn shaped by the metaphysical presumption that our existence has no purpose other than what we arbitrarily create.

In such a world it makes perfect sense to call physicians "health professionals" and patients "clients." Nevertheless, modern medicine has stuck with the anachronisms—which we think demonstrates the true pathos of medicine. For in fact the practice of medicine was formed under a quite different set of presumptions than those now so widely held. This is why at least some physicians still presume that they are to care for a patient even though they cannot cure, or even alleviate to any significant extent, the patient's malady.[10] This kind of behavior makes little sense if physicians are there for the sole purpose of repairing our bodies when they don't serve us as we like. Medical care, moreover, is still governed by the presumption that patients are to be cared for in a manner independent of and preceding all other considerations concerning their worth to wider society.

This pathos—whereby physicians and patients yet engage in practices that are unintelligible within our predominant modern self-descriptions—is one

10. We are acutely aware that this puts the issue too simply, since part of the power of modern medicine is constituted by its ability to name the "illnesses" that then become subject to medical intervention. For a more extended (but hardly exhaustive) discussion of these issues, see Hauerwas's SP.

of the reasons that medicine has seemed such a fertile ground for theological reflection. At the least, some of the practices of medicine continue to form a space where theological claims retain a semblance of intelligibility and persuasiveness. Ironically, however, theologians, propelled by the worry of their increasing irrelevancy to the newer trends in medicine and elsewhere, have been quick to shed their theological garments and join the ranks of the philosophical ethicists.[11] In this rush next to nothing has been said about the peculiar fact that medicine still calls its patients "patients." But what could it mean to be called "patient" given the impatience that so imbues the modern practice of medicine and the social order it serves?

3. The Christian Virtue of Patience

The recent retrieval of the virtues in modern ethics has even more recently begun to affect thinking in medical ethics.[12] However, it is not clear that

11. In an article in a special issue of the *Journal of Medicine and Philosophy* on theology and medicine edited by Hauerwas and James Gustafson, Alasdair MacIntyre issues the following challenge: "What we ought to expect from contemporary theologians in the area of medical ethics: First—and without this everything else is uninteresting—we ought to expect a clear statement of what difference it makes to be a Jew or a Christian or a Moslem, rather than a secular thinker, in morality generally. Second . . . we need to hear a theological critique of secular morality and culture. Third, we want to be told what bearing what has been said under the two headings has on the specific problems which arise for modern medicine" ("Theology, Ethics, and the Ethics of Medicine and Health Care: Comments on Papers by Novak, Mouw, Roach, Cahill, and Hartt," *Journal of Medicine and Philosophy* 4 [1979]: 435). MacIntyre's challenge was issued in 1979. Subsequent developments have made it clear that that issue did little to convince anyone that theology had or has anything distinctively important to say about these matters. MacIntyre challenges theologians to accent their differences, but in this time called modernity most theologians have attempted to downplay them. Their task has been to suggest that Christians believe pretty much what anyone would believe on reflection. For example, the call for theology to be a "public" discourse seems carried by the urge to show that theological convictions do in fact measure up to standards of truthfulness generally recognized in liberal democratic societies. Only if theology meets these standards can Christians enter into the public arena without apology. (For a succinct chronicle of these developments as well as some interesting comments about the rise of recent promising dissent, see Scott Giles and Jeffrey Greenmen, "Recent Work on Religion and Bioethics: A Review Article," *Biolaw: A Legal and Ethical Reporter on Medicine, Health Care, and Bioengineering* 2, nos. 7–8 [July–August 1994]: 151–60.)

12. See, for example, *Virtue and Medicine: Explorations in the Character of Medicine*, ed. Earl E. Shelp (Dordrecht: D. Reidel, 1985). Karen Lebacqz's essay, "The Virtuous Patient" (275–88), is particularly relevant for what we are trying to do here. Lebacqz argues that three virtues—fortitude, prudence, and hope—are central to the task of being a patient. Our only difficulty with her account is knowing from whence such virtues come. William May has also developed

medicine provides the kind of soil in which the virtues can take firm root. For while medicine usually gives us birth and surrounds us as we die, it does not form or mold us in the time in between. Indeed, when we meet medicine full in the face it comes to us as we or those we love are sick or dying. If, therefore, medicine attempts to form us into virtuous people on its own turf it will inevitably fail, for it will be too little too late. Indeed, if the first time we are called on to exercise patience is as patients, we will surely be unable, for there is no worse time to learn patience than when one is sick. So, if we are to understand the vital importance of patience as a virtue, we cannot begin by considering it in the context of medicine. For us, this will mean that before we can say much about being patient patients we will need to take the time to look at how and why patience is integral to the Christian life.

As a strategy this has its liabilities. For if the virtues in general have been ignored in modern Christian ethics, the virtue of patience has especially been ignored.[13] Happily, however, patience played a prominent role in much earlier Christian accounts of the moral life. It is to these we now turn for needed help in considering the shape of Christian patience.

Saint Cyprian begins his "On the Good of Patience" by observing that philosophers also claim to pursue the virtue of patience, but "their patience is as false as is their wisdom." How can anyone be either wise or patient unless he

---

the importance of the virtues in "The Virtues in a Professional Setting," in *Medicine and Moral Reasoning,* ed. K. W. M. Tulford, Grant Gillet, and Janet Martin Soskice (Cambridge, England: Cambridge University Press, 1994), 75–90. For an overview of recent work in medical ethics on the importance of virtue, see Hauerwas's "Virtue and Character" in *Encyclopedia of Bioethics,* rev. ed. Warren Thomas Reich, editor in chief (New York: Simon and Schuster Macmillan, 1995), 5:2525–532.

13. Typically out of step with his contemporaries, over twenty years ago John Howard Yoder observed that apparent complicity with evil, which the nonresistant stance allegedly involves, has always been a stumbling block to nonpacifists. In response, Yoder points out that "this attitude, leaving evil to be evil, leaving the sinner free to separate himself from God and sin against man, is part of the nature of *agape* itself, as revealed already in creation. If the cutting phrase of Peguy, *'complice, c'est pire que coupable,'* were true, then God Himself must needs be the guilty one for making man free and again for letting his innocent Son be killed. The Modern tendency to equate involvement with guilt should have to apply *par excellence,* if it were valid at all, to the implication of the all-powerful God in the sin of His creatures. God's love for men begins right at the point where he permits sin against Himself and against man, without crushing the rebel under his own rebellion. The word for this is divine *patience,* not complicity" (*The Original Revolution* [Scottdale, PA: Herald Press, 1971], 64–65). Drawing on Yoder, Hauerwas argued in PK that hope and patience are central Christian virtues. See especially 102–6.

knows the wisdom and patience of God? In contrast, Christians "are philosophers not in words but in deeds; we exhibit our wisdom not by our dress, but by truth; we know virtues by their practice rather than through boasting of them; we do not speak great things but we live them. Therefore, as servants and worshipers of God, let us show by spiritual homage the patience that we learn from heavenly teachings. For that virtue we have in common with God. In Him patience has its beginning, and from Him as its source it takes its splendor and dignity. The origin and greatness of patience proceeds from God its Author. The quality that is dear to God ought to be loved by man."[14]

According to Cyprian, God's patience is clearly shown by the way he endures profane temples, replete with earthly images and idolatrous rites meant to insult God's majesty and honor. Yet nowhere is God's patience more clearly exemplified than in the life of Christ. Tertullian likewise observes that the patience of God made it possible for him to be conceived in a mother's womb, await a time for birth, gradually grow up, and even when grown be less than eager to receive recognition, having himself baptized by his own servant. Throughout his ministry he cared for the ungrateful and even refrained from pointing out the betrayer who was part of his own company. "Moreover, while He is being betrayed, while He is being led up 'as a sheep for a victim' (for 'so He no more opens His mouth than a lamb under the power of the shearer'), He to whom, had He willed it, legions of angels would at one word have presented themselves from the heavens, approved not the avenging sword of even one disciple."[15]

Tertullian and Cyprian alike make much of Matthew 5:43–48, where the refusal to return evil for evil is highlighted as in the very character of God, and, through imitation, the way the sons and daughters of God are made perfect. As Tertullian says, "In this principal precept the universal discipline of

14. Cyprian, *De Bono Patientia: A Translation with an Introduction and Commentary,* by Sister M. George Edward Conway, S.S.J. (Washington, DC: Catholic University Press of America, 1957), 65. Cyprian's account of patience closely parallels Tertullian's earlier treatise "On Patience." The latter can be found in volume 3 of *The Ante-Nicene Fathers* (Grand Rapids, MI: Eerdmans, 1989), 707–17. Augustine drew on both Tertullian and Cyprian for his "On Patience," which can be found in *A Library of Fathers of the Holy Catholic Church, Anterior to the Division of the East and West,* trans. Members of the English Church (Oxford: John Henry Parker Press, 1937), 542–62. Sister Conway provides a very helpful comparison of these three treatments of patience. Augustine is careful to explain that just as God is jealous without any darkening of spirit, so He is patient without "thought of passion" (544).
15. Tertullian, 708.

patience is succinctly comprised, since evil-doing is not conceded even when it is deserved."[16] Such patience is not only in the mind, according to Tertullian, but in the body, for "just as Christ exhibited it in his body, so do we. By the affliction of the flesh, a victim is able to appease the Lord by means of the sacrifice of humiliation. By making a libation to the Lord of sordid raiment, together with scantiness of food, content with simple diet and the pure drink of water in conjoining fasts to all this; this *bodily* patience adds a grace to our prayers for good, a strength of our prayers against evil; this opens the ears of Christ our God, dissipates severity, elicits clemency."[17] Thus, that which springs from a virtue of the minds is perfected in the flesh, and finally, by the patience of the flesh, does battle under persecution.[18]

For the fathers of the church, bodily patience puts suicide out of the question. Job is the great exemplar in this regard as he resists his wife's suggestion that he should curse God and die. Augustine calls upon those who would kill themselves under persecution to look to "this man," meaning both Job and Christ. Like true martyrs who neither seek death nor invite it prematurely, we ought to bear all patiently rather than "to dare death impatiently." According to Augustine, all that can be said to those who have killed themselves under persecution is "Woe unto them which have lost patience!"[19]

Following Tertullian and Cyprian, Augustine maintains that only patience shaped by Christ is true patience. As he says, "Properly speaking those are patient who would rather bear evils without inflicting them, than inflict them without bearing them. As for those who bear evils that they may inflict evil, their patience is neither marvelous nor praiseworthy, for it is not patience at all; we may marvel at their hardness of heart, but we must refuse to call them patient."[20] Such patience cannot come from "the strength of the human will,"[21] but rather must come from the Holy Spirit. Behind it, of course, is the

16. Ibid., 711. Cyprian's reflections on Matthew are found on 68–69.
17. Ibid., 715.
18. Cyprian observes that the Christian should not hasten to revenge the pain of persecution, since vengeance is the Lord's. "Therefore, even the martyrs as they cry out and as they hasten to their punishment in the intensity of their suffering are still ordered to wait and to show patience until the appointed time is fulfilled and the number of martyrs is complete" (89).
19. Augustine, 550–51.
20. Ibid., 544. Aquinas uses this quote to counter the claim that patience is not a virtue, since it can sometimes be found in wicked men. See *Summa Theologica* (New York: Benziger Bros., 1947), II–II, 136, 1.
21. Augustine, 551.

greatest of all the Spirit's gifts, namely, charity. "Without [love] in us there cannot be true patience, because in good men it is the love of God which endureth all things, in bad men the lust of the world. But this love is in us by the Holy Spirit which was given us. Whence, of Whom cometh in us love, of Him cometh patience. But the lust of the world, when it patiently bears the burdens of any manner of calamity, boasts of the strength of its own will, like as of the stupor of disease, not robustness of health. This boasting is insane: it is not the language of patience, but of dotage. A will like this in that degree seems more patient of bitter ills, in which it is more greedy of temporal good things, because more empty of eternal."[22]

Following the fathers before him, Aquinas maintained that true patience comes from God. Like them, he was aware that many people display the semblance of patience without the gift of the Spirit. Yet patience taken as a "natural virtue" cannot be shaped by the appropriate sadness and joy constitutive of Christian patience. For Aquinas a true understanding of our place as creatures must include an insuperable sadness and dejection about our condition. Christ's suffering on the cross exemplifies the sorrow that must be present in every Christian's life.[23] Christians must "be saddened by their own

22. Ibid., 557–58. Augustine, like all the Christian fathers, makes constant appeals to Scripture in support of this argument—I Corinthians 13:4 being, of course, the central text. Charity must form patience, but it is equally the case that charity needs patience. In a remarkable passage Cyprian says:

> Charity is the bond of brotherhood, the foundation of peace, the steadfastness and firmness of unity; it is greater than both hope and faith; it excels both good works and suffering for faith; and, as an eternal virtue, it will abide with us forever in the kingdom of heaven. Take patience away from it, and thus forsaken, it will not last; take away the substance of enduring and tolerating, and it attempts to last with no roots or strength. Accordingly, the apostle when he was speaking about charity joined forbearance and patience to it, saying: Charity is magnanimous, charity is kind, charity does not envy, is not puffed up, is not provoked, thinks no evil, loves all things, believes all things, hopes all things, endures all things. By this he showed that charity can persevere steadfastly because it has learned how to endure all things. And in another place he says: bearing with one another in love, taking every care to preserve the unity of the Spirit in the union of peace. He proved that neither unity nor peace can be preserved unless brothers cherish one another with mutual forbearance and preserve the bond of unity with patience as intermediary. (81)

23. We are indebted once again to Lee Yearley's wonderful *Mencius and Aquinas: Theories of Virtue and Conceptions of Courage* (New York: State University of New York Press, 1990), particularly 136–43. Crucial for understanding Aquinas's views is the significance of his account of the passions and, in particular, sadness as a passion. See *Summa Theologica* I–II, 35–39. Yearley rightly observes that Aquinas thinks his understanding of the place of sadness in the Christian life is the crucial difference between Stoicism and Christianity. The Christian

frailty, by the suffering present in the world, and by their inability to change either fundamentally."[24]

From Aquinas's perspective, the problem is how to prevent the sadness, which we appropriately feel, from becoming depression, despair, or apathy. And this falls to patience. "Patience is to ensure that we do not abandon virtue's good through dejection of this kind."[25] It makes us capable of being rightly saddened without succumbing to the temptation to give up hope. A patience-formed sadness can be held together with joy, because each is the

---

cannot seek to be free of sadness, for without the appropriate sadness we lack the ability to be joyful.

The Stoics' understanding of the passions was much more complex than they are usually given credit for. See, for example, Martha Nussbaum's treatment of Stoicism in *The Therapy of Desire: Theory and Practice in Hellenistic Ethics* (Princeton, NJ: Princeton University Press, 1994), 359–438. Nussbaum, quoting Seneca, observes, " 'Where you take greatest joy you will also have the greatest fear.' Just as there is unity among the virtues, all being forms of correct apprehension of the self-sufficient good, just so there is a unity to the passions—and also to their underlying dispositional states. But this means, too, that there is a unity to the cure of the passions. 'You will cease to fear, if you cease to hope . . . Both belong to a soul that is hanging in suspense, to a soul that is made anxious by concern with the future.' The world's vulnerable gifts, cherished, give rise to the passionate life; despised, to a life of calm. 'What fortune does not give, she does take away' " (388–89). Against such a background the importance of Aquinas's insistence that Christians are the most passionate of people can be understood not only as a claim about what we must be as Christians, but also as a claim about the way the world is. If God, at least the God that Christians worship, does not exist, then our joy and our sadness, schooled by our hope, is a lie.

24. Yearley 137. This point should be qualified with the insistence that Thomas's account of patience does not entail passivity. Patience is a necessary component of fortitude, which, as Josef Pieper observes, seems incongruous for many people because for them patience

> has come to mean an indiscriminate, self-immolating, crabbed, joyless, and spineless submission to whatever evil is met with or, worse, deliberately sought out. Patience, however, is something quite other than indiscriminate acceptance of any and every evil: "The patient man is not the one who does not flee from evil, but the one who does not allow himself to be made inordinately sorrowful thereby." To be patient means to preserve cheerfulness and serenity of mind in spite of injuries that result from the realization of the good. Patience does not imply the exclusion of energetic, forceful activity, but simply, explicitly and solely the exclusion of sadness and confusion of heart. Patience keeps man from the anger that his spirit may be broken by grief and lose its greatness. Patience, therefore, is not the tear-veiled mirror of a "broken" life (as one might easily assume in the face of what is frequently presented and praised under this name), but the radiant embodiment of ultimate integrity. In the words of Hildegard of Bingen, patience is "the pillar which nothing can soften." And Thomas, following Holy Scripture (Luke 21:19), summarizes with superb precision: "Through patience man possesses his soul." (*The Four Cardinal Virtues* [South Bend, IN: University of Notre Dame Press, 1966], 129)

25. Aquinas, *Summa Theologica* II–II, 136, 4, 2. Yearley highlights this wonderful passage.

effect of charity. Holding such a joy we rightly "grieve over what opposes this participation in the divine good in ourselves, or in our neighbors, whom we love as ourselves."[26]

Lee Yearley suggests that Aquinas's account of patience combines two different, even apparently paradoxical attitudes. Christians must judge their earthly life according to the standard evident in God's goodness, yet they must also adhere to the future good of possible union with God and the present good evident in God's manifestations in the world and in people's lives. Neither side of such an attitude can be lost. We must persist in sadness, yet it must not be allowed to overwhelm the pursuit of the good, the accurate recognition of its forms, and a correct belief about the world's ultimate character. "This attitude is distinctive enough that it can arise, Aquinas thinks, only from the theological virtues. Charity's friendship with God is most crucial, but the attitude manifest in patience also rests on faith and displays the mean between presumption and despair that appears in hope."[27]

Like all the virtues that come from charity, Christian patience is a gift. As we noted earlier with courage [see "Courage Exemplified," essay 14 in this volume], there are always semblances of the virtues produced apart from charity; patience in particular is frequently confused with its semblances. For

---

26. Ibid., II–II, 28, 2. (This is Yearley's translation of this passage.) Crucial for sustaining such joy in the midst of sadness is the kind of materialism required in the Christian belief in the Incarnation and Resurrection. Our belief in the bodily Resurrection—that is, that the resurrection is not so much a throwing off of our human flesh but rather an exchanging of our present body for a new body so that we may dwell in a new heaven and a new earth—means that Christians' hope that "all manner of things shall be well" can never be a facile optimism that evades the reality of pain. As James Fodor observed to one of us (Hauerwas):

> Simply to encourage people to see things differently, while leaving things as they are, is to reinforce their slavery, the reinforcement of which is all the more insidious precisely because it is disguised as a proclamation of the truth to set us free. Christianity, in other words, is not merely a way of "regarding," "looking at," or "interpreting" reality. Christianity is not a "theory" but a way of life, a way of discipleship. And discipleship is concrete, specific; it occurs—or fails to occur—in particular practices and patterns of engagements, relations, suffering, and worship. Thus the importance of the practice of "bodily patience" for guarding against the tendency, all too common among many modern Christians, to affirm "the primacy of the spiritual" to the neglect of the material conditions of redemption. The practical, material display of Christian virtue necessary for patience is in finding a gift from God and not something we cultivate willfully or from our own strength, apart from God's help. In fact, patience is often something we reluctantly accept, if at all, and then only after a long and painful struggle to acknowledge our creaturely limits and the sense in which most things in our life remain out of our control.

27. Yearley, 139.

example, there is a kind of tempered optimism in which people "either rest too confidently on their past experiences of overcoming dejection or manifest a phlegmatic or unreflective disposition at inappropriate times. Their optimism, then, reflects a flawed hope that is close to dullness or presumption. It displays an intemperate attitude that expresses itself in the naive belief that all will turn out for the best."[28] Christians have no such wan hope, sustained as we are by a patience that looks to our misfortunes, even the misfortune of our illness and death, as part of our service to one another as God's people.

4. Christian Patience and Patients

The matter of whether true patience can be had without God is particularly relevant to our own time and especially to the medicine practiced within it. We suspect that those committed to living in the world without God will find no time for the patience described by the likes of Cyprian, Tertullian, Augustine, and Aquinas. Indeed, we moderns fill our lives with what Albert Borgmann characterizes as a kind of addiction to hyperactivity. Believing that we live in a world of infinite possibilities, we find ourselves constantly striving, restless for what, we are not sure.[29] We call our restlessness freedom, but more often than not our freedom seems more like fate, especially when we get what we have strived for only to discover that it does not satisfy—thus the peculiar combination in modern life of an attitude of metaphysical indeterminism with Stoic fatalism.

All this is what Christians might call impatience; we should not be surprised to discover it, for we live in a world governed by sin. Indeed, Tertullian

28. Ibid. Yearley notes that Aquinas did not examine the semblances of patience in the systematic manner in which he explored the semblances of courage. Yet, given patience's close relation to endurance, the crucial aspect of courage, Yearley rightly uses the semblances of courage to suggest analogies for how Aquinas might have understood the semblances of patience. Though the comparison of the semblances of patience with true patience (or the semblances of courage with true courage, or the semblances of prudence with true prudence) are usually negative, it is a mistake to assume that positive comparisons are not also a possibility. Since we are God's good creatures we should expect to find in those who are not Christians indications of God's patience. The problem, then, is not that non-Christians fail to exhibit any of the virtues, but that they do and because they do they are just as likely to display them in ways that may be destructive rather than constructive. The Christian advantage is to be part of God's people, which makes us vulnerable to the judgments of others who have acquired the wisdom necessary to understand the interrelation of the virtues.

29. Albert Borgmann, *Crossing the Postmodern Divide* (Chicago: University of Chicago Press, 1992), 97–102.

went so far as to attribute the creation of impatience to the devil, since he could not ensure the patience God exemplified in creation. According to Tertullian, the devil passed to Eve that same impatience when, through his speech, he "breathed on her a spirit infected with impatience: so certain is it that she would have never sinned at all, if she had honored the divine edict by maintaining her patience to the end."[30] She passed her impatience on to Adam, which in turn produced impatient sons. The very impatience that "had immersed Adam and Eve in death, taught their son, too, to begin with murder."[31] That murder was the fruit of impatience, as Cain impatiently refused his God-given obligation to his brother.

Surely medical care is one of God's gifts that it is our prerogative to use as a hedge against the impatience of the world. To care for one another when we cannot cure is one of the many ways we serve one another patiently. To be committed to alleviating the other's pain in a manner that makes all other considerations irrelevant makes no sense if we have not been made to be patient people. Yet, as we tried earlier to display, the powers of impatience have breathed heavily on the practice of modern medicine, leading it to promise more than it can or should deliver. Indeed, in the frustration of being unable to meet impatient expectations, we are threatened with a medicine that, in the name of relieving suffering, kills.

---

30. Tertullian, 710. Gerald J. Schiffhorst in a similar fashion argues that in *Paradise Lost* Milton "relies on patience to express the Christian's proper response to the divine will while ironically revealing the anti-heroism of Satan, whose blind impatience reverses what Milton called the 'better fortitude' of patience. Satan's struggle to fight God is undercut by the 'pleasing sorcery' of a false heroism whereas Adam learns to arm himself with patience 'to overcome by suffering' what God will unfold. The centrality of 'patience as the truest fortitude' (*Samson Agonistes*, 654) in revealing this fundamental contrast demonstrates the importance of the virtue in the poem" ("Satan's False Heroism in *Paradise Lost* as a Perversion of Patience," *Christianity and Literature* 38, no. 2 [winter 1984]: 13).

Schiffhorst provides a very helpful contrast of Christian patience with Stoic indifference by noting the difference between the Christian understanding of providence and the Stoic idea of fortune. He notes that "this basic Christian-pagan distinction helps us recall that Christ's victory over death was a victory over Fortune, and so the virtuous Christian can have everlasting life by imitating Christ's perfect patience. As Miles Coverdale says in his important Elizabethan treatise on patience, 'the impatient man complains against God and ascribes prosperity to his own wisdom, blaming blind Fortune for adversity.' Without ascribing dispassionate Stoic virtues to Satan, we can nevertheless say that his false heroism is rooted in a stubborn pride and that he exhibits all the passions of the impatient man: wrath, despair, grief, and envy" (14–15).

31. Tertullian, 710. As pacifists we find Tertullian's suggestion that our violence lies in our impatience as intriguing as it is persuasive.

We Christians are, of course, as implicated in this strange reversal as our non-Christian neighbors. But these issues are far too serious to play "Who is to blame?" The challenge is rather whether Christians have any contribution to make that would help us discover the proper limits of our care of one another through the office of medicine. It is not the unique task of Christians to suggest new and better theories about medical care, though some Christians engaged in that care undoubtedly have contributions to make. Rather, if Christians have anything to offer, it is to be patients who embody the virtue of Christian patience.[32]

To be patient when we are sick requires first that we learn how to practice patience when we are not sick. God has given us ample resources for recovering the practice of patience. First and foremost, we have been given our bodies, which will not let us do whatever we think we should be able to do.[33] We are our bodies and, as such, we are creatures destined to die. The trick is to

32. Our emphasis on patience as the virtue essential to the doctor-patient relationship may appear particularly perverse because it seems to make the patient even more powerless. There is rightly an asymmetry between the doctor and patient inasmuch as the physician has authority that the patient does not or should not have. However, once it is understood that medicine names an activity in which doctor and patient are jointly involved, patience can work in such a relationship to decrease rather than increase the abuse of power. Crucially, both Christian patience and obedience require the church for display. Without the kind of friendship, dependency, trust, and mutual nurturing imbedded in the worship of God, patience and obedience always risk the possibility of becoming malformed. That is why Hauerwas suggested in *SP* that institutionalized medicine requires a church for sustaining the kind of presence that physicians, nurses, and others in medical settings provide. The hospital is the best exemplification of the kind of care the church should make possible and sustain, although, as we suggested earlier, "the hospital," increasingly detached from the practices of the church which gave it birth, may be on its way to an entirely new sort of existence.

33. We are acutely aware, as anyone must be after the work of Foucault, that appeals to the "body" are anything but unproblematic. Recent historical work helps us better understand why Paul could say that nothing was more "spiritual" than the body. Moreover, understanding the body as peculiarly "spiritual" we think has great potential for helping us reexamine the relation of Christian practices and the practice of medicine. See, for example, Peter Brown's *The Body and Society: Men, Women and Sexual Renunciation in Early Christianity* (Boston: Faber, 1988), and Dale Martin's *The Corinthian Body* (New Haven: Yale University Press, 1995).

Particularly important is a better understanding of the "therapy of desire" characteristic of Christian practice in contrast to the assumptions of Galen and the other Hellenistic philosophical schools. For example, we need a Christian account parallel to Nussbaum's *The Therapy of Desire*. Brown's book is obviously a good beginning, but one has the feeling that we are just beginning to understand what Augustine and Aquinas grasped far better than we do about the nature of the passions. We are indebted to Thomas Harvey, a graduate student at Duke, for a paper in which he explored how Augustine provided an alternative to Galen's understanding of the body.

learn to love the great good things our bodies make possible without hating our bodies, if for no other reason than that the death of our bodies is our own death. To practice the patience of the body is to be put on the way to holiness as we learn that we are not our own creations.

Second, we have been given one another. To learn to live with the unavoidability of the other is to learn to be patient. Such patience comes not just from our inability to have the other do our will; more profoundly, it arises with the love that the presence of the other can and does create in us. Our loves, like our bodies, signal our deaths. And such love—if it is not to be fearful of its loss, a very difficult thing—must be patient. Moreover, patience sustains and strengthens love, for it opens to us the time we need to tell our own story with another's story intertwined and to tell it together with that other. So told, the story in fact constitutes our love.

Third, we have been given time and space for the acquisition of habits that come from worthy activities such as growing food, building shelters, spinning cloth, writing poems, playing baseball, and having children. Such activities not only take time but they create it by forcing us to take first one step and then another. These activities will outlive us, so long as we take the time to pass them on to future generations through shared activities and stories. So too, patience gives us the ability to engage in these activities with our children, to teach by doing, and to tell them worthy stories worthily so that we and they may be rightly entertained.[34]

These resources, these practices of patience, are not simply "there" but arise within the narrative of God's patient care of the world, which is but another way of insisting, with Aquinas, that it is impossible to have patience without charity—that is, without friendship with God. Put simply, our ability to take the time to enjoy God's world, when we are well as when we are sick, depends on our recognition that it is indeed God's world.

When we are sick, reminders of joy may seem to be the gestures of a false courage. Indeed, the Christian is charged with the responsibility of speaking truthfully about the sadness that riffles our lives. As Aquinas maintained, sadness must be recognized and lived with. But the acknowledgment of such sadness, upheld by patience, becomes integral to the Christian gift for sustaining the ill and those who care for them. Hence, those formed by the virtue of patience can be patients who do not believe that life is an end in itself. The

---

34. For a fuller development of how our practices not only take but also create time, see "Taking Time for Peace: The Ethical Significance of the Trivial," in CET.

patient patient knows—and can teach others, including physicians—that the enemy is neither the illness nor the death it intimates, but rather the fatalism these tempt us to as we meet our "bad luck"[35] with impatience.

If Christians could be such patient patients—and there is every reason to think that we can—we might well stand as witnesses to our non-Christian neighbor of the truth of the story of God's patient care of God's creatures. We might find we have something to say, not only about how illness and death can be met with grace and courage, but also about how those called to be physicians and nurses might care patiently for their patients, and perhaps even about the kind of training they will need to become capable of this high calling. To do this Christians will need to risk being different, but that should not be beyond a people who, having learned the patience of God, can find the time, even in the midst of a frenzied world, to give themselves over to such worthy work.

Further Reading

"The Nonresistant Church: The Theological Ethics of John Howard Yoder" (1974), in *vv*

"Pacifism: A Form of Politics," in *Peace Betrayed? Essays on Pacifism and Politics,* ed. Michael Cromartie (Washington, DC: Ethics and Public Policy Center, 1990), 133–42

"Tragedy and Joy: The Spirituality of Peaceableness" (1983), in *PK*

"Reflections on Suffering, Death, and Medicine" (1979), in *SP*

"The Servant Community: Christian Social Ethics" (1983), essay 19 in this volume

"The Testament of Friends: How My Mind Has Changed" (1990), *The Christian Century* 107, no. 7 (February 28, 1990): 212–16

---

35. We put quotes around this phrase to indicate its everyday usage but also to mark our unease. As we implied earlier, luck is a Stoic, not a Christian, notion that implies fortune, which is blind. Christians do not believe the world is ruled by fortune but rather by God's providential care.

PART III

New Intersections in Theological Ethics

The Church's Witness:

Christian Ethics after "Public Theology"

19. The Servant Community:
Christian Social Ethics (1983)

Two of Hauerwas's famous dictums present in this essay—"Every ethic must be a social ethic" and "The first social task of the church is to be the church—the servant community"—are paradigmatic exemplifications of his understanding of the nature of the Christian church and its relationship to the world. A third Hauerwas dictum, that a key task of the church is to "help the world understand itself as world," is not a sectarian view of the world, but a radically evangelistic one, where the church is called to witness what it means to be God's good creation in the context of practices such as baptism, Eucharist, and preaching. Hauerwas insists: "There is no ideal church, no mystically existing church more real than the concrete church of parking lots and potluck dinners." To the extent that the world pursues freedom and justice through violent means, it does not bear witness to God's kingdom. Thus, "the question of violence is the central issue for any Christian social ethic" if the church is to be "marked" as a servant community bearing witness to the peaceable Kingdom of God.

1. Social Ethics and Qualified Ethics

Christian ethics would be unintelligible if it did not presuppose the existence and recognizability of communities and corresponding institutions capable of carrying the story of God. The most general name we give that community is church, but there are other names for it in the history of Christianity. It is "the way," the body of Christ, people of God, and a plethora of images that denote the social reality of being Christian and what it means to be a distinctive people formed by the narrative of God. We should remember that the name "church" is no less an image than "people of God." In fact, one of the issues in

[From *PK* © 1983 by University of Notre Dame Press. Used by permission. It has been edited for length and clarity.]

theology is which images of the church are primary or controlling for the others.

Thus, the claim that there is no ethic without a qualifier itself implies that a Christian ethic is always a social ethic. Indeed, the notion that one can distinguish between personal and social ethics distorts the nature of Christian convictions, for Christians refuse to admit that "personal" morality is less a community concern than questions of justice, and so on. "Personal" issues may, of course, present different kinds of concern to the community from those of justice, but they are no less social for being personal.

At a general level there is much to be said for the contention that every ethic is a social ethic. The self is fundamentally social. We are not individuals who come into contact with others and then decide our various levels of social involvement. Our individuality is possible only because we are first of all social beings. I know who I am only in relation to others, and, indeed, who I am is a relation with others. The "self" names not a thing, but a relation.[1]

But the claim that Christian ethics is a social ethic is even stronger than those now commonplace observations about the self's sociality. We have seen that the content of Christian ethics involves claims about a kingdom. Therefore, the first words about the Christian life are about a life together, not about the individual. This kingdom sets the standard for the life of the church, but the life of the kingdom is broader than that of the church. For the church does not possess Christ; his presence is not confined to the church. Rather, it is in the church that we learn to recognize Christ's presence outside the church.

The church is not the kingdom but the foretaste of the kingdom. In the church the narrative of God is lived in a way that makes the kingdom visible. The church must be the clear manifestation of a people who have learned to be at peace with themselves, one another, the stranger, and of course, most of all, God. There can be no sanctification of individuals without a sanctified people. Like apprentices who learn their crafts by working alongside the master-craftsman, we Christians need exemplars or saints whose lives embody the kingdom way. If we lack such exemplars, the church cannot exist as a people who are pledged to be different from the world.

Therefore we see that contained in the claim that there is no ethic without a qualifier—a claim that at the beginning seemed to be primarily a methodological one—is a strong substantive assumption about the status and necessity of

1. The classic statement of this view remains G. H. Mead's *Mind, Self, and Society* (Chicago: University of Chicago Press, 1934).

the church as the locus for Christian ethical reflection. It is from the church that Christian ethics draws its ethical substance and it is to the church that Christian ethical reflection is first addressed. Christian ethics is not written for everyone, but for those people who have been formed by the God of Abraham, Isaac, Jacob, and Jesus, since Christian ethics presupposes a sanctified people wanting to live more faithful to God's story, and thus it cannot be a minimalistic ethic for everyone.

The story of God as told through the experience of Israel and the church cannot be abstracted from those communities engaged in the telling and the hearing. As a story it cannot exist without a community existing across time, for it requires telling and remembering. God has entrusted his presence to a historic and contingent community that must be renewed generation after generation. The story is not merely told but embodied in a people's habits that form and are formed in worship, governance, and morality.

Therefore the existence of Israel and the church is not accidentally related to the story but is necessary for our knowledge of God. You cannot tell the story of God without including within it the story of Israel and the church. Thus we affirm as part of the creed that we believe in the One Holy Catholic and Apostolic Church. We believe in the church in the sense that we know that it is not finally our creation, but exists only by God's calling of people. Moreover, it is only through such a people that the world can know that our God is one who wills nothing else than our good. To be sure, the church is often unfaithful, but God refuses to let that unfaithfulness be the last word. God creates and sustains a peaceable people in the world, generation after generation.

In a sense, the place of the Bible can be misleading in this respect, because it may appear that Scripture conveys the story independently of the existence of a historic people. You do not need an intergenerational community. All you need is the story told rightly in a book. But without a community of expounders, interpreters, and hearers, the Bible is a dead book.

Of course, Scripture stands over the community exerting a critical function, but that it does so is an aspect of the community's self-understanding. Scripture is the means the church uses to constantly test its memory. That is why it can never be content with using just one part of Scripture, but must struggle day in and day out with the full text. For the story the church must tell as well as embody is a many-sided tale that constantly calls us from complacency and conventions. Scripture has authority in the church; Scripture sets the agenda and boundaries for a truthful conversation. Those with true authority, then, are those who would serve by helping the church better hear and correspond to the stories of God as we find them in Scripture. Thus we are told, "A dispute also arose among them, which of them was to be regarded as the greatest. And he said to them, 'The kings of the Gentiles exercise lordship over them; and those in authority over them are called benefactors. But not so with you; rather let the greatest among you become as the youngest, and the leader as one who serves. For which is the greater, one who sits at table, or one who serves? Is it not the one who sits at the table? But I am among you as one who serves'" (Luke 22:24–27).

2. The Church Is a Social Ethic

But what does all this have to do with social ethics? What does this emphasis on the church tell us about what we should be doing in third-world countries? Or what we Christians ought to be doing in this country to ensure social justice? What should be our response to war? These are the kinds of questions that are most often thought to constitute social ethics, not questions about the place of Scripture in the church's life.

Furthermore, once we accept the neutrality of these questions for social ethics we feel the pull of natural law as the essential feature of Christian ethics. For to accomplish justice, to work for a more nearly free and equitable social order requires cooperation with non-Christians. If Christian social ethics depends on sources peculiar to Christians, then it seems that the prospects for achieving a more just society will be weakened. Even worse, it presents the specter of Christians seeking to form Christian states or societies (and we are well versed in the real and supposed histories of repression and coercion in such efforts). But surely in matters of social ethics there must be moral generalities anchored in our social nature that provide the basis for common moral commitment and action. Surely in social ethics we should downplay the distinctively Christian and emphasize that we are all people of good will as we seek to work for a more peaceable and just world for everyone.

Yet that is exactly what I am suggesting we should not do. I am challenging the very idea that the primary goal of Christian social ethics should be an attempt to make the world more peaceable or just. Rather, *the first social ethical task of the church is to be the church—the servant community.* Such a claim may well sound self-serving until we remember that what makes the church the church is its faithful manifestation of the peaceable kingdom in the world. *As such, the church does not have a social ethic; the church is a social ethic.*

The church is where the stories of Israel and Jesus are told, enacted, and heard. As a Christian people, there is literally nothing more important we can do. But the telling of that story requires that we be a particular kind of people if we and the world are to hear the story truthfully. That means that the church must never cease from being a community of peace and truth in a world of mendacity and fear. The church does not let the world set its agenda about what constitutes a "social ethic," but a church of peace and justice must set its own agenda. It does this first by having the patience amid the injustice and violence of this world to care for the widow, the poor, and the orphan. Such care, from the world's perspective, may seem to contribute little to the cause of justice, yet it is our conviction that unless we take the time for such care neither we nor the world can know what justice looks like.

By being that kind of community we see that the church helps the world understand what it means to be the world. The world is God's world, God's good creation, which is all the more distorted by sin because it still is bounded by God's goodness. For the church to be the church it must show what the world is meant to be as God's good creation. For the world has no way of knowing it is the world without the church pointing to the reality of God's kingdom. How could the world ever recognize the arbitrariness of the divisions between people if it did not have a contrasting model in the unity of the church? Only against the church's universality can the world have the means to recognize the arbitrariness of the national and racial divisions resulting in violence and war.

The scandal of the disunity of the church is even more painful when we recognize this social task. For all too often it appears that we who have been called to be the foretaste of the peaceable kingdom fail to maintain unity among ourselves. As a result we abandon the world to its own devices. The divisions I speak of in the church are not only those based on doctrine, history, or practices, important though they are. The deepest and most painful divisions afflicting the church in America are those based on class, race, and nationality that we have sinfully accepted as written into the nature of things.

We must remember that the "world" as that opposed to God is not an ontological designation. Thus, "world" is not inherently sinful; rather, its sinful character comes from its own free will. The only difference between church and world is the difference between agents. As Yoder suggests, the distinction between church and world is not between realms of reality, between orders of creation and redemption, between nature and supernature, but "rather between the basic personal postures of men and women, some of whom confess and others of whom do not confess that Jesus is Lord. The distinction between church and the world is not something that God has imposed upon the world by a prior metaphysical definition, nor is it only something which timid or pharisaical Christians have built up around themselves. It is all of that in creation that has taken the freedom not yet to believe."[2]

In this respect, moreover, it is particularly important to remember that the world consists of those, including ourselves, who have chosen not to make the story of God their story. The world in us refuses to affirm that this is God's world and that, as loving Lord, God's care for creation is greater than our illusion of control. The world is those aspects of our individual and social lives where we live untruthfully by continuing to rely on violence to bring order.

Church and world are thus relational concepts: neither is intelligible without the other. They are companions on a journey that makes it impossible for one to survive without the other, though each constantly seeks to do so. They are thus more often enemies than friends, an enmity tragically arising from the church's attempt to deny its calling and service to the world—dismissing the world as irredeemable or transforming its own servant status into a triumphalist subordination of the world. But God has in fact redeemed the world, even if the world refuses to acknowledge its redemption. The church can never abandon the world to the hopelessness deriving from its rejection of God, but must be a people with a hope sufficiently fervent to sustain the world as well as itself.

As Christians we will at times find that people who are not Christians

2. John Howard Yoder, *The Original Revolution* (Scottdale, PA: Herald Press, 1971), 110; see the revised version of this essay in Yoder's *The Royal Priesthood: Essays Ecclesiological and Ecumenical* (Grand Rapids, MI: Eerdmans, 1994), 171.

The reality designated "world" is obviously an extremely complex phenomenon. In the New Testament it is often used to designate that order organized and operating devoid of any reference to God's will. This is particularly true of the Johannine corpus. Yet the world is nonetheless described as the object of God's love (John 3:16) and even in 1 John, Jesus is called the "savior of the world" (4:14). Thus, even in the Johannine literature the world is not depicted as completely devoid of God's presence and/or good order. The great temptation is to assume that we have a clear idea of the empirical subject (i.e., government, society, etc.) that corresponds to the Johannine description. Yoder wisely locates the basis for the distinction between church and world in agents rather than ontological orders or institutions. To do so makes clear (1) that the distinction between church and world runs through every agent and thus there is no basis for self-righteousness on the part of those who explicitly identify with the church; and (2) that the "necessities" many claim must be accepted as part and parcel of being "world," such as violence, are such only because of our unfaithfulness. Thus the world, when it is true to its nature as God's redeemed subject, can be ordered and governed without resort to violence.

manifest God's peace better than we ourselves. It is to be hoped that such people may provide the conditions for our ability to cooperate with others for securing justice in the world. Such cooperation, however, is not based on a "natural law" legitimation of a generally shared "natural morality." Rather, it is a testimony to the fact that God's kingdom is wide indeed. As the church we have no right to determine the boundaries of God's kingdom, for it is our happy task to acknowledge God's power to make his kingdom present in the most surprising places and ways.

Thus the church serves the world by giving the world the means to see itself truthfully. *The first question we must ask is not "What should we do?" but "What is going on?"*[3] Our task as church is the demanding one of trying to understand rightly the world as world, to face realistically what the world is with its madness and irrationality.

Therefore, calling for the church to be the church is not a formula for a withdrawal ethic, nor is it a self-righteous attempt to flee from the world's problems. Rather, it is a call for the church to be a community that tries to develop the resources to stand within the world witnessing to the peaceable kingdom. The gospel is political. Christians are engaged in politics, a politics of the kingdom. Such a politics reveals the insufficiency of all politics based on coercion and falsehood, and it finds the true source of power in servanthood rather than domination.

This is not to imply that the church is any less a human community than other forms of human association. As with other institutions, the church draws on and requires patterns of authority that derive from human needs for status, belonging, and direction. The question is not whether the church is a natural institution, as it surely is, but how it shapes that "nature" in accordance with its fundamental convictions.[4] "Nature" provides the context for community but does not determine its character.

3. I am obviously drawing here on the work of H. R. Niebuhr. See in particular *The Responsible Self* (New York: Harper and Row, 1963).

4. James Gustafson's *Treasures in Earthen Vessels* (New York: Harper and Row, 1961) still provides the best analysis of the church as a "natural" institution. For the development of this insight, see Gustafson's too often overlooked *The Church as Moral Decision-Maker* (Philadelphia: Pilgrim Press, 1976).

The general position I am trying to defend is nicely summarized by Karl Barth: "The decisive contribution which the Christian community can make to the upbuilding and work and maintenance of the civil consists in the witness which it has to give to it and to all human societies in the form of the order of its own upbuilding and constitution. It cannot give in the world a direct portrayal of Jesus Christ, who is also the world's Lord and Savior, or of the peace and freedom and joy of the kingdom of God. For it is itself only a human society

While the church clearly is a polity, it is a polity *unlike* any other insofar as it is formed by a people who have no reason to fear the truth. They seek to exist in the world without resorting to coercion to maintain their presence. Their ability to sustain this presence depends to a large extent on their willing-ness to move—they must be "a moveable feast." For it is certain that much of the world is bound to hate them for truthfully naming the world. They cannot and should not wish to provoke the world's violence, but if it comes they must resist even if that resistance requires them to leave one place for another. For as Christians we are at home in no nation. Our true home is the church itself, where we find those who, like us, have been formed by a savior who was necessarily always on the move.

3. A Community of Virtues

For the church to *be* rather than to *have* a social ethic requires a certain kind of people to sustain it as an institution across time. They must be a people of virtue—specifically, the virtues necessary for remembering and telling the story of a crucified savior. They must be capable of being peaceable among themselves and with the world, so that the world sees what it means to hope for God's kingdom. In such a community, we are not free to do whatever we will but are called to develop our particular gifts to serve the community of faith.

James Gustafson has rightly argued that all human communities require virtues in order to be sustained. People in a community must learn to trust one another as well as trust the community itself.[5] Moreover, all communities

---

moving like all others to His manifestation. But in the form in which it exists among them it can and must be to the world of men around it a reminder of the law of the kingdom of God already set up on earth in Jesus Christ, and a promise of its future manifestation. *De facto,* whether they realise it or not, it can and should show them that there is already on earth an order which is based on the great alteration of the human situation and directed towards its manifestation" (Karl Barth, *Church Dogmatics,* IV/2, trans. G. W. Bromiley [Edinburgh, Scotland: T. and T. Clark, 1958], 72). A few pages later Barth suggests that "If the community were to imagine that the reach of the sanctification of humanity accomplished in Jesus Christ were restricted to itself and the ingathering of believers, that it did not have corresponding effects *extra muros ecclesiae,* it would be in flat contradiction to its own confession of its Lord" (723).

5. James Gustafson, *Christian Ethics and the Community* (Philadelphia: Pilgrim Press, 1971), 153–63. That all human relations require and engender some sense of trust indicates why the virtues require narrative construal. For without the latter the very skills necessary for us to be good can be made to serve our most destructive capacities. Sensing that, too often we try to

require a sense of hope in the future and they witness to the necessity of love for sustaining relationships. Therefore, there is a profound sense in which the traditional "theological virtues" of faith, hope, and love are "natural." As much as any institution the church is sustained by these "natural virtues." However, the kind of faith, hope, and love that must be displayed among Christians derives from the tradition that molds their community. Christians are the community of a new age that must continue to exist in the old age [2 Cor. 5:16–17]. As a people "on a way," they make certain virtues central.

Patience, for example, is a crucial virtue for Christians seeking to live amid this violent world as a peaceable people. Though we know that the kingdom has come in Jesus and is present in the breaking of bread, it is still to come. Sustained by the kingdom's having come and fueled by its presence, we hope all the more for its complete fulfillment, but this hope must be schooled by a patience, lest it turns into fanaticism or cynicism.

The church must learn time and time again that its task is not to *make* the world the kingdom, but to be faithful to the kingdom by showing to the world a community of peace. Thus we are required to be patient and never lose hope. But hope in what? Specifically, hope in the God who has promised that faithfulness to the kingdom will be of use in God's care for the world. Thus our ultimate hope is not in this world, or in humankind's goodness, or in some sense that everything always works out for the best, but in God and God's faithful caring for the world.

Especially with regard to questions of justice we see the importance of the interrelationship of hope and patience. For it is a matter of justice that those who are hungry should be fed, that those who are abandoned should be cared for, that those who have been oppressed and maltreated should be freed and respected. Yet we know that while justice demands all these things, we live in a world where injustice seems to dominate. For in this world, the hungry are fed, the abandoned cared for, the oppressed freed, it seems, only if it can be done without anyone's feeling the pinch.

When a people who have been trained to hunger and thirst for righteousness are confronted with this reality, especially if they are no longer poor, they may be sorely tempted to turn to violence. How can we continue to face the poor without allowing the possibility of coercion to see that at least minimal justice is done? For there is no question that violence "works" in some cir-

---

avoid trusting anyone or anything and as a result become subject to the most oppressive tyrant: ourselves.

cumstances to relieve the burden of the poor. Indeed, one of their primary weapons is violence, since they are a people with nothing to lose—and such people are the most threatening of all for those of us who have something to lose. Most of us would rather bargain away some of our possessions than have to deal with the threat of violence from those who have so little.

But the justice that the church seeks cannot be derived from envy or fear. Rather, we seek a justice that comes from a people who know their possessions are a gift in the first place. Therefore, Christians cannot support "justice" coming from the barrel of a gun, and we must be suspicious of that "justice" that relies on manipulation of our less than worthy motives. For God does not rule creation through coercion, but through a cross. As Christians, therefore, we seek not so much to be effective as to be faithful. We cannot seek "results" that require us to employ unjust means. Christians have rightly felt much in accord with those, such as Kant, who argue that there are some things we cannot do, no matter what good might accrue.

We must be a people who have learned to be patient in the face of injustice. But it may be objected: Surely that is too easily said if you are not the ones who are suffering from injustice. Precisely, but that does not mean that we ought to legitimize the use of force to overcome injustice. Such legitimation often comes from the attempt to have justice without risking the self, as when we ask the "state" or the "revolution" to see that justice is done, but in a manner that does not significantly affect our own material position. If we are to be a hopeful and patient people in a world of injustice, however, we cannot merely identify with the "cause" of the poor, we must become poor and powerless.

Too often, ideals and strategies for "social justice" are but formulas that attempt to make the poor and oppressed better off without requiring anything of us. Thus when we read that the poor, the merciful, the peacemakers, the meek, the persecuted, the pure in heart are blessed, we may well presume those descriptions of "blessedness" apply to anyone who would be a follower of Jesus. But the fundamental question we must address to ourselves as Christians is: How is it that we who are Christians are so rich? Furthermore, has our being rich led us to misread the gospel as essentially an apolitical account of individual salvation, rather than the good news of the creation of a new community of peace and justice formed by a hope that God's kingdom has and will prevail?

Moreover, the virtues of patience and hope are necessary to be a people who must learn to "live out of control." While not all senses of "living out of control" are relevant for determining the character of the Christian community, "living out of control" is important in that it suggests that Christians base their lives on the knowledge that God has redeemed his creation through the work of Jesus of Nazareth. We thus live out of control in the sense that we must assume God will use our faithfulness to make his kingdom a reality in the world.

To live out of control, however, does not mean that we do not plan and/or seek to find the means to promote justice in the world, but that such planning is not done under the illusion of omnipotence. We can take the risk of planning that does not make effectiveness our primary goal, but faithfulness to God's kingdom. To plan in such a manner involves breaking the cycle of self-deception that leads to the belief that justice can be achieved only through a power and violence that seeks to assure its efficacy.

Ironically, those who are most controlled are those who (mistakenly) assume that they are in control. Wealth is particularly insidious in giving its bearers the illusion of independence, separateness, and "being in control." But all of us in one way or another willingly submit to the illusion that we can rid our world of chance and surprise. Yet when we try to live securely rather than well, our world begins to shrink. For example, ironically, people in power often become controlled by their subordinates, who tell them only what they want to hear. They thus lose the capacity to deal with the unexpected except by ignoring it, suppressing it, or eliminating it. Such people do not yet understand that the trick to living well is learning to see the unexpected as our greatest resource.

To live out of control, then, is to renounce the illusion that our task as Christians is to make history come out right.[6] We do not write social ethics from the perspective of those who would claim to be in control and "in power." Rather, we believe that a more truthful account of what is really going on in the world comes from those who are "out of control." For those who are without control have fewer illusions about what makes this world secure or safe, and they inherently distrust those who say they are going to help through power and violence. The apropos perspective when writing Christian social

6. Thus, John Howard Yoder argues, "Any renunciation of violence is preferable to its acceptance; but what Jesus renounced is not first of all violence, but rather the compulsiveness of purpose that leads men to violate the dignity of others. The point is not that one can attain all of one's legitimate ends without using violent means. It is rather that our readiness to renounce our legitimate ends whenever they cannot be attained by legitimate means itself constitutes our participation in the triumphant suffering of the Lamb" (*The Politics of Jesus* [Grand Rapids, MI: Eerdmans, 1972], 243–44).

ethics, therefore, is not that of the secretary of state or the president, but the perspective of those who are subject to such people.

The task of the Christian people is not to seek to control history, but to be faithful to the mode of life of the peaceable kingdom. Such a people can never lose hope in the reality of that kingdom, but they must surely also learn to be patient. For they must often endure injustice that might appear to be quickly eliminated through violence. Moreover, they can never acquiesce in the injustice, for to do so would only leave the neighbor to his or her own devices. Those who are violent, who are also our neighbors, must be resisted, but resisted on our terms, because not to resist is to abandon them to sin and injustice.

Such resistance may appear to the world as foolish and ineffective for it may involve something so small as refusing to pay a telephone tax to support a war, but that does not mean that it is not resistance. Such resistance at least makes clear that Christian social witness can never take place in a manner that excludes the possibility of miracles, of surprises, of the unexpected. As Yoder frankly states, "Christian ethics calls for behavior which is impossible except by the miracle of the Holy Spirit."[7] But that is the way it must be for a people who believe their very existence is nothing less than a continuing miracle.

4. The "Marks" of the Church

For miracles happen here and there—indeed, we believe the very existence of the church to be a miracle. However, to speak of the church as a continuing miracle simply does not sound like any church we know or experience. The church is not just a "community" but an institution that has budgets, buildings, parking lots, potluck dinners, heated debates about who should be the next pastor, and so on. What do these matters pertaining to the institutional form of the church have to do with the church as the miracle of God's continuing presence in our midst?

The people of God are no less an empirical reality than the crucifixion of Christ. The church is as real as his cross. There is no "ideal church," no "invisible church," no "mystically existing universal church" more real than the concrete church with parking lots and potluck dinners. It is the church of

7. Yoder, *The Original Revolution*, 121. It is instructive to compare this with Michael Novak's critique of the Catholic bishops on nuclear disarmament. Novak explicitly asserts that the "Christian faith does not teach us to rely on the miraculous" ("Making Deterrence Work," *Catholicism in Crisis* 1, no. 1 [November 1982]: 5).

parking lots and potluck dinners that comprises the sanctified ones formed by and forming the continuing story of Jesus Christ in the world. There are certainly differences in the church that may even cause separation, but that too is part of what it means to call the church an extended argument over time about the significance of that story and how best to understand it. In this vein, this is a reason why the church should learn to value her heretics, since the church also learns what it believes by learning what it does not believe.

No conversation over differences is more important than that between Israel and the church. For it is from Israel that we learn of the God who is present to us in the life, cross, and resurrection of Jesus. It is from Israel's continuing willingness to wait for the Messiah that we learn better how we must wait between the times. The church and Israel are two people walking in the path provided by God; they cannot walk independently of one another, for if they do they both risk becoming lost.[8]

The church, therefore, is not some ideal of community but a particular people who, like Israel, must find the way to sustain their existence generation after generation. Indeed, there are clear "marks" through which we know that the church is church. These marks do not guarantee the existence of the church, but are the means God has given us to help us along the way. Thus the church is known where the sacraments are celebrated, the word is preached, and upright lives are encouraged and lived. Some churches emphasize one of these "marks" more than others, but that does not mean that they are deficient in some decisive manner. What is important is that these "marks" are exhibited by Christians everywhere, not that each particular body of Christians does all of these things.

In the sacraments we enact the story of Jesus and in so doing form a community in his image. We could not be the church without them. For the story of Jesus is not simply one that is told; it must be enacted. The sacraments are means crucial to shaping and preparing us to tell and hear that story. Thus baptism is that rite of initiation necessary for us to become part of Jesus' death and resurrection. Through baptism we do not simply learn the story, but we become part of that story. The eucharist is the eschatological meal of God's continuing presence that makes possible a peaceable people. At that meal we become part of Christ's kingdom, as we learn there that death could not contain him. His presence, his peace is a living reality in the world. As we

8. This way of putting the matter I have borrowed from Paul Van Buren's *Discerning the Way* (New York: Seabury Press, 1980).

partake we become part of his sacrifice, God's sacrifice, so that the world might be saved from sin and death.

These rites, baptism and eucharist, are not just "religious things" that Christian people do. They are the essential rituals of our politics. Through them we enact who we are. These liturgies do not motivate us for effective social work; rather, these liturgies are our effective social work. For if the church *is* rather than has a social ethic, these actions are our most important social witness. In baptism and eucharist we see most clearly the marks of God's kingdom in the world. They set our standard, as we try to bring every aspect of our lives under their sway.[9]

Baptism and eucharist are also our most fervent prayers and set the standard for all of our other prayers. For prayer is not our pleading to an unmoveable or unsympathetic but all-powerful God. Through these and other prayers, we learn to make ourselves open to God's presence. Prayer is the way we let God loose in the world.[10] As such, prayer is a dangerous activity, for God's presence is not easily controlled. God is a wild presence calling us to ways of life we had not previously imagined possible. Through baptism and the eucharist Christian people open themselves to that wildness. It is no wonder that throughout history various rulers and powers have sought to prevent Christians from praying, since there is no more powerful challenge to their power.

In addition to praying, Christians also preach. There is no story without witness, and it is through the preaching of God's good news and our willingness to hear it that we become a people of witness. Preaching involves not only "telling," but also hearing. Just as great art creates an audience capable of hearing or seeing in new ways, so the church's preaching creates an audience capable of being challenged in new ways by the story of Jesus and his kingdom.

---

9. As William Willimon says, "The Lord's Supper is a 'sanctifying ordinance,' a sign of the continuity, necessity, and availability of God's enabling, communal, confirming, nurturing grace. Our characters are formed, sanctified, by such instruments of continual divine activity in our lives. Sanctification is a willingness to see our lives as significant only as we are formed into God's image for us. According to Paul, that image is always ecclesial, social, communal. In our attentiveness and response to this call to be saints, we find our thoughts, affections, sight, and deeds qualified by this beckoning grace. We become characterized as those who attend to the world in a different way from those who are not so qualified. Gradually we are weaned from our natural self-centered, autonomous ways of looking at the world until we become as we profess. We are different" (*The Service of God: How Worship and Ethics are Related* [Nashville, TN: Abingdon Press, 1983], 125).

10. Enda McDonagh, *Doing the Truth: The Quest for Moral Theology* (Notre Dame, IN: University of Notre Dame Press, 1979), 40–57.

Our preaching, however, cannot be confined to ourselves, because we become witnesses to those who do not share our story. In fact, the very content of that story requires us to address the stranger. God has promised us that where the word is rightly preached (and heard), it will be fruitful. Through the witnessing to the story of Jesus Christ generation after generation, God will create a people capable of carrying into the world the story of Jesus and his kingdom.

Therefore, just as baptism and the eucharist are essential to the church's social ethic, so is our preaching. Our obligation to witness arises from the conviction that there are no people beyond the power of God's word. Christians know no "barbarians," but only strangers whom we hope to make our friends. We extend hospitality to God's kingdom by inviting the stranger to share our story. Of course, we know that the stranger does not come to us as a cipher, but also has a story to tell us. Through the stranger's reception of the story of Jesus (which may often take the form of rejection), we too learn more fully to hear the story of God. Without the constant challenge of the stranger—who often, interestingly enough, is but one side of ourselves—we are tempted to so domesticate Jesus' story that we lose the power of it.

But neither the marks of sacraments nor preaching would be sufficient if the church was not also called to be a holy people—that is, a people capable of maintaining a life of charity, hospitality, and justice. Thus the church must vigorously attend to mutual upbuilding and correction. We seek out the other because it is from the other that we learn how well or how poorly we have made the story of Jesus our story. For the church is finally known by the character of the people who constitute it, and if we lack that character, the world rightly draws the conclusion that the God we worship is in fact a false God.

It would be a mistake, moreover, to separate this emphasis on being a holy people from that of being a sacramental people. For I think it is not accidental that one of the classical eucharistic texts appears in the context of moral exhortation. In 1 Corinthians 11:17–26 Paul says:

> But in the following instructions I do not commend you, because when you come together it is not for the better but for the worse. For in the first place, when you assemble as a church, I hear that there are divisions among you; and I partly believe it, for there must be factions among you in order that those who are genuine among you may be recognized. When you meet together, it is not the Lord's supper that you eat. For in eating, each one goes ahead with his own meal, and one is hungry and another is drunk. What! Do

you not have houses to eat and drink in? Or do you despise the church of God and humiliate those who have nothing? What shall I say to you? Shall I commend you in this? No, I will not. For I received from the Lord what I also delivered to you, that the Lord Jesus on the night when he was betrayed took bread, and when he had given thanks, he broke it, and said, "This is my body which is for you. Do this in remembrance of me." In the same way also the cup, after supper, saying, "This cup is the new covenant in my blood. Do this, as often as you drink it, in remembrance of me." For as often as you eat this bread and drink the cup, you proclaim the Lord's death until he comes.

Our eating with our Lord is not different from our learning to be his disciples, his holy people. The kind of holiness that marks the church, however, is not that of moral perfection, but the holiness of a people who have learned not to fear one another and thus are capable of love. We do not just go ahead with our meals or our lives, but we wait for each other, so we may learn to live in the presence of others without fear and envy. We thus become a perfect people through the meal we share with our Lord. We learn that forgiveness of the enemy, even when the enemy is ourselves, is the way God would have his kingdom accomplished.

In his illuminating book about his missionary work with the Masai, Vincent Donovan powerfully illustrates the inherent relation between our holiness as a people and our eucharistic celebrations. One of the most significant gestures for the Masai is to offer one another a handful of grass as a sign of peace, happiness, and well-being. During arguments, for example, a tuft of grass might be offered by one Masai to another as an assurance that no violence would erupt because of the argument. "No Masai would violate that sacred sign of peace offered, because it was not only a sign of peace; it was peace."[11]

Donovan describes how the beginning of a Mass among the Masai would involve the whole village, as every activity of the village, from praying for the sick to dancing, would become a natural part of the Mass. Yet he says he never knew if the eucharist would emerge from all this. The leaders of the village were the ones to decide yes or no. "If there had been selfishness and forgetfulness and hatefulness and lack of forgiveness in the work that had been done, in the life that had been led here, let them not make a sacrilege out of it by calling it the Body of Christ. And the leaders did decide occasionally that, despite the

---

11. Vincent Donovan, *Christianity Rediscovered* (Maryknoll, NY: Orbis Books, 1982), 125. I am indebted to Philip Foubert for calling Donovan's fascinating book to my attention.

prayers and readings and discussions, if the grass had stopped, if someone, or some group, in the village had refused to accept the grass as the sign of the peace of Christ, there would be no eucharist at this time."[12]

The Masai understand well the relation between their eucharistic celebration and the demand to be a holy people, a peaceable people. For the eucharist and their baptism are not isolated acts separate from the kind of people they are meant to be. Rather, the eucharist is possible because they have become what they, and we, were meant to be: a people capable of passing grass, of forgiveness, in a world that would have us believe that human relations are ultimately determined by manipulation and violence.

5. The Social Ethics of the Church

It may be objected that all this still remains very abstract. Even if it is true that the church itself is a social ethic, surely it must also have a social ethic that reaches out in strategic terms in the societies in which it finds itself. That is certainly the case, but a social ethic in this latter sense cannot be done in the abstract. For there is no universal social strategy of the church that applies equally to diverse social circumstances. Indeed, different circumstances and social contexts require different responses and strategies. For example, the church's stance in the context of totalitarian governments is obviously different from its stance in liberal democratic regimes.

This does not mean the church must have a particular theory of government that can help it to understand the different ways it responds to totalitarian regimes as opposed to the more liberal democratic ones. The contemporary church has often assumed that it favors "democratic" societies because such societies have institutionalized the freedom of religion through legal recognition of the freedom of conscience. But the assumption that democracies are intrinsically more just because they provide more freedom than other kinds of societies is misleading at best. For "freedom" often functions as an abstraction that serves merely to direct our attention away from faithfully serving as the church. With regard to freedom, the crucial questions are What kind of freedom? and How do we plan to use it?

Yet it may be suggested that even if there is no one theory of government intrinsic to the church's self-understanding, surely there are some values, which may have diverse institutional forms, that the church has a stake in

12. Ibid., 127.

promoting. For example, Enda McDonagh speaks of "kingdom values," such as freedom, inviolability of the person, and equality, as necessary correlatives of the Christian commitment. Indeed, the church's promotion of these values in wider society is entailed by the Christian duty to promote more nearly just social orders. Christians, according to McDonagh, support these "values" as intrinsic to the kingdom, but they are not peculiar to Christians per se. Rather, the pursuit of justice "not only allows for cooperation with the non-believer, it opens up the non-believer and believer to an awareness of the human, the mystery of the human. . . . In this way the discernment and promotion of social justice provides a pedagogy of the faith, a learning experience that has the capacity, under the attracting power of the self-giving and revealing God whom we are encountering in the neighbor, to be transcended into explicit recognition of God, into faith. Not only does faith demand social justice, social justice finally demands faith—for the believer, increases in faith."[13]

It is extremely interesting to compare McDonagh's position in this respect with that of Yoder. For Yoder says:

> The ultimate and most profound reason to consider Christ—rather than democracy or justice, or equality of liberty—as the hope of the world, is not the negative observation, clear enough already, that hopes of this kind generally remain incomplete and disappointing, or that they can lead those who trust them to pride or brutality. The fundamental limitation of these hopes is found in the fact that in their search for power and in the urgency with which they seek to guarantee justice they are still not powerful enough. They locate the greatest need of man in the wrong place. . . . Those for whom Jesus Christ is the hope of the world will for this reason not measure their contemporary social involvement by its efficacy for tomorrow nor by its success in providing work, or freedom, or food or in building new social structures, but by identifying with the Lord in whom they have placed their trust.[14]

Yoder is not objecting to McDonagh's concern for justice, nor does he wish to deny that God requires that we seek justice for all people. Rather, he notices that "justice" can mean—and thus require—many different things, and not all are equally amenable to Jesus' proclamation of the kingdom. Furthermore,

---

13. Enda McDonagh, *Church and Politics* (Notre Dame, IN: University of Notre Dame Press, 1980), 27.
14. Yoder, *The Original Revolution*, 165–66. For Yoder's fuller analysis of the theological status of democracy, see his "The Christian Case for Democracy," *Journal of Religious Ethics* 5 (fall 1977): 209–24.

once "justice" is made a criterion of Christian social strategy, it can too easily take on a meaning and life of its own that is not informed by fundamental Christian convictions. For example, the appeal to "justice" can and has been used to justify the Christian's resort to violence to secure a more "relative justice." But is this the justice we are to seek as Christians?

Put differently, the problem with identifying, or at least closely associating, the meaning of the Gospel with the pursuit of "kingdom values" such as justice, freedom, and equality is that such values lack the specificity and concreteness of the kingdom as found in Jesus' life and death. It is not sufficient to interpret, as McDonagh does, the eschatological nature of freedom and equality by noting that they are ideals never fully realized.[15] The problem is not that the kingdom brought by Christ is too idealistic to be realized. The problem is just the opposite. The kingdom present in Jesus Christ is the ultimate realism that rightly calls into question vague, secular ideals of freedom, equality, and peace. In other words, we do not learn about the demands of the kingdom by learning about freedom and equality; rather, we must first experience the kingdom if we are even to know what kind of freedom and what kind of equality we should desire. Christian freedom lies in service, and Christian equality is equality before God, and neither can be achieved through the coercive efforts of liberal idealists who would transform the world into their image.

Put in terms that have now become familiar, freedom and equality are not self-interpreting, but require a tradition to give them specificity and content. For example, it is a truism of political theory that freedom of the individual and a more egalitarian society are not consistent ideals—that is, the pursuit of equality necessarily will qualify someone's sense of what it means to be "free." Indeed, I suspect that the current concentration on these two "values" keeps our society from pursuing the appropriate aims of a good society. Current understandings of "freedom" and "equality" tend to underwrite a view of society as essentially a collection of individuals who are engaged in continual bargaining procedures to provide mutual security without letting it cost too much in their personal freedom. Questions of the common purpose of such societies simply cannot be asked. Distinctions between society and state, while perfectly intelligible in a formal mode, make little empirical sense, because "society" lacks a sufficient narrative to give it moral substance. The church, to be sure, has a stake in a "limited state," but what keeps the state limited is not

15. McDonagh, *Church and Politics,* 34.

finally a theory about the place of the state within society but a people who have the power of discernment and know when to say "No."[16]

Thus, to say that the church must pursue societal justice is certainly right, but it is not very helpful or informative. For justice needs to be imaginatively construed and displayed by a people who have learned that genuine justice involves our receiving what is not due us! This justice is best served when such people exemplify in their own lives how to help one another—that is, how goods might be shared since no one has a rightful claim on them. A prerequisite for genuine justice is a sense of what might rightly be desired. Otherwise, justice remains formal and procedural. While there is much to be said for procedural norms, in themselves they can never sustain the conversation necessary for a people to survive as a good people.

Moreover, when freedom and equality are made ideal abstractions, they become the justification for violence, since if these values are absent or insufficiently institutionalized some conclude that they must be forced into existence. As McDonagh points out, "Most political orders are established by violence and certainly use violence to maintain themselves."[17] This is not without ethical justification, since, as McDonagh suggests, the state's hegemony of violence is at least in principle rooted in the just war rationale. The state uses violence to restrain those who have no respect for the lives and rights of other people in that society. Thus it seems the state can claim to use violence as the necessary means to preserve freedom and justice. And by further inference of this reasoning, when freedom and justice are missing, the Christian can resort to violence so that they may be achieved.

No one can deny the appeal of this position. Moreover, it certainly makes clear that the question of violence is the central issue for any Christian social ethic. Can Christians ever be justified in resorting to arms to do "some good"? Are Christians not unjust if they allow another person to be injured or even

---

16. McDonagh is quite right to stress the importance of the distinction between state and society, for there is no doubt it has proved crucial for securing more nearly just social orders. Moreover, there is every reason to think this distinction between state and society—that is, the assumption that society is a moral reality more primary than the organ of government, thus making the latter subordinate to, as well as in service to, the former—is the result of the Christian challenge to the authority of the Roman imperium. Yet it cannot therefore be concluded that the Church has more stake in social orders that seem to maintain in theory a "limited" state than in those that do not. For no state is more omnivorous in its appetites for our loyalty than one that claims it is protecting our freedom from "state control." See ibid., 29–39.

17. Ibid., 69.

killed if they might prevent that by the use of violence? Should not Christians call on the power of the state to employ its coercive force to secure more relative forms of justice? Such action would not be a question of using violence to be "in control," but simply to prevent a worse evil.

Although I have sympathy with this position and though it certainly cannot be discounted as a possibility for Christians, one problem with many efforts to demonstrate the necessity of the use of violence is that they often misrepresent the character of the alternatives. Violence used in the name of justice, or freedom, or equality is seldom simply a matter of justice: it is a matter of the power of some over others. Moreover, when violence is justified in principle as a necessary strategy for securing justice, it stills the imaginative search for nonviolent ways of resistance to injustice.[18] For true justice never comes through violence, nor can it be based on violence. It can only be based on truth, which has no need to resort to violence to secure its own existence. Such a justice comes at best fitfully to nation-states, for by nature we are people who fear disorder and violence and thus we prefer order (even if the order is built on the lies inspired by our hates, fears, and resentments) to truth. The church, therefore, as a community based on God's kingdom of truth, cannot help but make all rulers tremble, especially when those rulers have become "the people."

Further Reading
"The Gesture of a Truthful Story" (1985), in CET
"The Liturgical Shape of the Christian Life: Teaching Christian Ethics as Worship"
    (1995), in IGC
"The Church as God's New Language" (1986), essay 7 in this volume
"Peacemaking: The Virtue of the Church" (1985), essay 16 in this volume
"Worship, Evangelism, Ethics: Eliminating the 'And'" (1998) in BP
"The Politics of Salvation: Why There Is No Salvation Outside the Church" (1991)
    in AC
"Practicing Discipleship: Embodiment" (1996), in WRAL

18. To what extent can Christians participate in a society's government? Any response will necessarily depend on the character of individual societies and their governments. Most governmental functions, even within the military, do not depend on coercion and violence. It may be possible, therefore, for a Christian in some societies to be a policeman, prison warden, and so on. What is crucial, however, is that Christians work to help their societies develop the kind of people and institutions that make possible a government whose justice does not require resort to violence.

20. Should War Be Eliminated?
A Thought Experiment (1984)

In 1983 the National Conference of Catholic Bishops of the United States issued a pastoral letter entitled The Challenge of Peace: God's Promise and Our Response. *Hauerwas takes the occasion of its publication to engage in a "thought experiment" on Roman Catholic ambivalence to warfare more generally. Hauerwas shows how the pastoral letter's two viewpoints about war (i.e., just war and pacifism) issue from ethical perspectives (one beginning with the gospel vs. one beginning with the natural law) that have different starting points. Though not strictly incompatible, Hauerwas wonders "how one can hold both at once." Examining the defense of war on natural law grounds as presented in both* The Challenge of Peace *and the work of the Catholic theologian David Hollenbach, Hauerwas concludes that neither is successful at resolving the obvious tension between the just war and pacifist viewpoints. "Should war be eliminated?" is not the appropriate question because "war has been eliminated for those who participate in God's history." Drawing on the conception of "eschatological peace" developed by the Mennonite theological ethicist John Howard Yoder, Hauerwas argues that the church is properly understood as "God's sign that war is not part of his providential care of the world" and therefore as "the carrier of a history other than the history of war."*

On Getting the Problems Right

Large numbers of people are now convinced that we should eliminate all nuclear weapons. In their recent pastoral letter the Roman Catholic Bishops of America seem virtually to have joined these ranks. Still more people, while they do not call for the complete destruction of nuclear weapons, suggest that

[Originally published as the "1984 Pere Marquette Theology Lecture: Should War Be Eliminated?" By Stanley Hauerwas, Marquette University Press, 1984. Subsequently reprinted in AN. It has been edited for clarity.]

we should drastically reduce the kind and number of our nuclear stockpile. This latter group includes such highly respected persons as George Kennan and Robert MacNamara, the sort who cannot be accused of political naïveté. As yet, however, these many voices have precipitated no change in public policy and they seem unlikely to do so in the near future. Indeed, we are told that the peace movement threatens the peace, as peace can be guaranteed only through strength, which means more, not fewer, nuclear missiles. And so the stockpiles continue to grow.

Why do we seem caught in this dilemma? Why, when all admit that nuclear weapons threaten our very existence as nations, if not as a species, do we seem so unable to free ourselves from their power? Some suppose that people want peace, but our leaders, inspired by some nefarious motive, do not. Such explanations are far too simple; the problem is much more recalcitrant than a change in leadership can solve. We all, leaders and followers alike, seem caught in a web of powers that is one of our own making yet not under our control. We say we want peace, but we seem destined for war.

Why is this the case? Why do all our attempts to think morally about war often seem so futile in the face of war's irresistible inevitability? In spite of its horror and destructiveness, its insanity and irrationality, might it be that we have overlooked the fact that war has a moral purpose? Could that be the reason why, no matter how compelling the logic against nuclear weapons, we still seem defeated by those who say, "All that may be quite right, but . . ."? What are the moral presuppositions that make that "but" seem so powerful?

In order to try to understand these kinds of questions I am going to propose a thought experiment that may help us reconsider our assumptions about war and its place in our lives. The experiment is to provide the best negative answer I am able to the question: "Should war be eliminated?" We tend to think such a question absurd. After all, it is not a question of "should" at all, but of "can." We all know we should eliminate war; the problem is we cannot. Asking if we should eliminate war is like asking if we should eliminate sin. Of course we should, but the problem is that we cannot. Therefore, to ask such a question is to start us off in the wrong direction.

While I admit that there may be aspects of the question bordering on the absurd, I hope to show that by pressing it seriously we may be able to illuminate why war is such an intractable aspect of our existence. Moreover, by insisting on using the language of *should* I want to force us to consider what is at stake morally by the very fact that we describe some forms of violence as war. Too often those concerned to make moral judgments about war, whether they be pacifists or just war theorists, assume that the description of war is unproblematic: the only question is how to eliminate or control war. Yet that is exactly what I am suggesting cannot be assumed.

It may be objected that just war theory in fact does presuppose the kind of analysis of war I am suggesting. Rather than being a theory about the criteria necessary to determine if or how a war may be fought morally, the just war is an attempt to understand war as a moral enterprise. I have no reason to deny such an interpretation of the just war theory. Moreover, if in fact that is what just war theory is about, then the moral description of war I will try to develop can be seen as an attempt to expose some of the implicit assumptions entailed by just war thinking.

Ethical reflection about war, therefore, does not begin by asking what makes a war more or less just. Rather, a morality is already implied by the very fact that we call it war. For war is not simply another name for violence.

We must begin, therefore, by asking: Do we know what we mean by calling something a war? Certainly war entails violence, but yet the very description *war* seems to propose a different moral evaluation than violence. At the very least, *war* denotes purposive human activity that *violence* does not always imply. Perhaps that is why normal categories dealing with killing do not seem to apply in war. For example, we are taken aback by the suggestion that war is but legitimized murder on a mass scale. Our resistance to calling war murder indicates that we assume it has a moral legitimacy.

Indeed, some who argue currently against nuclear weapons do so in defense of war as an important moral institution. From their perspective war as a legitimate enterprise is being ruined by modern weapons of mass destruction. They deny that "nuclear war" is appropriately so called because war presupposes that good can be done through its prosecution. Thus George Kennan challenges "the thesis that these devices, the so-called nuclear weapons, are really weapons at all—that they deserve that designation. A weapon is something with which you try to affect the purposes and the concepts of an opponent; it is not something with which you blindly destroy his entire civilization, and probably your own as well."[1] We might say that Kennan, and others who argue like him, are trying to eliminate nuclear war in order to make the world safe for war. But we must ask if their position is coherent, for once the moral presuppositions underlying their acceptance of war are re-

---

1. George Kennan, *The Nuclear Delusion: Soviet-American Relations in the Atomic Age* (New York: Pantheon Books, 1983), 243.

vealed, it may be the case that nuclear weapons are but a new development in the institution of war.

If it is so important to save war as a significant moral option, we need an account that makes explicit war's moral status. In spite of all calls for peace, such an account might show us that if war were eliminated we would be morally the worse for it. By this I do not mean merely that we would miss the extraordinary individual heroics often associated with war, or lose the kind of comradeship war creates between soldiers and citizens.[2] It is undoubtedly true that war often provides the occasion for our most impressive moral behavior, but these good results are not contained within the very fabric of war itself. The issue is not whether war occasionally can have good results, but whether war, with all its horror, destructiveness, and brutality, is an institution that nonetheless serves moral purposes that we should not will to be without.

This is the issue I seek to address, although I honestly must say I am skeptical of the very possibility of a coherent response. In particular I fear that any abstract account of *war* risks lapsing into a false idealism. What we need to talk about is not war, but this or that war. Philosophical analysis of the kind I propose has the dangerous tendency to console by offering explanations for what is essentially inexplicable.

So why pursue it? First, I hope by proceeding in this manner that we will be able to get beyond some of the current rhetoric about nuclear war and deal with the basic issue of war itself. The current debate about nuclear weapons is beginning to resemble in a disturbing fashion the conflict over abortion. Both sides have arguments and responses to which the opponent does not listen. By directing our attention to war rather than simply the morality of nuclear weapons, I hope to raise new questions that will perhaps prevent our discussion from ending in a shouting match. I do not intend to solve the moral problems raised by nuclear deterrence strategy; rather, my purpose is to try to help us understand morally how we have arrived at a situation where our so-called safety can be ensured only if we are willing to will countless deaths and destruction. I want first to understand, not judge or offer solutions.

Second, by developing a moral case for war I hope to illuminate the ambiv-

---

2. The classic account of this perspective on war is J. Glenn Gray's *The Warriors: Reflections on Men in Battle*, 2d ed. (New York: Harper Torchbook, 1970). For a recent attempt to defend the vocation of the soldier, see Walter Benjamin, "In Defense of the Soldier, "*Christianity and Crisis* 43, no. 19 (November 28, 1983): 453–58; and my response in the same issue, "What Can the State Ask?"

alence Christians often exhibit about war. That ambivalence is at the heart of *The Challenge of Peace: God's Promise and Our Response*.[3] The kind of ambivalence with which I am concerned is not the bishops' unwillingness to condemn forthrightly all forms of deterrence. Rather, I wish to call our attention to the even more fundamental ambivalence concerning war itself. For in spite of the bishops' avowal that Christians are fundamentally a people of peace, they affirm that Christians can participate in war as a legitimate moral endeavor. I hope to show, in spite of the bishops' assertion that war is always the result of sin (a fact they continue to presume, and it is a presumption consistent with the natural law basis of the just war tradition), that war is a morally positive institution.

Finally, I want to develop as strong a case as I can for war because I am a pacifist. Too often pacifists try to win easy victories against those who support war by stressing war's irrationality and horror. The problem with such strategy is that, in spite of war's obvious irrationalities and horrors, it somehow is beside the point. It is so, I think, because it ignores the powerful moral presupposition that sustains war's viability in spite of its brutality. The significance of the pacifist's refusal to cooperate with war can be appreciated only by understanding why war has such a hold on our moral imagination.

Moreover, by proceeding in this way I hope we will also be able to better understand the theological disagreements between pacifist and just war thinkers.[4] For by developing a positive case for war I hope to show that pacifist and just war thinkers draw on quite different assumptions about eschatology. Both entail assumptions about how history should be told and the Christian role in it. By suggesting how war determines our history we can better understand why Christians cannot allow that history to define their existence. Pacifism, therefore, is not just an attitude about war, but it entails the belief that God,

3. *The Challenge of Peace: God's Promise and Our Response* (Washington, DC: United States Catholic Conference, 1983). All references to this pastoral letter appear in the text and refer to the numbered paragraph.
4. It is often alleged, moreover, that if one is a pacifist then one really has nothing to say of interest about war. The implication that pacifists simply have nothing to say about war or strategies of disarmament is a silent rebuke suggesting that pacifists simply do not face up to the hard issues. But the pacifist, no less than the just war advocate, must be concerned to find means to make war less likely and less destructive. After all, the pacifist refusal to participate in war does not mean that all wars are therefore morally on a par. Indeed, it is even more a moral imperative for the pacifist to be concerned with issues of how disarmament can take place since the pacifist knows that calls for peace apart from an account of how such peace might take place cannot but appear as utopian.

through Jesus Christ, has inaugurated a history that frees all people from our assumption that we have no moral alternative to war.

War in a Catholic Perspective

The suggestion that Christians have a moral ambivalence about war leads us to suppose that some explicit theological justification of war might be at work as well as the more generally accepted moral ones. Investigation of two significant documents, Pope John XXIII's *Pacem in Terris* and the recent Pastoral Letter of the American Roman Catholic Bishops, *The Challenge of Peace: God's Promise and Our Response,* shows this to be the case. In the following treatment of them it is not my intention to try to give a complete analysis, but rather to try to make explicit each document's understanding of war. For though each says much about the ethics of war, neither tries to explain what it understands war to be. By attending to how they make their ethical case I hope to show that their implicit understanding of war is more positive than their ethical pronouncements about war would lead one to believe.

I have chosen these documents because they are representative of a church's position rather than that of an individual thinker. Moreover, they bring to bear elements, some conflictual, from a Christian tradition that has developed the most sophisticated moral analysis of war. While the documents urge peace, they nonetheless continue to maintain war as a moral possibility, if not a duty, for Christians. I hope my criticism of these documents will expose these assumptions as well as generate some of the conceptual tools we will need to understand war in a more positive light.

Pacem in Terris was promulgated in 1963 and brought a new emphasis on peace by a church that in the past had generally been associated with the just war tradition.[5] In *Pacem in Terris* the just war theory is subordinated to a wider vision of peace. Thus John XXIII argues, "There will never be peace among men unless peace resides in the soul of each man—unless each person

---

5. John XXIII, *Peace on Earth* (Huntington, IN: Our Sunday Visitor, 1965); subsequent references are in the text. I am treating *Peace on Earth* not only because it provides the necessary background for understanding *The Challenge of Peace,* but because the bishops' appeal to just war seems to presuppose the kind of reasoning suggested by *Peace on Earth.* Indeed, Bryan Hehir suggests that *The Challenge of Peace* is an attempt to blend *Peace on Earth* with the methodology of the Second Vatican Council's *Pastoral Constitution on the Church in the Modern World (Gaudium et spes).* See his "From the Pastoral Constitution of Vatican II to the Challenge of Peace," in *Catholics and Nuclear War,* ed. Philip Murnion (New York: Crossroad, 1983), 71–86.

preserves within himself the order commanded by God" (165). That order is to be found in the natural law which can be known by all people. Its most basic principle is "that every human being is a person naturally endowed with intelligence and free will. Thus man has rights and duties flowing directly and conjointly from his very nature. These rights and duties are universal and inviolable and therefore inalienable" (9).

Every human right—the right of life, truth, conscience, family, work, private property, assembly, political participation—is connected with a corresponding set of duties. Since we are social by nature a well-ordered society is one where "every natural right of a man and the duties of others to acknowledge and foster that right is recognized" (30). In such a society authority is primarily a moral force as order is maintained by an "appeal primarily to the conscience of individual citizens . . . , to the duty of each one to work willingly for the common good of all. Since all men are naturally equal in human dignity, no one has the power to force compliance on another, except God alone, Who sees and judges the unseen thought of men's hearts" (48).

Thus the encyclical assumes an organic view of society where each nation contains elements of the common good by safeguarding the personal rights and duties of individuals (60). Society, and the state that serves it, is peaceful since by definition it seems there can be no conflict between rights if everyone is allowed to pursue those rights fairly. The more we cooperate, the less we will need to resort to violence.

This basic assumption is then applied to international affairs. Each state has "reciprocal rights and duties and the relations between States should be harmonized in truth, justice, active cooperation, and liberty. For the same natural law which governs the relations between individual men must also regulate those between states" (80). Thus the relations among states must be governed by truth. Truth calls for the elimination of every form of racism and recognition of the inviolable and immutable principle that all states are by nature equal in dignity. Each state therefore has the right to exist, to make progress, to possess the means for its development, and to bear the principal responsibility for bringing about and expanding its own progress and growth. Truth also demands that each nation have the right to its good name and to due honor (86).

It may be that the advantages each state seeks to acquire will lead to disagreements but those should be settled not by force of arms but by "appraisal of the arguments and attitudes of the opposing sides, a mature and objective weighing of the facts, and an equitable adjustment of the opposing views" (93). Peace, therefore, cannot be based on the stockpiling of weapons, but on mutual trust. "Justice, right reason, and an appreciation of the dignity of man urgently demand that the arms race stop; that weapons on hand in the various countries be reduced through parallel and simultaneous action by the parties concerned; that nuclear weapons be banned; and that all men finally come to an agreement on a suitable disarmament program with an effective system for mutual control" (112).

It is easy to accuse *Pacem in Terris* of naïveté, but I think such an accusation overlooks the substantive assumptions embodied in the encyclical. These assumptions are all the more powerful because they are widely shared. Like the encyclical, many assume that war is the result of a failure to give persons their right to pursue their interests. If each of us is satisfied in himself we would be at peace with one another; in like manner, nation-states would be at peace, having nothing to gain by aggression. War is not so much wrong, therefore, as it is plain irrational.

Yet the view that peace results from cooperation among free individuals is seriously flawed. Flawed not because we are more fundamentally depraved than the encyclical assumes (though I certainly think it is far too optimistic concerning human goodwill), but because the kind of violence embodied in the institution of war is not due to the pursuit of our interests at the expense of others but rather, as I hope to show, results from our moral commitment to the good of others. That the encyclical fails to confront this reality of war causes, I think, its calls for peace to appear flaccid. We thus dismiss it as but another idealistic call for peace in a world constituted by war.

The vision of peace articulated in *Pacem in Terris* is not limited to Catholic teaching. Indeed, this view of peace is also the working assumption of many schooled by the Enlightenment. It may seem odd to suggest that the Catholic Church, the great enemy of the Enlightenment, has now become its most prominent advocate, but I think this is what has happened. For the working assumption of the encyclical is something like this: There is a fundamental symmetry between establishing and maintaining a just constitution within a state and in establishing and maintaining a just relationship among states.[6] If

---

6. For an extremely helpful account of Enlightenment accounts of war and peace, see W. B. Gallie, *Philosophers of Peace and War: Kant, Clausewitz, Marx, Engels and Tolstoy* (Cambridge, England: Cambridge University Press, 1978). Of course, one of the crucial issues that too often goes unanalyzed in most of the literature dealing with war is whether we know what we mean when we say *state*. Obviously a *state* is not the same as a people, nor is it clear that a nation-state corresponds to what was classically meant by a "state"—that is, a subunit for the government of a society. One wonders if the Enlightenment accounts of *state*, which seem to be

we could instruct just states of autonomous moral agents then we could secure peace among them, reserving war for protection against unjust aggressor states.

The Challenge of Peace begins by asserting, quite contrary to these Enlightenment assumptions, that the Christians' longing for peace is based in the Gospel rather than natural law. The bishops suggest that there can be no question that Jesus was on the side of peace against war.[7] Indeed, Jesus not only taught peace but, as the full demonstration of the power of God's reign made present in his life and work, Jesus gives a peace beyond what is possible for relations among autonomous nation states (51). "Jesus gives that peace to his disciples, to those who had witnessed the helplessness of the crucifixion and the power of the resurrection (Jn. 20:19, 20, 26). The peace which he gives to them as he greets them as their risen Lord is the fullness of salvation. It is the reconciliation of the world and God (Rom. 5:1–2; Col. 1:20); the restoration of the unity and harmony of all creation which the Old Testament spoke of with such longing. Because the walls of hostility between God and humankind were broken down in the life and death of the true, perfect servant, union and well-being between God and the world were finally fully possible (Eph. 2:13–22; Gal. 3:28)" (51).

Nevertheless, the bishops go on to say, the peace and reconciliation Jesus left with the early Christians "were not yet fully operative in their world" (53). They assert on the one hand that "Jesus Christ is our peace, and in his death-resurrection he gives God's peace to our world" (54), but on the other hand, it is false to suppose that Jesus or the Scriptures provide us with a "detailed answer to the specifics of the questions which we face today. They do not speak specifically of nuclear war or nuclear weapons, for these were beyond the imagination of the communities in which the scriptures were formed. The sacred texts do, however, provide us with urgent direction when we look at today's concrete realities. The fullness of eschatological peace remains before us in hope and yet the gift of peace is already ours in the reconciliation effected in Jesus Christ" (55).[8]

---

accepted in *Pacem in Terris,* have any relation to what empirically counts for state in the modern world.

7. The bishops' account of war in the Hebrew Scriptures unfortunately is not well developed. It is as if they thought to themselves, War is a valid mode of God's way with Israel, but fortunately we have the New Testament to balance that emphasis. For an account with much stronger continuity between Israel and Jesus on the question of war, see Millard Lind's *Yahweh Is a Warrior: The Theology of Warfare in Ancient Israel* (Scottdale, PA: Herald Press, 1980).

8. There is an ambiguity in the bishops' position for it is unclear if the peace Jesus brought is

Thus the Christian must live between the vision of the reign of God and its concrete realization in history. Any ethical response to war must be worked out in light of this tension. Christians may take different stances about war as they move toward the realization of God's kingdom in history, but all Christians will "find in any violent situation the consequences of sin: not only sinful patterns of domination, oppression or aggression, but the conflict of values and interests which illustrate the limitations of a sinful world" (61). Therefore pacifism is a legitimate response by Christians to war, but it is not that which the bishops take. For while their letter is addressed "principally to the Catholic community, we want it to make a contribution to the wider public debate in our country on the dangers and dilemmas of the nuclear age."[9] Therefore, the ethical basis of *The Challenge of Peace* must be one that is not based on specifically Christian presuppositions.

---

not relevant for nuclear war because it is an eschatological peace or because Jesus did not speak explicitly about questions of nuclear war. I doubt the bishops would want to press the latter argument since there are many matters on which they want to speak authoritatively, such as contraception, on which Jesus did not speak explicitly.

9. Paragraphs 16 and 17 of *The Challenge of Peace* provide the most extended justification for the assumption that this pastoral letter should address the public policy debate on its own terms. Even with the presumption of the bishops, however, the matter is still fraught with ambiguity. For it is not clear if they want to enter the public debate because Catholics are "also members of the wider political community" and may thus be in positions of public responsibility about such matters; or if they want to address all people of goodwill. If the latter, then it seems they are right to think they must presuppose a natural law starting point—that is, "law written on the human heart by God"—that provides a moral norm all can agree on irrespective of their faith. If the former, it is not clear why they cannot continue to speak theologically without resorting to natural law. Such issues are important because it is not clear the bishops can have it both ways. For at least they want in principle to claim that while the norms of natural law do not "exhaust the gospel vision," neither are such norms in fundamental conflict with the obligation of Christians to follow Christ. Yet they also suggest that just war may be the kind of thinking necessary in a sinful world and thus less than the full demand of, and perhaps even a compromise with, the Gospel. This formal issue is reflected by the political ambiguity of *The Challenge of Peace*. For example, David J. O'Brien observes: "The bishops are caught in a classic bind. If they ground themselves exclusively in the spiritual imperative of love and withdraw from the effort to influence the public consensus and public policy, they may indeed mobilize considerable support for a critical, prophetic witness within the church, even if it costs the church many members and opens the community to charges of public irresponsibility. At the other extreme, they may stand too closely to the prevailing framework of responsibility, looking at issues through the lens of decision makers, become sympathetic to their dilemmas, and accept only the limited alternatives that seem to be presently available. If they move one way they seem utopian, unrealistic, and irresponsible. If they move the other they appear to have lost their integrity as Christian leaders acquiescing in a situation they themselves have defined as unjust and immoral" ("American Catholics and American Society," in *Catholics and Nuclear War*, 27).

In order to develop a position capable of providing such guidance, the bishops, in spite of their analysis of the New Testament, turn to the just war theory. That theory, they argue, is built on the fundamental assumption that "governments threatened by armed, unjust aggression must defend their people. This includes defense by armed force if necessary as a last resort" (75). We therefore have a "fundamental right of defense." Even more strongly put, the bishops quote Pius XII, who argued that "a people threatened with an unjust aggression, or already its victim, may not remain passively indifferent, if it would think and act as befits a Christian. Their defense is even an obligation for the nations as a whole, who have a duty not to abandon a nation that is attacked" (76).

Thus while recommending nonviolent means to fend off aggression, the bishops candidly suggest that "we must recognize the reality of the paradox we face as Christians living in the context of the world as it presently exists; we must continue to articulate our belief that love is possible and the only real hope for all human relations, and yet accept that force, even deadly force, is sometimes justified and that nations must provide for their defense" (78).[10]

10. In defense of the bishops on this point, Dennis McCann says:

> Lest the bishops be dismissed as at best muddled and at worst hypocritical we must recognize that within the Catholic tradition moral questions have never been exhausted by referring to the real or imagined ethic of Jesus. Later developments within the Christian ethos, beyond the time of Jesus and the early Christians, are regarded as themselves part of the promised "gift of the Spirit." Without preempting the discussion of the bishops' "quasi-theological beliefs," here I must point out that when Catholic tradition adopted the paradigm of just war theory and began to transform it according to its own agenda, the transition was not marked by tortuous equivocation but by a new sense of what "the call of Jesus" requires "in context of the world as it presently exists." The use of lethal force, in other words, came to be regarded as the most effective and the least unacceptable way "to prevent aggression against innocent victims." The paradigm of just war theory became morally necessary, as soon as Catholic tradition, following St. Augustine, admitted that war itself was not just the result of sin but also a "tragic remedy for sin in the life of political societies." ("The NCCB Letter and Its Critics: An Ethical Analysis," in *Christian Perspectives in Nuclear Deterrence*, ed. Bernard Adeney [In private correspondence, Prof. McCann indicated that this essay has never been published.])

Later, McCann says such a position is justified by the Trinitarian vision of *The Challenge of Peace*, as such a vision is obviously "larger than the words and deeds of Jesus of Nazareth. While such is and will ever remain the decisive moment of incarnation in history, that moment has meaning only in the context of the whole process. The mystery of God's Trinitarian presence thus is reflected in the overall pattern of meaning discerned in human life: we are to 'take responsibility for his work of creation and try to shape it in the ways of the kingdom.'" McCann thus seems to suggest that "just war" is a further development of the Spirit, but surely that is an extremely doubtful claim. It may be that the Trinitarian vision is

For it is an essential presupposition of Catholic teaching about war that "every nation has a right and duty to defend itself against unjust aggression" (iii).

For my purposes it is not necessary to pursue the bishops' detailed account of the just war theory, its implications for nuclear weapons, and their arguments against deterrence. The crucial issues have already been joined by their willingness to underwrite the presumption that the state has the right and duty to defend itself and yet maintains that, in principle, peace should be possible in our world. Once the former presumption has been granted, and it is not clear why they grant it, it is not easy to see how what they say about the Gospel's commitment to peace can be anything more than an unrealizable ideal.

Of course, it may be asked what is wrong about having such an ideal. Given the fact that we live in a war-ridden world, it would seem to be a good idea at least to keep the goal of peace ever before us. But I am not so sure that is the case. For such an ideal might well encourage us, if war is not only a necessary but morally necessary part of our lives, to self-deceptive explanations for our involvement with war. It may well be that war is "the result of sin and a tragic remedy for sin in the life of political societies," but even as such war can serve moral purposes.

Perhaps what we need to learn from this is that, while it sounds right to say war is due to sin, such claims are of little interest. For such a description does not help us understand what war is and why it seems such an inevitable part of our lives. Therefore I will try to give an account of war that goes beyond such broad categories in the hope that by it we will better understand why the bishops cannot bring themselves to deny war as an institution integral to the nation-state.

For there seem to be two different views of war in *The Challenge of Peace* that reflect its two different ethical perspectives—the one based on the Gospel, the other deriving from natural law assumptions. From the perspective of the former, war is the unambiguous sign of sin and can never be called a good. From the perspective of the latter, war can sometimes be a good, indeed a moral duty, necessary to preserve human community. While not strictly incompatible it is not clear how one can hold both at once.

---

larger than the words and deeds of Jesus, but I do not see how it can be claimed that that vision is not in essential continuity with all that Jesus said and did. In truth, the bishops seem torn between justifying just war as a necessary compromise for living responsibly in a sinful world and, as *Peace on Earth* suggests, as a position consistent with natural law.

This is particularly true if one continues to maintain, as the Pastoral does, there can be no incompatibility between nature and grace, reason and revelation (17). For if just war is based on natural law, a law written in the conscience of all men and women by God, then it seems that war must be understood as the outgrowth of legitimate moral commitments. If war, however, is the compromises we make with sin, then it is not clear on what grounds, given the Gospel ethic depicted by the Pastoral, Christians can participate in war. That is, it is not clear if one presumes that Christians should avoid intentionally cooperating with sin.

How Cooperation Results in War

Many, impressed with the universality of violence, attribute war to some fundamental aspect of human nature. The difficulty with such "explanations," however, is that they tell us little about the specific activity we call war. As Kenneth Waltz suggests, while human nature no doubt plays a part in bringing about war, it cannot "by itself explain both war and peace, except by the simple statement that man's nature is such that sometimes he fits and sometimes he does not."[11] In other words, to say that war is the result of some aspect of human nature is at once to say too much and too little. Too much is said because it is unclear what possibly could count against such a claim. Too little, because concentration on the "primary" cause of war directs our attention away from an analysis of the relation between states. Attempts to explain war by appeals to human nature mistakenly assume that war has a cause.

As I suggested at the beginning, war is not simply violence in a magnified form. Rather, it is an institution that arises among peoples who can claim sufficient commonality to transform violence into power. As Hannah Arendt reminds us, power is an instrument of rule and thus is the mitigation of violence.[12] Power implies the ability of people to cooperate so that explicit violence is not needed. Violence is that to which individuals, whether they be particular persons or foreign states, resort in order to challenge the legitimacy of power.[13] When power breaks down, violence is often the result. Therefore, according to Arendt, power is indeed the essence of all government, but

11. Kenneth Waltz, *Man, the State, and War: A Theoretical Analysis* (New York: Columbia University Press, 1959), 29.
12. Hannah Arendt, *On Violence* (New York: Harcourt, Brace, and World, 1970), 36.
13. Ibid., 47.

violence is not. While we might call war violent, its essence is not violence, for in a moral sense it is the enemy of violence.

War is an institution that occurs uniquely between agents of power. Currently we call such agents "nation-states," though war is by no means limited to that particular institution. War, for example, can occur between people who have not organized themselves into nations as we know them. War must be a continuing possibility between nation-states (or other communities), since there neither is nor does it seem there ought to be a system of law, of power, enforceable between them. Communities exist on the basis of shared public concern. Each state must judge its own interests and purposes in terms of its particular history and situation. As a result, to accept war is not to accept violence or anarchy; it is to accept commonality and cooperation.

In his now classic *Man, the State, and War: A Theoretical Analysis,* Kenneth Waltz develops the moral assumptions behind this account of war by calling attention to Rousseau's analysis of the nature and the cause of war. According to Rousseau, persons were originally dispersed sufficiently to make cooperation unnecessary. But numbers increased and contact with other humans posed the alternatives: cooperate or die. Rousseau illustrates this with the simplest example: "Assume that five men who have acquired a rudimentary ability to speak and to understand each other happen to come together at a time when all of them suffer from hunger. The hunger of each will be satisfied by the fifth part of a stag, so they agree to cooperate in a project to trap one. But also the hunger of any one of them will be satisfied by a hare so, as a hare comes within reach, one of them grabs it. The defector obtains the means of satisfying his hunger but in doing so permits the stag to escape. His immediate interest prevails over consideration for his fellows."[14]

The example, while obviously overly simple, conveys a significant but often overlooked point. Unlike most who link conflict casually to some imperfection of our nature, particularly of our reason, Rousseau tries to show that the "sources of conflict are not so much in the minds of men as they are in the nature of social activity."[15] Conflict arises not from our individual selfishness, though we may be selfish, but from the nature of cooperation whereby one person's immediate interest and the general long-term interest of the group are not the same. Yet the long-term interest can be served only when all individuals concerned forgo their immediate interest. Yet it is not merely that

14. Waltz, 167–68.
15. Ibid., 168.

each must forgo an immediate interest, but each must trust the others to do so as well. As Waltz points out, "The problem is now posed in more significant terms. If harmony is to exist in anarchy, not only must I be perfectly rational but I must be able to assume that everyone else is too."[16] But that is exactly what I cannot assume.

If the rational choice is to forgo the immediate good to cooperate, then rationality entails the acceptance of the possibility of coercion whereby the dissenting individual is forced to serve the common good. This is the moral importance of power; without it we could not justify our pursuit of the common good which in turn justifies all our attempts at cooperation. From such a perspective, society (and resulting states) is a remarkable moral achievement. For a state is a unit created by establishing habits of trust through which the citizen is encouraged to submit to a general will for the good of the whole. Whether the state is organic or only the name of some power that has so established itself so that its decisions are accepted as decisions for all, it is nonetheless a force for order. Compliance is rationally fortified by two considerations: one does have the power to change the decision; and one judges that in the long run it is to his or her advantage to cooperate with the state's decision and work for change in the accepted ways. According to Rousseau, the better the state the more prominent the second consideration.[17]

The distillation of a cooperative venture into a state allows for the further possibility of cooperation/conflict between states. Here unity is particularly important. For questions of foreign policy call for choices that are supported by the state as a whole. If a state is to have a foreign policy it must be able to speak at times with a single voice. War, therefore, is a particularly important time as, in war, states are most likely to be able to generate nearly unanimous backing. The unity of the nation, in fact, is partly derived from antagonism generated by international contact. Thus individuals participate in war because they are members of states and because only states can make war on other states.[18]

War is thus not to be immediately judged as good or evil any more than the man who pursues the hare. Contrary to the assumption of *Pacem in Terris*, Rousseau tried to show that even if all states were good states, that is, states that work to procure the uncoerced consent of their citizens, we would not neces-

16. Ibid., 169.
17. Ibid., 178.
18. Ibid., 179.

sarily have a world of peace. For the will of any one state is only a particular will in relation to another. The absence of any authority above states to prevent or adjust conflicts means that war is inevitable. Abstractly put, "That among particularities accidents will occur is not accidental but necessary."[19]

Theoretically, we can imagine two alternatives to war: (1) impose an effective control on separate states, or (2) remove states from the sphere of the accidental; that is, define a state that is not particularly constituted. The former possibility is fraught with its own dangers; the extent of the power necessary for such control is frightening to us. The latter is impossible since states by their very nature are formed and "maintained by nothing better than chance."[20] Indeed, our greatest danger comes when some states forget their particularity and claim universality and thus the right to determine the affairs of other states.[21]

The startling, simple implication of Rousseau's analysis is that war occurs because there is nothing to prevent it. As we cannot presume all individuals will comply uncoerced with the common good of the state, so we cannot assume states will subordinate their ends. If we seek cooperation we must accept the possibility of war. Of course, Rousseau's account does not purport to tell us how one or the other war is caused; surely in each case a wide range of circumstances and purposes is at work. Particular wars may be more or less justifiable, but war per se is never justifiably excluded as a possibility. War just is; it is neither good nor bad.

Perhaps from this perspective we can appreciate the ambiguity we often feel about war as an institution. We do not generally seek war; we think of it as something we choose when we have no other choice. Even though war is clearly a human endeavor, we tend to conceive it as an external agent, a fate that we had not willed but that we cannot but follow. It is just in the "nature" of things. War is finally no one's fault; it is an unsolicited yet unavoidable consequence of our shared activities. War in this sense is simply beyond good and evil.

Should War Be Eliminated?

Rousseau suggested that war is an unavoidable by-product of our cooperation. While in itself morally ambiguous, as a by-product of cooperation, its

19. Ibid., 182.
20. Ibid., 183.
21. I think it is not accidental that the two most imperialistic states of the twentieth century, the U.S.A. and the USSR, are both founded on the universalistic assumptions of the Enlightenment.

elimination would mean as well the extinction of cooperation. Therefore, we should not seek to eliminate war.

But there are perhaps other reasons why war should not be eliminated, which are related to this, yet distinguishable from it. These point to the moral purpose served specifically by war. We do not live in a world of a common morality. What goods we share are those that come to us through the achievement and sacrifices of our forebears. Our goods are inseparable from our histories and our histories can be preserved only as they are associated with states pledged to protect them. While no one wishes war, it may in some cases be the only way to preserve these goods.

Indeed, in war we learn to sacrifice ourselves for these goods. No morality is worthy that does not require sacrificing even our life. War also teaches us to preserve the common life, even to kill for it, precisely because the common life transcends the life of the individual. Indeed, to refuse to kill for the state would be to dishonor those who have given their lives for the morality that the state is pledged to protect. So when threatened, the good state cannot but ask us to be willing to kill in the name of the good we have achieved.

Indeed, the very achievements that we are often called upon to protect through the means of war are those that in the past have been achieved through war. We must pursue war exactly because not to do so dishonors those who have made us what we are through the sacrifices they have made in past wars. This is not simply to make the point that engagement in war breeds extraordinary camaraderie, although that is surely true. Rather, it is to say, with Hegel, that it is only in time of war that the state achieves its true universality. For only then are "the rights and interests of individuals established as a passing phase."[22]

Yet I do not think Hegel has put it quite right, for it is not a matter simply of our individual interests being qualified in times of war for the greater good. Rather, war reaffirms our history by offering us the opportunity to be worthy of our history by making similar sacrifices. We fight wars because our ancestors have fought wars. Wars provide us a way to realize our continuity with our ancestors, to locate ourselves within their continuing saga, and in the process, to give to that saga an otherwise absent coherence over time.

There is no question that war makes marvelous history to read. We like to read about war, I think, not simply because there are sometimes good and bad

---

22. Quoted in Michael Walzer, *Obligations: Essays on Disobedience, War, and Citizenship* (New York: Simon and Schuster, 1970), 184.

guys, winners and losers, but because war, unlike most of our lives, seems to be more coherent. To be sure, in the middle of a battle the participants seldom know what is going on or what they are doing, but looking back on the confusion, an order emerges that often reassures us that, whether we won or lost, we still have a damn fine story to tell. Not only to tell but to be. It is a particular story to be sure, and perhaps we tell it with a good deal of bias, but it is nonetheless ours.

In that respect I sometimes think there is a deep commonality between baseball and war. I am hesitant to make such a suggestion as it seems so frivolous, if not immoral. War is too serious for such comparisons. Yet just as baseball seems to be played not for the playing itself but for the gathering of statistics so that we may later tell the story, so wars seem to be fought so that we are able to place ourselves within a framework that gives us a place to be. We fear destruction, but even more we fear not having a niche within an ongoing history. War is our ultimate comfort in a world without a history, for it provides us with a story. To be sure, it may be a hard and even gruesome story, but such a story is better than no story at all.

I am not suggesting that we fight wars in order to have a story to tell. Rather, the stories that we learn to tell as peoples inextricably involve war as one of the major characters in the story. That this is the case perhaps helps us understand further why it is almost impossible to exclude war as an imaginative possibility from our lives. For if war is no longer a possibility, we fear we will lose the ability to locate ourselves in a worthy story or as participants in the ongoing life of a people.

In summary, I have suggested that war is to provide for as well as sustain the particular goods of particular peoples in a divided world. War is not anarchy existing between states, but rather it is anarchy's enemy insofar as it allows corporate entities, such as the nation-states, to perpetuate their own particular shared goods, to preserve their histories and moralities. Conflict in the international arena may arise not only as societies protect their histories but as they attempt to share them as well. Indeed, it sometimes appears that nations with the most in common war the most frequently and bitterly, much as within families conflict is often bitterest. As the ties of cooperation are strong so is the possibility of conflict; for, as I have argued, the two are inextricably related.

Such is the best case I can muster for the moral viability of war. It is obviously an ideal account, as the sheer stupidity, mendacity, and perversity that often gets us into war is missing. Moreover, the presumption of nation-states that their ambitions override all other interests, even those of the survival of the human species, is not taken into account. But the case I have tried to present is not meant to provide the discriminating judgments necessary to determine the wisdom of particular wars. Rather, all I have done is to suggest why some find it so hard to exclude war as a moral possibility in human affairs. You can accept my analysis and still condemn particular wars as irrational, imprudent, or immoral. What you cannot do, if this account is right, is condemn a war on the grounds that all war is fundamentally immoral.

Peace, Justice, and the Viability of Pacifism

In the preceding sections I have done my best to give an account of war as a moral institution. But in what ways has it helped us understand why Christians so often say they are advocates of peace but accept the necessity of war? Does it, for example, help us to understand why the bishops, in *The Challenge of Peace,* acknowledge the nonviolent character of the Gospel while continuing to support Christian participation in war?

As we have seen, the bishops suppose they must accept war as an inevitability in this time between the times. The peace brought by Jesus is an eschatological peace. It is God's gift and cannot be the work of humankind. While God's peace may provide the individual with a sense of future union with God, it cannot be the working principle for present relations among nations; it is but an ideal in a complex and fallen world. Some in the name of God's peace may personally renounce the use of all violence, but they can by no means stand as an example for nations or, for that matter, all Christians.

The peace that is already ours in Christ is a religious, not a political reality (*The Challenge of Peace* 55).[23] Committed as they are to this eschatological peace that is not just the absence of war but the peace that comes from justice, Christians cannot exclude the possibility of violence (68). So any pursuit of justice, any pursuit of a peace that is political, may require that Christians sadly use violence since "the struggles for justice may threaten certain forms of peace" (60).

For the bishops, Saint Augustine gave the clearest answer to the question of why Christians must resort to war even though they desire peace. Thus they

---

23. In light of the influence of liberation theology this claim seems a bit surprising; or at least one would have expected the bishops to provide a more elaborate defense. For if they wish to claim that the Gospel is political concerning matters of justice then I do not see how they can limit the Gospel's admonitions for peace to the "religious" realm.

tell us, "Augustine was impressed by the fact and the consequences of sin in history—the 'not yet' dimension of the kingdom. In his view war was both the result of sin and a tragic remedy for sin and the life of political societies. War arose from disordered ambitions, but it could also be used, in some cases at least to restrain evil and protect the innocent. The classic case which illustrated his view was the use of lethal force to prevent aggression against innocent victims. Faced with the fact of attack on the innocent, the presumption that we do no harm, even to our enemy, yielded to the command of love understood as the need to restrain an enemy who would injure the innocent. The just war argument has taken several forms in the history of Catholic theology, but this Augustinian insight is its central premise" (81–82).

In a similar manner, David Hollenbach has argued that for the just war theory the goods of peace and justice are interdependent: "Justice is regarded as the precondition of peace in the concrete political order. The pursuit of justice, even by force, can in some circumstances be the only way to fulfill the duty to promote both peace and justice."[24] Both Hollenbach and the bishops agree that the resort to war comes not from the counsel of Jesus, for to follow his nonviolent example would be to collapse the tension between the already and not yet of Christian eschatology. As long as we live in history there must exist an unresolved tension between justice and nonviolence. This tension requires the Christian to use violence in the cause of justice.[25]

The assumption that war can be a means for achieving justice entails a view of war very similar, I think, to the one I have developed. The bishops and Hollenbach assume a state has the responsibility to defend its people in the

24. David Hollenbach, *Nuclear Ethics: A Christian Moral Argument* (New York: Paulist Press, 1983), 22–23. I introduce Hollenbach's work at this point, as he has spelled out more fully the position the bishops have taken in *The Challenge of Peace*. I do not want to claim, however, that his viewpoint is identical with that of *The Challenge of Peace*.

25. Though the bishops and Hollenbach urge nonviolent forms of resistance in the interest of justice, they always hold out the possibility of violence if nonviolence does not work. Yet they fail to give any indication of how we are ever to know if nonviolence has not worked and thus we can turn to violence. I suspect behind their failure to press this issue is the assumption that war is of the essence of state action so the ability of a state to use nonviolence is extremely limited. They owe us an account, however, of how a Christian can do justice to the neighbor if we use the means that tell the neighbor that he is less obligated than we to love the enemy. For the "innocent" that we defend cannot be defended "justly" if the form of the defense belies our conviction, based on Jesus' way of dealing with the world, that the enemy is to be loved even as he attacks. Peace and justice are not equal "means" for the building of God's kingdom, but rather the justice that required the forgiveness of enemies that makes peace possible is the kingdom.

cause of justice. Yet what it means to "defend its people" is never made clear, as wars are seldom fought to protect the physical survival of a people but rather for the achievement of this or that political advantage. Behind this question are complex questions about the justification of just war thinking. For we are sometimes told that just war theory is derived from the analogy of self-defense and at other times the primary paradigm that justifies the use of violence is the defense of the innocent. While these may not be incompatible they can make a great difference to how one understands the nature and role of state power to prosecute war.[26]

However, if, as I have suggested, war is the means by which a people merely protect not their existence but their interpretation of their existence, then war in a sense does not need a "justification." Perhaps that is why some prefer to talk not about just war, but of justified war.[27] The justice war protects is the cooperative achievement by a people that often has been the result of their ancestors' waging war for limited moral goods.[28]

Aside from the individualistic analogy often employed, we are reminded in this context that just war theory is much more a theory of state action than a justification of individual response to attack. In other words, the primary actor required by just war thinking is not the individual, but the state acting on behalf of its society. Here the theory can be correlated with my previous account. In a sense, only the state has the right of self-defense for it alone has the responsibility of defending that history that makes a people a people. "The state" is the name we give to those charged with upholding the patterns of

26. Paul Ramsey has provided the strongest defense of just war logic on the paradigm of defense of the innocent. I suspect that is why Ramsey places so much emphasis on the principle of discrimination as the overriding criterion for the justifiability of war. The bishops, unfortunately, seem to move uncritically from appeals to self-defense to defense of the innocent without noting how they make a difference to how one derives the various criteria of just war or their priority. The analysis of war I have provided, however, is meant to provide them a way out of this difficulty. For in effect they can say the justification of just war for a nation-state can be put in the language of self-defense because its larger intention is to defend the innocent within the state. Therefore, the fundamental intention of just war at an individual level is defense of the innocent, but as a social policy it appears in the form of "self"-defense, but the "self" is a public agent.

27. See, for example, Paul Ramsey, *The Just War: Force and Political Responsibility* (New York: Scribner's Sons, 1968), 4–18.

28. Since the task is to protect the past goods achieved by war, the criteria of discrimination may not be overriding for a state's prosecution of war. Therefore, from a just war perspective, the bishops may be right to suggest that the principle of proportionality is just as, if not more, important than discrimination for determining the morality of nuclear warfare.

cooperation achieved by our society to preserve our particular shared goods. To preserve that cooperation and relative peace the state must be prepared to wage war against any who would threaten it. That is the "justice" that war protects.

This kind of interpretation of the "justice" of the state, I think, may be the necessary presumption to make clear why, in spite of a tacit affirmation of peace, the bishops continue to insist that nations have the right and duty to defend themselves against an unjust aggressor. But if this account is right, then I think the bishops need to be more candid than they have been about the status of peace. For I do not see how you can give nations the right to defend themselves and yet, at the same time, maintain that peace is not only the ideal but the normal state of affairs among nations. For are you not required to recognize that such a "peace" is but the justice dependent on the continued possibility of war?[29]

In this respect I do not see how the bishops can maintain, as they try to do, the right of some to be nonviolent. That they do so is, of course, extraordinary; *imagine* Roman Catholics ever hinting that pacifism is an option as appropriate for Christians as just war! Yet surely an affirmation of pacifism cannot but seriously qualify the bishops' defense of just war as not merely the means of peace but also as the form just peace must take in this "time between the times."

The bishops, however, are very careful in their support for the pacifist position. For they are very clear that their support is for the pacifist options for "individuals" (119). Moreover, they suggest that this "new moment" determined by our possession of nuclear weapons has meant an increasing convergence between pacifist and just war positions. For "they share a common presumption against the use of force as a means of settling disputes. Both find their roots in the Christian theological tradition; each contributes to the full moral vision we need in pursuit of a human peace. We believe the two perspectives support and complement one another, each preserving the other

---

29. In *The Just War: Force and Political Responsibility,* Paul Ramsey is admirably clear that the great task is to save war and politics for purposeful use by mankind. Therefore, the task is not to make war impossible, but to make it serve human ends through disciplining it through a politics formed by just war commitments. Therefore, just war is commensurate with the assumption that war is not the exception in international relations but the norm. The bishops, however, drawing on the assumptions of *Pacem in Terris,* seem to presume that war is the exception. I am simply suggesting that their position would be more consistent if they had followed Ramsey's lead.

from distortion" (120–21). At any rate, the bishops never propose, nor can they propose, pacifism as an option for statecraft.[30]

Hollenbach is even more adamant in his support of pacifism as an option for some Christians. Both pacifism and just war positions are necessary if

> the full content of Christian hope is to be made visible in history. Each of these ethical stances bears witness to an essential part of the Christian mystery. Each of them, however, is incomplete by itself. Within time it is simply not possible to embody the fullness of the kingdom of God in a single form of life or a single ethical standard. Thus if the Christian community is to be

30. Michael Novak, unlike the bishops, denies that pacifism, even of an individual sort, is required by the New Testament. The peace offered by Jesus is not the absence of war, but a form of knowing and being in union with God. It is a mistake, though one that is honored, to believe that we are called to imitate Jesus' nonviolence, as it is a misreading of Scripture as well as the Catholic tradition. Novak argues that we must "sharply distinguish between pacifism as a personal commitment, implicating only a person who is not a public figure responsible for the lives of others, and pacifism as a public policy, compromising many who are not pacifists and endangering the very possibility of pacifism itself. It is not justice if the human race as a whole or in part is heaped with indignities, spat upon, publicly humiliated, destroyed, as Jesus was. It is not moral to permit the human race so to endure the injustice of the passion and death of Christ" (*Moral Clarity in the Nuclear Age* [Nashville, TN: Thomas Nelson, 1983], 34). Novak's argument is to the point, but I think he has not pressed it consistently enough. For why does he not argue further that Jesus was wrong to allow himself to die at the hands of such injustice? Or why not argue that at least the disciples should have come to Jesus' aid since Jesus' teaching should have convinced them that their overriding duty was to aid the innocent against injustice? One cannot but feel that those who defend so strongly the use of violence in the service of justice are finally trying to rescue Jesus from the cross. See, for example, Carol Oglesby, "Rescuing Jesus from the Cross," *CoEvolution Quarterly* 39 (fall 1983): 36–41. [Eds. note: see also the beginning of essay 12 in this volume.]

It is not easy to characterize the difference between Novak's position and that of the bishops for it is not simply a difference about how to understand the facts and strategic alternatives. Rather, it involves profound assumptions about the status of the just war theory as well as where one begins reflection on the ethics of war. Novak, unlike the bishops, does not assume that you can begin with the just war criteria and then ask in a legalistic way whether nuclear strategy conforms or does not conform to those criteria. Rather, one must begin with an interpretation on the international situation that relativizes the status of the just war theory. Thus he says, "Virtually all arguments about the prevention of nuclear war hinge on judgments concerning the nature of the Soviet Union and its nuclear forces" (49). Even apart from the question of whether Novak's account of the Soviet Union and his depiction of the international situation is correct, he has not given us more reasons for why we should begin our ethical analysis of nuclear war with the international context. Indeed, given Novak's account, it is extremely unclear why he bothers to treat the just war theory at all. For a more detailed critique of Novak's views, particularly his rather odd view of "intention," see James Cameron, "Nuclear Catholics," *New York Review of Books* 30, no. 20 (December 22, 1983): 38–42.

faithful to the full meaning of the paschal mystery as the inauguration of the kingdom of God, there must be a pluralism of ethical stances represented within it. I would conclude, therefore, that both the pacifist and the just war ethic are legitimate and necessary expressions of the Christian faith. The necessity of such pluralism in approaching the morality of warfare is a particular case of the more general theological truth that the kingdom of God cannot be fully expressed in any single historical way of living or hierarchy of values. Pacifism and just war theory are both historical syntheses of a particular aspect of the Christian hope with an historical-political interpretation of how the basic values of justice and peace are related to each other within time. The fact that these two traditions have been present within the Christian community for millennia has not been an accident but a theological necessity.[31]

Thus those who adhere to just war need the pacifist to remind them of the centrality of nonviolence that is too easily lost amid the intricacies of public policy debates. Pacifists, on the other hand, need the just war representatives to remind them of the centrality of justice and that Christian responsibility can never be limited simply by avoiding evil but requires the positive promotion of both justice and peace.

It may seem terribly ungrateful for me as a pacifist to argue against this unusual acceptance of the pacifist position, but I think there are important reasons for doing so; or more accurately, I fear that the approval of pacifism as a stance for individuals may seem to put the bishops more firmly on the side of peace than they are. They seem to support pacifism when in fact the structure of their argument ought to lead them to be more candid about their support of war. If, as they maintain, it is not just a right but a duty of a state to defend itself through the force of arms, pacifists act irresponsibly insofar as they absent themselves from the joint moral undertaking that the state must perform.

Of course, in times of peace it may be that the state has the resources sufficient to give some the privilege to follow their conscience against war. Such a policy can make sense on a number of pragmatic grounds since such people may make poor soldiers, or to grant them exemption from military service may result in taking some of the moral heat off the military. Yet it is difficult to understand how a state can perpetuate such a policy when its existence is being threatened if in fact, as the Pastoral argues, a people threatened with unjust aggression "may not remain passively indifferent" (76).

31. Hollenbach, 31.

In spite of the general statements about peace in the Pastoral, it continues to assume that those who would take the pacifist stance, even as individuals, bear the burden of proof. They bear the burden of proof because, the bishops presume, states are the bearers of our history, and nations (as I have argued) rely upon war or the possibility of war to sustain our history. Indeed, the assumption that the state bears our history leads straight to the affirmation that war is not just a necessity caused by sin, but an institution morally necessary for the protection of the goods of a society. And if it is such, then those who refuse to go to war have made a decisive moral mistake.

Although Hollenbach tends to interpret the difference between just war and pacifist positions primarily in strategic terms, he must as well give a secondary status to pacifism. The pacifist tradition "argues the nontheological part of its case against the just war on a competing historical-political inter-pretation of the relation between nonviolence and justice. It maintains the use of force inevitably contributes to an escalating spiral of both violence and injustice."[32] While the advent of nuclear weapons has certainly given new weight to this pacifist position, nonetheless it cannot "be made the basis for a political ethic for a pluralist society."[33] In contrast, the just war is an attempt to consider how the "basic values of life, freedom, justice, etc., are related to each other in the light of our historical experience and our practical understanding of the political order."[34] Thus the ultimate problem with pacifists is that they are "prepared to tolerate injustice in the limit situation where justice cannot be attained by nonviolent means."[35]

Hollenbach's account, therefore, seems but another version of the sugges-tion that the pacifist is useful to remind those who are really concerned about justice that violence may finally be self-defeating, but pacifism cannot be a stance of the church. The crucial claim by Hollenbach is that pacifism cannot be made the political ethic for a pluralist society, that is, a society that has its

---

32. Ibid., 43. Hollenbach, therefore, at least seems to suggest that pacifism might be a social policy.

33. Ibid. Like the bishops, Hollenbach assumes that the church's social ethics must be one amenable to the non-Christian. Yet, he confuses that issue with the claims that Christian convictions must be capable of being construed in policy terms. The latter may be possible without those strategies being agreeable to non-Christians.

34. Ibid. The problem with such claims is that such values are so abstractly put that we cannot be sure what institutional form they may assume. It may be that some who argue against nuclear war because it threatens survival itself are right to remind us that values such as freedom can be idolatrous when they make our very survival problematic.

35. Ibid., 28.

being shaped and protected by war. For the "just war theory, the goods of peace and justice are interdependent, but justice is regarded as the precondition of peace in the concrete political order. The pursuit of justice, even by force, can in some circumstances be the only way to fulfill the duty to promote both peace and justice."[36]

The affirmation of pluralism, however, is not as free from cost as Hollenbach suggests. For it appears that by embracing both pacifism and just war theory he can provide the means to achieve justice in a pluralist society. He assumes such a society is so significant that the Gospel's command of peace can be qualified in the interest of the "justice" such a society represents.

I do not think, therefore, that Hollenbach can resolve the tension between pacifist and just war theories as easily as he suggests. On the one hand, Hollenbach and the bishops both want to say that just war is the attempt to set down the "conditions under which exceptions to the general obligation to nonviolence might be made," and there is certainly some truth to that.[37] But on the other hand, they want to maintain that war is the character of our lives "between the times," as the failure to go to war cannot but result in injustice. From this latter perspective the just war theory is not just a theory of exceptions, but an attempt to limit the destructive potential of war once it is recognized as a moral necessity. On this account the theory of just war denies pacifism; it does not attempt to make war impossible, but rather to make the moral necessity of war serve human purposes. As such, it would seem that the bishops and Hollenbach should welcome the account I have tried to give concerning why war cannot morally be eliminated from our lives.

The Elimination of War: A Theological Imperative

By developing a moral case for war I have tried to help us understand the ambivalence about war among Christians. We say we want peace yet we still hold out the possibility of war. I have taken *The Challenge of Peace* as a prime example of this ambivalence as the bishops, who strive to take the Gospel imperatives for peace so seriously, seem yet unable to free themselves from the assumption that Christians must still be willing to support war in the interest of justice. Such ambivalence takes form in eschatological appeals to our living between the times, when our ideals must be compromised by the recognition

36. Ibid., 23. Hollenbach's basic mistake is to think that justice and peace are the means to build the kingdom rather than the form of the kingdom itself.
37. Ibid., 37.

of our sinful condition. Thus, the bishops uphold the right, if not duty, of nations to defend themselves, thereby underwriting the hold war has over our imaginations. While we all want to minimize war in general, we will not relinquish the possibility of war for our national communities. We do so not simply because we believe we live in a sinful world, but because we believe that our nations are the bearer of commitments and goods that justice compels us to defend even if such defense requires war. We wish for peace but plan for war; and we get it.

My analysis, I believe, pushes the bishops in the direction that they clearly want to avoid. To this it may be objected that I have treated the bishops unfairly as they give every indication that they wish to rid the world of war.[38] Quoting John Paul II, they say, "Today, the scale and the horror of modern warfare—whether nuclear or not—makes it totally unacceptable as a means of settling differences between nations. War should belong to the tragic past, to history; it should find no place on humanity's agenda for the future" (219). Surely by criticizing nuclear weapons the bishops do not mean to encourage war. Moreover, they underwrite the concern to develop nonviolent ways for conflict resolution, rejecting the argument that pacifists have no response to violence (221–30). Yet one must question how seriously such suggestions are to be taken as long as the bishops unwaveringly affirm that Christians can in times of stress resort to violence. As long as the bishops entertain the moral possibility of war I cannot see how they can avoid its actuality.

But did they (and do we) have an alternative? I believe we do. It is an alternative to which the bishops point in their sensitive portrayal of the peace brought by Jesus' life, death, and resurrection. Such a peace, as the bishops quite rightly note, is not simply the absence of war, but rather it is a peace that is itself an alternative to a world at war. As such it is not some ideal, but an actual way of life among a concrete group of people. The bishops are quite right, it is an eschatological peace, but they are wrong to think it can be ours only on the "edge of history." Rather, it means that we must see peace as a possibility amid a world at war.[39] The decisive issue is how we understand the

---

38. I may have been particularly unfair to the bishops by treating what is essentially a political document as if it should be conceptually coherent. Indeed, in many ways the document is stronger exactly because it is a hodgepodge of different positions representing the different viewpoints of the various bishops. Yet the bishops say they want to be true to the intent of the Gospel and as much as I am able, I want to help them do just that.

39. For a marvelous account of a spirituality of peace, see Rowan Williams, *The Truce of God*

eschatological nature of God's peace. The bishops stress the "already but not yet" as a way of legitimating Christian participation in war. But, as the bishops also indicate, to view the world eschatologically does not mean simply to mark the kingdom as yet to come, for in fact the kingdom has been made present fully in Jesus Christ. That is why they rightly say that Jesus' words requiring us to forgive one another, the requirement to love our enemy more than all others, are not just ideals but possibilities here and now (45, 48). Thus Jesus "made the tender mercy of God present in a world that knew violence, oppression and injustice" (15).

God's "tender mercy" is not a sense of forgiveness that comes after we have had to use violence for justice, though such forgiveness certainly is not withheld, but rather his "tender mercy" makes it possible to stand against the world's tragic assumption that war can be the means to justice. To be sure, here a different understanding of eschatology from that of the bishops is at work, but I believe it is one that is closer to that of the New Testament. For the bishops seem to have accepted the view that the early Christians were nonviolent only because they had a mistaken apocalyptic idea that the world was soon to end. When that end failed to arrive Christians reluctantly took up the means of violence in the interest of justice. In fact, what we now know of the New Testament eschatology differs from such a view. To be sure, the early Christians looked for God's reign immediately to become a reality for all people, but that did not qualify their dedication to live in that reign here and now.[40]

(New York: Pilgrim Press, 1984). One of Williams's strongest themes is that peace is not simply what is left when social constraints have all vanished. Such a conception of peace he rightly criticizes as infantile, for the world created by such a peace is one where nothing happens and nothing is left to do. Rather, the peace that is identified with Christian reconciliation is that which requires change and newness of life, not only of the heart, but in the structures of politics and industry (58).

40. For a fuller defense of this view, see my PK.

In "The Moral Methodology of the Bishops' Pastoral," Charles Curran suggests that "much New Testament moral teaching is influenced by the eschatological coloring of the times; that is, many thought that the end of history was coming quickly, and such an understanding obviously colored their approach to moral questions. However, our understanding of eschatology is quite different. It is our understanding that the end-time has begun in Christ Jesus but will be completed only in his second-coming" (Catholics and Nuclear War, 47). While I doubt the simplicity of Curran's description of early Christian attitudes about eschatology, I still do not see why he thinks that makes a difference about how Christians are to understand the New Testament. For the early Christians did not think they refrained from

The eschatology of the New Testament rests not in the conviction that the kingdom has not fully come, but that it has. What is required is not a belief in some ideal amid the ambiguities of history, but rather a recognition that we have entered a period in which two ages overlap. As John Howard Yoder has observed, "These aeons are not distinct periods of time, for they exist simultaneously. They differ rather in nature or in direction; one points backwards to human history outside of (before) Christ; the other points forward to the fullness of the kingdom of God, of which it is a foretaste. Each aeon has a social manifestation: the former in the 'world,' the latter in the body of Christ."[41]

The Christian commitment to nonviolence is therefore not first of all an "ethic" but a declaration of the reality of the new age. Again, as Yoder puts it:

> Non-resistance is thus not a matter of legalism but of discipleship, nor "thou shalt not" but "as he is so are we in this world" (I Jn. 4:17), and it is especially in relation to evil that discipleship is meaningful. Every strand of New Testament literature testifies to a direct relationship between the way Christ suffered on the cross and the way the Christian, as disciple, is called to suffer in the face of evil (Mt. 10:38; Mk. 10:38f; 8:34ff; Lk. 14:27). Solidarity with Christ ("discipleship") must often be in tension with the wider human solidarity (Jn. 15:20; II Cor. 1:5; 4:10; Phil. 1:29). It is not going too far to affirm that the new thing revealed in Christ was this attitude to the old aeon including force and self-defense. The cross was not in itself a new revelation; Isaiah 53 foresaw already the path which the Servant of Yahweh would have to tread. Nor was the resurrection essentially new; God's victory over evil had been affirmed, by definition one might say, from the beginning. Nor was the selection of a faithful remnant a new idea. What was centrally new about Christ was that these ideas became incarnate. But superficially the greatest novelty and the occasion of stumbling was His willingness to sacrifice, in the interest of non-resistant love, all other forms of human solidarity, including the legitimate national interests of the chosen people. The Jews had been told that in Abra-

---

violence because the end of history was soon to come; rather, they refrained from violence because, as Curran suggests, they thought the end time had come.

One cannot but feel an uneasiness on the part of many Catholic moralists about the methodology of the Pastoral. The "conservatives" cannot but be worried about the implications for other questions of the moral life. For if you are willing to appeal to the ambiguity of the moral case caused by sin then why not apply the same moral logic to abortion? The "liberals" may rejoice in that result, yet they may at the same time wish the bishops had been more forthright in their condemnation of nuclear war.

41. John Howard Yoder, *The Original Revolution* (Scottdale, PA: Herald Press, 1971), 58.

ham all the nations would be blessed and had understood this promise as the vindication of their nationalism. Jesus revealed that the contrary was the case: the universality of God's kingdom contradicts rather than confirms all particular solidarities and can be reached only by first forsaking the old aeon. (Lk. 18:28–30)[42]

So, in spite of the bishops' (and Hollenbach's) attempt to clear a space for the pacifist, I cannot accept the terms of their acceptance. For pacifism and just war are not simply two ethical strategies for the achievement of God's justice in the world. Rather, they draw on different assumptions about history and its relation to God's kingdom. The debate between pacifism and just war thinking is a theological issue of how we are to read and interpret history. I have argued that war is part and parcel of societies' histories, a necessary part that provides them with their sense of moral purpose and destiny. The problem with those histories is not that they are devoid of moral substance, but that they are not God's history. They are not the way God would have his kingdom present in the world. The debate between pacifism and just war thinking is, therefore, a theological question of how we are to read and interpret history.

Christians believe that the true history of the world, that history that determines our destiny, is not carried by the nation-state. In spite of its powerful moral appeal, this history is the history of godlessness. Only the church has the stance, therefore, to describe war for what it is, for the world is too broken to know the reality of war.[43] For what is war but the desire to be rid of God, to claim for ourselves the power to determine our meaning and destiny? Our desire to protect ourselves from our enemies, to eliminate our enemies in the name of protecting the common history we share with our friends, is but the manifestation of our hatred of God.[44]

42. Ibid., 60–61.

43. The account of war I developed above is parasitic on Christian presuppositions insofar as a unity of history is presupposed from which war could be described. But, in fact, there is no such unity in history other than that provided by the church. Otherwise war is relative to each people's history. We thus often seek to deny to the other side the right to describe their violence as war. For example, barbarians cannot be warriors since they do not fight in a civilized manner; a bombing in London by the IRA is terrorism, not war. From this perspective, war can be seen as a progressive conversation between diverse peoples about the meaning of war itself. World war is a moral achievement as it suggests all sides have the right to describe their violence as war. Insofar as nuclear weapons force all to have a stake in war, they can be seen as a moral advance reflecting our increasing interdependence.

44. For an unrelenting account of war along these lines, see Dale Aukerman, *Darkening Valley*

Christians have been offered the possibility of a different history through participation in a community in which one learns to love the enemy. They are thus a people who believe that God will have them exist through history without the necessity of war. God has done so by providing the world with a history through the church. For without the church we are but a scattered people with nothing in common. Only through the church do we learn that we share the same creator and destiny. So the world's true history is not that built on war, but that offered by a community that witnesses to God's refusal to give up on his creation.

This does not mean that our existence is constituted by two histories. There is only one true history: the history of God's peaceable kingdom. Christians can admit no ultimate dualism between God's history and the world's history. The peace we believe we have been offered is not just for us but is the peace for all, just as we believe our God is the God of all. Thus we do not preclude the possibility that a state could exist for which war is not a possibility. To deny such a possibility would be the ultimate act of unbelief, for who are we to determine the power of God's providential care of the world?[45]

Christians, therefore, offer a "moral equivalent to war" in William James's sense by first offering themselves. James rightly saw that the essential problem for the elimination of war lies in our imagination. Under the power of history created by war we cannot morally imagine a world without war. But James's suggestion that we find new contexts to sustain the virtues that arise in war is too weak. What is required is not simply discovering new contexts to sustain martial virtues, but rather an alternative history. Precisely this God has offered

---

(New York: Seabury Press, 1981). Aukerman observes:

> The dual drives to be rid of God and the countering brother—the opposite of the dual loves to which we are called—coincided completely in the drama of the murder of Jesus. Malice toward the visible brother formed a continuum with the rejection of the unseen God; the judicial murder of the brother was at the same time an attempt to do away with God . . . Still, as Christians we can at times discern in ourselves the dual drives to be rid of God and our enemy. The desire to be rid of God lies behind all of my sinning; the desire to do away with the enemy is the identifiable extreme of what is wrong with me. This means that any manifestation of the drive to be rid of a fellow human being—the hostility-hatred-murder continuum—carries with it inseparably the drive to be rid of God and veers back across the centuries into that crucifixion of the Christ. (45)

45. I am indebted to Robert and Blanche Jenson for helping me put the matter this way. For the pacifist is tempted to condemn the state to the necessity of war, but if we do so we but become the other side of the just war position. Theologically we may not know how God can provide for the possibility of a nonviolent state, but neither can we act as if such were not a possibility.

through the life, death, and resurrection of Jesus of Nazareth. Such an alternative is not an unrealizable ideal. No, it is present now in the church, a real alternative able to free our imagination from the capacity of war.

For the imagination is not simply a container of images or ideas that we now entertain in preference to other images and ideas. Rather, the imagination is a set of habits and relations that can only be carried by a group of people in distinction from the world's habits. For example, nothing is more important for the church's imagination than the meal we share together in the presence of our crucified and resurrected Lord. For it is in that meal, that set of habits and relations, that the world is offered an alternative to the habits of disunity that war breeds.

In the practice of such a meal we can see that the morality that makes war seem so necessary to our lives is deeply flawed. For it is a morality that sees no alternative to war as the necessary means to sustain our particular loyalties. It leads us to suppose those loyalties can be protected, we think, only by eliminating the threat of the other, be it aggression or merely strangeness. But in the meal provided by the Lord of history we discover our particularity is not destroyed but enhanced by the coming of the stranger. In the church we find an alternative to war exactly because there we learn to make others' histories part of our own. We are able to do so because God has shown us the way by making us a new people through the life, death, and resurrection of Jesus Christ.[46]

From this perspective "Should war be eliminated?" is a false question. It is not a false question because the elimination of war is impossible or because war has a moral viability that means we should not eliminate it. Rather, it is a

---

46. Such a position is at least suggested by the bishops in *The Challenge of Peace*, as they say, "Building peace within and among nations is the work of many individuals and institutions; it is the fruit of ideas and decisions taken in the political, cultural, economic, social, military, and legal sectors of life. We believe that the Church, as a community of faith and social institution, has a proper, necessary, and distinctive part to play in the pursuit of peace. The distinctive contribution of the Church flows from her religious nature and ministry. The Church is called to be, in a unique way, the instrument of God in history. Since peace is one of the signs of that kingdom present in the world, the Church fulfills part of her essential mission by making the peace of the kingdom more visible in our time" (21–22).

In a manner similar to some of the criticisms I have made, Joseph Komonchak suggests that some may "wonder why the bishops do not make more of the redemptive role of Christ and the church as an instrument in history of his word and grace. The latter, of course, is not denied, but it certainly does not occupy a major role. If it had, it might have been possible to stress more than is now done the 'already' aspect of the Christian faith" ("Kingdom, History, and Church," in *Catholics and Nuclear War*, 109).

false question because war has been eliminated for those who participate in God's history. The miracle we call the church is God's sign that war is not part of his providential care of the world. Our happy task as Christians is to witness to that fact.

But perhaps all this misses the point. To say the church is the carrier of a history other than the history of war sounds lofty, but in fact we know we do not live in such a history. We continue to live in a history determined by nation-states, where war shows no signs of abating. Even worse, it is a world now threatened by nuclear annihilation. Do Christians, because of their commitment to peace, say that is too bad for the world and let others do their fighting for them? Or do they follow the Augustinian solution, noting that the two histories are hopelessly mixed together on this side of the eschaton so we are required to use the means of violence to support the history of the world?

Once again we have arrived at a false alternative. Christian commitment to nonviolence does not require withdrawal from the world and the world's violence. Rather, it requires the Christian to be in the world with an enthusiasm that cannot be defeated, for he or she knows that the power of war is not easily broken. Christians, therefore, cannot avoid, just as the bishops have not tried to avoid, attempting one step at a time to make the world less war-determined. We do that exactly by entering into the complex world of deterrence and disarmament strategy believing that a community nurtured on the habits of peace might be able to see new opportunities not otherwise present. For what creates new opportunities is being a kind of people who have been freed from the assumption that war is our fate.

Christian commitment to nonviolence is a way of life for the long haul. Exactly because we understand how morally compelling war can be we know what a challenge we face. That is why we offer the world not simply moral advice designed to make war less destructive, but a witness to God's invitation to join a community that is so imaginative, so rich in its history that it gives us the means to resist the temptation to give our loyalties to those that would use them for war. At Babel we were scattered, each having our own language and history, and even those who followed Jesus were scattered prior to his death, yet in his resurrection we have been gathered again to be part of God's history. In him we have our peace, by his grace we can be of good cheer since he has overcome the world (Jn. 16:32–33).[47]

47. I am indebted to David Burrell, James Burtchaell, and John Howard Yoder for reading and criticizing an earlier version of this chapter. Carol Descoteaux contributed much to the

Further Reading

"On Being a Church Capable of Addressing a World at War" (1988), essay 21 in this
     volume

"On Surviving Justly: Ethics and Nuclear Disarmament" (1984), in AN

"An Eschatological Perspective on Nuclear Disarmament" (1984), in AN

"Can a Pacifist Think about War?" (1994), in DF

"Whose 'Just' War? Which Peace?" (1992), in DF

"Tragedy and Joy: The Spirituality of Peaceableness" (1983), in PK

editing of this manuscript. I owe a special debt of gratitude to Charles Pinches for his close
critique of the manuscript. I only wish I knew how to respond to the many questions he
raised. Philip Rossi, S.J., and Michael Duffey of Marquette University also helped save me
from some obvious errors.

21. On Being a Church Capable of Addressing a World at War: A Pacifist Response to the United Methodist Bishops' Pastoral *In Defense of Creation* (1988)

This essay is Hauerwas's contribution to Speak Up for Just War or Pacifism, *coauthored with fellow Methodist Paul Ramsey. As committed Methodists, both found sorely inadequate the "survivalist" assumptions of* In Defense of Creation *(1985), the United Methodist Bishops' pastoral letter on nuclear war, for which both had been invited to be theological advisors. While holding significantly different viewpoints on the morality of war, Ramsey and Hauerwas shared the conviction that United Methodists deserved an articulation of the morality of war that more adequately engaged their tradition. Hauerwas seeks to articulate what difference it makes for Christians to understand the eschatological character of peace. Arguing that the bishops' views are largely shaped by the Christian realism of Reinhold Niebuhr, he argues that a "defensible Christian pacifism . . . derives its intelligibility not from any one set of teachings of Jesus, but rather from the very form of his life and death." In addition to responding to some of Ramsey's own challenges to Christian pacifism, Hauerwas concludes that the bishops should have reminded the church that "even in the face of the prospect of nuclear destruction, God has given us the time to be a people of peace."*

"Perhaps in this time of God's patience we should speak of the church for the church about being the church—no more, let that witness be overheard or not by the 'world of today.' "[1] Without overlooking the "perhaps," this is an extraordinary statement by Paul Ramsey. I suspect it will surprise many who know of Ramsey's writings on war. It is my own view that what Ramsey has written in his response to the United Methodist Bishops is not surprising

[Originally published as the epilogue to Paul Ramsey's *Speak Up for Just War or Pacifism: A Critique of the United Methodist Bishops' Pastoral Letter "In Defense of Creation: The Nuclear Crisis and a Just Peace"* (University Park: Pennsylvania State University Press, 1988), 149–82. Copyright 1988 by The Pennsylvania State University. Reproduced by permission of the publisher.]

1. [Paul Ramsey, *Speak Up for Just War or Pacifism*, 142.]

given his past work, but my primary concern is not to place this book within the context of Ramsey's reflection on the morality of war. Rather I, as a pacifist, must do what Ramsey has tried to do as a just war advocate—namely, say how I think our Bishops should have addressed our church and world.

Yet in doing so I cannot avoid making reference to Ramsey's arguments and specific challenges to me. I am convinced that Ramsey has written a remarkable book about a quite unremarkable statement by the Methodist Bishops. Indeed, I almost regret the quality of Ramsey's response, since it may give the Bishops' statement longer life than it deserves. As will be clear from what follows, I am in agreement with almost every criticism Ramsey has to make of *In Defense of Creation*. That is why I am writing this epilogue. I hope that our common criticism of the Bishops will help direct attention to the issues that make the continuing debate between pacifists and just war advocates so important for the life of the church. For it is Ramsey's and my common conviction that, contrary to the Bishops' claim, the nuclear crisis has not posed questions of faith that point beyond just war or pacifism.[2]

I must begin my response where Ramsey ended his. In the sentence quoted above, as well as in his "Almost thou persuadest me,"[3] Ramsey suggests that—due to the character of our current cultural and political situation, as well as the accommodated character of the contemporary church—it may be necessary for the church to speak to itself about ethics before it speaks to the world. I am sure Ramsey is right about this, but I need to explain why *what is for him a judgment about our current political and ecclesial situation is for me a continual problem* for the church in any age. For that is the challenge Ramsey thinks we pacifists have failed to address, namely, how a pacifist church can be the church and at the same time speak *to the point* on military questions. My quick response is that a pacifist church is not in principle prevented from so speaking. It just must do so the way porcupines make love: very, very carefully.

2. [The United Methodist Bishops, *In Defense of Creation: The Nuclear Crisis and a Just Peace* (Nashville, TN: Graded Press, 1986). Subsequent references are in the text. Alan Geyer, executive director of the Churches' Center for Theology and Public Policy, was the principal author of the document. The actual text of the bishops' pastoral letter is found on pp. 91–93. For the full context of the bishops' argument and policy recommendations, see the "foundation document," 11–22, 74–90.]

3. [Ramsey, *Speak Up*, 142. Ramsey's full statement reads: "Hauerwas, almost thou persuadest me that speaking up for real pacifism (and other Christian distinctives) is as apt to impress and work its way into the ethos of the United Methodist Church as speaking up for the imperatives and limitations of just war is to impress and work its way into the moral and political ethos of our nation."]

Yet Ramsey is right to raise the question, for as he well knows, in my testimony before the Methodist Bishops in Washington I urged them to refrain from addressing the wider society, and certainly to refrain from addressing issues of nuclear strategy and/or policy. I did not want our Bishops taking positions on the Strategic Defense Initiative and/or whether we ought or ought not to recommend a zero-option plan for Europe. The reasons I wanted our Bishops to refrain from such recommendations were not only the ones already set forth by Ramsey but because such strategic questions beg the theological issues to which the Bishops should direct our attention. But alas, it was soon clear to me that the Bishops and the drafting team could not hear or understand why I was making such a recommendation, so intent were they on making a "public" impact.

I feared that if our Bishops took as their audience the wider society they would wander into the wasteland of "crisis" language about nuclear war. In other words, I feared that the Bishops would give theological legitimacy to the widespread secular assumption that nuclear war must be condemned because it threatens the survival of the human species, if not the earth itself. Thus I (and Ramsey, even though we had written our testimony independent of one another) urged the Bishops to avoid such "survivalist" rhetoric, noting that what we must fear as Christians is not our deaths at the hands of an unjust aggressor but how as Christians we might serve the neighbor without resorting to unjust means. In urging such a strategy, I did not think I was asking our Bishops to take a pacifist stance. At the time I was unaware that in 1972 the Methodist Church had declared war incompatible with the teachings and example of Christ.[4] Rather, I was trying to ask the church to at least live up to the standards of a just war church that might prophetically challenge the nationalist and survivalist assumptions of our society and unfortunately of many in our churches.[5]

In all candor I must admit I had an ulterior motive informing this strategy.

4. [See the Social Principles statement on "Military Service" in para. 76.D of the 1972 edition of *The United Methodist Book of Discipline* (Nashville, TN: United Methodist Publishing House, 1973), 95, which states: "Though coercion, violence and war are presently the ultimate sanctions in international relations, we reject them as incompatible with the gospel and spirit of Christ." Although this statement has been amplified at a few points, the substance of the church's position on war has remained basically the same in all subsequent editions of the Book of Discipline, which is revised quadrennially.]

5. For my critique of the Bishops along these lines, see "A Pacifist Response to *In Defense of Creation*," *Asbury Theological Journal* 41, no. 2 (fall 1986): 5–14. I had developed this line of argument earlier in "An Eschatological Perspective on Nuclear Disarmament" (1982) in AN.

It has long been my suspicion that, if we could force just war thinkers (and churches) to recognize the disciplined kind of communities necessary to sustain the discourse and practices necessary for just war, it would make it increasingly difficult to accuse pacifists of being hopeless "idealists" or "sectarians." Therefore, in calling for our chief pastors to take as their primary audience the Methodist people, I was trying to remind them that the first word we as Christians have to say to the world about war is "church." In other words, as Christians we do not so much have an alternative ethic to the world's way of war—we are the alternative.

I wanted our Bishops to follow the example of the early Quakers who, in speaking against slavery, first spoke to their slave-owning brothers and sisters. I am not convinced that as a church we are ready to speak to the world about war. Thus recently, in the 1986 Duke Divinity School convocation, I asked a class of seventy-five pastors how many of them had even heard of just war prior to the Bishops' letter. Only a third raised their hands. And at a recent talk on the Bishops' letter at a Methodist church in Durham, I was told by the laity that it was unthinkable to ask Christians to qualify their loyalty to America by appealing to Christian convictions. As one man put it with no visible sign of shame, "Just look at us; we obviously do not follow Jesus."

Of course, it might be objected that these examples support the Bishops' assumption that they should write something to challenge Christians and non-Christians alike to awaken from their nuclear numbness. Without doubting the goodwill that underlies the Bishops' effort, I cannot help but think the project fundamentally misconceived. For when you have a church where the laity thinks it is legitimate to disavow in public the commitment to follow Jesus, then you do not draft statements about war. Rather, what is needed is a much more fundamental challenge to the Methodist people concerning the basic convictions and practices that make us Christians in the first place. Pacifism and just war (at least if Ramsey is right in his account of just war) are only intelligible against the background of faith in Jesus as the Lord's anointed. If that faith is missing, then pacifism and just war alike become hollow abstractions inviting casuistical games at best and ideological perversions at worst.

For this reason I found myself less than enthusiastic about the Bishops' plan to draft a statement on nuclear war. I am not convinced such statements foster the sort of moral discourse necessary for the church to sustain an ongoing witness. Indeed, I suspect there is almost an inverse ratio between the undisciplined character of the Methodist people and the radical nature of our social statements. We draft radical statements as a substitute for being a radical people pledged to witness to the world that God's peace is not just some ideal but a present possibility for us.

In the following I will try to indicate how I think a pacifist church can be the church and still speak to the society and state about war policy. But far more important for me is that the church must first be the church. As Ramsey rightly notes, I have no use for distinctions between visible and invisible church. The church can be no less real than he who was crucified. The church cannot be an ideal that is never quite realized. Rather, the church must be as real as the nation we confront if we are to be capable of challenging its imperial pretension.

That the contemporary church in America may seem to lack the discipline to be either pacifist or just war should not determine how we argue as theologians or how Bishops should exercise their pastoral duties. Ramsey and I would betray our church if we wrote as if God had abandoned the United Methodist Church. I do not believe that. So we rightfully claim our vocations as theologians, trusting that exposing the disagreements between one another and the Bishops may in some modest way be of service for the upbuilding of God's church and, perhaps, even his kingdom.

I begin my argument by examining the Bishops' understanding of pacifism and why they seem to think pacifism is deficient given the threat of nuclear war. In the process I try to suggest the kind of pacifism I wish the Bishops had espoused and to which they had called the church. Next, I will address more directly the issues between Ramsey and me. Finally, I conclude by making a few suggestions about where we should go from here.

Peace without Christology or Eschatology

In Defense of Creation is on the whole a quasi-pacifist document. It certainly seems to be for peace as an alternative to war. Moreover, it espouses a peace that is a present possibility for relations between nations. Thus Bishop Dale White in his preface states that the Bishops' purpose "is to encourage and equip our members to become knowledgeable witnesses to the power of God in Christ to bring peace to the human family" (6). Yet neither Bishop White nor the subsequent document makes clear exactly what is meant by that all-important word "peace."

Ramsey is right that the kind of pacifism the Bishops seem to adopt is one built more on a secular hope than on the eschatological hope made possible by Jesus Christ. The Bishops simply fail to see that genuine Christian pacifism, that is, pacifism that is determined by the reality of Christ's cross, assumes we must be peaceful not because such peace holds out the hope of a world free from war but because as followers of Jesus we cannot be anything other than peaceful in a world inextricably at war.

But I am getting ahead of myself. Before such charges can be sustained I must look more closely at what the Bishops actually say about pacifism. They treat pacifism in two separate sections, both rather brief and unfocused. On pages 30 to 32 a brief overview of the pacifist tradition is provided. They note that the early church, at least through the first three centuries, was pacifist. They suggest this was probably due to "scriptural seriousness" as well as to the "historical proximity to Jesus." The latter is no doubt thought decisive, because in the section just preceding we are told that Jesus never resorted to violence in his own defense and even at his death had the power to forgive his own killers: "The crucifixion is an eternal testimony to the transcendent power of forgiving love and nonviolence" (29). As I shall argue below, this kind of exchange model for the atonement is inextricably individualistic.

The Bishops continue their history by noting that the "pacifist tradition" outlived the Constantinian establishment: it was exemplified in the figure of St. Francis of Assisi and three centuries later in the "brilliant" Erasmus of Rotterdam. Noting that none of the magisterial reformers could be called pacifist, the Bishops nonetheless noted that the Reformation eventually generated the "historic peace churches." Finally, though Wesley was certainly not a pacifist, the Bishops suggested he had an ambivalent attitude toward the American Revolution and generally saw war as a prime example of sin. Moreover, many prominent Methodists of the twentieth century have been pacifist, which I am sure is a telling point, though I must confess I seem to be missing entirely the power of such an observation. After all, many Methodists of the twentieth century have also been racist.

The Bishops, of course, could not be expected in such a short document to provide a well-documented history of pacifism. But certainly we should have expected better than this. They write as if the "pacifist tradition" was just that: a single coherent set of convictions fairly consistently held over twenty centuries. But even the most cursory reading of church history cannot help but dispel that idea. In fairness to the Bishops, Bainton's typological method in his famous *Christian Attitudes to War and Peace*[6] can tempt one to read history as

---

6. [Roland Bainton, *Christian Attitudes to War and Peace: A Historical Survey and Critical Reevaluation* (Nashville, TN: Abingdon Press, 1960).]

the Bishops have done. But a closer reading of Bainton and, even better, a reading of Yoder's *Nevertheless*[7] reveal the extraordinary diversity and incompatibility among different forms of pacifism among Christians.

For example, a particularly glaring example of the distortions caused by the Bishops' lumping all who cry peace into one history is their connecting St. Francis and Erasmus in one paragraph. The former's understanding of peace was based on the presumption that Christians were to imitate as nearly as possible in their life the teachings and life of Jesus. Therefore, to restrain from using violence had little to do with calculations about the honor and/or stupidity of war. Yet that is exactly the basis of Erasmus's objections to war. For, as Michael Howard has shown, Erasmus is the beginning of the peculiarly modern assumption that war is wrong because it is so destructive.[8] No particular theological beliefs are required for such a position; nor is it in continuity with past forms of Christian pacifism. Erasmus was not a Christian pacifist; he was a pacifist who happened to be Christian.

Lest it is thought that little hangs on these historical issues, I should point out that the Bishops' failure to distinguish different kinds of Christian pacifism allows them to underwrite the vague generalization about Christians as a "shalom people." Shalom is characterized at such an abstract and ideal level that one never has the sense that it is a way of life that can be lived out in history. We are told that shalom is positive peace, more than the absence of war, denoting harmony, wholeness, health, and well-being in all human relations (24); or that in shalom there is no contradiction between justice and peace, peace and security, love and justice (25). It thus appears that what "pacifism" means throughout Christian history is the Christian's attempt to create a world so just that war is no longer a necessity. But as I have indicated, most Christian pacifism, at least before the Enlightenment, never assumed that the Christian commitment to peace promised a just or war-free world.

The Bishops rightly note that too often Christian discussions of war and peace have lost the breadth and depth of the "scriptural understanding of creation, God's action in history, the world of nations, and human destiny" (24). Though I would have been happier if they had included in their list Jesus' crucifixion and resurrection, they are no doubt right about this; or at least they are right about the kind of pacifism so often espoused by Christians since

7. [John Howard Yoder, *Nevertheless: The Varieties and Shortcomings of Religious Pacifism* (Scottdale, PA: Herald Press, 1971; revised and expanded edition, 1992).]
8. Michael Howard, *War and the Liberal Conscience* (New Brunswick, NJ: Rutgers University Press, 1978).

the Enlightenment. Yet one searches in vain for any account of peace in *In Defense of Creation* that has been informed by those theological realities. Instead, peace, or shalom, is simply assumed as a realizable ideal harmony among nature, people, and nations that our theological commitments under-write but play no decisive role in determining its content.

This interpretation of the Bishops' account of pacifism is only confirmed when we look at the second brief treatment of pacifism in chapter 2. They note that the production, possession, deployment, and use of nuclear weapons must appear illegitimate and immoral from a pacifist perspective. This seems plain enough if, as they assert, pacifism conscientiously repudiates all warfare and weapons of war (40). If knives and guns are out, I suppose we can regard it as a safe bet that nuclear bombs are also to be forbidden. They go on to observe that fidelity to this tradition points to two fundamental questions of the nuclear age: "Can any major war remain non-nuclear? If not, hasn't rejection of war itself become an imperative for all our churches?"

For the life of me, I cannot follow the Bishops' reasoning at this point. They seem to suggest that, since we have no guarantee that we can keep a war nonnuclear, then war itself is no longer a possibility. What puzzles me is why the Bishops think this has anything to do with pacifism. If war is wrong, then nuclear war is clearly wrong, but no conclusions about how to keep war nonnuclear need to be drawn to reach that conclusion. One cannot help but think the Bishops are trying to slip in a Jonathan Schell–like argument: namely, since war continues to protect a nation's right to build nuclear weapons, then war (and nations, according to Schell) must go.[9] This is clearly utopianism, but even at that it is not pacifism, much less Christian pacifism. Rather, it presupposes that if we could eliminate nuclear weapons then war might again be a viable institution. While I am sure at least some of our Bishops might recoil from such a conclusion, I see no way it can be avoided given the logic of this argument.

The Bishops want to be a little bit pacifist. But it is no easier to be a little bit pacifist than it is to be a little bit pregnant. The peace that is sought is not the peace that has been given by Christ. Instead it is a peace that encourages us to put our faith in the threat of nuclear war, for it is assumed that threat is frightening people to the extent that they may finally come to their senses and

9. [For an example of the kind of "survivalist" argumentation that Hauerwas has in mind, see Jonathan Schell's book *The Fate of the Earth* (New York: Avon Books, 1982). Hauerwas also responds to the "totalitarian" character of survivalist argumentation in "Taking Time for Peace: The Ethical Significance of the Trivial" (1986) in CET.]

realize they stand on the brink of annihilation. Yet a peace so built cannot be the "shalom" to which the Bishops appeal; it is a peace based on fear rather than on positive faith in God.

I do not want to be unfair to the Bishops, but I simply do not understand what position about war they are willing to defend. I understand they believe the nuclear crisis raises questions of faith that neither the pacifist nor just war position has "adequately addressed," but I remain unclear what kind of alternative they propose.

For example, they quote the United Methodist Social Principles: "We believe war is incompatible with the teachings and example of Christ. We therefore reject war as an instrument of national foreign policy and insist that the first moral duty of all nations is to resolve by peaceful means every dispute that arises between or among them."[10] That seems to be about as straightforward a pacifist position as one would want. Admittedly it is a confused one, in that it assumes that simply because war is incompatible with the "teachings and example of Christ" it is also a workable foreign policy for affairs between nations. Ramsey is quite right to chide the General Conference as well as the Bishops for failing to see that the kind of wars we particularly have to fear are those that are not under the political policy of a government. In the same manner I believe Ramsey is right when he says that to ask states to rid themselves of deterrence is to get rid of nations. Yet the Bishops seem to want it both ways.[11]

Because they want it both ways I find it hard to understand the Bishops' constant appeal for the church to be an alternative community. They note that, because of the Fall, government is not only a legitimate expression of creation's natural order but is also necessary because of human sinfulness. Governments can thus become destroyers of community. Yet, "Shalom discloses an alternative community—alternative to the idolatries, oppressions, and violence that mark the ways of many nations" (12). Later we are told it is the church that is to serve as an alternative community in an alienated and fractured world: "a loving and peaceable international company of disciples transcending all governments, races, and ideologies, reaching out to all enemies, ministering to all the victims of poverty and oppression" (20). They tell us we have hardly begun to imagine the church as a transnational community

10. [See n. 4 above.]

11. [For an account of origins of this statement—including Paul Ramsey's attempt to clarify the church's statements on war—see *Speak Up for Just War or Pacifism*, 7–10.]

that proclaims "the unsearchable riches of Christ" to the "principalities and powers" (Ephesians 3:8, 10) (82).

I could understand these appeals for the "church to be a redemptive model of peaceable diversity" (11) if the Bishops were consistently pacifist. If Christians are called to be peaceable in a world at war, no doubt such a community is required. But if it is assumed that the relations between nations can mimic that community, then I find it hard to understand why such a community is an "alternative." As Ramsey suggests, the Bishops seem to believe that nations are capable of repentance. While I am never one to limit the power of God's grace, I find such a position as a matter of policy naïve in the extreme.

Perhaps the clue to the ambiguity in the Bishops' position resides in their claim that, "In the roundness of shalom, a just-war ethic is never enough. Our churches must nurture a *new theology for a just peace*" (13). The phrase "just peace" is obviously loaded for the Bishops, though I remain unclear about its content and in particular why a "new theology" is called for. I thought a just peace was always what just war was about.

At least part of what the Bishops want to encompass with their use of this phrase is their belief that the nuclear crisis is as much a matter of social justice as it is war prevention (52). This legitimates their bringing into the discussion every social issue confronting the modern world in order to suggest how all injustice can be laid at the door of the nuclear challenge. I have no wish to doubt the Bishops' sincerity in trying to make such a linkage, but without showing actual empirical connections justice becomes a covering word with no content.[12]

Even more disquieting, now that the threat of nuclear war has made clear that the nations share only one earth, is the suggestion that a new vision of a just and peaceable human family imbued with the loving kindness of our Creator is made possible. Thus justice requires that we work for common institutions, shared sovereignty, and supernatural authority (73). Again the Bishops seem to assume that the threat of nuclear war—rather than the crucifixion and resurrection of Jesus Christ—is what has made a "just peace" possible. Moreover, they fail to understand how the cross challenges all worldly accounts of justice by God's willingness to submit to injustice so that the world might be justly redeemed.

12. For my general disquiet about the current enthusiasm of Christians for justice, see "Should Christians Talk So Much about Justice," *Books and Religion Review* 14, nos. 5–6 (May/June 1986): 5, 14–15.

I have only one other suggestion for trying to understand the Bishops' position. It is quite simply that in spite of their avowed preference for peace they finally do not want to exclude the use of violence as legitimate. They observe that the Old Testament is full of violence and warfare; for example, God's victory over Pharaoh to liberate Hebrew slaves discloses God's opposition to oppression and injustice (26). Yet we are told that "liberation from oppression is hardly on the same moral plane as the building up of standing armies for nationalistic expansion and oppression of weaker nations" (26–27). Do the Bishops mean to suggest that "liberation movements," which often look very much like standing armies, are in moral perspective different from the war making of established states? I confess I do not know whether the Bishops mean to hold out for this; but if they do, it helps to explain why they seem to be halfway pacifist.

In summary, the Bishops seem to have wanted to have it both ways: to be a little bit pacifist, yet holding out for the legitimate use of force by states and, possibly, liberation fronts. Yet their pacifism is not derived from any determinative Christological perspective but instead derives from the need to avoid nuclear destruction. In effect, the Bishops want to be Constantinian pacifists; that is, they want to be pacifists who continue to rule because now pacifism has become a viable foreign policy due to the threat of nuclear weapons. Yet such a position cannot but be both theologically and politically incoherent.

What a Christological Pacifism Looks Like

What the Bishops fail to appreciate is that the peace that sustains Christian pacifism is an eschatological notion. Christian pacifism is not based on the assumption that Jesus has given us the means to achieve a warless world, but rather, as John Howard Yoder suggests, peace describes the hope, the goal in the light of which the pacifist acts, "the character of his action, the ultimate divine certainty which lets his position make sense; it does not describe the external appearance or the observable results of his behavior. This is what we mean by eschatology: a hope which, defying present frustrations, defines a present position in terms of the yet unseen goal which gives it meaning."[13]

In his classic essay "Peace without Eschatology," John Howard Yoder cri-

---

13. John Howard Yoder, *The Original Revolution* (Scottdale, PA: Herald Press, 1971), 56. Subsequent references are in the text.

tiqued the kind of pacifism we find represented in *In Defense of Creation*.[14] For the pacifism of *In Defense of Creation* is not new but is simply an updated version of the liberal assumption (illusion) that church and world can be identified and that peace is imminent. What is new about the pacifism of the Bishops is that they think they have discovered the mechanism that will force that peace on the nation: the threat of nuclear destruction.

Ramsey is quite right to criticize the Bishops' eschatology and to ask me to elaborate my own eschatology. Of course, the latter, as Ramsey also rightly notes, is a correlative of Christology. To elaborate it I can do no better than to refer to Yoder's essay mentioned above. Like Ramsey, Yoder argues there is more than a slash between the words "already/not yet": the slash is (exactly as Ramsey suggests) aeonic. From the perspective of the New Testament, our present age—that is, the age from Pentecost to Parousia—is the time that these aeons overlap.

These aeons, therefore, exist simultaneously: the old points backward to history before Christ; the new points forward to the fulfillment of the king-dom of God made fully present in the life, death, and resurrection of Jesus of Nazareth. Moreover, each aeon has a social manifestation: the former in the "world," the latter in the church.

The "new aeon" came into the world through the work of Jesus, who is God's agape—self-giving, nonresistant love. Defensible Christian pacifism thereby derives its intelligibility not from any one set of teachings of Jesus but rather from the very form of his life and death. As Yoder says, "At the cross this nonresistance, including the refusal to use political means of self-defense, found its ultimate revelation in the uncomplaining and forgiving death of the innocent at the hands of the guilty. This death reveals how God deals with evil; here is the only valid starting point for Christian pacifism or nonresistance. The cross is the extreme demonstration that agape seeks neither effectiveness nor justice, and is willing to suffer any loss or seeming defeat for the sake of obedience" (59).

Christian nonresistance is a form of discipleship to Jesus, not in a legalistic way but rather "as he is, so are we in this world" (I John 4:17). Such disciple-ship is inherently eschatological, for only in relation to evil is it meaningful. Just as Christ suffered on the cross, so the Christian must suffer in the face of

---

14. [See John Howard Yoder, *The Royal Priesthood: Essays Ecumenical and Ecclesiological* (Grand Rapids, MI: Eerdmans, 1994), 143–67. Hauerwas is citing an earlier edition of this essay, published as "If Christ Is Truly Lord" in *The Original Revolution*, 52–84.]

evil. The "new thing" revealed by Christ was this attitude toward the old aeon: "The cross was not in itself a new revelation; Isaiah 53 foresaw already the path which the servant of Yahweh would have to tread. Nor was the resurrection essentially new; God's victory over evil had been affirmed by definition, one might say, from the beginning. Nor was the selection of a new faithful remnant a new idea. What was centrally new about Christ was that these ideas became incarnate. But superficially the greatest novelty and the occasion of stumbling was His willingness to sacrifice, in the interest of nonresistant love, all other forms of human solidarity, including the legitimate national interests of the chosen people" (61).

By being raised from the dead, Christ becomes not only head of the church but Lord of history reigning over the principalities and powers. Even the old aeon is now brought under the reign of Christ. The characteristic of Christ's reign is that evil, which still certainly exists, is now made to serve God's purposes in spite of itself. Thus vengeance, instead of creating chaos, is harnessed through the state to preserve order and to give room for the work of the church. Vengeance is not made good, but it is made subservient to God's purposes as an anticipation of the ultimate defeat of sin. What has changed is not that the state, for example, has changed since the coming of Christ but that now Christ takes primacy over the old order.

Put differently, Christ's victory on the cross sealed the victory of the kingdom over the world. The church's suffering, like that of Jesus, is the measure of her obedience to the new age. Thus nonresistance is right, "not because it works, but because it anticipates the triumph of the Lamb that was slain" (64). That such nonresistance may appear to let evil reign invites the charge of complicity with evil. Yet this attitude of leaving evil free to be evil is part of the nature of agape, as God's goodwill finally leaves sinners free to separate themselves from God. The word for God's involvement with sin through letting his innocent Son be killed is not "complicity" but "patience" (65). Such patience makes sense only eschatologically.

From this eschatological perspective Yoder criticizes those, like the United Methodist Bishops, who would seek peace without eschatology. For such a peace resolves the tension between the two aeons, confusing the providential purpose of the state to achieve a "tolerable balance of egoism" (Reinhold Niebuhr) with the purpose of the church, which is the rejection of all egoism in the commitment to discipleship: "This confusion leads to the paganization of the church and the demonization of the state" (67). Constantinian pacifism is but the other side of a Constantinian crusade mentality. Such a stance must seek to make the peace of Christ an ethic workable for all society, believer and nonbeliever alike.

Yoder therefore criticizes those pacifists who confuse eschatological pacifism with the optimistic political pacifism that thought that peace might be achieved through the action of unrepentant states. Neither Kellogg-Briand pacts nor the threat of nuclear annihilation is sufficient to force states to achieve peace. Yoder, like Ramsey, draws on Butterfield, who, as an honest historian, rightly saw that the function of the state is like the task of the architect in building a cathedral: "The force of gravity, like human egoism, is not in itself a constructive force. Yet if art and science combine to shape and properly place each stone, the result is a unity of balanced tensions, combining to give an impression not of gravity but of lightness and buoyancy. This sort of delicate balance of essentially destructive forces is what the political apparatus is to maintain under the lordship of Christ, for the sake not of the cathedral, but of the service going on within it" (77–78).

Thus the church does not ask the state to do more than it was meant to do. When Christians speak to the state, therefore, they use criteria that are intrinsic to the state's purpose: "The good are to be protected, the evildoers are to be restrained, and the fabric of society is to be preserved, both from revolutions and war" (78). On the same grounds the church condemns indiscriminate methods of war because such actions are wrong because of the state's commitment to prohibit murder. But a police action within a society cannot be condemned in principle. Rather, the only question is whether there are safeguards to prevent it from becoming something more. According to Yoder, modern war is to be condemned not on the basis of Jesus' ethic but on a realistic basis of the state's purpose.

From this perspective, Yoder considers the issue of whether the Christian as an individual should turn the other cheek for the neighbor. Does the Christian have responsibility for using societal means to protect his neighbor against his bad neighbor? That is, does not the Christian have responsibility to support the police function of the state? Yoder admits that such a view of the state coincides with the biblical view of the police function of the state. But the problem with the argument is that it is "based on a realistic analysis of the old aeon, knows nothing of the new. It is not specifically Christian and would fit into any honest system of social reality. If Christ had never become incarnate, died, risen, ascended into heaven and sent His Spirit, this view would be just as possible, though its particularly clear and objective expression results partly from certain Christian insights" (81).

Ramsey is right when he says that the difference between advocates of just war and pacifists is Christological. But when compared to the Christology of *In Defense of Creation,* that difference seems small indeed. We both take the life and teachings of Jesus with utmost seriousness, but I suspect the crucial difference between us lies in our understanding of Christ's work. Certainly neither Yoder nor I believe that Jesus simply exemplifies a way of life for us to follow. On the contrary, without the ontological change occasioned through Christ's resurrection, there would be no possibility of living as he did. Ramsey is quite right that there is forever a decisive distance between us and Jesus, insofar as Jesus and Jesus alone is the singular faithful Son that makes God's kingdom present. Our obedience to his life is possible only because of the Father's vindication of Jesus' obedience through the resurrection.

However, crucial to my (and I think Yoder's) views on these matters is a refusal to separate the person and the work of Christ. Attempts to develop theories of the incarnation separate from doctrines of atonement invariably result in individualistic accounts of salvation that distort Jesus' eschatological mission.

Jesus is not about saving the individual from sin. Rather, the salvation wrought in Christ makes present God's eschatological kingdom as a possibility for Jew and Gentile alike. All are called to this salvation as individuals, but the salvation itself is the socially embodied life of a community that knows it lives by forgiveness. Pacifism, therefore, is not some "teaching" about nonviolence but rather a way of talking about a community that has learned to deal with conflicts through truth rather than violence—and that truth is no general or universal teaching about agape but the concrete presence of a life. Such a truth requires the existence of a community, for it cannot be known separate from embodiment in concrete lives. If such a community does not exist, then I think Christians have few grounds to counter the challenge of unbelief or the violence it breeds.

So, in response to Ramsey's questions to me about Jesus' work, I must ask him, What exactly do you take Christ's salvation to be? I hope I have now made clear how I answer that question. It is an answer that is quite traditional: that is, Jesus saves us from sin and death. Yet sin and death are embodied in a history that requires an alternative narration of history (namely, "the new aeon") if our salvation is to be anything more than a vague hope. The name we give the social manifestation that makes that history present is church. We believe the church's history is the only true history of the world, but there is no way to establish that till God's kingdom comes in its fulfillment. In between the times we must live by faith. But such faithful living means we can live confident that God's victory has been accomplished forever through Jesus of Nazareth.

Ramsey is certainly right that Jesus is no less in the center of nonpacifist accounts of the Christian life. That I do not doubt. What I question, however, is whether such accounts properly describe the social and political character of Christ's work. For example, there is no question that Jesus is at the center of Reinhold Niebuhr's work, but the forgiveness Christ offers is primarily to the individual, for according to Niebuhr Jesus was the exemplification of the eternal truth of love as the law of our existence. He was not the irreplaceable Messiah who came to redeem Israel only to be rejected.[15]

At issue here is not only the reality of the redemption wrought in Christ but its continuing reality. Ramsey is quite right to characterize my pacifism as eucharistic, especially if he means by that a sense of how the church in all of its life is used by God as the social manifestation of his kingdom. I do not believe Reinhold Niebuhr thought our redemption is so really present or so embodied in community.

Ramsey may well respond that, given the first section of this epilogue, my position is in deep trouble, because there just are not that many empirical indications that the kind of redemption of which I speak is present among us. Yet God's church is not determined by number or influence. On the contrary, I am amazed at the continuing miracle of the many who live faithful to God's calling. Such witnesses are crucial, but we must finally remember that our affirmation of the church is not an empirical claim but a statement of faith. For just as I believe that God has surely made his kingdom present in Jesus Christ, I no less believe that it continues to be present in the church.

One final issue concerning this account of pacifism needs to be mentioned before I turn to the social and political implications of the position. I have not here attempted to provide the scriptural warrants for this position, partly because it has been done well elsewhere, but also because it is a mistake to assume that "pacifism" is a position to be found in the New Testament. I suspect the first Christians had no idea they were "pacifists." They just thought they were following Jesus. The very abstractions "pacifism" and "just war" tend to encourage an ahistorical reading of Scripture and Christian tradition.

I suspect one of the reasons, therefore, that those of us who count ourselves

15. [See, for example, Niebuhr's classic essay "Why the Christian Church Is Not Pacifist," in *Christianity and Power Politics* (New York: Scribner's Sons, 1940), 1–32.]

as "pacifists" have so much difficulty making the position intelligible is the widespread assumption that pacifism can easily be summed up as antiwarism or antiviolence. In the above I have tried to suggest that the kind of pacifism I hold, as well as the kind I wish the Bishops had embraced, is not so much a "position" as a way of life of a community. In James McClendon's words, Jesus is a pacifist insofar as he "evokes and guides a program of nonviolent action that transforms human conduct for its sharers. It is inwardly but also outwardly oriented, its theme is the love of enemies; its focus, in light of God's mighty signs and the inbreaking of the end, is the building of a community that can survive the dying of an old age while with its Lord it anticipates the new."[16]

Since Constantine it has been difficult to recapture conceptually this sense of pacifism. This is not just because pacifists are now seen as "irresponsible," given the assumption that Christians must take up the reins of power. The real difficulty is that pacifism has to be presented as if it were an alternative to just war—that is, as a principled position that is meant to determine the policy of states. As I have tried to show, that is simply not how Christian pacifism, when it is Christologically and eschatologically determined, works.[17]

Moreover, when pacifism becomes that kind of "position," we miss some of the most important features of war. Then war is treated entirely in terms of whether it serves or accomplishes certain political ends. The power of war as an occasion for societies to renew themselves through sacrifice is overlooked in our concern to make judgments of whether the war is legitimate or illegitimate. Insofar as Christian pacifism is a genuine alternative to war, it is because it captures our attention by providing us a truthful community that directs the human desire to sacrifice into service to God.[18]

As Yoder observes, to speak of the pacifism of the messianic community means the focus of attention is shifted from the individual asking about right or wrong "to the human community experiencing in its life a foretaste of God's kingdom. The pacifistic experience is communal in that it is not a life

---

16. James William McClendon Jr., *Systematic Theology: Ethics* (Nashville, TN: Abingdon, 1986), 1:308.

17. I am indebted to L. Gregory Jones for making this point clear.

18. What we must do is find ways to think "ethically" about war that do not repeat our past formulas. Just war and pacifism have become "positions" that are debated in and of themselves without helping us better to understand the complex phenomenon called war. That is what I was trying to do when I wrote "Should War Be Eliminated" [essay 20 in this volume]— namely, to suggest that more important than the principles used to judge war are the narratives through which we enact and interpret war.

alone for heroic personalities but for a society. It is communal in that it is lived by a brotherhood of men and women who instruct one another, forgive one another, bear one another's burdens, reinforce one another's witness."[19]

Once this is understood it becomes clear why I regard *In Defense of Creation* so negatively. For the Bishops have acted as if they can write for anyone. To the contrary, any serious Christian pacifist must recognize that such a way of life is possible only by the reorientation of the self through the repentance made possible by Jesus Christ. For those who have not begun that reorientation, we cannot anticipate what it would mean for them to live nonviolently. This is particularly true once nonviolence is understood not simply as the avoidance of violence but as the disciplined undertaking of living in the life together of a nonviolent community.

But Ramsey may well note that I do not seem to be talking about any United Methodist church he knows and that I am a theologian who is a United Methodist. Yet I cannot help but wish my Bishops had turned their attention to the church in the way I indicate—that is, that they had called us to take ourselves seriously as a genuine alternative to the world of violence. For we know as Christians that we *also* are world. We know we are possessed by the hate and envy that feed the fires of our violence. We know we desire to sacrifice ourselves and others in hope of securing a sense of worth. So we needed our chief pastors to refrain from addressing the world and instead first to address the church, hopefully calling us to be what we are: God's peace.

Moreover, I have the sense that, in spite of the obvious accommodation of the contemporary church to the world, God may well be winnowing us so that we might once again read the Gospel with non-Constantinian eyes. For the increasing irrelevance of the church—an irrelevance that fuels the desperation we feel—may well provide the opportunity for the church to discover again that God has made us an alternative to the world's violence. If only our Bishops had thought it possible to speak about a distinctively *Christian* pacifism, then they would have genuinely acted as our chief pastors.

How a Pacifist Can Serve the Neighbor in a Violent World

In trying to go beyond pacifism and just war, the United Methodist Bishops' position concerning Christian social responsibility is a hopeless muddle. For example, in the section "A Theology for a Just Peace: Guiding Principles," the

19. Yoder, *Nevertheless,* 124.

Bishops assert that "government is a natural institution of human community in God's creation as well as a requirement for the restraint of evil" (36). One assumes the Bishops mean to suggest by this that government would have existed if the Fall had never happened, but after the Fall the purpose of government has had to take on the added function of the use of force for the restraint of evil.

These sets of claims are not intrinsically incompatible. But we need to know more if we are to understand their relation to other positions the Bishops take in *In Defense of Creation*. Do the Bishops think it possible to have a state that can or has disavowed all violence? If so, what are we to make of their call for government to pursue justice on behalf of the poor, the weak, and the oppressed? Do the Bishops think that such justice can always be achieved without resort to violence?

It seems they are really of two minds in trying to respond to these questions. In Guiding Principle 16 they tell us that "all Christians, pacifists and nonpacifists alike, ought to share a strong moral presumption against violence, killing, and warfare, seeking every possible means of peaceful conflict resolution" (37). Yet in Principle 17 they maintain that "any just resort to coercive force must seek the restoration of peace with justice, refrain from directly attacking noncombatants, and avoid causing more harm than good." We are never told, however, when and on what grounds we might know such coercive force to be justified.

What the Bishops seem to have failed to understand is that you simply cannot mix just war and pacifism and have a consistent position. In this respect one can only wish that the Bishops had attended to Ramsey's arguments, made as early as *Basic Christian Ethics*, that just war is not simply a casuistical checklist to determine when violence might be used; it is a theory of statecraft. Thus Ramsey rightly reminds the Bishops that the first presumption of just war is not against violence, nor does it seek "peace"; rather, just war seeks the maintenance of ordered justice through which the innocent are protected.[20] Put as starkly as one can, Ramsey rightly notes that "justified-war Christians do *not believe* that killing is intrinsically wrong" (188).

While I do not wish to go over ground Ramsey has already well covered, I want to fill in some of the background for the position he takes here in order that I might make clear my disagreements not only with the Bishops but also

---

20. Paul Ramsey, *Basic Christian Ethics* (New York: Charles Scribner's Sons, 1950); see particularly 157–84. Subsequent references are in the text.

with Ramsey. Ramsey's position hinges on his interpretation of Jesus' ethic as an uncompromising, disinterested love of the neighbor. The crucial test case for such love is love for the enemy-neighbor, for it is only here, where the Christian can expect no good, that we can be sure we are not simply loving ourselves in loving our neighbor (98–99). I think it important to emphasize this; otherwise, one can miss the radical nature of Ramsey's position.

The problem, however, with Jesus' radical demand of love is how this "non-preferential love" can prefer some persons to others, which it must do in this time between the times: "How can non-resisting love take upon itself any responsibility for public protection or in support of just social reform through the vocation of legislator, judge, sheriff, hangman or soldier?" (157). Ramsey's answer is that Christian love remains absolutely nonresistant in one-to-one neighbor relations but may be required to change its tactic to resistance when more than one neighbor is involved. In other words, there may be a "neighbor-centered preferential love" that replaces "self-centered preferential loves" (159). Ramsey calls this love "enlightened unselfishness," in contrast to systems of ethics based on enlightened selfishness and/or mutual love of self-realization.

On this basis Ramsey develops a "preferential ethics of protection" without denying that Jesus, when it came to his own life, showed no preference for his own welfare and did not resist evildoers when evil fell upon him. Yet Ramsey suggests that in his denouncing of those who were evil Jesus manifested a preferential ethic of protection, which, while coupled with his "personal ethic" of nonresistance, suggests the beginning of an ethics of resistance (169).

Charity, therefore, remains the basis for a Christian ethic of (violent or nonviolent) resistance to evil. Thus, Ramsey argues that it was a work of charity for the Good Samaritan to help him who had fallen among thieves. It was also a work of charity for the innkeeper to receive the wounded man and to conduct his business well enough that he could extend credit to the Samaritan. Still a further step of charity, not justice alone, would be to maintain and serve in a police patrol on the Jericho road to prevent such things from happening. "By yet another step, it might well be a work of charity to resist, by force of arms, any external aggression against the social order that maintains the police patrol along the road to Jericho. This means that where the enforcement of an ordered community is not effectively present, it may be a work of justice and a work of social charity to resort to other available and effective means of resisting injustices. What do you think Jesus would have made the Samaritan do if he had come upon the scene while the robbers were still at their fell work?" (142–43). Ramsey thinks this illustrates the problem of how nonresisting un-self-defensive love must determine its responsibility when there is more than one neighbor to serve.

It is against this background that Ramsey argues that the change from pacifism to just war was a change only in tactics. Following Augustine, he maintains that Christians claim no right of self-defense, and thus it is a travesty to base just war on self-defense. Indeed, "self-defense is the worst of all possible excuses for war or for any other form of resistance or any sort of preference among other people" (173). (Ramsey later qualifies this by noting that we may have vocational responsibilities to defend ourselves.) Ramsey is quite critical of "modern pacifists" who reverse the relation between private and public defense and think that they obviously should defend themselves by going to law but doubt or deny that Christians may be called to service on behalf of national defense (181–82).

In contrast, Ambrose and Augustine argued that "no Christian should save his own life at the expense of another, yet when other persons than himself are involved in the decision, no Christian ought to fail to resist evil by effective means which the state makes available to him" (Ramsey 172). Thus, the primary motive for Christian participation in war was the same love that earlier impelled Christians (out of Christlike love) to reject the use of armed force. "Christians simply came to see that the service of real needs of all the men for whom Christ died required more than personal, witnessing action. It also required them to be involved in maintaining the organized social and political life in which all men live. Non-resisting love had sometimes to resist evil."[21]

Unlike those Catholics who continue to base just war on natural-law assumptions of self-defense, Ramsey has from the beginning argued that just war is the *disinterested love* taught by Christ now institutionalized in the state. Just war is love-transformed justice through which the justice of the earthly city is elevated. Whether this account of the state is compatible with Ramsey's realism about the state (also derived from Augustine) is a question worth exploring. Does this analysis, for example, apply to all states or only the ones that have been formed by people schooled in the Gospels? If the latter, then how would Ramsey counsel Christians to act in states that are not Christian?

This issue is crucial, for it should now be clear that for Ramsey just war is an attempt to provide Christians with a justification for our secular vocation. Just war is not just about war, but it is an account of politics that is nonutopian

---

21. Paul Ramsey, *War and the Christian Conscience* (Durham, ·NC: Duke University Press, 1961), xvii–xviii.

in the interest of keeping the political within humane limits. Ramsey thus argues, "Peace is not the only political good. It is rather that peace with justice and ordered liberty is a 'process,' a process that sometimes involves resort to non-peaceful means. It is not at all paradoxical that this should be the nature of international politics. In mankind's endless struggle for an ordered justice and peace, it is only realistic to expect (even if no one should hope for this) that 'the fact that there are different ideas of what constitutes *pacem in terris*' may be 'the final source of human division.' "[22] Thus Ramsey in *Speak Up for Just War or Pacifism* rightly notes that there is no "universal view" of justice, only "views of universal justice" that may mean that both sides in a just war may be fighting justly.[23]

This should help explain why Ramsey is so disappointed in *In Defense of Creation*. For it makes the mistake against which he has been arguing for three decades; namely, it argues in a utopian fashion that war can be eliminated from our lives, thus leaving us no means to contend against those who believe that war cannot be subject to or limited by moral purpose. As a result, we are robbed of the wisdom that Ramsey strongly believes has been at the heart of just war thinking: We should never fight war for peace but *only* for more ordered liberty.

While it is not something on which I wish to dwell, I think it is interesting how Ramsey has tried through his account of just war to argue for limited war without losing the realism of Reinhold Niebuhr. Indeed, in many ways Ramsey's development of just war thinking can be seen as an extended commentary on Niebuhr's sense of the inevitability of war, while saving Niebuhr from the consequentialism to which (without "justice more articulated") his account of violence seemed to commit him. Ramsey may not want to say with Niebuhr that "society is in a perpetual state of war" or to underwrite Niebuhr's tendency to justify violence primarily in terms of its effects without an explicit ethics of means, but Ramsey agrees with Niebuhr's claim that "once we have made the fateful concession of ethics to politics, and accepted coercion as a necessary instrument of social cohesion, we can make no absolute distinctions between non-violent and violent types of coercion or between coercion used by government and that which is used by revolutionaries."[24]

Ramsey, who is often his own best interpreter, explicitly says,

22. Paul Ramsey, *The Just War: Force and Political Responsibility* (New York: Scribner's, 1968), 38.
23. Ramsey, *Speak Up for Just War or Pacifism*, 91.
24. Reinhold Niebuhr, *Moral Man and Immoral Society* (New York: Scribner's, 1932), 19, 179.

All that I have ever written on the morality of war, I have been quite consciously drawing upon a wider theory of statecraft and of political justice to propose an extension within the Christian realism of Reinhold Niebuhr— an added note within responsibility ethics. There is more to be said about justice in war than was articulated in Niebuhr's sense of the ambiguities of politics and his greater/lesser evil doctrine of force. That "more" is the principle of discrimination; and I have tried to trace out the meaning of this as well as the meaning of warfare that Niebuhr never faced. Come to think about it, this may explain why I seem so alone in championing the recovery of the just war doctrine—since Protestant messianists rushed pell-mell to join forces with the new breed of Catholic messianists in jettisoning the elements of Christian political realism from their thinking.[25]

Therefore, like Niebuhr, Ramsey argues that pacifists cannot be involved in this cardinal feature of politics once we recognize that the use of power, and probably the use of force, are the *esse* of politics: "You never have good politics without the use of power, possibly armed force" (5). Armed conflict is an unavoidable feature of the life of nations, so that the attempt to banish force is not only impossible, but more important, if we are to be moral, undesirable (50). "Genuine sectarian Christian pacifists" therefore prescind from the history of nations insofar as they prescind from the history of warfare. As such they "radically even if still selectively withdraw from politics" (263). If they are to be consistent, they must cease advising citizens and statesmen concerning what they should do in the restraining function of their offices.

The Political Implications of Constantinian and Non-Constantinian Pacifism

It seems to be a no-win situation for me as a pacifist to be caught between the United Methodist Bishops and Ramsey. By arguing against the kind of Constantinian pacifism the Bishops seem to have embraced, I appear to conform to the stereotype that pacifists must withdraw from political engagement. If I argue against Ramsey's characterization, then I seem to have joined up with the Council of Bishops. It thus becomes my task to suggest how badly the Bishops understand the political implications of Christian pacifism as well as to indicate my disagreements with Ramsey.

Both the Bishops and Ramsey remain committed Constantinians. By that I

---

25. Ramsey, *The Just War*, 260–61. Subsequent references are in the text.

mean they argue presuming that Christians not only still rule but can and should rule. It is therefore their task to show that Christians can develop an ethic sufficient to sustain a civilization. This is a particular temptation for Christians (and even more for United Methodists) in America, where the idea has long persisted that there is a close connection between Christianity and democracy. The Bishops clearly assume that if they could simply get the American people concerned about the nuclear crisis the issue would be resolved, ignoring entirely that our current situation has little to do with the good or evil will of either the American or Russian people as people.

Ramsey is much less susceptible to such a criticism, having little illusion about the capacity of democracies to control their wars. Yet Ramsey's argument that just war is generated and sustained by Christian love would seem to commit him to the view that those civilizations and correlative states that are not formed by Christian presence cannot sustain the ethos necessary to make war an option for Christians; or that those states of modernity that have explicitly rejected their Christian heritage cannot command Christian conscience to fight in their wars since Christians can have no confidence that the wars of such states can be kept limited. Perhaps that is why Ramsey asserts in *The Just War* "that no Christian and no man who loves an ordered liberty should conspire with communism in coming to power. (This is a different question of whether it is possible to serve God in a communist land.)" (449).

It is extremely important that Ramsey not be misunderstood here. He is not uncritically siding with liberal democratic regimes against communism. Ramsey is no "cold warrior"; but even if he was tempted to be, his moral reflection is better than his political views. Indeed, given Ramsey's criticism about our society's adherence to the "heavenly city of the eighteenth century philosophers," he might well argue as a political judgment that it is increasingly hard to see how Christians can support Western societies' wars since they too cannot be kept limited.

More important than Ramsey's political judgments is his understanding of the role of nations. For while Ramsey maintains that "the nations also are creations of God; and the world would be poorer without any one of these creatures of His," he always insists that it is not nations but "first persons" that the Christian is concerned to serve through the strange work of love called war. As he says, "Christian love, expressed in principles of justice that suit it, does not first of all fashion itself in terms of regard for the fabric of community life, nor does Christian faith, going into political action, take effect primarily in fidelity to the recuperative powers of an enemy nation. Not nations but first persons are elevated to citizenship in another city and to a destiny kept between themselves and God which prohibits any man from reducing them wholly to the status of means useful in attaining some historical goal in the life of the kingdoms of this world. The neighbors and companions God has given us are primarily persons, within the separate national traditions" (163). (I suspect that this is the reason Ramsey abhors communism, because such societies, as policy, reduce persons to means. Of course, it can be asked if "liberal societies" do not in fact do the same thing in the name of the "protection of the individual.")

Thus Ramsey qualifies Robert Tucker's "initially profoundly true contention that no matter what are the higher values the state serves, and despite the hierarchy of values in human political communities, a 'realistic' state craft nevertheless holds true if only the state is a necessary condition to these higher human goods" (417). Tucker, as Ramsey notes, does not deny that the state may be only an instrumental value inferior to those it serves. Tucker nonetheless maintains that when the chips are down we must recognize or at least act "as if the state were the supreme value" since it is the necessary condition to the higher values it serves (417). Yet, against this, Ramsey argues that not only is the state today an insufficient condition for protecting the values it serves, but "because of the nature of the weapons into the use of which the politics of the nation-state today may extend, 'necessities of state' may quite readily contradict, frustrate, and destroy those very values which the state exists to serve. The state as necessary condition may become destructive of the goals to which it is ordinarily a condition" (418–19).

Therefore, Ramsey's whole program for recovering the authentic function of just war logic is to remind us that the state's *raison d'état* depends on the state's *raison d'être*. Of course, the latter, as we saw above, is how the state provides the institutional means to protect the neighbor from unjust attack. Moreover, Ramsey is unafraid to draw the radical conclusion from this: "In an age when the state in seeking its safety can prove positively dysfunctional as a condition (and not only insufficient), resort must be made again directly to those unconditional values and finalities which before or ordinarily warrant the exercise of statecraft as if the state were the supreme value" (419).

But one must ask exactly what are the concrete implications of this for our current situation. Even if the broad outlines of Ramsey's defense of the state as the embodiment of love-transformed justice are correct, we must ask if the concrete states we have in fact fit Ramsey's moral condition for sustaining a just war. My judgment is that they do not.[26]

In sum, unlike Ramsey and the United Methodist Bishops, I simply do not believe that Christians need any theory of the state to inform or guide their witness in whatever society they happen to find themselves. For the Bishops to say that the state is a natural institution as well as required for restraint of evil may be theologically useful, but it does little to help us understand how to negotiate how to live as Christians in America. For Ramsey to develop just war as a theory of statecraft is useful, but again it does not help us know how this or that state may command our loyalties, given the form of order it provides along the Jericho road.

As a pacifist, I—no less than just warriors like Ramsey—am called to be of service to the neighbor, and in particular the enemy-neighbor. But I do not assume the state as such is a special creature of God provided for that service. In that respect I think I assume a deeper realism than Ramsey (or Niebuhr). Like the Christians who gave us the New Testament, I simply believe that the state—which can take the form of any group that provides order, from Augustine's robber bands to North Carolina to the United States of America— exists. I do not need a theory about its existence or its penchant for making a war. Rather, what I need is a community schooled with skills provided by a truthful account of the world to give up the power to interpret the perversities and possibilities of the states that come and go.

Therefore, when I called for the United Methodist Bishops to address the church first, I meant for them to remind us of the kind of skills we need to be a people capable of discerning the illusions of a world that has created nuclear weapons. Wesley's "General Rules,"[27] of which Ramsey rightly reminds

---

26. [Here the editors have deleted four paragraphs where Hauerwas discusses questions and challenges posed by Michael Quirk and David Hollenbach.]

27. ["The General Rules of the United Societies" (London, 1739) are part of the canonical documents of the United Methodist Church as specified in para. 62 of the 1996 edition of *The Book of Discipline of the United Methodist Church* (Nashville, TN: Abingdon Press, 1996), 69– 73. The rules are presented in three sections prefaced by a condition specifying the need for conversion:

There is only one condition . . . required of those who desire admission into these societies: "a desire to flee from the wrath to come, and to be saved from their sins." But wherever this is really fixed in the soul it will be shown by its fruits.

It is therefore expected of all who continue therein that they should continue to evidence their desire for salvation.

us,[28] are to my mind not a bad place to begin insofar as they ask us to take on those personal disciplines and charitable acts that create the distance necessary for us to recognize the demonic. Only as the church becomes that kind of disciplined community do we have any possibility of discerning those forms of secular life that may provide us the opportunity to be of service to the neighbor.

Because I don't think I need a theory of the state and/or a justification for Christians' assuming secular vocations, I find Ramsey's insistence that I make clear my understanding of the relation of nonviolent or passive resistance to nonresistance less than urgent. I do so first because I do not believe that Ramsey's characterization of Jesus' teaching and life as one of absolute "nonresistance" is correct. Jesus' cross was a confrontation with powers that was meant to defeat those forces that hold us to the presuppositions of the old age. He did not restrain from fighting them—and that includes their embodiment in Rome—but rather refused to fight them on their terms. That is why he was victorious as he submitted to their power, trusting in God to vindicate his faithful service. This, of course, we believe to have happened through the resurrection, thus making it possible for us to fight as he fought in service to the neighbor—that is, nonviolently.

First: By doing no harm, by avoiding evil of every kind, especially that which is most generally practiced. . . .

Secondly: By doing good; by being in every kind merciful after their power; as they have opportunity, doing good of every possible sort, and, as far as possible, to all men. . . .

Thirdly: By attending upon all the ordinances of God; such are:

    a) The public worship of God.

    b) The ministry of the Word, either read or expounded.

    c) The Supper of the Lord.

    d) Family and private prayer.

    e) Searching the Scriptures.

    f) Fasting or abstinence.

These are the General Rules of our societies; all of which we are taught of God to observe, even in his written Word, which is the only rule, and the sufficient rule, both of our faith and practice. And all these we know his Spirit writes on truly awakened hearts. If there be any among us who observe them not, who habitually break any of them, let it be known unto them who watch over that soul as they who must give an account. We will admonish him of the error of his ways. We will bear with him for a season. But then, if he repent not, he hath no more place among us. We have delivered our own souls.]

28. [Ramsey's discussion of the General Rules can be found in *Speak Up for Just War or Pacifism,* where he cites this document in its entirety (143–44) and proceeds to discuss the implications of what it would mean to be a church of "mutual discipline" (143) in the final pages of his contribution to the book (144–47). This is significant because on this point, Hauerwas and Ramsey are in agreement.]

Connected to Ramsey's insistence that "non-resistance is incommensurable with any form of resistance" is his penchant for summarizing Jesus' ethic by the principle of disinterested or impartial love.[29] This kind of monistic characterization fails to do justice to the interrelation of Jesus' life and his teaching. Jesus is not the teacher of love; rather, he is the herald of the Kingdom whose life makes possible a new way of existence. I am certainly not denying that love is an important way to describe that existence, but it cannot be isolated in a way that seems to make necessary our asking how such nonpreferential love can take the form of violence in the name of preserving ordered liberty. When the question is put in that way, it no longer seems necessary that Jesus ever lived or died.

As Ramsey nicely notes, the pacifist avoidance of violence is not correlative with the assumption that violence is the name of a set of actions that are inherently evil. Rather, the pacifist avoidance of violence is derived from the positive discovery that God has made possible a new way of resolving disputes through the life of Christ that we find continued in the church. That is why the pacifist feels so strongly the contrast with the state. For the state is where violence is legitimated in the name of good. The Christian does not deny that often the state does some good through its violence; the point is rather that the sword of the state is outside the "perfection of Christ."[30]

So the issue again comes back to eschatology. For as I suggested above, the pacifist and the just warrior theologically understand the aeonic tension differently. For the pacifist, at least the kind I wish to defend, there is no reason we should be forced from the world of the state simply because we disavow violence. There is no reason we should not use just war claims as a means to try to help the state be as nonviolent as possible. But finally, it must be admitted that the rationale for pacifism is not our ability to make the world less violent, but rather our various assessments of Jesus of Nazareth, who taught us to trust in God's kingdom and not in ourselves.

This does not mean that the pacifist makes nonviolence more important

---

29. [Here Hauerwas is referring to Ramsey's fairly dense discussion and critique of the work of John Howard Yoder found in *Speak Up for Just War or Pacifism*, 96–123. For the comments about nonresistance, see 111–20.]

30. [Here Hauerwas (and Ramsey) are referring to the 1527 "Schleitheim Confession of Faith," translated by John C. Wenger in *The Mennonite Quarterly Review* 19, no. 4 (October 1947): 247–52. According to this original Anabaptist confession, whereas the "ban" (excommunication) was to be used "in the perfection of Christ," the sword (as an instrument of violence and coercive order) was to be used only "outside the perfection of Christ."]

than justice—that is, aid to the neighbor. The pacifist is not forced to disavow a concern for, as well as an involvement in, the attempt to secure justice in this context or that situation. The alternative of violence or acceptance of injustice is as false as the assumption that all state action partakes of or depends on violence. On the contrary, most states do not depend on violence for many of their activities; and even more strongly, when violence is used it tends to be antithetical to the social good being pursued.

So I do not agree with Ramsey that nonviolence as a political strategy is war by another means. That does not mean that I think all forms of political action that take nonviolent form are therefore justified. Rather, it means that all genuine politics—that is, politics in the sense of conversation necessary for a people to discover the goods they have in common—are nonviolent. Rather than denying the political, nonviolence requires that we become political by forcing us to listen to the other rather than destroy them.

Let me again illustrate this point. In a recent article, Michael Quirk borrows an example from the life of Mahatma Gandhi that is often cited by partisans of just war theory and "reasons of state" alike to indicate the moral bankruptcy of Gandhi's politics of nonviolent resistance. Shortly before his death, Gandhi was asked how he would deal with an atom bomb attack. He said he would not go into a shelter but would "come out in the open and let the pilot see I have not a trace of evil against him. The pilot will not see our faces from this great height, I know. But the longing in our hearts that he will not come to harm would reach him and his eyes would be opened."[31] Quirk notes that most people think this is no answer at all, thus revealing the fatal theoretical point against pacifism: that it prohibits statespersons from overcoming certain types of unscrupulous and energetic evil without recourse to violence.

I believe this interpretation of Gandhi misses the point because it makes Gandhi's social thought a compendium of tactical advice rather than "a vision of a different sort of political life where the use of violence is so antithetical to the shared identities of citizens that a violent political victory is a contradiction in terms." Gandhi was aware that, given the scenario, nonviolent tactics would be ineffective, but that is irrelevant because he endorses, as Quirk observes, a different criterion of "effective" political action.[32] The modern

31. Michael Quirk, "Just War, Theory, Nuclear Deterrence, and Reason of State," *International Journal of Applied Philosophy* 3, no. 2 (fall 1986): 56.
32. Ibid.

nation-state cannot conceive of an effective political act that dissolves the policy itself, but Gandhi could. He could because he refused to conceive of politics except as the creation of communities whose common good excludes violence. The extinction of such communities is not an unqualified tragedy since such communities do not believe the violent life is worth living.

Finally, Quirk observes: "What distinguishes Gandhi's pacifism from most contemporary versions is his wise conviction that pacifism as a political program is effective only in the context of a specific way of life, a community which is in part constituted by a belief that no violence is ever justified. It should be clear that modern states—built as they are around managerial rather than practical rationality—preclude such communities on the national scale."[33] But there is no reason for pacifists and/or just warriors to think such communities cannot therefore exist; we just need to have our imaginations freed to consider alternatives to the nation-state. We must act, as Yoder describes the early Quakers doing in Pennsylvania, to create social and political processes that make questions of violence irrelevant. As Yoder notes, the failure of the Quakers' "holy experiment" had as much to do with the fact that William Penn's charter was from the Crown, as it did with their failure to live faithfully.[34]

Even though I have refused to respond to Ramsey's demand to clarify nonresistance and nonviolent resistance, I (and I think Yoder) am in his debt for noting that pacifist reaction on this matter is often distorted by our responding to the charge of passivism or irresponsibility. In fact, Yoder agrees with him in a passage Ramsey did not quote from Yoder's *Christian Attitudes to War, Peace, and Revolution*. Yoder responds to a student's question about effectiveness by saying:

> The longer I look at the question of effectiveness, the less I trust that way to put the issue to be of any help. The longer you look, the more you see dimensions of the question that change the definitions of terms, so that it is less clear what you are asking about. Do we mean short range effectiveness or long range effectiveness? Do we mean guaranteeing a certain result, or just contributing to a statistical mix in which the chances of a derived outcome may increase by so much that you might come out with something? The interplay between an ethic which cares only about faithfulness regardless of

33. Ibid., 57.
34. John Howard Yoder, *Christian Attitudes to War, Peace, and Revolution: A Companion to Bainton* (Goshen Biblical Seminary, Elkhart, Indiana, 1983), 274.

cost, and another that is purely pragmatic is a caricature that nobody really will stay on one end of for long. The person who says, "You must give up some of your scruples in order to be effective" is still saying that because the goal for the sake of which to be effective is in principle a good goal. So the argument which takes the clothing of "principles versus effectiveness" really means this principle versus that principle. It really means that that goal, for the sake of which I want you to give up other scruples, is so overridingly important that those other things are less important. That's an ethic of principle. It differs only in that the choice of which things you are willing to give up for which other things will change. Likewise, the people who say "You must simply be true to God" . . . and "let the heavens fall" . . . really say that because of a conviction about Providence, trusting that if the heavens fall God has another better set of heavens ready, which is part of the process, so even that is not thumbing your nose at results. It's trusting God who gave us the rules to know more about the results than we know. So I am increasingly convinced that the debate between the effectiveness ethic and the principle ethic is a false debate.[35]

In the same way, I think Ramsey is right to call a halt to the charge that those who adhere to just war are trying to make "history come out right." At least he is right given his account of just war, which certainly does not appeal to lesser-evil consequences alone to justify and limit its use of violence. What we must both admit, Christian pacifist and Christian just warrior alike, is that there is no way either of us can avoid the tragic fact that at times there is no alternative than to have other people, who may not share our conviction, suffer for our commitment to nonviolence or to just limits upon the use of force. Speaking for Christian pacifists, we are pledged to serve the neighbor by doing all we can to create contexts and habits that make peaceable communities possible. But we cannot deny that in certain circumstances it may be necessary to watch others die unjustly—which is surely harder even than envisioning our own deaths. The only thing worse would be our failing to witness to our brother and sister that God's love took the form of a cross so that the powers that make our world so violent might be defeated. That our death and the death of others might be required if we are faithful to that cross cannot be denied, but it would only be more tragic if we died in a manner that underwrites the pagan assumption that nothing is more tragic than death

---

35. Ibid., 436–37.

itself. Without such an eschatological conviction, how the Christian pacifist serves the neighbor in a violent world cannot help but be unintelligible.

So What Should the Bishops Have Said?

Having come to the end of my substantive response to the United Methodist Bishops and Paul Ramsey, I still have to say what I wish the Bishops had done. I wish they had begun with a confession of sin in which they called on the church to ask God's forgiveness for our failure as a *church* over these many years to discipline ourselves so we might be capable of making a witness for peace. I am well aware that by God's grace extraordinary witnesses about war and peace have been raised up from out of United Methodism. But they were isolated and heroic rather than what might have normally been asked of Christians.

I would have then wanted our Bishops to address the issue of war rather than nuclear war. The Christological, eschatological, ethical, and political issues raised by the exchange between Ramsey and myself should have been brought to the attention of the Methodist people. Given the lack of discussion in the church about these matters, I think it would have been presumptuous for the Bishops to have taken a position either as pacifist, in spite of the General Conference resolution, or as just war. The time is not ripe for positions. Rather, what is called for is for the Bishops to exercise their pastoral office as teachers helping the Methodist people recover the moral resources of the past that we might better think about today.

To better help the Methodist people explore these issues, it would have been useful for the Bishops to suggest how various policy alternatives would look from the perspective of just war and pacifism. The kind of alternatives suggested by Ramsey would have helped people understand better the costs of taking a just war stance. In exploring the pacifist alternative, perhaps the Bishops should have spoken not quite so much to the point of military policy, but that in itself is an open question. Once the church is clear that it is a pacifist church, if it is going to be such, there is no reason it cannot urge the government to take what is judged to be the least destructive stand.

Intrinsic to the Christian pacifist tradition, or at least the one I have tried to defend, is the overriding commitment to the process of conversation by which a community discovers its true goals. I should like it if the United Methodist Church could speak as a peace church, but we are clearly not that. So in this time between the times, we must take the time for that part of the church called Methodist to discover its heart and mind about the issues of war and peace. If we do that, we just might recover a sense of being a people of the new age who believe that even in the face of the threat of nuclear destruction God has given us the time to be a people of peace.[36]

Further Reading

"Should War Be Eliminated? A Thought Experiment" (1984), essay 20 in this volume

"A Pacifist Response to *In Defense of Creation*," *The Asbury Theological Journal* 41, no. 2 (fall 1986): 5–14.

"Pacifism: A Form of Politics," in *Peace Betrayed? Essays on Pacifism and Politics*, ed. by Michael Cromartie (Washington, DC: Ethics and Public Policy Center, 1990), 133–41.

"The Gospel's Radical Alternative: A Peace the World Cannot Give," with Michael G. Cartwright, *The Other Side* (July/August 1987): 22–26, 45–46 [This article was one part of "A Dialogue on Christian Peacemaking in the Nuclear Age"; the contribution by Hauerwas and Cartwright was paired with an article by Jim and Shelly Douglass.]

"On Surviving Justly: Ethics and Nuclear Disarmament" (1983), in AN

36. I am indebted to Michael Cartwright and L. Gregory Jones for criticism of this and earlier drafts of the epilogue. Of course, my greatest debt is to Paul Ramsey, who not only read and energetically criticized my earlier draft, but who graciously suggested I should write this epilogue. His sense of fairness and colleagueship in this and throughout his life will, I hope, continue to serve as an example for all of us who attempt to be theologians.

[In addition to cuts noted earlier (see n. 26), the editors also deleted two extended notes in which Hauerwas addresses criticisms put forward by John Milbank in his review of Hauerwas's AN, and one extended note in which Hauerwas discusses Jean Bethke Elshtain's *Women and War* and Elaine Scarry's *The Body in Pain: The Making and Unmaking of the World.*]

22. A Christian Critique of Christian America (1986)

Hauerwas has never shied away from taking public stands (e.g., on abortion, capital punishment, American participation in war, prayer in public schools, gays in the military). Because many theologians (and American Christians in general) have difficulty understanding Hauerwas's "theological politics," Hauerwas constantly finds himself being "lumped with" (depending on the issue) either political conservatives or liberals. The assumption that being a "good Christian" on social issues involves being either a "liberal" or a "conservative" dates back to the turn of the century, when the dominant understanding of Christian social ethics came to be that Christians must take responsibility through the political process for the direction of American democracy. Hauerwas critiques this nineteenth-century assumption of a "spiritual oneness" between Christianity and democracy, arguing that this "Constantinian" approach confuses the "progress" of nation-states with the providence of God, confuses "effectiveness" with "faithfulness." A faithful Christian response to any of a variety of important moral issues may lead to conclusions similar to those of liberals or conservatives, but will not be based on the same reasoning.

1. Setting the Agenda: A Report on a Conversation

At a conference on narrative and virtue I had an encounter with a philosopher that raises the problem with which I wish to deal. My philosophical counterpart has been strongly influenced by C. S. Peirce and is also a committed Jew. In his paper he had argued that most of the rational paradigms accepted by contemporary philosophy cannot make sense of Judaism. We began by exchanging views about why current ethical theory seems so committed to foundationalist epistemological assumptions. We shared in general a sympathy with antifoundationalist arguments, though neither of us wanted to give

[Originally published in *The Cresset* 50, no. 1 (November 1986): 5–16. Used by permission. Subsequently reprinted in CET.]

up any possibility of some more modest realist epistemology. We also found we were equally critical of liberal political theory and in particular the ahistorical character of its methodology. Then our conversation suddenly took a turn for which I was completely unprepared. It went something like this:

Philosopher: Do you support prayer in the public schools?

Theologian: No, I do not, because I do not want the state sponsoring my faith.

Philosopher: That is not the real reason. You are just afraid to be for anything that Jerry Falwell is for. You really are a liberal in spite of your doubts about liberalism's philosophical adequacy.

Theologian: That is not fair. I did not say I was against school prayer because I think such prayer is coercive, though I think such considerations are not unimportant, but because state-sponsored prayer cannot help but give the impression that the state is friendly toward religion. Moreover, school prayers, insofar as they can pass muster in a religiously pluralistic context, are so anemic that they cannot help but give a distorted view of God. So I am against school prayer not because it is against the tenets of liberalism but because it is theologically a scandal.

Philosopher: That is not good enough. As a Christian you typically do not give a damn about the Jews. You want to create a civilization and society and then walk away from it when the going gets a little tough. Of course the prayers sponsored by public authorities are degraded but they still remind people that they are creatures. A vague god prayed to vaguely is better than no god or prayer at all. Otherwise we face the possibility of a neopagan culture for which liberal procedural rules of fair play will be no match.

Theologian: I am a bit surprised to hear you argue this way. After all, Christians have persecuted and killed Jews with as much enthusiasm as anyone. I would think you would feel safer in a secular culture than one that is quasi-Christian. Indeed, has that not been the dominant social strategy of Jews since the Enlightenment? The way to secure protection from the Christians is to create and support liberal societies where religion is relegated to the private sphere and thus becomes unavailable for public policy directed against the Jews or those of any other religious faith.

Philosopher: I do not deny that is the strategy of many Jews, but I think this century has shown it to be a decisive failure. Pagan societies kill us with an abandon that Christians can never muster. Christianity even in a degraded form at least has material convictions that can make the persecution and killing of Jews problematic. Paganism has no such convictions, so I will take my chances with the Christians and their societies. After all, we Jews do not ask for much. We just do not want you to kill our children. Living in quasi-Christian societies means we have to put up with a lot of inconvenience and prejudice—for example, Christmas as a school holiday—but we Jews have long known how to handle that. We flourish under a little prejudice. What we cannot stand is the false tolerance of liberalism which relegates us to the arena of being just one religion among others.

Theologian: So, if I understand you rightly, you are suggesting that you want me as a Christian to support school prayer, even if such prayers are but forms of degraded Christian religiosity, because at least that continues to underwrite the assumption that we are a "religious" society. Such an assumption allows an appeal to a higher standard of justice, which makes the survival of the Jewish people more likely.

Philosopher: That is about right. You Christians have to take responsibility for what you have done. You created a civilization based on belief in God and it is your responsibility to continue to support that civilization.

Theologian: But you know yourself that such a social strategy cannot help but lead to the continued degradation of Christianity. The more Christians try to make Christianity a philosophy sufficient to sustain a society, especially a liberal society, the more we must distort or explain away our fundamental beliefs. Therefore, in the name of sustaining a civilization Christians increasingly undercut the ability of the church to take a critical stance toward this society. Even when the church acts as a critic in such a context, it cannot be more than a friendly critic, since it has a stake in maintaining the basic structure of society.

Philosopher: Why should that bother me? Christians have always been willing in the past to degrade their convictions to attain social and political power (of course, always in order that they might "do good"). Why should they start worrying about being degraded now? On that score it seems a little late. For the church to start to worry about being pure is about as realistic as for the pop star Madonna to worry about being a virgin. It is just too late. So if you care anything about the Jews you ought to support school prayer.

Our conversation did not end at this point, but what I have portrayed is enough for my purposes. Even though I think most of what my philosopher friend has to say is right, for theological reasons I still cannot support school prayer. That I cannot puts me at odds with the social strategy of most Christians, both liberal and conservative, in America. In the next section I will try to explain why this is the case. Then the ground will be prepared for me to suggest what a more radical Christian critique of America entails, both in terms of its logic as well as political strategy.

2. Liberal Christianity and American Democracy, or Why Jerry Falwell Is Such a Pain

Since the turn of the century, one of the dominant themes in Christian social ethics has been the Christian's responsibility for societal affairs. Time and time again it is argued that faith and action cannot be separated. Our religious convictions cannot be relegated to one sphere of our lives and our social and political activities to another. Since the faith of Christians is a faith that does justice, there is no way we can avoid political activity. Whether the political realm is viewed in Lutheran terms as a realm of lesser evil, or more Calvinistically as the arena of the mediocre good, Christians cannot avoid involvement in the political process. That is especially the case in a democratic society in which the actions of individual citizens can make a difference.

Armed with this set of presuppositions, Christians in the "mainstream" denominations attacked those Christians who maintained no particular social or political responsibilities. This position, they argued, pietistically relegates salvation to the individual's relation to God and thus betrays the essential Christian claim that God is Lord of all creation. What must be remembered is that Jesus came preaching a Kingdom that makes it impossible for his followers to be indifferent to the injustices in their surrounding social orders. On these grounds mainstream churches, such as those that constitute the National Council of Churches, urged Baptist and other pietistic Christians to join them in the political struggle to make this a more just society. As is often pointed out, not to take a political stand in the name of being Christian is in fact to be taking a political stand.

Pietists, in defense of their position, sometimes responded by appealing not to their theological convictions but instead to what they considered the normative commitments of the American society—namely, that our constitution has erected a "wall of separation between church and state." In the name of maintaining the freedom of religion the church claims no competency in matters political. The difficulty with this position, however, is that it attributes a perspective to the Constitution that simply is not there. Neither the free exercise clause nor the nonestablishment clause prohibits Christians, either as organized in churches or as individuals, from seeking to influence their society or government. Just to the extent the free church tradition allows itself to be so excluded from the public arena, moreover, it underwrites an individualistic account of Christianity that is antithetical to its very nature.

Such was the state of the debate among Christians until recently. But now suddenly everything has changed, because the message finally got across to the pietistic Baptists. They have become politically active, seeking to influence our society and government to support causes in the name of making this a better society. Jerry Falwell represents the triumph of mainstream Christianity in America, as he is convinced, just like Martin Luther King Jr., that Christians cannot abandon the political realm in their desire for justice. They must seek through the constitutionally guaranteed means to influence our political representatives to prevent abortion, to support democratic regimes around the world, to support Israel, to provide support for the family, and so on.

Therefore, the mainstream won, but it is not a victory they are celebrating. For it turns out that once politically inactive Christians became active, the causes they supported were not those the mainstream wanted supported. The temptation is to try to defeat this new political activism by using the slogans of the past, that "religion and politics do not mix," or, that "one should not try to force one's religious views on anyone through public policy"—but to do so is to go against the position the mainstream has been arguing for years.

In order to understand how we have reached this point in American Protestantism I need to call your attention to some aspects of the history of Christianity in America. I do not mean I am going to give you a rendition of Puritan America or engage in the debate about how "Christian" America has been.[1] While such studies and questions are interesting and may still have some normative importance, they are not crucial for helping us understand why Falwell presents such a challenge to mainstream Christianity. To understand that we need to appreciate why Christian theologians and ethicists in

1. For an extremely interesting approach to this latter question, see Mark Noll, Nathan Hatch, and George Marsden, *The Search for Christian America* (Westchester, IL: Crossway Books, 1983). In summary, their position is that "a careful study of the facts of history shows that early America does not deserve to be considered uniquely, distinctively or even predominantly Christian, if we mean by the word 'Christian' a state of society reflecting the ideals presented in Scripture. There is no lost golden age to which American Christians may return. In addition, a careful study of history will also show that evangelicals themselves were often partly to blame for the spread of secularism in contemporary American life. We feel also that careful examination of Christian teaching on government, the state, and the nature of culture shows that the idea of a 'Christian nation' is a very ambiguous concept which is usually harmful to effective Christian action in society" (17).

America, especially since the nineteenth century, have assumed that Christianity and democracy are integrally related.

That they have done so is because America stands as the great experiment in what Max Stackhouse has identified as "constructive Protestantism." Stackhouse notes that in *The Social Teaching of the Christian Churches* Ernst Troeltsch argues that only two major Christian social philosophies have ever been developed: the Catholic and the Calvinist. Yet each of these as social philosophies no longer seems viable. "The vision of an organic, hierarchical order sanctified by objectified means of grace, and that of an established theocracy of elect saints who are justified by grace through faith, must both be judged as no longer live options for social reconstruction. This is not to suggest that these visions do not still hold power . . . But this is to suggest that these two forms of 'Christendom' have ended—or rather, have played their part and now must yield the stage after their immeasurable contribution to the drama of Christianity in modern culture."[2]

According to Stackhouse, the crucial question is whether Christianity can develop another "social philosophy." If it cannot, it would then seem that the social ethical power of Christianity is at an end. Stackhouse argues that American Christianity has, in fact, developed a third option, which he calls "conciliar denominationalism."[3] The character of this new form of social philosophy Stackhouse sees prefigured in Walter Rauschenbusch, who held together two conflicting motifs, sectarianism and Christendom, that constitute the unique blend of "conciliar denominationalism." "On the one hand, Rauschenbusch comes from an evangelical background from which he gained a sense of intense and explicit faith that could only be held by fully committed members. On the other hand, Rauschenbusch lived in the age of lingering hope for a catholic 'Christian culture' and in an age that, especially through the developing social sciences, saw the legitimacy of secular realms. He, like the developing 'conciliar denominations,' saw the necessity of the select body of believers anticipating the Kingdom in word and deed in good sectarian fashion, and of taking the world seriously on its own terms, as did all visions of Christendom. These motifs conspire in his thought to produce a vision of a revolutionized responsible society for which a socially understood gospel is the catalyst."[4]

Rauschenbusch, as the champion of liberal Christianity, could speak

2. Max Stackhouse, introduction to *The Righteousness of the Kingdom,* by Walter Rauschenbusch (Nashville, TN: Abingdon Press, 1968), 21.
3. Ibid., 22.
4. Ibid., 22–23.

straightforwardly of the need to "Christianize" social orders. "It is not enough to christianize individuals; we must christianize societies, organizations, nations, for they too have a life of their own which may be made better or worse."[5] On that basis he thought it quite possible to speak of saved and unsaved organizations: "The one is under the law of Christ, the other under the law of mammon. The one is democratic and the other autocratic. Whenever capitalism has invaded a new country or industry, there has been a speeding up in labor and in the production of wealth, but always with a trail of human misery, discontent, bitterness, and demoralization. When cooperation has invaded a country there has been increased thrift, education, and neighborly feeling, and there has been no trail of concomitant evil and no cries of protest."[6]

The difference between saved and unsaved social orders, from Rauschenbusch's perspective, is quite simple: saved social orders and institutions are democratic. As he says, "Social sciences confirm the correctness of Christ's protest against the stratification of society in ranks and classes. What is the general tendency toward democracy and the gradual abolition of hereditary privileges but history's assent to the revolutionary dogmas of Christ?"[7] The Kingdom of God is not a concept or ideal for Rauschenbusch; it is a historical force at work in humanity. The way it ultimately works its way out, moreover, is in the form of democracy. As he puts it, "Where religion and intellect combine, the foundation is laid for political democracy."[8]

If, as Stackhouse suggests, America is the great experiment in "constructive Protestantism," it seems what is Christian about that construction is democracy.[9] For in claiming a close interrelation between Christianity and democ-

---

5. Rauschenbusch, *The Righteousness of the Kingdom*, 102.

6. Walter Rauschenbusch, *Theology for the Social Gospel* (Nashville, TN: Abingdon Press, 1917), 112–13.

7. Rauschenbusch, *The Righteousness of the Kingdom*, 199.

8. Rauschenbusch, *Theology for the Social Gospel*, 165.

9. For Stackhouse's own constructive efforts to extend Rauschenbusch's program, only now in terms of human rights, see his *Creeds, Society, and Human Rights* (Grand Rapids, MI: Eerdmans, 1984). In defense of his position, Stackhouse provides a history of the joining of Puritanism and liberalism to create the universalistic creed of rights that culminated in the United Declaration on Human Rights. He notes that these "principles could not be articulated in the particular language of Christian piety which had shaped both the Christian and secular liberal philosophers who had first developed them. Representatives from many cultures and religions would have resisted overt theological formulations in christological or deist terms. The principles had to be stated in 'confessionally neutral' terms. But even at this point we see the triumph of the basic assumptions of the Liberal-Puritan synthesis. The state

racy, Rauschenbusch's work is hardly an isolated example. As Jan Dawson has recently argued, at the turn of this century there developed a "faith in the spiritual oneness of Christianity and democracy, based on the democratic theology of Christianity and concerned primarily with the survival of Christianity in troubled modern democracies."[10] To support democracy became a means of supporting Christianity and vice versa.

Dawson quotes Lyman Abbott, successor to Henry Ward Beecher, in the liberal Christian paper *Outlook* to the effect that "Democracy is not merely a political theory, it is not merely a social opinion; it is a profound religious faith. . . . To him who holds it, this one fundamental faith in the Fatherhood of God and in the universal brotherhood of man is the essence of democracy."[11] If democracy was seen as the institutionalized form of Christianity, it was no less true that democracy was dependent on religion to survive. Thus in 1907, the year following the publication of the article by Abbott, Robert Ashworth wrote in the *Chicago Divinity School Journal* that "the fate of the democratic movement rests ultimately upon religion. Religion is essential to democracy, and is, indeed, its foundation. It is based upon the New Testament principle of the equal value of every soul in the sight of the Divine Father."[12]

This kind of direct theological appeal in support of democracy becomes more muted as Christian thinkers become increasingly aware of the religious and social pluralism of America, but that does not lessen their enthusiasm for democracy as that form of society and government that best institutionalizes Christian social philosophy. Reinhold Niebuhr is certainly a case in point. Vicious in his critique of the theological and social optimism of Rauschenbusch and the other "social gospelers" ' defense of democracy, he never questioned the assumption that democracy was the most appropriate form of society and government for Christians. What was needed, according to Niebuhr, was to provide a more adequate basis for democracy in a realistic

---

itself should not be 'religious'! In this view the theologically and morally valid state is one limited by righteous principles and one that allows other organizations to define what is religiously valid. In brief, the 'godly state' is a secular state" (103). Stackhouse's account seems far too sanguine about how the obvious tensions between the Puritan sense of community can be reconciled with the individualism of liberalism. But even if that were not a problem, one cannot help but wonder what has happened that a "secular state" by definition can be called "godly."

10. Jan Dawson, "The Religion of Democracy in Early Twentieth-Century America," *Journal of Church and State* 27, no. 1 (winter 1985): 47.

11. Quoted in ibid., 48.

12. Ibid.

account of human nature. Such an account, he thought, was to be found primarily in the "Christian view of human nature [that] is more adequate for the development of a democratic society than either the optimism with which democracy has become historically associated or the moral cynicism which inclines human communities to tyrannical political strategies."[13]

In effect, from Rauschenbusch to the present Christian social ethics has had one agenda: to show why American democracy possesses distinctive religious status. The primary subject of Christian ethics in America has been America.[14] This has now even become the project for Roman Catholic social ethics, as exemplified in the work of John Courtney Murray. It was Murray's task to make America amenable to Catholic social theory by interpreting the separation of church and state as a confession by the state of its incompetence in matters of religion[15] and, at the same time, to make Catholics amenable to America by showing that Catholics can enthusiastically support democracy as an imaginative solution to the problem of religious pluralism.[16] Murray argued an even stronger case by suggesting that American democracy, whose political substance consists in an order of antecedent rights to the state,[17] can be sustained only by the Catholic theory of natural law as the only alternative to the destructive individualism of Locke and Hobbes.[18]

13. Reinhold Niebuhr, *The Children of Light and the Children of Darkness* (New York: Charles Scribner's Sons, 1944), xiii. In fairness to Niebuhr, it should be pointed out that he wrote *The Children of Light* at the end of World War II in the interest of trying to deflate some of the more enthusiastic celebrations of democracy the war had occasioned. Yet Niebuhr remained throughout his life a firm supporter of democracy as that social system that best embodies the Christian understanding of man. Richard Fox observes, "What is still surprising about *The Children of Light* is that the author of *Moral Man,* even if older and wiser, could have become so complacent about democratic processes in advanced industrial society. The book elevated gradualist experimentation and piecemeal reform to the level of a basic axiom" (*Reinhold Niebuhr: A Biography* [New York: Pantheon Books, 1985], 220).

14. For a more complete development of this claim, see "On Keeping Theological Ethics Theological" (1983), essay 2 in this volume.

15. This part of Murray's work is often, unfortunately, ignored. One of the reasons for this may be that these were articles published in *Theological Studies* 13 and 14 (1953) called "The Church and Totalitarian Democracy" and "Leo XIII: Separation of Church and State." They are still worth reading.

16. This is the main argument of Murray's *We Hold These Truths* (Garden City, NY: Image Books, 1964).

17. Ibid., 308.

18. In *An American Strategic Theology* (Ramsey, NJ: Paulist Press, 1982), John Coleman provides the best Roman Catholic attempt to continue Murray's project. Coleman, however, is much more interested in how Catholicism can act to renew the ethos or civil religion of America than the more strictly constitutional issues with which Murray was concerned.

It is only against this background that one can understand and/or appreciate the work of Richard Neuhaus. In his much publicized book, *The Naked Public Square: Religion and Democracy in America,* Neuhaus argues that we are facing a crisis in our society. Because religious discourse has increasingly been excluded from our public life, he fears that a moral vacuum has been created. This vacuum threatens constantly to be filled by totalitarianism, as the isolation of the individual from mediating structures gives us little power to stand against the omnivorous appetite of the bureaucratic state.[19] The only way out of this predicament is to mend the "rupture between public policy and moral sentiment. But the only moral sentiment of public effect is the sentiment that

19. Richard Neuhaus, *The Naked Public Square: Religion and Democracy in America* (Grand Rapids, MI: Eerdmans, 1984), 83–86. Charles Taylor rightly argues that no one saw this problem more clearly than did Hegel—namely, that

> absolute freedom requires homogeneity. It cannot brook differences which would prevent everyone participating totally in the decisions of the society. And what is even more, it requires some near unanimity of will emerge from this deliberation, for otherwise the majority would just be imposing its will on the minority and freedom would not be universal. But differentiation of some fairly essential kinds are ineradicable. Moreover they are recognized in our post-Romantic climate essential to human identity. Men cannot simply identify themselves as men, but they define themselves more immediately by their partial community, cultural, linguistic, confessional and so, on. Modern democracy is therefore in a bind. I think the dilemma of this kind can be seen in contemporary society. Modern societies have moved towards much greater homogeneity and greater interdependence, so that partial communities lost their autonomy, and to some extent, their identity. But great differences remain; only because of the ideology of homogeneity these differential characteristics no longer have meaning and value for those who have them. Thus the rural population is taught by the mass media to see itself as just lacking in some of the advantages of a more advanced life style. Homogenization thus increases minority alienation and resentment and the first response of liberal society is to try even more of the same: programs to eliminate poverty, or assimilate Indians, move populations out of declining regions, bring an urban way of life to the countryside. But the radical response is to convert this sense of alienation into a demand for "absolute freedom." The idea is to overcome alienation by creating a society in which everyone, including the present "out" groups, participate fully in the decisions. But both these solutions would simply aggravate the problem, which is that homogenization has undermined the communities or characteristics by which people formerly identified themselves, and put nothing in their place. What does step into the gap almost everywhere is ethnic or national identity. Nationalism has become the most powerful focus of identity in modern society. The demand for radical freedom can and frequently does join up with nationalism and is given a definite impetus and direction from this. (*Hegel and Modern Society* [Cambridge, England: Cambridge University Press, 1979], 114–15).

Neuhaus's point is profound, but I do not see how he provides an adequate response since he continues to support the political and economic presumptions that are the source of the difficulty.

is embodied in and reinforced by living tradition. There are no areligious moral traditions of public, or at least of democratic, force in American life. This is not to say that morality must be embodied in religion or that the whole of religion is morality. It is to say that among the American people, religion and morality are conjoined. Religion in our popular life is the morality-bearing part of culture, and in that sense the heart of culture."[20]

From this perspective Neuhaus is appreciative of the Moral Majority. For in spite of the crudeness with which they often put their position they have at least raised the issue of the public value of religion that at one time was the agenda of political liberals. Rather than condemning the Moral Majority, Neuhaus seeks to help them enter the public debate by basing their appeals to principles that are accessible to the public:

> Publicly assertive religious forces will have to learn that the remedy for the naked public square is not naked religion in public. They will have to develop a mediating language by which ultimate truths can be related to the penultimate and prepenultimate questions of political and legal content. In our several traditions there are rich conceptual resources for the development of such mediating language—whether concepts be called natural law, common grace, general revelation, or the order of creation. Such a civil engagement of secular and religious forces could produce a new public philosophy to sustain this American experiment in liberal democracy. The result may not be that we would agree with one another. Indeed there may be more disagreement. But at least we would know what we are disagreeing about, namely, different accounts of the transcendent good by which we might order our life together. Contra Justice Blackmun and legions of others, democracy is not served by evading the question of the good. Democracy becomes a political community worthy of moral actors only when we engage the question of the good.[21]

20. Neuhaus, 154.

21. Richard Neuhaus, "Nihilism without the Abyss: Law, Rights, and Transcendent Good," paper delivered at a conference on Religion and Law at Catholic University Law School, Washington, D.C., April 1985, 14–15. For a similar claim, see *The Naked Public Square*, 36. While agreeing with Neuhaus that religion needs to help our society discover or create a moral discourse for the public sphere, John Coleman rightly raises questions about the assumed neutrality or objectivity of that discourse. Thus he criticizes Brian Hehir for requiring Christians to come to the public arena shorn of their particularistic commitments. As Coleman says, he does not think it possible to escape "the 'permanent hermeneutical predicament' of particular languages and community traditions in a conflict of interpretive schemes through the emergence of a common universal language. I fear that this proposal could court the risk of a continuation of the pernicious intertwining of an ethics of deep concern with an ethic of

Neuhaus challenges mainline Protestant liberalism to live up to its rightful commitment to sustaining democracy as the socially specific form that Christianity should take.[22] As he puts it, "The main line of the mainline story was confidence and hope regarding the Americanizing of Christianity and the Christianizing of America."[23] Indeed, he argues that in spite of their fervor for disestablishing Christianity in America, most liberals remain committed to "Christianizing" the social order, only the synonyms for "Christianize" today "include terms such as justice, equality, and sustainability."[24]

That such is the case helps explain the enthusiasm for the work of John Rawls among those working in Christian ethics. Harlen Beckley puts the matter well as he notes that the emergence of a politically powerful Christian right has made vivid a dilemma that Christian ethics has still to resolve. "The

---

looking out for number one. But finally, and most persuasive for me, I simply do not know anywhere else to look in American culture besides to our religious ethical resources to find the social wisdom and ethical orientation we would seem to need if we are to face as Americans our new context of increasing interdependence at the national and international level" (*An American Strategic Theology*, 197–98). Thus Coleman, like many Protestant thinkers, calls us to renew the biblical and republican-virtue tradition against contemporary liberalism. (This is the main theme of William Sullivan's *Reconstructing Public Philosophy* [Berkeley: University of California Press, 1982].) It is a strange social order indeed that makes Catholics so committed to making America work that they accept the project of constructive Protestantism. For a provocative article of the destructive results this process has had on orthodoxy, see Vigen Guroian, "The Americanization of Orthodoxy: Crisis and Challenge," *Greek Orthodox Theological Review* 29, no. 3 (1984): 255–67.

22. Neuhaus, *The Naked Public Square*, 121.

23. Ibid., 220. In an unpublished paper, "Democratic Morality: A Possibility," Neuhaus responds to this essay and qualifies the starkness of this claim. As he says, "I count myself among the many Christians, perhaps the majority of Christians in America, who have the gravest reservations about the idea of 'Christian America.' It makes sense to speak, always cautiously, of America as a Christian society in terms of historical forces, ideas, and demography. But no society is worthy of the name of Christ, except the society that is the church, and then it is worthy only by virtue of being made worthy through the grace of God in Christ" (6).

24. Neuhaus, *The Naked Public Square*, 230. For one of the ablest critiques of Neuhaus, see George Marsden, "Secularism and the Public Square," *This World* 11 (spring–summer 1985): 48–62. Marsden challenges Neuhaus's contention that religion is the morality-bearing part of our culture, thus denying Neuhaus's statement of the problem. As Marsden says, "Nontheistic secularism also promotes a morality. The problem regarding public philosophy is not simply that of whether or not we have morality in public life. More basically, it is a problem of having competing moral systems and hence less of a consensus in public philosophy than we might like. Putting more religion into public life would not resolve this problem unless we decide first whose religion it would be. In fact, there is even less consensus regarding religion than there is on public philosophy; it is difficult to see how adding more religion would increase the needed consensus" (59).

dilemma is: How can an evaluation of the distribution of rights, duties, benefits, and burdens which society necessarily imposes upon all of its citizens be faithful to Christian beliefs without forcing others to accept the distinctive moral implications of beliefs they do not and should not be required to share?"[25] According to Beckley, "This dilemma can only be resolved if the justification for principles of justice is founded upon general beliefs and values that others hold, or can be reasonably expected to hold, and which Christians can affirm on the basis of their distinctive beliefs."[26] Beckley argues that to accomplish this resolution "the distinctively Christian moral ideal of love obligates those who adhere to it to embrace the beliefs which undergird John Rawls's idea of justice as fairness."[27] Rawls thus becomes the language of common grace that continues the project of Christianizing America.

Of course, there are disagreements among Christian ethicists on this score. Neuhaus, for example, thinks Rawls's theory threatens to destroy the individual "by depriving him of all those personal particularities that are the essence of being an individual."[28] As a result, Rawls's account is ahistorical, in contradistinction to the "Judeo-Christian tradition," which is "premised upon the concept of real history, real change, happening in an incomplete universe that is still awaiting its promised fulfillment."[29] What is needed, according to Neu-

25. Harlan Beckley, "A Christian Affirmation of Rawls' Idea of Justice as Fairness: Part 1," *Journal of Religious Ethics* 13, no. 2 (fall 1985): 210–11.
26. Ibid., 212.
27. Ibid.
28. Neuhaus, *The Naked Public Square,* 257.
29. Ibid., 258. Neuhaus's criticisms are broad strokes of the much more detailed and refined criticism of Rawls offered by Michael Sandel in *Liberalism and the Limits of Justice* (Cambridge, England: Cambridge University Press, 1982). Yet Neuhaus does not explain how he can at once criticize Rawls on such grounds and yet continue to underwrite America as the exemplification of what a Christian social order should look like. For whether Neuhaus likes it or not, the public philosophy of America is liberal and Rawls in many ways is its most eloquent spokesman. In recent essays Rawls has begun to reinterpret *A Theory of Justice* more in terms of political strategy for pluralist democracies that may at once make it less philosophically compelling for philosophers but more socially significant. See, for example, his "Justice or Fairness: Political Not Metaphysical," *Philosophy and Public Affairs* 14, no. 3 (summer 1985): 223–51. In spite of his qualifications, the question still remains whether any account of justice can be intelligibly abstracted from a conception of the virtues integral to the pursuit of goods in common. The very fact that many Christian theologians such as Beckley feel the need to adopt Rawls in order to have a comprehensive theory of justice may mean that something has already gone wrong in Christians' understanding of the social and political role of the church. Put overly simply, one needs a theory of justice when one no longer assumes that the very existence of the church is a social stance. Christian thinkers obviously must test various accounts of justice offered by different societies in order to find areas of common cause. But it

haus, is a recovery of some substantive account of the goods that make a good society possible through attending to the concrete desires of real people who are not required to leave their religious convictions behind when they participate in the public arena. This same set of issues is at the center of Robert Bellah et al.'s much discussed and praised book *Habits of the Heart*. The critique of "individualism" that is the hallmark of that book is part of a larger agenda that is in essential continuity with the hope of Christianizing America. As the authors suggest, in spite of our individualism,

> we have never been, and still are not, a collection of private individuals who, except for a conscious contract to create a minimal government, have nothing in common. Our lives make sense in a thousand ways, most of which we are unaware of, because of traditions that are centuries, if not millennia, old. It is these traditions that help us to know that it does make a difference who we are and how we treat one another. But if we owe the meaning of our lives to biblical and republican traditions of which we seldom consciously think, is there not the danger that the erosion of these traditions may eventually deprive us of that meaning altogether? We would argue that if we are ever to enter that new world that so far has been powerless to be born, it will be through reversing modernity's tendency to obliterate all previous culture. We need to learn again from the cultural riches of the human species and to reappropriate and revitalize those riches so that they can speak to our condition today.[30]

---

is quite another matter to assume that in order for Christians to act politically they need a theory of justice such as Rawls's that claims to order the basic structure of society. In that respect Beckley's contention that Rawls's theory does not pretend to comprehend all of morality fails to denote adequately the tendency of Rawls's account to render some goods, such as the family, problematic. See, for example, *A Theory of Justice* (Cambridge, MA: Harvard University Press, 1971), 511–12. I am indebted to L. Gregory Jones for helping me see this.

30. Robert Bellah et al., *Habits of the Heart: Individualism and Commitment in American Life* (Berkeley: University of California Press, 1985), 282–83. For Bellah's more explicit views, see "The Revolution and the Civil Religion," in *Religion and the American Revolution*, ed. Jerald Brauer (Philadelphia: Fortress, 1976), 55–73. There Bellah observes that when his original article on civil religion was published (1967), it came just as the existence of civil religion was becoming questionable. He observes, "Only the biblical religions can provide the energy and vision for a new turn in American history, perhaps a new understanding of covenant, which may be necessary not only to save ourselves but to keep us from destroying the rest of the world" (73). For a thorough discussion that raises doubts about the extent of the influence of civic republicanism in America, see John Patrick Diggins, *The Lost Soul of American Politics: Virtue, Self-Interest, and the Foundations of Liberalism* (New York: Basic Books, 1984). Equally

This sounds very much like a call for reconstituting Christian America.

I have no interest in trying to resolve the many disagreements among Neuhaus, Beckley, Bellah, and Falwell. Rather, what I have attempted to do is to show that the reason Falwell is such a challenge to the Christian mainstream in America is not because he is so different from them, but because he has basically accepted their agenda.[31] The Christian right and the Christian left do not disagree about the religious status of the American experiment. They just disagree about what language and/or political theory will allow them to accomplish their common goal of making American democracy as close as possible to a manifestation of God's Kingdom.

3. What a Christian Critique of Christian America Should Look Like

For most Christians in America, from the nominal Christian to the committed social activist to the theologian, it is unthinkable to theorize outside the tradition I have just tried to sketch. Yet I refuse to support prayer in the

---

interesting is Arthur Vidich and Stanford Lyman, *American Sociology: Worldly Rejections of Religion and Their Directions* (New Haven: Yale University Press, 1985). They document that the birth of sociology in America has been, even in its most secularized and scientific form, a continuation of the project to form civil society on the basis of religious values:

> The problems of American sociology emanate from the dilemma and contradictions in the relationship between God, the state, and civil society. In America's Puritan heritage there is envisioned a society composed of a voluntaristic covenant of believers, exercising mutual watchfulness over one another, acceding to legitimate civil authority but recognizing the ultimate sovereignty of God over all affairs. The nation would take form as a democratic commonwealth. However, in America the promise of this democratic commonwealth was threatened by new forms of worldly success and failure and new modes of social differentiation. American sociological thinkers were the moral successors to the earlier Puritan theologians. Convinced that America was destined to be the redeemer nation for the world, these sociologists took as their project the inner-worldly perfection of American social, economic, and political institutions. Implicit in this project was the belief that a covenanted national community could be established within the boundaries of the United States. Virtually all the American sociologists converted issues of theodicy into problems for sociology. Instead of vindicating the ways of God to man, they sought to justify the ways of society to its members. (281)

They point out also that as sociologists noted the inability of Protestant churches to provide a moral framework for civil society, sociologists tended to center on the state itself as the only institution with the moral authority to guide society. Sociology as a "policy science" thus becomes the new priestly craft necessary to help the modern bureaucratic state "manage" society.

31. Falwell is particularly interesting when he wanders into questions of international relations. Suddenly he no longer makes direct biblical appeals but, rather, sounds like any good American realist accepting consequential calculations for determining the right moral policy.

public schools because I *do* find myself outside that tradition. That I do so is because I do not believe that the universalism that is intrinsic to the Christian faith is carried by the culture of the West, but instead is to be found first and foremost in the church.[32] From this perspective something has already gone wrong when Christians think they can ask, "What is the best form of society or government?"[33] This question assumes that Christians should or do have social and political power so they can determine the ethos of society. That this assumption has long been with us does nothing to confirm its truth.

That assumption, in short, is the heritage of what John Howard Yoder has called "the Constantinian sources of Western social ethics." It is an assumption shared by Christians and non-Christians alike, for the very logic of most contemporary philosophical accounts of ethics and social theory accepts its essential rightness only in secular terms. By calling our attention to Constantine, Yoder has no stake in determining the sincerity of Constantine's conversion or whether it was exactly at that time that a decisive shift in Christian assumptions took place. Rather, Constantine is the symbol of the decisive shift in the logic of moral argument when Christians ceased being a minority and accepted Caesar as a member of the church. It is that logic we must understand if a genuine Christian critique of Christian America is to be made.

The most obvious consequence of the change occasioned by Constantine, according to Yoder, was the change in the composition of the church. Prior to that time Christians had been a minority who at least required some degree of loyalty. After that time everyone was a member. It now takes conviction to be a pagan. As a result, Christians are now forced to develop a doctrine of the "true church" that remains invisible (136).[34]

---

32. For an attempt to develop this position, see my cc and pk.

33. John Howard Yoder, *The Priestly Kingdom: Social Ethics as Gospel* (Notre Dame, IN: University of Notre Dame, 1984), 154. Subsequent references are in the text. When Christians ask such a question they assume a majority status. In contrast, Yoder's view, as well as my own, is that Christians cannot help but be a minority if they are being faithful to their basic convictions.

34. It should not be thought that Yoder is committing the genetic fallacy by his appeal to the early Christian community. He is not saying that because the early church was a minority it should always be a minority; rather, in this context he is working descriptively to show the change in the logic of moral argument when this occurred. Of course, he will argue that the form of the early church is normative for Christians, not because it was the early church but because what the early Christians believed is true and results in Christians taking a critical stance toward governmental authorities. I share that view but I cannot here adequately defend it.

This shift is of crucial importance for how ethics is now understood. Prior to the time of Constantine, Christian belief in God's rule of the world was a matter of faith. However, with Constantine the idea that providence is no longer an object of faith for God's governance of the world was now thought to be empirically evident in the person of the Christian ruler. With this changed eschatology, ethics had to change "because one must aim one's behavior at strengthening the regime, and because the ruler himself must have very soon some approbation and perhaps some guidance as he does things the earlier church would have perhaps disapproved" (137). As a result, the distinctive character of Christian life is now primarily identified with inwardness since everyone by definition is already Christian.

Once Christianity became dominant, moreover, it was now thought that moral discourse must be that which can direct the behavior of anyone. Servanthood and love of enemy, contentment and monogamy, cannot be expected of everyone. So a duality develops in ethics between "evangelical counsels" for the motivated and "precepts" for everyone else. Perhaps an even more significant change is the assumption that the decisive ethical questions become, to quote Yoder, "What would happen if everyone did it? If everyone gave their wealth away what would we do for capital? If everyone loved their enemies who would ward off the communists? This argument could be met on other levels, but here the only point is to observe that such reasoning would have been preposterous in the early church and remains ludicrous wherever committed Christians accept realistically their minority status. Far more fitting than 'What if everybody did it' would be its inverse, 'What if nobody else acted like a Christian and we did?' " (139).[35]

---

35. Connected with this reversal is what happens once the ruler is let into the church, for then the ruler, not the average or weak person, is the model for ethical reason. Thus, the rightness of truth telling or the wrongness of killing is tested first by whether a ruler can meet such standards. Yoder, however, does not mean to exclude rulers from the church, but rather he expects them to act like Christians. Thus,

Caesar would be perfectly free (for a while) to bring to bear upon the exercise of his office the ordinary meaning of the Christian faith. It might happen that the result would be that his enemies triumph over him, but that often happens to rulers anyway. It might happen that he would have to suffer, or not stay in office all his life, but that too often happens to rulers anyway, and it is something that Christians are supposed to be ready for. It might happen that he would be killed; but most Caesars are killed anyway. It might happen that some of his followers would have to suffer. But emperors and kings are accustomed to asking people to suffer for them. Especially if the view were still authentically alive, which the earlier Christians undeniably had held to and which the theologians in the age of Constantine were still repeating, that God blesses those who serve him, it might also have

With this new universalism comes an increasing need to test moral discourse by its effectiveness. Once the course of history is thought to be empirically discernible and the prosperity of our regime the measure of the good, efficacy becomes a decisive test for the moral rightness of our action. Self-sacrifice that is not tied to some long-term account of result becomes irrational. This is particularly important in assessing the validity of violence and the Christian's participation in war.

What is important about Yoder's depiction of the change in moral logic occasioned by the Constantinian turn is that the effects he describes are still with us. With the Renaissance and Reformation "Christendom" was replaced by the nation-state. Christians, however, did not respond to this change by maintaining the cosmopolitanism of the Holy Roman Empire, but rather now maintained that Christian societies could wage war on one another in the name of preserving their Christian culture. With the Enlightenment, the link between church and state was broken, but the moral identification of Christians with the state remained strong. This has been especially the case in America where "once the separation of church and state is seen as theologically desirable, a society where this separation is achieved is not a pagan society but a nation structured according to the will of God. For nearly two centuries, in fact, the language of American public discourse was not only religious, not only Christian, but specifically Protestant. Moral identification of church with nation remains despite institutional separation. In fact, forms of institutional interlocking develop which partly deny the story of separation (chaplaincies, tax exemptions)" (142).

If there is to be a genuine Christian critique of Christian America, I am convinced that this habit of thought, which Yoder calls Constantinianism, must be given up. Otherwise, we Christians remain caught in the same habits of thought and behavior that implicitly or explicitly assume that insofar as America is a democracy she is Christian. As a result Christians lose exactly the skills necessary to see how deeply they have been compromised by the assumption that their task is to rule, if not the government, at least the ethos of America. That is why Christian social strategy in America continues to be caught in a fateful ambiguity—namely, Christians claim that Christianity, or at least religion, should be more present in public life yet they want to make

---

been possible that, together with all of the risks just described, most of which a ruler accepts anyway, there could have been in some times and some places the possibility that good could be done, that creative social alternatives could be discovered, that problems could be solved, enemies loved and justice fostered. (146)

government itself religiously neutral. The history of the Supreme Court decisions on church/state issues should be enough to convince anyone that there is no easy way to resolve this tension in the American legal system, much less the social and political systems.[36]

Am I therefore suggesting that Christians must "withdraw" from the social, political, and legal life of America? I am certainly not arguing that; rather, I am trying to suggest that in order to answer questions of "why" or "how" Christians participate in the life of this country we do not need a theory about the Christian character of democracy. Rather, I am suggesting, with Yoder, that as Christians we would "be more relaxed and less compulsive about running the world if we made our peace with our minority situation, seeing this neither as a dirty trick of destiny nor as some great new progress but simply as the unmasking of the myth of Christendom, which wasn't true even when it was believed" (158).

As Yoder argues, since almost all rulers claim to be our benefactors in order to justify their rule, there is no reason that Christians cannot use that very language to call their rulers to be more humane in their ways of governing. Moreover, if we are lucky enough to be in a situation where the ruler's language of justification claims to have the consent of the governed, we can use the machinery of democracy for our own and our neighbor's advantage. But we should not, thereby, be lulled into believing that "we the people" are thereby governing ourselves. Democracy is still government by the elite, though it may be less oppressive since it uses language in its justification that provides ways to mitigate oppressiveness. But that does not make democracy, from a Christian point of view, different in kind from states of another form (158–59).

Perhaps the hardest habit to break deriving from our Constantinianism is the assumption that if we do not govern then surely society and/or government will fall into anarchy or totalitarianism. But I notice no shortage of people willing to rule nor any absence of ideologies for rule. The problem is not Christians disavowing ruling, but rather that when Christians rule they tend to create international and national disorder because they have such a calling to make things right. If Christians "claim for democracy the status of a social institution *sui generis*, we shall inflate ourselves and destroy our neighbors through the demonic demands of the claims we make for our system and

---

36. For a romp through church/state issues, see George Goldberg, *Reconsecrating America* (Grand Rapids, MI: Eerdmans, 1984).

we shall pollute our Christian faith by making of it a civil religion. If, on the other hand, we protect ourselves from the Constantinianism of that view of democracy, we may find the realistic liberty to foster and celebrate relative democratization as one of the prophetic ministries of a servant people in a world we do not control" (165–66).

I am aware that the position I have taken will be a surprise to most Christians schooled on the assumption that there is an intrinsic relation between Christianity and America. Yet I suspect the position will be equally unwelcomed by many who dislike calls like that of Neuhaus for a recovery of the role of religion in American life. They want people who still use their private time to entertain religious convictions to be willing to work to create a social order and corresponding government that relegates those convictions to the private sphere. That is done, of course, in the name of creating a democratic society that is based on universal claims justified by reason qua reason.[37] Constantinianism is a hard habit to break even for those who no longer understand themselves to be religious.

From this perspective the problem with Yoder (and Falwell) is their refusal to find a neutral or at least nonconfrontational way to state the social implications of their religious convictions.[38] That is not playing the game fairly, as it makes religion more public than is healthy for an allegedly pluralistic society. After all, there have to be some limits to our pluralism.

Of course, Yoder might well respond that he is willing on a case-by-case basis pragmatically to use the allegedly more universal language of our society. But for many, I suspect, such a pragmatic approach would be insufficient. It is not enough to be willing to play the game of the putative neutral or objective language and procedures of pluralist democracy: one must be willing to believe that such language and procedures are truly the form of the society any people anywhere would choose if they had the material means, institutional creativity, and philosophical acumen. To challenge that presumption, as Yoder

---

37. It is interesting to observe that most Americans, whether religious or secular, continue to take a missionary stance for democracy. Americans criticize our government's support for nondemocratic regimes around the world to the point of sometimes advocating intervention against nondemocratic regimes. As Yoder observes, "After the 'Christian west' has lost the naive righteousness with which it thought it should export its religion around the world, we still seem to have a good conscience about exporting our politics" (151).

38. By associating Yoder and Falwell at this point, I do not mean to deny their obvious differences. Yet they both use language about Jesus in the public arena without apology. The problem with Falwell is not that he uses Christian appeals but that his understanding of the Christian tradition is so attenuated.

has, is I think the necessary starting point for any genuine Christian critique of Christian America.

4. On Being Christian in America

But where does this leave us? If America is not the "new Jerusalem," does that mean Christians must seek to make America live consistent with secular presuppositions? In order to make the line between being Christian and being American clear, must we side with those who wish to force any religious phenomenon out of the public arena? Should we rejoice in the destructive kind of individualism that is so graphically displayed in *Habits of the Heart?* Do we not have a stake in sustaining a public ethos that might make the rise of paganism, which might well use the language of Christianity, less likely?

I see no reason that the position I have taken would make me give an affirmative answer to these questions. I believe that Christians should not will that secular society be more unjust than it already has a tendency to be. Therefore, we have a stake in fostering those forms of human association that ensure that the virtues can be sustained. Virtues make it possible to sustain a society committed to working out differences short of violence.[39] What I fear, however, is that in the absence of those associations we will seek to solve the moral anomie of the American people through state action or by a coercive reclaiming of Christian America.[40]

Therefore, if I refuse to support prayer in the public school it becomes all the more important that I urge Christians to learn to pray authentically as Christians. For if Christians reclaim prayer as an end in itself rather than a way to confirm the "Christian nature" of our society, we will perform our most important civic responsibility. As Origen argued, what more important public

---

39. Of course, some accounts of what it means to be virtuous require violence as a necessary correlative: the just person must envisage the possibility of using coercion if he or she is to be just and to do justice. To be persuasive, therefore, my claim requires a substantial account of the content of the virtues, for example, why the virtues of patience and forgiveness are central to the moral life. [Hauerwas would seek to provide such an account in, e.g., "Reconciling the Practice of Reason: Casuistry in a Christian Context" (1986) in *CET;* "Peacemaking: The Virtue of the Church" (1985), essay 16 in this volume; as well as *PK* in general.]

40. George Hunsinger, for example, has argued that we live in a time not unlike the situation that confronted those who produced the Barmen declaration. See his "Barth, Barmen, and the Confessing Church Today," *Katallagete* 9, no. 2 (summer 1985): 14–27. See also my response, "On Learning Simplicity in an Ambiguous Age," *Katallagete* 10, nos. 1–3 (fall 1987): 43–46.

service can we render than to pray that the emperor recognize his or her status as a creature of God? Such a prayer is no less significant in a society that believes "the people" have in fact become the emperor.

Further Reading

"The Democratic Policing of Christianity" (1993), in DF

"The Importance of Being Catholic: Unsolicited Advice from a Protestant Bystander" (1989), in IGC

"On Keeping Theological Ethics Theological" (1983), essay 2 in this volume

"Walter Rauschenbusch and the Saving of America" (2000), in BH.

"Remaining in Babylon: Oliver O'Donovan's Defence of Christendom" (1997), in WW

"The Politics of Witness: How We Educate Christians in Liberal Societies" (1991), in AC

"The Politics of Justice: Why Justice Is a Bad Idea for Christians" (1991), in AC

"The Kingship of Christ: Why Freedom of Belief Is Not Enough" (1992), in IGC

"Flight from Foundationalism, or, Things Aren't as Bad as They Seem" (1989), in WW

"Theology and the New American Culture" (1972), in VV

"The Reality of the Church: Even a Democratic State Is Not the Kingdom" (1985), in AN

"Virtue in Public" (1986), in CET

23. Sex in Public: How Adventurous
Christians Are Doing It (1978)

After examining a number of typical responses by both Catholic and Protestant theological ethicists to the sexual revolution of the 1960s, Hauerwas offers a genuine alternative to the naïveté of the romanticists and the cynicism of the realists. Hauerwas shows that viewpoints claiming that a sexual ethic should be based on criteria that "foster creative growth toward integration" turn out to be vacuous, serving conclusions arrived at on other grounds. More important, such viewpoints are destructive because they tacitly reject the inherently political nature of sexuality in the Christian tradition. In other words, Christian sexual ethics of the 1970s uncritically accepted the individualism of American culture and thus was unable to offer a compelling account of why sexual desire and activity should be ordered to the mission of the Christian church.

1. On Speaking Candidly and as a Christian about Sex

Candor is always to be striven for, but it is especially important for any discussion about sex; in particular, the morality of sex. And candor compels me to say that I cannot provide anything like an adequate ethic to deal with sex. This is, no doubt, partly because of my own moral and intellectual limitations. But it also reflects that generally Christians, and in particular Christian ethicists, are unsure what to say or how to respond to our culture's changing sexual mores (if in fact they are changing).[1]

[From CC © 1981 by University of Notre Dame Press. Used by permission. Originally titled "Sex in Public: Toward a Christian Ethic of Sex." It has been slightly abridged and edited for clarity.]
1. Indeed, I suspect that the "crisis" concerning sexual behavior in our society is not what people are actually doing or not doing, but that we have no way to explain to ourselves or to others why it is that we are doing one thing rather than another. Thus, people simply do not know why they do or do not have sexual intercourse before marriage, or even more disturbing, why they should or should not get married at all, or why they should or should not have

Current reflection about sexual ethics by Christian ethicists is a mess. That may seem an odd state of affairs, for it is generally thought that while the church may often be confused about issues of war or politics, we can surely count on Christians to have a clear view about sex. It has been assumed that the church and her theologians have seldom spoken ambiguously about sex and most of what they have had to say took the form of a negative.[2] No, you should not have sexual intercourse before marriage. No, you should not commit adultery. No, you should not practice contraception. And so on.

Indeed, the proscriptive nature of much of the church's teaching about sex (together with the assumption often associated with such strictures that there is something wrong with sex), seems to me the source of some of the confusion concerning current sexual ethics. By rights, theologians and ethicists should not be able to say enough good things about sex. Broad anthropological analysis has shown us that we are fundamentally sexual beings, and that is indeed a good thing. God has created us to be sexual beings and it seems nothing short of Manichaean for us to deny that aspect of our lives. But in our rush to show that Christians know that sex can be beautiful, Christian ethicists have often failed to talk candidly about sex. One suspects that if sex can be beautiful, it is as often likely to be messy or boring.

Many people are particularly disturbed when they are told that contemporary Christian ethics has little coherent to say about sexual ethics. We live in a cultural situation that is extremely confusing in regard to sex and we rightly feel we need some guidance from somewhere. Whether we are sexually faithful in our marriages or not, we feel at a loss to explain why we live that way rather than another. Thus, some stay faithful because they are fearful of women or men, or lazy, or fear the consequences if found out. If or how sexual fidelity is anchored in our fundamental Christian convictions remains unclear.[3]

---

children. In the absence of any such accounts, pragmatic considerations, which are often filled with wisdom and much good sense, rule the day. However, pragmatic reflection is not sufficient to guide our lives in a manner that helps us have a sense of worth necessary to sustain our own and our community's moral projects.

2. For an excellent brief overview of the historical development of sexual ethics, see Margaret Farley, "Sexual Ethics," *Encyclopedia of Bioethics* (New York: Free Press, 1978), 4:1575–89.

3. Even more disturbing is what appears to be the sheer sexual anarchy characteristic of much of our culture. For example, Paul Ramsey in a recent article cites Dr. Robert Johnson, director of adolescent medicine at the New Jersey College of Medicine, that two of every ten girls in junior and senior high school in New Jersey will get pregnant this year (see Paul Ramsey, "Do You Know Where Your Children Are?", *Theology Today* 36, no. 1 [April 1979]: 10–21). No

This is an area about which the church and Christian ethicists surely ought to have something to say, but I think what we should have to say will demand a more thorough rethinking of the nature of Christian life than most who call for a new "sex ethic" anticipate. For it is my thesis that the development of a sexual ethic and practice appropriate to basic Christian convictions must be part of a broader political understanding of the church. Put bluntly, there is no way that the traditional Christian insistence that marriage must be characterized by unitive and procreative ends can be made intelligible unless the political function of marriage in the Christian community is understood.[4] Sexual ethics cannot be separated from political ethics if Christians are to make sense of why sexual practices are to be determined by how they contribute to the good of the Christian community.

Methodologically, this means that attempts to base a Christian ethics of sex on natural law—whether natural law be understood as unexceptionable norms or broadly construed anthropological characterizations of human sexuality—must be abandoned. Ironically, the attempt to develop a sexual ethic based on natural law (i.e., the idea that the legitimacy of contraception can be determined by the nature of the act of sex considered in itself) has much in common with the current effort to liberalize sexual ethics through suggestions about what is necessary for the flourishing of human sexuality.[5] The attempt to base an ethic of sex on "nature" results in abstracting sex from those institutions that are necessary to make any ethic of sex intelligible. In contrast, I will try to show that the claim that a sexual ethic derives its form from marriage is a political claim, as it makes sense only in terms of the church's understanding of its mission. Therefore, a Christian ethic of sex cannot be an ethic for all people, but only for those who share the purposes of the community gathered by God and the subsequent understanding of marriage.

The thesis that the ethics of sex is a public and political issue seems to be odd or even absurd in our cultural context. We have been taught to understand that sex is private and is determined by two or more people with free

---

matter what one thinks about premarital sexuality, that is a shocking statistic, and we feel we need some ethical guidance on how to deal with such problems.

4. [Hauerwas's reference to the unitive and procreative ends of marriage show him in conversation with the Catholic tradition. For an example of the Catholic understanding of the ends of marriage, see the Vatican II document *Gaudium et Spes* (Pastoral Constitution on the Church in the Modern World), sections 47–52.]

5. [The natural law understandings of sex that Hauerwas has in mind are (a) readings of Pope Pius XI's encyclical *Casti Connubii* (1930) and (b) Kosnik et al., *Human Sexuality* (1977). See n. 13 regarding the latter document.]

consent. It is often assumed that you can do pretty much what you want as long as you do not "hurt" one another. What we have failed to note is that the claim that sex is a matter of private morality is a political claim dependent upon a liberal political ethos. Any attempt to reclaim an authentic Christian ethic of sex must begin by challenging the assumption that sex is a "private" matter.

Our current sexual ethics is largely made up of inconsistent borrowings from the various options provided by our culture, because by and large Christians have not lived or understood the political nature of their convictions about marriage and sex. Currently, realism and romanticism seem to be the two main cultural alternatives with regard to how people think about sex. These options appear to be fundamentally opposed, but I think on analysis they share some strikingly similar presuppositions. For realism is but chastened romanticism that seeks to "talk sense" about sex in order to prevent some of the worst excesses of romanticism. Yet like romanticism, realism continues to underwrite the assumption that sex is a private matter and is subject to public interest only when it has consequences (e.g., teenage pregnancy) that affect the public pocketbook. A brief analysis of realism and romanticism will make evident that they have set the agenda for the current discussion of sexual ethics among Christians.

1.1 Realism

As the term suggests, realism has the virtue of dealing with sex without illusion or cant. Realists often claim to be amoral, but that does not mean the realist vision lacks depth. For the realist simply assumes that it is too late to raise "moral issues" about sex, one way or the other. We live in a situation where two out of ten young girls in New Jersey are going to get pregnant this year. The realist may deplore the implications but assumes the situation as a fact and concentrates on the task of information: how to get knowledge and techniques to young people who have become "sexually active"[6] so some of the consequences of their behavior can be checked.

The realist position is also often coupled with an attempt to help people have a more healthy attitude toward sex. In particular, the realists stress that

6. Of course, the very phrase "sexually active" already embodies realist assumptions, since it tries to describe what many assume is a serious moral issue in morally neutral language. And of course, the "realist" may be right that such language is more appropriate because it avoids the "moralistic" language of the past, but it must be recognized that this kind of language-transforming proposal assumes substantive moral presuppositions.

sex is simply one human activity among others—it can be a profound human expression or it can just be fun—but what is important, no matter how sex is understood, is that it be demystified. The realist thus suggests to young people that they may not be as ready for sex as they think they are, for as the sexually experienced often discover, sex is not easy to keep just fun.

Realism is a position I often find myself tempted to assume. I still remember vividly when in 1970, my first year of teaching at the University of Notre Dame, I was asked by a delegation of students from the college's student senate what the "Christian ethical position" should be concerning whether doors in the dorms could be shut during visiting hours by members of the opposite sex. Completely taken aback by what seemed to be the triviality of the issue, all I could think to say was that I supposed closing the door was better than getting grass stains. My response was meant to be realistic. I assumed that those students who were going to have sex were going to do so whatever rules one thought up about parietals. And like most realists, I thought that the most important thing anyone could do when confronted by such an issue was to speak candidly.

Yet, in spite of the kind of "worldly wisdom" that makes the realist position attractive, it is doomed to failure. What realists fail to recognize is that, in spite of claims to being amoral or at least nonmoralistic, their position in fact presupposes an ethical recommendation. Realists cannot help but assume that the way things are is the ways things ought to be. In so doing, realists accept as morally normative the liberal assumption that sexual activity should be determined by what each individual feels is good for him or her.

By accepting such an assumption, moreover, realism fails to provide an adequate response to our other primary cultural alternative, romanticism. For many teenagers get pregnant exactly because of their romantic notion that sex should be a significant gesture denoting the level of commitment between two people. In an ironic way the phenomenon of teenage pregnancy, which no doubt is often the result of ignorance and an absence of proper contraceptive techniques, is the sign of how deeply conservative assumptions about the significance of sex are ingrained in our culture.

1.2 Romanticism

Like realism, romanticism is less a coherent position than a general stance about the place of sex and marriage in our lives. The basic assumption of romanticism is that love is the necessary condition for sex and marriage. How love is understood can and often does vary greatly among different versions of romanticism. Yet for all romantics, the quality of the interpersonal relation between a couple is the primary issue for considering sexual involvement. Even the arguments that criticize romanticism structurally may accept the assumption that the primary issue is the "depth" of commitment between the couple.

Examples of this kind of thinking in our society are almost endless, but by way of illustration let me call your attention to the position of Nena and George O'Neill as developed in their best-selling 1972 book, *Open Marriage.*[7] Though I do not think the O'Neills provide a particularly profound version of romanticism, I suspect that they represent broadly shared views and judgments about sex and marriage in our culture.

Ironically, theirs is essentially a conservative position, written in the spirit of saving marriage as a worthwhile activity. To save marriage, however, they argue that the meaning of marriage "must be independently forged by a man and a woman who have the freedom to find their own reasons for being, and for being together. Marriage must be based on a new openness—an openness to one's self, an openness to another's self, and openness to the world. Only by writing their own open contract can couples achieve the flexibility they need to grow. Open marriage is expanded monogamy, retaining the fulfilling and rewarding aspects of an intimate in-depth relationship with another, yet eliminating the restrictions we were formerly led to believe were an integral part of monogamy" (41).

Open marriages must necessarily avoid being controlled by presupposed roles denoted by the terms "husband" and "wife." What we do and do not do as husbands and wives should be determined by what we feel as individual human beings, not by some predetermined set of restrictive codes (148). Thus, in an "open marriage, each gives the other the opportunity, the freedom, to pursue those pleasures he or she wishes to, and the time they do spend together is fruitfully and happily spent in catching up on one another's individual activities" (188). Crucial to such a marriage is trust, as only trust provides the possibility for a marriage to be a "dynamic, growing relationship" (224). But it must be an "open trust," in contrast to those forms of trust built on dependability and assured predictability. To have open trust "means believing in your mate's ability and willingness to cherish and respect your honesty and your open communications. Trust is the feeling that no matter

---

7. Nena and George O'Neill, *Open Marriage* (New York: Avon Press, 1972). Subsequent references are in the text.

what you do or say you are not going to be criticized" (231). "Trust then is freedom, the freedom to assume responsibility for your own self first and then to share that human self in love with your partner in a marriage that places no restrictions upon growth, or limits on fulfillment" (235).

This seems an attractive ideal. After all, who could be against trust? And who would deny the importance of each partner's continuing to develop as his or her own person in and outside marriage? For it is surely true that the strength of any marriage is partly judged by the ability of each partner to rejoice in the friendships of the other. Indeed, such friendships can be seen as necessary for the enrichment of any marriage.

Yet, ironically, the O'Neills' account of "open marriage" requires a transformation of the self that makes intimate relationships impossible in or outside of marriage. Many conservative critics of proposals like "open marriage" tend to overlook this element, because all their attention is directed to the sexual implication—namely, that premarital and extramarital sex is not condemned. But that element has long been written into the very structure and nature of romanticism.

What the "conservative" must recognize is that prior to the issue of whether premarital or extramarital sexual intercourse is wrong is the question of character. What kind of people do you want to encourage? Hidden in the question of What ought we to do? is always the prior question What ought we to be? The most disturbing thing about such proposals as the O'Neills' is the kind of person they wish each of us to be. On analysis, the ideal candidate for an open marriage turns out to be the self-interested individual presupposed and encouraged by our liberal political structure and our capitalist consumer economy.

Perhaps this is best illustrated by calling attention to the O'Neills' discussion of adultery. Of course, the O'Neills see no reason why adultery should be excluded from open marriage. After all, most people "now recognize sex for what it is: a natural function that should be enjoyed for its own earthy self without hypocrisy" (247). Indeed, extramarital sexual experiences "when they are in the context of a meaningful relationship may be rewarding and beneficial to an open marriage" (254). But the O'Neills do provide a word of caution; they suggest that to have an extramarital affair without first "developing yourself to the point where you are ready, and your mate is ready, for such a step could be detrimental to the possibility of developing a true open marriage" (254).

I have thought a lot about this very interesting suggestion, namely, that we develop ourselves to be ready to engage in an extramarital affair. What could that possibly mean? Would it mean that we each date and then come home and compare notes on our experience to see how it makes the other feel? And what would be the object of such a project? Surely it is nothing less than for us to learn to devalue sexual expression between ourselves in order to justify it with other people.

But even more interesting, such training would also require that we learn to control, if not destroy entirely, that primitive emotion called jealousy. What is involved in proposals such as the O'Neills' are extremely profound—yet unrecognized—assumptions about the kind of person each of us ought to be. And the O'Neills are quite explicit about this, as they argue that jealousy is but a learned response determined by cultural attitudes dependent on our assumptions about sexually exclusive monogamy. But such possession of another only "breeds deep-rooted dependencies, infantile and childish emotions, and insecurities. The more insecure you are, the more you will be jealous. Jealousy, says Abraham Maslow, 'practically always breeds further rejection and deeper insecurity.' And jealousy, like a destructive cancer, breeds more jealousy. It is never, then, a function of love, but of our insecurities and dependencies. It is the fear of a loss of love and it destroys that very love. It is detrimental to and a denial of a loved one's personal identity. Jealousy is a serious impediment, then, to the development of security and identity, and our closed marriage concepts of possession are directly at fault" (237). Alas, if only Othello could have had the opportunity to have read *Open Marriage,* the whole messy play could have been avoided.

The irony is that romanticism, which began as an attempt to recapture the power of intimate relation as opposed to the "formal" or institutionalized relationship implied by marriage, now finds itself recommending the development of people who are actually incapable of sustaining intimate relationships. For intimacy depends on the willingness to give of the self, to place oneself in the hands of another, to be vulnerable, even if that means we may be hurt. Contrary to Maslow, jealousy is the emotion required by our willingness to love another at all. Indeed, I suspect that part of the reason the church has always assumed that marriage is a reality that is prior to love is that genuine love is so capable of destruction that we need a structure to sustain us through the pain and the joy of it. At least one reason for sex being limited to marriage, though it is not a reason sufficient to support an intrinsic relation between sex and marriage, is that marriage provides the context for us to have sex, with its often compromising personal conditions, with the confidence that what the other knows about us will not be used to hurt us. For never are we more vulnerable than when we are naked and making the clumsy gestures necessary to "make love."

It is true, of course, that romanticism cannot be defeated simply by calling attention to some of the implications inherent in the O'Neills' argument. Indeed, romanticism has become far too complex a phenomenon for it to be easily characterized or criticized. I am content at this point simply to suggest that the romantic assumption that sexual expression is a "private" matter in fact masks a profound commitment to the understanding of society and self sponsored by political liberalism. Thus, human relations are increasingly understood in contractual terms and the ideal self becomes the person capable of understanding everything and capable of being hurt by nothing.

2. The Current State of Christian Reflection about Sexual Ethics

I suggested above that current Christian reflection about sexual ethics has been limited to trying to adjudicate among various versions of realism and romanticism in order to establish the "Christian" ethics of sex. What Christian ethicists have been unable to do is provide an account of sexual ethics that is clearly based on an agenda central to the Christian community's own self-understanding. They have been unable to do so because they have failed to see that any discussion of sex must begin with an understanding of how a sexual ethics is rooted in a community's basic political commitments.

As a result sexual ethics, though often very insightful, betrays a fatal abstractness. For example, it is often claimed that it is a mistake to begin reflection about sexual ethics by trying to determine if certain kinds of genital sex are right or wrong. Instead, we must begin by recognizing that sexuality is a matter that involves the "whole person," or that "sexuality" so understood must be affirmed as a manifestation of the goodness of God's creation. While all of this is no doubt true, we are not sure how such claims give direction to or help us think better about genital sexual activity. Put bluntly, such analysis does little to help us to answer a teenager who wants to know what is wrong with fooling around before marriage.

The directness of such questions tends to frustrate many ethicists as these questions refer to a specific sort of genital activity. Instead, ethicists prefer to call attention to the importance of the presence of love for wholesome sex. Rather than answering yes or no, we say things like "The physical expression of one's sexuality with another person ought to be appropriate to the level of loving commitment present in that relationship,"[8] or that any one act of "genital sexual expression should be evaluated in regard to motivations, intentions, the nature of the act itself, and the consequences of the act, each of these informed and shaped by love."[9]

For instance, like the O'Neills, James Nelson does not believe that the question of infidelity in marriage can be limited to the issue of adultery, but rather is the rupture of the bonds of "faithfulness, honesty, trust, and commitment between the spouses."[10] He therefore thinks we must remain open to the possibility that people can be maritally faithful without being sexually exclusive. My difficulty with such arguments is this: How would you ever have any basis to know if you are in fact "faithful" or not? It is certainly the case that often married people harm one another in more profound ways than by having sex with someone else. But it is also the case that sexual fidelity may be the way we learn to be faithful in other aspects of our lives together. I am aware that some couples may have sustained impressive marriages without the commitment to sexual fidelity, but that is not the issue. The issue is what kind of marriage Christians want to encourage as essential to the purposes of their community. All of which may be true, but is a lot for teenagers in the back seat of a car to remember.

This last comment, while rhetorically clever, is in some ways deeply unfair. For no ethic, not even the most conservative, should be judged by its ability to influence the behavior of teenagers in the back seat of a car. What happens there will often happen irrespective of what "ethic" has been officially taught. Yet I think in a more profound sense people are right to expect ethicists to be concerned about how their "ethic" might be understood or misunderstood for providing guidance about our actual sexual conduct.

"What is wrong with a little fooling around?" is a frustrating and direct question. But such questions are necessary to remind us that often our attempts to provide sophisticated and nuanced accounts of sexuality are misleading and perhaps even corrupting for our children. That is not to say that any ethic of sex should be written from the perspective of only what is good for adolescents or relative to what they are capable of understanding, but I am sure any ethic of sex that does not provide direction for how adolescents should learn to understand and govern their sexual behavior cannot be suffi-

8. James Nelson, *Embodiment* (Minneapolis: Augsburg, 1978), 127.
9. Ibid. Again, the difficulty with such "criteria" is that one has no idea what would count for or against whether certain forms of activity should be considered shaped by love.
10. Ibid.

cient.[11] Perhaps one of the crucial tests for any ethics of sex and sexual behavior is that we be able to explain it honestly and straightforwardly to our children.

To provide that kind of account for our children, however, requires that we are able to presuppose a community with the practices and convictions that make such an ethic intelligible. Our children have to see that marriage and having children, and the correlative sexual ethic, are central to the community's political task. For only then can they be offered a vision and an enterprise that might make the disciplining of sex as interesting as its gratification.[12]

3. One Catholic Attempt at Sexual Ethics

Most current attempts at formulating a Christian ethics of sex continue to assume the apolitical nature of sexual practice and ethics. Nowhere is this clearer than in the 1977 study entitled *Human Sexuality,* commissioned by the Catholic Theological Society of America. The romantic ideal clearly dominates the report, as the authors argue that sexuality must be understood morally as serving the development of persons by calling them to constant creativity, that is, to full openness to being, to the realization of every potential within the personality, to a continued discovery and expression of authentic selfhood. Procreation is one form of this call to creativity, but by no means is it the only reason for sexual expression. Sexuality further serves the development of genuine personhood by calling people to a clearer recognition of their relational nature, of their absolute need to reach out and embrace others to achieve personal fulfillment.[13] In the light of this "richer" understanding of "sexuality" the authors of the *Report* argue that we should abandon the traditional language of "unitive and procreative" and instead ask whether acts of sexual intercourse are "creative and integrative." "Wholesome human sexuality" is that which should "foster a creative growth toward integration" (86).

The authors of the report find it "woefully inadequate" to evaluate any human sexual behavior "based on an abstract absolute predetermination of

11. I owe this point to Anne Harley Hauerwas.
12. [For an elaboration of this point, see "The Radical Hope in the Annunciation: Why Both Single and Married Christians Welcome Children," essay 24 in this volume.]
13. Anthony Kosnik et al., *Human Sexuality* (New York: Paulist Press, 1977), 85. Subsequent references are in the text. It should be noted that though their report was published by the Catholic Theological Society of America the board of that society took pains to make clear that this action implied neither approval nor disapproval of the report.

any sexual expressions as intrinsically evil and always immoral" (89). The fact that they refuse to find contraception morally unacceptable is not surprising on such grounds, but they also suggest that while it is hard to see how adultery could be good for all involved, the "principle" of "creative growth toward integration" needs also to be applied in these cases (148). Thus, even though some suggest that "co-marital sexual relations"—that is, situations that involve sexual activity with one or more persons beyond the "primary pair bond" with the consent or encouragement of the marriage partner—appear to contradict the "characteristics of wholesome sexual interrelatedness," empirical data do "not as yet warrant any solid conclusions on the effects of such behavior, particularly from the long-range point of view" (149).

On the same grounds the report concludes that no moral theologian has yet succeeded in producing convincing proof why in every case sexual intercourse must be reserved to marriage (158). Yet in no way does this imply an approval of promiscuity, as casual sex "robs human sexuality of its deepest and richest meaning as an expression of intimacy and love" (164). In casual sex the sexual act is separated from the deeper intrapersonal meaning necessary if it is to realize its creative and integrative potential. Yet the report is careful to remind us that on many of these questions we still lack the empirical data to make an informed and objective judgment.

On that criterion one might well argue that it is the moral responsibility of Catholics to experiment with "comarital sexual relations" in the hopes of generating the appropriate data. Or that some take as their moral mission to find forms of extramarital sexual relations that will help us determine if such relations always rob human sexuality of its "deepest meaning."

In fairness it should be said that the CTSA report is not always so tentative, as it states clearly that there is no question that bestiality "renders impossible the realization of the personal meaning of human sexuality" (230). I question, however, if this is consistent with the *Report*'s methodology, as such a summary judgment has all the appearance of the biased judgment of city people who have had little experience with country life. At the very least it seems as though the report could have suggested that in these matters, like other forms of sexuality that seem to these writers unusual, we simply need more "data" before we can make a summary judgment.

The difficulty with the *Report*'s recommendations is not just that the criteria "creative and integrative" are so abstract we have no idea what they might exclude, but the *Report* ironically continues to assume, like more conservative sexual ethics of the past, that a sexual ethic can be formulated in abstraction from how it contributes to the upbuilding of the political task of the church. The conservative sexual ethics of the past seemed to be harsher as they not only said no more readily, but also seemed to care little for the welfare of persons who were having to live such an ethic. In some ways the conservative was right that a sex ethic was not to be judged by whether it produced integrated persons, but the conservative, as well as the authors of the *Report*, equally fail to understand that the kind of "person" we should be is a prior question, answered only by the nature of the Christian community.[14]

4. The Public Character of Sex: Marriage as a Heroic Institution

The recovery of a political vision of marriage and appreciation for the public character of sexuality are conceptually and institutionally interdependent. By calling attention to the public context for sexual behavior and ethics I am not simply reasserting the traditional concern that sex should only take place in a publicly recognizable institution, though I certainly think that is important, but I am making the stronger claim that any sex ethic is a political ethic.[15] This

14. It is, of course, true that *Human Sexuality* does not represent the general consensus of Catholic attitudes about the morality of sexual conduct. But I suspect what it does accurately represent is the confusion of Catholic thought about sex—not just judgments about particular forms of sexual expression but confusion about where one should even begin thinking about the ethics of sex. For once the connection between sexual intercourse and procreation is broken, and it has been broken in theory and practice for many Catholics, then it is by no means clear what basis you have for maintaining other judgments about the rightness or wrongness of certain forms of sexual expression. No amount of rethinking of natural law will be able to show that every act of sexual intercourse must be procreative; rather, what must be recaptured is that the connection between the unitive and procreative ends of marriage is integral to the Christian understanding of the political significance of marriage.

15. For a more extensive analysis of this point, see my "Sex and Politics: Bertrand Russell and 'Human Sexuality,'" *Christian Century* 95, no. 14 (April 19, 1978): 417–22. The church's traditional condemnation of "secret marriages" involves substantive assumptions that can be too easily overlooked. For the significance of maintaining that sex should occur in publicly sanctioned contexts (which might well include "engagements") suggests that we should not trust our declaration of love unless we are willing to commit ourselves publicly. For there is surely no area where we are more liable to self-deception than in those contexts where love is mixed with sexual desire. Of course, there is nothing wrong with love or sexual desire except that we may often confuse the two. The problem with the suggestion that sexual expression should be relative to the level of loving commitment is that it is simply too hard to test the latter. I would suggest instead that the form and extent of our sexual expression is best correlated to the extent we are willing to intermix our finances. It may sound terribly unromantic, but I am convinced that one of the best tests of "love" is the extent to which a couple are willing to share a common economic destiny. As John Howard Yoder has suggested, "The

is particularly true of Christian marriage. The vision of marriage for Christians requires and calls forth an extraordinary polity for the very reason that Christian marriage is such an extraordinary thing.

Whereas most recent theories about sexual ethics are individualistic, since they focus primarily on how persons should deal with their bodies and private actions, William Everett has argued that we must see that sexuality is shaped by humanly created institutions and that this formation works for good as well as for evil. But the question is not whether "the social formation of our sexuality is good or bad, but whether the institutions in which we live are rightly ordered. An ethics of sex must, therefore, be coordinated with an ethic governing the relations among institutions—familial, economic, ecclesial and political."[16]

To illustrate his claim, Everett notes that the development of Christian sexual ethics was not merely a part of the quest for a general social order.

> While Augustine was laying the theological basis for a familist social order, counter-currents were also developing to avoid submerging the Church in that order. As the Church was increasingly drawn into the orbits of the princes, a sexual ethic had to be evolved to separate it from the family-based power of the princes. In the wake of Hildebrand (Gregory VII), celibacy finally became mandatory for clergy in order to separate the Church from the

---

ethical question is not whether the sex-with-true-love is by definition sinful, but whether true love can be honest, can be true love if it dodges the honest outward expressions which are its normal social form. . . . Therefore what is questionable about 'pre-marital sex' is not that it is sex, nor that it is pre-marital, but that the maintenance of secrecy, the avoidance of legality, the postponement of common residence and finances, the withholding of public pledge, constitute both a handicap for the marriage's success and *prima facie* evidence that the love is not true. This is not sex-without-marriage but marriage without honesty. It is not that the hasty youngsters sin against backward cultural mores while fulfilling themselves and consummating their own love: it is that they sin against themselves, their lives and their marriage, by depriving their love of the social consummative, the orderly cohabitative, the fresh air, without which it is stunted or amputated" ("When Is a Marriage Not a Marriage," unpublished manuscript, 12). [Though never published, this essay is available, as of July 1999, online at Yoder's Web site at www.nd.edu/~theo/jhy/writings.]

16. William Everett, "Between Augustine and Hildebrand: A Critical Response to *Human Sexuality*," *Proceedings of the Catholic Theological Society of America* 33 (1978): 78. Subsequent references are in the text.

hereditary powers of the princes. Celibacy was as important to the Church's integrity in a familistic social order as constitutional separation of Church and state has become under nationalism. The Augustinian accommodation required a Hildebrandine distance. Celibacy was and is an institutional policy evolved for the sake of the institution. Moreover, this policy had a legitimate purpose—to enable the Church to carry out its mission as a critical and prophetic agent in human affairs. (79)

The church's restraints on various forms of sexual activity were intelligible only to the extent that the church could be a "counterfamily" to the princes. But as Everett points out, in our time, when family order is no longer the model of societal order or authority, "it becomes very difficult to transfer this self-restraint in order to conform to the demands of other institutions" (79).[17] The family, having lost its political, social, and economic functions, apart from being a unit of consumption, is only intelligible as the context that provides for "creative integration" through intimate relationship. Thus increasingly the family becomes understood as a voluntary society justified by its ability to contribute to the personal enhancement of each of its members.[18] Everett is not surprised that such an accommodation has occurred, but he wonders if the correlative understanding of sexuality, as that which functions primarily within the private sphere of emotional and ego-related needs, is sufficient to provide a prophetic perspective on our society. For he claims:

It is not enough to see the pressures of advertising and bureaucratic life as a natural given, for behind these immediate forces lie the needs of a capital-intensive economy seeking to maintain a high level of consumption for essentially useless products. Our sexual life is shaped by the fundamental workings of this kind of economy. It is not enough, therefore, to invoke [as *Human Sexuality* does] "social responsibility" or "the common good" as a consideration in sexual decisions, without a more critical analysis of the nature of that society and its conception of the good. We need to be able to see how the pursuit of "creative integration" in our bedrooms might depend on the sacrifices of primary-producing nations to the south of us who keep our economy fueled with metals and oil. We need to see how the pleasures and disciplines

17. Indeed, the church's shift to "personalist" accounts of marriage and sexual conduct is an attempt to baptize the transformation of the family occasioned by a capital-intensive economy that needs fewer but better trained workers.
18. See, for example, Christopher Lasch's account of the effect of liberalism on the family in *Haven in a Heartless World* (New York: Basic Books, 1977).

of mobile individuality are tied to the expressways and housing developments devouring our agricultural land.

The capacity to see those connections is essential to any kind of prophetic
or biblical ethic of sex. Not to see the whole is to be victimized by the parts.
The CTSA study has comforted those who have adapted to the dominant
North American patterns, but it does little to challenge that society or to
support those left on the margins. It has met the demands of realistic accom-
modations but has not gone far enough to provide Christian distance. We
have yet to move, in our own time, from Augustine to Hildebrand. (82)

Everett maintains that the development of such a critical ethic awaits an
adequate ecclesiology. The ecclesiology of most of the more liberal sexual
ethics assumes that the church is a voluntary association that exists for the
spiritual enrichment of the individuals composing it. While admitting that
such a voluntaristic theory of church is inextricably bound up with a pluralist
social context, Everett doubts that voluntarism can provide the countervailing
power we need to counter the tremendous powers that shape and often destroy our lives.[19]

Following Everett, I believe that we cannot expect to begin to develop an
adequate Christian sexual ethic without starting with the insistence that sex is
a public matter for the Christian community. For our sexual ethic is part and
parcel of our political ethic. How we order and form our lives sexually cannot
be separated from the necessity of the church to chart an alternative to our
culture's dominant assumptions. Indeed, it is my contention that Christian

19. Even granting that God's hand is at work in the dialectic among these massive institutions,
can a purely voluntaristic vision of Christian life provide an adequate ecclesiology that relates
our sexuality to our society? Is that kind of community enough to protect our fragile psyches
from these potent cultural forces? I think not. A sexual ethic that doesn't place the dilemmas
of sexuality in this kind of societal context will never reach "the Hildebrandine moment"
(Everett, 83).

Having said this, I disagree with particular points of Everett's position. In particular, I think
that Everett is incorrect in implying that the only way the church challenged the empire was
through celibacy. It is extremely important to recognize that the kind of family the church
started to create from the beginning was a means to gain a critical edge against its wider
society.

Moreover, even though Everett is right to suggest that no church, not even "the Catholic
church, in our current pluralist context can provide a total ritual environment in which
people grow up with their sexual activities already integrated into the symbolism of Church
and family" (83), I suspect that a more normative form of sectarianism will be required if we
have any hope of articulating and institutionalizing a form of sexual life appropriate to
Christians. Having said this, the structure of Everett's argument seems to me to be right.

conviction concerning the place of singleness and the family is perhaps the most important political task of the church in our society.

4.1 Sex and the Church's Mission

The political nature of the church's sexual ethic is perhaps most clearly illuminated by calling attention to the alternative of singleness as a legitimate form of life among Christians. Indeed, in the strongest possible language the basis and intelligibility of the Christian understanding of marriage makes sense only in relation to the early Church's legitimation for some of "singleness."[20] This is often forgotten, as the church is prone, for apologetic reasons, to simply underwrite the broad assumption that marriage is a natural and primary context in which to "locate" sex. Thus most Christians assume that marriage is the first mode of sexual life and that the single therefore must justify his or her mode of life rather than vice versa. But Christian marriage is not a "natural" institution but rather the creation of a people who marry for very definite purposes. The constant institutional reminder of this fact is the assumption of the early Christians that singleness was as legitimate a form of life as marriage.

It is worth pointing out that the New Testament seems to have little to say about sex and marriage. And what it does say has a singularly foreign sound for those of us brought up on romantic notions of marriage and sex. We are thus struck by the stark realism of the Pauline recommendations in I Corinthians 7 and more than a little embarrassed by the Haustafeln passages in Ephesians, Colossians, and I Peter.[21] As a means to soften these passages, many call attention to I Corinthians 13 and Ephesians 5:21–33 to stress that love really is crucial to Christian marriage. Yet this attempt to rescue the New Testament views on marriage and sexuality seem to involve creative forms of exegesis. I am particularly struck by the supposition that Ephesians 5:22ff can be used to justify the importance of "happy" marriages for Christians. There seems to be

20. I am using the locution "singleness" rather than celibacy, as it is by no means clear that they are the same. Celibacy denotes a life-long vocation, while "singleness" may be a form of life assumed for a while without excluding the possibility of marriage. While both may be sexually celibate, the rationale for their celibacy is not necessarily of the same order. For an extremely insightful article on singleness that criticizes the church's limitation of the category to the religious, see Mary Jo Weaver, "Singleness and the Family," *Commonweal* (October 26, 1979): 588–91.

21. For an extremely interesting interpretation of the *Haustafeln,* see John Howard Yoder, *The Politics of Jesus* (Grand Rapids, MI: Eerdmans, 1972), 163–92.

nothing in the text itself to suggest that Christ's love and unity with the church implies that unity is without discord.[22]

More important, however, than the interpretation of particular New Testament texts about marriage and sex is the recognition that the church's sexual ethic cannot be determined through examination and collation of individual texts. Of course, the individual texts are significant for helping us understand the early church's sex ethic, but they must be understood in the broader context of the early Christians' understanding of their mission. Ironically, in that respect singleness is a better indication than marriage of the church's self-understanding.

The early church's legitimation of singleness as a form of life symbolized the necessity of the church to grow through witness and conversion. Singleness was legitimate, not because sex was thought to be a particularly questionable activity, but because the mission of the church was such that "between the times" the church required those who were capable of complete service to the Kingdom. And we must remember that the "sacrifice" made by the single is not that of "giving up sex," but the much more significant sacrifice of giving up heirs. There can be no more radical act than this, as it is the clearest institutional expression that one's future is not guaranteed by the family, but by the church. The church, the harbinger of the Kingdom of God, is now the source of our primary loyalty.[23]

Extraordinary moral commitments are involved in a community that encourages us to form particular attachments that are morally legitimated to override concern for the general welfare of the community. Christians have legitimated such commitments because they believe that the "good" that con-

22. Many interpret Ephesians 5:21–33 to mean that marriage is a paradigm of the unity of Christ and his church, but in the passage itself the analogy works the other way, as the relationship between Christ and his church is the paradigm for marriage.

23. And of course such loyalty involves the gravest dangers, as we have recently had tragically displayed at Jonestown. Jones was right that Christianity in some fundamental ways challenges how we "naturally" think about the family. His "solution" to the problem of the family in Christianity reveals the depth of apostasy his peculiar account of Christianity involved, but Jonestown helps us understand what extraordinary assumptions were involved in the early Christians' commitment to marriage and the family. For they too knew they were involved in a revolutionary struggle, yet they continued to sponsor particular commitments and the having of children who were the responsibility of particular parents. For a fuller development of this point, see my "Self-Sacrifice as Demonic: A Theological Response to Jonestown," in *Violence and Religious Commitment*, ed. Ken Levi (University Park: Penn State University Press, 1982), 152–62, 189–91. [See also "On Taking Religion Seriously: The Challenge of Jonestown" (1985), in *AN.*]

stitutes the church is served only by our learning to love and serve our neighbors as we find them in our mates and children. The sexual exclusiveness traditionally associated with the Christian understanding of marriage is but a form of the church's commitment to support exclusive relationships.[24]

In this respect there is a certain tension in the church's sponsoring of singleness and marriage as equally valid modes of life. But both singleness and marriage are necessary symbolic institutions for the constitution of the church's life as the historic institution that witnesses to God's Kingdom. Neither can be valid without the other.[25] If singleness is a symbol of the church's confidence in God's power to affect lives for the growth of the church, marriage and procreation are the symbols of the church's understanding that the struggle will be long and arduous. For Christians do not place their hope in their children, but rather their children are a sign of their hope, in spite of the considerable evidence to the contrary, that God has not abandoned this world. Because we have confidence in God, we find the confidence in ourselves to bring new life into this world, even though we cannot be assured that our children will share our mission.[26] For they, too, must be converted if they are to be followers of the way.

From this perspective marriage (as well as the family) stands as one of the central institutions of the political reality of the church, for it is a sign of our faithfulness to God's Kingdom come through the providential ordering of history. By our faithfulness to *one* other, within a community that requires, finally, loyalty to God, we experience and witness to the first fruits of the new creation. Our commitment to exclusive relations witnesses to God's pledge to his people, Israel and the church, that through his exclusive commitment to them, all people will be brought into his Kingdom.

4.2 Marriage as a Heroic Role

Marriage so understood is a heroic task that can be accomplished only by people who have developed the virtues and character necessary for such a task.

24. [For other discussions of "exclusive relationships," see Hauerwas's "Clerical Character" in *CET*, and "Friendship and Fragility" in *CAV*.]

25. Donald Goergen argues this well in *The Sexual Celibate* (New York: Seabury Press, 1975), 107.

26. It must be remembered that for Christians parenting is not simply a biological role, but an office in a community that everyone in the church shares to some extent. That biological parents bear a particular responsibility for the rearing of children is but one of the ways Christians are reminded of how deeply we are anchored in "nature," and it manifests the church's stake in exclusive commitments.

The development of such virtues and character is a correlative of a narrative that helps us understand that struggle in which we are involved. But it is exactly such a narrative that we have been lacking, or, perhaps more accurately, our primary problem is that our experience of marriage has been captured by narratives that have done little for, and have perhaps even perverted, the role of marriage in the Christian community.

Contrary to the romanticism so prevalent in our culture, Rosemary Haughton has argued for a "heroic" view of marriage. Marriage is heroic for Christians because "the couple must dedicate themselves, not simply to each other, but to work together at something greater than I imagine."[27] Haughton is not suggesting that such an understanding of marriage will necessarily produce a "better" marriage than the romantic ideal, but rather that the "criteria" of success are simply different. "The point is that the qualities that make people stick out a hard life together, not stopping too much to wonder if they are fulfilled, are the qualities people need if they are to develop the hero in marriage, which is what being married 'in the Lord' is about" (143).[28]

There is one particular quality Haughton finds especially important for the hero: fidelity. The virtue of fidelity is often ignored or attacked by advocates of the romantic model, as romantic love seeks intensity, not continuity. And fidelity seems to contradict the fact that people develop and change, and in doing so it seems unjust that they should remain attached to past commitments. But, as I suggested above, such fidelity makes sense only if it occurs in a community that has a mission in which marriage serves a central political purpose. And marriage has such a purpose for Christians, as it is a sign that we are a community sustained by hope. Marriage is a sign and source of such hope, "for as long as there are people loving and working together, and

---

27. Rosemary Haughton, "Marriage: An Old, New Fairy Tale," in *A Curious Tradition: Marriage among Christians*, ed. James Burtchaell, C.S.C. (Notre Dame, IN: Ave Maria Press, 1977), 142. Subsequent references are in the text.

28. Traditionally all that marrying "in the Lord" meant was simply that Christians should marry other Christians. See, for example, the discussion by E. Schillebeeckx in *Marriage: Secular Reality and Saving Mystery* (London: Sheed and Ward, 1956), 192–202. Schillebeeckx rightly emphasizes that the early Christians did not think they were "spiritualizing" marriage, but rather that their Christian commitment gave marriage a new intentionality. Thus, Christian marriage did not happen in spite of the human institution of marriage, but in it. That does not mean that Christian marriage can be justified because it involves some special magic that ensures domestic bliss and happiness. Rather, Christian marriage is justified because it is what Christians are called to do for the building up of the community of the faithful.

bringing up children, there is a chance of new life. To take conscious hold on that life, to realize oneself at the heart of it, for others also, is a tremendously vitalizing spiritual experience" (150).

5. Practical Implications

"Vitalizing spiritual experience" seems a long way away from answering the query concerning what is wrong with messing around a little before or during marriage. Moreover, there is the added problem that whether the argument above is right or not seems of little relevance to our concrete experience. For the truth of the matter is that few of us had that understanding of what we were doing when we got married; nor has our sexual conduct been formed by or lived out in such terms. As a result, most of what has been said may seem but one more idealistic account of marriage and sex that should properly be dismissed by those of us who have to live in this life.

Yet I think my argument, incomplete as it is, at least provides some means of response. While few of us have been trained to view our marriage in the adventurous ways described above, the perspective I have developed should at least help us deal with the fact that even though we may not have known what we were doing when we got married, we find ourselves married. The important issue is how we are to understand what has happened through marriage. Surely it is not just that we have undervalued or overvalued the significance of sex in our lives, but that we have had no sense that this way of understanding sex represents a destructive alternative.

From the perspective I have tried to develop we can now see why realism is insufficient to provide us with ethical guidance about sex. For realism, as I have argued, turns out to be but a chastened form of romanticism that continues to reflect a culture that insists that sex and marriage have no public function. A true realism requires a community that forms our loyalties in such a manner that both the costs and hopes of marriage can be properly held in balance. Only from such a perspective can we reach a more profound sense of the relation of love and marriage, as it is only within such a context that we can begin to understand that the love properly characteristic of marriage is not a correlative of the attractive qualities of our mates. Only a love so formed has the capacity to allow the other freedom to be other without resentment.[29]

29. Christians have far too readily underwritten the romantic assumption that people "fall"

I think also that the account I have tried to sketch out helps explain aspects of our lives that are simply anomalous given our culture's understanding of marriage and the family. I am thinking of such common matters as our deep commitment to our particular children and their care, or of the extraordinary efforts some couples go through to save their marriages, or why we continue to care about having children at all. To be sure, many are finding that it is possible to train ourselves not to have such "irrational" desires, but there is the lingering feeling that we are poorer for it. Sadder still is that many spouses who remain committed in the midst of difficult marriages and continue caring for children in very difficult circumstances are only able to explain these commitments as an expression of their own peculiar desires. It is as if such commitments were merely a matter of taste.

What we forget is that such "peculiar desires" are the product of centuries of Christian insistence and training that the family is central to what the church means in this time between the times. To be sure, the church often forgets its own best insights and justifies its practice on grounds that appear more amenable or "natural" to its cultural context, but it continues to have the advantage of having to deal with the necessity of men and women struggling to figure out what they are doing by being married "in the Lord." Such a "necessity" means that the church can never forget for long that marriage among Christians involves commitments not readily recognized by the world.

---

into love and then get married. We would be much better advised to suggest that love does not create marriage; rather, marriage provides a good training ground to teach us what love involves. Indeed, one of the assumptions that Christians should challenge is the general belief that love is an intrinsic aspect of "natural" marriage. There is simply no good reason to think that, as many cultures provide very acceptable forms of marriage without requiring the couple to "love" one another. The relation between love and marriage is not necessarily peculiar to Christians, though I suspect the kind of love characteristic of Christian marriage has distinctive aspects. Moreover, I think we should be hesitant to identify this distinctiveness with "self-sacrifice," as no marriage can long survive as a truthful relation built on "self-sacrifice." Rather, the distinctiveness of love between Christians must rest on the fact that they share a commitment in common that provides the basis not to fear the truth about themselves or their relation.

It has been suggested to me that my positing of Hauerwas's Law, "You always marry the wrong person," though meant to challenge romanticism, presupposes romanticism. That may be, but the deeper intent of the "law" is to suggest that marriage among Christians requires an account that allows us to form a life together where fidelity and love are required without assuming "common interests." We learn to love the other not because they are like us but because they are not. See, for example, my "Love and Marriage," *The Cresset* 40, no. 8 (June 1977): 20–21.

But I think the perspective I have tried to develop does more than simply help us to interpret our past. It also helps us ask the right question for giving direction to our future. For the issue is not whether x or y form of sexual activity is right or wrong, as if such activity could be separated from a whole way of life. Rather, such questions are but shorthand ways of asking what kind of people we should be to be capable of supporting the mission of the church. The question of sexual conduct before marriage is thus a question of the kind of preparation necessary so that we may well play the roles and perform the tasks that we are called to by the Christian community. It is through coming to understand the roles and tasks to which we are called by God that we learn whether we may be called to a life of singleness or marriage.[30]

The issue is not whether someone is chaste in the sense of not engaging in genital activity, but whether we have lived in a manner that allows us to bring a history with us that contributes to the common history we may be called upon to develop with one another. Chastity, we forget, is not a state but a form of the virtue of faithfulness that is necessary for all who wish to serve a role in the community.[31] As such, it is as crucial to the married life as it is to the single life.

Of course, we need to remind ourselves again, that is still quite a bit to remember in the back seat of a car. But, as I suggested, there is no "ethic" that in itself can solve all the problems involved in such behavior. Rather, what the young properly demand is an account of life and the initiation into a community that makes intelligible why their interest in sex should be subordinated to other interests.[32] What they, and we, demand is the lure of an adventure that captures the imagination sufficiently that for Christians "conquest" comes to mean something other than the sexual possession of another. I have tried to suggest that marriage and singleness for Christians should represent just such

30. There are many roles in the church, but the roles of singleness and marriage are particularly fundamental, since they derive immediately from what the community is about. However, we must remember that "singleness" is not ultimately justified because of the requirements of certain tasks or functions, but because it is symbolically crucial to the church's understanding of itself as an eschatological community.

31. Goergen, 98–99.

32. I suspect that part of the current difficulty of developing a sexual ethic for young people is the absence of any other signs and rituals for becoming an adult. Thus, sexual experimentation and/or involvement become the signs in the youth subculture that one has "grown up." Of course, rituals of initiation into adulthood only make sense when being an adult involves special privileges and responsibilities because of the tasks it requires.

an "adventurous conquest," which provides us with the skills necessary to know when, how, and with whom to have sex in public.

Further Reading
"The Politics of Sex: How Marriage Is a Subversive Act" (1991), in AC
"Self-Deception and Autobiography: Reflections on Speer's *Inside the Third Reich*" (1974), essay 10 in this volume
"The Radical Hope in the Annunciation: Why Both Single and Married Christians Welcome Children" (1998), essay 24 in this volume
"A Story-Formed Community: Reflections on *Watership Down*" (1981), essay 9 in this volume
"The Insufficiency of Scripture" (1993), essay 12 in this volume
"Why Truthfulness Requires Forgiveness" (1992), essay 15 in this volume
"The Servant Community: Christian Social Ethics" (1983), essay 19 in this volume
"A Guide to Sexual Adventure," *The Reformed Journal* 36, no. 11 (1986): 12–16.
"Love and Marriage," *The Cresset* 40, no. 8 (June 1977): 20–21.
"Love's Not All You Need" (1972), in VV

24. The Radical Hope in the Annunciation: Why Both Single and Married Christians Welcome Children (2001)

Occasioned by the birth of his first grandchild, Hauerwas returns to an early theme of his work, giving his account of why "the family" has become such a precarious institution in American society. Here Hauerwas argues that the penchant of some Christians to idealize the family of a bygone era serves only to mask the problems presented by the successful economic obsolescence of the family. With children no longer an economic boon (as they are in preindustrial societies), accounts of the significance of children as a means to "domestic" happiness need all the more to be challenged. Hauerwas argues that Christian marriages and families are to be understood in terms of their contribution to the growth and development of the church. Their significance can be adequately comprehended only when analyzed in conjunction with the complementary Christian calling to singleness.

1. "Families and Family Values": Do We Know Why We Want Them?

I begin with an announcement: On the Feast of the Annunciation, March 25, 1998, Joel Adam Hauerwas was born. I am a grandfather. Nothing is more hopeful than the birth of a child. Such births defy the unknown, claiming that we can in fact trust in God. So I stand before you as one representing the hope *that is named by the family* and in gratitude to Adam and Laura Hauerwas for opening their lives and thus Paula's and my lives to this new life.

It may not be fair to begin with this announcement. Why should you care whether Joel has been born? It is a nice thing, of course, that he has been born, but such matters are "personal." This essay is supposed to address the family qua family, not the family Hauerwas. Yet, given some of what I have said in the

[This is an edited version of a lecture delivered at the Catholic University of America, April 28, 1998. The lecture title was "Should Catholics Support Family Values? Christian Marriage, Sex, and Singleness."]

past about the family, namely, that the first enemy of the family is Christianity, I want to make clear that I care deeply that Joel has been born.

I am hesitant to speak about the family because I am not altogether happy with what I have to say. The family in America is in profound trouble. I think I know why the family is in profound trouble, but I have no answer that will "fix" the family. Indeed, I fear my theological understanding of the place of the family can make things worse. I do not want to make things worse. I want Joel Adam Hauerwas born and I want him to have the confidence to have children. However, I also want Joel's wants to be shaped by the hope that is of God so that they will not be demonic. How to say that in a society like ours that fears having children is not easy.

Thus, readers of this essay who assume that the roles of marriage and/or singleness are coherent in this society, and that this essay constitutes advice on "how to do family" or "how to do marriage," may well be disappointed. For we live in a time when we must ask more basic questions, like "What is marriage?" and "Why would anybody want to do it?" One of the things I will try to show is that if Christians are going to "do" marriage and family faithfully, they need to overcome their "romantic" individualistic fantasies about them, which is no easy matter.[1]

2. The American Family

Let me try to explain these last remarks by giving you an overview of why, in spite of the celebration of the family by most Americans, the family that we celebrate is in such profound trouble. Indeed, what I hope to show is that the very celebration of the family—the fact that Americans so desperately cling to the family as our anchor in the storms of life—is but an indication of the trouble in which the family in America finds itself. The more we are forced to make the family the end-all and be-all of our existence, the more the family becomes a problem not only for American society generally, but more particularly a problem for Christians.

In order to appreciate just what Christians are up against in thinking about "family" and how we might adequately respond, I need to outline what I take to be the two most destructive developments in the past few centuries for the current understanding of the family. I name these two developments "The

---

1. For more on this last point, see Hauerwas, CC, 156–57.

Economic Marginalization of the Family," and its flip side "The Romantic Idealization of the Family."

2.1 The Economic Marginalization of the Family

To understand how the role of the family has changed in the past two hundred years, I want to summarize what I understand to be the viewpoint of the philosopher who perhaps has had the greatest influence on our current social and economic order. His perspective on the family can be summarized in three points: First, he advocates the Stoic view that individuals are best able to take care of themselves and should be committed principally to their own care. Why? Because "every man feels his own pleasures and his own pains more sensibly than those of other people."

Second, after ourselves, our families are the most important object of our affection, because our own happiness is greatly influenced by their happiness and/or misery. More specifically, nature directs our sympathies more to our children than to our parents. Why? Because from the eye of nature "a child is a more important object than an old man; and excites a much more lively, as well as a much more universal sympathy. It ought to do so. Everything may be expected, or at least hoped, from the child. In ordinary cases, very little can be expected or hoped from the old man. The weakness of childhood interests the affections of the most brutal and hard-hearted. It is only to the virtuous and humane, that the infirmities of old age are not the objects of contempt and aversion" (219). A sobering observation, perhaps, but one in which we cannot help but see ourselves.[2]

---

2. It is fascinating to compare this account with Aquinas's account of charity. Aquinas's discussion of the order of charity is framed by his presumption that we are first to love God above all else. In this context, note his understanding of the relation between love of self and love of neighbor: "God is loved as the principle of good, on which the love of charity is founded; while man, out of charity, loves himself by reason of his being a partaker of the aforesaid good, and loves his neighbor by reason of his fellowship in that good. Now fellowship is a reason for love according to a certain union in relation to God. Wherefore just as unity surpasses union, the fact that man himself has a share of the Divine good is a more potent reason for loving than that another should be a partner with him in that share. Therefore man, out of charity, ought to love himself more than his neighbor: in sign whereof, a man ought not to give way to any evil of sin, which counteracts his share of happiness, not even that he may free his neighbor of sin" (St. Thomas Aquinas, *Summa Theologica* [New York: Benziger Bros., 1946], II–II, 26, 4). As for love of family in relation to others, Aquinas suggests that love of kindred must come first since we are commanded thus by the Decalogue. He even suggests we ought to give priority to our love of our parents over our children because the father is the source of our origin, "in which respect he is a more exalted good and

Third, in countries where the rule of law is strong, such that even the poorest and weakest members of that state have relative security, family ties are weaker. Why? Because in a society where the rule of law gives individuals a sense of safety, "the descendants of the same family, having no such motive for keeping together, naturally separate and disperse, as interest or inclination may direct. They soon cease to be of importance to one another; and, in a few generations, not only lose all care about one another, but all remembrance of their common origin, and of the connection which took place among their ancestors. Regard for remote relations becomes, in every country, less and less, according as this state of civilization has been longer and more completely established. It has been longer and more completely established in England than in Scotland; and remote relations are, accordingly, more considered in the latter country than in the former, though, in this respect, the difference between the two countries is growing less and less every day" (223).

Who is the philosopher who so clearly saw the decline of the extended family? It was Adam Smith, and he noted all these things in *The Theory of Moral Sentiments* first published in 1759.[3] Smith's aim was to articulate the philosophical presuppositions and institutional arrangements necessary for the creation of societies in which the poorest man of a clan could survive without need for the regard of the chieftain. Such a system would no longer require individual acts of charity (though of course neither would it exclude such acts, but would render them "voluntary") since the system itself would supply the wants of each individual through free exchange. The family would still exist, but it would increasingly be understood as but another instance of exchange relation.

As for what follows from Smith's *Theory of Moral Sentiments,* the rest, so to speak, is history. For I take it that Smith's observations about how the family is reshaped by the growth of a society governed by law (what Max Weber called a "legal-rational social order") have come to pass. Scotland did and has become England and now the whole world will soon be California. Of course, Smith thought this to be a good thing. Indeed, the whole point of *The Theory of Moral Sentiments* was to show how the weakening of familial ties would increase the necessity of sympathy between strangers and result in cooperative forms of behavior that had not previously been realized.

---

more like God" (II–II, 26, 9). While Aquinas's account of the order of charity is not without problems, what makes it so interesting is that it is determinatively ordered by our love of God.
3. Adam Smith, *The Theory of Moral Sentiments*, ed. D. D. Raphael and A. L. Macfie (Oxford: Clarendon Press, 1979); page numbers in the text.

Moving from Smith's account to the contemporary situation in which we find ourselves, I see two main efforts to respond to the profound changes with regard to the family that Smith both prophesied and helped bring about. First, it is not difficult to see that much of the current social and psychological literature, which is often written in the interest of saving the family or at least making the family "work," merely reproduces Smith's understanding of "sympathy," the dominance of which has brought us to our current predicament. From my perspective these social workers and psychologists are but trying to cure the illness by infecting more people with the disease.

Second, the same is true for those who want to save the family by appealing to the intervention of the state. That is surely to have the fox guard the hen house. That the state has increasingly taken over the functions of the family is the result of the changes Smith at once named and championed. For example, I think few developments have been more deleterious for the family in America than what we now call "public education" and its supporting services. The development of such bureaucracies, legitimated by their commitment to "help" children, inevitably result—in spite of their best intentions—in making parents feel incompetent to raise children. Indeed, a 1977 Carnegie Council Report suggested that the primary role of the parents should be that of a manager coordinating the care their children receive through the appropriate experts.[4] As the report puts the matter, "No longer able to do it all themselves, parents today are in some ways like the executives in a large firm—responsible for the smooth coordination of the many people and processes that must work together to produce the final product."[5]

One of the curiosities of our time is how many conservatives in America— that is, people who support the capitalist economic arrangements championed by Adam Smith—believe the family can be protected, despite its ever diminishing role in the face of such economic arrangements. Some "communitarians" attempt to respond to this problem by appealing to the importance of "intermediate institutions" like the family, the church and synagogue, and various other civic and social organizations. However, in stressing the importance of these intermediate institutions, most communitarians usually fail to appreciate that to call the family an intermediate institution is to have already accepted the presuppositions of a legal-rationalistic social order that presup-

4. The Carnegie Council, *All Our Children: The American Family under Pressure* (1977).
5. I discuss this report extensively in "The Moral Value of the Family" (1978), in cc. The direct quote I use can be found on page 17 of the Carnegie report.

poses the quest to make all relationships exchange-relations. Having all too often accepted this capitalist presumption, many of those who make the loudest calls for "family values" assume the family exists primarily as the place from which we receive and learn affection. This is what Adam Smith called "sympathy."

2.2 The Romantic Idealization of the Family

Formerly, the strength of the family had been its social, economic, and political significance. The fact that the economic and political significance of the family is now secondary has the ironic effect of making an idealized account of the family too important in our lives. In a world of strangers, we cling to the family as the one place that supplies us with relationships that we have not chosen. As a set of relationships that are a "given" rather than ones we can choose to opt into or out of, family relationships at least seem to promise to give our lives, if not purpose, at least an "anchor." The problem, however, is that the family is generally unable to bear the burden of such intense psychological and moral expectations. We have seen that when one attaches such intense psychological importance to the family, what results is the spawning of whole industries of counselors of the family (e.g., social workers, psychologists, and educators), who now take as their task to "save" the family or "save us from" the family. Furthermore, these projects of saving the family (or saving us from the family) are undertaken in terms largely shaped by the economic concerns of Adam Smith. Even further, it is not clear that these "family counselors" have any significant alternative to offer us. I fear that too often, the alternative offered is little more than stressing to us the importance of a "career."[6]

Following Robert Nisbet, I do not believe that familial kinship can be sustained on solely interpersonal and psychological grounds. To sustain the family, there must be a set of traditions and practices that are passed on from generation to generation.[7] "But, to the extent the family today is not even seen

6. That "career" too often becomes the alternative to the family indicates the class nature of much of these discussions. The role money has in the destruction of the family I think has not been appropriately appreciated. For a discussion of how privacy concerning money subverts efforts to have a disciplined church, see Hauerwas, AC, 99–101.

7. The relation between my reflections on the family and my overall project has been poorly understood. One happy exception to this is a wonderful footnote by Grady Scott Davis in *Warcraft and the Fragility of Virtue: An Essay in Aristotelian Ethics* (Moscow: University of Idaho Press, 1992), 25. Davis rightly sees that my reflections on these matters constitute my most sustained critique of liberalism. As Davis puts it, "It is in coming to grips with the constitutive institutions of the community—marriage, family, religion, political participa-

as the bearer of tradition—whether it be the tradition of a nation, religion, or the family itself, the children are not raised or initiated by the family to be worthy of carrying forward the work of their ancestors. Rather, they are to be raised to make intelligent choices when they are adults. Perhaps the crassest form of this attitude is exemplified by those parents who raise their children to be able to choose to be 'religious or not' when they grow up. To do otherwise is to 'impose one's own views' on children, which would be, it is suggested, a violation of their autonomy."[8] I will return to the difficulties inherent in these "romantic" or psychological views of family and marriage a little later in this presentation.

3. The Christian Family

My extreme dissatisfaction with the above two alternatives—the family as necessary starting point that we must leave behind in the interest of being free (the project of Adam Smith), or the family as "everything" (i.e., its romantic idealization)—is the reason I have tried to remind Christians that for us the family is constituted by a quite different politics from the world that was aborning when Smith wrote *The Theory of Moral Sentiments*. In particular, I have objected to the view of some Christians that the greatest virtue of Christianity is the bulwark it supposedly provides for some form of defense of the family. That seems to me to be nothing short of idolatrous. After all, Christianity has been and will continue to be, if we are serious as Christians, a challenge to familial loyalties.

For example, my friend Will Willimon notes that during the time he has been Dean of the Chapel at Duke, he has received four angry phone calls from parents. All the calls have taken the same form. The parent says, "We sent Suzy to Duke with her head on straight. She was to major in economics and go on to law school. But she has become so involved in the Wesley Fellowship that she has now decided she is going to become a missionary to Honduras. How could you let this happen? You have ruined her life." That as pale a form of Christianity as Methodism can still produce this kind of result indicates pretty definitively that the Gospel is not altogether friendly to the family. I am sure that campus ministers at the Catholic University of America could tell similar

---

tion, and health care, for example—that the limits of the contractarian tradition become clearest and Hauerwas' writings on these topics more telling in their critical implications than even the best of Rawls' more 'philosophical' critiques."

8. Quoted from "The Family: Theological Reflections," in CC, 169.

tales of discussions with parents whose son or daughter has found a call to priesthood or religious life while an undergraduate here.

Of course, the Christian challenge to the family goes deeper than the difference in expectations that may occur between parents and children. I take it that nothing embodies the Christian challenge to the family more determinatively than the presumption that Christians do not have to have children to be Christians. The most decisive difference between Christianity and Judaism is to be found here. God has not willed the church to be reproduced through biology but through witness and conversion. We must remember that the most significant thing the single give up is not sex. What the single give up are heirs, grandchildren named Joel Adam Hauerwas, and they do so because they now understand that they have been made part of a community that is more determinative than the biological family.[9]

3.1 Christian Singleness

Singleness is the one practice of the Church that most profoundly shows that it has accepted and wishes to participate in the hope that God secured through Christ's cross, resurrection, and ascension. Singleness embodies the Christian hope that God's kingdom has come, is present, and is still to come. Accordingly, we cannot help but witness this good news to others. These "others" may indeed be our own children, but are more likely to be children who have come from families who have never heard the name of Christ. When the church loses the significance of singleness, I suspect it does so because Christians no longer have confidence that the Gospel can be received by those who have not been, so to speak, "raised in it." Put differently: Christian justifications of the family may often be the result that Christians no longer believe the Gospel is true or joyful.

That singleness is the first way of life for Christians does not imply that marriage and the having of children is in any way a less worthy way to be Christian. Quite the opposite. The fact that marriage is for Christians a vocation rather than a requirement gives it a new dignity. For the Christian, marriage cannot and must not be seen as a necessary means for self-fulfillment. Christians are not called to marriage for "fulfillment," but for the upbuilding of that community called church. This has the remarkable implication that what it means for Christians to "love" in marriage can be properly understood

9. For a further discussion of this, see "Sex in Public: How Adventurous Christians Are Doing It," essay 23 in this volume.

only in relation to the love that we share with our brothers and sisters in Christ. For Christians, marriage is not ultimately where one learns what love is about; indeed, the "love" that Christians share in marriage is made possible because we have first been loved by God.

3.2 Christian Marriage

I realize such a view seems quite bizarre in a culture dominated by romantic accounts of marriage. We assume a couple falls in love and comes to the church to have their love publicly acknowledged. One problem with this romantic view is that it tends to the presumption that if the love that was initially present in the relationship is no longer present, the marriage no longer exists. Romantic accounts of marriage simply cannot comprehend the church's view that marriage names the time created through a faithful promise that makes possible the discovery of love. Marriage is God's gift to the church through which the hope born by the gift of the kingdom patiently learns to wait in the time made possible by the presence of children.[10]

If this is not the fundamental theological presumption that sustains Christian marriage, then I do not see how we can make sense of the Church's acceptance of arranged marriages. I am aware that we tend to look on the institution of arranged marriage as a cultural mistake we are well rid of, but such a view assumes "arranged marriage" is a far narrower category than in fact it is. As I often observed when I taught at the University of Notre Dame, the very existence of Notre Dame and its sister institution Saint Mary's was dependent on the continuing belief in arranged marriages. Those institutions were rightly used by Catholic families who sent their sons and daughters in the hopes that they would meet someone of approximately the same social class and religious background to marry. That is arranged marriage under the illusion of choice.

Moreover, that is why I always taught "Hauerwas's Law" to my classes in marriage and the family at Notre Dame: "You always marry the wrong person." Like any good law it is, of course, reversible. You also always marry the right person. My law was not intended to instill in students a cynical view of marriage, but rather to help them see that the church rightly understands that we no more know the person we marry than we know ourselves. However, that we lack such knowledge in no way renders marriage problematic, at least

10. For my critique of recent Catholic sexual ethics which accept the presumptions of romantic accounts of sex and marriage, see AC, 113–15, 125–27.

Does not marriage exist for the non-Christian?

not marriage between Christians; for to be married as Christians is possible because we understand that we are members of a community more determinative than marriage.[11]

That the church is a more determinative community than a marriage is evidenced by the fact that it requires Christian marriage vows to be made with the church as witness. This is a reminder that we as church rightfully will hold you to promises you made when you did not and could not fully comprehend what you were promising. How could anyone *know* what it means to promise life-long monogamous fidelity? From the church's perspective the question is not whether you know what you are promising; rather, the question is whether you are the kind of person who can be held to a promise you made when you did not know what you were promising. We believe, of course, that baptism creates the condition that makes possible the presumption that we might just be such people.

Only against this background is Christian reflection about sex intelligible. Christians do not have a sexual ethic based on some general account of human sexuality. Rather, we have marriage as a practice that governs how we think about sex. For Christians there is nothing called premarital sex because we believe that all sex is marital. The problem with sex outside publicly acknowledged marriages is not that it is not sex, but that it is without the purposes that come only from marriage. To name such purpose unitive and procreative is obviously shorthand for a very complex relation, but such a shorthand has its purpose in a time when people think they get to make up what sex is for.[12]

11. In other words, baptism makes marriage possible.

12. My difficulty with the Roman Catholic argument against contraception is that it may involve the abstraction of sex from marriage. The argument that every act of sexual intercourse must be open to conception I fear tries to read too much off the act itself, thus divorcing the act from marriage. It is one thing to maintain that marriage as an institution must be open to procreation; it is quite another to maintain that every act of sexual intercourse must be open to conception. The problem is how to make clear that marriage is a practice whose telos is children in a world in which marriage has been spiritualized in the name of love. If nothing else, the prohibition of contraception reminds Christians that sex has a purpose inseparable from our bodies.

A significant reason why Catholic sexual ethics are currently in such deep trouble is that so many Catholics have such a negative view of the church that they could not imagine sacrificing their personal sexual satisfaction as what might be required to be part of the adventure of what it means to be part of the body of Christ called "church" (see *Hauerwas Reader*, 503). Their inability to see this adventure as worthwhile is not even primarily due to "lust" (though it may be!), but more profoundly a sense of loneliness and the need for power in their lives (see AC, 131).

The Christian refusal to separate marriage and the having of children can be usefully contrasted with Adam Smith's account of the place of children. Smith simply assumed the having of children was a natural process that resulted in a particularly intense form of sympathy. Yet what he does not provide is an answer to the question as to why having children is a good thing to do. Indeed, I think there is no greater sign of the incoherence surrounding the having of children in our culture than the pagan assumption that biology makes children "ours." Such an assumption seems to draw on Smith's view that it is necessary for the child to be "like us" in order to create bonds of sympathy. That children are born of our bodies, that children can be the bodily form of the unity of a marriage, is no doubt a great gift. But it is not, from a Christian perspective, a necessary condition to account for our responsibility for children.

Christians, single and married, are parents. "Parent" names an office of the Christian community that everyone in the community is expected faithfully to fulfill. Those called to marriage are presumed to accept the call and responsibility to have and care for particular children in the name of the community. But the goods and the burdens of that office cannot be restricted just to those that "have" children. That is why the church rightly expects parents to bring up children in the faith. No responsibility is more important.[13]

Accordingly, the church has rightly resisted state authorities when they attempt to educate children in a manner contrary to parental desires. The church does so because the church expects parents to represent Christ for our children. Having said that, it is also important to remember that the parental rights of those who have their children baptized are not primary but derivative, since they draw their intelligibility from the church's command that parents bring their children up in the faith. Christian parents do not own their children; rather, those of us who are Christian parents are called to serve our children by recognizing that the children of our bodies are gifts of God, not our possessions. That is the "right" the church protects in the name of parental care of children. Of course, the problem in America is that Christians have come to believe the public authorities are but an extension of the care we are to give our children.[14]

13. For examples of how the faithful activity of a church creates possibilities for parenting that are not possible given the individualistic assumptions about marriage and family in our culture, see Hauerwas and Willimon, *RA*, chaps. 4–6.

14. In *AC*, I use Bertrand Russell's account of marriage to show how the contractual version of marriage and sexual relations, contrary to Russell's desires, must lead to the growth of the state.

I am aware that the account I have just given of the Christian family may strike many as extreme. Surely the business of marriage and having children is a more straightforward affair. Indeed, there seems to be something distinctly "unnatural" about my account of Christian marriage. My account may even seem to risk creating a gulf between God's good creation of marriage and family as we generally know it and how marriage and the family are institutionalized in the church. Or, to put the objection in more Catholic terms: I may seem to risk divorcing nature from grace.[15]

I cannot deny that Christian singleness represents a challenge to what we may well consider "normal." But then again, "normal" is scarcely a good indication of what is "natural." Singleness does not deny the natural, but rather is a reminder that nature "naturally" has an eschatological destiny. In that respect, singleness is no different from marriage. With this account of "natural," I can think of nothing more "natural" than life-long monogamous fidelity.[16] I can think of nothing more "natural" than the desire for children even in a world as dark as this one. What Christians have discovered about singleness or marriage is not unique to us. It is simply our privilege and responsibility to be for others what God has made it possible for us to be. Indeed, I think Christians can do few things more important in a world like ours than to be a people capable of welcoming children.

4. Where Do We Go from Here?

Which brings me back to how I began this essay. You may remember I expressed the worry that my critique of those that make Christianity a "good thing" for the family may play into the hands of the forces that are about the destruction of the family. Put more accurately: I am not at all sure how we as Christians can sustain the practices of singleness, marriage, and the having of children in a world that makes those practices a matter of individual satisfaction. The account I have just given of the Christian family which I think is true is also, I fear, too ethereal. Nisbet is right. The family, and in particular the Christian family, cannot survive unless the family in fact is necessary for our survival.[17]

15. For my extensive reflections on the relationship between nature and grace, see "The Truth about God: The Decalogue as Condition for Truthful Speech" (1998) in STT.

16. For a wonderful argument to this effect, see Catherine M. Wallace, For Fidelity: How Intimacy and Commitment Enrich Our Lives (New York: Knopf, 1998).

17. While this essay has emphasized how a Christian conception and practice of the family requires the church, American Christians live in a culture whose individualistic assumptions

It is quite interesting in this respect to think about the poor. The poor go on having children in our society in a manner that those with money seem to think irresponsible. But I wonder if the poor are not prophetic just to the extent they understand the having of children is not a matter of our being able to make sure the world into which children are born will be safe. What we are about as Christians is the having of children. That must come first, and then we must subject other aspects of our lives to that reality. I am not suggesting that children become an end in themselves, but rather that children are the way we remember that it is God that matters, not making the world safe or rich.

At stake in all this is the survival of the church. I am often accused of tempting Christians to withdraw from the world. I have no wish for that, nor, for that matter, any idea how that might be done. Yet I am convinced that if the church is to be able to discipline marriage in the name of that politics called church, we are going to find ourselves as Christians in tension with the world—at least the world as envisaged by Adam Smith—in which we find ourselves. My claim that the first task of the church is to be the church may, in other words, be exactly what is required if Christians are to be a people capable of bringing children into the world. Moreover, for the church to be a community capable of sustaining the having and care of children, we must also be a people who are not bent on the control of our economic destinies. No attitude is more destructive of children or the family than the presumption that the having of children is a zero-sum game. This is but a reminder that nothing is easier or harder to remember than that, when all is said and done, we must remember that children are a gift from God. Thank God for Joel Adam Hauerwas.

Further Reading
"The Moral Value of the Family" (1981), in CC
"The Family: Theological and Ethical Reflections" (1981), in CC

---

affect not only themselves but also the practices of the church. (For more on this, see CC, 160.) This is especially a situation of pathos for American Catholics. Whereas the church was once a central component for Catholic belief and practice, Catholics are now becoming increasingly Protestant in granting no more epistemological claim on their lives to the church than they give to any other institution, and often less. Whereas most Americans do not really think twice about the possibility that their country might ask them to die to protect it, we Christians find it hard to imagine the church requiring anything similarly demanding of us, or responding if it did. If so, the church has just become another institution for voluntary association that we are happy to abandon when it fails to meet our consumer needs.

"Taking Time for Peace: The Ethical Significance of the Trivial" (1986), in CET

"The Politics of Sex: How Marriage Is a Subversive Act" (1991), in AC

"The Fourth Commandment," with William H. Willimon (1999), in TG

"The Ninth and Tenth Commandments," with William H. Willimon (1999), in TG

"The Retarded, Society, and the Family: The Dilemma of Care" (1982), in SP

"Abortion, Theologically Understood" (1991), essay 31 in this volume

"Must a Patient Be a Person to Be a Patient? Or, My Uncle Charlie Is Not Much of a Person but He Is Still My Uncle Charlie" (1975), essay 30 in this volume

"A Child's Dying" (1990), in NS

"Medicine as Theodicy" (1990), in NS

"Communitarians and Medical Ethicists: Why I Am None of the Above" (1994), in DF

"Hating Mothers As a Way to Peace" (1993), in US

25. Why Gays (as a Group) Are Morally Superior to Christians (as a Group) (1993)

Satire [handwritten annotation]

Originally appearing in the Charlotte Observer _newspaper during the controversy over whether gays should be allowed to serve in the military, this polemical editorial seeks to expose some of the inevitable incoherencies of moral positions staked out under the assumptions of political liberalism. Drawing on the example of traditional Catholic just war theory, Hauerwas challenges his fellow Christians to acknowledge some of the radical demands of the Christian Gospel, including those that may well conflict with the reigning ethos of their society. In this respect, this essay is as much about what it means to be the church in a secular world as it is a response to public policy debate about gays and lesbians in the military._

I am ambivalent about recent discussions concerning gays in the military. I see no good reason why gays and lesbians should be excluded from military service; as a pacifist I do not see why anyone should serve. Moreover, I think it a wonderful thing that some people are excluded as a group. I only wish that Christians could be seen by the military to be as problematic as gays.

The groundswell of reaction against gays serving in the military is no doubt due to many factors. The response is not due, however, to the threat that gays might pose to our moral or military culture. Discrimination against gays grows from the moral incoherence of our lives; people who are secure in their convictions and practices are not so easily threatened by the prospects of a marginal group acquiring legitimacy through military service.

Gay men and lesbians are being made to pay the price of our society's moral incoherence not only about sex, but about most of our moral convictions. As a society we have no general agreement about what constitutes

[This essay was originally published as "Christian Soldiers" in the _Charlotte Observer,_ May 31, 1993, and in other newspapers subscribing to the Religious News Service. Subsequently it was included in DF.]

marriage and/or what goods marriage ought to serve. We allegedly live in a monogamous culture, but in fact we are at best serially polygamous. We are confused about sex, why and with whom we have it, and about our reasons for having children.

This moral confusion leads to a need for the illusion of certainty. If nothing is wrong with homosexuality then it seems everything is up for grabs. Of course, everything is already up for grabs, but the condemnation of gays hides that fact from our lives. So the moral "no" to gays becomes the necessary symbolic commitment to show that we really do believe in something.

But in some way this prejudice against gays has worked in their favor. They at least know more about who they are and who their enemy is. If only Christians could be equally sure of who they are. If only the military could come to view Christians as a group of doubtful warriors.

What if Catholics took the commitment to just war seriously as a discipline of the church? Just war considerations might not only raise questions about targeting strategies of nuclear weapons, but also question whether we should even have a standing army. A just war stance requires discussion in order to secure genuine conscientious participation. The very fact of our standing army means too often such discussion is relegated to politicians who manipulate the media to legitimate what they were going to do anyway. If Catholics challenged the presumption of a standing army, or at least one the size of the American army, they might not be so quickly received into the military.

Consider the implications of Catholic Christians trained to press issues of discrimination in terms of battlefield strategy. Would the military welcome pilots who worried if bombing drops might incur civilian casualties? Even concern with the distinction between direct and indirect intention for dealing with such a matter is, I suspect, more than the military wants to address on a daily basis.

Imagine Catholics, adhering closely to just war theory, insisting that war is not about killing but only incapacitating the enemy. They could participate only in wars designed to take prisoners and then, if that is not a possibility, only to wound. Killing the enemy is a last resort. What would military training look like if that were institutionalized?

Concentration on just war reflection is probably too abstract a way to imagine how Christians as a group might become suspect for military service. Far more likely are Christian behaviors and practices. Christians, for example, might be bad for morale in barracks. For example, non-Christians may find it disconcerting to have a few people gathering nightly holding hands with heads bowed. God knows what kind of disgusting behavior in which they might be engaged.

Even more troubling is what they might say to one another in such a group. Christians are asked to pray for the enemy. Could you really trust people in your unit who think the enemy's life is as valid as their own or their fellow soldier? Could you trust someone who would think it more important to die than to kill unjustly? Are these people fit for the military?

Prayer, of course, is a problem. But even worse is what Christians do in corporate worship. Think about the meal, during which they say they eat and drink with their God. They do something called "pass the peace." They even say they cannot come to this meal with blood on their hands. People so concerned with sanctity would be a threat to the military.

Having them around is no fun. They think they ought to keep their promises. They think that fidelity matters. They do not approve of the sexual license long thought to be a way of life and legitimate for those facing the danger of battle. Their loyalty is first to God, and then to their military commanders. How can these people possibly be trusted to be good soldiers?

Finally, consider the problem of taking showers with these people. They are, after all, constantly going on about the business of witnessing in the hopes of making converts to their God and church. Would you want to shower with such people? You never know when they might try to baptize you.

If gays can be excluded as a group from the military, I have hope that it could even happen to Christians. God, after all, has done stranger things in the past.

However, until God works this miracle, it seems clear to me that gays, as a group, are morally superior to Christians.

Further Reading

"Gay Friendship: A Thought Experiment in Catholic Moral Theology" (1996–97), in STT

"Understanding Homosexuality: The Viewpoint of Ethics," in *Pastoral Psychology* 24, no. 3 (spring 1976): 238–42.

"The Politics of Witness: How We Educate Christians in Liberal Societies" (1991), in AC

"The Politics of Sex: How Marriage Is a Subversive Act" (1991), in AC

"Life in the Colony: The Church as the Basis for Christian Ethics" (1989), in RA

"The Christian Difference, Or: Surviving Postmodernism" (1999) in BH

26. Christianity: It's Not a Religion: It's an Adventure (1991)

While some of the issues covered here are particularly pertinent to Catholics in the United States (e.g., issues of authority and of the effort of Catholics to "make it" in a Protestant country), this popular interview addresses many of the key challenges for Christians living in a liberal democratic culture. Here in capsule form Hauerwas argues why our notions of individualism, liberalism, and pluralism have their own tyrannical and totalitarian tendencies. Hauerwas here rejects the common charge that his rejection of liberalism requires a Christian "withdrawal," and explicates alternative modes of engagement with the culture within which we find ourselves. Interviewed in the aftermath of the Persian Gulf War of 1991, Hauerwas makes pointed remarks about a society that so enthusiastically engaged the war, as well as one that continues to abort its children. Here Hauerwas argues that Christian discipleship is not about happiness through desire fulfillment, but about becoming part of a community that transforms our desires toward things we did not know we wanted.

What does it mean to be Christian?

Being Christian is a way of life; it's being part of God's story. To be Christian is to appreciate what God has done for us through Jesus of Nazareth. Being Christian doesn't mean following a set of rules or principles; Christianity depends on the character of people's lives. The Gospel has no meaning unless it can be lived out and embodied in people's lives. That's why the lives of the saints are so important. To be Christian means to praise and glorify God. The lives of Christians look different from other people's lives. When Christians try to look the same as everyone else, they find themselves in all sorts of quandaries.

[Originally published in *U.S. Catholic* 56, no. 6 (June 1991), 6–13. Reprinted with permission from *U.S. Catholic*, Claretian Publications, www.uscatholic.org, 800-328-6515.]

What do you mean?

For example, when Catholics came to the United States, their deep concern was to be at home in their new country. They were ethnics who wanted to show they were good Americans. Thus, Catholics became super-Americans, who wanted to make sure their morality would conform to the best insights of the American way of life. But much of their Catholic character got lost in the process, and they found themselves in all sorts of unprecedented dilemmas.

Such as?

First and foremost, Catholics lost their sense of authority. The United States is a social order built upon the presumption that each person gets to be his or her own tyrant—that's called the pursuit of happiness. Each person gets to make up his or her own mind based on the presumption that choices are made free from an overarching influence.

When Catholics came to the United States, they were told, "This country is based on the neutral principle of the separation of church and state." Catholics said, "That principle doesn't sound neutral to us." So they built their own schools. But they had deep moral reticences about forming their own schools because they didn't believe in the separation of church and state. They had no sense that people could divide their lives in that way.

Catholics thought of themselves as Catholics. They had no concept of what it meant to be individuals. In fact, they believed that one couldn't be free if one wasn't ultimately loyal to the church. Without a sense of legitimate authority, Catholics believed that one would simply serve one's own conscience, which would be a terrible thing if that conscience hadn't been well formed. The Catholic Church understood that, prior to one's having a choice, a person had to be trained to want the right things rightly. The Catholic school system's goal was to inform consciences.

Unfortunately, the Catholic school system has for the most part simply become the carbon image of the public school system because Catholics are deathly afraid of their children not being successful in U.S. society. How will Catholics maintain their distinctiveness without distinct institutions? That is a real challenge for North American Catholics in the future.

What's wrong with the trend toward individualism in the United States?

One of the deep difficulties for people in the United States is what I call the Groucho Marx Principle. Groucho Marx said he wouldn't want to belong to a country club that would have him as a member. The same problem holds true in making moral choices. Would you want a moral life that you've created?

Most people wouldn't, so cynicism has become the primary virtue of U.S. public life. Cynicism ensures that there's absolutely nothing worth dedicating one's life to in a way that totally encompasses it. One always wants to be able to disassociate oneself from one's engagements at any given moment.

A way to counter this cynicism is to point out some of the delusions we have about choice in our lives. For example, in a marriage course I used to teach at the University of Notre Dame, I always gave the students one absolute that they could write down and put in their pockets; when times got tough, they could pull it out and say, "God, it's great to have an absolute to guide my life." My absolute was that you always marry the wrong person. It's a reversible absolute, though: you also always marry the right person. The point is you don't know who you're marrying.

That absolute is meant to challenge the presumption that a person's life is fundamentally a matter of choice. It is a matter of choice, but often one doesn't know what one is choosing. That's where fidelity comes in. A couple marrying must be willing to make a promise although neither person knows exactly what kind of promise is being made.

How do we know what choices to make?

That's what the church is all about. It says that we really don't know what powers and what stories have a hold on us until our lives have become one with the life of the church. The church says to us, "We're not giving you a story that you can choose. We're making you part of a story you didn't choose: God's story. You don't get to make God; God gets to make you. You are made by being brought into this community through which you discover your story. And your story is that you have been created to praise and glorify God—all moral life derives from that truth. Therefore, there is a distinct difference between you and those who have not been made part of God's story."

So there isn't one morality that guides everyone whether they know it or not?

One of the difficulties of Catholic moral theology has been its assumption that it is rooted in so-called natural law. Christian ethics, then, is said to be about certain presumptions that all people share. Being Christian, according to this way of thinking, is merely icing on top of ordinary human nature—a sort of super nature if one is endowed with all the Christian virtues.

Saint Thomas Aquinas's account of natural law is quite different from these presumptions. Aquinas didn't think that natural law meant all people really believed the same thing about the moral life. He knew they didn't. Natural law for Aquinas was a way of saying that all people have the same destiny in God.

But the way people understand and interpret their lives is different depending on the story they embrace. This is a way of saying, "Outside the church there's no salvation." But it's also a way of saying, "Only within the church is there damnation."

What sets Christians apart?

Christians are put in jeopardy in a special way because they have been made part of God's creation and providential care. What God does with a Muslim, a Hindu, a Buddhist, and so on is God's business. All a Christian knows is that God has given him or her a special mission as a witness to the kingdom brought by Jesus.

This kind of talk doesn't sit well with Christians who are constantly trying to make it as good citizens in the United States. But Christians should be in contention with what is called modernity because modernity is in contention with the Christian belief that an individual's freedom comes from being engrafted into a community and into a narrative that he or she did not create or choose.

So how should Christians live in society?

Very carefully; but, I would also say, joyfully. That's the most important thing Christians can do. They should live in the United States, for example, without pretending that they are at home here because they are not at home anywhere. Every social order is going to give Christians peculiar challenges. Christians belong to a worldwide church that has great and varied resources; they're not trapped in any one country. Their home is part of a movable feast.

Christians in the United States must know how to be contentious within the democratic social order. They must know how to make it count that they're Christian. They shouldn't believe in words like *pluralism*. Words like *pluralism* are used by the powerful, who want to determine people's lives. Citizens in the United States do not live in a pluralist culture—at best they live in a highly fragmented one for which there's very little possibility of genuine disagreement. Nobody questions or argues; they tolerate.

What's wrong with tolerating others?

Look what happened to Catholics in the United States. They struggled like hell to make it and finally saw John F. Kennedy elected president. Any Catholic of that generation will tell you how important it was that Kennedy became president. Catholics all over the world rejoiced, but I say it was their day of shame—particularly when Kennedy told a group of Southern Baptists in

Houston, Texas, that he would follow his conscience and not the Roman Catholic Church. Catholics said, "See, it is possible to be American and Catholic."

But then what happened? Abortion happened. Catholics were forced to ask themselves, "What is this society that we just bought into?" It turned out to be a society that is going to kill its kids. Abortion is not some little mistake. Abortion is a reflection of who Americans are: people in the United States are supposed to concentrate on themselves and pursue happiness; thus, they ask themselves, "Why should we bother having children?"

As a Catholic growing up after Vatican II, I was under the impression that we should be more ecumenical and see the good in all faiths. What would you say about that?

I would say you were being corrupted. I'm absolutely serious about that. You were corrupted because what that did was put compassion in the place of the crucified Savior. The great enemy of the church today is not atheism but sentimentality; and there's no deeper sentimentality than the presumption by Christians and nonbelievers alike that they should be able to have children without their children suffering for their convictions.

In the name of compassion, in the name of justice, Christians accepted the ideology of liberalism. They began to say that their task was to create societies where no one ever has to die for what they believe; therefore, Christians became identified with people of goodwill—wishing everyone well. And that is exactly to buy into the liberal presumption that there really is a common morality that we all share and that we all know how to work for. But that's the message of imperialism, not Christianity. For example, if you were a nonbeliever, would you want a Christian to say to you, "You're such a good person; I'm so impressed with you; you're really just like me—you're really a Christian." Such a statement would be terribly arrogant on the Christian's part.

Pagans aren't Christians either. Christians in the early church knew that; they knew it was a matter of life or death to defeat the pagans, and when they finally did defeat them, Christians said to the pagans, "You've got to be converted; you're murderers. You need at least three years of confessional practice."

What Christians did back then was good. That's what modern Christians ought to tell someone like President Bush. Bush's war against Iraq was murder. His soul is in jeopardy. Christians ought to tell Bush he needs to be converted.

Would it be better for Christians to separate themselves from society?

Absolutely not. Christians shouldn't be sitting in a corner sucking their thumbs in self-righteous indignation about the corruption of the wider society. Christians shouldn't withdraw; they should live in society as Christians. They should have the courage to identify themselves as Christians. The problem is that the guiding principle in the United States is to sublimate differences so that we won't have to face up to conflict. As a result, society imposes on people a kind of peace that is really violent order.

The church believes that it is always under the judgment of truth. The ideology of democracy believes that somehow truth is discerned and carried by the majority. But we must never forget that the most democratically elected leader of modern times was Adolf Hitler.

So I stand here in my position as a Christian and someone else stands there in his or her position as a Jew. How do we get anything done in society?

You may not. Why do you think that your first task as a Christian is to make society work?

Because I want to eat.

I quite appreciate that response. You may have to learn to cooperate with people to figure out how to do that. Yet, in our society, eating is the source of our deepest injustices. For Christians, one of their great challenges is to figure out how they can eat and provide for themselves without reinforcing the powers that Christ defeated. The problem with affluent Christians in the United States today is that they want to eliminate the otherness of poverty. They say everybody can be rich. That is the vision of justice for Christians in the United States. It's an elitist vision that makes the lives of anyone who isn't poor easier because they've already won. They can sit back, wish others well, and never deal with any of the injustices of poverty or admit that they're part of the problem.

Middle-class Christians assume they have a common language with the poor. But they don't. The rich, the poor, and the middle class don't speak the same language because they don't have the same practices. Our nation is made up of separate tribes. Christians must face up to the fact that they, too, should see themselves as a tribe and work toward establishing a common language through shared practices.

How should Christians, particularly Catholics, respond to injustice within the church?

Listening to the weakest member is the kind of church government that is at the very heart of the Gospel. One of the deep problems in Catholicism is when the weakest member is shut up. The weakest brother or sister is always there to speak as a Christian and to be a witness to Jesus Christ. Giving power to those weakest members is necessary; otherwise, the entire community is always dependent on the good nature of the leadership.

Politically speaking, within the church, Catholics, particularly in the United States, are perpetual adolescents. They want to kick the hell out of Daddy—that is, criticize the Pope and the clergy, but they don't want to take responsibility for the perpetuation of the institution or any of the other responsibilities of the church. My basic view is that the Vatican has written off the church in the United States. It's not that Rome doesn't want the U.S. church to survive; but on the whole, Rome thinks that people in the United States have been deeply corrupted by bourgeois liberalism—and Rome is right.

Sure, the battle about authority and discipline that concerns U.S. Catholics needs to be fought; but U.S. Catholics better not think they're going to win over Rome just by saying "We need to get more democratic representation." The church as an institution is not just about providing for greater participation; it's about being a people in a hostile environment capable of sustaining the witness to Jesus of Nazareth, who has brought to us a way of life that we know to be life-giving.

Hasn't liberalism in the United States helped Christianity in any way?

Once in the United States, Christians certainly discovered things about themselves that had been repressed during the Enlightenment. When I critique liberalism, I don't assume that it's bad. I assume that we've created it and now must figure out how to live with it. You see, the more entrenched this social order becomes—where everyone is automatically defined as moral—the more morality looks like law; and eventually virtues and holiness are no longer determined by the community.

It's a little like this analogy: I used to be a bricklayer. My father was a bricklayer. When I was eight, I was taken out on the job, put up on scaffolds, and taught to catch brick. The next summer I learned to stir the mud after it hardened. Eventually I learned how to pitch brick, build scaffolds, and chop mud. I mastered all the necessary skills. I didn't actually lay a brick until I was eighteen.

If bricklayers were never to go through all the steps, then, when laying bricks, they wouldn't know whether they had the right consistency of mud or how to spread the mortar. They had to be initiated into the craft. And that's how one needs to think about the virtues. To become virtuous one must subject oneself to a master, become initiated into the moral life, and undergo a transformation.

For example, the only way that one becomes just is to act the way a just person acts. Each Christian needs to apprentice himself or herself to moral people. But it isn't enough just to copy them. One has to be moral in the way they are moral, that is, with the right emotions and right judgments. These are nuances that take years to master. Morality isn't something you can force on people.

How can we bring up our children to be moral?

Start with baseball and also teach them to read. Don't teach kids a bunch of rules. Help them submit their lives to something that they find to be a wonderful activity that transforms them. Activities such as baseball and reading are where the virtues are inculcated with a seriousness that is hard to match in other areas of our lives.

Christians also ought to go to church. That's where you learn to practice religion and be virtuous. It's unnatural at first, but that's what virtue is all about. For example, we aren't naturally truthful. It's hard to learn to be truthful because truthfulness as a virtue requires transformation by being made humble, by letting oneself be transformed by what is strange to us.

What's the proper way to hand on the faith?

By example and by teaching the basics of the faith along the line. Christians should say to their children such things as "We Christians marry for a lifetime," and they should tell the stories of people they know who have lived Christian lives. I talk a lot about the importance of stories because what most people identify as morality—the do's and don'ts—make no sense out of context. They don't help people become moral because people need to see how do's and don'ts are intelligible within a whole way of life. People get a sense of a whole way of life through examples they've witnessed and stories they've heard.

As a family, there's nothing more important Christians can do than worship together. I saw that time after time while I was teaching at Notre Dame. The students could be in awful shape—mad at their parents, the church, or whomever, but they'd still attend Mass. The liturgy provided the students with substance and perspective. Taking young kids to the liturgy helps them learn its importance. If ever my own son said, "I don't want to go to Mass this Sunday," I'd say, "It doesn't matter; it's our duty; we go." Oftentimes, I'd say, "Jeez, I just don't know whether or not I believe in God today. But we're still going to Mass." Attending liturgy is a Christian's duty because it's true. It's what makes life make any sense at all.

So that's how one learns about Christian character and the moral life— through common practices like the liturgy. Practices and rituals help the story of one's life take shape. One learns that as a Christian one is here to be a glorifier of God; one's whole life depends upon that.

So the Christian message isn't something like "Live the good life and you'll be happy."

No. That's an awful message to be sending children. Never let someone say, "We don't want our education to be indoctrination." Of course Christians want their education to be indoctrination, and of course it's going to make the students unhappy. How can one be happy in a world of such violence? Christians are going to make people feel guilty, but let's hope it's about the right things. We live in a hard, harsh world. We've just finished killing a lot of people in the Persian Gulf. That's real. That's not joking. And that action is in deep tension with who Christians are.

What we do when we educate kids to be happy and self-fulfilled is to absolutely ruin them. Parents should say to their kids, "What you want out of life is not happiness but to be part of a worthy adventure. You want to have something worth dying for." It's awful when all we have to live for is ourselves; that's what the Gospel reveals to us. The Good News tells of the adventure that humans have been made part of through God's grace, through Christ, and through the church. God made each Christian part of God's sacrificial life so that the world might know that it is not abandoned and that there is salvation. That's who Christians are. Doesn't that sound like a joyful thing? I use the language of joy because happiness is just too pale to describe this adventure.

Christianity is the proclamation that God gives Christians a gift that they don't know they need. The gift then transforms their lives so that they are trained to want the right things rightly. Christmas has absolutely destroyed this understanding of the Good News. It's trained people to believe that Christianity is fundamentally about giving and receiving and that our happiness is in giving and getting what we want. But, in fact, the best Christmases are often the ones in which one doesn't get what one wants.

Remember when you got a chemistry set rather than a bicycle and you thought, "I hate this thing." But one wintry day you started playing with the chemistry set and discovered that it was really interesting. Suddenly you were trained to have wants you didn't know you should have. That's what Christianity is all about: it's an adventure we didn't know we wanted to be on.

What are some of the everyday situations where being Christian is going to make a difference?

Christians don't start off trying to be different. Difference isn't a virtue in and of itself. In a little book that Will Willimon and I wrote called *Resident Aliens*, all our examples come from everyday life. Regular people are meant to exemplify truthful living and truthful speech. What does it mean for us to be able to sustain people capable of truthful speech in a world where most people don't even know what truthful speech is?

One example we used in our book was about a teenage student who, through a parish program, was being mentored in catechism by a young man in his twenties. The two had a good relationship; however, one time the student went over to his mentor's house and found the young man sleeping with his girlfriend. The teenager raised a question about it, and the first response by the young man was "It's none of your business."

But the point is, it is the teenager's business. That's part of what it means to be a church—that we have claims on one another's lives. I like to quote Chuck Primus, who taught Judaica at Notre Dame when I was teaching there. He says, "Any religion that doesn't tell you what to do with your pots and pans and genitals can't be interesting."

Of course, pots and pans have to do with our economic relationships as well. I was giving a lecture several years ago at the business school at Houston Baptist University. Since they're Southern Baptist, they're deeply concerned about being moral. After I finished critiquing the concept of business ethics, one of the deans of the business school asked, "What can we do to be better Christians?" I said, "One thing I would do before I let people join a Southern Baptist church is have them declare in public what they make. They should say, 'I make $75,000 a year, and I want to be a member of your church.' That would show you very quickly how we have let capitalism privatize our economic lives in a way that's detrimental to the public character of the church."

These examples are very simple things that Christians can do to recapture what living our lives together means.

When you say another Christian's business is my business, that scares me because I can see it quickly going from someone's business to someone's judgment.

That's right. But that makes you nervous. Why?

Because I don't trust a lot of other people's judgment.

Allowing people to make judgments creates the discourse necessary to make those judgments less arbitrary. You're always living by somebody's judgments; unfortunately, most of the time, they're your own. We need ways to have matters tested by other people.

When it comes to marriage, for example, the church still holds some power and influence—and I say rightly so. Many churches require that the couple be part of the community for at least a year before they can marry there. It's not because the community will know the couple any better but the community will get some sense that the couple is capable of being faithful to a promise. So that's a judgment others are making about a person's life. I understand that the thought of such judgments is frightening, especially for those brought up in the liberal tradition; but without them Christians are lost.

Why?

Christians have an obligation to love one another as followers of Christ. Let's say I'm married and having an affair. Someone must say to me, "What you're doing to your spouse is unfaithful. I'm calling you from the life of adultery." Christians need to be judged in that way. Or, for example, they should say to their pastor or to the bishop who has lost perspective, "The way that you're exercising power in your office is not for the good of the church; it's for your personal ambition, and we call you from it." Matthew 18 is crucial for a good governance of the church. If we believe one of our brothers or sisters has wronged us, we are to *confront* him or her. People think that pacifists believe in avoiding conflict, but actually pacifists attempt to enhance conflict because they really believe in something, namely, peace.

Christians need to speak the truth about what is right and wrong and good and evil in our society. They need to establish a context where they can have real disputes with others. The conflicts will hurt, and not everyone will always be happy with the results; but at least people will be talking about things that really matter.

Does forgiveness fit into all of this?

Forgiveness is crucial for having truthful accounts of ourselves. We think that we should be able to turn our evils into goods, to right our wrongs; but there's no way that we can. Forgiveness is a necessary element in being able to name our sins, without forgetting them, and go on.

The deep difficulty, however, is not in forgiving but in being forgiven. One has to be trained to be a sinner. Sin is not a natural category. The Christian story trains a person to understand the ways in which he or she shows hatred toward God. Once a Christian realizes his or her need for forgiveness, he or she discovers that God is capable of forgiving and that Christians are, in fact, forgiving people who know how to give and receive forgiveness.

What are some of the hallmarks of being a Christian that are not often recognized?

Well, first of all, Christians can't tell their story separate from the Jews. For Christians, Israel and the continuing presence of Jews in the world is of absolute significance. Christians believe that Jesus is the Messiah of the Jews; therefore, Christians are locked in an eternal battle with Jews about how Jesus can be considered the Messiah when, in fact, the world remains. Israel and the church are side by side as communities narrating the world as God's creation. It's absolutely crucial to the telling of the story to understand that Christians are Jews. Christians can't tell their story without telling the story of the Jews. The Gospel is engrafted into this particular community of people.

Another hallmark of Christianity is that salvation is not individualistic—it's not something one person receives for himself or herself alone. Salvation is the reign of God. It is a political alternative to the way the world is constituted. That's a very important part of the story that has been lost to accounts of salvation that are centered in the individual. But without an understanding that salvation is the reign of God, the need for the church to mediate salvation makes no sense at all.

Another important point is that Jesus' death was a political death. If you ask one of the crucial theological questions—Why was Jesus killed?—the answer isn't "Because God wants us to love one another." Why in the hell would anyone kill Jesus for that? That's stupid. It's not even interesting. Why did Jesus get killed? Because he challenged the powers that be.

The church is a political institution calling people to be an alternative to the world. That's what the cross is about. The first social task of the church is not to make the world more just; it's to identify the world as the world. George Bush, for example, doesn't know he's the world.[1] He thinks he's a Christian. He needs to be told he's the world. The world isn't out there ready to be seen. Christians create the world by being a different people with different habits and practices

---

1. [This interview took place in 1991, in the wake of the Persian Gulf War. Hauerwas's references (both here and on p. 526) to George Bush (U.S. President from 1989 to 1993) are largely an indictment of President Bush's actions during that war.]

from that of the world. Then it becomes the task of the Christian to say, "World, you need converting because you're not part of the Christian story."

Is there a particular point in people's lives when they decide to accept or reject the Christian story?

I resist the notion that conversion is a sudden change at a particular point in one's life. Now, people clearly have had overwhelming religious experiences of which I stand in awe. But conversion is the name for the lifelong process of discovering that one's life has been constituted by a good God in ways one could never have imagined. Read Saint Teresa of Avila; Teresa never had any sudden conversion. She was just born knowing God and knowing that God knew her.

Basically, what it means to be Christianly formed is to be confronted by a witness who brings me news that I wouldn't have known unless I had that witness in front of me. That's the way the church grows. One person tells another. There is no account of Christianity that makes sense without evangelization. Don't give up on missions. Christians are a missionary people. Let's hope some African Christians will soon be sending missionaries to the United States. People in the United States need missionaries; they need people willing to help make them better than they are.

How do Christians go about helping people be better?

I often say to people that I'm a pacifist; but, as you can see, I'm very violent in my language and in many other ways. I'm a smart person, and smart people often use their minds as weapons. I'm always thinking three moves down a conversational ladder of how I can gain the upper hand. Therefore, when I say to people I'm a pacifist, I don't have any hope at all in being able to will my life that way. But by creating expectations in other people, I hope they will keep me truthful to the way I know I ought to live.

That's why Christians need the church. I don't have any faith in myself of living a virtuous life; but if I am surrounded by other people who are also formed by the same commitments, then we've got a better chance. We need one another to live up to the wonderful invitation we've been given to be other than we are.

Further Reading

"*The Door* Interview: William Willimon and Stanley Hauerwas," *The Door* 129 (May/June 1993): 6–11.

"What Would Pope Stanley say? Conversation with Stanley Hauerwas. An Interview with Rodney Clapp," *Books and Culture* 4, no. 6 (November/December 1998): 16–18.

"Salvation as Adventure" (1989), in *RA*

"A Story-Formed Community: Reflections on *Watership Down*" (1981), essay 9 in this volume

"A Homage to Mary and the University Called Notre Dame" (1994), in *IGC*

"The Importance of Being Catholic: Unsolicited Advice from a Protestant Bystander" (1989), in *IGC*

"Living in Truth: Moral Theology as Pilgrimage" (1994), in *IGC*

"Casuistry in Context: The Need for Tradition" (1995), essay 13 in this volume

"Should War Be Eliminated?: A Thought Experiment" (1984), essay 21 in this volume

The Church's Hospitality:

Christian Ethics after "Medical Ethics"

27. Salvation and Health:
Why Medicine Needs the Church (1985)

Modern medicine seems always to be prone to the temptation to separate medicine from religion, limiting medicine to the "mechanical understanding and care of the body." Although medicine has traditionally had a role in caring for the body, the development of ever increasing possibilities of "cure" has burdened medicine with expectations bordering on the idolatrous. But as Paul Ramsey has noted, the moral commitment made by doctors is not to care for bodies or "the population" but for the individual patient before them. Challenging both the "mechanical" and "sacralizing" views of medicine, Hauerwas changes the question, arguing that the appropriate starting place is to ask what kinds of communities are necessary to sustain long-term care of the ill. Pain and illness alienate us from others and from ourselves. It is the commitment of physicians, nurses, and chaplains to be present to those in pain. How can this commitment be maintained without caregivers either hardening in the face of it (sometimes called "physician's distance") or being overwhelmed by it? The church claims to be a community that has the resources to develop and sustain such habits, guided as it is by a God who is always faithful to us, in our sin, our suffering, and our pain. Medicine needs the church "as a resource of the habits and practices necessary to sustain the care of those in pain over the long haul."

A Text and a Story

While it is not unheard of for a theologian to begin an essay with a text from the Scripture, it is relatively rare for those who are addressing issues of medicine to do so. However, I begin with a text, as almost everything I have to say is but a commentary on this passage from Job 2:11–13: "Now when Job's friends

[Reprinted from *Theology and Bioethics*, D. Reidel Publishers, 1985, ed. Earl Shelp, 205–24, with kind permission from Kluwer Academic Publishers. Subsequently reprinted in *SP*. It has been slightly abridged and edited for clarity.]

heard of all this evil that had come upon him, then came each from his own place, Eliphaz the Temanite, Bildad the Shuhite, and Zophar the Na'amathite. They made an appointment together to come console with him and comfort him. And when they saw him from afar, they did not recognize him; and they raised their voices and wept; and they rent their robes and sprinkled dust upon their heads toward heaven. And they sat with him on the ground seven days and seven nights, and no one spoke a word to him, for they saw that his suffering was very great."

I do not want to comment immediately on the text. Instead, I think it best to begin by telling you a story. The story is about one of my earliest friendships. When I was in my early teens I had a friend, let's call him Bob, who meant everything to me. We made our first hesitant steps toward growing up through sharing the things young boys do—double dating, athletic activities, and endless discussions on every topic. For two years we were inseparable. I was extremely appreciative of Bob's friendship, as he was not only brighter and more talented than I, but also came from a family that was economically considerably better off than my own. Through Bob I was introduced to a world that otherwise I hardly would have known existed. For example, we spent hours in his home playing pool in a room that was built for no other purpose; and we swam in the lake that his house was specifically built to overlook.

Then very early one Sunday morning I received a phone call from Bob requesting that I come to see him immediately. He was sobbing intensely but through his crying he was able to tell me that they had just found his mother dead. She had committed suicide by placing a shotgun in her mouth. I knew immediately I did not want to go to see him or confront a reality like that. I had not yet learned the desperation hidden under our everyday routines and I did not want to learn of it. Moreover, I did not want to go because I knew there was nothing I could do or say to make things even appear better than they were. Finally, I did not want to go because I did not want to be close to anyone who had been touched by such a tragedy.

But I went. I felt awkward, but I went. And as I came into Bob's room we embraced, a gesture that was almost unheard of between young men raised in the Southwest, and we cried together. After that first period of shared sorrow we somehow calmed down and took a walk. For the rest of that day and that night we stayed together. I do not remember what we said, but I do remember that it was inconsequential. We never talked about his mother or what had happened. We never speculated about why she might do such a thing, even though I could not believe someone who seemed to have such a good life would want to die. We did what we always did. We talked girls, football, cars, movies, and anything else that was inconsequential enough to distract our attention from this horrible event.

As I look on that time now I now realize that it was obviously one of the most important events in my life. That it was so is at least partly indicated by how often I have thought about it and tried to understand its significance in the years from then to now. As often as I have reflected on what happened in that short space of time I have also remembered how inept I was in helping Bob. I did not know what should or could be said. I did not know how to help him start sorting out such a horrible event so that he could go on. All I could do was be present.

But time has helped me realize that this is all he wanted—namely, my presence. For as inept as I was, my willingness to be present was a sign that this was not an event so horrible that it drew us away from all other human contact. Life could go on, and in the days to follow we would again swim together, double date, and generally waste time. In retrospect, I think God granted me the marvelous privilege of being a presence in the face of profound pain and suffering even when I did not appreciate the significance of being present.

Yet the story cannot end here. For while it is true that Bob and I did go on being friends, nothing was the same. For a few months we continued to see one another often, but somehow the innocent joy of loving one another was gone. We slowly found that our lives were going in different directions and we developed new friends. No doubt the difference between our social and cultural opportunities helps explain to some extent our drifting apart. Bob finally went to Princeton and I went to Southwestern University in Georgetown, Texas.

But that kind of explanation for our growing apart is not sufficient. What was standing between us was that day and night we spent together under the burden of a profound sadness that neither of us had known could exist until that time. We had shared a pain so intense that for a short period we had become closer than we knew, but now the very pain that created that sharing stood in the way of the development of our friendship. Neither of us wished to recapture that time, nor did we know how to make that night and day part of our ongoing story together. So we went our separate ways. I have no idea what became of Bob, though every once in a while I remember to ask my mother if she has heard about him.

Does medicine need the church? How could this text and this story possibly help us understand that question, much less suggest how it might be answered? Yet I am going to claim in this essay that it does. Put briefly, what I will try to show is that if medicine can be rightly understood as an activity that trains some to know how to be present to those in pain, then something very much like a church is needed to sustain that presence day in and day out. Before I try to develop that thesis, however, I need to do some conceptual groundbreaking to make clear exactly what kind of claim I am trying to make about the relationship of salvation and health, medicine and the church.

Religion and Medicine: Is There or Should There Be a Relation?

It is a well-known fact that for most of human history there has been a close affinity between religion and medicine. Indeed, that very way of putting it is misleading, since to claim a relation suggests that they were distinguished, and often that has not been the case. From earliest times, disease and illness were not seen as matters having no religious import but rather as resulting from the disfavor of God. As Darrel Amundsen and Gary Ferngren have recently reminded us, the Hebrew Scriptures often depict God promising "health and prosperity for the covenant people if they are faithful to him, and disease and other suffering if they spurn his love" (Exod. 15:26).[1]

This view of illness was not associated only with the community as a whole, but with individuals. Thus in Psalm 38 the lament is "There is no soundness in my flesh because of thy indignation; there is no health in my bones because of my sin. . . . My wounds grow foul and fester because of foolishness. . . . I am utterly spent and crushed; I groan because of the tumult of my heart. . . . Do not forsake me, O Lord! O my God, be not far from me! Make haste to help me, O Lord, my salvation!" (vv. 3, 5, 8, 21–22). Amundsen and Ferngren point out this view of illness as accompanied by the assumption that acknowledgment of and repentance for our sin was essential for our healing. Thus in Psalm 32: "When I declared not my sin, my body wasted away through my groaning all day long. For day and night thy hand was heavy upon me; my strength was dried up. . . . I acknowledged my sin to thee, and I did not hide

---

1. Darrel Amundsen, and Gary Ferngren, "Medicine and Religion: Early Christianity through the Middle Ages," in *Health, Medicine and the Faith Traditions*, ed. M. Marty and K. Vaux (Philadelphia: Fortress Press, 1982), 92.

my iniquity; I said, 'I will confess my transgressions to the Lord'; then thou didst forgive the guilt of my sin" (vv. 3–5).[2]

Since illness and sin were closely connected it is not surprising that healing was also closely associated with religious practices; or, put more accurately, healing was a religious discipline. Indeed, Amundsen and Ferngren make the interesting point that since the most important issue was a person's relationship with God, the chief means of healing was naturally prayer. That clearly precluded magic and thus the Mosaic code excluded soothsayers, augurs, sorcerers, charmers, wizards, and other such figures who offered a means to control or avoid the primary issue of their relation to Yahweh.[3] They also suggest that this may have been why no sacerdotal medical practice developed in Israel particularly associated with the priesthood. Rather, the pattern of the Exodus tended to prevail, with illness and healing more closely associated with prophetic activity.

The early Christian community seems to have done little to change these basic presuppositions. If anything, it simply intensified them by adding what Amundsen and Ferngren call the "central paradox" in the New Testament: "Strength comes only through weakness. This strength is Christ's strength that comes only through dependence upon him. In the Gospel of John Christ says: 'I have said to you, that in me you may have peace. In the world you have tribulation; but be of good cheer, I have overcome the world' (16:33). 'In the world you have tribulation.' It is simply to be expected and accepted. But for the New Testament Christian no suffering is meaningless. The ultimate purpose and meaning behind Christian suffering in the New Testament is spiritual maturity. And the ultimate goal in spiritual maturity is a close dependence upon Christ based upon a childlike trust."[4] Thus illness is seen as an opportunity for growth in faith and trust in God.

Because of this way of viewing both the positive and negative effects of illness, Amundsen and Ferngren note that there has always been a degree of tension in the way Christians understand the relation between theology and secular medicine, between the medicine of the soul and the medicine of the body:

> According to one view, if God sends disease either to punish or to test a person, it is to God that one must turn for care and healing. If God is both the

2. Ibid., 93.
3. Ibid., 94.
4. Ibid., 96.

source and healer of a person's ills, the use of human medicine would circumvent the spiritual framework by resorting to worldly wisdom. On another view, if God is the source of disease, or if God permits disease and is the ultimate healer, God's will can be fulfilled through human agents, who with divine help have acquired the ability to aid in the curative process. Most Christians have asserted that the human agent of care, the physician, is an instrument of God, used by God in bringing succor to humankind. But in every age some have maintained that any use of human medicine is a manifestation of a lack of faith. This ambivalence in the Christian attitude, among both theologians and laity, has always been present to some degree.[5]

Nor is it possible to separate or distinguish religion and medicine on the basis of a distinction between soul and body. For as Paul Ramsey has reminded us, Christians affirm that God has created and holds us sacred as embodied souls.[6] Religion does not deal with the soul and medicine with the body. Practitioners of both are too well aware of the inseparability of soul and body; or, perhaps better, they know the abstractness of both categories. Moreover, when religion too easily legitimates the independence of medical care by limiting medicine to mechanical understanding and care of the body, it has the result of making religious convictions ethereal in character. It may be that just to the extent Christianity is always tempted in Gnostic and Manichean directions it accepts too willingly a technological understanding of medicine. Christians, if they are to be faithful to their convictions, may not ever be able to avoid at least potential conflict between their own assumptions about illness and health and how the ill should be cared for and the assumptions of medicine. One hopes for cooperation, of course, but structurally the possibility of conflict between church and medicine cannot be excluded, since both entail convictions and practices concerned with that same subject.

Put differently, given Judaism's and Christianity's understanding of humankind's relation with God—that is, how we understand salvation—health can never be thought of as an autonomous sphere. Moreover, insofar as medicine is a specialized activity distinguished from religious convictions, you cannot exclude the possibility that there may well be conflict between religion and medicine. For in many ways the latter is constantly tempted to offer a form of salvation that religiously may come close to idolatry. The ability of modern medicine to cure is at once a benefit and a potential pitfall. Too often

---

5. Ibid.
6. Paul Ramsey, *The Patient as Person* (New Haven: Yale University Press, 1970), xiii.

it is tempted to increase its power by offering more than care, by offering in fact alleviation from the human condition—for example, the development of artificial hearts. That is not the fault of medical practitioners, though often they encourage such idolatry; rather, the fault lies with those of us who pretentiously place undue expectations on medicine in the hope of finding an earthly remedy to our death. But we can never forget that the relation between medicine and health, and especially the health of a population, is as ambiguous as the relation between the church and salvation.

In the hope of securing peace between medicine and religion, two quite different and equally unsatisfactory proposals have been suggested. The first advocates a strong division of labor between medicine and religion by limiting the scope of medicine to the mechanism of our body. While it is certainly true that medicine in a unique way entails the passing on of the wisdom of the body from one generation to another, there is no way that medical care can be limited to the body and be good medicine.[7] As Ramsey has reminded us again and again, the moral commitment of the physician is not to treat diseases, or populations, or the human race, but the immediate patient before him or her.[8] Religiously, therefore, the care offered by physicians cannot be abstracted from the moral commitment to care based on our view that every aspect of our existence is dependent upon God.

By the same token the clergy, no less than physicians, are concerned about the patient's physical well-being. No assumption about technical skills and knowledge can legitimate the clergy's retreating into the realm of the spiritual in order to claim some continued usefulness and status. Such a retreat is as unfaithful as abandoning the natural world to the physicist on the grounds that God is a God of history and not of nature. For the church and its officeholders to abandon claims over the body in the name of a lack of expertise is equivalent to reducing God to the gaps in scientific theory. Such a strategy is not only bad faith but it results in making religious convictions appear at best irrelevant and at worse foolish.

The second alternative to accepting the autonomy of medicine from our religious convictions seeks to maintain a close relationship by resacralizing medical care. Medicine requires a "holistic vision of man,"[9] because the care it brings is but one aspect of salvation. Thus the church and its theology serves

7. For fuller treatment of this set of issues, see Hauerwas, "Authority and the Profession of Medicine" (1982) in SP.
8. Ramsey, 36, 59.
9. Bernard Haring, *Medical Ethics* (South Bend, IN: Fides Publishers, 1973), 9.

medical care by promoting a holistic view of man, one that can provide a "comprehensive understanding of human health [that] includes the greatest possible harmony of all of man's forces and energies, the greatest possible spiritualization of man's bodily aspect and the finest embodiment of the spiritual. True health is revealed in the self-actualization of the person who has attained that freedom which marshals all available energies for the fulfillment of his total human vocation."[10]

Such a view of health, however, cannot help but pervert the kind of care that physicians can provide. Physicians rightly maintain that their skill primarily has to do with the body, as medicine promises us health, not happiness. When such a general understanding of health is made the goal of medicine, it results only in making medical care promise more than it can deliver. As a result, we are tyrannized by the agents of medicine because we have voluntarily vested them with too much power. It is already a difficult task in our society to control the expectations people have about modern medicine; we only compound that problem by providing religious legitimacy to this overblown understanding of health. Certainly we believe that any account of salvation includes questions of our health, but that does not mean that medicine can or ever should become the agency of salvation. It may be a fundamental judgment on the church's failure to help us locate wherein our salvation lies that so many today seek a salvation through medicine.

Can Medical Ethics Be Christian?

The already complex question of the relation between religion and medicine only becomes more confusing when we turn our attention to more recent developments in medical ethics. For even though religious thinkers have been at the forefront of much of the work done in the expanding field of "medical ethics," it is not clear that they have been there as religious thinkers. Joseph Fletcher, Paul Ramsey, James Gustafson, Charles Curran, Jim Childress,[11] to name just a few, have done extensive work in medical ethics, but often it is hard to tell how their religious convictions have made a difference for the

---

10. Ibid., 154.
11. For example, see the following works: Joseph Fletcher, *Morals and Medicine* (Boston: Beacon Press, 1954); Ramsey, *The Patient as Person*; James Gustafson, *The Contributions of Theology to Medical Ethics* (Milwaukee: Marquette University Press, 1975); Charles Curran, *Issues in Sexual and Medical Ethics* (Notre Dame, IN: University of Notre Dame Press, 1978); and James Childress, *Priorities in Biomedical Ethics* (Philadelphia: Westminster Press, 1981).

methodology they employ or for their response to specific quandaries. Indeed, it is interesting to note how seldom they raise issues of the meaning or relation of salvation and health, as they seem to prefer dealing with questions of death and dying, truth telling, and so on.

In calling attention to this fact by no means do I wish to disparage the kind of reflection that has been done concerning these issues. We have all benefited from their careful analysis and distinctions concerning such problems. Yet one must wonder if, by letting the agenda be set in such a manner, we have already lost the theological ballgame. For the very concentration on "issues" and "quandaries" as central for medical ethics tends to underwrite the practice of medicine as we know it, rather than challenging some of the basic presuppositions of medical practice and care.

We tend to forget that the development of "Christian ethics" is a relatively new development.[12] It has only been in the past hundred years that some have styled themselves as "ethicists" rather than simply theologians. It is by no means clear that we know how to indicate what difference it makes conceptually and methodologically to claim our ethics as Christian in distinction from other kinds of ethical reflection. In the hope of securing greater clarity about their own work many who have identified their work as Christian have nonetheless assumed that the meaning and method of "ethics" was determined fundamentally by non-Christian sources. In a sense the very concentration on "medical ethics" was a godsend for many "religious ethicists," as it seemed to provide a coherent activity without having to deal with the fundamental issue of what makes Christian ethics Christian.[13]

Pain, Loneliness, and Being Present: The Church and the Care of the Ill

I think we will make little headway on this issue as long as we try to address the questions in terms of the dichotomies of religion and medicine or the relation between medical ethics and theology. Rather, what is needed is a restatement of the issue. In the remainder of this essay, I will show how the stories of Job and Bob remind us that more fundamental than questions of religion and

12. For more about the development of Christian ethics, see "How Christian Ethics Came to Be" (1997) and "On Keeping Theological Ethics Theological" (1983), essays 1 and 2 in this volume.

13. [An extended discussion of the nontheological character of the debate between Fletcher and Ramsey as to whether Christian moral reasoning is primarily "teleological" or "deontological" has been omitted.]

morality is the question of the kind of community necessary to sustain the long-term care of the ill.

Indeed, part of the problem with discussing the question of "relation" in such general terms as "medicine" and "religion" is that each of those terms in its own way distorts the character of what it is meant to describe. For example, when we talk in general about "religion" rather than a specific set of beliefs, behaviors, and habits embodied by a distinct group of people, our account always tends to be reductionistic. It makes it appear that underlying what people actually believe and do is a deeper reality called "religion." It is as if we can talk about God abstracted from how a people have learned to pray to that God. In like manner we often tend to oversimplify the nature of medicine by trying to capture the many activities covered by that term in a definition or ideological system. What doctors do is often quite different from what they say they do.

Moreover, the question of the relation of theology to medical ethics is far too abstract. For when the issue is posed in that manner it makes it appear that religion is primarily a set of beliefs, a worldview, that may or may not have implications for how we understand and respond to certain kinds of ethical dilemmas. While it is certainly true that Christianity involves beliefs, the character of those beliefs cannot be understand apart from its place in the formation of a community with cultic practices. By focusing on this fact I hope to throw a different perspective on how those who are called to care for the sick can draw upon and count on the particular kind of community we call the church.

I do not intend, for example, to argue that medicine must be reclaimed as in some decisive way dependent on theology. Nor do I want to argue that the development of "medical ethics" will ultimately require the acknowledgment of, or recourse to, theological presuppositions. Rather, all I want to try to show is why, given the particular demands put on those who care for the ill, something very much like a church is necessary to sustain that care.

To develop this point I want to call attention to an obvious but often overlooked aspect of illness—namely, that when we are sick we hurt and are in pain. I realize that often we are sick and yet not in pain (e.g., with hardening of the arteries) but that does not ultimately defeat my general point, since we know that such an illness will lead to physical and mental pain. Moreover, I am well aware that there are many different kinds of pain, as well as intensity of pains. What is only a minor hurt for me may be a major trauma for someone else. Pain comes in many shapes and sizes. For example, suffering, which is not the same as pain since we can suffer without being in pain, is nonetheless akin to pain inasmuch as it is a felt deficiency that can make us as miserable as pain itself.[14]

Yet given these qualifications, it remains true that there is a strong connection between pain and illness, an area of our lives in which it is appropriate to call upon the skills of a physician. When we are in pain we want to be helped. But it is exactly at this point that one of the strangest aspects of our being in pain occurs: namely, it is impossible for us to experience one another's pain. That does not mean we cannot communicate to one another our pain. That we can do, but what cannot be done is for you to understand or experience my pain as mine.

This puts us under a double burden because we have enough of a problem learning to know one another in the normal aspects of our lives, but when we are in pain our alienation from one another only increases. For no matter how sympathetic we may be to the other in pain, that very pain creates a history and experience that makes the other just that much more foreign to me. Our pains isolate us from one another as they create worlds that cut us off from one another. Consider, for example, the immense gulf between the world of the sick and the world of the healthy. No matter how much we may experience the former, when we are healthy or not in pain we have trouble imagining and understanding the world of the ill.

Indeed, the terms we are using are still far too abstract. For we do not suffer illness in and of itself, but we suffer this particular kind of illness and have this particular kind of pain. Thus even within the world of illness there are subworlds that are not easily crossed. Think, for example, of how important it is for those suffering from the same illness to share their stories with one another. They do not believe others can understand their particular kind of pain. People with heart disease may find little basis of communion with those suffering from cancer. Pain itself does not create a shared experience, only pain of a particular kind and sort. Moreover, the very commonality thus created separates the ill from the healthy in a decisive way.

Pain isolates us not only from one another, but even from ourselves. Think how quickly people with a terribly diseased limb or organ are anxious for surgery in the hope that if it is just cut off or cut out they will not be burdened by the pain that makes them not know themselves. This gangrenous leg is not

---

14. For a fuller account of the complex relation between pain and suffering, see Hauerwas, "Reflections on Suffering, Death, and Medicine" (1979), in SP.

mine; I would prefer to lose the leg rather than face the reality of its connection to me.

The difficulties pain creates in terms of our relation with ourselves is compounded by the peculiar difficulties it creates for those close to us who do not share our pain. For no matter how sympathetic they may be, no matter how much they may try to be with and comfort us, we know they do not want to experience our pain. No matter how goodwilled we may be, we cannot take another's pain as our pain. Our pains divide us and there is little we can do to restore our unity.

I suspect this is one of the reasons that chronic illness is such a burden. For often we are willing to be present and sympathetic with someone with an intense but temporary pain; that is, we are willing to be present as long as they work at being "good" sick people who try to get well quickly and do not make too much of their discomfort. We may initially be quite sympathetic with someone with a chronic disease, but it seems to be asking too much of us to be compassionate year in and year out. Thus the universal testimony of people with chronic illnesses that their illnesses often results in the alienation of their former friends. This is a problem not only for the person who is ill but also for those closely connected with that person. The family of a person who is chronically ill often discovers that the very skills and habits they must learn to be present to the one in pain creates a gulf between themselves and their friends. Perhaps no case illustrates this more poignantly than a family that has a retarded child. Often they discover it is not long before they have a whole new set of friends who also happen to have retarded children.[15]

Exactly because pain is so alienating, we are hesitant to admit that we are in pain. To be in pain means we need help, that we are vulnerable to the interests of others, that we are not in control of our destiny. Thus we seek to deny our pain in the hope that we will be able to handle it within ourselves. But the attempt to deal with our pain by ourselves or to deny its existence has the odd effect of only increasing our loneliness. For exactly to the extent I am successful, I create a story about myself that I cannot easily share.

No doubt more can be and needs to be said that would nuance this account of pain and the way it tends to isolate us from one another. Yet I think I have said enough that our attention has been called to this quite common but all the more extraordinary aspect of our existence. Moreover, in the light of

15. For more on this set of issues, see Hauerwas, "The Retarded, Society and the Family: The Dilemma of Care" (1982) in SP.

this analysis I hope we can now appreciate the remarkable behavior of Job's friends. For in spite of the bad press Job's comforters usually receive (and in many ways it is deserved!), they at least sat on the ground with him for seven days. Moreover, they did not speak to him, "for they saw that his suffering was very great." That they did so is truly an act of magnanimity, for most of us are willing to be with sufferers, especially those in such pain that we can hardly recognize them, only if we can "do something" to relieve their suffering or at least distract their attention. Not so with Job's comforters. They sat on the ground with Job doing nothing more than being willing to be present in the face of his suffering.

Now if any of this is close to being right, it puts the task of physicians and others who are pledged to be with the ill in an interesting perspective. For I take it that their activity as physicians is characterized by the fundamental commitment to be, like Job's comforters, in the presence of those who are in pain.[16] At this moment I am not concerned to explore the moral reason for that commitment, but only to note that in fact physicians, nurses, chaplains, and many others are present to the ill as none of the rest of us are. They are the bridge between the world of the ill and the world of the healthy.

Certainly physicians are there because they have been trained with skills that enable them to alleviate the pain of the ill. They have learned from some sick people how to help other sick people. Yet every physician soon learns of the terrible limit of his or her craft, for the sheer particularity of the patient's illness often defies the best knowledge and skill. Even more dramatically, physicians learn that using the best knowledge and skill they have on some patients sometimes has terrible results.

Yet the fact that medicine through the agency of physicians does not and cannot always "cure" in no way qualifies the commitment of the physician. At least it does not do so if we remember that the physician's basic pledge is not to cure, but to care through being present to the one in pain. Yet it is not easy to carry out that commitment on a day-to-day, year-to-year basis. For none of us has the resource to see too much pain without that pain's hardening us. Without such a hardening, something we sometimes call by the name of professional distance, we fear we will lose the ability to feel at all.

Yet physicians cannot help but be touched and, thus, tainted by the world of the sick. Through their willingness to be present to us in our most vulner-

16. I am indebted to a conversation with Dr. Earl Shelp for helping me understand better the significance of this point.

able moments they are forever scarred with our pain—a pain that we the healthy want to deny or at least keep at arm's length. They have seen a world we do not want to see until it is forced on us, and we will accept them into polite community only to the extent they keep that world hidden from us. But when we are driven into that world we want to be able to count on their skill and their presence, even though we have been unwilling to face that reality while we were healthy.

But what do these somewhat random and controversial observations have to do with helping us better understand the relation between medicine and the church and the story of my boyhood friendship with Bob? To begin with the latter, I think in some ways the mechanism that was working during that trying time with Bob is quite similar to the mechanism that works on a day-to-day basis in medicine. For the physician, and others concerned with our illness, are called to be present during times of great pain and tragedy. Indeed physicians, because of their moral commitments, have the privilege and the burden to be with us when we are most vulnerable. The physician learns our deepest fears and our profoundest hopes. As patients, that is also why so often we fear physicians, because they may know us better than we know ourselves. Surely that is one of the reasons that confidentiality is so crucial to the patient-physician relation, since it is a situation of such intimacy.

But just to the extent that the physician has been granted the privilege of being with us while we are in pain, that very experience creates the seeds of distrust and fear. We are afraid of one another's use of the knowledge gained, but even more deeply we fear remembering the pain as part of our history. Thus every crisis that joins us in a common fight for health also has the potential for separating us more profoundly after the crisis. Yet the physician is pledged to come to our aid again and again, no matter how we may try to protect ourselves from his or her presence.

The physician, on the other hand, has yet another problem, for how can anyone be present to the ill day in and day out without learning to dislike, if not positively detest, our smallness in the face of pain? People in pain are omnivorous in their appetite for help, and they will use us up if we let them. Fortunately, the physician has other patients who can give him or her distance from any patient who requires too much. But the problem still remains. How do physicians—who are pledged to be with the ill—maintain their ability to see patients' humanity, which often comes close to being obliterated by their suffering? For the physician cannot, as Bob and I did, drift apart and away from those whom he or she is pledged to serve. At least they cannot if I am right that medicine is first of all pledged to be nothing more than a human presence in the face of suffering.

But how can we account for such a commitment—the commitment to be present to those in pain? No doubt basic human sympathy is not to be discounted, but it does not seem to be sufficient to account for a group of people dedicated to being present to the ill as their vocation in life. Nor does it seem sufficient to account for the acquiring of the skills necessary to sustain that presence in a manner that does not alienate or become the source of distrust in a community.

To learn how to be present in that way we need examples, people who have so learned to embody such a presence in their lives that it has become the marrow of their habits. The church claims to be such a community, a people called out by a God who is always present to us, both in our sin and in our faithfulness. Because of God's faithfulness we are supposed to be a people who have learned how to be faithful to one another by our willingness to be present, with all our vulnerabilities, to one another. For what does our God require of us other than our unfailing presence in the midst of the world's sin and pain? Thus our willingness to be ill and to ask for help, as well as our willingness to be present with the ill, is no special or extraordinary activity but a form of the Christian obligation to be present to one another in and out of pain.

Moreover, it is such a people who should have learned how to be present with those in pain without that pain having driven them further apart. For the very bond that pain forms between us becomes the basis for alienation, as we have no means to know how to make it part of our common history. Just as it is painful to remember our sins, so we seek not to remember our pain, since we desire to live as if our world and existence were pain-free. Only a people trained in remembering, and remembering as a communal act, their sins and pains can offer a paradigm for sustaining across time a painful memory so that it acts to heal rather than to divide.

Thus medicine needs the church not to supply a foundation for its moral commitments, but rather as a resource of the habits and practices necessary to sustain the care of those in pain over the long haul. For it is no easy matter to be with the ill, especially when we cannot do much for them other than simply be present. Our very helplessness too often turns to hate, both toward the ones in pain and toward ourselves, as we despise them for reminding us of our helplessness. Only when we remember that our presence is our doing, when sitting on the ground seven days saying nothing is what we can do, can we be saved from our fevered and hopeless attempt to control others' and our own existence. Of course, to believe that such presence is what we can and should do entails a belief in a presence in and beyond this world. And it is certainly true that many today no longer believe in or experience such a presence. If that is the case, then I do wonder if medicine as an activity of presence is possible in a world without God.

Another way of raising this issue is to ask the relation between prayer and medical care. Nothing I have said about the basic pledge of physicians to be present to the ill entails that they should not try to develop the skills necessary to help those in pain and illness. Certainly they should, as theirs is an art that is one of our most valuable resources for the care of one another. But no matter how powerful that craft becomes, it cannot in principle rule out the necessity of prayer. For prayer is not a supplement to the insufficiency of our medical knowledge and practice; nor is it some divine insurance policy that our medical skill will work; rather, our prayer is the means that we have to make God present whether our medical skill is successful or not. So understood, the issue is not whether medical care and prayer are antithetical, but how medical care can ever be sustained without the necessity of continued prayer.

Finally, those involved in medicine need the church, as otherwise they cannot help but be alienated from the rest of us. Unless there is a body of people who have learned the skills of presence, the world of the ill cannot help but become a separate world both for the ill and for those who care for them. Only a community that is pledged not to fear the stranger—and illness always makes us a stranger to ourselves and others—can welcome the continued presence of the ill in our midst. The hospital is, after all, first and foremost a house of hospitality along the way of our journey with finitude. It is our sign that we will not abandon those who have become ill simply because they currently are suffering the sign of that finitude. If the hospital, as too often is the case today, becomes but a means of isolating the ill from the rest of us, then we have betrayed its central purpose and distorted our community and ourselves.

If the church is the kind of people who show clearly that they have learned to be with the sick and the dying, then we will better understand the relation of salvation to health, of religion to medicine. Perhaps even more significantly, we will better understand what kind of medicine we ought to practice, since too often we try to substitute "doing" for presence. Paul Ramsey rightly reminds us that "not since Socrates posed the question have we learned how to teach virtue. The quandaries of medical ethics are not unlike that question. Still, we can no longer rely upon the ethical assumptions in our culture to be powerful enough or clear enough to instruct the profession in virtue; therefore the medical profession should no longer believe that the personal integrity of physicians alone is enough; neither can anyone count on values being transmitted without thought."[17] What I have tried to do is remind us that in order to transmit such "values" we need a people who believe in and live trusting in God's unfailing presence.

Further Reading

"How Christian Ethics Became Medical Ethics: The Case of Paul Ramsey" (1997),
    in *ww*

"Authority and the Profession of Medicine" (1982), in *sp*

"Theology, Theodicy, and Medicine" (1990), in *ns*

"Sinsick" (2000), in *bh*

"Medicine as a Tragic Profession" (1977), in *tt*

"Practicing Patience: How Christians Should Be Sick" (1997), essay 18 in this
    volume.

17. Ramsey, xviii.

28. Should Suffering Be Eliminated?
What the Retarded Have to Teach Us (1984)

Should we attempt to prevent retardation? Hauerwas explores this question within a broader context of questions concerning suffering, medicine, and human nature. We are tempted to say retardation should be prevented because it seems all suffering should be prevented. But is this really the case? While not interested in providing explanations of pain and suffering—the essay has no theodicy to offer—Hauerwas argues that suffering is intimately connected to our being "inherently creatures of need." We "suffer" simply by being creatures; thus to eliminate all suffering might imply the elimination of the sufferers. Hauerwas argues that the retarded are profoundly threatening to us, not least because they expose our own fear of weakness and dependence on others. Though we should be careful not to sentimentalize the retarded, they offer us "an opportunity to see God," for they point to our essential dependence on the suffering God of the cross.

A Short Movie and a Question

The movie begins. A man and woman stand looking into a baby crib. The baby is never shown. The room is dark and the countenance of the couple is yet darker. They have obviously been through a trauma and are still in shock. The joy and excitement associated with the birth of a child has been crushed from their lives. Their high expectations have been transformed to absolute despair.

They turn toward us and the man speaks: "Don't let this happen to you. Our child was born retarded. He will never play the way other children play. He will not be able to go to school with other children. He will never have an

[Originally published in *The Deprived, the Disabled, and the Fullness of Life,* ed. Flavian Dougherty (Collegeville, MN: Michael Glazier, 1984). Subsequently reprinted in *SP*. Originally entitled "Suffering the Retarded: Should We Prevent Retardation?" It has been slightly abridged and edited for clarity.]

independent existence and will require us to care for him throughout his and our lifetime. Our lives have been ruined. It is too late for us but not for you."

The mother speaks: "Don't let what happened to us happen to you. Be tested early if you think you are pregnant. Maintain good prenatal care under the direction of a physician. Do not smoke, drink, or take any drugs except those absolutely necessary for your health. Please do not let this happen to you—prevent retardation."

A film very much like this was sponsored a few years ago by the American Association of Retarded Citizens. No doubt the film was made with the best of intentions and concern. Surely we ought to prevent retardation. Certainly as many couples as can ought to be encouraged to maintain good prenatal care. Moreover, the Association of Retarded Citizens is probably right to assume they will stand a better chance of getting research funds for the retarded if they can convince the public, and thus the government, that their long-term policy is to eliminate retardation, as is the case for cancer. For if retardation can be eliminated, then the amount of money needed for constant care will be significantly reduced. Better a short-term outlay now than a continuing cost.

Nevertheless, there seems to be something deeply wrong, something disturbing about this film and its message, "Prevent retardation." Perhaps part of the difficulty involves the disanalogy between preventing retardation and preventing cancer, polio, or heart disease, as these latter diseases exist independent of the subjects having diseases. The disease can be eliminated without eliminating the subject of the disease. But the same is not always true of the retarded. To eliminate retardation may sometimes mean to eliminate the subject.

Yet surely this point is not decisive. The film, after all, is not suggesting that we kill anyone who is presently retarded. On the contrary, those who produced the film have dedicated their lives to enhancing the lives of retarded citizens. They have led the war on unjust forms of discrimination against the retarded. They surely do not seek to make the lot of the retarded worse than it is already; rather, they simply seek to prevent some from being born unnecessarily retarded. What could be wrong with that?

Still, I think something is wrong with a general policy that seeks to prevent retardation, but to say what is wrong with such a policy involves some of the most profound questions of human existence, including our relationship to God. In particular, assumptions about the nature and necessity of suffering, and our willingness to endure it in our own and other's lives, will need to be addressed. For the very humanity that causes us to cry out against suffering, that motivates us to seek to eliminate retardation, is also the source of our potentially greatest inhumanity.

By trying to understand why this is the case, moreover, I hope to illumine how our moral and religious presuppositions shape our medical care. Too often medicine becomes the means by which, in the name of humanity, we eliminate those who suffer. Thus it has become common in our society to assume that certain children born with severe birth defects who also happen to be retarded should not be kept alive in order to spare them a lifetime of suffering. But why do we assume that it is the role of medicine to save us from suffering? By exploring whether we ought to try to eliminate the retarded I hope therefore to make explicit a whole set of assumptions about suffering and medicine's role in its alleviation.

Setting the Issues

Before addressing these large issues, however, I think it wise to discern more exactly some of the problems raised by the film as well as some of the problems of the film. It is obvious that the film is in serious conflict with the convictions of many who belong to and support the Association for Retarded Citizens. The film gives the impression that there is nothing more disastrous, nothing more destructive, than for a child to be born retarded, but the sponsoring organization for the film maintains that the retarded are not significantly different from the so-called normal. Indeed, the Association for Retarded Citizens believes that with appropriate training most retarded people can become contributing members of a society even as complex as our own. Thus, the negative impression of retardation that the film conveys is not one that those sponsoring the film believe or think warranted. And it could have the unintended effect of reinforcing our society's largely negative attitude toward the retarded.

Perhaps equally troubling is the indiscriminate use of the notion of "retardation" in the film. Not only does the film fail to denote the wide variety of retardation—some types much less serious than others—but even more it fails to make clear that our very conception of retardation may be due as much to our prejudices as it is the assumed limits of the retarded. It has become increasingly recognized that disease descriptions and remedies are relative to a society's values and needs. Thus, "retardation" might not "exist" in a society that values cooperation more than competition and ambition.

Yet the increasing realization that retardation is a social designation should not blind us to the fact that the retarded do have some quite specifiable problems peculiar to them and that their difference requires special forms of care. It is extremely important how we frame our very relation to the "retarded" if we are to avoid two different perils.

The first, assuming that societal prejudice is embodied in all designations of retardation, seeks to aid the retarded by preventing discriminatory practices in a manner similar to the civil rights campaigns for blacks and women. Because the retarded are said to have the same rights as anyone, in this view all they require is to be treated "normally." Without denying that the retarded have "rights" or that much good has been done under the banner "normalization," I believe this way of putting the matter is misleading and risks making the retarded subject to even greater societal cruelty.[1] Would it not be unjust to treat the retarded "equally"? Instead, retardation ought to be so precisely understood that those who are thus handicapped can be accommodated as they need. (But that may be a reason for avoiding the word retardation altogether. As I have already noted, there are so many different ways of being retarded, so many different kinds of disabilities and corresponding forms of care required that to isolate a group as "retarded" may be the source of much of the injustice we perpetrate on those whom we identify as "not normal.")

The second peril is that of oppressive care, a kind of care based on the assumption that the retarded are so disabled they must be protected from the dangers and risks of life. Such a strategy subjects the retarded to a cruelty fueled by our sentimental concern to deal with their differences by treating them as something less than human agents. Too often this strategy isolates the retarded from the rest of society in the interest of "protecting" them from societal indifference. As a result they are trained to be retarded.

The challenge is to know how to characterize retardation and to know what difference it should make, without our very characterizations being used as an excuse to treat the retarded unjustly. However, we see this is not just a problem for the retarded, but a basic problem of any society, since societies are possible only because we are all different in skills and different in needs.[2] Societies must find ways to characterize and institutionalize those differences so that we see

1. For an excellent critique of the use of "rights" language in relation to retardation, see Barry Hoffmaster, "Caring for Retarded Persons: Ideals and Practical Choices," in *Responsibility for Devalued Persons: Ethical Interactions between Society, the Family, and the Retarded,* ed. Stanley Hauerwas (Springfield, IL: Charles Thomas Press, 1982), 24–38.
2. See, for example, Hauerwas, "Community and Diversity: The Tyranny of Normality" (1977), in SP.

them as enhancing rather than diminishing each of our lives. From this perspective the retarded are a poignant test of a society's particular understanding of how our differences are relevant to and for achievement of a common good.

The various issues I have raised can be illustrated by pointing to one final fallacy that the film underwrites. It gives the impression that retardation is primarily a genetic problem recognized at, or soon after, birth. But that is simply not the case. Half the people who bear the label "retarded" do so as the result of some circumstance after their conception or birth. Many are retarded due to environmental, nutritional, and/or accidental causes. To suggest, therefore, that we can eliminate retardation by better prenatal care or more thorough genetic screening and counseling is a mistake. Even if we were all required to have genetic checks before being allowed to marry, we would still have some among us that we currently label as "retarded."

We must ask what the "Prevent retardation" campaign would mean for this group. If a society were even partially successful in "eliminating" retardation, how would it regard those who have become retarded? Since retardation was eliminated on the grounds of being an unacceptable way of being human, would the retarded who remain live in a society able to recognize the validity of their existence and willing to provide the care they require? Of course, it might be suggested that with fewer retarded there would be more resources for the care of those remaining. That is no doubt true, but the question is whether there would be the moral will to direct those resources in their direction. Our present resources are more than enough to provide good care for the retarded. That we do not provide such care can be attributed to a lack of moral will and imagination. What will and imagination there is comes from those who have found themselves unexpectedly committed to care for a retarded person through birth or relation. Remove that and I seriously doubt whether our society will find the moral conviction necessary to sustain our alleged commitment to the retarded.

To reckon whether this is mere speculation, consider this thought experiment. We live at a time when it is possible through genetic screening to predict who has the greatest likelihood of having a retarded child, particularly if that person marries someone with similar genetic characteristics. It has become a general policy for most of the population to have such screening and to choose their marriage partner accordingly. Moreover, amniocentesis has become so routine that the early abortion of handicapped children has become the medical "therapy" of choice.

How would such a society regard and treat a couple who refused to be genetically screened, who refused amniocentesis, and who might perhaps have a less than normal child? Would such a society be happy with the increased burden on its social and financial resources? Why should citizens support the birth and care of such a child when its existence could easily have been avoided? To care for such a child, to support such "irresponsible" parents, means only that the "truly" needy will be unjustly deprived of care in the interest of sustaining a child who will never "contribute to societal good." That such an attitude seems not unreasonable to many people also suggests that in our current situation a campaign to "prevent retardation" might have negative implications for those who are retarded, as well as those who may have the misfortune to be born retarded or become retarded in the future.

Suffering and the Retarded

But surely there is something wrong with these observations, as they seem to imply that since we can never ensure that no one will be born or become retarded, then we should not even try to prevent retardation. On such grounds it seems we cannot change our lives to ensure that few will be born retarded so that those who are retarded now and in the future will not be cruelly treated and may even receive better care. That is clearly a vicious and unworthy position. We rightly seek to prevent those forms of retardation that are preventable. To challenge that assumption would be equivalent to questioning our belief that the world is round or that love is a good thing. Like so many things that seem obvious, however, if we ask *why* they seem so, we are often unable to supply an answer. Perhaps they seem obvious precisely because they do not require a reason for holding them.

I suspect that at least part of the reason it seems so obvious that we ought to prevent retardation is the conviction that we ought to prevent suffering. No one should will that an animal should suffer gratuitously. No one should will that a child should endure an illness. No one should will that another person should suffer from hunger. No one should will that a child should be born retarded. That suffering should be avoided is a belief as deep as any we have. That someone born retarded suffers is obvious. Therefore, if we believe we ought to prevent suffering, it seems we ought to prevent retardation.

Yet, like many other "obvious" beliefs, the assumption that suffering should *always* be prevented, if analyzed, becomes increasingly less certain or at least involves unanticipated complexity. Just because it implies eliminating subjects who happen to be retarded should at least suggest to us that something is wrong with our straightforward assumption that suffering should always be avoided or, if possible, eliminated. This is similar to some justifications of suicide: namely, in the interest of avoiding or ending suffering a subject wills no longer to exist. Just because in suicide there is allegedly a decision by the victim does not alter the comparison with some programs to prevent retardation: both assume that certain forms of suffering are so dehumanizing that it is better not to exist.

As I have indicated above, this assumption draws upon some of our most profound moral convictions. Yet I hope to show that our assumption that suffering should *always* be prevented is a serious and misleading oversimplification. To show why this is the case a general analysis of suffering is required. We assume we know what suffering is because it is so common, but on analysis suffering turns out to be an extremely elusive subject. Only once that analysis has been done will we be in a position to ask if the retarded suffer from being retarded or whether the problem is the suffering we feel the retarded cause us.

The Kinds and Ways of Suffering

"To suffer" means to undergo, to be subject. But we undergo much we do not call suffering. Suffering names those aspects of our lives that we undergo and that have a particularly negative sense. We suffer when what we undergo blocks our positive desires and wants. Suffering also carries a sense of "surdness": it denotes those frustrations for which we can give no satisfying explanation and that we cannot make serve some wider end. Suffering thus names a sense of brute power that does violence to our best laid plans. It is not easily domesticated. Therefore, there can be no purely descriptive account of suffering, since every description necessarily entails some judgment about the value or purpose of certain states.

No doubt the intensity of our own suffering or of our sympathy for others' suffering has reinforced our assumptions that we have a firm grip on its meaning. Yet it is certainly not clear that the kind of suffering occasioned by starvation is the same as that of cancer, though each is equally terrifying in its relentless but slow resolution in death. It is interesting that we also use "suffer" in an active sense of bearing with, permitting, or enduring. While such expressions do not eclipse the passive sense associated with suffering, they at least connote that we do not associate suffering only with that for which we can do nothing. Perhaps this is the clue we have been needing to understand better the nature of suffering. We must distinguish between those forms of suffering that happen to us and those that we bring on ourselves. We not only suffer from diseases, accidents, tornadoes, earthquakes, droughts, and floods—all those things over which we have little control—but we also suffer from other people, from living here rather than there, from doing this kind of job—all matters we might avoid. Some suffering that befalls us is integral to our goals, only we did not previously realize it. In these instances we see what we suffer as part of a large scheme. This latter sense of "suffer," moreover, seems more subjective, since what may appear as a problem for one may seem an opportunity for another. Not only is what we suffer relative to our projects, but how we suffer is relative to what we have or wish to be.[3]

Without denying the importance of the distinction between forms of suffering that happen to us and those that we instigate as requisite to our goals, we would be mistaken to press it too hard. Once considered, it may not seem as evident or as helpful as it first appeared. For example, we often discuss how what at the time looked like something that happened to us—something we suffered—was in fact something we did, or at least chose not to avoid. Our increasing knowledge of the relation of illness to lifestyle is enough to make us think twice before drawing a hard and fast distinction between what happens to us and what we do.

But the situation is even more complex. We often find that essential in our response to suffering is the ability to make what happens to me mine. Cancer patients frequently testify to some sense of relief when they find out they have cancer. The very ability to name what they have seems to give them a sense of control or possession that replaces the undifferentiated fear they had been feeling. Pain and suffering alienate us from ourselves. They make us what we do not know. The conceptual task is to make mine that which is happening to me—to interpret its presence (even if such an interpretation is negative) as

---

3. The relation between suffering and luck certainly would be fruitful to explore. Like suffering, luck involves aspects of life over which we have no control, yet we persist in thinking some forms of good and bad luck are "deserved." The latter judgment seems to imply that someone has "tempted fate" and thus got what he or she deserved. We therefore tend to assume that certain kinds of suffering, like certain forms of luck, go with particular forms of life. For extremely interesting discussions of luck, see Thomas J. Nagel, *Mortal Questions* (Cambridge, England: Cambridge University Press, 1979), 24–38, and Bernard Williams, *Moral Luck* (Cambridge, England: Cambridge University Press, 1981).

something I can claim as integral to my identity. No doubt our power to transform events into decisions can be the source of great self-deception, but it is also the source of our moral identity.

Please note: I am not suggesting that every form of pain or suffering can or should be seen as some good or challenge. Extreme suffering can as easily destroy as enhance. Nor do I suggest that we should be the kind of people who can transform any suffering into benefit. We rightly feel that some forms of suffering can only be acknowledged, not transformed. Indeed, at this point I am not making any normative recommendations about how we should respond to suffering; rather, I am suggesting that the distinction between the suffering that happens to us and the suffering that we accept as part of our projects is not as clear as it may at first seem. More important is the question of what kind of people we ought to be so that certain forms of suffering are not denied but accepted as part and parcel of our existence as moral agents. In viewing our life narrowly as a matter of purposes and accomplishments, we may miss our actual need for suffering, even apparently purposeless or actively destructive suffering. The issue is not whether retarded children can serve a human good, but whether we should be the kind of people, the kind of parents and community, that can receive, even welcome, them into our midst in a manner that allows them to flourish.

But it may be objected that although this latter way of putting the issue seems to embody the highest moral ideals, in fact it is deeply immoral because the suggestion that all forms of suffering are capable of being given human meaning is destructive of the human project. Certain kinds of suffering— Hiroshima, Auschwitz, wars—are so horrible we are able to preserve our humanity only by denying them human significance. No "meaning" can be derived from the Holocaust except that we must do everything we can to see that it does not happen again. Perhaps individuals can respond to natural disasters such as hurricanes and floods in a positive manner, but humanly we are right to view these other destructions as a scourge that we will neither accept nor try to explain in some positive sense.

Our refusal to accept certain kinds of suffering, or to try to interpret them as serving some human purpose, is essential for our moral health. Otherwise we would far too easily accept the causes of suffering rather than trying to eliminate or avoid them. Our primary business is not to accept suffering, but to escape it, both for our own sake and our neighbor's. Still, in the very attempt to escape suffering, do we not lose something of our own humanity? We rightly try to avoid unnecessary suffering, but it also seems that we are never quite what we should be until we recognize the necessity and inevitability of suffering in our lives.

To be human is to suffer. That sounds wise. That sounds right—that is, true to the facts. But we should not be too quick to affirm it as a norm. Questions remain as to what kind of suffering should be accepted and how it should be integrated into our lives. Moreover, prior to these questions is the even more challenging question of why suffering seems to be our fate. Even if I knew how to answer such questions, I could not try to address them in this essay. (Indeed, I suspect that there can be no general answer that does not mislead as much as it informs.) But perhaps by directing our attention toward the retarded we can better understand why and how suffering is never to be merely "accepted" and yet why it is unavoidable in our lives. In preparation for that discussion, I need to try to suggest why it is that suffering seems so unavoidable.

On Why We Suffer

To ask why we suffer makes the questioner appear either terribly foolish or extremely arrogant. It seems foolish to ask, since in fact we *do* suffer and no sufficient reason can be given to explain that fact. Indeed, if it were explained, suffering would be denied some of its power. The question seems arrogant because it seeks to put us in the position of eating from the tree of the knowledge of good and evil. Only God knows the answer to such questions.

Without denying that the question of why we suffer can be foolish and pretentious, I think it is worth asking since it has one obvious answer: we suffer because we are incomplete beings who depend on one another for our existence. Indeed, the matter can be put more strongly, since we depend upon others not only for our survival but also for our identity. Suffering is built into our condition because it is literally true that we exist only to the extent that we sustain, or "suffer," the existence of others, and the others include not just others like us, but mountains, trees, animals, and so on.

This is exactly contrary to cherished assumptions. We believe that our identity derives from our independence, our self-possession. As Arthur McGill suggests, we think "a person is real so far as he can draw a line around certain items—his body, his thoughts, his house—and claim them as his own."[4] Thus death becomes our ultimate enemy—the intimation involved in every form of

---

4. Arthur McGill, *Suffering: A Test Case of Theological Method* (Philadelphia: Westminster Press, 1983), 89.

suffering—because it is the ultimate threat to our identity. Again, as McGill suggests, that is why what we suffer so often seems to take proportions: our neediness seems to make us helpless to what we undergo. In this sense, our "neediness represents a fundamental flaw in our identity, a basic inability to rest securely with those things which are one's own and which lie inside the line between oneself and the rest of reality. Need forces the self to become open to the not-self, it requires every man to come to terms with the threats of demonic power."[5]

The irony is, however, that our neediness is also the source of our greatest strength, for our need requires the cooperation and love of others from which derives our ability not only to live but to flourish. Our identity, far from deriving from our self-possession or our self-control, comes from being "depossessed" of those powers whose promise is only illusory. Believing otherwise, fearful of our sense of need, when we attempt to deny our reliance on others we become all the more subject to those powers. As we shall see, this has particularly significant implications for our relations with the retarded, since we "naturally" disdain those who do not or cannot cover up their neediness. Prophetlike, the retarded only remind us of the insecurity hidden in our false sense of self-possession.[6]

It may be objected that such an account of suffering is falsely subtle, since it is obvious why we suffer: bad things happen to us. We are injured in accidents; we lose everything in a flood; our community is destroyed by a tornado; we get cancer; a retarded child is born. These are not things that happen to us because of our needs, but rather they happen because they happen. Yet each does relate to concrete needs: the need for security and safety, the need for everydayness, the need for health, the need for new life.[7] If we try to deny any of these needs, as well as many others, we deny ourselves the necessary re-

---

5. Ibid., 90.

6. This sense of the prophetic character of the retarded I learned from Dr. Bonita Raine. See in particular "Care and Mentally Retarded People: Pastoral Dimensions Appropriate to Christian Ethical Convictions" (Ph.D. diss., University of Notre Dame, 1982).

7. I suspect this is one of the reasons the ARC film appeals to parents, for all parents are frustrated by the presence of a retarded child. Most parents suffer willingly for their children if they think such suffering will make their children "better." The problem with the retarded is they seem to offer little hope of ever being decisively better. So we are tempted to eliminate retarded children because of our unwillingness to suffer for a child who will never get better. Of course, parents of retarded children soon learn, as, finally, all parents of normal children also learn, that they can rejoice in their children's "progress" even if such progress fails to correspond to their original ambitions for their children's "betterment."

sources for well-lived lives and make ourselves all the more subject to the powers who draw their strength from our fears.

I have not tried in this brief and inadequate account of why we suffer to offer anything like a theodicy. Indeed, I remain skeptical of all attempts to provide some general account or explanation of evil or suffering. For example, it is by no means clear that evil and suffering raise the same questions, since certainly not every form of suffering is evil. Moreover, as I have suggested above, I do not think any explanation that removes the surdness of certain forms of suffering can be right. Much in our lives should not be made "good" or explained.

All I have tried to do is to state the obvious: we suffer because we are inherently creatures of need. This does not explain, much less justify our suffering or the evil we endure. But it does help us understand why the general policy to prevent suffering is at least odd as a general policy. Our task is to prevent unnecessary suffering, but the hard question, as we have seen, is to know what constitutes unnecessary suffering. It is even more difficult when that question concerns another, as it does in the case of the retarded. It is just that question to which we now must turn.

Do the Retarded Suffer from Being Retarded?

I suggested above that behind the claim that we ought to prevent retardation lies the assumption that we ought to prevent suffering or, in particular, unnecessary suffering. I have tried at least to raise some critical questions about that assumption. But there is another issue that requires equal analysis: Are we right to assume that the retarded are suffering by being retarded? Certainly they suffer retardation, but do they suffer from being retarded?

No doubt, like everyone, the retarded suffer. Like us, they have accidents. Like us, they have colds, sores, and cancer. Like us, they are subject to natural disasters. Like us, they die. But the question is whether they suffer from being retarded. We assume they suffer because of their retardation, just as we or others suffer from being born blind or deaf. Yet it is by no means clear that such cases are similar or even whether those born blind or deaf suffer from blindness or deafness. It is possible that they are in fact taught by us that they are decisively disabled, and thus learn to suffer. If that is the case, then there is at least some difference between being blind and being retarded, since the very nature of being retarded means there is a limit to their understanding of their disadvantage and thus the extent of their suffering. That may also be true of being blind or deaf, of course, but not in the same way.

Do the retarded understand that they are retarded? Certainly most are able to see that they are different from many of us, but there is no reason to think they would on their own come to understand their condition as "retardation" or that they are in some decisive way suffering. They may perceive that there are some things some people do easily that they can do only with great effort or not at all, but that in itself is not sufficient reason to attribute to them great suffering. Of course, it may be objected that if we are to care for them, if we are to help alleviate some of the results of their being retarded, we cannot help but try to make them understand their limits. We have to make them conscious of their retardation if we are to help them be free from some of the effects of their condition. But again, this is certainly not as clear as it first appears, for it by no means follows that by learning to confront their limits in order to better their life, the retarded necessarily understand they are thereby suffering from something called "retardation," "Down syndrome," or the like.

Yet we persist in the notion that the retarded are suffering and suffering so much from being retarded that it would be better for them not to exist than to have to bear such disability. It is important I not be misunderstood. I am not suggesting that retardation is a minor problem or that nothing should be done to try to prevent, alleviate, or lessen the effects of being retarded; I have tried, rather, to suggest that the widespread assumption that the retarded suffer from being retarded is by no means obviously true.

Perhaps what we assume is not that the retarded suffer from being retarded but rather, because they are retarded, they will suffer from being in a world like ours. They will suffer from inadequate housing, inadequate medical care, inadequate schooling, lack of love and care. They will suffer from discrimination as well as cruel kidding and treatment from unfeeling peers. All this is certainly true, but it is not an argument for preventing retardation in the name of preventing suffering; rather, it is an argument for changing the nature of the world in the interest of preventing the needless suffering we impose on the retarded.

It may be observed that we have very little hope that the world will or can be changed in this respect, but even if that is the case it would be insufficient grounds for the general policy of eliminating the retarded. On such grounds anyone suffering injustice or ill-treatment would be in jeopardy. If justice comes to mean the elimination of the victim of injustice rather than the cause of injustice, we stand the risk of creating admittedly a less troubled but deeply unjust world.

The need to subject this set of assumptions to rigorous analysis is particularly pressing in relation to the care of children born retarded or otherwise handicapped. A policy of nontreatment is often justified as a means of sparing a child a life of suffering. I by no means wish to argue that every child should receive the most energetic medical care to keep it alive, but if such care is withheld it cannot be simply to spare the child a life of suffering. On such grounds few children with any moderately serious chronic health problem would be cared for at birth. We all, healthy and nonhealthy, normal or abnormal, are destined for a life of suffering.

Some will say that this is surely to miss the point behind the concern to spare certain children a life of suffering. The issue is the extent and intensity of the suffering. But again such a judgment is a projection of our assumptions about how we would feel if we were in their situation. But that is exactly what we are not. We do not know to what extent they may suffer from their disability. We do not know how much pain they will undergo, but we nonetheless act to justify our lack of care in the name of our humane concern about their destiny. We do so even knowing that our greatest nobility as humans often derives from the individual's struggle to make positive use of his or her limitations.

I am not suggesting that the care we give to severely disabled children (or adults) will always result in happy results for themselves or those around them. But to refrain from such care to spare them future suffering can be a formula for profound self-deception. Too often the suffering we wish to spare them is the result of our unwillingness to change our lives so that those disabled might have a better life. Or, even more troubling, we refrain from life-giving care simply because we do not like to have those who are different from us to care for.

Our Suffering of the Retarded

Why, therefore, do we persist in assumptions that the retarded suffer from being retarded? At least something of an answer comes from a most unlikely source: Adam Smith's *Theory of Moral Sentiments*. In that book Smith endeavors to provide an account for why, no matter how "selfish a man may be supposed, there are evidently some principles in his nature which interest him in the fortune of others, and render their happiness necessary to him, though he derives nothing from it except the pleasure of seeing it."[8] Such a sentiment, Smith observes, is by no means confined to the virtuous, since even the most "hardened ruffian" at times may derive sorrow from the sorrow of others.

Still, according to Smith, this is something of a puzzle. Since we have no "immediate experience of what other men feel, we can form no idea of the manner in which they are affected, but by conceiving what we ourselves should feel in the like situation. Though our brother is upon the rack, as long as we ourselves are at our ease, our senses will never inform us what he suffers. They never did, and never can, carry us beyond our own person, and it is by the imagination only that we can form any conception of what are his sensations."[9]

It is through our imagination, therefore, that our fellow feeling with the source of others is generated. But our sympathy does not extend to every passion, for there are some passions that disgust us; thus the furious behavior of an angry man may actually make us more sympathetic with his enemies. That this is so makes us especially anxious to be people capable of eliciting sympathy from others. Thus, "sympathy enlivens joy and alleviates grief. It enlivens joy by presenting another source of satisfaction; and it alleviates grief by insinuating unto the heart almost the only agreeable sensation which it is at that time capable of receiving."[10] By knowing our sorrow is shared by another we seem to be less burdened with our distress. Moreover, we are pleased when we are able to sympathize with one who is suffering, but we look forward more to enjoying another's good fortune.

Because we seek to sympathize as well as be the object of sympathy, Smith observes: "Of all the calamities to which the condition of mortality exposes mankind, the loss of reason appears, to those who have the least spark of humanity, by far the most dreadful, and they behold that last stage of human 'wretchedness' with deeper commiseration than any other. But the poor wretch, who is in it, laughs and sings perhaps, and is altogether insensible of his own misery. The anguish which humanity feels, therefore, at the sight of such an object, cannot be the reflection of any sentiment of the sufferer. The compassion of the spectator must arise altogether from the consideration of what he himself would feel if he was reduced to the same unhappy situation,

---

8. Adam Smith, *The Theory of Moral Sentiments,* ed. D. D. Raphael and A. L. Macfie (Oxford: Oxford University Press, 1976), I.I.I.1 (p. 9).
9. Ibid., I.I.I.2 (p. 9).
10. Ibid., I.I.II.2 (p. 14).

and, what perhaps is impossible, was at the same time able to regard it with his present reason and judgment."[11] We thus persist in our assumption that the retarded suffer from being retarded not because we are unsympathetic with them but because we are not sure how to be sympathetic with them. We fear that the very imagination that is the source of our sympathy, on which our fellow feeling is founded, is not shared by them. To lack such an important resource, we suspect, means they are fatally flawed, for one thus lacks the ability to be the subject of sympathy. We seek to prevent retardation not because we are inhumane but because we fear the retarded lack the means of giving and receiving sympathy, and thus we cannot imagine how they feel. Exactly because we are unsure whether they have the capacity to suffer as we suffer we seek to avoid their presence in order to avoid the limits of our own sympathy.

As Smith observes, we have no way to know what the retarded suffer as retarded. All we know is how we imagine we would feel if we were retarded. We thus often think we would rather not exist at all than to exist as one retarded. As a result, we miss the point at issue. For the retarded do not feel or understand their retardation as we do, or imagine we would, but rather as they do. We have no right or basis to attribute our assumed unhappiness or suffering to them.

Ironically, therefore, the policy of preventing suffering is one based on a failure of imagination. Unable to see like the retarded, to hear like the retarded, we attribute to them our suffering. We thus rob them of the opportunity to do what each of us must do: learn to bear and live with our individual sufferings.

Need, Loneliness, and the Retarded

In many respects, however, our inability to sympathize with the retarded—to see their life as they see it, to suffer their suffering—is but an aspect of a more general problem. As Smith observes, we do not readily expose our sufferings, because none of us is anxious to identify with the sufferings of others. We try to present a pleasant appearance in order to elicit fellow feeling with others. We fear to be sufferers, to be in pain, to be unpleasant, because we fear so desperately the loss of fellow feeling on the part of others. We resent those who

11. Ibid., I.I.I.11 (p. 12).

suffer without apology, as we expect the sufferer at least to show shame in exchange for our sympathy.

As much as we fear suffering, we fear more the loneliness that accompanies it. We try to deny our neediness as much, if not more, to ourselves as to others. We seek to be strong. We seek to be self-possessed. We seek to deny that we depend on others for our existence. We will be self-reliant and we resent and avoid those who do not seek to be like us—the strong. We will be friends to one another only so long as we promise not to impose seriously our sufferings on the others. Of course, we willingly enter into some of our friends' suffering—indeed, to do so only reinforces our sense of strength—but we expect such suffering to be bounded by a more determinative strength.

That we avoid the sufferer is not because we are deeply unsympathetic or inhumane, but because of the very character of suffering. By its very nature suffering alienates us not only from one another but from ourselves, especially suffering that we undergo, that is not easily integrated into our ongoing projects or hopes. To suffer is to have our identity threatened physically, psychologically, and morally. Thus our suffering even makes us unsure of who we are.

It is not surprising, therefore, that we should have trouble with the suffering of others. None of us willingly seeks to enter into the loneliness of others. We fear such loneliness may result in loss of control of our own life. We feel we must be very strong to be able to help the weak and needy. We may be right about that, but we may also fail to understand the kind of help they really need. Too often we seek to do something rather than first simply learn how to be with, to be present to, the sufferer in his or her loneliness. We especially fear, if not dislike, those whose suffering is the kind for which we can do nothing.

The retarded, therefore, are particularly troubling for us. Even if they do not suffer by being retarded, they are certainly people in need. Even worse, they do not try to hide their needs. They are not self-sufficient, they are not self-possessed, they are in need. Even more, they do not evidence the proper shame for being so. They simply assume that they are what they are and they need to provide no justification for being such. It is almost as if they have been given a natural grace to be free from the regret most of us feel for our neediness.

That such is the case, however, does not mean that the retarded do not suffer from the general tendency of wanting to be self-sufficient. Like us they are more than capable of engaging in the self-deceptive project of being their own person. Nor is such an attempt entirely wrong, for they, like us, rightly seek to develop skills that can help them help themselves as well as others. Yet we perceive them as essentially different from us, as beings whose condition has doomed them to a loneliness we fear worse than suffering itself, and, as a result, we seek to prevent retardation.

That we are led to such an extreme derives partly from our frustration at not being able to cure the retarded. We seek to help them overcome their disability, but we know that even our best efforts will not result in the retarded's not being retarded. After all, what we finally seek is not simply to help the retarded better negotiate their disability but to be like us: not retarded. Our inability to accomplish that frustrates and angers us, and sometimes the retarded themselves become the object of our anger. We do not like to be reminded of the limits of our power, and we do not like those who remind us.

We fervently seek to help the retarded, to do for the retarded, to make their lot less subject to suffering. No doubt much good derives from such efforts. But our frenzied activity can also be a failure to recognize that our attempts to help, our attempt to "do for" the retarded must first be governed by our ability to "be with" the retarded. Only as we learn to be and do with the retarded do we learn that their retardation, our projection of their suffering, need not create an unbridgeable gap between them and us. We learn that they are not incapable of fellow feeling with us and, just as important, that we are not incapable of fellow feeling with them.

That such fellow feeling is possible does not mean that they are "really just like us." They are not. They do not have the same joys we have nor do they suffer just as we suffer. But in our joys and in our sufferings they recognize something of their joy and their suffering, and they offer to share their neediness with us. Such an offer enables us in quite surprising ways to discover that we have needs to share with them. We are thus freed from the false and vicious circle of having to appear strong before others' weakness, and we are then able to join with the retarded in the common project of sharing our needs and satisfactions. As a result we discover we no longer fear them.

I am *not* suggesting that such sharing comes easily. Few of us are prepared to enter naturally into such a life. Indeed, most of us, cherishing the illusion of our strength, must be drawn in reluctantly. But miraculously, many are so graced. Day in and day out, through life with their retarded child, brother, or friend, they learn to see themselves through the eyes of the other who happens also to be retarded. Moreover, by learning not to fear the other's retardation, they learn not to fear their own neediness.

Thus if we are to make a movie to help others avoid unnecessary risks that can result in retardation, let us not begin soon after the birth. To begin there is grossly unfair, because it catches us before we are even sure what has happened to us. Let the film begin several years after the birth, after the parents of a child born retarded have discovered, like all parents must, that they are capable of dealing with this. It is not the child they would have willed, but then all children turn out to be different from our expectations. This child, to be sure, raises particular challenges, but let the film show the confidence of the couple that comes from facing those challenges. Unless suggestions for avoiding retarded children are bounded by such confidence, we cannot help but make the life of the retarded that much more difficult. But even more destructive, such a campaign is bound to make our own illusory fears of the retarded and our own needs that much more powerful.

An Inconclusive Theological Postscript

It may well be asked what all this has to do with our religious convictions as Christians. Of course, some obvious connections can be drawn. Christians are alleged to be concerned with the weak and the downtrodden. The retarded seem to fit that description. Since the position developed generally supports the ideal of help for the retarded, it seems consistent with such a religious sentiment.

Or it may be suggested that Christians are a people who have learned to accept that life is under God's direction. They attribute to God the bad as well as the good. Parents, in particular, think it presumptuous to try to determine the quality of their offspring. They accept their retarded as well as their more nearly normal children as God's will. They do not presume arrogantly to ask why or to what purpose retarded children are born.

There is some truth to each of these positions, but they have to be stated much more carefully. Concern with the downtrodden can too easily result in sentimental acceptance and care of the retarded that fails to respect the integrity of their existence. It condemns the retarded to being "weak" so that they might receive our "charity" rather than acknowledging them to be essential members of our community. The second position, God's will, has been and is used wrongly to justify acceptance of avoidable suffering and injustice.

Yet these more obvious theological connections are not the most significant for helping us understand how we as Christians should respond to the retarded. Quite simply, the challenge of learning to know, to be with, and to care for the retarded is nothing less than learning to know, be with, and love God. God's face is the face of the retarded; God's body is the body of the retarded; God's being is that of the retarded. For the God we Christians must learn to worship is not a god of self-sufficient power, a god who in self-possession needs no one; rather, ours is a God who needs a people, who needs a son. Absoluteness of being or power is not a work of the God we have come to know through the cross of Christ.[12]

Arthur McGill has perceptively interpreted the classical trinitarian debate in this fashion:

> The issue between Arius and Athanasius has nothing to do with whether God is one or two or three. It has to do with what quality makes God divine, what quality constitutes his perfection. From the perspective of self-contained absoluteness and transcendent supremacy, Arius can only look upon God's begetting a Son as grotesque blasphemy. God, he observed, must be very imperfect if he must generate a Son in order to become complete. But from the perspective of self-communicating love, Athanasius can look upon the dependent derived Son, not as a blot upon God's divinity, but as a mode of its perfection. Love and not transcendence, giving and not being superior, are qualities that mark God's divinity. Since giving entails receiving, there must be a receptive, dependent, needy pole within the being of God. It is pride—and not love—that fears dependence and that worships transcendence.[13]

That is why in the face of the retarded we are offered an opportunity to see God, for like God they offer us an opportunity of recognizing the character of our neediness. In truth, the retarded in this respect are but an instance of the capacity we each have for one another. That the retarded are singled out is only an indication of how they can serve for us all as a prophetic sign of our true nature as creatures destined to need God and, thus, one another.

Moreover, it is through such a recognition that we learn how God would have the world governed. As we are told in the Epistle to Diognetus in answer to the question of why God sent his Son: "To rule as a tyrant, to inspire terror and astonishment? No, he did not. No, he sent him in gentleness and mildness. To be sure, as a king sending his royal son, he sent him as God. But he sent him as to men, as saving and persuading them, and not as exercising

12. McGill, 75.
13. Ibid., 78.

force. For force is no attribute of God."[14] But if force is no attribute of God's governance, suffering is. Unlike us, God is not separated from himself or us by his suffering; rather, his suffering makes it possible for him to share our life and for us to share his.

Learning to share our life with God is no doubt difficult: it must be at least as demanding as learning that we can share life with the retarded. But that such a sharing of our sufferings as well as our joys is necessary cannot be doubted. For a world where there is no unpatterned, unpurposeful suffering would be devoid of the means for us to grow out of our selfishness and into love. That is why those who worship such a God are obligated to be confident that we can live well with those whose difference from ourselves we have learned to characterize by the unfortunate label "retarded." For if we did not so learn to live, we know we would be decisively retarded: retarded in our ability to turn ourselves to others' needs, regardless of the cost.[15]

Further Reading
"Killing Compassion" (1994), in DF
"Practicing Patience: How Christians Should Be Sick" (1997), essay 18 in this
    volume
"A Child's Dying" and "Medicine as Theodicy" (1990), in NS
"Reflections on Suffering, Death and Medicine" (1979), in SP
"Timeful Friends: Living with the Handicapped" (1998), in STT
"The Moral Challenge of the Handicapped" (1981), in SP
"Having and Learning to Care for Retarded Children: Some Reflections" (1975),
    in TT

14. Quoted in ibid., 82.
15. Much in this paragraph I have learned from Rev. James Burtchaell. I also need to thank Mr. Phil Foubert, Rev. Paul Wadell, and Dr. Bonita Raine for reading and criticizing an earlier draft of this essay and making valuable suggestions for its improvement.

29. Memory, Community, and the Reasons for Living: Reflections on Suicide and Euthanasia (1976)

with Richard Bondi

In this early essay analyzing suicide and euthanasia, Hauerwas shows how the "grammar" of these notions betrays deeper commitments about what is important in human life. Hauerwas's fundamental point is that an adequate discussion of the questions of suicide and euthanasia must bring to the surface these underlying commitments. Christians, by their refusal to consider suicide or euthanasia, witness to their convictions about the nature of life as a gift, and this sustains them even in the "homely" face of tragedy and death. Even under trying circumstances, Christians know that their obligation to witness to life as a gift from God is more significant than their ease, and so refuse to end their own lives.

If suicide is allowed then everything is allowed. If anything is not allowed then suicide is not allowed. This throws a light on the nature of ethics, for suicide is, so to speak, the elementary sin.—WITTGENSTEIN, *NOTEBOOKS*, 1914–1915

1. Suicide and Euthanasia as Moral Problems

Ethicists do not need to provide a reason to describe suicide and euthanasia as moral problems. Everyone seems to agree that if anything is a moral problem suicide and euthanasia are prime examples and thus ready grist for the ethicist's mill. As Wittgenstein suggests, we seem to be on fundamentally moral grounds when dealing with the taking of one's own life.

Yet we feel it is by no means clear why it is assumed that suicide and euthanasia raise moral issues, or indeed, what those issues are and how the ethicist might relate to them. At the very least people have begun to realize that "acts" of suicide and euthanasia are often ambiguous. We suspect, however,

[Originally published in the *Journal of the American Academy of Religion* 44, no. 3 (September 1976). Used by permission of Oxford University Press, publisher of the *Journal of the American Academy of Religion.* Subsequently reprinted in TT.]

that the unanimous agreement that suicide and euthanasia constitute moral problems is not connected with such practical cases. Rather, it reflects an increasingly prevalent judgment that the traditional assumption that suicide and euthanasia are morally questionable has itself become problematic.[1] Some are suggesting that suicide and euthanasia are not only morally ambiguous, but that they represent positive moral goods or rights. This is particularly true in relation to euthanasia, which often appears a kind and humane act.[2] Thus, while the place of suicide and euthanasia on a list of "moral problems" is still secure, how the notions are to be understood is no longer clear.

We do not believe that the way out of this difficulty lies in constructing ever more comprehensive typologies of suicide and euthanasia. Rather, we must try to get at the grammar of the notions. In this essay we will examine suicide and euthanasia as heuristic notions to see how they may be displayed in a given community. We are specifically interested in how these notions relate to the story that forms the Christian community. Indeed, we will suggest that the notions of suicide and euthanasia are incompatible with and subversive of some fundamental elements of the Christian story. At the same time our investigation should have wider appeal. Our attempt represents a model of how the moral notions and practical behavior of any people relate to the story that constitutes it as community. In this way we also hope to open up the possibility for challenges to the Christian tradition being made intelligible themselves in terms of the use of moral notions within a story that they embody.

1.1 The Ambiguity of Suicide and Euthanasia as Moral Notions

If this is true, it should make us wary of the "hard case" approach, which proceeds by examining certain instances of actual or potential suicide or euthanasia.[3] The assumption is that we already know what euthanasia or suicide is and the task is to find counterexamples that will let us ask what is wrong with suicide or euthanasia under x or y circumstances. We are suggest-

---

1. For example, see R. B. Brandt, "The Morality and Rationality of Suicide," in *A Handbook for the Study of Suicide,* ed. Seymour Perlin (New York: Oxford University Press, 1975), 61–75.
2. See, for example, Marvin Kohl, "Voluntary Beneficent Euthanasia" in the book edited by him, *Beneficent Euthanasia* (Buffalo: Prometheus Books, 1975), 130–44. Kohl argues that euthanasia is a positive moral duty insofar as we have an obligation to be kind. That seems a bit odd, as it is not clear why we have an obligation to be kind, kindness usually being associated with those aspects of the moral life that are commendable but not obligatory.
3. On "hard cases," see Sissela Bok, "Euthanasia and the Care of the Dying," in *The Dilemmas of Euthanasia,* ed. John A. Behnke and Sissela Bok (New York: Anchor Books, 1975), 1–25.

ing instead that the ambiguity is in the notions of suicide and euthanasia themselves, and more particularly in the role they play in relation to the story that shapes our moral vocabulary.

The hard case approach, with its emphasis on discrete acts, is backwards, as it assumes that the moral life is primarily concerned with decisions. Yet prior to the question of What should we do? is the question What should we be? For "what we are" is the context that makes moral notions such as suicide and euthanasia work at all. Suicide and euthanasia are not just descriptions of individual acts, but notions that form intentionality to have one kind of character rather than another. It is this latter kind of problem that is our concern in this essay, namely, not what we should do in certain contexts, but what kind of character we should have in order to see certain contexts one way rather than another. Or, even more accurately, we are concerned with what kind of communities we should be to encourage people to view their death as a humane ending that we need not hasten through our own power. We are concerned with what kind of story a community needs to hold about life that provides the skills to display the notions of suicide and euthanasia in a morally accurate way. Put differently, when the moral question is limited to whether certain assumed acts are suicide or euthanasia, and thus to be praised or blamed, we often fail to see the positive commitments embodied in such notions. Suicide and euthanasia as notions that help individuate certain behavior involve background beliefs without which their descriptive value is limited or perhaps misleading.[4]

This can be illustrated by considering what we mean by suicide. "The taking of one's own life" is clearly insufficient. We would not wish to admit to a moral vocabulary so impoverished as to lump together Saul or those who died at Masada with the student who plunges from an eighth-story window after failing to make fraternity rush. Yet if we begin to make distinctions we must ultimately appeal, not to the physical description of the act, but to the meaning it has in the larger social, moral, and cultural context. In other words, we are back to examining the formal notions of suicide and euthanasia

---

4. For this sense of "background beliefs," see Phillipa Foot, "Moral Beliefs," in *Ethics*, ed. Judith Thompson and Gerald Dworkin (New York: Harper and Row, 1968), 239–60. We use the language of "story" rather than belief because of its richer connotations. It is not just the "beliefs" we hold about life that form our attitudes toward suicide, but our attitudes are skills that result from the stories that form our lives; that is, beliefs are not self-involving in the same manner as stories.

in relation to the stories that shape our communities. As Jack Douglas has pointed out, the social meaning of suicide is in part constructed by the person committing the act, but is fundamentally in the hands of the community where the formation of the moral notions and vocabulary that the person committing suicide uses in "constructing" his or her act takes place.[5]

We may assume that euthanasia is easier to describe than suicide since it seems to be a more limited case. That this is not the case can be seen in the contrast between the etymology of the word and its present usage. The word originally meant simply "good death."[6] However, it currently means the ending of life in order to secure the release from pain and suffering; or more rigorously put, it is the deliberate, intended putting to death of someone in pain in order to secure his or her release from pain. It is obvious that this description attempts to qualify some acts of putting ourselves or someone to death from all the material acts of death that involve release from pain. In other words, not all cases that look like euthanasia carry the moral weight normally associated with the judgment implied in the notion of euthanasia.[7] In the case of both suicide and euthanasia, only an examination of the stories that form the notions can help us understand and use them properly.[8]

5. Jack Douglas, *The Social Meanings of Suicide* (Princeton, NJ: Princeton University Press, 1967). See especially the appendix, "Formal Definitions of Suicide," where Douglas demonstrates the fundamental dimensions of meaning in definitions of suicide. For a more psychological approach to suicide, see Edwin Shneidman, ed., *On the Nature of Suicide* (San Francisco: Jossey Bass, 1973). We are aware that the reasons or motives for suicide can be as various as the individuals who commit suicide. The question, however, is how each of us should learn to train our intentions in accordance with the moral commitments involved in the notion of suicide. In other words, the notion, suicide, involves what kind of intentionality we should have about life. The fact that people who commit suicide often have a wide range of reasons does not defeat the meaningfulness of suicide as a moral notion, but rather is a reminder of how important it is that we know how to use the notion at all.

6. Arthur Dyck has coined the word "benemortasia" to mean "the ethical framework that one adopts in order to interpret what it is to experience a good death, or at least what would be the most morally responsible way to behave in the face of death, either one's own or that of others." See "Beneficent Euthanasia and Benemortasia: Alternative Views of Mercy," in Kohl, ed., *Beneficent Euthanasia*, 117–29.

7. It is particularly at this point that we suggest we cannot evade tragedy and suffering. See the argument in the final section (3.2).

8. It should be clear that nothing we have said or will say indicates whether attempted suicide should or should not be against the law. We have no "in principle" objection to laws against suicide as this may be one of the ways a society gestures its concern for its members as a society of trust. Of course, some societies may have become so much like societies of strangers that it makes no sense to have such laws. The legal situation with regard to euthanasia is more complicated. See section 3 for a discussion of the relevant problems.

1.2 The Importance of Attitudes toward Life-taking

It is impossible to understand suicide or euthanasia apart from our attitudes toward life itself. We should not view these issues as special cases of death but as the result of certain attitudes toward life. It is this that ties the two issues together: if we learn to think morally about suicide in terms of our willingness to live we will have gained the necessary skills to talk about euthanasia.

When an ethicist takes on issues such as euthanasia or suicide, it looks like his or her primary interest is to tell us whether a particular set of actions are right or wrong, to be encouraged or discouraged. Rather, our job is to help the communities we serve to keep their language pure; in other words, the ethicist is more like a poet than anything else. Our primary interest in this essay is to help Christians get the meaning of suicide and euthanasia right in terms of how those notions help them to understand the basic story that defines the kind of community they are.

Thus, identifying the grammar of suicide and euthanasia entails discriminating the story that the notions play a role in. Our notions, our descriptions, our very actions are held fast by stories, by the narratives that are our context for meaning.[9] Ethics is the attempt to help us remember what kind of story sustains certain descriptions. It is, therefore, a discipline rather like history, in that we are forced to tell stories in order to capture our past, sustain our present, and give our future direction.[10]

It may be that the meaning of suicide and euthanasia for Christians is the same as that found in our wider society, but that is certainly not self-evident. As Christian ethicists, we may well share a story that you do not, though we

9. Thus within the Japanese tradition the taking of life is not necessarily suicide until we know more about the kind of story that informs their actions.

10. This view of ethics owes much to the work of Alasdair MacIntyre. In particular, see his *A Short History of Ethics* (New York: Macmillan, 1966), and *Against the Self-Image of the Age* (New York: Schocken Books, 1971). In several essays not yet published MacIntyre has developed this position, arguing persuasively that we are inheritors of "fragments" of past moral stories in a manner that makes it impossible to develop any one coherent account of morality. MacIntyre argues that those attempts to provide a formal definition of morality that can in some manner assume the objectivity of moral judgments are, in fact, opting for one moral fragment against others. He suggests, therefore, that in order to know the sense of such notions as suicide, murder, or stealing, or such virtues as justice, courage, or humility, you must know the narrative context in which they are displayed. For example, see his "How Virtues Became Vices: Values, Medicine, and Social Context," in *Evaluation and Explanation in the Biomedical Sciences*, ed. H. T. Engelhardt and S. Spicker (Utrecht, Holland: Reydal, 1975), 97–111. [The views of Alasdair MacIntyre discussed here would be published in complete form in his epochal work *After Virtue* (1981).]

hope that our story may at least help enliven those different from ours, and vice versa. We think that part of the problem with suicide and euthanasia has been that we have all assumed we know what the notions mean, while the story that should underlie the Christian understanding of suicide and euthanasia is not that of wider society.

For example, it is often assumed that the background belief or story that displays the meaning and reasons against suicide and euthanasia is the "natural desire to live" that is grounded in our justified fear of dying or our love of life. The "natural desire to live" is thus taken to be a universal story that somehow sustains or is the basis of any particular account of suicide or euthanasia. But on reflection it is clear that there is no such universal desire, for the very meaning of "to live" depends on particularistic commitments of a people's form of life. Of course, the "natural desire to live" can be interpreted as an instinct of moral significance, but when this is done we lack adequate skills to see whether and why suicide is a morally destructive practice. In an attempt to articulate the story that informs the Christian use of suicide and euthanasia we are really beginning with a very different question, namely, Do we have an obligation to live, and if so, what kind of obligation is it? Or, perhaps more fundamentally still, What are the moral reasons that should form our interest in continuing our existence?

2. Memory, Community, and the Reasons for Living

Most of what is important to our moral existence is not what causes us problems, but what is behind those problems and never raised as a question. Our failure to notice what we are about often makes us reach for theories to explain our moral judgments that fail to do justice to our convictions. Anthropologists and historians of religion, for example, remind us that in primitive cultures, the gravest transgressions a person can make are those that challenge or deny the sustaining story of his or her community.[11] The most disruptive practices or acts in a community are those that abandon or deny the virtues and skills that the character of a community makes available and incumbent on the members of that community. In theological terms, we call such forgetfulness "sin," as we literally forget what we are about as people who have been created by a God who sets our way.

11. The work of Adolf Jensen, Mircea Eliade, and Claude Lévi-Strauss provides ample evidence of the close relationship between memory and community.

The role of the theological ethicist is to continually call us back to and seek a greater understanding of our sustaining story and the moral skills it provides for those people called Christian. Theology, therefore, is the attempt to keep us faithful to the character (the story and skills) of our community lest we forget who and why we are. It charges the imagination by helping us to notice those images that provide convictions that will truthfully form our existence.

2.1 Memory and Community

When forgetfulness is sin, memory becomes a prized virtue. But memory cannot be understood simply along the lines of "remembering the past" or even "preserving an identity." Such "memories" can too easily become confused, are often open to widely divergent interpretations, and have the potential for being dangerously conservative. If memory is to be a useful concept in discussing ethical theory it must be distinguished from the simpler senses of "remembering."

For example, almost any American would name as crucially formative periods in our history the American Revolution and the Civil War. There is, however, a considerable difference of opinion on what these periods mean, that is, how we should remember them today. The kind of memory that truly shapes and guides a community is the kind that keeps past events in mind in a way that draws guidance from them for the future. The questions we should ask about the American Revolution and the Civil War are: Do we want to be identified as a people with the kind of nation that fought such a revolution and such a civil war? What are the images and skills found in our stories about our past that would enable us to answer and carry out that question?

Memory must not concentrate on events but on character, or it can become perverted into a pathological force. In a commonsense way we call this situation "living in the past." The anthropologist Jules Henry has given us a dramatic illustration of this use of memory. He speaks of those people who live only through memories of past triumphs or hopes, defiantly rejecting the present or the future that does not match up to their remembrances.[12] Viewing the present through the strong images of the past, they cannot interpret their surroundings correctly. Memory has bound them to the past, warped the present, and robbed the future of reality apart from their delusions. Henry concludes by quoting Kierkegaard: "Memory is emphatically the real element

12. Jules Henry, *Pathways to Madness* (New York: Vintage Books, 1973), 200–203, 249–51, 313–16.

of the unhappy. . . . In order that the man of hope may be able to find himself in the future, the future must have reality."[13]

The Christian should have a particular aversion to the use of memory that shuts out the future. This use of memory shows a distrust of the mercy, power, and love of the God who is the source of all time and creation. For instance, Wolfhart Pannenberg speaks of man's "enmity toward the future" as sin: "When man asserts himself against the future, he misses his authentic existence, betrays his destiny to exist in full openness toward what is to be, and abdicates his participation in God's creative love."[14]

Instead of trying to understand "memory" through the model of "remembering," we should take memory to mean "being present in mind." "Presence" is the fundamental meaning of memory. We are truly present when we are living aware of the past and the future, knowing that "the present time" is only a moment's flow toward the future. When we are present, we are "fully here," and to have something "present in mind" through memory is to have it here with us in all its creative force. Memory has creative force when it reminds us not of past events but of the character that produced them and when the memory of that character challenges us to renounce it or be true to it in the present moment.

The problem with suicide is that it eradicates the presence of the other and results in the other's loss in our memory. For we are suggesting that our very existence—that is, our willingness to be present—has moral significance that we seldom notice. It is like the importance of being physically present at a moment of grief or tragedy, and of the power and support generated toward those we love by our "mere" presence. We seldom know what to say on such occasions, but we know we should be there. In the same manner we know we must be here and be willing to die in a manner that makes it possible for us to be present in memory.

2.2 Convictions and the Cultural Configuration

Different communities will have different "stories" to keep present in memory, but none exists cut off from the wider world. If we have no convictions, our culture will provide them for us; and if our convictions are poorly understood or weakly held, the cultural configuration will override them. It is only

13. Ibid., 314. The quotation is from *Either/Or* (New York: Doubleday, 1959), I:221.
14. Wolfhart Pannenberg, *Theology and the Kingdom of God* (Philadelphia: Westminster Press, 1969), 69.

by continual recourse to the sources of the strength of our convictions that we can articulate and hold them in the world.

This is not a concession to determinism, but the recognition of the complexity of human culture. The customs, symbols, and even the values of a culture must be learned by all in order to survive in the civilization. Failure to do so is not a sign of individuality so much as of "madness," or what the culture will call madness.[15] Unless we replace our culture's convictions and reasons for action and belief with those that get their power from a different story, we will live our lives for good or evil in the sphere of the convictions and customs in which we were raised. A little reflection shows this is the case in mundane and serious areas of our lives. Witness the "fear" most people have of snakes, the dark, or revealing intimate feelings in public. Or consider the attitudes toward sexuality from which many have felt a need to be "liberated." Or, perhaps even more fundamentally, look at our conceptions of what constitutes a normal child and the problems in having and caring for retarded children (let alone "normal" children) that these attitudes engender.[16] The theological ethicist seeks ways to form behavior and belief by the convictions that represent faithful expressions of the story that forms our Christian character.

2.3 The Reasons for Living: Life as a Gift

Earlier, we discussed the importance of attitudes toward life-taking, and said that suicide and euthanasia are properly seen not as forms of death but as the outcome of certain attitudes toward life. For the Christian the reasons for living begin with the understanding that life is a gift.

We are not our own creators. Our desire to live should be given shape in the affirmation that we are not the determiners of our life, God is. We Christians are people who must learn to live, as we have learned that life is a gift. We thus live not as if survival is an end in itself, but rather because we know that life allows us the time and space to live in the service of God. We should view time not as something to be lived through, nor life as an end in itself, but rather see life as the gift of time enough for love.[17]

It is important that this language of "gift" not be understood as a poetic

15. See Henry, *Pathways to Madness,* especially the account of the Wilson family.
16. See, for example, Stanley Hauerwas, "The Demands and Limits of Love: Ethical Reflections on the Moral Dilemma of Neonatal Intensive Care" (1975) and "Having and Learning How to Care for Retarded Children: Some Reflections" (1975) both in *TT*.
17. The last phrase is the title of a novel by Robert Heinlein, *Time Enough for Love* (New York: G. P. Putnam's Sons, 1974).

expression of a matter that could be more "literally" expressed—we mean that life is a gift. Recently, Eike-Henner W. Kluge strongly objected to this language in his book, *The Practice of Death*.[18] He argues that the concept of "life as a gift" is logically incoherent because: (1) a gift that we cannot reject is not a gift, and (2) though a gift can only be given to someone, it seems that here we have a case where the gift and the one receiving it are the same.

However, it is of course true that we can reject the gift of life. That was what the traditional condemnation of suicide was all about. Kluge quite rightly points out that the problem with the language of gift comes when one attempts to draw immediate ethical conclusions from it. The language of "gift of life" does not mean that life is never to be taken. Properly understood, the language of "gift of life" is not meant to direct our attention to the gift, but rather to the nature of the giver and the conditions under which it is given. Life is not a gift as an end, in and of itself. God is the giver who would have men and women have an independent existence from the source of all creation. Life is a gift exactly because the character of the giver does not require that the gift be given at all.

Second, Kluge fails to see that the language of gift in relation to life is an analogical term. The gift of life is not like other gifts inasmuch as the gift and the recipient are one—but that is to indicate that this is a gift that is not a property to possess (Kluge's version of the analogy), but a task to live out, a task where freedom follows upon responsibility. Indeed, the whole point of learning to talk of life as a gift is to see ourselves as not our own possession nor anyone else's. Rather, we owe our existence to others who sustain us and finally to the one without whom we could not be at all. As James Gustafson suggests, the language of gift is not just a description of what God has done for us, but an indication of the way we can accept the gift of life in a nondestructive manner. "The experience of gratitude is a pivot on which our awareness of God's goodness turns toward our life as moral men and communities. What is given is not ours to dispose of as if we created it, nor ours to use to serve only our own interests, to mutilate, wantonly destroy, and to deprive others of. Rather, if life is given in grace and freedom and love, we are to care for it and share it graciously, freely and in gratitude to him we have reason enough to seek the good of others, and are moved to do so."[19]

18. Eike-Henner W. Kluge, *The Practice of Death* (New Haven: Yale University Press, 1975), 124–26.
19. James Gustafson, *Theology and Christian Ethics* (Philadelphia: Pilgrim Press, 1974), 170.

The Christian understanding of life as a gift of time enough for love is more fundamental for determining our stance toward life preservation than the language of sanctity or of a right to life. The right-to-life language has understandably been prominent among Christians today in relation to the abortion problem, but it is important to recognize that it is not the language offered by our primary convictions. If Christians use this language, they must keep in mind that they do so only as a political device since only such language offers them a way into the political discourse on this issue. We should nonetheless recognize that right-to-life talk is a foreign language for us, and that the seeming necessity of our using it is a sign of the tension we are now in with our surrounding culture.

Second, there is the question of whether "right-to-life" language makes conceptual sense. We probably do have a "right" not to be put to death, but it is unclear that we have a right to life. "Rights" language implies corresponding duties. It is extremely problematic whether anyone has a duty to keep me alive—to provide life-enhancing acts over and above refraining from life-taking acts.

More problematic still from a theological point of view is that rights language suggests we should be able to determine our lives, when our life will end, and what we shall do with it.[20] But it is fundamental to the Christian manner that our lives are formed in terms not of what we will do with them, but of what God will do with our lives, both in our living and our dying. Life is not sacred as if we Christians had an interest in holding onto it to the last minute. Christians are a people who are formed ready to die for what they believe. Our beliefs are as precious to us as our lives—indeed, they are our lives. Life for us, therefore, is not an absolute, for that which we think gives our life form will not let us place unwarranted value on life itself.

At the very least this means that accepting the fatedness of our ending is a way of affirming the trustworthiness of God's care for us. It means I will not fight my death nor the death of others when it cannot be avoided.[21] Dying is not the tragedy but, from our point of view, dying for the wrong thing. As H. Tristram Engelhardt has suggested, what we need is "a language of finitude,

20. This, of course, raises the larger question of to what extent the language of "rights" can be used in Christian ethical discourse. For a good analysis of this problem, see Joseph Allen, "A Theological Approach to Moral Rights," *Journal of Religious Ethics* 2, no. 1 (spring 1974): 119–41. See also Hauerwas, "Rights, Duties, and Experimentation on Children" in *SP* (1977).

21. Admittedly this last phrase is extremely ambiguous. We will try to give it more clarity in the final section (3.2).

a way of talking decently about the limits of human life, a way of saying why and under what circumstances death is natural."[22] Such a language would not deny that early death or painful death are matters we wish to avoid if possible, but it would give us the skill to know that our purpose is not existence but "the pursuit of a rich but finite life";[23] or, in language closer to our everyday speech, it would give us the means to talk of what a "good death" involves.

In this respect we Christians must rethink our relation to modern medicine. For we have been taught that natural death means the death that occurs when doctors can no longer do anything for us,[24] but it may be that we must be willing to die a good deal earlier. For we may well have accepted in the medical imperative a Promethean desire to control death or extend life that is finally incompatible with our basic Christian convictions.

2.4 The Reasons for Living: The "Miracle" of Trust

Beside these theological convictions that should form our attitudes toward how we desire to live, our lives should also be formed to embody our existence as social creatures. At the same time our existence as members of the Christian community should enliven and strengthen our natural social existence. The area where this interplay can perhaps most clearly be seen can be called the "miracle" of trust.

Insofar as we are human we exist and are sustained by communities of trust and care. In his book, *The Ethical Demand,* Knud Logstrup reminds us that "it is a characteristic of human life that we naturally trust one another. . . . This may indeed seem strange, but it is part of what it means to be human. Human life could scarcely exist if it were otherwise."[25] Our dependence on trust may indeed seem strange, especially to people living in modern cities, dealing with politicians and Madison Avenue. It may seem stranger still to those who have had shattering experiences of lack of trust and confidence in others close to them,[26] or have become aware of their own weakness and capability for untrustworthiness. Yet a moment's reflection will show that we do usually trust people to be honest, not to cheat us, not to crash the airplane in which we are riding, and so on.

---

22. H. Tristram Engelhardt, *The Hastings Center Report* 5, no. 2 (April 1975): 32.
23. Ibid., 34.
24. Ivan Illich, "The Political Uses of Natural Death," *Hastings Center Studies* 2, no. 1 (January 1974): 3–20.
25. Knud Logstrup, *The Ethical Demand* (Philadelphia: Fortress, 1971), 8.
26. See Henry, *Pathways to Madness,* especially "The Jones Family."

A certain minimal level of trust is necessary for the very functioning of this social creature, the human being, but it can easily be degraded to the level of the minimal trust in gravity that makes us confident we will not fall up. It takes purpose and conviction to turn minimal trust into a positive creative force. Trust, like all aspects of human culture, is a luxurious skin stretched taut over the bones of survival.[27] We must work to create conditions for the "miracle" of positive, creative trust to occur. Of these conditions, one of the most important is our very willingness to live. It represents our continued affirmation that basic human trust has been strengthened and given positive force through the story that sustains our communities—that in spite of the danger, terrors, and apathy of this life the goodness of our communities is more basic. We exist in a network of relations that our death helps affirm symbolically. Just as we can survive because we can trust others, so should we choose to live because we also need to be counted on by others.

This can be seen in everyday life by our use of words like "sacrifice." All too often, when we describe our actions for another as a sacrifice it is at the least a sign that trust has failed and at most an effort to replace trust with a mercantile reciprocity by placing the other "in our debt." This comes to a head most dramatically at the death of another person, when we are left in a wave of guilt and responsibility as our untrustworthiness to the person in life becomes clear to us in his or her dying. The problem of guilt at the death of one of our friends is not whether to be guilty or not, but that we be guilty for the right thing and that our recovery from the wounds of this guilt be a sign that we have recognized the valid sacrifice so necessary to create the miracle of trust.

In this way our death itself speaks to and is constitutive of the presence and quality of trust in our community. Just as we work to live in a manner that continues our communities of trust, so we must die in a way that provides for healthful and morally sound grief for those we leave behind. The miracle of trust is both a reason for living and a reason for dying in one way rather than another. There is no question of denying grief at death, but rather that we die in a way that leaves behind us a morally healthy community of grief. This is what makes a proper funeral so important; it is a means of forming and expressing grief that at the same time makes the ending of grief ritually appropriate.

---

27. See Colin Turnbull's *The Mountain People* (New York: Simon and Schuster, 1972) for a frightening description of a society that is forced to abandon luxuries like trust and love.

3. Suicide, Euthanasia, and the Affirmation of Life

These theological and ethical considerations provide the context that makes intelligible the reason that suicide has generally been prohibited, and particularly so for those who share the Christian story. The prohibition against suicide is a way of affirming how we should die in our communities in a nondestructive way for those who continue after us. It is a symbolic claim that insists we remember our primary business is about living, not dying. The moral prohibition against suicide is not meant to point a judgmental finger at the one who does or attempts to commit suicide;[28] rather, it is a notion meant to awaken us to the convictions needed to shape the character of our communities in such a way as to enhance the trust that must pertain if life is to be worth living.

Just as with suicide, we think that euthanasia should be morally prohibited. Some of the reasons for this are purely pragmatic, such as (1) knowing if a disease is really fatal; (2) the possibility of new cures being developed; (3) the difficulty of obtaining informed consent under the influence of pain or drugs; (4) legal problems with distinguishing euthanasia from murder; and (5) controlling it as a medical practice and its effect on the ethos of medicine.[29]

These pragmatic reasons are important from the perspective of public policy, but they are not morally why euthanasia is rightly thought to be problematic; indeed, we suspect that euthanasia could be pragmatically controlled if we wished to do so. Rather, it is a matter of not killing ourselves, even if we are in pain, as a way of affirming our continued contribution and affirmation of the goodness and care of the community in which we exist. In other words, our unwillingness to kill ourselves even under pain is an affirmation that the trust that has sustained us in health is also the trust that sustains us in illness and distress; that our existence is a gift ultimately bounded by a hope that gives us a way to go on; that the full, present memory of our Christian story is a source of strength and consolation for ourselves and our community. Community, of course, is not a warm feeling or an ever-retreating ideal. It is that group of people whose lives are shaped by a common story. Thus, "erosion of communities" is not simply the progressive blunting of our feelings of other regardingness, though this may be involved. Rather, it

28. That judgmental finger might just as often be brought against the society in which the one committing suicide lived.
29. See Yale Kamisar, "Some Non-Religious Views against Proposed Mercy Killing Legislation," in *Euthanasia*, ed. A. B. Downing (London: Owen, 1974), 85–133.

is the pernicious dissolution of the order, coherence, and power of a story to make an issue like "other regardingness" even significant.

With this in mind, we must be especially careful that euthanasia, though often supported by the most humane arguments, does not become a way of doing away with those who bother us rather than giving them care. It may be that the demand for euthanasia comes because we lack the skills humanely to know how to be with and care for the dying, especially when we are the one doing the dying. Humans never kill more readily than when we kill in the name of mercy. We must be careful that the mercy we dispense, especially when it takes the form of ending life, is not necessary because of our original uncare.

3.1 Suicide, Euthanasia, and the Erosion of Community

Suicide and euthanasia contribute to the erosion of community. They can both be signs of pathogenic abandonment, and they undermine our notions of living bravely in the face of suffering as individuals and as communities.

Pathogenic abandonment in euthanasia was mentioned earlier; euthanasia can be a sign that our failure to care has triumphed. Pathogenic abandonment in regard to suicide is more complex, and has two principal forms. From the perspective of the one committing suicide, his or her act can be one of the most perverse forms of moral manipulation, as it abandons those left behind to their shame, guilt, and grief. Suicide is something like a metaphysical "I gotcha!" It is often an attempt to kill or wound others.

We all know that our lives are shot through with trying to gain power over others. We want power not so much for itself, but because we fear the loss of those we love and thus try to gain power to ensure and protect ourselves from the loss of their love. We thus are often engaged in running exchanges of power through love and our relationships with others. Most of the time these tradeoffs are balanced out, and while they are potentially very destructive they are often simply perverse in their covertness, often even being concealed from ourselves. It is one of the messier and less noble things about being human.

Now suicide is the ultimate revenge, the unanswerable tradeoff, the metaphysical "I gotcha." There is nothing we can do to pay back the moral debt. We are left with a guilt that cannot be formed in a useful manner. Its negativity in this regard is even self-defeating, if we can speak of the defeat of a person dead by his or her own hand, for all that is left for those left behind is to reject their guilt and in the process the memory of the one that committed suicide. Suicide does horrible damage to memory, for it eradicates a history that is the same as the self.

Yet perhaps just as common, and certainly mingled with revenge suicide, is the pathogenic abandonment of the individual by his or her community. Many of the suicides that occur are not occasions for blaming the agent, but rather the final affirmation and sealing of a long process of abandonment by the community, the dramatic expression of an abandonment experienced across a person's lifetime. Even though we often think of suicide occurring under conditions of extreme stress or constant threat of life, Eugene Genovese reminds us in *Roll, Jordan, Roll* that slaves never committed suicide in large numbers; though abandoned by the white society, they found a sustaining faithfulness in their own community. "The assertion that slaves frequently committed suicide, quaintly put forward by some historians as a form of 'day-to-day resistance to slavery,' rests on no discernible evidence. The strong sense of stewardship in the quarters—of collective responsibility for each other— probably accounts for the low suicide rate more than does any other factor."[30]

Suicide understood against this background is a sign of failure of community. This is especially cogent in our society, where "abandonment" is often called the pursuit of life, liberty, and happiness, and hallowed by the ethics of individualism. We may well have a "right," within the framework of libertarian ethics, to commit suicide.

In this connection, MacIntyre reminds us that the concept of rights, which we have learned to take for granted, only emerges in the modern age: "The central preoccupation of both ancient and medieval communities was characteristically: how may men together realize the true human good? The central preoccupation of modern men is and has been characteristically: how may we prevent men interfering with each other as each of us goes about our own concerns? The classical view begins with the community of the polis and with the individual viewed as having no moral identity apart from the communities of kinship and citizenship; the modern view begins with the concept of a collection of individuals and the problem of how out of and by individuals social institutions can be constructed."[31] It is therefore not surprising, but indeed a correlative of liberal political theory, that one should have the "right" to commit suicide. We must ask ourselves whether in accepting that right we have unwittingly affirmed a society that no longer wishes to provide the conditions for the miracle of trust and community.

30. Eugene Genovese, *Roll, Jordan, Roll* (New York: Pantheon Books, 1974), 639–40.
31. The quotation from MacIntyre appears in his essay "How to Identify Ethical Principles," prepared for the National Commission for the Protection of Human Subjects of Biomedical and Behavioral Research. [This essay was never published. See editor's note in n. 10.]

If we are right about this, then those who would redescribe suicide as a sickness rather than a moral problem are leading us up a blind alley. To call suicide a sickness, even though some who commit suicide may be sick, is an attempt to take the moral onus off those who commit suicide.[32] We fail to see that at the same time you take the moral onus off the society that failed to provide the forms of care and trust necessary to sustain a commitment to life.

Suicide and euthanasia also undermine our notions of what it is to live bravely in the face of suffering; they tempt us to take on a story that will pervert our manner not only of dying but of living. When this paper was given as a lecture, a man once violently objected to our position. He did so because he felt that suicide must remain a constant option, for he never wanted to grow so old that he became a burden to anyone, in particular to his children. But that is exactly our primary concern, namely, that the voluntary taking of one's own life has itself become a way of life in order to let people play out false stories of bravery and heroism, to sustain the hollow sense of sacrifice referred to earlier. There is nothing wrong with being a burden! The care of the elderly is a crucial act for witnessing our celebration of their lives and ours.

Indeed, living does require bravery. It is not, however, the bravery of ending life but of continuing it. This position obviously involves some assumptions about the moral role of suffering; that is, suffering is not always an evil to overcome but often part of life we must learn to live with. Suffering is a highly relative matter that we should be willing to bear for the good and with the aid of the community—so we will not put our friends and lovers in the position of having to kill us. Some would fear boredom and uselessness even more than suffering. But it is not our right to end our life prematurely because we fear boredom. As Chesterton pointed out, only children, old folks, and God understand how much energy it takes to sustain repetition.[33] It certainly takes extraordinary commitments to sustain our lives, but they are not different commitments from those we must make when we are young.

3.2 "Letting Die" and the Homeliness of Tragedy
Having said this, we are sure that there are cases we would not describe as suicide even though they look very much like suicide, Saul and those who died at Masada having already been mentioned as examples. We are even surer that there are cases that may call for actions that look very much like euthanasia.

32. For example, see Thomas Szasz's defense of suicide as a moral category in "The Nature of Suicide," *Antioch Review* 31 (spring 1971): 7–17.
33. G. K. Chesterton, *Orthodoxy* (London: Fontana Books, 1963), 58–59.

There is no point in keeping someone alive beyond all reason, especially when "death" is being kept at bay by means over which the agent has little control.[34] Justice demands that we give to one what we would have for all, but that may not mean we must always do everything we can do for the dying. We would question, however, if such instances are properly described as euthanasia. For here we think the distinction between putting to death and letting die makes sense. If we have entered the dying process there are times that we can actively intervene to help ourselves die. We doubt that most cases will require such active intervention. The issue at stake here is not whether we are putting ourselves to death, but rather our right to refuse medical care.[35] We do not have an obligation to use dialysis, especially when we are old and few depend on us. We have the right to die as we have lived. We would agree with any who wished to object that having said this there seems to be little difference between active intervention and refraining from giving care. Yet the moral reason not to actively intervene, but rather to refrain from acting, is to show the one who suffers the continuing trustworthiness of his or her existence. Our refraining from acting or our refraining from extraordinary care, may be a symbolic act of the trustworthiness of our existence.

It seems to us that cases such as that of Captain Oates[36] are instructive in this respect. For what Oates did was allow those that were left alive to describe what happened as "The blizzard killed him." Their refusal to use their own

34. See the discussion in "The Ethics of Death: Letting Die or Putting to Death" (1974) in vv.
35. On this issue, of course, hangs much of the tragedy of the Quinlan case. For a particularly useful analysis of the ethical issues involved in that case, see Paul Ramsey's, "Prolonged Dying: Not Medically Indicated," *Hastings Center Report* 6, no. 1 (February 1976): 14–17. Ramsey argues, we think correctly, that the language of ordinary and extraordinary should be abandoned, "and that instead we should speak of (1) a comparison of treatments that are medically indicated and expected to be helpful, and those that are *not* medically indicated. In the case of the dying, that includes in all cases, or in most or many cases, a judgment that further curative treatment is no *longer* indicated. Instead of the traditional language, still current among physicians, we should talk about (2) a patient's right to refuse treatment" (15). Thus, Ramsey suggests that the "treatments" given Ms. Quinlan should not be prolonged because they act only to prolong her dying. For this kind of analysis applied to those only new in life, see Hauerwas, "The Demands and Limits of Care: Ethical Reflections on the Moral Dilemma of Neonatal Intensive Care" (1975) in TT.
36. Oates was a member of Scott's Antarctic expedition. He had been severely injured. Knowing that the others would refuse to leave him and yet would be dangerously delayed in taking him along, he told the others he was going out for a walk and disappeared into a blizzard. R. F. Holland gives a persuasive account of why this is not suicide in his article "Suicide" in *Moral Problems*, ed. James Rachels (New York: Harper and Row, 1971), 345–59.

hand to kill him, even in the sense of leaving him behind, was a way of symbolically gesturing their care for him.

Finally, we feel that to end one's own life, either by one's own hand or by requesting the hand of another to do it, places too great a burden on those who are left, as it asks us to cooperate in a process we should keep distant from. To ask us to passively or actively cooperate in the ending of life opens us to temptations best kept at bay: that we should determine for others whether they will live or die. To help another die invites us far too readily to justify our action by turning it into a policy, by saying that euthanasia is an act of mercy, a policy that is hard to control and even harder to adopt if we are to learn to look on life as a gift.

We are aware that our position may well result in some tragic circumstances. But then, finally, that is what the moral life is all about. Tragedy is a homely thing; the heart adapts and copes, if we are to live humanely.

Further Reading

"The Ethics of Death: Letting Die or Putting to Death" (1974), in *vv*

"Rational Suicide and Reasons for Living" (1981), in *sp*

"On Taking Religion Seriously: The Challenge of Jonestown" (1985), in *an*

"Should Suffering Be Eliminated? What the Retarded Have to Teach Us" (1984), essay 28 in this volume

"Remembering as a Moral Task: The Challenge of the Holocaust" (1985), essay 17 in this volume

"Courage Exemplified" (1993), essay 14 in this volume

"Practicing Patience: How Christians Should Be Sick" (1997), essay 18 in this volume

30. Must a Patient Be a Person to Be a Patient?
Or, My Uncle Charlie Is Not Much of a Person,
But He Is Still My Uncle Charlie (1975)

In the early 1970s, a number of the most serious issues in medical ethics came to be thought to turn on the question of "personhood": Is the fetus a person? Are profoundly handicapped infants persons? Are those in a persistent vegetative state still persons? While the notion of "personhood" was initially invoked to protect the weak and helpless, others in turn argued that certain classes of human beings are not yet or are no longer persons, and hence do not deserve the kinds of protections given to persons. In this brief reflection Hauerwas argues that defenses of the unborn and dying that rely on "personhood" (or any other generalized notion) are bound to fail. Such concepts cannot be expected to do work that requires not only a broader and richer theological account of "the way of life with which we wish to identify," but also an account of practices embodying and sustaining the story of a particular community.

As a Protestant teaching at a Catholic university, I continue to learn about problems I had no idea even existed. For example, recently I was called down for referring to Catholics as "Roman Catholics." I had been working on the assumption that a Catholic was a Roman Catholic; however, it was pointed out to me that this phrase appeared only with the beginning of the English Reformation in order to distinguish a Roman from an Anglo-Catholic. A Catholic is not Roman, as my Irish Catholic friend emphatically reminded me, but is more properly thought of simply as a Catholic.

I recount this tale because I think it has something to do with the issue I want to raise for our consideration. For we tend to think that most of our descriptions, the way we individuate action, have a long and honored history that can be tampered with only with great hesitation. Often, however, the supposed tradition is a recent innovation that may be as misleading as it is helpful.

[Reprinted from *Connecticut Medicine* 39:815–17 © 1975. Subsequently reprinted in *TT*. It has been edited for clarity.]

That is what I think may be happening with the emphasis on whether someone is or is not a "person" when this is used to determine whether or what kind of medical care a patient should receive. In the literature of past medical ethics the notion of "person" does not seem to have played a prominent role in deciding how medicine should or should not be used vis-à-vis a particular patient. Why is it, then, that we suddenly seem so concerned with the question of whether someone is a person? It is my hunch we have much to learn from this phenomenon as it is an indication, not that our philosophy of medicine or medical ethics is in good shape, but rather that it is in deep trouble. For it is my thesis that we are trying to put forward "person" as a regulative notion to direct our health care as a substitute for what only a substantive community and story can do.

However, before trying to defend this thesis, let me first illustrate how the notion of "person" is being used in relation to some of the recent issues of medical ethics. Paul Ramsey, in his book *The Patient as Person*,[1] uses the notion of person to protect the individual patient against the temptation of physician-researchers, especially in experimental medicine, to use one patient for the good of another or society. According to Ramsey, the major issue of medical ethics is how to reconcile the welfare of the individual with the welfare of humankind when both must be served. Ramsey argues that it is necessary to emphasize the personhood of the patient in order to remind doctors or experimenters that their first responsibility is to their immediate patient, not humankind or even the patient's family. Thus, Ramsey's emphasis on "person" is an attempt to provide the basis for what he takes to be the central ethical commitment of medicine, namely, that no one will be used as a means for the good of another. Medicine can serve humankind only as it does so through serving the individual patient.

Without the presumption of the inviolability of the "person," Ramsey thinks that we would have no basis for "informed consent" as the controlling criterion for medical therapy and experimentation. Moreover, it is only on this basis that doctors rightly see that their task is not to cure diseases, but rather to cure the person who happens to be subject to a disease. Thus, the notion of "person" functions for Ramsey as a Kantian or deontological check on what he suspects is the utilitarian bias of modern medicine.

However, the notion of "person" plays quite a different function in other literature dealing with medical ethics. In these contexts, "person" is not used

1. Paul Ramsey, *The Patient as Person* (New Haven: Yale University Press, 1970).

primarily as a protective notion, but rather as a permissive notion that takes the moral heat off certain quandaries raised by modern medicine. It is felt that if we can say with some assuredness that x, y, or z is not a person, then our responsibility is not the same as it is to those who bear this august title.

Of course, the issue where this is most prominent is abortion. Is the fetus a human person? Supposedly on that question hangs all the law and the prophets of the morality of abortion. For if it can be shown that the fetus is not a person, as indeed I think it can be shown, then the right to the care and protection that modern medicine can provide is not due to the fetus. Indeed, the technological skill of medicine can be used to destroy such life, for its status is of no special human concern since it lacks the attribute of "personhood."

Or, for example, the issue of *when* one is a person is raised to help settle when it is morally appropriate to withdraw care from the dying. If it can be shown, for example, that a patient has moved from the status of person to nonperson, then it seems that many of the difficult decisions surrounding what kind and extent of care should be given to the dying become moot. For the aid that medicine can bring is directed at persons, not at the mere continuation of our bodily life. (Since I will not develop it further, however, it is worth mentioning that this view assumes a rather extreme dualism between being a person and the bodily life necessary to provide the conditions for being a person.)[2]

Or, finally, there are the issues of what kind of care should be given to defective or deformed infants in order to keep them alive. For example, Joseph Fletcher has argued that any individual who falls below the 40 IQ mark in a Stanford-Binet test is "Questionably a person," and if you score 20 or below you are not a person.[3] Or Michael Tooley has argued that young infants, indeed, are not "persons" and, therefore, do not bear the rights necessary to make infanticide a morally questionable practice.[4] Whether, or what kind, of medical care should be given to children is determined by whether children are able to meet the demands of being a person. You may give them life-sustaining care, but in doing so you are acting strictly from the motive of charity since nothing obligates you to do so.

2. For a more extended analysis of this point, see "The Ethics of Death: Letting Die or Putting to Death?" (1974), "Towards an Ethic of Character" (1972), and "Situation Ethics, Moral Notions, and Moral Theology" (1972), in vv.

3. Joseph Fletcher, "Indicators of Humanhood," *Hastings Center Report* (November 1972): 1–3; also see my response in "The Retarded and the Criteria for the Human" (1973) in TT.

4. Michael Tooley, "A Defense of Abortion and Infanticide," in *The Problem of Abortion*, ed. Joel Feinberg (Belmont, CA: Wadsworth, 1973), 51–91.

As I suggested at the first, I find all this rather odd, not because some of the conclusions reached by such reasoning may be against my own moral opinions, or because they entail practices that seem counterintuitive (e.g., infanticide), but rather because I think this use of "person" tends to do violence to our language. For example, it is only seldom that we have occasion to think of ourselves as "persons"; when asked to identify myself, I do not think that I am a person, but I am Stanley Hauerwas, teacher, husband, father, or, ultimately, a Texan. Nor do I often have the occasion to think of others as persons. I do sometimes say, "Now, that Joe is one hell of a fine person," but so used, "person" carries no special status beyond the naming of a role. If I still lived in Texas, I would, as a matter of fact, never use such an expression, but rather say, "Now there is a good old boy."

Moreover, it is interesting to notice how abstract the language of person is in relation to our first-order moral language through which we live our lives and see the kinds of issues I have mentioned above. For example, the reason we do not use one man for another or society's good is not that we violate his "person," but rather because we have learned that it is destructive of the trust between us to do so. (Which is, in fact, Ramsey's real concern, as his case actually rests much more on his emphasis on the "covenant" between doctor and patient than on the status of the patient as a "person.") For example, it would surely make us hesitant to go to a doctor if we thought he or she might actually care for us only as a means of caring for another. It should be noted, however, that in a different kind of society it might well be intelligible and trustworthy for the doctor rightly to expect that his or her patient be willing to undergo certain risks for the good of the society itself. I suspect that Ramsey's excessive concern to protect the patient from the demands of society through the agency of the doctor is due to living in an extraordinarily individualistic society where citizens share no good in common.

Even more artificial is the use of "person" to try to determine the moral decision in relation to abortion, death, and the care of the defective newborn. For the issues surrounding whether an abortion should or should not be done seldom turn on the question of the status of the fetus. Rather, they involve why the mother does not want the pregnancy to continue, the conditions under which the pregnancy occurred, the social conditions into which the child would be born. The question of whether the fetus is or is not a person is almost a theoretical nicety in relation to the kind of questions that most abortion decisions actually involve.

Or, for example, when a man is dying, we seldom decide to treat or not to treat him because he has or has not yet passed some line that makes him a person or a nonperson. Rather, we care or do not care for him because he is Uncle Charlie, or my father, or a good friend. In the same manner, we do not care or cease to care for a child born defective because it is or is not a person. Rather, whether or how we decide to care for such a child depends on our attitude toward the having of and caring for children, our perception of our role as parents, and how medicine is seen as one form of how care is to be given to children.[5] (For it may well be that we will care for such children, but this does not mean that medicine has some kind of overriding claim on being the form that such care should take.)

It might be felt that these examples assume far too easily that our common notions and stories are the primary ones for giving moral guidance in such cases. The introduction of the notion of "person" as regulatory in such matters might be an attempt to find a firmer basis than these more historically and socially contingent notions can provide. But I am suggesting that is just what the notion of "person" cannot do without seriously distorting the practices, institutions, and notions that underlie how we have learned morally to display our lives. More technically, what advocates of "personhood" have failed to show is how the notion of person works in a way of life with which we wish to identify.

Yet, we feel inextricably drawn to come up with some account that will give direction to our medical practice, exactly because we sense that our more immediate moral notions never were, or are no longer, sufficient to provide such a guide. Put concretely, we are beginning to understand how much medicine depended on the moral ethos of its society to guide how it should care for children, because we are now in a period when some people no longer think that simply because a child is born to them they need regard it as their child. We will not solve this kind of dilemma by trying to say what the doctor can and cannot do in such circumstances in terms of whether the child can be understood to be a "person" or not.

As Paul Ramsey suggests, we may have arrived at a time when we have achieved an unspeakable thing: a medical profession without a moral philosophy in a society without one either. Medicine, of course, still seems to carry the marks of a profession inasmuch as it seems to be a guardian of certain values—that is, the unconditional commitment to preserve life and health, the

5. For an extended analysis of these issues, see my "The Demands and Limits of Care: Ethical Reflections on the Moral Dilemma of Neonatal Intensive Care" (1975), in *TT*.

responsibility for justifying the patient's trust in the physician, and the autonomy of the physician in making judgments on others in the profession. But, as Alasdair MacIntyre has argued, these assumed virtues can quickly be turned to vices when they lack a scheme, or, in my language, a story that depends on further beliefs about our true nature and end.[6] But such a scheme is exactly what we lack, and it will not be supplied by trying to determine who is and is not a "person."

The language of "person" seems convenient to us, however, because we wish to assume that our medicine still rests on a consensus of moral beliefs. But I am suggesting that is exactly what is not the case and, in the absence of such a consensus, we will be much better off to simply admit that morally there are many different ways to practice medicine. We should, in other words, be willing to have our medicine as fragmented as our moral lives. I take this to be particularly important for Christians and Jews, as we have been under the illusion that we could morally expect medicine to embody our own standards or, at least, standards that we could sympathize with. I suspect, however, that this may not be the case, for the story that determines how the virtues of medicine are to be displayed for us is quite different from the one claimed by the language of "person."[7] It may be, then, if we are to be honest, that we should again think of the possibility of what it might mean to practice medicine befitting our convictions as Christians or Jews. Yet, there is a heavy price to be paid for the development of such a medical practice, as it may well involve training and going to doctors whose technology is less able to cure and sustain us than current medicine provides. But, then, we must decide what is more valuable: our survival or how we choose to survive.[8]

6. Alasdair MacIntyre, "How Virtues Become Vices: Values, Medicine and Social Context," *Evaluation and Explanation in the Biomedical Sciences* (Dordrecht, Netherlands: Reidel, 1975), 97–111.

7. For I would not deny that advocates of "person," or the regulatory notion of medical care, are right to assume that the notion of person involves the basic libertarian values of our society. It is my claim that such values are not adequate to direct medicine in a humane or Christian manner.

8. For an analysis of the political theory implications of my argument here, see Robert Paul Wolff, "There's Nobody Here But Us Persons," in *Women and Philosophy: Toward a Theory of Liberation,* ed. Carol Gould and Marx Wartofsky (New York: Putnam's Sons, 1976), 128–44. Wolff points out that there is a paradox of ideology in modern America:

Radical critics of American life and society attack racism, sexism, discrimination against the old, and other injustices of the public realm. They argue that the work world, and the political world, should be blind to a person's sex, or race, or age, or religion. These same critics—among whom I include myself—condemn the inhumanity of capitalism, the de-

Further Reading

"The Christian, Society and the Weak: A Meditation on the Care of the Retarded" (1972), in *vv*

"Memory, Community, and the Reasons for Living: Reflections on Suicide and Euthanasia" (1976), essay 29 in this volume

"The Retarded, Society, and the Family: The Dilemma of Care" (1982), in *sp*

Naming the Silences: Reflections on God, Medicine, and the Problem of Suffering (1990)

"The Retarded and the Criteria for the Human" (1973), in *tt*

---

struction of the human character of work, the alienation of the worker from his labor, from his product, from his fellow workers, and from his own human essence. But the very same principle of political philosophy and social organization is at work in the causes we champion and in the alienation we condemn. To ignore the sex, race, age, culture, religion, or personality of a person when hiring, or paying, or electing, or admitting that person, is to accept the public/private split, and to shove into the private sphere, out of sight and out of consideration, everything that makes a person a human being and not merely a rational agent. I am not a person who just happens, accidentally and irrelevantly, to be a man, forty years old, the husband of a professor of English literature, the son of two aging and sick parents, the father of two small boys six and four, a comfortable well-off member of the upper-middle class, American-Jewish born and raised in New York. I am *essentially* such a man. . . . To demand that the public world of work and politics be blind to age, sex, race, and so forth precisely is to equate the most essential facts of my human self with relatively trivial facts of my tastes and preferences, and to consign them to the private world where they will have no influence on *important* public policies and decisions. (136–37)

31. Abortion, Theologically Understood (1991)

In 1990 the Evangelical Fellowship of the North Carolina Conference of the United Methodist Church invited Hauerwas to address the body at its annual gathering. Not part of the official agenda, the lecture was not able to begin until 10 P.M. What follows is an edited transcription of Hauerwas's remarks and responses to questions that followed. Hauerwas challenges the dominant catego-ries for discussing abortion in American society (e.g., appeals to "rights," "life," "choice," or "wanted children"), pointing out the misleading character of these descriptions from a Christian theological perspective. Hauerwas calls on Chris-tians (here, specifically United Methodists) to name abortion in relation to their most formative practices of worship. He believes that this is the way the privatiza-tion of abortion can best be overcome. Such moral privatization not only kills children, but also abandons women and encourages male promiscuity. Painfully aware that the church has often not had an integrity of conviction and practice necessary to successfully resist the secular presuppositions on the question of abortion, Hauerwas challenges the church to show the hospitality inherent in its own baptismal promises.

Every once in a while you get a wonderful gift. Recently, the Reverend Terry Hamilton-Poor, a former student who is now a Presbyterian minister, mailed to me a copy of a sermon on abortion. The text for the sermon is Matthew 25:31–46, from the Revised Standard Version.

[An earlier version of this selection was first delivered at a meeting of the Evangelical Fellow-ship during the North Carolina Annual Conference of the United Methodist Church in June 1990. Published as a booklet by Lifewatch: The Taskforce of United Methodists on Abortion and Sexuality, 1991. Reprinted with permission of The Taskforce of United Methodists on Abortion and Sexuality. Subsequently reprinted in *The Church and Abortion: In Search of New Ground for Response* (Nashville, TN: Abingdon Press, 1993), 44–66.]

"When the Son of man comes in his glory, and all the angels with him, then he will sit on his glorious throne. Before him will be gathered all the nations, and he will separate them one from another as a shepherd separates the sheep from the goats, and he will place the sheep at his right hand, but the goats at the left. Then the King will say to those at his right hand, 'Come, O blessed of my Father, inherit the kingdom prepared for you from the foundation of the world; for I was hungry and you gave me food, I was thirsty and you gave me drink, I was a stranger and you welcomed me, I was naked and you clothed me, I was sick and you visited me, I was in prison and you came to me.' Then the righteous will answer him, 'Lord when did we see thee hungry and feed thee, or thirsty and give thee drink? And when did we see thee a stranger and welcome thee, or naked and clothe thee? And when did we see thee sick or in prison and visit thee?' And the King will answer them, 'Truly, I say to you, as you did it to one of the least of these my brethren, you did it to me.' Then he will say to those at his left hand, 'Depart from me, you cursed, into the eternal fire prepared for the devil and his angels; for I was hungry and you gave me no food, I was thirsty and you gave me no drink, I was a stranger and you did not welcome me, naked and you did not clothe me, sick and in prison and you did not visit me.' Then they also will answer, 'Lord, when did we see thee hungry or thirsty or a stranger or naked or sick or in prison, and did not minister to thee?' Then he will answer them, 'Truly, I say to you, as you did it not to one of the least of these, you did it not to me.' And they will go away into eternal punishment, but the righteous into eternal life."

As a Christian and a woman, I find abortion a most difficult subject to address. Even so, I believe that it is essential that the church face the issue of abortion in a distinctly Christian manner. Because of that, I am hereby addressing not society in general, but those of us who call ourselves Christians. I also want to be clear that I am not addressing abortion as a legal issue. I believe the issue, for the church, must be framed not around the banners of "pro-choice" or "pro-life," but around God's call to care for the least among us whom Jesus calls his sisters and brothers.

So, in this sermon, I will make three points. The first point is that the gospel favors women and children. The second point is that the customary framing of the abortion issue by both pro-choice and pro-life groups is unbiblical because it assumes that the woman is ultimately responsible for both herself and for any child she might carry. The third point is that a

Christian response must reframe the issue to focus on responsibility rather than rights.

Point number one: the gospel favors women and children. The gospel is feminist. In Matthew, Mark, Luke, and John, Jesus treats women as thinking people who are worthy of respect. This was not, of course, the usual attitude of that time. In addition, it is to the women among Jesus' followers, not to the men, that he entrusts the initial proclamation of his resurrection. It is not only Jesus himself who sees the gospel making all people equal, for Saint Paul wrote, "There is neither Jew nor Greek, there is neither slave nor free, there is neither male nor female; for you are all one in Christ Jesus" (Galatians 3:28 RSV).

And yet, women have been oppressed through recorded history and continue to be oppressed today. So when Jesus says, "As you did it to one of the least of these my brethren, you did it to me" (Matthew 25:40 RSV), I have to believe that Jesus includes women among "the least of these." Anything that helps women, therefore, helps Jesus. When Jesus says, "As you did it to one of the least of these my brethren, you did it to me," he is also talking about children, because children are literally "the least of these." Children lack the three things the world values most—power, wealth, and influence. If we concern ourselves with people who are powerless, then children should obviously be at the top of our list. The irony of the abortion debate, as it now stands in our church and society, is that it frames these two groups, women and children, as enemies of one another.

This brings me to my second point. The usual way of framing the abortion issue, by both pro-choice and pro-life groups, is unbiblical because it assumes that the woman is ultimately responsible both for herself and for any child she might carry. Why is it that women have abortions? Women I know, and those I know about, have had abortions for two basic reasons: the fear that they cannot handle the financial and physical demands of the child, and the fear that having the child will destroy relationships that are important to them.

An example of the first fear, the inability to handle the child financially or physically, is the divorced mother of two children, the younger of whom has Down syndrome. This woman recently discovered that she was pregnant. She believed abortion was wrong. However, the father of the child would not commit himself to help raise this child, and she was afraid she could not handle raising another child on her own.

An example of the second fear, the fear of destroying relationships, is the woman who became pregnant and was told by her husband that he would leave her if she did not have an abortion. She did not want to lose her husband so she had the abortion. Later, her husband left her anyway.

In both of these cases, and in others I have known, the woman has had an abortion not because she was exercising her free choice but because she felt she had no choice. In each case the responsibility for caring for the child, had she had the child, would have rested squarely and solely on the woman.

Which brings me to my third point: the Christian response to abortion must reframe the issue to focus on responsibility rather than rights. The pro-choice/pro-life debate presently pits the right of the mother to choose against the right of the fetus to live. The Christian response, on the other hand, centers on the responsibility of the whole Christian community to care for "the least of these."

According to the Presbyterian Church's *Book of Order* of 1983–1985, when a person is baptized, the congregation answers this question: "Do you, the members of this congregation, in the name of the whole Church of Christ, undertake the responsibility for the continued Christian nurture of this person, promising to be an example of the new life in Christ and to pray for him or her in this new life?" We make this promise because we know that no adult belongs to himself or herself, and that no child belongs to his or her parents, but that every person is a child of God. Because of that, every young one is our child, the church's child to care for. This is not an option. It is a responsibility.

Let me tell you two stories about what it is like when the church takes this responsibility seriously. The first is a story that Will Willimon, the dean of Duke University Chapel, tells about a black church. In this church, when a teenager has a baby that she cannot care for, the church baptizes the baby and gives him or her to an older couple in the church that has the time and wisdom to raise the child. That way, says the pastor, the couple can raise the teenage mother along with the baby. "That," the pastor says, "is how we do it."

The second story involves something that happened to Deborah Campbell. A member of her church, a divorced woman, became pregnant, and the father dropped out of the picture. The woman decided to keep the child. But as the pregnancy progressed and began to show, she became upset because she felt she could not go to church anymore. After all, here she was, a Sunday School teacher, unmarried and pregnant. So she called Deborah. Deborah told her to come to church and sit in the pew with the Campbell family, and, no matter how the church reacted, the family would support her. Well, the church rallied around when the woman's doctor told her at her six-month checkup that she owed him the remaining balance of fifteen hundred dollars by the next month; otherwise, he would not deliver the baby. The church held a baby shower and raised the money. When the time came for her to deliver, Deborah was her labor coach. When the woman's mother refused to come and help after the baby was born, the church brought food and helped clean her house while she recovered from the birth. Now the woman's little girl is the child of the parish.

This is what the church looks like when it takes seriously its call to care for "the least of these." These two churches differ in certain ways: one is Methodist, the other Roman Catholic; one has a carefully planned strategy for supporting women and babies, the other simply reacted spontaneously to a particular woman and her baby. But in each case the church acted with creativity and compassion to live out the gospel.

In our scripture lesson today, Jesus gives a preview of the Last Judgment:

"Then the King will say to those at his right hand, 'Come, O blessed of my Father, inherit the kingdom prepared for you from the foundation of the world; for I was hungry and you gave me food, I was thirsty and you gave me drink, I was a stranger and you welcomed me, I was naked and you clothed me, I was sick and you visited me, I was in prison and you came to me.' Then the righteous will answer him, 'Lord, when did we see thee hungry and feed thee, or thirsty and give thee drink? And when did we see thee a stranger and welcome thee, or naked and clothe thee? And when did we see thee sick or in prison and visit thee?' And the King will answer them, 'Truly, I say to you, as you did it to one of the least of these my brethren, you did it to me'" (Matthew 25:34–40 RSV).

We cannot simply throw the issue of abortion in the faces of women and say, "You decide and you bear the consequences of your decision." As the church, our response to the abortion issue must be to shoulder the responsibility to care for women and children. We cannot do otherwise and still be the church. If we close our doors in the faces of women and children, then we close our doors in the face of Christ.

I begin with this sermon because I suspect that most ministers avoid preaching about abortion. They do so because they have not had the slightest idea about how to do it in a way that would not make everyone in their congregations mad. And the reason they have not known how to preach a sermon on abortion is that they thought they would have to take up the terms that are given by the wider society.

Above you have a young minister cutting through the kind of pro-choice and pro-life rhetoric that is given in the wider society. She preached a sermon on abortion that derives directly from the gospel. The sermon argues that the church must refuse to use society's terms for the abortion debate. The church must address the abortion problem as church. Abortion is not fundamentally a question about the law, but about what kind of people we are to be as the church and as Christians.

Beyond Rights

Christians in America are tempted to think of issues like abortion primarily in legal terms such as "rights." This is because the legal mode, as Tocqueville pointed out long ago, provides the constituting morality in liberal societies. In other words, when you live in a liberal society like ours, the fundamental problem is how you can achieve cooperative agreements between individuals who share nothing in common other than their fear of death. In liberal society the law has the function of securing such agreements. That is the reason why lawyers are to America what priests were to the medieval world. The law is our way of negotiating safe agreements between autonomous individuals who have nothing else in common other than their fear of death and their mutual desire for protection.

Therefore, rights language is fundamental in our political and moral context. In America, we oftentimes pride ourselves, as Americans, on being a pragmatic people that is not ideological. But that is absolutely false. No country has ever been more theory-dependent on a public philosophy than America.

Indeed, I want to argue that America is the only country that has the misfortune of being founded on a philosophical mistake—namely, the notion of inalienable rights. We Christians do not believe that we have inalienable rights. That is the false presumption of Enlightenment individualism, and it opposes everything that Christians believe about what it means to be a creature. Notice that the issue is inalienable rights. Rights make a certain sense when they are correlative to duties and goods, but they are not inalienable. For example, when the lords protested against the king in the *Magna Carta*, they did so in the name of their duties to their serfs. Duties, not rights, were primary.

Christians, to be more specific, do not believe that we have a right to do whatever we want with our bodies. We do not believe that we have a right to our bodies because when we are baptized we become members of one another; then we can tell one another what it is that we should and should not do with our bodies. I had a colleague at the University of Notre Dame who taught Judaica. He was Jewish and always said that any religion that does not tell you what to do with your genitals and pots and pans cannot be interesting. That is exactly true. In the church we tell you what you can and cannot do with your genitals. They are not your own. They are not private. That means that you cannot commit adultery. If you do, you are no longer a member of "us." Of course, pots and pans are equally important.

I was recently giving a talk at a very conservative university, Houston Baptist University. Since its business school has an ethics program, I called my talk, "Why Business Ethics Is a Bad Idea." When I had finished, one of the business school people asked, "Well goodness, what then can we Christians do about business ethics?" I said, "A place to start would be the local church. It might be established that before anyone joins a Baptist church in Houston, he or she would have to declare in public his or her annual income." The only people whose incomes are known in the United Methodist Church today are ordained ministers. Why should we make the ministers' salaries public and not the laity's?[1] Most people would rather tell you what they do in the bedroom than how much they make. With these things in mind, you can see how the church is being destroyed by the privatization of individual lives, by the American ethos. If you want to know who is destroying the babies of this country through abortion, look at privatization, which is learned in the economic arena.

Under the veil of American privatization, we are encouraging people to believe in the same way that Andrew Carnegie believed.[2] He thought that he

1. [Here Hauerwas is referring to the disciplinary requirement that the salaries of all ordained ministers must be made public (See *The United Methodist Book of Discipline 1988*, para. 725). Unlike early Methodism, where all members of the societies and all members of the conference of preachers were held to be accountable to the same standards of holiness and discipline (see "The General Rules of the United Societies" for the rules about buying, selling, and spending), contemporary United Methodists appear to have drifted into a kind of "two-level ethic" in matters of financial accountability, requiring accountability of the clergy but not even bothering to ask the question of the laity. When confronted with "The General Rules of the United Societies" (a document that remains a part of the Constitution of the United Methodist Church), many United Methodists respond with "Well, thank God we don't do that!"]
2. [Andrew Carnegie's "Gospel of Wealth" summarizes four fundamental laws: individualism,

had a right to his steel mills. In the same sense, people think that they have a right to their bodies. The body is then a piece of property in a capitalist sense. Unfortunately, that is antithetical to the way we Christians think we have to share as members of the same body of Christ.

So, you cannot separate these issues. If you think that you can be very concerned about abortion and not concerned about the privatization of American life generally, you are making a mistake. So the problem is: How, as Christians, should we think about abortion without the rights rhetoric that we have been given—right to my body, right to life, pro-choice, pro-life, and so on? In this respect, we Christians must try to make the abortion issue our issue.

Learning the Language

We must remember that the first question is not, Is abortion right or wrong? or Is this abortion right or wrong? Rather, the first question is, Why do Christians call abortion *abortion*? And with the first question goes a second: Why do Christians think that *abortion* is a morally problematic term? To call abortion by that name is already a moral achievement. The reason why people are pro-choice rather than pro-abortion is that nobody really wants to be pro-abortion. The use of *choice* rather than *abortion* is an attempt at a linguistic transformation that tries to avoid the reality of abortion, because most people do not want to use that description. So, instead of *abortion,* another term is used, something like *termination of pregnancy.* Now, the church can live more easily in a world with "terminated pregnancies," because in that world the church no longer claims power, even linguistic power, over that medically described part of life; instead, doctors do.

One of the interesting cultural currents that is involved is the medicalization of abortion. It is one of the ways that the medical profession is continuing to secure power against the church. Ordained ministers can sense this when they are in hospital situations. In a hospital today, the minister feels less power than the doctor, right?

My way of explaining this is that when someone goes to seminary today, he can say, "I'm not into Christology this year. I'm just into relating. After all,

---

private property, accumulation of wealth, and competition. See Carnegie's article "Wealth" in *North American Review* 391 (June 1889): 653–64. For a provocative assessment of the patterns of self-deception in Carnegie's gospel of success, see Roger Betsworth, "The Gospel of Success in America," in *Social Ethics: An Examination of American Moral Traditions* (Louisville, KY: Westminster/John Knox, 1990), 53–80.]

relating is what the ministry is really about, isn't it? Ministry is about helping people relate to one another, isn't it? So I want to take some more Clinical Pastoral Education (CPE) courses." And the seminary says, "Go ahead and do it. Right, get your head straight, and so on." A kid can go to medical school and say, "I'm not into anatomy this year. I'm into relating. So I'd like to take a few more courses in psychology, because I need to know how to relate better to people." The medical school then says, "Who in the hell do you think you are, kid? We're not interested in your interests. You're going to take anatomy. If you don't like it, that's tough."

Now what that shows you is that people believe incompetent physicians can hurt them. Therefore, people expect medical schools to hold their students responsible for the kind of training that's necessary to be competent physicians. On the other hand, few people believe an incompetent minister can damage their salvation. This helps you see that what people want today is not salvation, but health. And that helps you see why the medical profession has, as a matter of fact, so much power over the church and her ministry. The medical establishment is the counter-salvation-promising group in our society today.

So, when you innocently say "termination of pregnancy," while it sounds like a neutral term, you are placing your thinking under the sway of an increasingly large segment of the medical profession. In contrast to the medical profession, Christians maintain that the description "abortion" is more accurate and determinative than the description "termination of pregnancy." That is a most morally serious matter.

Morally speaking, the first issue is never what we are to do, but what we should see. Here is the way it works: you can act only in the world that you can see, and you must be taught to see by learning to say. Steadfastly maintaining the language of abortion is one way of training ourselves as Christians to see and to practice its opposite: hospitality, and particularly hospitality to children and the vulnerable. "Abortion" reminds us of how Christians are to envision life: we are a baptizing people ready to welcome new life into our communities.

In that sense, "abortion" is as much a moral description as "suicide." Exactly why does a community maintain a description like "suicide"? Because it reminds the community of its practice of enhancing life, even under duress. The language of suicide also works as a way to remind you that even when you are in pain, even when you are sick, you have an obligation to remain with the people of God, vulnerable and yet present.

When we joined the United Methodist Church, we promised to uphold it with "our prayers, our presence, our gifts, and our service." We often think that "our presence" is the easy one. In fact, it is the hardest one. I can illustrate this by speaking about the church I belonged to in South Bend, Indiana. It was a small group of people that originally was an E.U.B. (or Evangelical United Brethren) congregation. Every Sunday we had Eucharist, prayers from the congregation, and a noon meal for the neighborhood. When the usual congregation would pray, we would pray for the hungry in Ethiopia and for an end to the war in the Near East, and so on. Well, this bag lady started coming to church and she would pray things like, "Lord, I have a cold, and I would really like you to cure it." Or, "I've just had a horrible week and I'm depressed. Lord, would you please raise my spirits?" You never hear prayers like that in most of our churches. Why? Because the last thing that Christians want to do is show one another that they are vulnerable. People go to church because they are strong. They want to reinforce the presumption that they are strong.

One of the crucial issues here is how we learn to be a people dependent on one another. We must learn to confess that, as a hospitable people, we need one another because we are dependent on one another. The last thing the church wants is a bunch of autonomous, free individuals. We want people who know how to express authentic need, because that creates community.

So, the language of abortion is a reminder about the kind of community we need to be. Abortion language reminds the church to be ready to receive new life as church.

The Church as True Family

We, as church, are ready to be challenged by the other. This has to do with the fact that in the church, every adult, whether single or married, is called to be a parent. All Christian adults have a parental responsibility because of baptism. Biology does not make parents in the church. Baptism does. Baptism makes all adult Christians parents and gives them the obligation to help introduce these children to the gospel. Listen to the baptismal vows; in them the whole church promises to be parent. The minister addresses the church with these words:

> Will you nurture one another in the Christian faith and life and include [those being baptized] now before you in your care?
> With God's help we will proclaim the good news and live according to the example of Christ.

We will surround [those being baptized] with a community of love and forgiveness, that they may grow in their service to others.

We will pray for [those being baptized], that they may be true disciples who walk in the way that leads to life.[3]

By these vows the church reinvents the family.

When I taught a marriage course at the University of Notre Dame, I used to read to my students a letter. It went something like this: "Our son had done well. He had gone to good schools, had gone through the military, had gotten out, had looked like he had a very promising career ahead. Unfortunately, he has joined some eastern religious sect. Now he does not want to have anything to do with us because we are people of 'the world.' He is never going to marry because now his true family is this funny group of people he associates with. We are heartsick. We do not know what to do about this." Then I would ask the class, "Who wrote this letter?" And the students would say, "Probably some family whose kid became a Moonie or a Hare Krishna." In fact, this is the letter of a fourth-century Roman senatorial family about their son's conversion to Christianity.

From the beginning we Christians have made singleness as valid a way of life as marriage. What it means to be the church is to be a group of people called out of the world, and back into the world, to embody the hope of the Kingdom of God. Children are not necessary for the growth of the Kingdom, because the church can call the stranger into her midst. That makes both singleness and marriage possible vocations. If everybody has to marry, then marriage is a terrible burden. But the church does not believe that everybody has to marry. Even so, those who do not marry are also parents within the church, because the church is now the true family. The church is a family into which children are brought and received. It is only within that context that it makes sense for the church to say, "We are always ready to receive children. We are *always* ready to receive children." The people of God know no enemy when it comes to children.

Why "When Life Begins" Is Not the Fundamental Question

Against the background of the church as family, you can see that the Christian language of abortion challenges the modern tendency to deal with moral di-

---

3. ["Baptismal Covenant I," *The United Methodist Hymnal* (Nashville, TN: Abingdon, 1989), 35.]

lemmas and discrete units of behavior. If that tendency is followed, you get the questions, What is really wrong with abortion? and Isn't abortion a separate problem that can be settled on its own grounds? And then you get the termination-of-pregnancy language that wants to see abortion as solely a medical problem. At the same time, you get abortion framed in a legalistic way.

When many people start talking about abortion, what is the first thing they talk about? When life begins. And why do they get into the question of when life begins? Because they think that the abortion issue is determined primarily by the claims that life is sacred and that life is never to be taken. They assume that these claims let you know how it is that you ought to think about abortion.

Well, I want to know where Christians get the notion that life is sacred. That notion seems to have no reference at all to God. Any good secularist can think life is sacred. Of course, what the secularist means by the word *sacred* is interesting, but the idea that Christians are about the maintenance of some principle separate from our understanding of God is just crazy. As a matter of fact, Christians do not believe that life is sacred. I often remind my right-to-life friends that Christians took their children with them to martyrdom rather than have them raised pagan. Christians believe there is much worth dying for. We do not believe that human life is an absolute good in and of itself.[4] Of course, our desire to protect human life is part of our seeing each human being as God's creature. But that does not mean that we believe that life is an overriding good.

To say that life is an overriding good is to underwrite the modern sentimentality that there is absolutely nothing in this world worth dying for. Christians know that Christianity is simply extended training in dying early. That is what we have always been about. Listen to the gospel! I know that today we use the church primarily as a means of safety, but life in the church should actually involve extended training in learning to die early.

When you frame the abortion issue in sacredness-of-life language, you get into intractable debates about when life begins. Notice that is an issue for legalists. By that I mean the fundamental question becomes, How do you avoid doing the wrong thing?

In contrast, the Christian approach is not one of deciding when life has

4. [This is also the view expressed by Pope John Paul II in *Evangelium Vitae* (The Gospel of Life) AAS 87 (1995), (Washington, DC: National Conference of Catholic Bishops, 1995), section 47. "Certainly *the life of the body in its earthly state is not an absolute good* for the believer, especially as he may be asked to give up his life for a greater good." (Italics in original.)]

begun, but hoping that it has. We hope that human life has begun! We are not the kind of people that ask: Does human life start at the blastocyst stage, or at implantation? Instead, we are the kind of people that hope life has started, because we are ready to believe that this new life will enrich our community. We believe this not because we have sentimental views about children. Honestly, I cannot imagine anything worse than people saying that they have children because their hope for the future is in their children. You would never have children if you had them for that reason. We are able to have children because our hope is in God, who makes it possible to do the absurd thing of having children. In a world of such terrible injustice, in a world of such terrible misery, in a world that may well be about the killing of our children, having children is an extraordinary act of faith and hope. But as Christians we can have hope in the God who urges us to welcome children. When that happens, it is an extraordinary testimony of faith.

Why "When Personhood Begins" Is Not the Fundamental Question

On the pro-choice side, you also get the abortion issue framed in a context that is outside of a communitarian structure. On the pro-choice side, you get the question about when the fetus becomes a "person," because only persons supposedly have citizenship rights. That is the issue of *Roe v. Wade.*

It is odd for Christians to take this approach since we believe that we are first of all citizens of a far different kingdom than something called the United States of America. If we end up identifying persons with the ability to reason—which, I think, finally renders all of our lives deeply problematic—then we cannot tell why it is that we ought to care for the profoundly retarded. One of the most chilling aspects of the current abortion debate in the wider society is the general acceptance, even among antiabortion people, of the legitimacy of aborting severely defective children.[5] Where do people get that idea? Where do people get the idea that severely defective children are somehow a less valuable gift from God? People get that idea by privileging rationality. We privilege our ability to reason. I find that morally indefensible.

We must remember that as Christians we do not believe in the inherent sacredness of life or in personhood. Instead, we believe that there is much

5. One of the earliest and most strident advocates of aborting defective children is Joseph Fletcher. See his "Four Indicators of Humanhood: The Inquiry Matures," *Hastings Center Report* 4 (December 1975): 4–7; reprinted in *On Moral Medicine,* first edition ed. Stephen Lammers and Allen Verhey (Grand Rapids, MI: Eerdmans, 1987).

worth dying for. Christians do not believe that life is a right or that we have inherent dignity. Instead, we believe that life is the gift of a gracious God. That is our primary Christian language regarding abortion: life is the gift of a gracious God. As part of the giftedness of life, we believe that we ought to live in a profound awe of the other's existence, knowing that in the other we find God. So abortion is a description maintained by Christians to remind us of the kind of community we must be to sustain the practice of hospitality to life. That is related to everything else that we do and believe.

There is the argument that if you let abortion start occurring for the late-developed fetus, sooner or later you cannot prohibit infanticide. Here you are entering the slippery slope argument. There is a prominent, well-respected philosopher in this country named H. Tristram Engelhardt who wrote a book called *Foundations of Bioethics.* In the book Engelhardt argues that, as far as he can see, there is absolutely no reason at all that we should not kill children up to a year and a half old, since they are not yet persons. *Foundations* is a text widely used in our universities today by people having to deal with all kinds of bioethical problems.

I have no doubt that bioethical problems exist. After all, today you can run into all kinds of anomalies. To understand the incoherence of liberal societies, consider for example what is happening in hospitals; on one side of the hall, doctors and nurses are working very hard to save a five-hundred-gram prema-ture infant while, on the other side of the hall, they are aborting a similar premature infant. There are many of these anomalies. There is no question that they are happening. You can build up a collection of such horror stories. But listen, people can get used to horror. Also, opposition to the horrible should not be the final, decisive ground on which Christians stand while tackling these kinds of issues. Instead, the issue is how we as a Christian community can live in positive affirmation of the kind of hospitality that will be a witness to the society we live in. That will open up a discourse that otherwise would be impossible.

Now I know that you probably feel a bit frustrated by this theological approach to abortion—especially when you are trying to deal with concrete, pastoral problems, as well as the political problems that we confront in this society. In some ways what I am asking you to think about regarding abortion and the church is a little like what the Quakers had to go through regarding slavery. Some of the early abolitionists, as you know, were Quakers. Then somebody pointed out to them, "There are a lot of slaveholding Friends." So the Quakers had to turn around and say, "Yes, that's right." Then they had to start trying to discipline their own ranks, and, as a result, they ended up creating a bunch of Anglicans in Philadelphia.[6]

One of the reasons why the church's position about abortion has not been authentic is because the church has not lived and witnessed as a community in a way that challenges the fundamental secular presuppositions of both the pro-life side and the pro-choice side. We are going to have to become that kind of community if our witness is to have the kind of integrity that it must.

Why Abortion Is about the Ethics of Sex and Power

When addressing abortion, one of the crucial questions that we must engage is the question of the relationship between men and women, and thus sexual ethics. One of the church's mistakes—all too common for denominations like ours in liberal social orders—has been to allow the issue of abortion to be isolated from the issue of sexual ethics. We cannot do that.

For example, the church has to make it clear that sexual relations are relations of power.

Unfortunately, one of the worst things Christians often do is underwrite romantic presuppositions about marriage. Many Christians even think that we ought to marry people simply because we are "in love." This romantic view underwrites the presumption that, because people are in love it is therefore legitimate for them to have sexual intercourse, whether they are married or not. Contrary to this is the church's view: marriage is the public declaration that two people have covenanted to live together faithfully for a lifetime.

On this view, we see how the church can be effective in making men take responsibility for their progeny. It is a great challenge for any society to get its men to take up this responsibility. The United Methodist Church must start condemning male promiscuity. Our church cannot have a valid voice on abortion until she attacks male promiscuity with the ferocity it deserves. We have got to get over our fear of appearing prudish.

Male promiscuity is nothing but the exercise of reckless power. There is no compromise. Otherwise, it ends up with high school kids having sexual intercourse because they think they love one another. Often we must say that that is rape. Let us be clear about it. No fourteen-year-old, unattractive woman who is not part of the social clique of a high school, who is suddenly dated by some

6. [Hauerwas's use of the example of Quakers to remind United Methodists that disciplined action on abortion may cause division is particularly poignant in light of the fact that American Methodists split in 1845 over "the General Rule on Slavery."]

male, who falls all over herself with the need for approval, and who ends up in bed with him can be said to have had anything other than rape happen to her. Let the church speak honestly about these matters and quit pussyfooting around. Until we speak clearly against male promiscuity, we will continue to make the mistake of constructing quandaries as problems of teenage pregnancy and abortion as private choice issues.

Should Christians "Want" Children?

There is one other issue that I think is worth highlighting. It concerns how abortion in our society has dramatically affected the practice of having children. In discussions about abortion, one often hears that no "unwanted child" ought to be born. But I can think of no greater burden than having to be a wanted child.

When I taught the marriage course at the University of Notre Dame, the parents of my students wanted me to teach their kids what the parents did not want them to do. The kids, on the other hand, approached the course from the perspective of whether or not they should feel guilty for what they had already done. Not wanting to privilege either approach, I started the course with the question, "What reason would you give for you or someone else wanting to have a child?" And I would get answers like, "Well, children are fun." In that case, I would ask them to think about their brothers and sisters. Another answer was, "Children are a hedge against loneliness." Then I recommended getting a dog. Also I would note that if they really wanted to feel lonely, they should think about someone they had raised turning out to be a stranger. Another student reply was, "Kids are a manifestation of our love." "Well," I responded, "what happens when your love changes and you are still stuck with them?" I would get all kinds of answers like these from my students. But, in effect, these answers show that people today do not know why they are having children.

It happened three or four times that someone in the class, usually a young woman, would raise her hand and say, "I do not want to talk about this anymore." What this means is that they know that they are going to have children, and yet they do not have the slightest idea why. And they do not want it examined. You can talk in your classes about whether God exists all semester and no one cares, because it does not seem to make any difference. But having children makes a difference and the students are frightened that they do not know about these matters.

Then they would come up with that one big answer that sounds good. They would say, "We want to have children in order to make the world a better place." And by that, they think that they ought to have a perfect child. And then you get into the notion that you can have a child only if you have everything set—that is, if you are in a good "relationship," if you have your finances in good shape, the house, and so on. As a result, of course, we absolutely destroy our children, so to speak, because we do not know how to appreciate their differences.

Now, who knows what we could possibly want when we "want a child"? The idea of want in that context is about as silly as the idea that we can marry the right person. That just does not happen. Wanting a child is particularly troubling as it finally results in a deep distrust of mentally and physically handicapped children. The crucial question for us as Christians is what kind of people we need to be to be capable of welcoming children into this world, some of whom may be born disabled and even die.

Too often we assume compassion means preventing suffering and think that we ought to prevent suffering even if it means eliminating the sufferer. In the abortion debate, the church's fundamental challenge is to challenge this ethics of compassion. There is no more fundamental issue than that. People who defend abortion defend it in the name of compassion. "We do not want any unwanted children born into the world," they say. But Christians are people who believe that any compassion that is not formed by the truthful worship of the true God cannot help but be accursed. That is the fundamental challenge that Christians must make to this world. It is not going to be easy.

Common Questions, Uncommon Answers

What about abortion in American society at large? That is, in your opinion, what would be the best abortion law for our society?

The church is not nearly at the point where she can concern herself with what kind of abortion law we should have in the United States or even in the state of North Carolina. Instead, we should start thinking about what it means for Christians to be the kind of community that can make a witness to the wider society about these matters.

Once I was giving a lecture on medical ethics at the University of Chicago Medical School. During the week before the lecture, the school's students and faculty had been discussing abortion. They had decided that, if a woman asked them to perform an abortion, they would do it because a doctor ought to do whatever a patient asks. So I said, "Let's not talk about abortion. Let's talk about suicide. Imagine that you are a doctor in the emergency room at Cook County Hospital, here on the edge of Lake Michigan. It's winter; the patient they have pulled out of the lake is cold, and he is brought to the E.R. He has a note attached to his clothing. It says, 'I've been studying the literature of suicide for the past thirty years. I now agree completely with Seneca on these matters. After careful consideration, I've decided to end my life. If I am rescued prior to my complete death, please do not resuscitate.' "

I said, "What would you do?"

"We'd try to save him, of course," they answered.

So I followed, "On what grounds? If you are going to do whatever the consumer asks you to do, you have no reason at all to save him."

So they countered, "It's our job as doctors to save life."

And I said, "Even if that is the case, why do you have the right to impose your role, your specific duties, on this man?"

After quite a bit of argument, they decided that the way to solve this problem would be to save this man the first time he comes into the E.R. The second time they would let him die.

My sense of the matter is that secular society, which assumes that you have a right to your body, has absolutely no basis for suicide prevention centers. In other words, the wider secular society has no public moral discourse about these matters.

In this kind of a setting, Christians witness to wider society first of all not by lobbying for a law against abortion, but by welcoming the children that the wider society does not want. Part of that witness might be to say to our pro-choice friends, "You are absolutely right. I don't think that any poor woman ought to be forced to have a child that she cannot afford. So let's work hard for an adequate child allowance in this country." That may not be entirely satisfactory, but that is one approach.

Should the church be creating more abortion-prevention ministries, such as homes for children?

I think that would be fine.

Let me add that I have a lot of respect for the people in Operation Rescue. However, intervention in an abortion clinic context is so humanly painful that I'm not sure what kind of witness Christians make there. But if we go to a rescue, one of the things that I think we ought to be ready to say to a woman considering an abortion is, "Will you come home and live with me until you have your child? And, if you want me to raise the child, I will." I think that that kind of witness would make a very powerful statement. The homes are good, but also I think that Christians should be the kind of people who can open our homes to a mother and her child. A lot of single people are ready to do that.

How should the church assist a woman who was raped and is pregnant? Where is justice, in a Niebuhrian sense, for her?

First, I am not a Niebuhrian. One of the problems with Niebuhr's account of sin is that it gets you into a lesser-of-two-evils argument. Because I am a pacifist, I do not want to entertain lesser-of-two-evils arguments. As you know, Christians are not about compromise. We are about being faithful.

Second, I do know some women who have been raped and who have had their children and become remarkable mothers. I am profoundly humbled by their witness.

Now, stop and think. Why is it that our church has not had much of a witness about abortion, suicide, or other such matters? We must face it: moral discourse in most of our churches is but a pale reflection of what you find in *Time* magazine. For example, when the United Methodist bishops drafted their peace pastoral, they said that most Methodist people have been pacifists or just-war people. Well that was, quite frankly, not true. I sat in on a continuing education session at Duke right after the peace pastoral came out. I asked how many of the ministers present had heard of just war prior to the pastoral. Two-thirds of the approximately one hundred ministers indicated that they had never heard of just war. The United Methodist Church has not had disciplined discourse about any of these matters.

When was the last time you preached or heard a sermon on war? Furthermore, when was the last time you preached or heard a sermon on abortion? When was the last time you preached or heard a sermon on the kind of care we ought to give to the ill? When was the last time you preached or heard a sermon on the political responsibilities of Christians? The problem is that we feel at a loss about how to make these kinds of matters part of the whole church. So, in effect, preaching betrays the church. I do not mean to put all the blame on preaching, but ministers do have opportunities to address moral issues that almost no one else in this society has—except for television. It is not much, but it is something. At least preachers can enliven a discourse that is not alive anywhere else, and people are hungering to be led by people of courage.

One of the deepest problems about these kinds of issues is that ministers fear their own congregations. But as the above sermon makes clear, this kind of sermon can be preached. And people will respond to it even when it makes them uncomfortable. And it will enhance a discourse that will make possible practices that otherwise would not be there.

Further Reading

"The Radical Hope in the Annunciation: Why Both Single and Married Christians Welcome Children" (2001), essay 24 in this volume

"Should Suffering Be Eliminated? What the Retarded Have to Teach Us" (1984), essay 28 in this volume

"Abortion: The Agent's Perspective" (1974), in *vv*

"The Demands and Limits of Care: On the Moral Dilemma of Neonatal Intensive Care" (1977), in *TT*

"Abortion: Why the Arguments Fail" (1981), in *CC*

"Why Abortion Is a Religious Issue" (1981), in *CC*

"Christianity: It's Not a Religion, It's an Adventure" (1991), essay 26 in this volume

"Killing Compassion" (1994), in *DF*

"Situation Ethics, Moral Notions, and Moral Theology" (1971), in *vv*

"The Liturgical Shape of the Christian Life: Teaching Christian Ethics as Worship" (1995), in *IGC*

"Abortion and Normative Ethics," (1991) in *vv*.

Afterword: Stanley Hauerwas's Essays in Theological Ethics: A Reader's Guide

Michael G. Cartwright

I. Learning to Read Hauerwas

Readers who have read some or all of the essays in this collection no doubt will have discovered some difficulty in reading Stanley Hauerwas's essays in theological ethics. Reading Hauerwas is not easy precisely because this theological ethicist does not condescend to his readers; indeed, he makes demands of his readers that most contemporary ethicists do not make. In addition to the fact that he reframes the questions readers bring to the subject matter, readers soon discover that they "did not know what they did not know" prior to reading Hauerwas's work. Hauerwas has an uncanny ability to penetrate the veil of unthinking ignorance that surrounds the use of clichés, slogans, and catchphrases and in so doing call his readers' attention to the fact that our moral language has "gone on holiday" (to use the words of Ludwig Wittgenstein). Other readers discover in the course of reading Hauerwas that there are other literatures and writers they need to consult, not for the purpose of understanding what Hauerwas has written, but to follow up on the connections he has helped them to see.

In the process, some readers report that reading Hauerwas's work has changed the way they think about the moral life as well as the way they think about the moral significance of the practices of Christian communities. To cite but one example: "Reading Hauerwas made me see that God genuinely intended the Church: and that the resources for its renewal lay in the habits and practices it had neglected."[1] The assertion embedded in this testimonial must not be overlooked. If contemporary Christian congregations have overlooked the significance of their most central practices, then most readers of the essays in this volume will discover that the author actively reframes the theological task. It so happens that this reader's discovery converges with Hauerwas's own sense of the proper focus of theological ethics: "Our theological task is to help

---

1. Samuel Wells, *Transforming Fate into Destiny: The Theological Ethics of Stanley Hauerwas* (Carlisle, England: Paternoster Press, 1998), xvii.

Christians discover that practices as common as praying for the sick during our common worship have implications that are as wonderful as they are frightening. I do not presume that such a theological task will best be done by theologians, but I at least want to try" (STT 7).

Herein lies one of the greatest *challenges* of reading Hauerwas's work. For serious Christian inquirers who find themselves confronting an ever wider menu of options for how to "do church" in the context of *late modern* capitalism—including gatherings where scripture is no longer read and the sick are no longer prayed for—to read that a Christian ethicist thinks the sacraments and other practices of the church provide the most significant theological context for explaining what it means for would-be Christian communities to *be* the church may stretch their credulity at the same time that they find themselves uncomfortably reminded of their own complex captivity to practices that are alien to the Christian tradition.

As one who has been reading Hauerwas's work for almost two decades, and who for the greater part of that time has been teaching undergraduates, I think I understand some of the problems that readers initially encounter in reading his work and therefore recognize the need to provide some guidance. Though I do not claim to offer a definitive reader's guide,[2] I do think that some conceptual obstacles can be identified, if not removed, making it possible for readers to engage the substance of Hauerwas's theological ethics with as few impediments as possible. In so doing, I hope to provide a kind of map of the constellation of theological interconnections that readers would encounter in any essay written by Stanley Hauerwas. As the five sections of this

2. Writing a "Reader's Guide" to Stanley Hauerwas's theological ethics feels a bit presumptuous to me for several additional reasons. First, I am well aware of the fact that there are a variety of readers and readings of Hauerwas's work, some of which are no doubt more discerning than my own. To point to three such works: "Taking Time for the Trivial: Reflections on Yet Another Book by Hauerwas," Philip Kenneson's review essay of *Christian Existence Today* in *The Asbury Theological Journal* 45, no. 1 (spring 1990): 65–74; Arne Rasmusson's *The Church as Polis: From Political Theology to Theological Politics as Exemplified by Juergen Moltmann and Stanley Hauerwas* (Notre Dame, IN: University of Notre Dame Press, 1995); and Samuel Wells's *Transforming Fate into Destiny: The Theological Ethics of Stanley Hauerwas.*

Second, there is the sheer volume of Hauerwas's work. Try as one might, it seems impossible to take into account all that he has written, and is writing even now. Third, Hauerwas has commented extensively on his own work in various books. When taken together, these "introductions" constitute a kind of running commentary that provides guidance to readers. In what follows, I will be drawing directly from Hauerwas's writings with the objective of bringing together many of these explanations within the framework of this reader's guide.

"Reader's Guide" suggest, to map these conceptual connections can *hardly* be accomplished in a linear mode—as if Hauerwas's theological ethics unfolds as a deductive mode of logic. In some sense, what I try to do in this "Reader's Guide" can best be described as a kind of spiral. Each of the five sections discusses a cluster of issues that lie at the heart of Hauerwas's project, albeit from different altitudes and directions, some of which are "above" and others "below"—and still other perspectives offered as it were *alongside*—the discourse of Hauerwas's essays. In the process, I try to provide readers with the kinds of orientation that will help them grasp the internal coherence of Hauerwas's essays. At the same time, I try to avoid giving the impression that there is some overriding systematic focus to the essays. Let it be said at the outset: there is no "system" to be found in Hauerwas's theological ethics.

Having stated that caveat, nevertheless there is a danger that I may make Hauerwas's work appear to be more consistent than it is. Indeed, to construe Hauerwas's work as a body of writing feels a bit odd because Hauerwas does not regard *anything* that he has written as being set in stone, as if there will ever be—from him or from anyone—a "last word" on the matters of theological ethics. Not only is there no one definitive volume of Hauerwas's work, readers should know that one will not be forthcoming. Nor could there be a canonical Hauerwas.

Indeed, in ways both subtle and unmistakable, Hauerwas's approach to theological ethics is deliberately *unfinished* (see pp. 654–71). But, as Hauerwas himself recognizes, the best analogy for what it means to do theological ethics is that of *learning a new language* for describing the moral world (*IGC* 12–13). There may be some value, therefore, in providing the kind of conceptual map that helps readers (new and old) to locate some of the most significant topics, strategies of argument, and implications of Hauerwas's approach. In what follows, I have tried as much as possible to use Hauerwas's own images, metaphors, and locutions. At some points, I have incorporated generous quotations from his essays not found in this collection, which I hope will serve the purpose of directing readers to other essays that they will want to read to explore these issues further. I also hope to show in what senses Hauerwas's work can be said to be *more than* "an eclectic synthesis of improbably diverse influences"[3] precisely because of the way these essays actively *reshape* the

---

3. Richard Hays, *The Moral Vision of the New Testament: Community, Cross, New Creation; A Contemporary Introduction to New Testament Ethics* (New York: HarperSanFrancisco, 1996), 254.

questions that many readers bring to his various books and essays in theological ethics and "thought experiments" in moral theology.

Doing Theology "One Brick at a Time": How Hauerwas Writes Christian Ethics
I begin by calling attention to the shape of Hauerwas's theological ethics. With a few notable exceptions, most of Hauerwas's work has been in the form of *essays*. It is important to notice the exploratory—even provisional—nature of Hauerwas's writing at the outset to account both for its provocative quality and its deliberately *unfinished* character. Drawing on a metaphor taken from his father's occupation as a bricklayer, Hauerwas has described what he does as a theological ethicist this way:

> In a sense, I am a theologian who still works like a bricklayer. You can only lay one brick at a time. Moreover, each brick you lay is different. Though bricks look quite uniform, and they often are, there are always variations that force the bricklayer to cut head joints in a manner necessary for the bond to be true. In other words, you have to adjust how you lay the next brick because of what happened when you laid the previous brick and, at the same time, in anticipation of the one to come. Moreover bricklayers may work from a blueprint, but the way the brick must be laid often means the relations between what is originally drawn and what results defies easy comparison.
>
> That much of my work is done in the form of essays is, therefore, not accidental. Composing essays is something like doing theology one brick at a time. Just as laying bricks requires as well as allows for exploration and experimentation, so does the writing of essays. Having to work in such an experimental yet conscientious fashion seems to me to be particularly appropriate, given the ecclesial challenges before us. Such work can only be done in communion. (STT 9)

I will say more about what it means to Hauerwas to read and write "in communion," but for the moment I want to explore further the metaphor of doing theology "one brick at a time." As essay 4 of this collection indicates, Hauerwas, looking back in 1986 on what he did in the late 1960s and early 1970s, now wishes that he had begun with *a different brick* than that of "character" (the subject of his dissertation later published as *Character and the Christian Life*). Such a comment should not be taken to be a retraction, but this retrospective assessment does indicate that Hauerwas takes seriously the historical—and therefore provisional—nature of all human discourse even as he takes seriously the necessity of doing theology in communion with the church.

Hauerwas's approach to doing theological ethics "one brick at a time" also takes place in the awareness that he is *reconstructing* the task of theological ethics even as he is *practicing* the craft of the theologian. The "bricks" he has chosen to use have shifted over time, and so the conceptual vocabulary of his essays has also shifted. Whereas the early essays discuss "vision" and "character," Hauerwas's more recent explorations discuss the "timefulness" of Christian existence in relation to the eschatological character of Jesus' proclamation of the Kingdom of God. Although some conceptual tools—narrative, for example—appear frequently in essays he has written since 1980, it is also true that his usage of these tools has shifted[4] in discernible ways as he has engaged the uses to which other theologians and ethicists have put these ideas. (For an explanation of Hauerwas's own shifting use of "narrative" in relation to the proclamation of the church see essays 7, 8, and 9 in this volume.) It is not possible here to chart the full significance of this and other conceptual shifts in Hauerwas's theological ethics, but readers should be aware of the fact that the essays found in this collection do display these shifts, to greater and lesser degrees, given the fact that the essays were written over a thirty-year period.[5]

The choice of the essay also can be said to indicate something significant about Hauerwas's disposition to his subject matter. Unlike many other twentieth-century Christian ethicists, Hauerwas has "never felt the need to react against Christianity in the way many seem to do whose background provided more confidence that they knew in fact what Christianity involved both as belief and behavior." Early in his intellectual pilgrimage, he came to believe that he "did not understand Christianity well enough to deserve an opinion. Indeed I still often feel that this is the case. . . . For me it has always been more a matter of trying to understand what we Christians should believe

4. Wells, *Transforming Fate into Destiny.* Chapters 1–8 of Wells's book chart seven shifts in Hauerwas's essays in theological ethics: *from quandary to character, from character to story, from story to community, from community to church, from space to time, from tragedy to irony,* all of which work together to refocus theological ethics *from fate to destiny.*

5. Although each of these conceptual tools is subject to precise definition in the context of his usage in particular essays, the editors of this anthology have chosen not to provide a glossary of the terms—as if the terms could be "frozen in time" or to suggest a consistency of use that Hauerwas has neither claimed for himself nor sought. Indeed, discerning readers will notice that Hauerwas himself describes his own reservations about "narrative theology" and "postmodernism" as well as other intellectual moods, currents, and theological trends of the past three decades.

and do" (PK, xix). Because Hauerwas does not approach his task with the presupposition that he *already knows* "what Christianity is," he writes from the perspective of the "semi-Christian," disposed to discover the truth of what it would mean to live the truth of Christianity. Hauerwas invites the reader to inquire with him and therefore to acquire a certain set of dispositions, including the intellectual virtue of truthfulness. It may or may not be the case that Hauerwas actively "constructs" his intended reader (as truthful explorer of what Christianity might be about),[6] but there can be no doubt that he disconcerts many readers with his audacious humor, acute analytic ability, and ingenious argumentation.

Back to "the Rough Ground": Unfolding Hauerwas's Theological Project

If the way Hauerwas gets to where he is going is through essays, what is the destination? At various points along the way, Hauerwas has provided explanations for his way of construing the theological task. For example, in the introduction to *Sanctify Them in the Truth,* he states: "If the way I do theology is in any sense new, and I certainly do not desire to do anything unique, it is my conviction that theologically we have to get back to the rough ground" (STT, 7). What is "the rough ground" to which Hauerwas is referring, and where is it that theological ethicists have been that they must get back to the rough ground?

Although Hauerwas provides several different answers to this question—in some sense, the whole body of his work serves as the only full answer—at minimum it involves a profound shift in focus about what is important about the activity or endeavor of doing theology. As Hauerwas states with clarity: "Theology is always a matter of finding the interconnections in a manner that helps our lives not to be distorted by overemphasis on one aspect of faith. . . . That theology works like a web helps us understand why the work of theology is never done. Webs, after all, are fragile. They must constantly be redone." For this reason, Hauerwas resists those who urge him to "pull it all together" in a grand system of theological ethics, because he believes that "attempts to do so impose false unity on the wonderful anarchy of life called church" (STT 2,4). This comment is instructive. Hauerwas's theological project is one of reconstruction in the midst of contesting claims that would seek to eliminate the

---

6. Hauerwas has observed that he first discovered this way of engaging the reader in the context of a course taught by Paul Holmer that he took his first year at Yale Divinity School in which he read Kierkegaard's reflections about his point of view as an author with respect to the kind of readers he wanted to cultivate for his theological writings.

"wonderful anarchy" of the church in favor of one or another regime. By contrast, Hauerwas prefers to spend his time reconstructing the "web" of Christian theology in the awareness that this task will never be complete and must always take place with an awareness of the provisionality and fragility of the interconnections that are made.

For this reason, Hauerwas refuses to abide by the disciplinary distinctions that inform the work of many other Protestant, Catholic, and Orthodox theological ethicists. "Theologians must attempt to help those of us who worship God make the connections that such worship requires but also makes possible. The stories we will need to tell in order to make such connections will require that we defy current academic specializations, particularly those that presently dominate theological curricula" (STT 4). This is no idle comment coming from Stanley Hauerwas. More than most essays by theological ethicists working today, his essays engage a wide array of disciplines, ranging from literary criticism and social theory to anthropology and the history and philosophy of science. Hauerwas's work calls for nothing less than the *reshaping* of the curricula of seminaries, and more broadly of universities.

Hauerwas's theological project also involves questioning the institutions, practices, dispositions, and habits that have been formed under the conditions of Christendom, which imaged the unity of church and world under the (official or unofficial) sponsorship of so-called Christian governments from Constantine to so-called Christian America. The name of the first Christian emperor has come to be associated with the complex of institutional changes and alliances that led Christians in the West to see churches and nation-states to be aligned within a God-given order within which Christians would exercise leadership. The vestiges of this "Constantinian synthesis," while obviously weakened and unstable, continue to tempt contemporary Christians to believe that they don't have to take responsibility for the church's own discourse and practices because the powers that be (whether the Emperor Constantine or the latest incumbent of the White House) are "Christian" and Christianity is on the side of Western "progress." But then, as Hauerwas has observed on more than one occasion, "Constantinianism is a hard habit to break. It is particularly hard when it seems that we can do so much good by remaining 'in power.' It is hard to break because all our categories have been set by the church's establishment as a necessary part of Western civilization" (AC 19).

One way to think about what Hauerwas does is to consider that each of the bricks he lays (essays he writes) constitutes an attempt to *reconstruct* what Christianity can be—*apart from* (or in opposition to) the conditions imposed by the Constantinian context in which Western Christians for the most part have lived. In *Resident Aliens* (1989), Hauerwas and Willimon provide an evocative description of the era (before 1963) when Christians in America believed that "The church was the only show in town." Rather than lamenting the demise of the Constantinian worldview, Hauerwas sees this as an opportunity to celebrate: "The decline of the old, Constantinian synthesis between the church and the world means that we American Christians are at last free to be faithful in a way that makes being a Christian today an exciting adventure" (*RA* 16–18). As this statement suggests, Hauerwas's conception of freedom *for obedience* is very different from the sense of freedom *from constraint* that is so pervasive in American culture in general and the academic context of universities in particular (see, for example, the interview with Hauerwas in essay 26). This adventurous sense of freedom displayed by Hauerwas in the midst of the ruins of "modernist" paradigms of Christian existence is an appropriate place to begin in trying to explain in which ways Hauerwas's essays can be said to "reframe" the questions of theological ethics.

II. Reframing Theological Ethics by Changing the Questions

The Church as God's New Language

Frequently, readers of Stanley Hauerwas's essays in Christian theological ethics find themselves astonished to discover the power of the questions that Hauerwas encourages Christians to ask when they reembark on the quest for truth. Readers particularly notice the probing nature of Hauerwas's questions as they begin to realize the implications of the "flight from authority"[7] that describes modern Christianity's quest to establish the foundations of Christianity through the use of Enlightenment conceptions of autonomous reason. As essay 1 in this collection explains, from Hauerwas's angle of vision the history of "how Christian ethics came to be" cannot be told apart from confronting the issue of the authority of Christian discourse in relation to Christian practices. Properly understood, Hauerwas argues (see essay 7 in this collection) that the Church itself is to be the truthful company of sanctified people whose lives refer to—that is, bear witness to the truth of—the Triune God.

Hauerwas is fully aware of the revolutionary implications of what he is

---

7. Here I borrow the title of Jeffrey Stout's brilliant study of moral reflection prior to and during the Enlightenment, *The Flight from Authority: Religion, Morality, and the Quest for Autonomy* (Notre Dame, IN: University of Notre Dame Press, 1981).

doing, as he indicated in his 1995 introduction to *In Good Company:* "I am trying to foment a modest revolution by forcing Christians to take themselves seriously as Christians. Such an ambition means that I am not simply trying to give new answers to old questions, but I am trying to change the questions. . . . To change the questions involves nothing less than learning to speak differently. To learn a language, as anyone knows who teaches or has learned a second language, requires repetition" (*IGC* 12–13). Readers of the essays in this volume, then, should not be surprised to discover thematic repetitions. This should not be mistaken as mere redundancy. In line with Hauerwas's metaphor of learning a new language, the repetition of themes, images, and arguments in his essays has the pedagogical purpose of helping the reader to learn to think *theologically* about ethics.

Questioning the Standard Account(s) of Ethics

Much of twentieth-century ethics, religious and nonreligious alike, has been a contest between deontological (duty-oriented) and teleological (consequence-oriented) approaches to ethics. The effect of this contestation has been to focus attention on various "ethical dilemmas" without questioning the account of Enlightenment rationality that underwrites this moral framework. Throughout his career, Hauerwas has questioned this "standard account of rationality" as it can be discerned in the works of such diverse moral philosophers as Immanuel Kant, R. M. Hare, William Frankena, and John Rawls.[8] The chain of neo-Kantian reasoning that informs the account of morality that Hauerwas opposes can be stated in its most elemental form this way: "People have different genes, different upbringings, different traditions, different motives. But they all do pretty much the same actions. By grounding morality in actions, and by chiefly discussing the rightness of actions, a rational debate can continue, and people of all traditions can meet without the constant threat of violence."[9]

By contrast, Hauerwas argues that *there is no foundation* to be abstracted from moral reflection. As a result, he rejects the contention that there is (or needs to be) a "common ground" constituting the descriptive and prescriptive

8. Two essays where Hauerwas offers extended argumentation against the standard account of morality are "Obligation and Virtue Once More" and "From System to Story: An Alternative Pattern for Rationality in Ethics," in *TT*.

9. Wells, *Transforming Fate into Destiny,* 14. Wells draws on the summary of neo-Kantian principles articulated by Gregory Trianosky in his essay "What Is Virtue Ethics All About?" in *American Philosophical Quarterly* 27, no. 4 (October 1990): 335.

dimensions of ethics. Hauerwas's counterargument can be summarized this way: "What is the use of discussing the rightness of actions, if two people can do the same 'action' with hugely differing aspirations, purposes, styles, colleagues, antagonists, and with very different descriptions and understandings of what they are doing?"[10] Not content with reifications and left-right political and theological oppositions, Hauerwas charts *a third way* that is not so much the mean between the extremes as it is a *redefinition of the field* of moral debate as such. His tack in such a circumstance is to offer such a powerful set of moral exemplars that the framework of conversation itself starts to shift.

The Embodiment of Christian Virtues

The kinds of moral examples that Hauerwas offers typically involve one or more *virtues,* which he understands to be embodiments of moral excellence that are enacted in the context of the exercise of practical reason. Unlike some religious ethicists whose use of virtue language is formal, Hauerwas typically calls attention to the complex but well-defined ways that virtues are embedded in the practices of historical communities. Thus, it is not uncommon to discover Hauerwas offering theological reflections about the virtues of peaceableness, patience, and hope as well as the moral significance of the practice of justice, temperance, and prudence, especially as the latter are informed by the substance of the Christian faith. The formation of moral excellence (virtue) in the lives of Christian communities constitutes a very significant aspect of Hauerwas's reconfiguration of theological ethics (for more on this topic, see pp. 639–54). This emphasis on the virtues informs one of the most prominent reframing arguments found in his books and essays; Hauerwas has repeatedly stated, "The church does not *have* a social ethic, but *is* a social ethic."[11]

What does he mean by this claim? As Hauerwas explains, it involves refocusing what we think Christian "social ethics" is as a form of moral inquiry: "The claim . . . is an attempt to remind us that the church is the place where the story of God is enacted, told, and heard. Christian social ethics is not first of all principles or policies for social action but rather the story of God's calling Israel and of the life of Jesus. That story requires the formation of a corresponding community which has learned to live in a way that makes it

10. Ibid. (Wells paraphrasing Hauerwas.)
11. The essay where Hauerwas provides the fullest programmatic discussion of this dictum is "The Gesture of a Truthful Story," *CET,* 101–10.

possible for them to hear that story" (CET 101). (For more on this set of issues, see essays 5 and 9 in this volume.)

THE SKILLS AND GESTURES OF THE CHURCH Some readers might object that at its best the kind of church that Hauerwas is talking about exists as little more than a set of gestures. But such readers might be surprised to learn that Hauerwas agrees, and then proceeds to show that the problem is that we need to pay more attention to the moral significance of these very gestures: "I am ready to concede that the church and Christian social ethics as I have tried to depict it are but gestures, but I do not think that to be a damaging admission. Nothing in life is more important than gestures, as gestures embody as well as sustain the valuable and significant. Through gestures we create and form our worlds. Through gestures we make contact with one another and share common tasks. Through gestures we communicate and learn from each other the limits of our world. . . . In this sense, the church is but God's gesture on behalf of the world to create a space and time in which we might have a foretaste of the kingdom" (CET 106).

This discussion of gestures, narrative, and the church as a social ethic also has important implications for the role of practical reason in Christian ethics—as Hauerwas's discussion of baptism and eucharist makes very clear: "Through baptism and eucharist we are initiated into God's life by our becoming part of Jesus' life, death, and resurrection. These are essential gestures of the church; we cannot be church without them. They are, in effect, essential reminders for the constitution of God's people in the world. Without them, we are constantly tempted to turn God into an ideology to supply our wants and needs rather than have our needs and wants transformed by God's capturing our attention through the mundane life of Jesus of Nazareth" (CET 107). The sacraments of baptism and eucharist, then, must be understood to be "essential gestures" through which we learn *the skills* to be Christians, but they are not the only such gestures. Hauerwas argues that the gestures Christians embody that constitute the proper focus of Christian social ethics are precisely the kinds of gestures that can be done with the mentally handicapped.[12] (For more on this theme, see essays 27 and 28 in this volume.)

---

12. Ibid., 107–10. This is but one reason why, over and over again, Hauerwas has pointed to Jean Vanier's L'Arche community and other Christian communities that offer hospitality to the mentally handicapped as an example of what it means to be church. For a profound discussion of the practice of foot washing in the context of the L'Arche community that is convergent with Hauerwas's discussion of the gestures of the church's liturgy, see Jean Vanier's *The Scandal of Service: Jesus Washes Our Feet* (New York: Continuum Books, 1998).

Thus, the skills required for "Christian existence today" can be acquired by children, adults, and the mentally handicapped through participation in the church's liturgy. "Thus liturgy is not a motive for social action, it is not a cause to effect. Liturgy is social action. Through liturgy we are shaped to live rightly the story of God, to become part of that story, and are thus able to recognize and respond to the saints in our midst. Once we recognize that the church is a social ethic—an ethic that is, to be sure, but a gesture—then we can appreciate how every activity of the church is a means and an opportunity for faithful service to and for the world. We believe that the gesture that is the church is nothing less than the sign of God's salvation of the world" (CET 107).

WITTGENSTEINIAN EMPHASIS ON VISION   Hauerwas has said that his essays are supposed to work like Ludwig Wittgenstein's epigrams. That is to say, his theological ethics focuses attention on what appears to be the ordinary commonplaces of life, and reminds his readers of the significance of the way they use language to describe the moral life. In a sense, Hauerwas's dictum "The church does not *have* a social ethic, but *is* a social ethic" has the same logical force as Wittgenstein's dictum "*Don't think; look!*" That is to say, it *reorients* the discussion by calling attention to the mistaken focus of the question(s) being asked. Thus, Hauerwas contends over and over again: "To be a Christian in effect is learning to see the world in a certain way and thus become as we see" (*VV* 29). *To become as we see,* however, requires that we *learn the moral language* of Christian discipleship. From this it follows: "The task of Christian ethics is to help us see how our convictions *are* in themselves a morality" (*PK* 16). In sum, Hauerwas argues that we must ask a different set of questions. As he learned from H. Richard Niebuhr, we must ask *What is going on?* before we can intelligibly engage the question *What must we do?*

Hauerwas observes that when we stop to ask ourselves *What is going on?* with respect to the ordinary practices of contemporary social life, one of the most notable problems for which we must account is *the absence of memory* which results in the church's incapacity to reinterpret its own most sacred texts. "That we no longer consider remembering as an ethical or political task manifests our questionable assumption that ethics primarily concerns decisions whereas politics brokers power" (CC 53). In such a circumstance, the nature of moral authority (in relation to traditions and communities) is obscured by a politics of *amnesia,* which leaves people without the moral skills to combat self-deception not only with respect to one's own existence (see essays 10 and 11), but also in relation to the Holocaust (27), war (19 and 20), and euthanasia and suicide (29).

The Morality of Remembering: Authority, Politics, and Tradition

Even after taking into account the fact that Hauerwas engages contemporary ethical issues with a set of philosophical and theological assumptions very different from what they have encountered elsewhere, many readers nevertheless find themselves puzzled by the distinctive way Hauerwas engages and uses scripture, reason, tradition, and experience in his essays in theological ethics. In many instances, readers find themselves wrestling with the way Hauerwas understands the complex relationship of authority, politics, and tradition before they are able to grasp what he is doing with respect to scripture, reason, and experience.

HAUERWAS'S CRITIQUE OF LIBERALISM   The struggle that readers experience with this aspect of Hauerwas's work has everything to do with his external critique[13] of liberalism as the regnant political theory that informs the social context of contemporary American life. Unfolding this nexus of complex issues will involve several steps. First, it must be said that Hauerwas discusses liberalism as "a many-faced and historically ambiguous phenomenon" (CC 77). This said, he is also aware of the pervasive influence of this political theory in the United States, a nation where the citizenry has assumed that "unlike other societies, we are not creatures of history, but that we have the possibility of a new beginning. We are thus able to form our government on the basis of principle rather than the arbitrary elements of tradition" (CC 78).

Hauerwas regards this as a profound distortion of American history, but he does not doubt the power of the mythology that enfolds the American people.[14] "Liberalism is successful exactly because it supplies us with a myth that seems to make sense of our social origins. . . . In the absence of any shared history we seemed to lack anything in common that could serve as the basis

---

13. This comment is not intended to suggest that Hauerwas does not employ internal critiques of liberalism—indeed, his critiques of Rousseau et al. in essay 20 provide abundant evidence that he does do so with acute effect—but simply to point out that those arguments that bear the primary thrust of his critique are external to the terms and assumptions of liberal political theory. Hauerwas's critique of liberalism is external in at least three senses: (1) Part of his critique of liberalism can be sustained whether you are a Christian or not, and in that sense he can be said to write on behalf of a variety of "outsiders" in American culture for whom the policies and procedures of liberalism simply do not work; (2) his critique of liberalism is not always theologically specific in the ways that it might be; (3) the critique is not internal to the constructive position he is trying to develop with respect to the church as a polis.

14. See "Tale of Two Stories: On Being a Christian and Being a Texan" in CET for a fascinating example of the way Hauerwas analyzes the clashing myths of the Old South and West in relation to the identity formation of southern white males in Texas.

for social cooperation . . . . liberalism provided that philosophical account of society designed to deal with exactly that problem: a people do not need a shared history; all they need is a system of rules that will constitute procedures for resolving disputes as they pursue their various interests. Thus liberalism is a political philosophy committed to the proposition that a social order and corresponding mode of government can be formed on self-interest and consent" (CC 78).

According to Hauerwas's analysis, then, the "moral adventure" projected by liberalism has been to develop a culture and government that left the individual to his or her own desires by rendering the coercive nature of the state and society so diffuse as to be invisible. As a result the coercive aspects of our social order are hidden, since they take the appearance of being self-imposed. Yet the distrust of the other inherent in liberal social and political theory cannot help but create powers that claim our loyalties and destructively run our lives. "Ironically, the most coercive aspect of the liberal account of the world is that we are free to make up our own story. The story that liberalism teaches us is that we have no story, and as a result we fail to notice how deeply that story determines our lives. Accordingly, we fail to recognize the coercive form of the liberal state, as it, like all states, finally claims our loyalty under the self-deceptive slogan that in a democracy the people rule themselves because they have 'consented' to be so ruled" (CC 84).

These are but a few of the reasons why Hauerwas regards the politics of liberalism as *inherently* self-deceptive. In teaching us to "flee" from all moral authorities other than the self, liberalism actually leads toward the self-deception of those enslaved to slogans and simulacra in the name of a "freedom" that actively undermines our capacity to seek the good truthfully.

THE POLITICS OF AUTHORITY   In contrast to the morally impoverished self portrayed in liberal political theory, Hauerwas operates with an enriched "political" understanding of authority that engages some of the best work in political theory and social and political philosophy. Drawing on the theories of political philosopher Yves Simon,[15] Hauerwas argues that "the very meaning of authority is community-dependent. Though authority is often confused with power or coercion, it draws its life from community in a quite

15. Those readers who are interested in following up on Hauerwas's critique of liberalism would do well to start by reading Yves Simon's book *A General Theory of Authority* (Notre Dame, IN: University of Notre Dame Press, 1962, 1980). Like Simon, Hauerwas has refused to dwell on the all too familiar *symptoms* of the political-intellectual crises of our time. Instead, he has devoted his intellectual gifts to penetrating the *causes* of these crises.

different manner. Like power, authority is directive; unlike power, however, it takes its rationale not from the deficiencies of community, but from the intrinsic demands of a common life. The meaning of authority must be grounded in a community's self-understanding, which is embodied in its habits, customs, laws, and traditions; for this embodiment constitutes the community's pledge to provide the means for an individual more nearly to approach the truth" (cc 60).

What is truth? What Hauerwas has in mind here is extricably theological at the same time that it is political. In *The Truth about God,* Hauerwas makes this point clear with respect to the Ten Commandments. He contends that "before the Ten Commandments are about us, they are about God" (TG, 19). Later he states that the Commandments are "a chief means by which our lives are bent toward the way and will of God. This is not a bad definition of worship in spirit and truth—*bending life toward God*" (TG 22). According to Hauerwas, the justifiability of the truth claims embedded in such practices is to be displayed, not via philosophical "certitude" allegedly founded on Enlightenment conceptions of "autonomous" reason, but rather with respect to the grammar of specifically theological convictions—convictions like the affirmation that "Jesus Christ is Lord"—as displayed in the character of actual *lives that are lived.* For Hauerwas, theology is futile unless it is "governed by the witness" of such lives as Martin Luther King Jr., Dietrich Bonhoeffer, and Dorothy Day. Hauerwas declares that "there is no 'foundation' more sure than the existence of such lives" (IGC, 49).[16] For this reason, Hauerwas tends to speak of the "truthfulness" of the characters of persons who have bent their lives toward God in the context of living traditions where practices are socially embodied in ways that make the display of moral virtues and moral vices intelligible.

The active pursuit of the truth, then, according to Hauerwas takes place in communal contexts of conversation and struggle that reveal the "fundamentally political" relationship of tradition and authority. "Although revolutions may occur without tradition, politics depends upon tradition, for politics is

16. For a provocative account of the conditions of the truth claims of Christian theology, see Hauerwas's essay "The Church's One Foundation Is Jesus Christ Her Lord; Or, In a World Without Foundations: All We Have Is the Church," in *IGC,* 49. At the beginning of this same essay, Hauerwas cites with approval the seminal book by James Wm. McClendon Jr. and James M. Smith, *Understanding Religious Convictions* (Notre Dame, IN: University of Notre Dame Press, 1975). This book has been reissued in a revised edition under the new title *Convictions: Defusing Religious Relativism* (Valley Forge, PA: Trinity Press International, 1994).

nothing else but a community's internal conversation with itself concerning the various possibilities of understanding and extending its life. In fact, the very discussion necessary to maintain the tradition can be considered an end in itself, since it provides the means for the community to discover the goods it holds in common. Without the authority of the tradition to guide such a discussion there would be no possibility of the community drawing nearer to the truth about itself and the world" (cc 61). Thus, the need to bend. Given this position, it is intriguing to observe that some of Hauerwas's most probing discussions of the failures of liberalism turn out to be his essays in medical ethics (see essays 27 and 28, as well as "Authority and the Profession of Medicine" in sp 39–62).

In contrast with those who propose to regard authority according to theories of deficiency, Hauerwas (following Simon) proceeds with the plurality of moral choices in full view: "Authority is required, not because there is any one perception of the common good that controls all others, but because there are many ways of seeking such a good. The necessity of authority grows from the fact that morality unavoidably involves judgments that by their nature are particular and contingent—that is, they could be otherwise. Tradition is but the history of a community's sharing of such judgments as they have been tested through generations. Authority is not, therefore, an external force that commands against our will; rather it proceeds from a common life made possible by tradition. Authority is not only compatible with freedom, but requires it, since the continued existence and excellence of the community is possible only by forming and perfecting new members. Yet freedom is not an end in itself, but the necessary condition for a community to come to a more truthful understanding of itself and the world" (cc 62). Here is where Hauerwas's disagreement with liberal political theory is most pointed: the relationship of freedom to moral authority. Hauerwas's considered response to those who accuse him of being a "sectarian" is that they do not grasp the significance of his understanding of the common good. If, as he argues, the common good for Christians is rightly understood as God, then it would be more apt to charge Hauerwas with being a theocrat without a state.

Hauerwas draws on this *positive* conception of freedom and authority for the purpose of describing the moral and political challenge of what it means "for the church to be a 'contrast model' for all politics that know not God" (cc 84). The theme of the church as a polis becomes even more prominent in Hauerwas's later essays (see essays 19 through 26). Over and over Hauerwas stresses that Christians in American culture already "have a language to de-

scribe the problems of liberalism, but we have become hesitant and embarrassed to use it" (cc 85–86). This is part of what has concerned Hauerwas
about the use of natural law rhetoric to engage the powers that be in this
cultural context. Where Christians (Catholic or Protestant) use the language
of "natural law" in such a way as to bless the status quo while neglecting to
engage the immoral structures of political communities, natural law reasoning is self-deceived.[17] These statements at the level of political theory inform
Hauerwas's way of engaging scripture and the Christian traditions as well as
the way he reasons about and in relation to narratives of human experience.

III. The Church as Polis: Reconstructing Ecclesial Authority

Though not all readers of Hauerwas's work are equally interested in the issues
of political theory that surround his objections to political liberalism's account of the self as an individual, many readers do find Hauerwas's way of
discussing scripture, reason, experience, and tradition to be provocative precisely because he does not treat these topics in the ways that most mainline
Protestant theologians have discussed these sources of Christian theology.
Indeed, it is precisely the way that Hauerwas reconfigures the interaction of
these sources in the course of reconstructing ecclesial authority that gives his
work its radical distinctiveness as neither "liberal" nor "conservative" (in the
usual ways those terms are used), while also converging in new and provocative ways with affirmations found in various Catholic, Orthodox, and Protestant traditions of Christian theology.

Not Sola Scriptura But Reading in Liturgical Community

It has become a commonplace for Christian ethicists to discuss the "problem"
of the use of scripture in Christian ethics as if the problem lies in the *meaningful appropriation of the text* of the Bible *as we attempt to apply it* to the context
of human experience at the beginning of the third millennium. Thus Christian ethicists often distinguish between "what it means" and "what it meant,"
as if the problem lies in the text of the books of the Christian Bible. By con-

17. As Hauerwas has also shown in such essays as "Gay Friendship: A Thought Experiment in
Catholic Moral Theology" (stt), he is actively interested in natural law discussions that are
not determined by the politics of liberalism and Constantinian presuppositions but that seek
to spell out theological accounts of "the natural." In this respect, Hauerwas sees himself as not
in fundamental conflict with Thomistic accounts of natural law, but rather he objects to the
role played by Kant's conception of natural law in twentieth-century Catholic moral theology.

trast, Hauerwas declares that "the problem is not in our scriptures but in ourselves" (cc 238 n.5). This simple statement redirects readers away from decades of mainstream Protestant and American Catholic debate about the moral authority of scripture, and toward the context of the gathered community at worship, a context that Hauerwas argues is inextricably *political* in character.

Instead of wrapping himself in methodological knots about how to "use" scripture, Hauerwas calls attention to the distortions already embedded in the question of what it means to "use" scripture in Christian ethics. It is not that we must first clarify the meaning of the text and only then are we able to inquire about its moral implications for how we are to live our lives. Rather, Hauerwas says, the authority of scripture is already *political* in nature. "By 'political' I do not mean . . . that Scripture should be used as an ideology for justifying the demands of the oppressed. The authority of Scripture derives its intelligibility from the existence of a community that knows its life depends on faithful remembering of God's care in his creation through the calling of Israel and the life of Jesus" (cc 53).

The "politics" of memory, then, involves the very way in which a community of faith is constituted. Drawing on the work of John Howard Yoder, Hauerwas invokes the "free church alternative" to the oppositions of classical Protestantism's tendency to locate authority in the perspicuity and objectivity of the words of scripture and Catholicism's tendency to cede authority to those who hold ecclesial office at any given time: "The free church alternative . . . recognizes the inadequacies of the text of Scripture standing alone uninterpreted and appropriates the promise of the guidance of the spirit throughout the ages, but locates the fulfillment of that promise in the assembly of those who gather around Scripture in the face of a given real moral challenge. Any description of the substance of ethical decision-making criteria is incomplete if this aspect of its communitarian and contemporary form is omitted" (cc 57).[18] Although Hauerwas does not spell out *all that he could have said* about this "free church understanding of the significance of community" (cc 54), what he does say in this context is consistent with his contention that Christian ethics must counter the Constantinian habits of the past. "The scripture's authority for that life consists in its being used so that it helps to

18. Hauerwas is quoting Yoder, "Radical Reformation Ethics in Ecumenical Perspective," *Journal of Ecumenical Studies* (fall 1978): 657. See also Yoder's *Priestly Kingdom: Social Ethics as Gospel* (Notre Dame, IN: University of Notre Dame Press, 1984), 117.

nurture and reform the community's self-identity as well as the personal character of its members" (CC 55). For Hauerwas, this is a claim about the *narrative* character of scripture, but it would be a mistake to think that this is a formalistic claim. Rather, he contends that reading scripture in community serves a constitutive purpose by *shaping* the way persons-in-community come to see the world and themselves. In sum, the church is the *irreplaceable locus* of authority for reading scripture.

In this respect, Hauerwas's work sometimes rings familiar bells for Catholic readers; that is, he sees the liturgy as shaping the lives of those who would be disciples. Indeed, part of what he understands it to mean for Christians to live "under authority" is to be willing to accept the discipline of the church's practices of preaching and the sacraments. In these and other respects, Hauerwas clearly understands scripture and Christian tradition to be in relation to one another, although it would be a mistake to think that his position is in any simple sense identical with that of the Roman Catholic Church, as some critics have charged.[19] Although Hauerwas has clearly not worked through all the implications of the claim, he has made clear that the interpretive enterprise of reading scripture is always located in the web of ecclesial practices, skills, and gestures.

This also partially explains why Hauerwas typically sees fundamentalists and biblical critics as reflecting the same interpretive defect.

> Fundamentalists and biblical critics alike fail to acknowledge the political character of their account of the Bible, and they fail to do so for very similar reasons. They want to disguise how their "interpretations" underwrite the privileges of the constituency that they serve. Admittedly, such realities may also be hidden from themselves, convinced as they are of the "objectivity" of their method. Accordingly, fundamentalism and biblical criticism are Enlightenment ideologies in the service of the fictive agent of the Enlight-

---

19. In this respect, I think Richard Hays's discussion of Hauerwas's use of tradition in *The Moral Vision of the New Testament* is misleading when he claims that "the logic of Hauerwas's hermeneutical position should require him to become Roman Catholic" (265). Although Hauerwas does discuss the Catholic Church's view of the role of scripture and tradition in *Unleashing the Scriptures,* 22–24, he also discusses the role of tradition in the Orthodox Church as well. The point in both cases is the hermeneutical necessity of the church as the social embodiment of the text. Hays appears to have forgotten that Hauerwas's original claim about the importance of the interpretative community was made in the context of explicating the "free church" vision of the church. In sum, the hermeneutical logic of Hauerwas's position is compatible with at least two Christian traditions.

enment—namely the rational individual—who believes that truth in general (and particularly the truth of the Christian faith) can be known without initiation into a community that requires transformation of the self. In this sense, fundamentalism and biblical criticism are attempts to maintain the influence of Constantinian Christianity—now clothed in the power of Enlightenment rationality—in the interest of continuing Christianity's hegemony over the ethos of North American cultures. (*us* 35)

Hauerwas's account of the political dimension of the moral authority of scripture has significant implications for the interpretation of the Bible inside (and outside) the context of the church's use: "I suspect that hermeneutics becomes the preoccupation of theology when the text of Scripture is divorced from particular practices of the church that makes it make sense in the first place" (*us* 18). As a result, Hauerwas observes that ironically both the fundamentalist and the biblical critic "share the assumption that the text of the Bible should make sense (to anyone), apart from the uses the Church has for Scripture" (*us* 18). In contrast to this assumption that has arisen under the social conditions of modernity, Hauerwas pointedly calls attention to the kinds of "communal presuppositions necessary for a Christian use of Scripture," which include, but are not limited to, the celebration of the eucharist by people who are in communion with one another through Christ (*us* 22). Hauerwas agrees with the contention of Orthodox theologian Georges Florovsky that "the sin of the Reformation" has been to cut off scripture from its sacred source, thereby making the church *incidental* to interpretation (*us* 27).

Hauerwas does not pretend to have resolved all the questions about authority and tradition that begin to surface once one moves beyond the fundamentalist-modernist controversies that have distorted the memory of mainstream Protestant Christianity in American culture. But he does recognize that this requires both a stronger conception of "accountable discipleship" than is found in most liberal Protestant congregations and/or a stronger conception of the bishop's "teaching office" than most episcopal leaders are able to embody in mainline Protestant denominations like the United Methodist Church. By attending to the kinds of *communal* presuppositions and specifically *ecclesial* practices that are still present in Catholic, Anabaptist, and Orthodox practices of interpreting the Bible, Hauerwas's essays have challenged mainline Protestants to begin to recognize the potential significance of their own worship practices for the interpretation of scripture. But to do so involves exploring the ways in which the interaction of scripture and liturgy in such practices as the eucharist engage strata of the Jewish and Christian traditions that are quite radical indeed. Liturgical embodiments of scripture involve gestures and practices the moral significance of which is inextricably related to the ways Jews and Christians tell the story of God's way with Israel and the church. Moreover, Hauerwas understands that to state the matter this way calls him (and his readers) to reengage the conflicted conversation with the Jewish tradition(s) while also taking more seriously the radical implications of the practices of interpretation that are embedded in Christian liturgies.

Reengaging Judaism and Christianity as Radical Traditions

As the foregoing discussion makes clear, Hauerwas advocates nothing less than a "return to the text" of the Bible, which means "a commitment to displaying the richness and wisdom of traditions that are at once text-based, hermeneutical, and oriented to communal practice."[20] This statement already signals that Hauerwas thinks it is a mistake to discuss biblical texts *as if* they exist apart from traditions and practices. An even more significant indicator about Hauerwas's conception of tradition is that he *does not* treat Christianity as existing apart from Judaism because for Hauerwas the story that Christians claim about Jesus *cannot be separated* from the story of Israel as narrated in the Christian canon of the Old Testament (see essay 6 in this volume).

Accordingly, Hauerwas understands scripture texts as existing fundamentally in relation to the Jewish and Christian liturgies. At one point, he speculates that "part of the reason for the misuse of the scripture in matters dealing with morality is that the text was isolated from the liturgical context. There is certainly nothing intrinsically wrong with individuals reading and studying scripture, but such reading must be guided by the use of the scripture through the liturgies of the church. For the shape of the liturgy over a whole year prevents any one part of scripture from being given undue emphasis in relation to the narrative line of scripture. The liturgy, in every performance and over a whole year, rightly contextualizes individual passages when we cannot read the whole . . . 'the liturgy is scripture's home rather than its stepchild, and

---

20. See the editors' statement coauthored by Stanley Hauerwas and Peter Ochs in ww, iii. This same statement describes the strategic goal of the Radical Traditions: Theology in a Postcritical Key series of books: to assemble "a promising matrix of strategies, disciplines, and lines of thought that invites Jewish, Christian, and Islamic theologians back to the word, recovering and articulating modes of scriptural reasoning as that which always underlies modernist reasoning and therefore has the capacity—and authority—to correct it."

the Hebrew and Christian bibles were the church's first liturgical books' " (cc 240 n.9).[21]

According to Hauerwas then, the coexistence of Judaism and Christianity in relation to the Hebrew scriptures and the New Testament makes for a highly complex relationship surrounded by several sets of questions. First, although the question of what Christians mean by identifying God as "Triune" has not always seemed important given the challenge of Jewish survival in a world dominated by Christians, the fact that the doctrine of the Trinity is used to identify the character of God described in the writings of the Old Testament means that Christians and Jews will continue to have reason to contest one another's readings of scripture. Thus, Hauerwas's explorations of the moral significance of the Ten Commandments for Christian living proceeds with the Trinitarian character of God clearly in view.[22] In no sense does Hauerwas attempt to eliminate the tension between Jewish and Christian ways of characterizing the identity of God.

Second, Hauerwas reminds Christians that "our ethics cannot be abstracted from our conviction that Jesus Christ is God's messiah—very God and very man. The church may have decisively rejected Marcion, but that doctrinal result may well have hidden from Christians that we continue in our politics and ethics to live as if the law, and the materiality of our faith that the law represents, can be left behind. Ironically, docetic Christologies that fail to acknowledge the full reality of Jesus' humanity—a humanity that is unavoidably Jewish—are often implied in natural law accounts of Christian ethics that separate what is required of Christians from the salvation into which we have been incorporated through the work of Jesus Christ."[23]

Finally, however complex and difficult it may be for both Jews and Christians to explain to one another, Hauerwas contends that "Christians must struggle to understand our Jewishness."

> Christians in the West are just beginning to learn to live the way Jews have had to live since Christians took over the world by making Caesar a member

---

21. Hauerwas is quoting from Aidan Kavanaugh's book *The Shape of Baptism: The Rite of Christian Initiation* (New York: Pueblo, 1978), xiii.

22. See Hauerwas's essay "The Truth about God: The Decalogue as Condition for Truthful Speech," in STT, and *The Truth about God: The Ten Commandments in Christian Life* (Nashville, TN: Abingdon Press, 1999).

23. Hauerwas, "Christian Ethics in Jewish Terms: A Response to David Novak," *Modern Theology* 16, no. 3 (July 2000): 294. This essay has been republished in *Christianity in Jewish Terms*, ed. Tikva Simone Frymer-Kensky, Peter Ochs, and David Sandmel (Boulder, CO: Westview Press, 2000), 135–40.

of the church. Put simply, we must learn from Jews how to survive in a world that is not constituted by the recognition, much less the worship of our God. In the process Christians may not only learn from the wisdom Jews have hewn from their struggle to survive Christianity, but we may even learn that our destiny is inseparable from the destiny of the Jews. I am convinced, however, that Christians cannot learn that lesson if, in an attempt to appear tolerant, we pretend our ethics can be divorced from the conviction that God through Jesus' life, death and resurrection has made us nothing less than heirs of Abraham. Accordingly, I believe Jewish theological readings of Christianity must face the challenge that the existence of Christianity is not a mistake, but rather one of the ways God desires to make His covenant with Israel known to the nations.[24]

Although these three issues already can be said to constitute a challenging agenda for contemporary Jews and Christians in assessing one another's traditions of moral and theological inquiry, this agenda for reengagement hardly exhausts the kind of moral and political *remembrance* that Hauerwas contends must be the case for Christians. Hauerwas dares to claim that, rightly understood, Christians cannot practice the eucharist without remembering the Jews as the chosen people of God.[25]

With all of this in view, there is probably some truth to the contention that "Hauerwas places the greatest weight" on the hermeneutical role of tradition.[26] However, accounts of Hauerwas's theological ethics that fail to explore the complexity of his engagement with *both* Judaism and Christianity—as living traditions that exist in a complex interrelationship and conflict—are one-dimensional at best. This is where Hauerwas's different set of assumptions about tradition are most telling. He has been influenced by the moral philosopher Alasdair MacIntyre's contention that "Traditions, when vital, embody continuities of conflict." Like MacIntyre, Hauerwas understands moral traditions to be "historically extended, socially embodied argument[(s)]" about the goods that constitute such traditions.[27]

But in what sense(s) does one think about Christianity as a "living tradition" (in Alasdair MacIntyre's sense of the phrase), given that we are now

24. Ibid., 294.
25. See Hauerwas's sermon on Jews and the eucharist in "The Church's One Foundation Is Jesus Christ Her Lord" (1994) in *IGC*, 34–38.
26. Hays, 263.
27. Alasdair MacIntyre, *After Virtue: A Study in Moral Theory*, 2d ed. (Notre Dame, IN: University of Notre Dame Press, 1984), 222.

living "*after* Christendom"? As I have already indicated, the nature of Hauer-was's project is that he does not assume that he already knows what Christianity is about, but rather, "It has always been more a matter of trying to understand what we Christians should believe and do" (PK xix). As a result, Hauerwas does not write self-consciously as a Protestant or a Catholic. In part, this is because Hauerwas recognizes that the proper "object of the theologian's inquiry is God—not Catholicism or Protestantism" (PK xxvi). At the same time, he pointedly reminds readers that "Christian ethics is not a distinct discipline but varies from time to time and from one to another ecclesial tradition" (PK 50). And in that sense, Hauerwas takes seriously that as a member of the United Methodist Church, he engages a particular legacy of Christian faith and practice (see pp. 665–70) that continues to exist in a conflicted relationship with respect to other Protestants (black and white, etc.) as well as with the Catholic and Orthodox communions, not to mention with respect to Judaism.

What constitutes an ecclesial tradition, then, turns out to have everything to do with the habits, practices, and conversation about goods of a given (set of) community(s) in space and time. Ecclesial traditions are not hermetically sealed from one another but exist in conversation. Hauerwas certainly is conscious of his own roots as a "Southern Methodist" and/or "evangelical Methodist." He has also been known to confess that he is "by training and habit a liberal Protestant." In part, as he muses in *Wilderness Wanderings,* this may account for the continued existence of the "agonized I" in his work (xii).

Hauerwas's awareness of his own struggles to "break back into Christianity" as *something other than* a mainline liberal Protestant also accounts for the broad range of conversation partners. Many of his essays are coauthored (including three in this analogy). For example, in his early years, Hauerwas collaborated with people like David Burrell, c.s.c. In the late 1980s, he worked on projects with Paul Ramsey. And of course, he has written many essays with current and former students. More striking still are his conversations with philosophical ethicists such as Tristram Engelhardt and Jewish theologians such as Peter Ochs and David Novak. For some readers, the "conversational" dimensions of Hauerwas's writing make his work at one and the same time intriguing and baffling to the first-time reader. Clearly, this theological ethicist is engaged in an ongoing argument with *several* traditions—Catholic, Methodist, Anabaptist, and others—at the same time.

The contested nature of Christian theological ethics extends, for Hauerwas, to taking seriously the fact that Christian existence "only makes sense as we recognize God's presence in the people of Israel, that is the Jews. Just to the extent that Christians are tempted to tell our story separate from the story of Israel we become something less than God's body" (*IGC* 38). Similarly, as essay 17 in this volume displays, the Holocaust is an issue for Christians not only because of the atrocities committed against Jews, but also for the very credibility of Christian witness. According to Hauerwas, whether Christians will develop the capacity to rightly remember the Holocaust depends upon our capacity to resist Constantinianism while at the same time *rediscovering* what it means for us to live as a *diaspora* people. This emphasis on the particularity—and radical power—of the Jewish and Christian traditions has everything to do with Hauerwas's refusal to give assent to universalistic accounts of religion anchored in Enlightenment conceptions of reason.

Not "Autonomous Reason" but Practical Reasoning

Unlike those Christian ethicists who understand the task of Christian ethics as based on foundationalist assumptions as influenced by the Enlightenment, Hauerwas claims to "begin in the middle"; that is, he claims that "Christian ethics is not what one does after one gets clear on everything else, or after one has established a starting point or basis of theology; rather it is at the heart of the theological task. For theology is practical activity concerned to display how Christian convictions construe the self and world" (*PK* 55). This way of doing theology "in a world without foundations" has everything to do with how Hauerwas reasons theologically, and, as the following section will explain, has significant implications for how Hauerwas engages questions about human experience.

As the preceding discussion makes clear, Hauerwas's way of reasoning in theological ethics is not isolated from the Jewish and Christian traditions. If by reason, then, one has in mind an Enlightenment conception of "autonomous human reason" that stands outside of the constraints of human history, then it is fair to say that reason plays no role in Hauerwas's theological ethics. However, if by reason one has in view the notion of practical reasoning about everyday existence with a view toward engaging the struggle for the truth in the context of a given community in relation to the pursuit of the good, then the answer is quite different. (In fact, he has been known to describe himself as a "rationalist" in contexts where it is possible to make that claim meaningfully with respect to its Aristotelian, Thomistic, and patristic backdrop.) In some well-defined contexts, Hauerwas describes his project as "postcritical" theology.

Influenced by Barth's critique of "monotheism" in *Church Dogmatics* II/1, Hauerwas believes that ethics has been "artificially separated from the theological task" due to the way secondary discourse about nature, grace, creation, and redemption (secondary discourse) has come to be regarded—under the conditions of modernity—as more primary than "the story of the man who was nothing less than the God-appointed initiator of the new kingdom" (PK 57). More particularly, he strongly dissents from the "theological abstractionism" that passes for theological ethics in Protestant and Catholic traditions alike. When theological concepts like nature and grace are taken "as the 'meat,' the point of Christian convictions," they become *reifications*. "But as abstractions both 'nature' and 'grace' require more determinative narrative display. There is no creation without the covenant of Israel, there is no redemption that does not take its meaning from Jesus' cross. Neither are they general concepts that straightforwardly describe or gain their meaning from human existence per se; rather the concepts of both creation and redemption are aids to train us to be creatures of a gracious God who has called us to be citizens of the community of the redeemed" (PK 57).

This emphasis on training has much to do with Hauerwas's use of the notion of "skill" in relation to the conception of consciousness as knowing how. Drawing on Herbert Fingarette's work on the phenomenology of self-deception, Hauerwas contends that consciousness is "more like an ability to say than the power to see." Hauerwas explains what an "operating skill" is and how it elaborates on the sense of being explicitly conscious: "To become explicitly conscious of something is to be exercising a certain skill. Skills, of course, are learned but need not be routinized. We are born with certain general capacities, which we shape, by learning, into specific skills, some of them being quite sensitive and artful. The specific skill I particularly have in mind as a model for becoming explicitly conscious of something is the skill of saying what we are doing or experiencing. I propose, then, that we do not characterize consciousness as a kind of mental mirror, but as the exercise of the learned skill of 'spelling out' some feature of the world we are engaged in." This account leads Hauerwas to observe that a self-deceived person is someone of whom "it is a patent characteristic that even when normally appropriate he persistently avoids spelling out some features of his engagement with the world" (TT 86; see essay 10).

Hauerwas's discussion of self-deception in essay 10 provides a useful example of the purpose of explaining the relationship of practical reasoning to the stories we tell ourselves about what we are doing in our lives. He begins from the presumption that "to be is to be rooted in self-deception. The moral task involves a constant vigilance: to note those areas where the tendency has taken root. . . . Our ability to [recognize] our deceptions is dependent on the dominant story, the master image, that we have embodied in our character. Through our experience we constantly learn new lessons, we gain new insights, about the limit of our life story. But 'insights are a dime a dozen' and even more useless unless we have the skills—the images and the stories—which can empower those insights to shape our lives. It is not enough to see nor is it enough to know; we must know how to say and give expression to what we come to see and know. 'Understanding what something is demands more than insight or vision—it requires appropriate discipline.' " (*TT* 95).

Invoking familiar images of exploration and adventure, Hauerwas describes the quest to overcome self-deception this way: "Like Columbus, we all have encounters that we do not know how to describe. Our basic stories and images determine what we discover, but often like Columbus, we insist on describing our engagements with an image that misleads us. To the extent that we cannot make anything of what we are doing, we fail to make our lives into anything. Columbus could not understand what he had done because he did not have the skills to get it right. Fortunately, we can keep sending out our ships to explore the coastlines of our engagements and learn the limits of our past descriptions; and on the strength of our previous failures, we can develop more adequate skills to say what we have done. Too often, however, we adopt the first coherent description of what we have done and it leads to greater self-deception" (*TT* 96). Developing the skills to reason in relation to the biblical narratives is then a matter of discipline that is developed in the context of the moral communities and traditions of which one is a part.

Many of the essays in "New Intersections in Theological Ethics" can be said to display Hauerwas's distinctive signature of this kind of practical reasoning. For example, essay 28, "Eliminating Suffering Is Not the Purpose of Medicine," has everything to do with the practice of medicine as a moral endeavor in which physicians and nurses face the challenge of caring for people who are born mentally handicapped. Similarly, the brief essay 30, "Must a Patient Be a Person to Be a Patient?," shows how reliant we are on moral traditions to be able to understand the moral significance of what it means to describe someone as a "person." In such essays as these, Hauerwas repeatedly draws our attention to the moral significance of our own capacities to articulate what is going on in the moral life.

Not Individual Experience but Eschatological Existence

As various critics have noted, the role of experience in Hauerwas's theological essays is complex *and* conflicted.[28] It is not uncommon for readers to wonder about the place of human experience (as a self-constituting authority) for theological ethics without questioning the assumption that we have unmediated access to our lives simply because we are conscious selves. To this kind of assumption Hauerwas responds with a set of comments, which are illuminating not only for what they say about Hauerwas's own religious background and affiliation, but for the more specific question of moral reflection on human experience.

> I was raised a Methodist. That means before I was twelve I had already had all the experience I could take. That is the reason I sometimes suggest that there are some words that certain religious traditions should never be allowed to use. Anglicans should never be allowed to say "Incarnation" because they usually mean by that "God became human and said, 'Say, this is not too bad.'" In like manner, Methodists should not be allowed to use the word "experience" because they usually mean that salvation consists in having the right feelings at the right time and in the right place. Rather than our confrontation with God being an occasion for challenging our endemic narcissism, the emphasis on experience thus only underwrites our fatal narcissism.
>
> All of which is to say I am not all that happy with an emphasis on experience for moral reflection as an end in and of itself. I feel about experience as I do about talk about values; namely I do not want to know what you value—tell me what you want. So do not tell me about the importance of experience, but rather name the experience you think is important. What is important is not that we attend to experience, but whose experience, where they had it, and how they understand it. More important than having had an

---

28. For example, Richard Hays observes that the role played by experience in Hauerwas's work is a "more complex matter" than his conception of reason. "On the whole . . . it seems that Hauerwas accords to experience only the role of confirming the truth of Scripture. . . . The experience of the individual Christian is in any case a matter of small importance; it is the experience of the church through time that carries hermeneutical weight. But when the matter is put in these terms, the distinction between scripture and experience becomes elusive or inconsequential" (263–64).

experience is whether we know how to describe it or name it. (from essay 13, pp. 267–68)

Behind this contention, of course, lies Hauerwas's critique of the theological and philosophical underpinnings of Protestant liberalism as well as his constructive account of the communal character of Christian existence in the church as polis.

According to Hauerwas, then, questions about the place of religious experience in the moral life must be *reframed*. How can we come to see our existence as human beings and Christians so that we learn to narrate that existence *truthfully*? The problem of self-deception arises (again) at precisely this point. Is it possible to offer an account of our human experience that does not involve some kind of narrative account of ourselves as human beings and as Christians? This is where the existence of the saints and the opportunity for Eucharist sharply qualify the horizon of how human experience is to be narrated by Christians.

Suffice it to say that Hauerwas *does not believe* that any of us have unmediated access to our own experience. That places him in unalterable opposition with Enlightenment accounts of the self that presume that "I" am the author of my own destiny and the arbiter of what is "good" for me. When combined with the Enlightenment conception of the primacy of the subject, these problems lead to "the flight from authority" that has distorted Christian witness. Hauerwas wants no part of the Enlightenment project of the free and autonomous individual—the individual unencumbered by the constraints of church, tradition, and scripture.

Instead, he stresses the *narrative* character of our knowledge of God in relation to the narrative of the Bible as enacted by the church in worship (PK 62). "First and foremost, the community must know that it has a history and tradition which separate it from the world" (CC 68). For Christians, the history and tradition that orients human existence is the life, ministry, death, and resurrection of Jesus as witnessed to in the liturgy of the church year which provides the basis for the eschatological emplotment of human existence *coram deo*. In essay 9 in this volume, Hauerwas recounts the story of "Cowslip's Warren" in *Watership Down*, a community that forgets that it has a story. The significance of this example is not limited to the fact that it serves as a parable of American liberal democracy. Absent the biblical narratives of human destiny as part of God's creative intention for the world, Christians are bound to be disoriented, Hauerwas argues.

It is certainly relevant—but hardly determinative—to inquire about the relationship of Hauerwas's life to the account he presents. Readers who are interested in following up on Cavanaugh's biographical essay are encouraged to read "Tale of Two Stories: On Being a Christian and Being a Texan" (CET). There they will discover Hauerwas sifting through the stuff of Southern myth and tradition. Certainly, it is true that Hauerwas grew up with vestiges of "the religion of the lost cause" with its distinctive conception of honor as displayed in the practices of cowboys and bricklayers. Probably more significant still is the fact that many of these narratives reflect the decay, disintegration, and disappearance of various moral traditions in the context of the American Southwest. Hauerwas's own reading of William Humphrey's novel *The Ordways* about life in a Northeast Texas small town provides an insightful account of the ways shifting myths shape the identity of white Texan males:

> Lee surrendered to Grant on April 9, 1865. The news was two months reaching Texas. I did not hear about until 1931. . . . The moment when he discovers the Civil War is lost comes to every Southern boy and proud Texan though I was, it was perhaps less shattering for me than for most. I had, right on my doorstep, another myth to turn to. When the last bugle call went echoing off into eternity and the muskets were stacked and the banners lowered and that star crossed flag hauled down—in short, when Appomattox came to me and I was demobilized and disarmed and returned home, filled with wounded pride and impatient with peacetime life—like many another veteran—I began to face about and look the other way, towards Blossom Prairie, where the range was open and the fancy free to roam. In my fashion I was repeating not only the history of my family, but of the country. For the West provided America with an escape from the memory of the Civil War. (92–93)

It would be reductionistic and inaccurate to say that Hauerwas's essays in theological ethics are written in response to his cultural situation, but it is true that he does see the social conflict of the American South and West as being one site for reflecting about the multiple conflicts with liberal political theory particularly as it has achieved institutional expression in the United States.

It is not uncommon for critics of Hauerwas to launch their critiques from the vantage point of human experience. For example, some feminist theologians and ethicists have criticized Hauerwas's construal of a "master narrative" from his reading of Christian sources as well as for failing to recognize the historical and social location of his own theological production.[29] In particular, he has been faulted for relating his own life story (as a white male from Texas who is a Christian) as if it were a "universal human tale." But as Debra Dean Murphy has argued, this is a misreading precisely Hauerwas uses the particular narrative of "A Tale of Two Stories: On Being a Christian and a Texan" to point "to the particularity of all human stories."[30]

Here, even more than in the case of the three previous discussions of authority, the problem of reification is salient. In response to reifications of "women's experience" in the name of advocating feminist concerns, Hauerwas contends that we must get back to the "rough ground" of particular human experiences without claiming some kind of privilege for his own experience—or, for that matter, the experience of any other theologian.[31] Given the fact that over the past decade feminism's own inner struggles have created a space where the very critiques Hauerwas makes of liberalism are now being offered by feminists themselves, Debra Dean Murphy poses the possibility that Hauerwas and feminist theologians could find "common ground" in the task of reconstructing ecclesial authority for Christian theology.[32]

Having learned from H. Richard Niebuhr that the most important moral question to ask is not *What must I do?* but *What is going on?*, Hauerwas has also drawn on Niebuhr's work to explore the complex ways in which narratives shape the character of human communities and their respective ends. As he once observed, "[H. Richard] Niebuhr is right to point us to the fact that most of us are simply 'fated' to be Christian, or Texan, but . . . the former,

29. I am indebted to Debra Dean Murphy's paper "Feminist Responses to Stanley Hauerwas: Past and Present," presented at the Southeastern Regional Meeting of the American Academy of Religion, Chapel Hill, NC, March 12, 1999.

30. Ibid., 6.

31. In this respect, it is worth noting the cautionary remarks that Hauerwas offers in his essay "A Tale of Two Stories": "I have used the nature of autobiographical literature to try to enliven the grammar of religious convictions, but I have studiously avoided any suggestion that the strength or weakness of theological argument was in any manner relative to the limits or richness of my or any theologian's biography. Indeed, I find those theologians who argue about what they are prepared or not prepared to believe in accord with their own experience, which they often claim represents 'modern man,' take their own subjectivities far too seriously. The important question is not what I do or do not believe but the convictions I should have if I am to have the skills to deal with this existence in a truthful manner" (26–27).

32. I am grateful to Debra Dean Murphy for helping me to clarify this set of contested issues about the significance of Hauerwas's work with respect to contentions by some feminist theologians and ethicists.

unlike the latter, provides us with the skills to turn our fate into destiny. Both stories 'fate' us, but the story of God involves in the way the story of being a Texan does not, a painful training that enables me to make my life my own" (*CET* 43 n.11). This enigmatic set of statements encapsulates one of the most seminal themes in Hauerwas's work: *the reconfiguration of time* in relation to (the narratives of) human existence made possible by the life, ministry, death, and resurrection of Jesus of Nazareth. Thus, Christian existence is to be lived within the eschatological horizon of the Kingdom of God, and it is in relation to that conception of ecclesial destiny that moral reflection on all human experience is to take place.

IV. The Unfinished *Character of Hauerwas's Theological Ethics*

By now it should be clear to the reader that Stanley Hauerwas not only is not "bound" by the wooden reasoning of Enlightenment conceptions of the relationship of scripture, reason, tradition, and experience. In significant respects he engages the theological task in a way that is at one and the same time *more indebted* to the history of Christianity, *more critical* of post-Enlightenment conceptions of reason and experience, and *more radically disposed to engage* the text of scripture than most other liberal Protestant theologians, while at the same time contending that we rightly engage scripture when we read it in the context of Christian practices.

Exercising Practical Reason: Casuistry and Liturgy
The previous discussion of the ways Hauerwas reframes the problem of the use of scripture, reason, tradition, and experience as "sources" for theological ethics has great significance for how he approaches casuistry, which he understands to be "the reflection by a community on its experience to test imaginatively the often unnoticed and unacknowledged implications of its narrative commitments" (*PK* 120). "What I mean by casuistry, then, is not just the attempt to adjudicate difficult cases of conscience within a system of moral principles, but is the process by which a tradition tests whether its practices are consistent (that is truthful) or inconsistent in light of its basic habits and convictions or whether these convictions require new practices and behavior. Those implications become apparent only through the day-to-day living of a people pledged to embody that narrative within their lives" (*PK* 120). Here it also may be useful to call attention to Hauerwas's pedagogy as one who is charged with the responsibility of teaching Christian ethics in a university-

related divinity school where most students are preparing for pastoral ministry. For almost an entire decade (1985–1994) Hauerwas taught a course structured around the pattern of the liturgy of worship:

> Worship and Life
> Gathering and Greeting
> Confession and Sin: Race, Class, Gender
> Scripture and Proclamation: Virtues and the Ministry
> Baptism: Marriage, Sex, and the Family
> Offering, Sacrifice, and Eucharist: Economic Justice, War and Peace
> Sending Forth (*IGC* 164)[33]

Among the readings he used over the years are works as diverse as Sharon
Welch's *A Feminist Ethic of Risk* and Anne Tyler's novel *Saint Maybe* alongside
his own book *The Peaceable Kingdom*. This course attempts to teach seminarians the "skills" of practical reasoning through their experience with the
"practices they have been put through in the course" (*IGC* 163). "Insofar as
ethics has a task peculiar to itself, that task is to assemble reminders from the
training we receive in worship that enable us to rightly see the world and to
perceive how we continue to be possessed by the world" (*IGC* 156). Hauerwas
rightly chooses to describe this approach as "ecclesial ethics" as a way of
naming the fact that such casuistry is "only intelligible in an ongoing tradition" (*HR* 271).

So, from Hauerwas's vantage point, it is not that experience plays no role in
theological ethics, but that we have to take into account *which community's experience* we are talking about (*HR* 279) precisely because our capacity to
describe the world in which we live depends in large part on the communities
in which we find ourselves living. In this regard, Hauerwas chides Albert Jonsen and Stephen Toulmin for *not providing* "an adequate account of the close
interaction between the flourishing of the virtues and casuistry" (*HR* 281):

> From this perspective, casuistry is less an attempt to find the minimum
> requirements for the Christian life than it is the imaginative mode for the
> Christian community to locate the innovative aspects of our convictions. No
> one can anticipate what being formed virtuously may require. I may well
> discover that if I am to be courageous in one aspect of my life, I am required
> to confront matters in other areas I had not even anticipated. Casuistry is the

---

33. See the syllabus for *CHE* 33 Christian Ethics that Hauerwas taught at the Divinity School of
Duke University in the fall semester of 1993, as listed in *IGC*, appendix 1, 164.

mode of wisdom developed by a community to test past innovations as well as to anticipate future challenges.

Put differently, the ultimate test of casuistry is how well our reasoning embodies as well as witnesses to the lives of the saints. Casuistry done rightly is meant to call Christians to attend to the innovative lives that we believe help us to know better what our convictions entail. That does not mean we are called to slavishly imitate the saints, but rather they provide the paradigms to help us know what we are to reason about. (HR 282)

Oddly enough, Hauerwas's critics have failed to recognize this aspect of his work, perhaps because this account of experience presumes the possibility that wisdom may develop over time *within* human communities that can interact with and be engaged by tradition.[34]

One of Hauerwas's most accessible and well-developed accounts of the role of practical reason in relation to the particularities of Christian traditions is found in his essay "Reconciling the Practice of Reason" in CET. In that essay, Hauerwas recounts an incident that happened in Shepshewana, Indiana, explaining why a Mennonite businessman named Olin Teague did not sue another businessman for failing to pay his debts. Hauerwas's exposition of the casuistry involved in this example involves unfolding practices of reconciliation that have developed among Anabaptists and Mennonites in relation to the Apostle Paul's admonitions to the church at Corinth found in I Cor. 6:1–11. While it might be of interest to provide extended historical critical analysis of the background of the text, Hauerwas argues that this background is not necessary for explaining why Teague does not resort to the legal option of suing fellow businessman Jim Burkholder. Practical reasoning in this case has everything to do with the question of "the kind of community [Mennonites understand] Christians are meant to be in order to hear and live according to this text" (CET 76).

The admonition not to take one another to court, therefore, is placed against the background of their being a particular kind of people with a distinct set of virtues. Therefore, unlike most Christians who have tried to run such passages into a legal regulation so one can start to find exceptions to it, Mennonites understand the admonition to be but a logical extension of

34. In this respect, Hauerwas's work has affinities with James Tunstead Burtchaell's essay "Community Experience as a Source of Ethics," in *The Giving and Taking of Life: Essays Ethical* (Notre Dame, IN: University of Notre Dame Press, 1989), 3–50.

their commitment to be a people of peace. Their reading of this text and the significance they give it are not because they think every command of the Bible should be followed to the letter, but rather reflects their understanding that the fundamental ministry of Christians in the world is reconciliation.

So their reading of the text and the behavior it prohibits is informed by their understanding of the virtues necessary to be Christian. But it is important to note that they have no "individualistic" conception of virtues; rather their conception is communal. Reconciliation is a central virtue because it denotes the communal reality that joins Mennonites in a common story and tradition. No doubt at times in their history the prohibition against litigation may have become lawlike for some Mennonites, but even as such it stands as a reminder of the kind of people they are to be.

Because Mennonites read th[e] text [of I Cor. 6:1–11] as but an extension of their general commitment to peacemaking, they extend its significance beyond the bare requirements of the text. The text says they are not to take one another to court. Note that this is not because they do not make any moral judgments about right and wrong. Obviously, Paul is more than willing to make such judgments and in rather harsh terms, at that. This is no easy ethic of tolerance. Indeed, Paul even suggests that Christians are ultimately to judge the world rather than vice versa. So not going to court has little to do with overlooking wrong, but rather has to do with discovering a way that Christians can respond to wrongs that builds up rather than destroys community. (CET 76–77)

The Mennonite assumption, then, that the early Christians were right to make the question of appearing in court "prismatic for determining the nature of their community," makes sense only, Hauerwas argues, when located in the complex practice of reconciliation, which itself conditions the practice of reason in communities of faith seeking to embody "sanctified peoplehood."

This emphasis on the *holiness* of the church, as embodied in particular practices of ethics and liturgy, is reflected in the way Hauerwas teaches Christian ethics to seminarians: "The formation of Christians through the liturgy makes clear that Christians are not simply called to do the 'right thing,' but rather we are expected to be holy. Such holiness is not an individual achievement but comes from being made part of a community in which we discover the truth of our lives. And 'truth' cannot be separated from how the community worships, since the truth is that we are creatures made for worship" (IGC 155). This emphasis on liturgy is part of what has led Hauerwas (and others) to think of his approach as in some sense "Catholic,"[35] but as Hauerwas has taken pains to state in several different contexts, although there are distinctions that can be drawn between liturgy, evangelism, and ethics, ultimately the "conceptual 'and' " must be eliminated if Christians—Protestant and Catholic alike—are to grasp the power of what it means to be a holy people.[36]

This orientation to practices of worship displays why Hauerwas is resolutely committed to the *holiness* of the church but refuses to entangle himself in the standard Protestant debates about the experience or appropriation of holiness. Indeed, although Hauerwas does write about justification and sanctification, he does so in a way that shows that the meaningfulness of such notions is dependent on practices. "When they are separated from Jesus' life and death, they distort Christian life. 'Sanctification' is but a way of reminding us of the kind of journey we must undertake if we are to [make] the story of Jesus our story. 'Justification' is but a reminder of the character of that story—namely, what God has done for us by providing us with a path to follow" (PK 94).

Happiness, Friendship, and the Life of Virtue

The path that we follow as Christian disciples is also the path in which happiness is (to be) found, but as Hauerwas reminds us, without the exercise of the virtues in the context of Christian friendship we are unlikely to discover the happiness that God intends for us as inheritors of the Kingdom of God. As Hauerwas warns his readers, the relation between happiness and virtue "is not simple, and the connection cannot be hurried" (CAV 17). Hauerwas follows the lead of Aristotle insofar as the virtues are not so much the means to happiness as they constitute the *form* of felicity.[37] That is to say that "we cannot know what kind of happiness we desire until we have acquired the virtues" (CAV 20).

"Yet if Christians affirm the ultimate unity of the virtues it must be an eschatological affirmation" (CAV 50). That the affirmation is eschatological

35. For a full discussion of this point, see Hauerwas's "Worship, Evangelism, Ethics: On Eliminating the 'And' " in BH.

36. Ibid., 104. Writing about his own tradition of Christianity, Hauerwas notes: "The name we Methodists have used to indicate the inseparability of worship, evangelism and ethics is holiness." As this statement suggests, Hauerwas does have a stake in the way the United Methodist tradition is narrated.

37. Whereas Hauerwas learned about the moral significance of friendship from Aristotle, it is to Saint Thomas Aquinas that he is most indebted for the theological significance of friendship for the moral life.

reminds us that "Christians look, not for individual happiness, but for the kingdom of God."

> While they must always refrain from specifying the exact shape of this kingdom, they can begin to imagine it in their present life in the church. For the church, no description holds more authority than that reiterated so often in the Epistles, namely that the church is a body with many parts, each with its own beauty and difference. As gifts of the Spirit, these differences are less learned in a virtue friendship, more supplied directly from God, who is building the kingdom through the church. Yet they do not exist separate from the friendship—indeed, they inhere in it, for as Paul sees them, they include gifts such as exhortation, wisdom, diligence, and even cheerfulness. . . .
>
> The introduction of the gifts cannot but change how we will view differences among friends. While I expect to grow in wisdom as I grow in virtue, if I also suppose another might have a special gift of wisdom, I cannot suppose that my acquired wisdom need not remain open to her correction. Indeed, I must see that we need this friend's wisdom to live well together, and since . . . our living is my living well, I must see that I cannot live without this other's guidance. So it is that I need her friendship for happiness, and for virtue. And in needing her I need something essentially different from myself. (CAV 50–51)

In sum, according to Hauerwas, we cannot live out the virtues in the absence of friends who help us to see the truth of what we are doing. For Christians, such friendship takes shape in relation to the life of the Church in time and space. Although it might initially seem to the reader that no one essay in *The Hauerwas Reader* discusses friendship in a focal way, the essay on peacemaking as the "virtue of the church" (essay 16) does provide a thick account of how Christian friendship unfolds in the context of reconciliation. Correlatively, Hauerwas would argue that the vision of what it might mean for a given community to embody peaceableness (corporately) is precisely the context of moral excellence in which Christian happiness becomes most intelligible. The fact that Christianity exists in such a separated state at this time in human history is a sad reminder that the virtues must be exercised in the midst of the ongoing reconstruction of the church as a set of practices. For Hauerwas, the scandal of such division lies in the fact that Christians fail to discern the social and moral significance of their own practices.

Discerning the "Christian Difference" While Living amid Fragments

As many of the essays in part 3 of *The Hauerwas Reader* demonstrate, Hauerwas's essays display a different stance toward pluralism than that of most mainline Protestants in American culture. As Hauerwas has explained elsewhere, he began to learn this different stance as he discovered the theological ethics of John Howard Yoder. "Yoder taught me that the mainstream's celebration of pluralism is the way the mainstream maintains its assumption of its superiority. Thus 'we' understand, and perhaps appreciate, the 'sects' better than they can appreciate themselves. The one with the most inclusive typology wins the game."[38] By contrast, like Yoder, Hauerwas proceeds in a way that is largely ad hoc but at the same time radically receptive to a variety of questions posed from within as well as outside the Christian traditions. If anything, Hauerwas explodes the myths of "mainstream pluralism" by engaging a *wider range* of concerns, including those of the mentally handicapped, to take but one example.

This kind of openness to questions from a variety of places and persons has everything to do with Hauerwas's *nonfoundationalist* approach. To invoke Rowan Williams's pithy phrase, there is a sense that Hauerwas deploys "the suspicion of suspicion" in dealing with the literatures of *both* modernity and postmodernity. This is not only because of what he has learned from Ludwig Wittgenstein, but also because of the overstated value of postmodernist critiques: "Most postmodern thinkers style themselves as radicals. As a style of thought, postmodernism is allegedly suspicious 'of classical notions of truth, reason, identity, and objectivity, of the idea of universal progress or emancipation.' Postmodernism seems, in other words, to call into question the Enlightenment project and surely that is a good thing. Yet I am not convinced that postmodernism, either as an intellectual position or a cultural style, is post-anything."[39] Hauerwas argues that Christians are not postmodernist because they "have a stake in history."

> Christians must be able to narrate postmodernism in a manner that postmodernism cannot narrate Christianity. Or more adequately, we must show how Christianity provides the resources for a critique of its own mistakes in a way that modernity or postmodernity cannot provide. Such narration will

38. Hauerwas, "Testament of Friends," 214.
39. Hauerwas, "The Christian Difference; Or, Surviving Postmodernism" in *BH*, 37. This essay also has been published in *Cultural Values* 3, no. 2 (April 1999): 164–81. The essay originated at a conference on "Anabaptists and Postmodernity" held at Bluffton College in August 1998.

require Christians to develop accounts . . . that are more powerful than either modernist or postmodernist can muster. Indeed, one of the illusions of post-modernism is to give a far too intelligible and, thus, comforting account of where we are. Our world and our lives are far too fragmentary and disordered to know where we are, but at least Christians owe it to themselves and their neighbors to confess that such disorder is but a reflection of the failure of the churches to be faithful. Modernity, and its bastard offspring, postmodernity, are but reflections of the Christian attempt to make God a god available without the mediation of the church. Such a god cannot help but become some "timeless thing" necessary to insure the assumed truth of Christianity in service to the growth of secular power. Postmodernism, in short, is the outworking of mistakes in Christian theology correlative to the attempt to make Christianity "true" apart from faithful witness.[40]

This critique, complete with a critique of the modernist approach to Christian theology, provides a good example of the philosophical force of many of Hauerwas's essays.[41]

While having no stake in the "Christianizing" of philosophy as such, Hauerwas is quite candid that he has never regarded philosophy and theology as discrete discourses. Rather, as he indicates in essay 4, "I do not think in terms of clearly delineated disciplines, one called 'philosophy,' the other 'theology' . . . I simply do not think that clear lines can be drawn between what philosophers and theologians do. Too often it seems we are concerned with the same set of issues and require quite similar conceptual skills to explore how and what we should think. Both philosophy and theology are activities that come in many shapes and sizes. As such each may well lead its practitioners into areas they had not anticipated." As Hauerwas indicates at various points in his career, "I found I could not avoid these issues if I was to develop an adequate account" of vision, virtue, character, community, narrative, ecclesiology, and so on.

On occasions, Hauerwas's argumentative rigor extends to the use of ad hominem argument, which he is known to defend as "the ultimate form of argument," given that arguments are embedded in practices, which are embod-

---

40. Ibid., 37–38.
41. For example, it is not an accident that Hauerwas's essay "On Keeping Theological Ethics Theological" (essay 2 in this volume) has been anthologized as an example of philosophical reasoning despite the fact that the essay decries the misplaced focus of theological ethics among Christian ethicists in American culture.

ied in the lives of those who hold the convictions being put forward in argumentation.[42] Friends and critics alike of Hauerwas have raised questions about what might be best described as his "contrarian" style of argumentation or polemical engagement. What they have in mind is his tendency to engage his opponents' arguments as if those arguments mask ends other than what they claim to be and therefore that they mask an unannounced political agenda.

In his book *In Good Company,* Hauerwas addresses this concern directly. After acknowledging that being a "contrarian" probably has some basis in his personality, Hauerwas goes on to explain that to some extent his contrarian style is "necessitated both by [his] polemic against theological and political liberalism. The liberal, of both kinds, is committed to englobing all positions into liberalism. To resist being 'explained' or, worse, 'appreciated' by liberals you have to resist their characterizations" (*IGC* 224 n. 32). Hauerwas's response to such charges is useful to consider given that it helps to locate the conversations within which such argumentation occurs and also helps to explain why there are essays that do not display such contrarianism even where he is also every bit as committed to reframing the questions.

Hauerwas's commitment to resisting such attempts to *domesticate* Christian convictions is entirely consistent with his view of his work as "incomplete." His comments in the introduction to *In Good Company* are revealing in this regard: "I do not try to write the 'the last word' about anything. That is partly because I do not believe in the last word about anything, but also because I find the politics of such scholarship offensive. 'Perfection' kills community. To try to write to anticipate all possible criticism, to qualify all strong claims in the name of 'scholarship,' protects authors but too often produces work that serves to defeat the necessity of community. That it does so is not surprising, since that is exactly what it is meant to do. In contrast, I assume the point is to write in a manner that invites others to care about what I write about because they sense there is so much to do given the incompleteness of what I have done" (13–14). Readers may or may not find this statement to be believable, but it does display Hauerwas's own sensibility with respect to the ongoing need for theologians to open up "new intersections" in theological ethics (see, for example, the essays in part 3 of this anthology).

---

42. Charles Taylor makes the case for ad hominem as the ultimate form of the practical argument in an essay entitled "Explanation and Practical Reason" in *The Quality of Life,* ed. Martha Nussbaum and Amartya Sen (Oxford: Oxford University Press, 1993), 231–40.

For Hauerwas, then, theological arguments will always be ongoing because argumentation about goods internal to the practice of Christianity is *necessary* if Christian theological ethics is to continue to be a *living* tradition. For argumentation to have ceased could mean only that there is no longer any telos worth contesting. That is another way of explaining why it is a mistake to ask what Hauerwas's theological "method" is. As he has boldly stated elsewhere, "there can be no 'method' for theology in a world without foundations. All we can do is follow at a distance."[43] Of course, it is one thing for Hauerwas to avoid what Yoder once described as the excesses of "methodologism" in theological ethics; it is another thing to act as if Hauerwas's way of doing theological ethics cannot be put into the context of intellectual and ecclesial traditions within which he works. To that task I now turn in the final section of this "Reader's Guide."

V. Reading Hauerwas in the Context of Traditions of Argument

Even with the extensive discussion of the four preceding parts of this "Reader's Guide," several questions are left unanswered. This final section describes those senses in which Hauerwas is a participant and an antagonist in various traditions as a way of displaying the coherence of his project with respect to the ongoing arguments about theological ethics and ecclesial existence. Although the intention is *not* to suggest that there are only two such traditions in which one can locate Hauerwas's discourse, I hope that the following explications of his participation in the tradition of North American theological ethics and the United Methodist tradition can serve as the basis for drawing analogies with regard to his involvement with other traditions of moral inquiry.

Hauerwas and the "Tradition" of North American Christian Social Ethics

No doubt, there is some truth to Samuel Wells's claim that Hauerwas's work can most accurately be located in relation to conversations and arguments of "the tradition of North American Christian social ethics. . . . Like a great-grandson, [Hauerwas] chafes at the traditions, quarrels with the rules, and distances himself from the grandees; but he can never leave the family."[44]

43. "The Church's One Foundation Is Jesus Christ Her Lord," 162.
44. Wells, *From Fate to Destiny*, 2. See also William Werpehowski's discussion of Hauerwas's work in the context of North American theology in his contribution "Theological Ethics," in *The Modern Theologians: An Introduction to Christian Theology in the Twentieth Century*, 2d ed., ed. David F. Ford (Cambridge, MA: Blackwell Publishers, 1997), 320–24.

Wells's image is a useful way to account for the work of someone like Stanley Hauerwas, whose conflictedness about his ecclesial background and academic pedigree is evidenced throughout his body of work. But I would suggest that there are limits to the "great-grandson" metaphor as well.

First, there is a sense in which Hauerwas has *redirected* the tradition. There is no question that Hauerwas's initial theological moves were learned from H. Richard Niebuhr's *The Meaning of Revelation* and *The Responsible Self.* One can also chart the influence of James Gustafson on Hauerwas's early essays. Further, Hauerwas readily acknowledges that he learned from Reinhold Niebuhr how you have to write across a wide range of issues and different discourses. Although he and Reinhold Niebuhr had different theological purposes, Hauerwas readily acknowledges that he learned the importance of the compelling phrase of simplification (the ability to state significant claims in pithy ways) from him. But this set of influences having been acknowledged, it is also the case that what Hauerwas ultimately learned from Barth and Wittgenstein *made it impossible* for him to continue to be part of the mainstream tradition of Christian ethics. If there is a sense in which the education that Hauerwas received at Yale can be said to have enabled him to recognize the significance of John Howard Yoder's work, it is also true that Hauerwas's bold way of displaying Yoder's influence has also cut him off from what remains of the tradition that for so many years was anchored at Yale. As the new century opens, the discontinuities are more evident than the continuities with the "tradition" of North American Christian social ethics. (See for example, Hauerwas's exchange with James Gustafson in essay 4 in this collection.)

Second, Wells's family image does not convey the wide array of persons (pastors, laypeople, philosophers, skeptics, graduate students, lawyers, doctors, and mentally handicapped persons) with whom Hauerwas continues to be engaged in correspondence, and in relation to which his essays can be said to be a kind of ongoing response. On the one hand, Hauerwas maintains correspondence with pastors like Kyle Childress at Austin Heights Baptist in Nacagdoches, Texas, while at the same time he continues to engage Aristotelian philosophers like Mike Quirk. Over the years, many undergraduates, seminarians, graduate students, and would-be theologians have found Hauerwas to be an encouraging as well as challenging conversation partner as they have honed their skills in theological discourse. The radical pluralism of Hauerwas's friendships and conversations, then, should be seen as another significant factor that has informed his essays in reconstructing theological ethics over the past thirty years.

Although Hauerwas has resisted facile characterizations of how his mind has changed[45] over the past three decades, he has readily acknowledged that teaching in particular contexts (Augustana, Notre Dame, and Duke) has had an effect on his work throughout his career as a theologian. For example, he agrees that in some sense the focus of some of his work in theological ethics did shift as a result of moving to Duke University in 1984. At Duke, he has been responsible for teaching seminarians. As he has indicated elsewhere (*IGC* 154–55), he found himself having to give much more attention to the question of how a basic Christian ethics course should be structured precisely because he was going to be teaching seminarians (most of whom are United Methodists). At about the same time Hauerwas moved to Duke, he began to receive more invitations to engage issues being discussed by the Council of Bishops and other leaders of the United Methodist Church (see, for example, essay 21 in this volume). Hauerwas's Methodist colleagues at Duke Divinity School have also provided him with a new set of conversation partners in relation to which he has had the opportunity to reengage his own conflicted heritage as a Christian in the United Methodist tradition.

The Unfinished Church of a "High Church Mennonite"

Though he finds himself living in the midst of fragments of Christian tradition(s), Hauerwas continues to participate in the project called the Church, even when, as in the case of his own denomination, it often seems to him to betray its own apostolate as "an evangelical order in the church catholic" rather than to embody such an ecumenical vocation. His various descriptions of himself as a "high church Mennonite" (*cc* 6) or an "evangelical Catholic" (*STT* 77) have puzzled more than they have clarified for those readers who are unfamiliar with the strange sojourn of "the people called Methodist" in American culture. Yet, as the context of such remarks bears out, both of these descriptions are Hauerwas's way of stating what he believes it means to be a Christian in the United Methodist tradition. To grasp the significance of this claim requires further explanation.

Although raised in a congregation strongly influenced by revivalist pietism, early on in his undergraduate education Hauerwas discovered the more theologically potent strands of the Methodist tradition that survive, among other

45. For an extended discussion of why "How My Mind Has Changed" is *the wrong question* to ask about Hauerwas's theological ethics, see Hauerwas's essay "The Testament of Friends: How My Mind Has Changed" in *The Christian Century* (February 28, 1990): 212.

places, in the writings of John and Charles Wesley.[46] As he has repeatedly avowed, "I have no desire to rid myself of my particular background as an evangelical Methodist. Rather it is my conviction that Methodism, like other Christian traditions, with its limits and possibilities, helps awaken all of us to being members of Christ's whole church" (CC, xxvi). Hauerwas contends that Albert Outler's description of Methodism as " 'an evangelical order' in the church catholic" describes the "true character of Methodism" (STT 77), but he also understands that this particular ecclesial vision is "inherently unstable, particularly in modernity" (STT 78).[47]

The ecclesiological *instability* of the United Methodist Church has concerned Hauerwas throughout his career.[48] Contemporary congregations of the United Methodist Church could well serve as "Exhibit A" on the list of the most accommodated mainline Protestant denominations. Although Hauerwas has often subjected the UMC to criticism (see essays 21 and 31, for example), he has not given up hope that theological discourse might yet be rehabilitated in the congregations of mainline Protestantism. At the same time, he takes seriously the fact that (as noted earlier) "Constantinianism is a hard

46. Hauerwas was first exposed to the work of John Wesley through his mentor and college teacher John Score. Score had written his dissertation at Duke University (under Dean Robert Cushman) on the issue of why John Wesley's so-called Aldersgate experience was *not* the center of Wesley's life and thought. Score had argued that *the real center* of the Wesleyan movement was the practice of field preaching, not revivalism. In retrospect, Hauerwas realizes that through Score he was introduced to a "catholic reading" of Wesley. Later, as a graduate student at Yale, he did a readings course on John Wesley and early Methodism as part of which he continued to discover the *catholicity* of John Wesley's life and work. His study of *Character and the Christian Life* displays his critical edge toward—and his appreciation of—the Wesleyan tradition's understanding of sanctification.

47. Methodism's evangelical zeal for spreading "scriptural holiness across the land and reforming the continent" has always existed in tension with early Wesleyan practice of sacramental renewal. Indeed, as Albert Outler once stated, John Wesley's own most mature ecclesiological reflections constituted "an unstable blend of Anabaptist and Anglican ecclesiologies." See Outler's editorial preface to John Wesley's sermon "Of the Church" in *The Works of John Wesley*, 3 (Nashville, TN: Abingdon, 1987), 46. By this Outler meant that the emphasis on discipline and the emphasis on sacramental piety were uneasily conjoined in life and practice. What was already unstable about Wesley's ecclesiological synthesis of eighteenth-century England continued to deteriorate in the American context, where a progressive identification between "Methodist" and "American" emerged during the nineteenth century. In the twentieth century as "mainline Protestant" denominations have declined, so has the distinctiveness of early Methodist ecclesiology.

48. Oddly enough, Hauerwas's career parallels the existence of the United Methodist Church, which came into being with the merger of the Methodist Church and the Evangelical United Brethren Church in 1966–1968.

habit to break." In a cultural context where the "triumph" of the Methodist Church coincided with the era of late nineteenth- and early twentieth-century American imperialism, the degree of habituation to Constantinian practices can hardly be overestimated.

What this means with respect to the UMC is that United Methodists have to be reminded of what they have forgotten about their own tradition, including the distinctive patterns of ecclesial authority that arise out of that tradition. On more than one occasion, a United Methodist bishop has discovered that Hauerwas has a stronger conception of the "teaching office" of the episcopate in United Methodism than the bishops do! In fact, one way of making sense of Hauerwas's famous comment that he was a "high-church Mennonite . . . that is to say that I am a Methodist" is that *the very practices* that constituted early Methodism are almost entirely absent from the contemporary United Methodist churches. Yet, such practices as "giving and receiving counsel" which were familiar to early Methodists do survive in many Mennonite/Anabaptist congregations, and the practice of the weekly celebration of the eucharist, which was mandated by John Wesley, still survives in most Catholic and Episcopalian practices. From Hauerwas's vantage point, United Methodists have forgotten what should be most constitutive of their apostolate as an evangelical order in the church catholic.

In these senses, then, Hauerwas's reading of the cultural situation in American culture with respect to the politics of remembering fits his own denomination very well. A case in point is the popular use of the locution "Wesleyan quadrilateral" as a way of negotiating the ideological differences that exist in the United Methodist Church, especially since 1968. Variously described as "sources" and "criteria" for theological and moral reflection, scripture, reason, tradition, and experience are known as the quadrilateral: "This fourfold locus of religious authority has gained remarkable acceptance as a tool for theological analysis."[49] The so-called Wesleyan quadrilateral[50]— the conceptual model by which scripture, tradition, reason, and experience

---

49. Ted Campbell, "The 'Wesleyan Quadrilateral': The Story of a Modern Methodist Myth," in *Doctrine and Theology in the United Methodist Church*, ed. Thomas A. Langford (Nashville, TN: Kingswood Books, 1991), 154. As Campbell goes on to note, the quadrilateral is also used "as a starting point for the recovery of the Wesleyan theological tradition in a modern ecumenical context" (154).

50. Albert Outler is widely credited with having coined this term in such essays as "The Wesleyan Quadrilateral: In John Wesley," *Wesleyan Theological Journal* 20 (spring 1985): 7–18. Ted Campbell has argued that this phrase is best understood as a "modern Methodist myth."

are deployed for contemporary doctrine and discipline—is often cited by pastors, theologians, and church leaders as a way to approach moral issues *as if* they exist outside the constraints of human history in some ideal framework. It is not uncommon for United Methodists to refer to "reason" or "experience" as if these sources were to be used as moral trumps to contradict interpretations of the Bible or the Christian tradition. In sum, it often appears as if one can talk about ethics in the United Methodist Church *without* standing within the particularities of any given human community or tradition, much less the Wesleyan or Evangelical United Brethren traditions.

This "modern Methodist myth," as Ted Campbell has described the "quadrilateral," came into use (through the influence of Albert Outler) as a way of giving "the rejection of uncritical views of scriptural primacy the weight of Methodism's deepest roots."[51] Unfortunately, this stratagem for achieving tolerance has succeeded in pushing back the tide of fundamentalism in the UMC at the price of forgetting the strong role played by scripture and tradition in early Methodism. In other words, the issues that Hauerwas writes about with respect to questions of the relationship of authority to tradition and community are precisely the issues that Hauerwas confronts in the typical congregation of the UMC. Reifications like "reason" and "experience" have replaced practices of discipleship, and no one seems to realize how much has been forgotten or how disconnected the "project" of Methodism has become from the moral adventure of the Kingdom of God. What initially seems as if it describes a strange split in Hauerwas's psyche—his self-description as a "high church Mennonite"—turns out, on examination, to demonstrate the *forgetfulness* of American liberal Protestantism about why Christian discipleship is an adventure.[52]

Remembering the Marks of the Church: the Adventure
of Christian Discipleship
In this respect, Hauerwas regards the conflictedness displayed by American Protestant communions about ecclesial authority to be a reflection of the

---

51. Campbell, "The Wesleyan Quadrilateral," 154.

52. Hauerwas is part of an ecumenical group of scholars, pastors, and activists known as The Ekklesia Project. For more about this adventure in radical discipleship, see Stanley Hauerwas and Michael Budde, "The Ekklesia Project: A School for Subversive Friendships" *The Ekklesia Project: Pamphlet #1* (Eugene, OR: Wipf and Stock Publishers, 2000), 1–12. In addition to the essay, this pamphlet includes an appendix "A Declaration and An Invitation to All Christians" (16–21) and a list of those persons who have endorsed this document (22–27).

individualistic culture that surrounds them. Like the warrens of rabbits in *Watership Down* which experienced amnesia about their own history and practices (see essay 9, Hauerwas's parable of American political liberalism), Christian congregations must recover the capacity to remember before they can begin to resolve the host of vexing questions about how authority is to be exercised in the context of the community of faith. As he tries to make clear to the editors of *U.S. Catholic* (see essay 26), this begins when Christians recover the sense of Christianity's being an adventure. With this end in view, Hauerwas repeatedly tells stories of what happens when congregations like Broadway United Methodist Church (South Bend, Indiana) and Aldersgate United Methodist Church (Chapel Hill, North Carolina) learn to live peaceably with neighbors through rediscovering the transformative power of the sacraments of baptism and eucharist. He also tells narratives about congregations of the black church rediscovering the possibility of extending hospitality to the stranger, including unwanted children. Other stories are historical, such as the powerful narrative of what happened in the village of Le Chambon during World War II when members of a Protestant church gave shelter to Jewish refugees while loving enemies (the Nazis) as well.

The point of such narration is *not* to idealize the church, but rather to call attention to what *some* of the "marks" (of excellence) of the church are when they are embodied (see essay 19). By narrating the stories of communities of character that display patience and hope as well as the courage and humility of those who know the grace of God in Jesus Christ, Hauerwas makes visible what it means to be "the servant community." By narrating the moral excellence displayed in the lives of such diverse persons as Dorothy Day, Andre and Magda Trocme, Martin Luther King, Jr., and Olin Teague, Hauerwas *renders visible* the possibility of sanctification, understood not as an abstract set of doctrines but as a practical reality that characterizes persons of character. Finally, when Hauerwas gives a commencement address (see essay 15) that uses portions of Anne Tyler's novel *Saint Maybe* as a way of depicting "The Church of the Second Chance," he helps the students to understand in what senses Goshen College is a Mennonite institution, and he calls attention to how they have embarked on an adventure of Christian discipleship that requires the "skills" of truthfulness and forgiveness.

The particularity of each of these narratives is instructive. Hauerwas would never claim to have isolated *all* of the "marks" of the church, or to have provided an exhaustive description of all of the forms of moral excellence that might be displayed in any given community of faith. Nor is he interested in providing some kind of ecclesiological theoretic that would anchor a particular version of the Protestant tradition as opposed to the traditions of Catholicism or Orthodoxy. On the contrary, Hauerwas argues that it is only as we are able to narrate the lives of holy people within the constraints of human history that we can begin to grasp what it means to combat our own inveterate tendency to self-deception and learn—as apprentices and companions of the holy ones—the skills of truthfulness as both the *intellectual virtue* most appropriate for the task of theological ethics and as the *moral virtue* necessary for the development of practical wisdom in living out the demands of the gospel in the context of the practices of everyday life.

None of these remarks should be taken to suggest that Hauerwas thinks he has resolved all conundrums about ecclesial authority that exist for Christians who find themselves confronting the liberal social order of the United States at the beginning of the third millennium. The fact that Hauerwas offers a more acute analysis of the problem of authority in mainline Protestant context should not be taken to mean that he thinks he has resolved all such questions. In fact, on more than one occasion, Hauerwas has also admitted to being puzzled about issues of ecclesial authority that have direct implications for his own life and work.[53] All of which is to say that, for Hauerwas as well as for his readers, the "adventure" of Christianity will continue to involve a set of contested arguments within (as well as among) the various Protestant, Catholic, and Orthodox traditions. Simply put, what Hauerwas has done is to have "developed a position from which such an argument [about ecclesial authority] can be meaningfully carried out"[54] by Christians in any of these traditions.

Conclusion

What import Hauerwas's essays in theological ethics *may yet have* for a world in which Stoic notions of fate are still more prevalent than Jesus' vision of the Kingdom as "an ecclesial space for peace" is not clear. What can be stated with assurance is that Hauerwas's essays in theological ethics provide a powerful explanation of the moral significance of the gathered church where would-be Christians take the time to worship the Triune God in the hope that this is not only what it means to be followers of the Way, but that their gathering as a people also points to the destiny of the world as God's creation.

53. For example, see his remarks about the authority of preaching in the foreword to *us*, 10.
54. Here I invoke the concluding line from one of Hauerwas's early essays "Toward an Ethics of Character" as published in *vv*, 67.

Further Reading

"The Moral Authority of Scripture: The Politics and Ethics of Remembering" (1981), in CC

"How Christian Ethics Came to Be" (1997), essay 1 in this volume

"On Keeping Theological Ethics Theological" (1983), essay 2 in this volume

"Tale of Two Stories: On Being a Christian and a Texan" (1988), in CET

"A Testament of Friends: How My Mind Has Changed," *The Christian Century* 107, no. 7 (February 28, 1990): 212–16.

See also the following (sections of) introductions from Hauerwas's books:

"Why the 'Sectarian Temptation' Is a Misrepresentation" (1988), essay 4 in this volume

"On What I Owe to Whom" and "My Ecclesial Stance" (1983), from introduction to PK

"Positioning: In the Church and University but Not of Either" (1994), in DF

"Church Matters" and "The Church as Polis" (1995), from introduction to IGC

"Theological Interventions and Interrogations" (1997), in WW

"The Rough Ground of Theology" (1998), from the introduction to STT

Selected Annotated Bibliography: 1971–2001
John Berkman and James Fodor

"The Nonresistant Church: The Theological Ethics of John Howard Yoder" (1971), in *vv*.

This is Hauerwas's first and most important essay on the significance of the work of the Mennonite historian and theologian John Howard Yoder. As a graduate student in the 1960s, Hauerwas had accepted a version of Reinhold Niebuhr's "Christian realism" as the way to justify Christians resorting to violence. Hauerwas finds in Yoder's writings an argument for Christian nonviolence that Niebuhr's analysis does not address, and an articulation of a theologically compelling form of Christian social criticism. The conclusions that Hauerwas draws in this essay have profoundly shaped all of Hauerwas's work.

"Situation Ethics, Moral Notions, and Moral Theology" (1971), in *vv*.

Drawing on the philosophical insights of Wittgenstein and Kovesi, this essay reframes the debate among Fletcher, Ramsey, and Evans over the status of moral principles, arguing that virtuous moral decisions ultimately depend more on skilled moral descriptions than on adequate grounding of moral principles. One of Hauerwas's earliest and most programmatic essays on moral theory, which influences all his later work.

"Love's Not All You Need" (1972), in *vv*.

Challenging the underlying assumption in the situation ethics debate that "love" is the central moral notion in Christian ethics, Hauerwas argues that such "love-monism" typically presupposes an inadequate Christology, one that evacuates the political significance of Jesus' proclamation of the Kingdom of God. Without the broader gospel context, "love" ends up as little more than a sentimental affirmation of the political status quo rather than a prophetic challenge to it.

"The Future of Christian Social Ethics," in *That They May Live: Theological Reflection on the Quality of Life,* ed. George Devine (Staten Island, NY: Alba House, 1972), 123–31.

Originally a response to Charles Curran at the College Theology Society. This essay shows why comparing Pope Leo XIII and Karl Marx can be mutually illuminating. Both were conservative radicals critiquing industrial capitalism, as they saw it destroying forms of community necessary for sustaining human solidarity. They differed in that Leo XIII assumed, whereas Marx did not, that "any [adequate] account of human solidarity depended on the acknowledgment that what we share in common is our worship of God."

"The Significance of Vision: Toward an Aesthetic Ethic" (1972), in *vv*.

Inspired by the work of Iris Murdoch, this essay criticizes the tendency of contemporary ethicists to focus almost exclusively on humans as actors and self-creators, especially to the extent that it ignores the indispensability of vision for the moral life. Though not diminishing in any way the importance of action description for ethics, this corrective underscores the sense in which any adequate account of the moral life presupposes a vision of the true and the good. See also "Murdochian Muddles: Can We Get Through Them If God Does Not Exist" (1996) in *ww*.

"The Self as Story: A Reconsideration of the Relation of Religion and Morality from the Agent's Perspective" (1973), in *vv*.

Whereas some philosophical ethicists (e.g., Strawson, Braithwaite, Gert) have argued that morality is necessarily distinct from religious beliefs, "The Self as Story" argues that one's religious convictions (or lack thereof) inevitably influence the form and substance of one's morality. For one can act only in a world one can envision, which in turn is partially determined by the kind of person one is becoming through the stories learned and embodied in a particular life plan. Though provisional and underdeveloped, this essay reveals some of Hauerwas's early interlocutors.

"Aristotle and Thomas Aquinas on the Ethics of Character" (1975), in CCL.

The starting point for Hauerwas's groundbreaking work in the recovery of virtue for theological ethics begins here. While primarily a historical analysis of Aristotle and Aquinas on character, Hauerwas considers their accounts of the self (particularly how it is formed in the interrelationship among practical reason, the passions, and the virtues) to be the most adequate systematic account in the history of ethics. Hauerwas's readings of Aristotle and Aquinas continue to develop in "Character, Narrative, and Growth in the Christian Life" (1980), essay 11 in this volume, "Courage Exemplified" (1993), essay 14 in this volume, "The Truth about God" (1998) in *STT,* and especially "Theological Reflections on Aristotelian Themes" (1997), in *CAV.*

"A Critique of the Concept of Character in Theological Ethics" (1975), in *CCL*.

Why did character and virtue have so little place in Protestant ethics in the mid–twentieth century? Hauerwas examines the work of two very different theologians: Karl Barth and Rudolf Bultmann. While Barth and Bultmann rightly seek to preserve the action of God as "the first word" for theological ethics, it must not be "the only word." These theologians share an emphasis on the priority of the command of God, leaving little space for the complexity of human response to God. Hauerwas argues that the formal features in the ethics of Barth and Bultmann (unwittingly) prepared the way for the development of the situation ethics of the 1960s. While a perversion of their thought, "situation ethics easily translates the ethics of command into an ethics of individual fulfilment by assuming the problematic status of God's command."

"Having and Learning to Care for Retarded Children" (1975), in *TT*.

For Christians to welcome mentally handicapped children into their lives without self-pity or false courage requires two things of them: first, they must disabuse themselves of the assumption that they "choose" their children and thus are responsible for them; and second, they must truly see and love these children as gifts from God. They must acquire—with the church's aid—the necessary childrearing practices and virtues of care (e.g., patience, honesty, trust, and humor).

"Story and Theology" (1976), in *TT*.

The emphasis on story as the grammatical setting for religious convictions reminds Christians of (1) the interrelatedness and interdependency of Christian convictions; (2) their inherently practical character; (3) the peculiar kind of cognitive claims such convictions entail; and (4) the sense in which the stories of God, self, and the world are analogically connected. See also "From System to Story" (1976) in *TT*, "Self-Deception and Autobiography" (1974), essay 10 in this volume, and "The Self as Story" (1973) in *VV*.

"From System to Story: An Alternative Pattern for Rationality in Ethics," with David B. Burrell (1976), in *TT*.

Contrasts the "standard account of moral rationality" with its appeals to neutrality and universality (system) with an account that acknowledges the narrative embeddedness of moral agents and communities (story). Appealing to Aristotle's account of practical rationality and the narrative in Augustine's *Confessions,* the authors argue that only a narrative-dependent account of moral reflection allows the significance of the distinctive convictions of Christians and Jews to be adequately displayed.

"Learning to See Red Wheelbarrows: On Vision and Relativism" (1977), in *Journal of the American Academy of Religion* 45, no. 2 (Supplement, June 1977): 643–55.

In this early and hard-to-find article, Hauerwas responds to J. Wesley Robbins's criticism (published in the same issue) that Hauerwas's refusal to make the Kantian principle of universalizability central for his ethical reflection leads to moral subjectivism or relativism. This exchange was part of an ongoing debate about relativism in relation to the "standard account" of morality. Robbins's "Narrative, Morality, and Religion," *Journal of Religious Ethics* 8, no. 1 (spring 1980), and Hauerwas's "From System to Story: An Alternative Pattern for Rationality in Ethics" (1977) in *TT* and "The Church in a Divided World: The Interpretative Power of the Christian Story" (1980) in *CC* were all contributions to the analysis of this important issue.

"Hope Faces Power: Thomas More and the King of England," with Thomas Shaffer (1978), in *CET*.

Possessing the virtue of hope, Thomas More is able to see the possibilities, limits, and seductions of power in an unusually truthful manner. Theologically, hope is a sign of a deep trust in God's truth and love. When exercised in a way that confronts political powers, those with such power may well unleash violence against the hopeful.

"Jesus: The Story of the Kingdom" (1978), in *CC*.

Challenging those ethicists who would separate Jesus' teaching from social ethics (e.g., Reinhold Niebuhr) as well as those theologians who would separate Jesus' teaching from Christology, this essay explores Jesus' identity as the narrative display of the reign of God. Hauerwas resists any strong separations between the person and work of Christ or between Christ and his community. Jesus' story can only be understood rightly by the community willing to make his story their own. Thus, Hauerwas advances one of his most tenacious convictions—that witness is more determinative than epistemology. The church, then, is that community, shaped as Christ's disciples, that is able to tell his story faithfully because it is the ongoing embodiment of that story.

"The Moral Value of the Family" (1978), in CC.

The so-called crisis of the family is the result not of the absence or even the breakdown of a moral ethos but precisely the outgrowth and logical result of a particular ethos. Family kinship has always been an anomaly for the liberal tradition. In the Christian tradition, its crucial moral importance lies in its ability to help Christians "bind time," to learn to be historic, tradition-dependent people.

"Abortion: Why the Arguments Fail" (1980), in CC.

Perhaps Hauerwas's most powerful and well-known analysis of this issue. Given the dominant ethos of liberalism, arguments in our culture concerning abortion are intractable. The current impasse is also an indictment of the church for failing to challenge that ethos with regards to its own form of argumentation about abortion. Hauerwas advocates the centrality of forms of hospitality, care, and support to the unborn child, without which the practice of abortion in a culture informed by liberal presumptions assumes the form of a necessity.

"The Moral Authority of Scripture" (1980), in CC.

The authority of Scripture is dependent on the existence of a church community willing and ready to live by the story it tells. Hauerwas follows Frei, Kelsey, and Auerbach in asserting that Scripture "creates a world," but he adds that this world must be borne by a community of disciples shaped by traditions of reading and practice. Scripture's authority, then, is a political claim. That is, it does not depend on something that inheres in the text itself (e.g., inerrancy or inspiration) but rather on the memory of a community that is faithful to the God of Scripture. Hauerwas's appeal to the language of "classic" in this essay stands in some tension with the rest of his argument; he later critiques the appeal to the "classic" in "A Non-Violent Proposal for Christian Participation in the Culture Wars," *Soundings* 75, no. 4 (winter 1992): 477–92.

"The Church in a Divided World" (1980), in CC.

A defense of Hauerwas's theological project against charges of relativism and tribalism (i.e., irresponsible withdrawal from the world). In particular, he questions the assumption that "relativism" is itself an intellectually stable or coherent notion, much less one that somehow needs to be "overcome." Modern "relativism" is typically a correlate of equally problematic foundationalist epistemologies, which, however, are useful to legitimate liberal social orders. See also "The Non-Violent Terrorist: In Defense of Christian Fanaticism" (1998), in STT.

"Resurrection, the Holocaust, and the Obligation to Forgive" (1980), in US.

Far from marking God's retreat from the world, the resurrection of Jesus announces that Christians can do nothing to alienate God's steadfast will to forgive and love them. The Holocaust presents a profound challenge to this. Like the Apostle Thomas, the painful lesson to be learned is that the resurrected Lord is also the crucified Messiah. The God Christians worship is one whose power resides in steadfast graciousness, not in making the horrible reality of the crucifixion or the Holocaust come out right. Freed to live as Easter people—not triumphalistically, but chastened by the history of suffering of the Jews, which is thus their history—Christians recognize their obligation to accept and to ask for forgiveness.

"A Tale of Two Stories: On Being a Texan and a Christian" (1981), in CET.

In the midst of a then burgeoning interest in (and emerging disagreements about) "narrative theology," Hauerwas seeks to illumine (and enliven) the grammar of Christian convictions through narrative display of being a Texan and a Christian. Among other things, the essay narrates a particular example of the interrelationship of ideology, self-deception, truth, and nonviolence taken from Hauerwas's own life. In particular, it challenges the false story at the heart of American liberal culture, namely, that individuals may create their own story, part of the wider false story that America is beholden to no determinative past and hence uniquely open to future possibilities.

"The Church and Liberal Democracy: The Moral Limits of a Secular Polity" (1981), in CC.

An examination of various challenges a liberal democratic polity presents for Christian social ethics. Within such polities, Christian enthusiasm for political involvement is too often correlative with Christians forgetting the church's more profound political task—namely, to be herself in order that secular polities might recognize their own possibilities and limits. The challenge is always for the church to be a "contrast model" for polities that do not know God, reminding them that the church must serve the world on her own terms.

"The Virtues and Our Communities: Human Nature as History" (1981), in CC.

An influential milestone for the recovery of "virtue" for theological ethics. Although appreciative of the accounts of the virtues in Aristotle and Aquinas for understanding the formation of the self, Hauerwas seeks to emphasize the relationship between habituation (i.e., virtue) and history. In other words, accounts of the "unity of the virtues" often fail to recognize the necessarily "historic" character of theological virtues (e.g., hope and patience), whose expression require a timeful church that lives "between the times." See also "The Truth about God" (1998) in *STT*.

"Why Abortion Is a Religious Issue" (1981), in *CC*.

The abortion debate in America has been too narrowly circumscribed, which in part accounts for its intractability. Seeking to reframe the debate, this essay argues that moral notions like "abortion" require narrative display. In a Christian context, this requires a normative account of how parenthood contributes to the ends of the church's communal life under God. Christian attitudes and practices regarding sexual behavior generally and abortion in particular must be determined by the form of life required to be open to the gift of children and to appropriately provide for their care.

"God the Measurer," *Journal of Religion* 62, no. 4 (October 1982): 402–11.

An evaluation of James Gustafson's critique of anthropocentrism. It is argued that the best antidote to anthropocentric tendencies is not Gustafson's "theocentrism," but a more Trinitarian perspective. See also "A Trinitarian Theology of the Chief End of All Flesh" (1992), in *IGC*.

"On Keeping Theological Ethics Imaginative," with Philip Foubert (1982), in *AN*. Originally published under the title "Disciplined Seeing: Imagination and the Moral Life."

Imagination is a requirement for Christians who wish to live morally. The truly imaginative person necessarily possesses certain virtues. Conversely, the exercise of the moral life requires virtues that compel the imagination. The "imaginative" are precisely those who have the courage and hope to see beyond the "necessary" or "available" options, and in so doing broaden our vision and enlarge the limits of faithfulness, especially with regard to the temptation to use violence to control our history.

"On Taking Religion Seriously: The Challenge of Jonestown" (1982), in *AN*.

Jim Jones and the mass suicide of nine hundred people of the People's Temple in Guyana provides the occasion for this reflection on the character of Christian martyrdom. In addition, the disappearance of apocalyptic from mainstream American Christianity results in the latter's inability to understand movements such as Jonestown. Whereas the typical critique of such movements is to label them "fanatical," this essay argues that what must be shown is the falsity of the beliefs held.

"The Reality of the Church: Even a Democratic State Is Not the Kingdom" (1982), in *AN*.

A rebuttal to then current attempts (e.g., Richard Neuhaus's "Christianity and Democracy") to theologically legitimate democracy per se. When the church lives true to itself as the only true polity Christians know in this life, it witnesses to God's sovereignty over all nations, thereby enabling Christians to resist the false dilemma of choosing either democratic or totalitarian political arrangements.

"A Qualified Ethic: The Narrative Character of Christian Ethics" (1983), in *PK*.

An argument for the necessarily "qualified" character of Christian ethics contra the quest of modern ethical theory for a universal foundation that would free moral judgments from dependence on historically contingent communities.

"Constancy and Forgiveness: The Novel as a School for Virtue" (1983), in *DF*.

Modern, realistic novels function as an excellent resource for displaying the kind of redescriptions necessary to live as Christians in liberal societies. Through reference to the novels of Anthony Trollope, constancy is shown to be unsustainable without forgiveness.

"On Being Historic: Agency, Character, and Sin" (1983), in *PK*.

An appreciation of the historic, narrative character of human existence is integral to understanding the truth claims of the Christian story, the complexity of which requires parsing in terms of agency, character, and sin. Agency names one's ability to locate one's action within an ongoing community of language users; character is the form one's agency takes in one's beliefs and intentions; sin names the resultant self-deception when one seeks to construe one's life fundamentally as an achievement rather than as a gift.

"On Surviving Justly: Ethics and Nuclear Disarmament" (1983), in *AN*.

An analysis and critique of four responses to the threat of nuclear war: pacifist, just war, survivalist, and sovereign-state deterrence. What all four responses share in common is an insufficient or false eschatology, which confuses peace with order and thus offers false consolation, which trades in abstract ideals and thus cannot sustain concrete practices of actual communities. Although American culture lacks a coherent moral account to sustain an antinuclear stance, a Christian eschatology can relativize the importance of survival, in light of its overriding commitment to fidelity.

"Tragedy and Joy: The Spirituality of Peaceableness" (1983), in PK.

Here Hauerwas presents an example of how Christians embody the Gospel, namely, through the practice of "the spirituality of peaceableness." Beginning with an analysis of the 1932 exchange between the brothers H. Richard and Reinhold Niebuhr over the appropriate response to the Japanese invasion of Manchuria, Hauerwas argues that the road to peaceableness begins with "the grace of doing one thing." We must begin by taking one step toward learning the ascetic disciplines (i.e., the formation necessary to hear God's word for our particular lives) necessary in our day. By learning to wait, to contentedly rest, to be a friend and to be loved, we show our desire to live at peace with ourselves, our neighbors, and most of all God. This path—living with the assurance of God's redemption—is the route to joy. The central themes of this essay are elaborated in "Taking Time for Peace: The Ethical Significance of the Trivial" (1986), in CET.

"Work as Co-Creation: A Critique of a Remarkably Bad Idea" (1983), in IGC.

While Hauerwas welcomed the renewed focus on economics in a Papal social encyclical, he critiqued the 1981 encyclical Laborem Exercens for an understanding of "work" that fails to adequately show how it is at once distorted by sin and yet a means God gives humans to serve one another. Instead of producing an economic theory that in the end fails to name and thus fails to confront the key economic challenges of our day, what was needed in this encyclical was analogically appropriate economic reflection on specific issues (e.g., just wage, usury) that could challenge sinful economic arrangements. See also "In Praise of Centesimus Annus" (1992) in IGC and "A Trinitarian Theology of the Chief End of all Flesh" (1992), in IGC.

"Characterizing Perfection: Second Thoughts on Character and Sanctification" (1985), in STT.

An attempt to balance individualistic and Catholic accounts of the church's holiness. On the one hand, individualistic/pietistic accounts of sanctification are refused. On the other hand, the Christian doctrine of holiness and sanctification is kept from devolving into a form of narcissistic fascination with one's own peculiar status before God by the insistence on practices of self-examination (set within a worshipful life of prayer and confession).

"God as Participant: Time and History in the Work of James Gustafson" (1985), in WW.

An examination of the moral methodology of James Gustafson. Beginning with general claims about philosophical anthropology rather than particular theological claims (e.g., the place of Israel or Christological claims), Gustafson leaves little conceptual space for the kind of temporal and historical "participation" he at times advocates. One apparent implication of his methodology is a politics that cannot account for radical change.

"Reconciling the Practice of Reason: Casuistry in a Christian Context" (1986), in CET.

Unlike current philosophical moralities (e.g., utilitarianism, Kantianism, contractarianism), Christian ethics begins not with a theory but with a God revealed in scripture and an accountable community. Displaying the differences that follow by attending to the question of Christian use of law courts in the Mennonite tradition, this essay shows the community-specific nature of practical reasoning (casuistry). Attending to this specific casuistical question reveals the interrelationship between Christian convictions about reconciliation and the community's practice of reconciliation. An important essay that has received little attention.

"Some Theological Reflections on Guttierrez's Use of 'Liberation' as a Theological Concept," *Modern Theology* 3, no. 1 (1986): 67–76.

While affirming Guttierez's attempts to link salvation and social practice, Hauerwas suggests that liberation theology too often underwrites an account of liberation that is at odds with the Christian promise of freedom in service to God. "At times," he writes, "[Guttierez's] account of liberation sounds far more like that of Kant and the Enlightenment than it does the Kingdom established by Christ." Without a correlative account of equality and power, liberation proves to be inadequate as a social analysis and strategy. More important, Guttierez's use of liberation seems to function at a level of abstraction that conceals the distinctive substance of Christian freedom as a form of service in community that cannot be reduced to mere autonomy.

"Taking Time for Peace: The Ethical Significance of the Trivial" (1986), in CET.

With the (then) threat of nuclear war, or the reality of world starvation and neighborhood poverty, how can we justify any activity that is not directly responding to such tragedies? Hauerwas argues that the proper response to such a totalitarian outlook on life is to reclaim the significance of the trivial, that is, of reading novels, playing sports, building communities, and, most important, worshipping God. But this is possible only if one recognizes that God's power is not the coercive power of the totalitarian, but is manifest in his patience. Our patient God creates the time for us to learn that our lives are distorted as long as we think we, rather than God, rule this world. Hauerwas displays these claims in the exemplary "trivial" activities of raising lemurs, maintaining universities, and especially by opening our lives to children.

"On Honor: By Way of a Comparison of Karl Barth and Trollope" (1988), in DF.

Whereas Trollope's novelistic accounts of honor are largely complementary to Barth's theological analysis of the same, Trollope's attention to particular communities allows him to show how honor is developed and sustained in a way Barth's more abstract account cannot. Though acknowledging accounts of honor that are not self-consciously Christian, the essay seeks to show the difference that Christian practices make for understanding honor (and constancy), and how the practice of such virtues are integral to the whole of the Christian life.

"Flight from Foundationalism, or Things Aren't as Bad as They Seem," with Phil Kenneson (1989), in ww.

An internal critique of Jeffrey Stout's moral bricolage that claims to avoid both foundationalism and relativism and to escape both nihilism and communitarianism. The crucial weakness in Stout's "modest pragmatism" is that its resources cannot be rendered fully intelligible insofar as they remain abstracted from specific communities of memory necessarily formed by a people of virtue.

"The Importance of Being Catholic: Unsolicited Advice from a Protestant Bystander" (1990), in IGC.

This address to Californian Catholics on ecumenical ethics is the context for this constructive account of how a "natural law ethics" can assist Catholics in a "pluralistic" society. Criticizing ahistorical accounts of the natural law advanced by "Americanist" Catholic ethicists (e.g., McCann, Hollenbach, Weigel), Hauerwas argues that a natural law advocated by Catholics is unavoidably tradition-dependent. If Catholics do not recognize this—and correlatively fail to attend to the distinctive habits and practices of their Church—they will become increasingly incapable of the disciplined moral practice and discourse necessary to avoid widespread capitulation to the general societal ethos called "America."

"Interpreting the Bible as a Political Act," with D. Stephen Long, *Religion and Intellectual Life* 6, nos. 3–4 (spring/summer 1989): 134–42.

Hauerwas argues that fundamentalist and historical-critical interpretations of the Bible are but two sides of the same coin, sharing the common assumption that the

Bible is an "object" of investigation whose meaning is intrinsic to the text and plain to the open, unbiased individual. Both are offshoots of the common heretical seedbed of a misunderstood doctrine of *sola scriptura*. In contrast, Hauerwas and Long draw on the work of Stanley Fish to show that reading the Bible is always a political act and thus must be understood in terms of community, power, and authority. With reference to the Vatican II *Dogmatic Constitution on Divine Revelation* and Georges Florovsky's account of Orthodox hermeneutics, they make the case that right understanding of Scripture requires the communal and liturgical context of the gathered people of God. This essay may be seen as working out implications of "The Servant Community" (1983), essay 19 in this volume. Also, the thesis of this essay shapes Hauerwas's 1993 book *US*.

"Medicine as Theodicy" (1990), in *NS*.

Embedded in this narrative of children dying from leukemia is a critique of the inevitable failure of political liberalism to provide an adequate rationale for medical practice. Though acknowledging no shared conception of death, liberalism presumes that the fear of death constitutes an adequate basis for medical practice. But without a shared conception of death we all die "alone," and medicine thus falls prey to the unconstrained desires of the liberal ethos to either forestall or at least control death. In this context, Christians need to recover and proclaim in word and practice an alternative and truthful narrative that comprehends and relativizes the power that death exercises over us.

"Pacifism: A Form of Politics," in *Peace Betrayed? Essays on Pacifism and Politics,* ed. Michael Cromartie (Washington, DC: Ethics and Public Policy Center Publication, 1990), 133–41.

Any compelling account of nonviolence as an ongoing practice of the church must address the question of how those who have fought in war nonetheless remain part of God's kingdom. See also "Should War Be Eliminated?" (1984), essay 20 in this volume, and "Whose 'Just' War? Which Peace?" (1992) in *DF*.

"The Testament of Friends: How My Mind Has Changed," *The Christian Century* 107, no. 7 (28 February 1990): 212–16.

Undoubtedly the clearest and best account of development in Hauerwas's thought through the first half of his career. In particular, it unselfconsciously narrates the shift in Hauerwas's work that can roughly be timed with his move from Notre Dame to Duke in 1984. Around that time, Hauerwas becomes less interested in theoretical analyses of the self or of the virtues, and more interested in their display in the context of concrete Christian communities. As he puts it, it is the discovery that "Christian beliefs do not need translation but should be demonstrated through Christian practice, not the least of which is friendship of and in a concrete community." Hauerwas sees his task as a theologian—"one of the lesser services the church provides"—to take what friends both living and dead have given him to faithfully serve the wonderful adventure called Kingdom.

"Honor in the University," *First Things* 10 (February 1991): 26–31.

Modern universities find it difficult to sustain honor codes to the degree that the kinds of practices necessary to make honor intrinsic to the university's own task have been abandoned by both the professors and the students.

"The Politics of Justice: Why Justice Is a Bad Idea for Christians" (1991), in AC.

Though on the surface challenging "justice" and "rights," the point of this essay is to challenge construals of the notion of justice that presume the fundamentals of political liberalism. Only by questioning these presumptions can Christians recover the significance of the gospel as a social alternative and thereby serve the wider society by bearing witness to the righteousness of God as embodied in the church's own politics.

"The Politics of Salvation: Why There Is No Salvation Outside the Church" (1991), in AC.

The awkwardness and ambiguity of our times presents a challenge to Christians to recover the peculiar political locality of salvation known as church, outside of which there is no salvation. Far from exclusionary, this traditional Augustinian doctrine rather positively affirms the church as the only true political society inasmuch as it rightly orders our desires and directs our worship to the one true God. The church therefore redefines the public itself, exposing life outside the Christian community as inauthentically political, something less than truly public.

"Why Resident Aliens Struck a Chord," with William Willimon (1991), in IGC.

An analysis of the reason for the extraordinary popularity (approaching 100,000 copies sold) of *Resident Aliens* (1988). Rejecting the temptation to bask in its "success," the authors see it as a contribution to a broader movement to renew the life of the church. By understanding discipleship as becoming part of a peaceable people on a journey to God, the authors hope to help American Christians disengage from the habits of a (potentially or actually) violent citizenry necessitated by the modern state.

"A Homage to Mary and to the University Called Notre Dame" (1992), in *IGC*.

Drawing on personal reminisces about the fourteen years he taught at the University of Notre Dame (1970–1984), this humorous and yet serious essay constitutes a series of reminders to Catholics of how their practices—particularly their Marian devotional practices—serve to protect them from giving ultimate allegiance to the nation-state or any particular ethnic group.

"A Trinitarian Theology of the Chief End of All Flesh," with John Berkman (1992), in *IGC*.

A theological understanding of the proper relationship between humans and other animals begins with the confession that all creaturely life is ordered to serve God's pleasure, and that creation is an eschatological, Christological, and ecclesial confession. As our chief end is to become signs of God's present and coming kingdom, vegetarianism may constitute a witness—on analogy with pacifism—to the peace of God in a world of violence.

"In Praise of *Centesimus Annus*" (1992), in *IGC*.

Pope John Paul II's encyclical *Centesimus annus* (1991) signals a return to the radical ecclesial vision of Leo XIII's 1891 encyclical *Rerum novarum*. Both encyclicals contend that the worship of God is the church's foremost social witness for the world. By resisting the temptation to advocate a particular "model" of economics, the church stands in witness as an alternative to all such models. It does so by attending to and confronting the contingencies of history. By engaging in theological commentary on specific, concrete histories of peoples (e.g., the writings of Leo XIII, John Paul II and Vaclav Havel), the church shows how its worship of God is integral to habits of truth-telling. Such habits are in turn crucial for the formation of a good society. Originally paired with an essay by the British Christian ethicist R. H. Preston in the journal *Theology*.

"The Church and/as God's Non-Violent Imagination," with Philip Kenneson, *Pro Ecclesia* 1, no. 3 (fall 1992): 76–88.

The skills, habits, and practices of the church are an imaginative embodiment of the character of God. That imaginative embodiment is shown especially in the interrelationship between practices of nonviolence and care for the weak. The God whom Christians worship will not settle for a "peace" that is created with violence, nor will this God have our lives made "better" through the elimination of the mentally handicapped.

"The Irony of Reinhold Niebuhr: The Ideological Character of 'Christian Realism,'" with Michael Broadway (1992), in ww.

A critique of Niebuhr's Christian realism. Historicizing claims notwithstanding, Niebuhr offers an ahistorical ontology of conflict purporting to deliver timeless truths about the "human condition." Because Niebuhr's account of politics renders Jesus irrelevant and distrusts casuistical use of natural law, this "Christian realism" seems less a faithful explication of a political theology rooted in scripture and tradition and more a legitimating ideology for America's balance-of-power politics. For a fuller analysis of Niebuhr's theological assumptions, see chs. 4 and 5 of wgu.

"The Kingship of Christ: Why Freedom of Belief Is Not Enough," with Michael Baxter (1992), in igc.

Setting out to dispel the notion that Christians require a theory of church-state relations, the authors argue that the "separation" clause of the American Constitution presents a challenge to the church insofar as the latter's alliance is first and foremost to the kingship of Christ. Availing themselves of the work of Stanley Fish, John Courtney Murray, Charles Taylor, and Pope Pius XI, the authors contend that church-state relations in the United States are marked by irresolvable conflict and that Christian theologians are profoundly mistaken in advocating harmony between the two. In conclusion, they remind their readers that Christians are formed by practices such as celebrating the Feast of Christ the King, that direct them to their true allegiance. See also "Abortion: Why the Arguments Fail" (1980).

"A Non-Violent Proposal for Christian Participation in the Culture Wars," *Soundings* 75, no. 4 (winter 1992): 477–92.

Hauerwas critiques both sides of the political correctness and multiculturalism debates, as their shared context of liberalism tends to deflate all such conflicts into matters of personal opinion. Against advocates of a Western canon, Hauerwas argues that "classics" are neither obvious nor universally meaningful but rather gain their intelligibility from being read within a tradition. There is no alternative to university curriculums being politicized because they always already are. Hauerwas also critiques the multiculturalists for welcoming "the other" only when his or her otherness has been disarmed as private preference. The shared liberal assumptions of both sides make these "wars" innocuous as well as irresolvable. A truly Christian educational vision will refuse to simply reinforce liberalism, but rather witness to the forms of knowledge particular to the church.

"Whose 'Just' War? Which Peace?" (1992), in DF.

In the aftermath of the Persian Gulf War, most Christian theological attempts to evaluate it according to just war criteria were inadequate to the extent that they failed to notice the difference it makes as to who is asking the question, for what reason(s), and thus what constitutes the "justice" of the war in question. Such efforts are illusory and sinful, in that they hide Christian complicity in patterns of domination and violence.

"Christian Practice and the Practice of Law in a World without Foundations," *Mercer Law Review* 44, no. 3 (spring 1993): 743–51.

An exploration of the theological and ethical implications of accounts of the law that take as their overriding goal the preservation of social order.

"Communitarians and Medical Ethicists or 'Why I Am None of the Above' " (1993), in DF.

An analysis of the limits to communitarian "celebration" of virtue as a good in and of itself. By comparing and contrasting the kind of training currently undertaken by those becoming physicians and those becoming ministers, Hauerwas shows how Christians face just as many difficulties with communitarian as with liberal alternatives in how they ought to care for one another through the office of medicine. In the absence of a theologically informed account of rational practices, institutional authority, and a hierarchy of goods, current medical care increasingly approximates a form of bureaucracy. For if no goods beyond survival are held in common, then there are no criteria by which we place limits on the good that medicine serves. See also "Medicine as Theodicy" (1990).

"Can a Pacifist Think about War?" (1994), in DF.

A "conversation" with Bainton, Ramsey, and Yoder, arguing that our very descriptions of violence are shaped by our practices of (or failure to practice) peace. Through being shaped by Christian practices of forgiveness and reconciliation, Christians may come to see how nonviolence is integral to all their convictions and communities. See also "Casuistry in Context," essay 13 in this volume.

"The Church and the Mentally Handicapped: A Continuing Challenge to the Imagination" (1994), in DF.

Taking his cue from Garrett Green's reflections on the indispensability of imagination to theology (*Imagining God: Theology and Religious Imagination*), Hauerwas argues that the gift of the handicapped to the Christian church is precisely their challenge to "normal people" to form communities that include the handicapped and thus know how to be with and care for one another in such a way that we become God's imagination for the world. The handicapped are a reminder, therefore, that the God we worship is not easily domesticated.

"Jews and the Eucharist," *Perspectives* 9, no. 3 (March 1994): 14–15.

"There are many reasons why Protestant churches do not regularly celebrate Eucharist, but I think the main reason is most of us no longer believe our salvation comes through the Jews." So Hauerwas begins this essay in which he summons an overly "spiritual" Christianity to a renewed appreciation of materiality—in creation, in the flesh of Israel, and in the elements of the eucharist. A spiritualized Christianity threatens to become irrelevant and extraneous in the material realms of politics, economics, and social life. Hauerwas argues that Israel's witness to the materiality of God's salvation is precisely what Christians must hear in order to appreciate the materiality of their own practice of the eucharist.

"Killing Compassion" (1994), in DF.

One of Hauerwas's most compelling analyses of the central virtues of liberal society, he here draws on Charles Taylor's account of the ascendancy of instrumental rationality in modernity. Under liberal society's "technological imperative," compassion has become modernity's cardinal virtue. This new ethic of "compassion" seeks to rid the world of unnecessary suffering. However, having abandoned the virtue of patience and its concomitant practices, it easily turns destructive, especially in the evolving practices of medicine. Without the continued practices of worshipping a God whose patience is quintessentially demonstrated in the cross, Christians are without the necessary resources to dwell faithfully in a world of deep agony and suffering. See also "Practicing Patience: How Christians Should Be Sick" (1997), essay 18 in this volume and "Should Suffering Be Eliminated?" (1984), essay 28 in this volume.

"Living in Truth: Moral Theology as Pilgrimage," with David Burrell (1994), in IGC.

An evaluation of *Veritatis splendor*, Pope John Paul II's encyclical on methodology in moral theology. Sympathetic to the encyclical's critiques of, for example, proportionalism and introspective accounts of conscience, the essay applauds the encyclical's call to forge an "intrinsic and unbreakable bond between faith and morality," a bond made possible by its appeal to Jesus as a compassionate guide along the way of Christian pilgrimage. *Veritatis splendor*'s method is commensurate with its message: beginning with scripture, it shows how rational argument contributes to faith seeking understanding, only to return to the life and practice of the church informed by scripture.

"Practice Preaching" (1994), in *STT*.

An analysis of preaching as a practice of the Christian church. Drawing on a category of Alasdair MacIntyre, the essay argues that being a Christian is well understood as a "craft-bound" activity, that is more a matter of being initiated into a community of skilled practitioners than embracing a set of beliefs. Although the activity of preaching exhibits qualities of a craft, it is a practice with authority in that it is not the possession of any one individual. Because the practice of preaching is a community possession—belonging to hearers and proclaimers alike—it is truly a political activity, one through which the church may discover its common good.

"The Church's One Foundation Is Jesus Christ Her Lord; Or, In a World without Foundations All We Have Is the Church" (1994), in *IGC*.

A contribution to a Festschrift for the Baptist theologian James McClendon. Drawing on McClendon's work, this essay displays the shape and significance of faithful Christian practice when one rejects foundationalist epistemologies. Emphasizes the "epistemological importance" of those lives God has chosen and whom the church has named "saints." See also "Reading James McClendon Takes Practice" (1997), in *WW* and "What Could It Mean for the Church to Be the Body of Christ? A Question without a Clear Answer" (1995) in *IGC*.

"The Democratic Policing of Christianity" (1994), in *DF*.

One of the crucial reasons why mainline Protestantism is dying in America is because in appointing themselves guardians of the "public" (i.e., democracy), these churches have ended up curtailing and compromising their (theological) convictions in the interests of what would seem to "sustain" this social order. Ironically, in the process of seeking to lend such "Christian" support to the prevailing social ethos, these churches find themselves imploding, as their form of Protestant Christianity assumes the form of "gnostic knowledge" rather than a set of ecclesial practices and habits disciplined by the Gospel. Two (unwitting) twentieth-century examples of this approach are Walter Rauschenbusch and Reinhold Niebuhr. See also "A Christian Critique of Christian America," essay 22 in this volume.

"Whose Church? Which Future? Whither the Anabaptist Vision?" (1994), in *IGC*.

Fifty years after the publication of Harold Bender's *The Anabaptist Vision*, the demise of Christendom and the characteristics of late modernity require a different narration of an ongoing Anabaptist vision. In an age when emphasis on "ecclesial identity" is symptomatic of a desire to commodify one's history to make it more appealing in the religious marketplace, the traditionally radical Anabaptist emphasis on "voluntary church membership" cannot help but appear as an affirmation of the secular commitment to autonomy. To faithfully appropriate Bender's vision will involve leaving behind the comfort of what may no longer be helpful categories and to learn anew what constitutes a witness and what martyrdom might look like today.

"Creation as Apocalyptic: A Tribute to William Stringfellow," with Jeff Powell (1995), in *DF*.

Apocalyptic fundamentally challenges a prevailing view of our contemporary social world as a sealed network of causally determined functions. Whereas such a world discloses no possibilities for hope or radical transformation, apocalyptic discloses a world created by a God who rules the principalities and powers and who always creates new possibilities. Through its apocalyptic narration of existence, the eucharistic community of the church constitutes the epistemological prerequisite for understanding "how things are." See also "Christian Practice and the Practice of Law in a World without Foundations" (1993) and "On Taking Religion Seriously" (1982), in *AN*.

"How Christian Ethics Became Medical Ethics: The Case of Paul Ramsey" (1995), in *WW*.

An analysis of the role (or lack thereof) of theological convictions in Paul Ramsey's important and influential work in medical ethics. Ramsey was the first of a generation of theological ethicists who became, in one sense or another, "medical ethicists." Taking on the role of medical ethicist, Ramsey bracketed all but a very limited place for theology, as can be seen in the preface to Ramsey's *The Patient as Person* (1970). What remained (e.g., Ramsey's "ethic of neighbor love") is in the end insufficient to show how Christian practice might make a difference for understanding, let alone forming, the practice of medicine. Unwittingly, Ramsey contributed his part to that great tradition of Protestant liberalism, preparing the ground to weed out distinctive theological convictions from medical ethics.

"Remembering Martin Luther King Jr. Remembering" (1995), in ww.

Christian peace and unity entails a process of remembering that is integrally related to being engrafted into a set of ecclesial practices. Comparing and contrasting the different ways in which Martin Luther King Jr. is remembered (e.g., by African Americans, by the state, by the church), this essay argues for the significance of the difference between how "remembering" goes on in a liberal state and how it goes on in Christian anamnesis.

"The Liturgical Shape of the Christian Life: Teaching Christian Ethics as Worship" (1995), in IGC.

An outline of and rationale for the course in theological ethics that Hauerwas teaches to students preparing for ministry at Duke Divinity School. Structuring its topics around the liturgy of the United Methodist Church, the course makes "praise" the overriding theological motif. Since Christians are from first to last constituted by praise, the course can make no sharp distinction between liturgy and ethics, between what Christians think and what Christians do. By holding this course "accountable" to the liturgy, Hauerwas hopes to "de-school" his students in the intellectual habits of liberalism, making the course an exercise in theology as tradition-determined craft.

"What Could It Mean for the Church to Be the Body of Christ? A Question without a Clear Answer" (1995), in IGC.

Responding to frequent criticisms, here Hauerwas articulates his ecclesiology. The essay emphasizes two key characteristics of the church: the eucharistic character and the Jewish character. The eucharistic character emphasizes the church's temporal (i.e., as a mode of gift and promise) as opposed to its spatial (i.e., as a geographical, inhabitable place) character. The Jewish character emphasizes that any faithful explication of the church must be rendered in relation to Israel and the ongoing existence and witness of the Jewish people. See also "In Defence of Cultural Christianity: Reflections on Going to Church" (1998), in STT.

"For Dappled Things" (1996), in STT.

In this 1996 Duke Ph.D. commencement address, the modern university is praised for the way it encourages, through its patient work of exactness and attending to minute details, a sense of the inexhaustible depth of things. In so doing, the university reflects the truthful difference that makes God's world so beautiful.

"Gay Friendship: A Thought Experiment in Catholic Moral Theology" (1996), in *STT*.

Through themes of bodily agency, the indivisibility of the virtues and friendship, this essay engages in a "thought experiment" as to whether, and if so how, Christian commitment to the practices of singleness and marriage might be reconciled with sexual relationships among gay Christians. Originally published with the title "Virtue, Description, and Friendship: A Thought Experiment in Catholic Moral Theology."

"Going Forward by Looking Back: Agency Reconsidered" (1996), in *STT*.

That our moral lives are constituted more by retrospective rather than prospective judgments provides the basis for Hauerwas's reexamination and more careful qualification of "agency" than was the case in his earlier work, particularly *Character and the Christian Life*. Against accounts that construe agency in terms of a rationality that enables agents to make right decisions so as not to leave them determined by their past, Hauerwas argues that agency rather names those skills necessary to make our past our own. Theologically, the accent falls on habituation, which means that no formal account of "agency" or the "self" is necessary for the acquisition of the virtues. Indeed, there is no agency more determinative than the skills the Christian story itself makes possible.

"Living with Dishonest Wealth" (1996), in *STT*.

A sermon on the correlation between dishonesty and wealth in contemporary American society, underscoring the extent to which "white, middle America" is held in a tenacious grip by the practices of capitalism. Beginning with Jesus' Parable of the Unjust Steward, Hauerwas contends that rather than deceiving ourselves that we can choose between being honest or dishonest in how we handle our wealth, we are better off accepting Jesus' presumption that we are all in fact enslaved. Salvation, then, begins with the confession of the sin of our dishonesty, that we cannot help but be possessed by dishonest habits and unjust systems—which is another way of saying that practices of confession are commensurate with practices of truth-telling.

"History as Fate: How Justification by Faith Became Anthropology (and History) in America" (1997), in *WW*.

A critique of the largely Stoic outlook of Reinhold Niebuhr's anthropology and theology of history. Niebuhr's presentation of "the problem of history" renders the historicity of Christian convictions virtually irrelevant to truth claims about salvation. For Niebuhr, history is a playground of ideas and theology's task is to use them to sustain—in the case of America—the liberal political order. See also Hauerwas's analyses of Niebuhr's theology in wGU.

"How to Go On When You Know You Are Going to Be Misunderstood, or How Paul Holmer Ruined My Life, or Making Sense of Paul Holmer" (1997), in ww.

In this tribute to one of his teachers, the Yale philosopher of religion Paul Holmer, Hauerwas analyzes the (often implicit) significance of the work of the philosopher Ludwig Wittgenstein (1889–1951) for his own work. Wittgenstein's influence is seen not only in Hauerwas's attention to issues of description, but also to such central themes as virtue, narrative, memory, and vision.

"Reading James McClendon Takes Practice: Lessons in the Craft of Theology" (1997), in ww.

Invoking James McClendon's novel way of "structuring" systematic theology, Hauerwas makes the case that no reading (or writing) is innocent but that "reading is a soul-making activity" insofar as being able to read well demands that we form new habits through which our lives are changed and transformed. In short, the language and form of theology is integral to the practice of soul formation through reading.

"Remaining in Babylon: Oliver O'Donovan's Defense of Christendom," with James Fodor (1997), in ww.

An appreciative and critical engagement with Oliver O'Donovan's *The Desire of the Nations: Rediscovering the Roots of Political Theology.* Argues that an adequate political theology in a post-Christendom time requires learning to live by one's wits—a prospect made possible only insofar as Christians learn to do what Jews have done for centuries: discover how to survive without ruling.

"Theological Reflections on Aristotelian Themes," with Charles Pinches (1997), in cav.

This is Hauerwas's most extended commentary showing the significance of Aristotle for theological ethics. An earlier version, entitled "Happiness, the Life of Virtue, and Friendship: Theological Reflections on Aristotelian Themes," was published in the *Asbury Theological Journal* 45, no. 1 (spring 1990): 5–48. That same issue included a response by University of Notre Dame philosopher Philip Quinn entitled "Athens Is a Long way from Jerusalem" and a further response from Hauerwas entitled "Athens May Be a Long Way from Jerusalem, but Prussia Is Even Further."

"Christians in the Hands of Flaccid Secularists: Theology and 'Moral Inquiry' in the Modern University" (1998), in STT.

An examination of the legitimating discourses of the modern university and the conditions under which theology and ethics are produced. Hauerwas argues that understandings of contemporary theology that do not account for their institutional settings are apt to distort the character and obscure the task of theology.

"God's Grandeur" (1998), in STT.

A sermon on the relation among creation, church, eschatology, and the triune character of God, arguing that the modern proclivity to speak of creation in terms of nature exposes the extent to which we live without hope. To the extent that we desire to be in control, to be our own creators, we turn creation into "nature," thereby losing the joy of being creatures whose true end is the enjoyment of God's good creation.

"On Not Holding On or Witnessing the Resurrection" (1998), in STT.

The ambivalence of many modern Christians toward the resurrection of Jesus reflects the extent to which they do not want to believe that their world has been turned upside down. Many Christians would rather "hold on" to Jesus by "explaining" the resurrection. Jesus, however, refuses to let his disciples hold on, rather making them witnesses. Thus, the vital connection between the life of the church and Jesus' life, crucifixion, and resurrection is not lost or obscured as anything less than the inauguration of God's kingdom of forgiveness.

"'Salvation Even in Sin': Learning to Speak Truthfully about Ourselves" (1998), in STT.

Sin and redemption are properly named, not by being mapped over a generalized anthropology (e.g., which is typical of much of Protestant liberalism) but by affirming, incorporating, and thus becoming part of the narrative of Israel and the law. Ephesians 4:25–5:2 is exegeted as a scriptural illustration of the necessity of the ecclesial practices of confession, penance, and reconciliation for this incorporation to go on.

"The Cruelty of Peace" (1998), in STT.

This sermon contends that God's patience is but another name for God's peace and that, concomitantly, Advent names the Christian practice whereby Christians become a people capable of waiting peaceably and eucharistically for the Kingdom of God. Without such practices, through which Christians become for the world God's very body, peace is no longer a lived reality but quickly degenerates into an ideal for which Christians are willing to do almost anything. Hence the cruelty of a peace not rooted in Advent and the Eucharist.

"The Sanctified Body: Why Perfection Does Not Require a 'Self'" (1998), in *STT*.

Originally presented at Point Loma Nazarene University and published with a series of responses in *Embodied Holiness: Toward a Corporate Theology of Spiritual Growth*, ed. Samuel M. Powell and Michael E. Lodahl (Downers Grove, IL: InterVarsity Press, 1999). Refusing individualistic and pietistic conceptions of sanctification and holiness, this essay develops an alternative conception of the holiness of the whole church through a renewed understanding of the body. Any theologically adequate account of sanctification is also an account of truth, and vice versa, for both entail the display of certain ecclesial practices by which the body of Christ is shaped/ transformed.

"The Truth about God: The Decalogue as Condition for Truthful Speech" (1998), in *STT*.

The degree to which Christians can tell the truth about God is concomitant to their ability to speak the truth about the world. Reflecting on "the grammar of the Decalogue" with reference to the accounts of Aquinas and Luther, the essay critiques the abstract form of the peculiarly modern distinction between nature (natural law) and grace (revealed law). It also seeks to show why the attendant attempts to ground morality on the basis of the so-called second table of the Decalogue is a theological mistake.

"Timeful Friends: Living with the Handicapped" (1998), in *STT*.

A meditation on the "gifted," historically contingent, and timeful character of Christian truth and holiness that attends to the ways in which God, through baptism, shapes the whole body of Christ by means of one part of the body called "handicapped." Not only are the handicapped exemplary in this respect, they are paradigmatic insofar as they underscore the way in which God's holiness is quintessentially constituted through the vulnerability of the presence of the other.

"Worship, Evangelism, Ethics: On Eliminating the 'And'" (1998), in *BH*.

An argument that attempts to help the church recover its liturgical integrity by exposing some of the historical and theological reasons for the fragmentation of theological studies that resulted in the disciplinary separation, and ultimately isolation, of worship, evangelism, and ethics from theology.

"The Christian Difference, Or: Surviving Postmodernism" (1999), in *BH*.

In this essay Hauerwas places himself as an enemy of postmodernism's enemy (modernity), while being no friend of postmodernism. Though showing appreciation for those like Foucault who have helped unmask the principalities and powers of the age, Hauerwas finds postmodernism generally to be a far too comfortable account of the fragmentation of advanced capitalism. In contrast to postmodernism, Christianity still has (or ought to have) a stake in history, even though it was Christianity's attempt to make its truth known ahistorically that created the possibility of both modernity and postmodernity. Christians can survive postmodernism by "out-narrating" the postmodernists as well as by nurturing practices of resistance to global capitalism.

WGU—With the Grain of the Universe: The Gifford Lectures for 2001 (Grand Rapids, MI: Brazos Press, 2001).

The primary problem confronting the Christian church in a postmodern world is not one of *logos,* whether Christian claims about God and the world can be debated with alternative accounts. Rather, it is one of *ethos,* whether a church of Christians can produce and sustain the kind of witness to God in which bearing the cross is not a confession peculiar to them, but a revelation to all that these witnesses are "working with the grain of the universe."

The argument of these eight lectures begins with an evaluation of the very possibility of giving the kind of lectures in natural theology demanded in Lord Gifford's will. Here the project of the lectures is established: to analyze the responses of three previous Gifford lectures (James, Niebuhr, and Barth) to Gifford's instruction that these "scientific" lectures were to overcome the vicissitudes of any particular religious or cultural tradition. Hauerwas's question: Can the project initiated by Gifford as absolutely necessary for understanding the truth about God avoid undermining the truth it seeks to find?

William James's *Varieties of Religious Experience* (Gifford Lectures of 1901–1902) claims to find the necessary objectivity for a scientific natural theology—through a fascinating combination of Darwinism and pragmatism—in religious psychology. In so doing, natural theology—the discovery of God in God's creation—becomes the discovery of humanity's worth in human subjectivity.

Reinhold Niebuhr's *The Nature and Destiny of Man* (Gifford Lectures of 1941) follows James's approach for a scientific natural theology in empirical observations of human experience. Niebuhr's natural theology thus begins with an analysis of human nature. This natural theology leads to a paradoxical God who, while being the ultimate fulfillment of human needs, makes such demands on human beings that attempts to meet them cannot but be a new form of egoism.

Karl Barth's *The Knowledge of God* (Gifford Lectures of 1937), while also seeking an understanding of human nature, overturns the "epistemological prejudices of modernity" in denying that natural theology can *begin* with human reason or religious experience. Rather, natural theology must (as all theology must) begin with what God reveals about human nature and the concomitant claims that such revelation makes on the lives of the people of God. The *Church Dogmatics*, Barth's magnum opus, is best understood as an extended effort to display the language of faith in a manner that continually resists the epistemological prejudices of modernity, functioning instead as a witness without end.

Hauerwas concludes by arguing that Barth's refusal to submit theological claims to "scientific" or any other supratheological standards does not necessarily lead to a self-referential and self-justifying Christian theology. For while rational argument is one form of Christian witness, it is a form of witness dependent on the preceding commitment of Christians to witness. Two contemporary Christian witnesses who have challenged the presumptions of modernity within as well as outside the precincts of the university are John Howard Yoder and Pope John Paul II. The primary significance of both witnesses lies not in their being "intellectuals," but in their being representative figures of churches who have challenged the epistemological prejudices of modernity. Here, the "first post-Constantinian pope" and an ecumenical neo-Anabaptist theologian display the difference Christian practice entails: that there can be no argument to the truth about God in Jesus Christ without witnesses.

Scripture References

Name Index

Subject Index

Intratextuality, 155. *See also* Narrative(s);
Reading(s); Scripture, Holy

Israel, 49, 107–108, 111, 121, 160, 198, 234, 251,
324, 340; calling of, 122, 640, 647; and the
church, 383; covenant of, 129, 336, 499,
543, 645; and Jesus, 122–123, 147, 400n; offices (prophet, priest, king), 103, 123, 127–
129, 543; people of, 109, 122, 129, 339; redemption of, 122, 149; 260; story of, 145,
261, 339, 643. *See also* Church; God, Jesus
of Nazareth; Kingdom of God; Yahweh

Jesus of Nazareth, 5, 11, 225, 234, 251, 310,
321–322, 333, 343, 378n, 381, 388, 422n, 429,
522, 525, 605; Atonement, 431, 440;
Christology, issues of, 20–21, 42, 63, 85,
108–109, 111, 117–118, 161, 342, 344, 345n,
436, 440, 457, 465n, 470n, 610, 644; crucifixion and resurrection of, 219, 256–258,
260, 263–264, 383, 432, 435, 512, 526, 533;
disciples and followers of, 258, 315; ethic
of, 402n, 445, 453; God with and as, 344,
647; as forerunner of the kingdom, 8, 109,
119–121, 440, 453; healings and miracles,
256–257, 453; life, death, and resurrection
of, 400, 418, 423–424, 640, 645, 651, 654; as
Lord, 253, 375, 439, 637; as Messiah
(anointed), 45, 119–120, 125–127, 198, 259–
262, 344, 441, 533, 644; presence of, 259;
peace of, 410, 418, 424; repentance made
possible by, 443; as savior, 317, 376n;
story(s) of, 342, 383, 385, 643; as suffering
servant, 261–262; as stranger, 256–257,
260, 265–266; teachings and example of,
117, 297, 402n, 426, 434, 612; as "very God
and very man," 109, 117, 255. *See also* Israel; Kingdom of God; Word of God

Jews, 146, 219, 255, 340, 344, 440, 459, 605; in
(American) liberal society, 20, 329, 338;
and Christians, 96, 109, 149, 328, 334–335,
341, 343n, 346–347, 460, 533, 644–645, 647;
nationalism of, 337, 420–421, 438; persecution and killing of, 208, 210–211, 332,
460–461, 647; social strategies of, 460–461

Judaism, 52, 100, 109, 134, 166, 334–336, 342;
contested identity, 328, 332n, 336n; laws

of, 129, 328; messianic hope of, 343n, 345n,
383; as particular people, 327–328, 332n; as
"radical tradition," 642–643; survival of,
327, 335, 338, 669; synagogue, 509; theological issues of, 343, 544, 644, 646. *See
also* Holocaust; Israel; Judaism

Journey, 173, 184, 186, 188, 299, 341n, 343n,
554. *See also* Discipleship

Joy, 300, 360n, 361, 365, 530, 570. *See also*
Happiness; Friendship(s)

Judgment(s), of God, 607; moral, 30, 231–
232, 277, 427, 492–493n, 532, 581n, 582,
601, 638

Just war, 8, 390, 416, 422, 428, 453, 621; Catholic commitment to, 520; and the church,
303n; as defense of the innocent, 280n; direct and indirect, 520; as elimination of
the victim of injustice, 568; form just
peace must take, 413; as further development of Spirit, 402n; "history come out
right" charge, 456; and pacifism, 392; protection of neighbor, 450; sustained by
Christian love, 449; theory(s) of, 394, 397,
402n, 403, 411, 412, 414n, 417, 444, 454, 519

Justification by faith, 658; of beliefs, 71–72;
of moral assertions, 71. *See also* Sanctification

Justice, 96, 173, 235, 238, 241, 243, 262, 336,
371, 375, 398–399, 414n, 416, 435, 461, 526;
that the church seeks, 380; commitment
to nonresistance, 230; as criterion of
Christian social strategy, 389; denies pacifism, 417; education for, 237; of God, 252;
John Rawls's understanding of, 67; in a
Niebuhrian sense, 621; ordered, 444;
peace with, 417; principles of, 288, 449,
471; role of revolution in, 380; role of
"state" in, 380; social, 66–67, 106, 288, 374,
380; theories of, 471n; and injustice, 178,
239, 427

Killing, avoidance of, 280; categories of, 394,
444; innocent, 256

Kingdom of God, 45, 116–120, 124, 159, 251,
264, 344, 375, 378n, 414, 420, 430, 525, 604,
659; American democracy as manifesta-

Peace/peaceableness *cont.*
requires change of structures of politics and industry, 419n; and resurrection of Jesus, 135; shalom, 432–434; spirituality of, 418; as truthful, 322; wider vision of, 397; "without eschatology," 438; without truthfulness, 322; working for, 320

Peacemaking, 12, 27, 196, 318–320, 324–325; as demanding task, 321, 326; as form of the church, 318, 324; practice(s) of, 321, 657; as (temporal) virtue of church, 320, 322–324, 659

Penance, rite of, 39, 43, 281n, 307

Pentecost, 143, 146–150

People, of God. *See* Church; Israel

Perseverance, 301; virtue of, 299–300

Person(s), 240, 602, 648; abstract regulative language of, 596–600

Philosophy, 19, 46, 91, 246, 269, 395, 508, 544, 664; and ethics, 43, 62–63, 545; moral, 165–166, 228–229, 268, 277, 469; and theology, 79–83, 459, 661

Physician(s), 272n, 611, 616, 664; analogous to "princes," 350; autonomy of, 601; care offered by, 545; care of, 354, 649; cure, inability to, 353–354; and need to act, 353; patience of, 364n, 366; patients, 283, 270, 273, 349, 364n, 539, 544, 551, 552, 554, 601, 620; personal integration not enough, 555; and professional distance, 539, 546, 551; skills of, 354, 546, 551

Pietism, 24, 43, 463; and individualism, 23, 462. *See also* Baptist tradition; United Methodist tradition

Pluralism, 92, 184, 417, 496, 522, 525, 660

Poetry, 167, 191. *See also* Literature; Metaphor(s)

Polis, classical and modern views of, 592. *See also* Church

Politics, 105, 172, 174, 212–213, 215, 316, 447–448, 459, 489, 635, 637; of amnesia, 634; 454–455; theological, of SMH, 459; theory(s) of, 25, 390, 639, 652

Postmodernism, 10, 660–661

Poverty, 380, 517, 527

Power, 172–173, 215, 388, 406, 591, 637; as co-ercion, 195, 404; as "essence" of politics, 404, 448. *See also* Pacifism; Politics; War

Practical reasoning, 274, 276n, 281n, 647, 655–656

Practices, 6, 290n, 297, 314, 365n, 520, 624, 627, 641, 643, 646, 649, 652, 659, 662, 667; and communities, 8, 23, 291n, 429, 623; and descriptions, 277–278; and narratives, 20, 527; ordinary, of everyday life, 20, 670

Prayer(s), 22, 28, 219, 358, 452n, 612, 643; healing for the sick, 265, 543, 554, 624; and military service, 520–521; and power of rulers, 384, 480; practice of, 308–309; in public schools, 460–461, 474, 479

Preaching (the Word), 40, 142–151, 159–160, 255, 334, 371, 384–385, 452, 530, 622, 641, 666, 670n; about abortion, 603–608, 621; of Peter at Pentecost, 146–147; on political responsibilities of Christians, 621; on war, 621. *See also* Church: "marks" of excellence; Holy Spirit; Narrative(s); Sacraments

Pregnancy, 350n, 557, 605; teenage, 482n, 484–485, 606, 618; "termination" of, 610–611, 614. *See also* Abortion; Sexual ethics; Women

Presence, gift of, 541, 554

Pride (vice of), 280n, 575

Priesthood, 24, 512. *See also* Pastors

"Principalities and powers," conflict with, 22, 312–313, 435, 438, 452, 524, 527

Principles, 165–166, 216, 245n, 269, 277, 456, 492, 523; moral, 221, 252, 272n, 281, 288, 320; and moral rules, 272–273, 281, 291n

Professions, 94, 212–215, 272n, 349; legal, 96, 105, 608; medical, 96, 600

Promiscuity, 492, 521, 603

Prophesy(ing), eschatological practice of, 146–147. *See also* Church; Israel; Pentecost; Witness

Propriety (virtue), 293–294

Protestantism, 18–19, 22–23, 47, 334n, 337, 448, 639, 654, 670; in America, 463, 476; debates, 640, 658; evangelicals, 30, 314, 596; "mainline," 3, 470, 660; Reformation, 42–43, 55, 431, 642; revivalism, 666; theo-

Dr. Stanley Martin Hauerwas is the Gilbert T. Rowe Professor of Theological Ethics at the Divinity School of Duke University. Prof. Hauerwas has been co-editor with Alasdair MacIntyre of the Revisions Series published by the University of Notre Dame Press and associate editor of the *Encyclopedia of Bioethics*. Among his numerous publications are *The Peaceable Kingdom: A Primer in Christian Ethics*; *Against the Nations: War and Survival in a Liberal Society*; *Resident Aliens: Life in the Christian Colony*, with Will Willimon; and its sequel of 1996, *Where Resident Aliens Live*; *Naming the Silences: God, Medicine and the Problem of Suffering*; *Dispatches from the Front: Theological Engagements with the Secular* (Duke University Press, 1994); *Christians among the Virtues: Theological Conversations with Ancient and Modern Ethics*, with Charles Pinches; *Wilderness Wanderings: Probing Twentieth-Century Theology and Philosophy*; *Sanctify Them in the Truth: Holiness Exemplified*; *The Truth About God*; *The Ten Commandments in Christian Life*, with Will Willimon.

John Berkman teaches moral theology in the Department of Theology at The Catholic University of America. He has contributed to a variety of books and academic journals, including *The Thomist, Christian Bioethics, Theology Today, New Blackfriars, Communio, Theology and Philosophy*, and the *Josephinum Journal of Theology*.

Michael Cartwright is Associate Professor of Philosophy and Religion at the University of Indianapolis. He is the editor of the *Royal Priesthood: Essays Ecclesiological and Ecumenical*.

Library of Congress Cataloging-in-Publication Data
Hauerwas, Stanley
The Hauerwas reader / Stanley Hauerwas ; edited by John Berkman and Michael Cartwright.
p. cm.
Includes bibliographical references and indexes.
ISBN 0-8223-2680-9 (cloth : alk. paper)—ISBN 0-8223-2691-4 (pbk. : alk. paper)
1. Christian ethics. I. Berkman, John. II. Cartwright, Michael G. III. Title.
BJ1251 .H326 2001
241'.0404—dc21   00-047709